Black.
Queer.
Southern.
Women.

Black.
Queer.
Southern.
Women.

AN ORAL HISTORY

E. Patrick Johnson

THE UNIVERSITY OF NORTH CAROLINA PRESS
Chapel Hill

This book was published with the assistance of the
Z. Smith Reynolds Fund of the University of North Carolina Press.

Manufactured in the United States of America

Cover photograph © Getty Images / Jim McGuire.

The University of North Carolina Press has been a member
of the Green Press Initiative since 2003.

LIBRARY OF CONGRESS CATALOGING-IN-PUBLICATION DATA
Names: Johnson, E. Patrick, 1967– author.
Title: Black. Queer. Southern. Women. : an oral history / E. Patrick Johnson.
Description: Chapel Hill : The University of North Carolina Press,
[2018] | Includes bibliographical references and index.
Identifiers: LCCN 2018018514 | ISBN 9781469641096 (cloth : alk. paper) |
ISBN 9781469641102 (pbk : alk. paper) | ISBN 9781469641119 (ebook)
Subjects: LCSH: African American lesbians—Southern States—Biography. |
African American lesbians—Southern States—History—20th century. |
African American lesbians—Southern States—History—21st century.
Classification: LCC HQ75.6.U52 S684 2018 | DDC 306.76/6308996073075—dc23
LC record available at https://lccn.loc.gov/2018018514

In memory of

JOAN GARNER

and

LENORE STACKHOUSE

Contents

· ·

Acknowledgments *xi*

Introduction *1*

Part I G.R.I.T.S.: Stories of Growing Up
Black, Female, and Queer *19*

1 It's Thick Here: Race, Gender, and
Sexuality in the South *21*

2 Does Your Mama Know? Motherhood and
Mother-Daughter Relationships *77*

3 Walk like a Man, Talk like a Woman:
Gender Nonconformity *137*

4 I Found God in Myself and I Loved Her
Fiercely: Religion and Spirituality *165*

5 A Taste of Honey: Sex among Women
Who Love Women *215*

6 I'm Sweet on You: Stories of Love,
Courtship, and Intimacy *280*

7 The Work My Soul Was Called to
Do: Art and Activism *323*

Part II My Soul Looks Back and Wonders:
Stories of Perseverance and Hope *391*

8 Salsa Soul Sister: Aida Rentas *393*

9 Being Human Is a Dangerous Thing:
Cherry Hussain *417*

10 I'm Happy as Hell: Gwen Cubit *443*

11 I'm Just a Black Woman in America:
Lori Wilson *473*

12 I'm Alright with Who I Am:
"Ida Mae" 508

13 Books Saved My Life:
Mary Anne Adams 534

Epilogue: A Poet's Response 559

Notes 563

Bibliography 567

Index of Narrators 571

General Index 573

Illustrations

Dedra and Laurinda, 2014 291

Cherry and Pat Hussain, waiting for their marriage license in Connecticut 305

Rose and Priscilla in Anguilla, 2016 307

Keturah and Shetikka at Yellow River Park in Stone Mountain, Georgia, 2014 318

Cherry at age six 418

Gwen at her college graduation from the University of Texas 465

Lori in San Antonio, 2015 474

Gwen and Lori in San Antonio, 2016 503

Acknowledgments

....

There are so many people to thank for making this book possible that I know that I will inevitably leave someone off this list! First, I would like to thank the Sexualities Project at Northwestern (SPAN) for two grants, without which this research could have never taken place. I especially want to thank SPAN directors Steven Epstein and Héctor Carrillo and the anonymous readers who vetted my grant applications. Additional financial support came from the Northwestern University Research Grants Committee and the Center for Interdisciplinary Arts for making a staged reading of this work possible. After receiving financial support, I had to find women to share their stories, and there were several people who assisted me with locating potential interviewees. Shean Atkins not only hosted me at his home in Atlanta but also introduced me to several of his "sorors." Also in Atlanta were Mary Anne Adams and Duncan Teague, whose networks provided me with numerous contacts for potential interviews. Thanks to Sharon Bridgforth and Omi Osun Joni L. Jones who put me in touch with women in Austin, Texas. Kevin Anderson of the T.R.U.T.H. Project in Houston, Texas, and Harold Steward, formerly of the South Dallas Cultural Center, for helping me find women in their respective cities. Lisa Moore was extremely helpful in getting the word out to women on various electronic mailing lists and in the DC-Maryland-Virginia area. Dwayne Jenkins and Melissa Smith recruited women for me in Nashville, and Roderick Hawkins put me in touch with women in Baton Rouge. My good friend Lamar Garnes in Tallahassee was a godsend in getting me tapped in to the community at Florida A&M University. I would also like to thank Zakiyya Lord, for contacts of other GRITS (girls raised in the South), especially those in Birmingham.

It really does take a village to transcribe and code close to two hundred hours of recorded interviews! Thanks to my undergraduate research assistants Gillian Levy and Lindsay Amer and to my graduate research assistants Nathan Lamp, Rhaisa Williams, Shoniqua Roach, and Tay Glover, who worked diligently to make sure that every word and theme was accounted for.

It was quite an honor to have a staged reading of some of these narratives through the Process Series at the University of North Carolina at Chapel Hill. Joseph Megel was an incredible collaborator, and Sibby Anderson-Thompkins, Kyra Jones, Omi Osun Joni L. Jones, Stacey Robinson, and Yolanda Rabun were incredible performers who brought these narratives to life. Also, thanks to Richard Joseph, director of the Sonja Haynes Stone Center for Black Culture and History, for providing a space for the staged reading.

I would be remiss if I did not acknowledge all of my colleagues at Northwestern and around the country who have supported this work through encouragement or inviting me to give talks at their institutions. They include D. Soyini Madison, Ramón Rivera-Servera, Joshua Chambers-Letson, Marcela Fuentes, Shayna Silverstein, Michelle Wright, Martha Biondi, Mary Pattillo, Sylvester Johnson, Darlene Clark Hine, Sherwin Bryant, Deborah Thompson, Celeste Watkins-Hayes, Nitasha Sharma, Jennifer Nash, Janice Radway, Steven Epstein, Héctor Carrillo, Gregory Ward, Ivy Wilson, Aymar Christian, Juan Battle, Renée Alexander-Craft, Tommy DeFrantz, Jill Dolan, Joseph Roach, Trudier Harris, Lauren Berlant, Lisa Duggan, Gayatri Gopinath, Kareem Khubchandani, John Jackson Jr., Deborah Thomas, Valerie Traub, Holly Hughes, Susan Lanser, Robin Bernstein, Bill Leap, Kai M. Green, Joanne Braxton, Leisa Meyer, Della Pollock, Patricia Parker, Patrick Horn, Beverly Guy Sheftall, and Nicole Fleetwood.

Having the time and space to write is such a privilege, which is why I have to thank Eric Dishman and Ashley Armstrong for being the first people to open up their home in Portland, Oregon, for me to do nothing but read, write, and eat fresh food from their garden. It was such a wondrous experience! And to my dear friends down under, Nicky Solomon and Glen McGillivray, who have welcomed me into their home in Sydney, Australia, for over fifteen years, I say, you remain my writing inspiration. Thank you for allowing me to escape to the other side of the world and for always providing me inspiration, great food, and an opportunity to cook! I'm sure you hold the record for the most books written by an acquaintance in your home.

To my editor, Mark Simpson-Vos, I cannot say how thankful I am for your steady hand during this process. You have kept me true to my own voice and scholarly endeavors and pushed me to think outside the box. This goes for the entire University of North Carolina Press family. You continue to take care of me and show me the southern hospitality that families in the South are known for!

As always, Stephen J. Lewis, my "Mr. Sweet Tea," put up with me being on the road for weeks on end to collect these stories and never locked the door when I returned. Thank you for always being my ride or die! I love you.

And, finally, I want to thank all of the women who opened up their lives to me for this book. You made me laugh and cry often, but more important, you shared with the world stories that I know will help transform many lives.

Black.
Queer.
Southern.
Women.

Introduction

. . . .

This oral history of southern black women who love women has been a long time in the making—twelve years, to be exact. When I first conceived of and began conducting oral history interviews for *Sweet Tea: Black Gay Men of the South (2008)*, I intended to include the stories of women. And, as with most things, the men took over the book! While I suggest in the introduction to *Sweet Tea* that my rationale for not including the stories of black southern lesbians had to do with my lack of exposure to their communities and because of my personal interest in homing in on a specific community with which I was intimately familiar, the ultimate decision not to combine the stories was—and for reasons that I hope will become clearer below—a prudent one.[1] The lessons I learned from conducting research for *Sweet Tea* has so benefited the current research, but more important, the women deserved to have their own book, for their experiences and perspectives vary drastically from those of black gay southern men.

During the question-and-answer session of a performance based on the stories in *Sweet Tea,* someone once yelled from the audience, "When are you going to write 'Pink Lemonade'?! When are you going to tell our story?!" Besides being a wonderful title (and one that I strongly considered for this book), the question, which came from a self-identified same-sex-loving woman, took me by surprise. *Sweet Tea* had already been out for two years, and I had assumed that someone—one of my colleagues in the field of black queer studies, perhaps—would write a book on the topic. After several more years passed and after hundreds more women kept asking me when I was going to collect their stories, I decided to do so.

But there were also other compelling reasons for collecting the oral histories for this book. I actually wanted to learn more about the interior lives of southern black lesbians and their journey toward selfhood in the South. As a child, the concept of "lesbian" was not in my consciousness, or necessarily in the lexicon of my western North Carolina black community. The typical slang of "funny," "that way," and "sissy" were certainly common but mostly were spoken in reference to men who were thought to be gay. I sometimes heard at the barbershop the oblique reference to a woman as a "bulldagger," but I had no idea the meaning of that term, only that it was negative. In hindsight, I realize that I actually grew up with quite a few black lesbians, one of whom is Anita, whose narrative I include in this book. In fact, it was not until I was much older that I realized just how many women in my community were "sweet" on other women. Thus, I was curious to hear the stories about same-sex desire from these women's early childhood to see if there were overlaps with black southern gay men with whom I have spoken and my own story, or if there were significant differences based on gender. For example, a few of the young girls with whom I was friends growing up were what many would refer to as "tomboys," girls who were more interested in climbing trees, building hotrods, and playing basketball than they were in playing with dolls, playing house, or making mud pies, as I so loved to do. I don't recall them being teased about being tomboys, however. I, on the other hand, was often called "sissy" because of my soft, soprano voice, big butt, noticeable lisp, and interest in art and "girly" things. What explains this difference in treatment based on gender expression and play interests? Conducting these interviews gave me some insight and perspective on that question, as many of the women in *Black. Queer. Southern. Women. (BQSW)* revealed that they believe that tomboyish girls are generally tolerated—at least until they are a certain age and expected to become southern "ladies."

And even after adulthood, some women—at least in my community growing up—were not bound by a narrow sexual identity when they engaged in nonnormative sexual behavior or expressed same-sex desire. While folks may have whispered about them, their dalliances with the same sex did not necessarily make them "lesbian" as much as it did just another eccentric whose membership in and contributions to the community outweighed their sexual behavior.

One humorous story in this regard involves my now deceased uncle, Johnny "Shaw Man" McHaney. For all intents and purposes, Uncle Johnny would have been considered a "dirty old man." Although he was married, I can't remember a time when he wasn't flirting with or coming on to a woman—any woman: old, young, fat, skinny, toothless, what have you. He never seemed to discriminate in his attraction for the other sex, but he definitely had a quare[2] sensibility about him—both in his attraction to nonnormative women (i.e., women who did not fit within or even aspired to traditional standards of beauty within the white or black communities) and in his linguistic play with gender when he added "Baby Doll" to the end of my brothers' and my names when he greeted us, as in, "How you doin' today, Pat, Baby Doll?" While it was mostly an infantilizing gesture, it also queered us in a specific way—and in a way that I loved, but my brothers, not so much.

Uncle Johnny was always taking pictures at family gatherings and holidays with his Polaroid camera. Unsurprisingly, many of the photos were of women guests at our family events or of women whom he had met at his favorite barbershop where he hung out every day after work and on the weekends. Several years ago my mother asked him to bring some of his pictures over to our house so that she could look through them and find ones that she could possibly use as part of a photo collage for an upcoming family reunion. Uncle Johnny arrived with two mega-sized trash bags full of Polaroid pictures and dumped them onto the kitchen table. My mother, who has always had a flair for the dramatic, responded in her off-the-scale, high-pitched voice that starts high and falls dramatically low at the end of a sentence, "Johnny! Where in the world did you get all of those PICT-tures?" Only offering a Mr. Grinch grin, Uncle Johnny ignored my mother's question and proceeded to smooth the pictures out on the table. Mama, my sister, Pam, my aunt, Mary Lee, Uncle Johnny, and I sat around the table looking through the pictures, often gasping or giggling at the images emerging from the pile. Mixed in with the photos from past family reunions were pictures of various women—some in compromising positions, scantily clad, or nude (including some of my high school classmates!). Aunt Mary Lee stumbled across a picture of Sylvia, a woman who I remembered lived up the road from us when I was a child and who was the mother of two daughters close to my age. Trying to needle Uncle Johnny, she asked in a voice almost as shrill as her sister's, "Johnny, ain't this a picture of Sylvia?" Uncle Johnny slipped the picture out of Aunt Mary Lee's hand, studying it as if lost in an erotic reverie: "Yeah, that's Syp. You know she's half and half," he replied. "Well, if she half and half, what YOU doin' wit' 'er then?" Aunt Mary Lee responded incredulously. "I was with the half I could be wit,'" Uncle Johnny quipped without missing a beat. Although totally scandalized and clutching her pearls,[3] even my mother gave in and joined the rest of the room in the uproar of gut-busting laughter.

It was my memory of Aunt Mary Lee's and Uncle Johnny's repartee and description of Sylvia as "half and half," meaning that she had sex with both men and women, that brought into clarity the ways in which black southern women's sexual desire, sexual practice, and sexual identity are not always one and the same. As a scholar of gender and sexuality, of course I know intellectually that this is not the case, but I had not thought about it *experientially* in the context of my own upbringing and family history until now. "Half and half" in this context signifies quare sexual *desire* rather than bisexual or lesbian *identity* per se, for the phrase exemplifies the verbal play of black folk vernacular that eschews fixed meanings. Aunt Mary Lee already knew that Uncle Johnny did not discriminate when it came to women; thus, she already assumed what he was "doing" with Sylvia, and especially given some of the other photos of women sprawled across my mother's kitchen table (e.g., a picture of Uncle Johnny and a woman with one breast and another of a naked woman with a very large behind standing in front of Uncle Johnny's television). And Uncle Johnny's coy response about being with only one "half" of Sylvia also cannot be read literally in terms of him denying a lesbian side of Sylvia in order to be with a straight side. More likely, the half to which Uncle Johnny referred was nonnormative sex, given his proclivities for kink. The point here is that Sylvia did not refer to herself as a lesbian, and the community did not project that identity onto her; they only knew that she engaged in quare sex without the encumbrance of a label or identity to accompany this behavior or desire. And, as I detail later in the book, this was common among many of the women that I interviewed. While the same phenomenon was true for some of the men I interviewed for *Sweet Tea*, it certainly was not the dominant narrative, as many of the men typically did identify under some label or category. This phenomenon made me think differently about the particularly vexing problem of how to conduct research on sexuality beyond identity "in order to produce a more complex accounting of the history of sexuality and sexual communities."[4] Ultimately, this is why the title of the book does not include the word "lesbian."[5]

Another reason for writing this book is that my coming to terms with and into consciousness about my own sexuality was facilitated by the writings of feminist women of color, specifically black lesbian feminist criticism, and black women's literature, such that I am invested in paying homage to black lesbians through the amelioration of their lived experiences. Indeed, the critical writings of black and Latina lesbian feminists, such as Barbara Smith, Beverly Smith, Cheryl Clarke, Audre Lorde, Cherríe Moraga, and Gloria Anzaldúa, and black women writers like Toni Morrison, Gloria Naylor, and Alice Walker, among others—all introduced to me in D. Soyini Madison's course Performance of Women of Color in the late 1980s—exposed me to and gave me insight into a world I had only begun to discover. For instance, Toni Morrison's novel *Sula* still stands as my favorite novel of all time. And it was Barbara Smith's essay "Toward a Black Feminist Criticism," in which she reads *Sula* as a "lesbian" text based on the title character's and her best friend Nel's level of intimacy, that I discovered that the close bonds between people of the same gender can be considered quare despite the absence of sex within that bond. While it was the relationship between the couple Lorraine and Theresa in Naylor's *The Women of Brewster Place* that exposed me to an overtly lesbian couple in fiction, it was Walker's Celie and Shug in *The Color Purple* that provided a *southern* example of black same-sex-loving women that I had not been exposed to at that point. Later on, I would discover Ann Allen Shockley's lesbian cult classic, *Say Jesus and Come to Me*. All of these writings, as well as others, provided a *feminist* foundation for me to become more comfortable with my own sexuality and, more important, provided examples of how to do antisexist and antihomophobic work despite being a man who benefits from patriarchy. Thus, it is for these as well as many other reasons that I chose to write *BQSW*.

Black. Queer. Southern. Women. An Oral History focuses on the oral histories of African American women who express same-sex desire and who were born, reared, and continue to reside in the US South. It is meant as a companion text to *Sweet Tea: Black Gay Men of the South—An Oral History*. As with *Sweet Tea*, my desire in *BQSW* is that the oral histories collected account for not only the way the narrators embody and relay historical material about race, region, class, sexuality, and gender but also how storytelling as a mode of communication is simultaneously a quotidian form of self-fashioning and theorizing. *BQSW* allows women whose identities and/or sexual desires have positioned them on the margins of society to have a platform to speak on their own terms about what it means to be black, southern, and expressive of same-sex desire. Ultimately, the narratives collected in *BQSW* evince larger questions regarding identity formation, community building, and power relations as they are negotiated within the context of southern history. As a result, the aim of *BQSW* is to fill a void in the historical accounts of black women's sexual history in the South; highlight the richly complex communities of black women who desire women; account for the ways that black lesbians negotiate their sexual, gender, class, and racial identity with their southern cultural identity; and highlight the ways in which southern black lesbians' lives diverge from those of black gay male southerners.

As I suggest above, despite experiencing homophobia and sexism, black same-sex-loving women like Sylvia from my hometown are an integral part of their black communities. And, based on the gender politics of the South in general, and within black queer southern spaces in particular, many of the women narrate stories of both common bonds and tensions with black gay men; thus, their life histories give rise to a complex and contested narrative about the life experiences of southern black lesbians compared to black gay men. In response to the question about whether it is harder for lesbians growing up in the South than it is for gay men, for example, all but a few of the women believe that life in the South is harder for gay men, and especially for those who are effeminate. "It's much harder to be a sissy in the South than it is to be a tomboy," a few told me. And yet, these same women also address the misogyny and sexism found within black gay male circles that excludes them from community. Accordingly, *BQSW* narrates a different history based on gendered relationships that position women as "other" within a sexist and patriarchal culture. As with any oppressed or marginalized group, however, these women resist victimhood in ways that inspire and challenge the status quo. While they do not always overcome the challenges of being black quare southern women, their oral narratives stand as testaments to the power of voicehood, self-determination, and tenacity in how one navigates and mediates the conflicting, complicated, and confounding ideologies of the South.

The image of the southern black woman is embedded in the American imaginary despite that image being contradictory and contested. Interestingly, the racialized, gendered, and classed representations of black southern women as asexual mammies, oversexed jezebels, and sassy sapphires are still framed through a heteronormative lens—as women who are sexually available to *men*. The narratives I have collected complicate this imagery by chronicling how same-sex desire exists among and between southern black women and how they maneuver within these long-held racist and sexist stereotypes to enact their own sexual agency around same-sex desire. Patriarchy, sexism, and misogyny necessarily distinguish the difference between these women's experiences and those of their gay male counterparts.

Until *Sweet Tea* was published in 2008, there were no books solely devoted to black queer southern life. While the impact of *Sweet Tea* has been immeasurable, there is still a void in scholarship on black southern lesbian history. Several books chronicle queer southern history and include sections on black lesbians, most notably Lillian Faderman's *Odd Girls and Twilight Lovers: A History of Lesbian Life in Twentieth-Century America* (1991); John Howard's *Carryin' On in the Lesbian and Gay South* (1997); James T. Sears's *Growing Up Gay in the South: Race, Gender, and Journeys of the Spirit* (1991), *Lonely Hunters: An Oral History of Lesbian and Gay Southern Life, 1948–1968* (1997), and *Rebels, Rubyfruit, and Rhinestones: Queering Space in the Stonewall South* (2001); and Brock Thompson's *The Un-natural State: Arkansas and the Queer South* (2010)—but the major focus of these texts is still decisively on white gay men and lesbians. Nonetheless, each of these texts in their own way is instructive about what it means for sexual dissidents to maneuver within southern culture across various periods in time (1930s to the present), class positions, and rural and urban spaces.

Black women fiction and nonfiction writers—both heterosexual and lesbian—have produced the most work on southern black lesbians, including Ann Allen Shockley's *Loving Her* (1974) and *Say Jesus and Come to Me* (1987); Alice Walker's *The Color Purple* (1982); Shay Youngblood's *The Big Mama Stories* (1989); Catherine McKinley and L. Joyce DeLaney's *Afrekete: An Anthology of Black Lesbian Writing* (1995); and Lisa C. Moore's *Does Your Mama Know? An Anthology of Black Lesbian Coming Out Stories* (1997). The novels, short stories, poems, and testimonials are invaluable resources for *BQSW*, both for their insights and for their methodologies. The novels and short stories in particular present a nuanced portrait of how black lesbians negotiate their identity in rural southern black communities—from the canonical story of the naïve Celie and blues woman Shug Avery in Walker's *The Color Purple* to the lesser known butch-femme melodrama of Myrtle Black and Travis Lee of Shockley's *Say Jesus and Come to Me*. These representations of black lesbian life provide a range of experiences reflected in the lives of the narrators of *BQSW* and thus provided me with some guidance about what themes to focus on during the interviews. The oral histories collected in this book stand in comparison to these works of fiction (and nonfiction) and tell us something about the current material history and conditions of black southern lesbian lives that sometimes mirror and sometimes disavow those depicted in these fictive and nonsouthern representations.[6]

While it took me two years to collect seventy-seven narratives for *Sweet Tea*, in fourteen months I conducted the same number of interviews for *BQSW*. I initially posted a call for participants on Facebook and on a few electronic mailing lists, and within a matter of weeks I was inundated with inquiries about participating. I conducted the very first interviews in August 2012, mostly in North Carolina and Georgia. Between August and September of that year I conducted over thirty interviews—sometimes three in one day—and then had to take a break because I became physically and emotionally exhausted. I was not prepared for the number of stories about sexual abuse and trauma, about which I speak more in chapter 5. The final interview was conducted in September 2014, for a total of seventy-nine—seventy-six of which are included in the book. The women range in age from eighteen to seventy-four and hail from states below the Mason-Dixon Line: Texas, Arkansas, Louisiana, Mississippi, Alabama, Oklahoma, Georgia, Florida, South Carolina, North Carolina, Tennessee, Kentucky, Virginia, Washington, DC, and Maryland. They occupy a range of social classes: factory workers, local government administrators, entrepreneurs, counselors, professors, librarians, schoolteachers, musicians, writers, community organizers, disc jockeys, truck drivers, housewives, and unemployed. Educational background also differed, but most of the women had completed high school, many had had some college education, and a few had postgraduate and professional degrees. The criteria for being interviewed was that the woman be born in a southern state, meaning a state that was below the Mason-Dixon Line, be primarily reared in the South for a significant portion of her life, and be currently living in the South. I made a few exceptions to these criteria if a woman had not been born in the South as I have defined it but who had been reared there as an infant to toddler onward. I also made one exception about what constitutes the "South" and expanded the boundaries of "blackness" by including the narrative of a woman born in Puerto Rico.

The interviews with women were longer than those I conducted with gay men, with most lasting at least ninety minutes and some as long as five hours over two sessions. They were all conducted face to face and audiotaped but not videotaped. Each narrator had the option of remaining anonymous, in which case I have given her a pseudonym, have changed names of people she mentioned, and do not include the specific place where she was born. When a pseudonym is used, the name appears in quotation marks. For those who chose to use their real names, I use their first name only, unless they requested that I use their first and last name—which some women did, as a matter of pride.

Most of the interviews took place at the women's homes or at a mutual friend's house. Unlike the men in *Sweet Tea*, I was never asked to "do" anything during the visit like help cook dinner or run errands. This may have been due to the gendered ways in which women in the South are socialized to "serve" men or, particularly with some of the older women I interviewed, to treat me like one of their own children or nephews. Nonetheless, a few of the women prepared dinner in anticipation of my visit, like Lenore Stackhouse, one of the last women I interviewed, who unfortunately passed away unexpectedly just three months after I interviewed her. She prepared a lovely "Sunday dinner" for me comprised of potato salad, collard greens, baked chicken, rolls, and, of course, sweetened iced tea.

I capture some of these interactions in my introduction to each narrator when she speaks for the first time. In addition to providing her place and year of birth, I provide background information about the circumstances under which we met, a little history about her hometown, and sometimes anecdotes about our meetings—the *mise-en-scène* of the oral history interview itself. Excerpts of some narrators' stories appear in more than one chapter.

Subsequent appearances are introduced only by the narrator's name, place of birth (if given), and birth date.

In general, my interactions with these women—most of whom I was meeting for the first time—were familial and familiar, not in the sense that I *knew* them but in the sense that we were kin based on our southern roots, our queerness, and, I believe, my "soft" masculinity. In fact, during some of the exchanges a few women would refer to me as "girl" or "honey" when responding to a question and then become embarrassed by the slip of tongue. I was heartened by these easy interactions, given the warnings from friends and colleagues that I might not be able to secure women to talk to me for the book and, if I did, they would not be forthcoming about the intimate details of their lives because I am a man. I did have a few women cancel at the last minute or stand me up altogether, but this happened only in Tallahassee, Florida—this was the only city where this happened, and I have no explanation for it. A total of four women failed to follow through with the interview there after agreeing to being a part of the book. They have yet to respond to my follow-up calls to find out what happened or to reschedule.[7]

Before embarking on the research for this book, I understood that the stakes were different because of the gender difference between the researcher and the subjects. Rather than view this as an obstacle, however, I viewed it as an opportunity to engage questions of gender, sexuality, and region across the gender divide. Moreover, I grew up in a single-parent home with a mother who instilled in her children southern manners, grace, and respect for others. And, as I stated above, it was lesbian of color feminism that brought me into my consciousness around my own sexuality. So, it was not a matter of me not knowing how to *act* around these women. It was more about me understanding how my male privilege—despite my upbringing and personal politics—might influence not only how I collected these oral histories but also how my gender might reinscribe some of the very structures and institutions that these women critique in their narratives. Thus, I want to take some time here to walk through my process of collecting these narratives as a way of engaging what Bryant Keith Alexander calls "critical reflexivity," which he defines as "both a demonstration and a call for a greater sense of implicating and complicating how we are always already complicit in the scholarly productions of our labor, and the effects of our positions and positionalities with the diverse communities in which we circulate."[8]

In this respect I am an "outsider/within," to borrow Patricia Hill Collins's phrase,[9] since my interlocutors share many of the same identity markers (e.g., queerness, southernness) and not others (e.g., gender and class position). This experience of conducting research within a community within which I belong but across gender boundaries was not new to me, as I conducted an oral history of my grandmother's life as a live-in domestic worker for my doctoral dissertation research. The power dynamic between the two of us shifted variously as I negotiated being "scholar in charge" and "deferential grandson" and she negotiated being "subject of study" and "grandmother in charge." These power dynamics are inescapable within the context of oral history and ethnographic research. It is a matter of the researcher being aware of such dynamics and approaching and working through them with a sense of ethics and moral responsibility. Alexander perhaps sums it up best when he writes: "These are the moral issues of avoiding egoism and promoting cultural knowledge as a mechanism for generating critical reflexive processes in/for audiences. And the moral issues of dealing with voice as cultures of thought."[10] Thus, my methodology for collecting these oral histories was guided by a sense of ethics and a moral obligation to render these women's lives in a way that acknowledges my male privilege—not just in the interview setting but also in the world. This latter point, however, is again one of the reasons that I chose to do this work in the first place: as an act of male feminist praxis.

Indeed, much of my work as a scholar has been about the celebration and promotion of women's lives—the research on my grandmother's life as a domestic worker, drawing on her black folk feminism to critique the field of queer studies,[11] providing a platform for black women solo artists to showcase their work, and collaborating with black feminist colleagues to team-teach courses on feminism and queer studies.[12] My scholarly and political praxis, therefore, is decidedly feminist. But not in the sense that Joy James critiques what she calls "opportunistic feminism" by "profeminists," (straight) male scholars of color who are seemingly (in James's estimation) down with the female cause but who nonetheless "see most women as supporting helpmates or damsels to be succored."[13] James's suspiciousness about the motivations of male academics that identify as feminist is well warranted, based on the usurpation of black women scholars' control over their own work by their male colleagues. And while all of James's examples of such poaching are by self-identified heterosexual men, I know, too, that gay men also engage in sexist and misogynist behavior—even those who presume to be in solidarity with their lesbian sisters. In fact, I remember a gay male couple who are friends of mine sharing a story about socializing on another friend's sailboat in which a lesbian guest and they got into a discussion about the AIDS epidemic, in which she suggested that, if the disease had infected and affected lesbians more disproportionately than gay men, gay men would have "stepped over women's diseased bodies to get to the club instead of helping them." My friends thought her comment was appalling and an exaggeration, but I don't know that she was too far off the mark, for the gay male community benefits from patriarchy and does not always work to dismantle it—even in solidarity with those with whom they share a common sexual identity or affinity or despite the fact that patriarchy and misogyny undergird homophobia. Nonetheless, this does not mean that all men—straight, gay, or queer—are beyond doing ethical, self-reflexive, antisexist work. I can never totally "undo" my male privilege—a privilege, a might add, that is never absolute, as it is contingent in various contexts in relation to my race, class, and sexuality. But what I can do is the work that my soul was called to do: to work to destroy oppressive institutions of power, including patriarchy.

Within the context of the oral history interviews for *BQSW*, my disavowal of patriarchy consisted of me taking a feminist approach to oral history. An example of this was eschewing what Kristina Minister calls the "standard oral history frame," which "denies women the communication form that supports the topics women value."[14] Although Minister recommends that only women should conduct interviews of other women to truly honor women's communication patterns (a point that I think has an essentialist component), I believe that the ways in which I conducted the interviews with the women in this research allowed for more flexibility in terms of having a set of questions but not necessarily privileging getting through the questions as the most important aspect of the interview. Many times I only got to ask a question every fifteen or twenty minutes, such as when I interviewed Iris in Atlanta. I might have asked Iris a total of ten questions, despite the interview lasting five hours over two meetings! Further, Minister argues that male oral historians focus more on "activities and facts" than on "feelings and attitudes," which women value more. This was definitely not the case with this research. In fact, many of the questions asked the women to describe how they felt about a particular event in their lives or their beliefs about something. For example, one of the questions I asked was, How do you *feel* about the life choices that you have made in light of being a black lesbian? Another was, Do you *feel* a sense of community among black lesbians here in your town? These, among other questions, that asked the women about their *thoughts* actually privilege the women as feeling and thinking subjects rather than as objects from which facts and information are extracted and abstracted.

Moreover, I believe the fact that I express a soft, quiet masculinity that is sometimes read as effeminacy allowed me to connect with these women in ways that I would not have otherwise been able to do. I am soft-spoken, polite, and a good listener—all self-effacing attributes that helped set a tone of openness and vulnerability. Paradoxically, my being a man with these attributes provided a space for some of the women to be even more open about their experiences. When I shared with "Lisa" that a few of my academic colleagues were skeptical about women opening up to me because of my gender, she said that the opposite was true for her. She revealed that she agreed to the interview *because* I am a man, for she felt that a woman interviewer would judge some of the decisions she had made in her life, like having an abortion or being sexually promiscuous with men. I also suspect that women shared certain things with me because they would assume that women would already know some of these experiences because they are women. This was one advantage to being an "outsider/within."

Similar to performance scholar Della Pollock, who theorizes the power dynamic between researcher and researched in her work on birthing narratives, I entered each interview with a sense of humility and vulnerability. Pollock writes: "I made myself . . . vulnerable to being moved. Listening and writing, I saw myself as the register of someone else's power. Against the grain of current obsessions with the power of the researcher to shape, tame, appropriate, and control the worlds he or she investigates . . . I more often than not felt unnerved and overwhelmed, 'othered,' interrogated, propelled into landscapes of knowing and not knowing I would not otherwise have dared enter."[15] This vulnerability Pollock describes was key to the empathetic connection I had with many of my interlocutors. Indeed, there were moments when I was so enraptured by a powerful story being told that time seemed to be suspended as I entered the life world being created before my eyes. I can think of two instances in which I became so emotional due to the intensity of the story—both about sexual trauma—that the narrator actually began to comfort me: "It's alright, Baby. I'm okay. I done worked through this"—all the while rubbing my back and handing me a tissue. In another instance, the narrator and I just sat in silence for what seemed an eternity, while we both sobbed and comforted each other. These are examples of a feminist practice of oral history and ethnography in which the researcher emphasizes empathy, collaboration, intersubjectivity, and a sharing of the emotional labor to tell the story. As Linda Shopes reminds us, "The peculiar intimacy available to strangers who share an important experience seems to create in at least some interviews a social space where normal power relations perhaps get blunted."[16]

Feminist sociologist Judith Stacey questions, "Can there be a feminist ethnography?" While she is dubious about a "fully" feminist ethnography, she concedes: "There can be (indeed there are) ethnographies that are partially feminist, accounts of culture enhanced by the application of feminist perspectives. There also can and should be feminist research that is rigorously self-aware and therefore humble about the partiality of its ethnographic vision and its capacity to represent self and other."[17] Given my position as a male oral historian and ethnographer, and keeping in mind the critique of male scholars who do research on women as posed by Joy James and others, I, too, concede that *BQSW* is a "partially feminist" ethnography, yet despite its feminist partiality, I believe that the benefits of the research far outweigh the potential pitfalls, for to not conduct this research based *simply* on the fact that I am a man would be to fall prey to what the late performance ethnographer Dwight Conquergood called the "skeptic's copout," a pitfall of ethnographic research that retreats to quietism, paralysis, and cynicism based on "difference." According to Conquergood, this position is the most morally reprehensible on his moral map of performative stances toward the other, which also includes the "custodian's rip-off," "curator's exhibitionism," and "enthusiast's infatuation," because the skeptic's copout forecloses dialogue altogether.[18] On the contrary, I engaged this research and these women's narratives not just to initiate a dialogue but also to create a living archive of black women's sexual history in the South.

I wish now to pivot from my role as a male oral historian and ethnographer to discuss oral history and performance as key methods for collecting the oral history of black southern women who love women. I could have chosen from a number of methods to chronicle the history of black lesbians from and living in the southern part of the country, including a more traditional archival project whereby I spent time poring over ephemera, newspaper articles, diaries, and other historical documents to piece together a historical narrative of southern black same-sex-loving women. My desire to use oral history, however, was undergirded by my investment and training in performance studies, which privileges the body and the body necessarily as archive.[19] In the act of performing one's life history, the self is affirmed through the interaction with another who bears witness to the story being told. As Madison suggests in her summary of Kristin Langellier and Eric Peterson's theorization of embodiment in oral history, "Narrative as *embodied* emphasizes the living presence of bodily contact. Bodies are within touch, not simply representing, displaying, or portraying a past moment."[20] Zora Neale Hurston's character Janie in the novel *Their Eyes Were Watching God* comes into voice through the telling of her story to her best friend, Phoeby.

In her description of Janie and Phoeby on Janie's back porch, Hurston makes note of the two women's proximity—their closeness—that provides a safe space for Janie to share her tale: "They sat there in the fresh young darkness close together, Phoeby eager to feel and do through Janie, but hating to show her zest for fear it might be thought mere curiosity. Janie full of that oldest human longing—self revelation."[21] I played Phoeby to many of my interlocutors' Janie as I bore witness to their affirmation of self, their trials, tribulations, and trivialities, their reveries, repulsions, and recollections. Through laughter, tears, and contemplation, I witnessed these women reveal themselves to me and to themselves—sometimes for the first time. For black women this is an important feature of finding their own voice, as historically they have been silenced. Gwendolyn Etter-Lewis argues, "It is oral narratives that is ideally suited to revealing the 'multilayered texture of black women's lives.'"[22] And if this is true for heterosexual black women, it is especially true for black women with same-sex desire. There exists a tradition of heterosexual black women's storytelling, but that has not been the case for black lesbians outside of fiction.[23]

I do not wish to overstate or romanticize oral history as a method for archiving southern black lesbian history. I am keenly aware of the paradox of oral histories since its transmission occurs through text. As Claudia Salazar points out, "Once discourse becomes text, its openness as dialogue, together with its evocative and performance elements, are lost: the punctuation and silences of speech are gone . . . it is edited, translated, and, finally, given a title."[24] Despite this conundrum I am not just interested in translation of these women's words from oral to written text; I am also interested in the value of what the oral history does for the storyteller herself, as well as detailing the ethnographic process—the relationship between teller and listener. This is not to say that I am not interested in the actual historical content of what the narrator shares, but not in a way that suggests an investment in the "truth," rather, more about the validation of the narrator's subjectivity. Madison suggests that

> oral history performances . . . do not function as factual reports or as objective evidence, nor are they pure fictions of history. Instead, they represent to us one moment *of* history and how that moment *in* history is *remembered* through a *particular* subjectivity. . . . It is at the matrix of materiality, memory, subjectivity, performance, and imagination, and experience that memory culminates in oral history performance, a culmination of layers that are all mutually formed by each other.[25]

Thus, unlike some oral histories, I am more invested in "what the narrator remembers and values and how . . . she expresses memory" than the validity of the narrative itself. This is why I do not offer an analysis of the narratives, for I want them to stand as quotidian forms of theorizing. As black feminist critic Barbara Christian writes, "Our [people of color] theorizing is often in narrative forms, in the stories we create, in riddles and proverbs, in the play with language, because dynamic rather than fixed ideas seem more to our liking."[26] The dynamism of these black same-sex-loving women's narratives, therefore, not only offers insight into ways of knowing that legitimize their own lives but also helps us understand the complexities and contradictions of race, sexuality, region, gender, and class more generally. What I offer by way of analysis, then, is more of the ethnographic encounter—the sight, sound, smell, taste, and touch of the interview scene, to amplify context and "refigure the small details and the taken for granted."[27]

Unlike in *Sweet Tea*, I have been a bit more judicious in editing the narratives in *BQSW*. Part of this was because the interviews were much longer, requiring me to distill them to discrete stories. Sometimes this required me to piece together various parts of the narrative, especially if the narrator discussed a topic in various parts of the interview. I indicate jumps in the narrative with a line of asterisks. I have also edited some of the narratives for clarity and continuity. For instance, I have deleted words and phrases such as "um," "you know," and "like" when they were not a part of the narrator's typical speech pattern and used as vocal fillers. I also edited stammers or incomplete thoughts. These deletions are indicated by ellipses in brackets, while unbracketed ellipses indicate a narrator's own pauses while thinking. Where possible I have tried to honor the vernacular colloquialisms and cadences of southern speech through nontraditional spellings of words.

Sometimes stories are like honey: slow to pour. Once it gets started, though, it's hard to stop. Its stream of luscious gold covers lots of ground, ignoring boundaries as it sticks to and spreads over surfaces. So, too, did the narrators of *BQSW* speak their stories, smoothly gliding between and underneath the crevices of their lives. Thus, the chapters I have chosen are not neat categories of themes that emerged across the narratives as much as they are signposts for the direction of the honey pour. In other words, while themes of "coming out," "religion," and "sex" are prevalent in the narratives, those subjects are often covered within a broader context of subjects and themes. As with *Sweet Tea*, I focus not solely on the narrators' sexuality but on their sexuality in the context of their whole lives in the South.

I have divided the book into two parts. Part I focuses on growing up in and living in the South and comprises seven chapters organized around themes that emerged across various narratives, with the understanding that there is considerable overlap. The chapters include excerpts from the longer oral history interviews. This curatorial decision allowed me to include a range of perspectives on a particular topic based on the narrator's age, place of birth, social class, and so on. Chapter 1 covers stories of early childhood in the South, including poverty, racism, and educational experiences. Chapter 2 covers stories of motherhood and mother-daughter relationships. Chapter 3 highlights stories of gender nonconformity. Chapter 4 engages the theme of religion, church, and spirituality. The narratives in this chapter diverge from common stories of religion in the South in terms of the church being a "safe haven" as narrated by black gay southern men. In these narratives the women speak about church as obligation rather than as a place of enjoyment, and about how as they got older they found other forms of spiritual affirmation. Chapter 5 covers the broad topic of sexuality. Eschewing hard-and-fast categories of sexual identity, the narratives in this chapter disaggregate sexual behavior, sexual desire, and sexual identity. The chapter is divided into subsections of sexual awakening, sexual pleasure, and sexual violence and trauma. Chapter 6 features love stories and female friendship. From young couples who are still finding their way to couples who have been together for decades, this chapter covers the joy and pains of courtship among these women, as well as the platonic but no less intimate relationships these women form between and among one another. Chapter 7 engages the art, activism, and political views of the narrators. As many of the women are artists, they discuss how their art reflects their sexuality, but also their politics. Some of the stories provide a bird's-eye view of current black lesbian organizations to which they belong, while others provide a historical overview of organizations that used to be in existence in their communities.

Part II of the book showcases the stories of six extraordinary women whose lives, when taken as a whole, stand out from the others. I do not mean this in the sense that their lives are more important, only that these particular life histories narrate overcoming extraordinary circumstances or challenges. Each of these women is the focus of a singular chapter. Chapter 8 provides insight into a woman born in Puerto Rico and reared in Spanish Harlem who lived in Atlanta for a major part of her life before retiring to San Juan to care for her mother. Chapter 9 focuses on a woman who overcame sexual and physical abuse, dyslexia, and colorism to find a partner with whom she found her true self. Chapter 10 is the first of two chapters that record the lives of women who battle their way back from drug addiction and incarceration. In this chapter, the narrator chronicles how she first succumbed to and then rebounded from drug addiction, but not before being incarcerated and losing her children. Chapter 11 is the bookend to the previous chapter, sharing the story of a woman who also battled drug and alcohol addition, incarceration, and the loss of a child but found her way back to sobriety and to a healthy relationship with her daughter and grandchildren. Chapter 12 follows the adventures of a gender-nonconforming sexagenarian who defies the southern conventions of self-presentation to stand in her own truth. And chapter 13 chronicles the life story of a woman who found refuge in books early in life as a way to cope with abject poverty, familial dysfunction, and prematurely being saddled with the responsibility of raising four of her younger siblings after her mother's death.

These women's tales have laid bare both the injustices of being black, queer, southern, and a woman and the joys of finding a home in the bountiful bosom, curvaceous hip, or soft midriff of womanly sameness. Together, these stories of love, laughter, loss, and longing till the soil of southern landscapes, creating fertile ground from which other stories may emerge and grow. My journey back to the South to speak to my sisters has occasioned my own growth as a scholar, black gay man, and southerner and affirmed for me that bearing witness to these others who are not so other is, perhaps, one of the most important gifts one human can give to another. Let the journey begin.

G.R.I.T.S.

Stories of Growing Up Black, Female, and Queer

....

I "You looking for some more grits to interview?" Zakiya yelled to me across Barcelona, a tapas restaurant and bar in Inman Park in Atlanta. She knew that I was stumped by the question as much as I was stunned to run into her, especially because the last time I had seen her was in Chicago almost a year before. A mutual friend had introduced us when she moved to Chicago from Birmingham, Alabama. After living in Chicago for less than a year, she moved back to Atlanta. She now lives in Brooklyn. After greeting her with a hardy hug, I asked her to repeat the question. "I knew you didn't know what the hell I was talking about," she laughed. "G.R.I.T.S. Girls raised in the South. Get it?" She was right—I had no clue what she meant. "Oh! That's what that means. You know I'm going to have to use that in the book," I replied.[1] She then went on to provide me with the contact of an ex-girlfriend of hers in Birmingham who might be willing to be interviewed—a lead I followed up the next day.

Like grits, these women's lives are substantive but seemingly bland for those who don't know their complexity once condiments like butter, sugar, salt, pepper, and even ketchup are added. The point is the narrators whose lives are chronicled here reflect the broad range of experiences of black southern women regardless of sexual desire, but like adding anything to grits, their lives take on a more nuanced flavor once sexual desire is taken into account. Gender, too, is a key component that distinguishes these narrators' experiences from those of gay men. The expectations for women coming of age within southern culture dramatically diverge from those for their male counterparts, which include gendered dress codes, chores, language, career trajectory, and a whole host of other behavioral and cultural expectations. There social and cultural mores are also inflected through class, which, for some women who grew up in abject poverty, meant that their exposure to sexual violence (chronicled in chapter 5) increased exponentially due to their proximity to male family members with whom they shared sleeping quarters. Class also shaped how their families dealt with their same-sex attraction—but not always in ways that align with stereotypical notions of a higher socioeconomic status equating with sexual liberalism or a working-class status equating with sexual conservatism. As many of the narrators attest, familial bonds often ran deeper than homophobia. Indeed, one of the more surprising discoveries in many of these stories was the number of women who shared close bonds with their mothers—some of whom also revealed their same-sex desire but for whatever reason chose not to act on it.

The narrators' responses to these different codes of expectation also run the gamut from submission to full-on defiance. Unsurprisingly, many of their responses hinge on the region of the South in which they were reared—that is, rural versus urban, East Coast versus Deep South. For instance, those women who were reared in or in close proximity to urban cities like Washington, DC, or Atlanta experienced less pressure to necessarily follow a traditional career path based on their gender than those who were reared in more rural areas. On the other hand, those women from small towns actually were freer to transgress traditional dress codes, such as wearing dresses, because some gendered clothing was not conducive to working on a farm or performing other chores.

The stories are divided into seven categories: "It's Thick Here: Race, Gender, and Sexuality in the South," "Does Your Mama Know? Motherhood and Mother-Daughter Relationships," "Walk like a Man, Talk like a Woman: Gender Nonconformity. "I Found God in Myself and I Loved Her Fiercely: Religion and Spirituality," "A Taste of Honey: Sex among Women Who Love Women," "I'm Sweet on You: Stories of Love, Courtship, and Intimacy," and "The Work My Soul was Called to Do." These categories are not rigid, as some of the narratives bleed into one another or into topics addressed in later chapters. They merely provide a general organization to themes that arose across stories when I asked women to talk about their early childhood memories and their lives later in life. I have not included stories from all of the narrators who spoke to me; in some instances, there is more than one excerpt from a narrator's story. I provide background information about each narrator when they are first introduced in the book but reference only an abbreviated form of that information when they appear thereafter.

It's Thick Here
Race, Gender, and Sexuality in the South

1

Many of the narrators in this book come from working-class backgrounds, even if they are currently securely middle class. Despite their socioeconomic status then or now, race played a major role in their life experiences. Whether having to attend segregated schools in the 1950s or experiencing racism at predominately white institutions now, these women's class position did not mitigate the structural and institutional forms of racism that impact every aspect of their lives. For black southern women who love women in particular, the by now "holy trinity" of academic humanities and social science research—race, class, and gender—is no less pertinent here. And yet, as discussed above, region and sexuality complicate racial, class, and gender experience when one adds to the discussion the history of a region (the South) and the history of sexuality (of African Americans generally and African American women specifically). The title of this chapter quotes one of the narrators: "it's thick here"; the "it" indexes the racism, sexism, homophobia, and classism they experience throughout their lives. Like southern humidity, the thickness of these oppressions can be suffocating at times. These women's survival strategies under these conditions, therefore, take many different forms—drugs, alcohol, education, bearing children, art, and so on—all of which reflect the pains and joys of being black, female, queer, and southern.

Anita

I have known Anita practically all of my life. We were born and raised in Hickory, a small town located in the foothills of western North Carolina. She was born in 1964. She and her partner live in a home that Anita purchased on her modest salary from working the overnight shift in a T-shirt factory and working as a DJ on the weekends. Growing up, Anita was what most would describe as a tomboy, but neither my childhood friends nor I necessarily equated tomboyish girls with sexuality. It was not until I was much older that I began to note that Anita might be "that way." She comes from a large family, the sixth of ten children by her father. She has a sister who is just one year older than her who started bringing a female "friend" home with her from college in the late 1980s. Anita watched how her parents dealt with her sister's same-sex relationship, which was basically not to acknowledge it for what it was, and decided that she would not reveal her own attraction to women. It was not until after her mother's death that she began living with a woman herself. I reconnected with Anita in 2012 after hearing her on National Public Radio speaking against Amendment 1, the North Carolina anti-gay marriage legislation that defined marriage between one man and one woman. Anita's father, with whom she is very close and who is supportive of her personally, was a proponent of the legislation and was also featured in the NPR story. I reached out to Anita after hearing the story to ask her if she would be willing to be a part of this book, and she happily agreed. The interview took place on August 28, 2012, at her home.

Any place would provide a better life for me as a gay person other than the South. [Laughter] It don't have to be a region. It could be another state out of the South. Out West, anywhere out of the South, anywhere away from this place. The South is just Baptists, religion, [and] the Bible Belt. And they just so stuck in their ways and beliefs and traditions. And the further north . . . or out west you go, that starts to break down fast. Tradition goes out the window when the Bible Belt stops.

But yet you feel a certain level of comfort here?

I do. The comfort here is my family. The comfort here is this area, being born and raised in this area. Once I get out of this area and I go on the other side of that [railroad] track, it becomes disturbing and hateful, and then that makes me want to leave. It makes me want to just say, "Man, I hate this place because of what I see on the other side of the tracks." And it doesn't necessarily have anything to do with being gay; it's just being black. They used to say being black and being a man was two strikes in the South, but it's being black and being gay now.

And when you say the other side of the tracks, you mean on the north side of Hickory where the white folks live?

Yeah. It's when I go on that side I develop this sense of hatred not only for Hickory, but just for the state, for the state of North Carolina. [. . .] It never dawned on me until I did this party [on] Saturday in Maiden. I go to work, I come to the stop, I come past the fire department, and I make a left, and when I come to a stop sign my job is facing me. But I have to make a left to go into the parking lot. And when I make a left to go into the parking lot, I cross over the railroad track and I go park in the parking lot. And it didn't dawn on me—I never even thought about it until Saturday—that on the other side of that railroad track is predominantly black, and on that side of that railroad track, it's predominantly white. And when I did that party Saturday it made me dislike North Carolina even more. I heard that saying as a child years ago: "Any time you cross over the tracks, the neighborhoods change." I didn't know that and I mean Saturday when I crossed over there, when I went to the other side of that railroad track, I couldn't believe it. I was like, "Oh my gosh, man, please don't tell me this is true." . . . I don't know anything about Maiden. All I've ever seen in Maiden was white people. I didn't know black people lived in Maiden. But right behind that mill: all blacks.

. . . .

Darlene Hudson

Darlene was born the eldest of three children in 1961 in Las Vegas, Nevada and reared from a very early age in Fordyce, Arkansas. Fordyce is located in the southeast corner of Arkansas and has a population less than five thousand, half of which are African American. One of several activists I interviewed in Atlanta, Darlene is a force of nature. She has a big personality, infectious laughter, and a very engaging storytelling style. This made sense after she revealed that she is a musician and served as a choir director and minister of music for many years. Indeed, her relationship to religion and spirituality diverges from that of many of the other women I interviewed, owing mostly to her close ties to her Pentecostal upbringing in the church and especially the choir. She lives with her Buddhist partner in Atlanta. The interview took place on August 9, 2012, at her home.

F-O-R-D-Y-C-E. I can see it in my head. Fordyce, Arkansas. And depending on where you're staying in Arkansas it can be *Foe-dice*. That's how they say it. But you know, just for reading, it's "Fordyce." [. . .] I can remember first grade in Arkansas, and probably maybe until about the second or third grade or something. My mother got married and then we lived in Jefferson City, Missouri. And I think I stayed there right until about the fifth grade. My mother and my stepfather moved to Arkansas and set up in Pine Bluff, Arkansas. My mother had some level of education in terms of postsecondary education, but she didn't complete it. I remember she worked for the Internal Revenue Service one time. One time she worked in a factory, so she worked where she could work. But my stepfather was a chef, so that had a little bit to do with why we kind of moved because working for the Cotton Belt at that time—I don't know if anybody remember the Cotton Belt—but the Cotton Belt was a train and it had like business men. They had a car and that's how they traveled, the railroad men. And so [my stepfather] was the cook. [. . .] That's how he made his living. He was a lot of other things too, security, whatever he had to do to make it work. So anyway, I consider Arkansas home, and I spent fifth grade until I graduated in Pine Bluff, Arkansas.

[. . .] The interesting thing about my family that we all take a little pride in, that could be controversial, is that they were bootleggers. They sold whiskey, and I can remember as a child [being] in the kitchen and all the windows were painted white. That was to keep folks from looking in to see what they was doing. I didn't understand that as a child, but when I got older, that's what my mama told us. She said, "Yeah, that was to keep the people from looking in on the bootleggers."

This was in Pine Bluff?

This was in Fordyce, my grandparents' place. Pine Bluff came fifth grade. We're modernized now. [Laughter] Down in the country, my folks were bootleggers. They were the first one with indoor plumbing and the first to have a car. And in Fordyce, you know how you have like Stone Mountain [suburb of Atlanta], they had the same kind of little setup but just in a rural way. So, in Mount Tabor, sitting up on this hill, my folks were kind of respected because they were bootleggers, they had a little bit more money and access to resources than most [. . .]. But as kids, all of us, my cousin could really tell it. He said, "You know [. . .] we really didn't come up like poor." But we came up with the understanding that you had to work to get what you want, and I can honestly tell you every member in my family that's age-wise has a job, even some of them who didn't have jobs, they working now. My little old niece, she thought she was going to ride welfare. But honey, she soon found out welfare wasn't taking her nowhere, so that girl got her a little job and she's in school. So, everybody knows the value and importance of working to achieve so you can be stable. Everybody has a home. [. . .]

Do you remember where you went to elementary, middle school, and high school?

I most certainly do. I sure do. When I was in elementary I went to what they call, now you said that, and then I can't even think of the name of it. But I'm going to tell you how they framed me. This is in rural Arkansas. It was a white school and a colored school. And when I started school, that's when they first started letting blacks go to the white school, so I went to "the white school" and that's what we always called it. I'm sure it has a real name, but that's what we called it.

You called it "the white school"?

Yeah. "Oh, you going to the white school." And I remember doing my first grade year and I had a white teacher. I sure did. My second year, I had *another* white teacher. And then, like I said, we moved. My mother got married and then we moved to, you know what? I have. I should run up and get that. Can I run up and get that just to reference some things because my mother is a great historian. [Goes to get a box of papers that her mother has kept on her.] But anyway that's just a caveat. Just a little extra thing. But my mother gave me like all of these papers [when] she was cleaning up [. . .]; this woman has kept up with everything, from my kindergarten school in Fordyce, Miss Bradley, and then every report card you can think of. I mean, just about every [paper], from the first grade all the way through. So yeah, I can tell you it was Fordyce Elementary School. But when we were coming up we called it "the white school," and I had to look on here to tell you just what was it called: Fordyce Elementary School. Because J. E. Wallace was the colored school. That's where everybody went. That's where my mother graduated from, J. E. Wallace, and even before that it was called the Dallas County Training School that she actually graduated from.

Now what year would this have been?

For me?

Yes. Because you said you were the first class to integrate?

[Studies the pictures closely and talks to herself] This year right here this is my first year of school? Oh no, this is grade two. Here's grade one, so this was in '68 that I went there.

And was that the first year that black kids went to that school?

You know I'm the first, yeah.

And so that would have been well after Brown v. Board of Education.

Right. It moved slow. So I think that's how that history go, but I just remember so distinctly that it was the white school. We were going to the white school, so that's where we went: to the white school. It was actually Fordyce Grammar School. [. . .]

What were your family's attitudes about people that were different from you either racially, religiously, sexual orientation? Was there talk about people who were different from you in your household growing up?

We didn't know anything about anything different. I'm serious. Even in the world of the whole gay thing. My first encounter with the possibility of there could be same-gender-loving people was they were referencing one of the guys from the church and somebody said, "He's like this." So, whatever "this" was, that's what it was. [. . .] But now in terms of black and white and racial things, my parents, my mother, my grandfather, and even my grandmother, they really kept us like this [puts her hands on her chest]. [. . .] Our community was all black. And if you went in another direction it was all white, so there wasn't any kids playing together, and we didn't really think anything about it. I didn't think anything about it, even when I would go to school and I had my teacher and classmates were white. I guess I kind of got . . . a little bit of an awakening, just a little bit when we lived in Missouri and we had a Jewish friend next door. And me and Eddie became very good friends, and another guy, his name was Daniel, and they were both white . . . the neighborhood was very mixed, and you know the little kids all played together. But now my mother was real clear. You don't go up in their house, and they don't come up in your house, and that was the difference, and we just was like, "okay." I was scared, and the big thing was they didn't invite us in either. But my mama was clear. You don't go up in their house. Y'all can play outside, and they don't come up in your house. I guess she was like, "Let's keep it even," and that's what we did, but it was not like, "Oh mama, why can't we?" It was like, okay, cool, long as we could play. We wasn't trying to be up in the house. We were just trying to play as kids.

· ·

Dedra

Dedra was born in 1966 in Prentiss, Mississippi. Although the population of Prentiss is less than fifteen hundred, it is birthplace to a number of famous people, including songwriter and record producer Clyde Otis, boxer Toxey Hall, and professional basketball player Al Jefferson. Located sixty miles southeast of Jackson, Prentiss is typical of many small towns in Mississippi where everyone knows everyone and race relations are strained. Dedra is a soft-spoken woman with a spirit of fire. She's quite an outspoken person in the community who actually ran for city coroner in 1995. She runs her family funeral home, the only black funeral home in Prentiss. She and her wife, Laurinda (also interviewed this book; see chapter 2), were married in New York before it was legal in every state and live openly as spouses in Prentiss. During my visit, Dedra and Laurinda took me to the one "fancy" restaurant in Prentiss, known for its seafood buffet, Country Fisherman, which has since closed. As we sat eating our fried fish and hush puppies, Dedra commented how some folks were staring at us, "but they better not say anything," she warned. This quiet, no-nonsense attitude is indicative of how Dedra runs her business and her life. The interview took place on August 22, 2013, at her family's funeral home.

My father died when I was eight, and of course they had the business.
And what was the business?
Johnson Funeral Home. And after he died my mother took over the business, and I had six brothers and one sister. My sister was the oldest, and she was a nurse, and she had moved away to Jackson and had a family up there. My oldest brother kind of stepped in as the backbone. He was in medical school when my father died. After my father died he had a nervous breakdown, came out of medical school, and came back to work in the funeral home, went to mortuary science school to run the funeral home for my mother. My mother must've been in her forties. My daddy was like forty-four when he died. She had all of us, so seven children, one in college, and the rest in high school, and I was in third grade. So, the competition, it's a small town. The competition took an opportunity to hit her below her knees as far as business. They put on a lot of rumors that she was gonna close down, she was a woman, she couldn't run the business, she couldn't do it, and she's from Alabama, scared of the white man. And she fought relentlessly [with] the white people. And when I say white people, [I mean] bill collectors, not white people coming to take the business, but bill collectors. She fought relentlessly [with] black people talking about her. Just, you name it, they did it. I watched her from eight years old just struggle with the business but . . . once my oldest brother got his mortuary science license he came and he stayed probably about four years and helped her get the business kind of leveled out . . . after the impact of my father dying. And once he did that then he went back to Ole Miss to pharmacy school and he finished and he was a pharmacist. He was her backbone. [. . .]
Where did you fall in the [family]?
I was a baby. Yeah, I was a baby; I was right behind her every day watching her struggle. I used to wonder. I used to hear her say, "Lord have mercy," and [as] an eight-year-old, it frightened me because my father had just died and not knowing what she meant by "Lord have mercy." I thought she was

going to die, so that stayed with me years and years and years and years, and just to watch her just have to deal with this. So I didn't have a childhood, basically. I didn't have a childhood because my brothers . . . went out into the world and experienced drugs and alcohol, and they come back and they want her to give them money, and they want to use the vehicles that she used for the funeral services, and just kind of took advantage of her. And I watched that, but she still stayed strong. So, everything kind of leveled out then, that was in '75. So, her son in '93 died. He was gay. He was HIV positive, so we took another hit, but at this point I knew that the responsibility was going to be on me because I was her right hand and kind of expected that. So in '91, she retired. Two years before he passed away she actually retired to take care of him, and in '93 he passed away, and I took over the business and that's my job.

What are your best memories of growing up in the South?

Going with my father before he died out to the pasture to feed the cows, when he would get out the truck and he would say "Woo" they would all come to him, and riding in the truck with him. I think that's why I have a love for trucks. But the little time that I remembered of him, if he had lived, wouldn't be in Prentiss. I wouldn't be here. So that and just being out, being able to go outside and just kind of be free. After he died then of course I had an aunt that stayed next door, and her husband had a farm that's probably about four or five miles down, and in the evening times I would go down with him and we get on the tractor and go feed the cows and ride, you know, out in the countryside.

What are your worst memories?

My brothers being on drugs and alcoholics. It wasn't segregation or anything like that because I wasn't really exposed to that. Them being on drugs. All of them went through a period of being that way but they survived. They went to recovery and one had to go twice but they finally got it together, but to watch that, and I think even though I was gay that helped to turn me further against men. It did. [. . .]

So, you associated being on drugs with being a man?

Alcoholic: I associated that with men. I associated the way they took advantage of my mother. I associated that with a man because she couldn't drive and it was either she give them the keys to what they want, or they were raising a fuss or threatening to do things all because it was something they want to go to do. And all the same time she's trying to run a business so she could feed them. [. . .]

I've still got to go back to my mama. Watching her . . . struggle helped me to be humble, helped me to appreciate [things] because even though she had a business, there were times where—now our lights were never turned off, water was never turned off—but there were times that she didn't have money to do other things, and it made me humble, [taught me how] to appreciate, and not look down on people that don't have. And try to at least give everybody a fair shot and try to kind of understand what the next person is going through because even though [they knew] my grandfather, [people thought] the Johnsons . . . had everything. The Johnsons were so high up on this pole that when I would go out in different places when I was young they'd say, "Oh you're a Johnson, you're one of them Johnsons, y'all got this, y'all got that." When I got grown, I was looking for what the Johnsons had, and guess what? The Johnsons didn't have nothing. They didn't have nothing. And to live under that Johnson facade: "The Johnsons, oh you one of them Johnsons. You one of them Johnsons with that good hair. Y'all got [everything], your granddaddy had this, your granddaddy had that, y'all got that." You know when you go in the store, "Let me have five dollars. You a Johnson, you got money. You got this. You got that." And to grow up, no we didn't have that. We didn't have it so probably . . . watching my mother . . . helped me to be humble . . . I probably could hold a conversation with anybody. I don't know if it was so much the South or if it was just her.

. . . .

Kate
Kate was born in Winston-Salem, North Carolina, in 1981, the eldest of four children. Winston-Salem is located in what is known as the Piedmont of North Carolina and is the fourth largest city in the state, with a population of 230,000. It is the home of R. J. Reynolds Tobacco Company and the famous Krispy Kreme donut. Kate now lives in Durham, North Carolina, and has her own bowtie company called Distinguished Cravat. A self-described "southern belle," Kate's gender and sartorial presentation put a twist on that stereotypical image, as she appears more as what one might think of as a dandy. Her story is filled with traumatic experiences of growing up poor, sexual violence, and exposure to drugs. Nonetheless, hers is a tale of resilience as she narrates how she worked around her life circumstances to become an entrepreneur. The interview took place on August 29, 2012, in Durham.

Even though we were a close-knit community, you still had people killing one another. And I think as a child I saw so many people killed, which is why in my older days I deal with death different than a lot of my friends. They've never—a lot of my friends today other than their grandparents or something, great grandparents, they've never really had an experience. But I mean you look out your window as a kid and there's a guy laying on the ground and he's been shot and he was one of your uncle's friends. And now he's dead. I would just cry. [. . .] But the community as a whole, it was one of those communities where if you needed some ketchup you could knock on your neighbor's door and ask for some ketchup. The one thing I will say, my house was clean. We always had food. My mom always washed our clothes. Some of my other friends, they weren't that fortunate. I would go to their house and there would only be an ice tray in the freezer. I remember this. And so, like I said those were the kids with the ice trays in there, those were the houses where we could chill at. Because either their parents were on drugs and they were gone like all the time, or either they would just party or they would drink and it was like we weren't even there, if you will. But like I said, there were a lot of people who killed each other because of drugs, and so that was one thing that really made me question just how much did they love one another. I remember my next-door neighbor; he walks up the street and shoots the guy in the head who was like his best friend. And I see the police going up the street and I ask, "What happened?" And my friend tells me, "You know Jonathan killed [man's name]." He just walked up the street and blew his brains out. Just a lot of death. [. . .]

. . . .

Kerrie
Born in Fort Lauderdale, Florida, in 1970, Kerrie is the youngest of two children. Her older brother and father were killed in a plane crash when she was an infant. At the age of five she moved to Atlanta with her mother and her stepfather. Though currently married to a woman, Kerrie's first marriage was to a man who asked her to marry him soon after she graduated from college. Like many women I interviewed, Kerrie followed a path of least resistance when it came to partnering with men because, according to her, "It was an easy path to go from not being married to being married. I didn't have to work very hard at it." The interview took place on August 7, 2012, at the Auburn Avenue Research Library.

Well, I was born in Florida. My mother, Gwendolyn, was born in Mobile, and my father, Frederick, was born in DC. But I never knew my father. My father and my brother who was . . . I believe he was six years old at the time or eight, died when I was six months old. He was eight; I was six months old. In a plane crash. And so, my father liked to fly planes. But I didn't know very much of that until much later. So, what I remember about my childhood, growing up in, like, Florida, was that a lot of people took care of me. So, I remember vaguely my grandmother, and then I had babysitters who always gave me candy. [Laughter]

And I remember playing in the backyard by myself, picking up mangos from the backyard and oranges and just being in Florida. I remember that physical space, although I was really young. I was like maybe four when I left Florida. But I remember like just the physical . . . like the . . . I didn't call it geography at the time, but I remember the trees and I remember the grass and I remember it being hot and I remember the fruit. And then my mother remarried when I was five and we moved here to Atlanta. And so most of my childhood memories come from Atlanta.

Did you move into the city proper?

We moved . . . I think we did. I think we lived . . . I think we lived in the hood. [Laughter] But we didn't stay there long. I just remember moving into an apartment. I think it was my father's apartment. My father, John, I think it was his apartment. And then like a year later we moved out to the suburbs, southwest Atlanta, which I think we were the second black family on the street. There were no blocks, we don't have blocks here in southwest Atlanta. And so, I remember there was one other black family across the street from me, and eventually more black families came in and the white families moved out. But there was this . . . this store that was down the street from us. We used to go to like all the time on the weekends and in the summer, and the family that owned the store owned a lot of the property in that area.

Mmm-hmm. It was a white family?

It was a white family. Campbell. Campbell's Store. And I remember my mother telling us all the time, "You always get a bag, don't ever walk out the store with just whatever you bought." And I never understood it. And then she said, "Well, they could always say you stole it." So, we used to always go there, get our candy and ask for a bag.

And this would have been in the midseventies.

It was in the seventies. [. . .]

And so, your family was the second family to integrate this neighborhood.

Mmm-hmm. Mmm-hmm.

Wow.

Yeah. And I remember crying going there because it just seemed so far out. When we went to go look at . . . I remember looking at houses with them or they were looking at houses and I just went. But everything just seemed so far. Like there was a horse farm and . . . and the families, the . . . I never saw the families, the white families, but I remember my mother saying it was just white families. We didn't play with [. . .] those kids.

Oh, you didn't?

No.

So who did you play with?

The black kid. [Laughter]

[Laughter] The one in the black family.

The one in the black family, yes. They had two kids and then eventually three and then some . . . uh, another family moved in next door to us. This was all in maybe a two- to three-year period. And then . . . my brother was born. He's five years younger than I am. And I went to elementary school. It was an integrated . . . obviously, integrated elementary school, but it was diverse. It was diverse in terms of black and white. And so that was, you know, I guess cool until I went to high school, then I was bussed to the north side of Atlanta, by my . . . actually, I chose that.

Oh really?

Mmm-hmm.

Okay. Why?

I play the violin and . . . they had a really good orchestra. The thing is, I never got into it once I got there, but they had a really good orchestra, it was a good academic school, and my thought was I wanted to have a diverse experience. But it wasn't diverse, it was predominantly white in Sandy Springs. And then I said, well, then I'll go to a black college, so I guess I had diversity in segregated ways.

. . . .

"Laura"

"Laura" was born in 1976 in Charleston, Mississippi, the eldest of three children. Charleston sits on the Tallahatchie River in north central Mississippi. Although its population is less than twenty-two hundred residents, the majority—60 percent—are African American. Despite the population, the city is highly segregated and was infamous for its segregated prom tradition. In 2008 the town held its first integrated prom—funded by actor and local resident Morgan Freeman—which became the subject of an

HBO documentary film, Prom Night in Mississippi, *released in 2009. "Laura" attended and graduated from that high school. The interview took place on August 24, 2013.*

Was your town segregated when you were growing up?
Very.
Really?
Very.
How? Like was it by a railroad track, or a road, or—?
[. . .] I guess the best way to describe it is it was just an understood segregation. And I don't know if you ever saw a documentary with Morgan Freeman about the black prom or having a separate prom—
Oh, yeah, yeah—.
—that's actually my hometown.
(Gasps) Oh, wow.
Yeah.
Oh wow. Wow.
So not to say that I didn't have white friends or we didn't hang out and we weren't close, because I think things significantly changed over the years. I mean, I graduated from high school in '95 but it still was understood, this is separate. The black kids had to go to the National Guard—no, they had to go to like an out-of-town hotel to have our prom, like in a barroom. Whereas the white kids were having theirs at the National Guard Armory in town. As I look back on it, some of it was a lot of limited support to me on the end of the black children because I feel like if somebody had stood up for us and allowed us to do it, then possibly they would have allowed us to. But there's a lot of fear when it comes to racial issues, and that's something that's still there.
So, did you go to high school with white people?
Mmm-hmm.
Oh, you did?
Yes. I mean, it wasn't like technically segregated at the school, because you'd have a combination. But here's the thing, there wasn't just a prom queen. [. . .] They would have a white prom queen and a black prom queen certain years. Yeah. Not just the prom queen but [laughter] . . . as I look back on that, it kind of makes me wonder if they had a black queen to kind of appease black people, as well. Because maybe there wouldn't be a chance of anybody ever being prom queen if they were black, I don't know.

"Mary"

"Mary" is one of the few narrators I interviewed who is also a professor. She has published essays on her experience of being a self-identified black lesbian from the South. A practicing Buddhist and actress, she is the mother of a teenage son from a previous marriage to a man. She was born in Tuscaloosa County in Alabama in 1975. The interview took place August 6, 2012, at her home in Atlanta.

Was your town segregated?

It was. It was segregated to a certain extent. [. . .] There's Main Street. For us it was Main Street. And I lived in an area called The Heights and [there were] no white people [who] lived in The Heights. And whenever we saw white people in The Heights, we knew that they were either there . . . it was either gonna be white girls that were there because they were sneaking to see their black boyfriends or the white dudes who were coming to buy drugs. So, that was the only reason that we would see them there in The Heights. So yeah, it was very much segregated, and I remember my mom calling . . . you know, she had her professional voice on. I wouldn't say talking white, I would say she was being professional. There was a house on Main Street for sale, and she called and asked about the house. And she gets there and it was just sold. And, I mean, when I say she gets there, it's like me leaving out of my driveway and walking to that stop sign up there because it was a very small area, and it was just sold. And I think it's still pretty much kind of that way. There are certain areas where the black people live and certain areas where the white people live.

What were the racial politics of your town growing up? Did blacks and whites get along? Were there riots or . . .

We got along until February. We did. Why, I don't know. [Laughter] I remember being in high school, something happened in high school and I remember we all just walked out. I can't remember what it was that happened, but it was in February. It was just like for some reason, I don't know if we had some internal clocks or whatever to say, hey, it's February, let's get it crunk around here, like we're . . . we're not taking it. But it was a very interesting racial dynamic. I think it's changed a little bit now. There was a lot of interracial . . . I wouldn't even say it was interracial dating as much as it was just interracial sexing. It was a lot of that going on behind closed doors. I remember there was this house we used to call the pink house. I can't remember who owned it, but I remember sitting outside the pink house one day as the lookout. Now, the white girls were a little more, I wouldn't even say they were open with it, but it was just a little more obvious with them as opposed to the white guys that were there. So, the pink house was where the white guys met the black girls they were having sex with.

Were they having sex in the house?

Yeah, in the house. In the house.

Who owned this house?

I don't know. I don't know who owned the house. I think it was maybe owned by one of the white guys. [. . .] I don't know. But that's where that went down. There was always racial tension. [. . .]

I remember the first time a black girl won valedictorian. She won valedictorian clearly and somehow they tried to finagle it into giving it to someone else. And her mother came up to the school with every assignment she had completed from ninth grade on and was like, "You know, if you want to sit here and calculate it, I'll wait." And she said she did that because she knew it was going to be an issue. So, it was a lot of those little scenarios going on. I even had my own little experience and, ironically, I just talked to him via Facebook the other day. There was a guy who I liked and we were in the same graduating class and we had hung out a little bit, but nothing really serious. And we hung out one night, I think, like maybe on a Friday or Saturday night. We hung out but it was very hush-hush.

This was a white guy?

Yes. Apparently, somebody told somebody or something like that, so I was at my locker and he was a couple of feet away from me, but his back was turned to me, so he didn't see that I was at my locker. And the whole football player crew crowded around and said, "What did you do this weekend?" And he was very hush-hush about it, like, "Why you worrying about it?" that type thing. And so, one of them said something to the effect of, "Oh, so, I heard once you go black you never go back," and they just all started laughing and just kind of making fun of him because they found out that he was with me that weekend. And he didn't join in, but he didn't say anything in my defense, either. So, needless to say, that was the last weekend that I spent talking to him. This was when I was like seventeen, so this was when I was in eleventh grade. We'd see each other here or there after I graduated and left, and he e-mailed me one day on Facebook and we kind of had this conversation via Facebook. And, you know, I said something about him and his friends joking and about me being the black girl. And he was like, "You know, to be honest with you, you were never just the black girl, but I didn't know what else to do, what else to say." I told him I understood. I really felt like he did like me, but it was one of those places where if he did he would have had to stand alone, you know what I mean? So he had to make a choice, and at seventeen I'm sure that's the choice that most people would make.

. . . .

Nancy

I was connected to Nancy through a mutual friend and colleague at Davidson College, who upon hearing about my research for this book said, "Oh, you must talk to Nancy. She definitely has a story." My friend was correct! Nancy was born in Maxton, North Carolina, in 1950. Located in eastern North Carolina southwest of Fort Bragg Army Base, Maxton's population is twenty-five hundred, with close to 65 percent of them African American. Nancy is an anthropology professor who pulls no punches when it comes to speaking her mind. While she is not closed about her sexual identity, she is clear about her sexuality being less important than her race. As described in chapter 2, she also has a daughter, Malu, who is same-sex loving. The interview took place on July 30, 2013.

Well, I grew up in the segregated South, so white people were not a part of my daily experience, so you knew racism existed but you created another world. Your parents had more racist encounters than you did, than you would have as a child, because I lived in a black community and went to all-black schools. The racial experiences that I had would be like a white boy exposing his penis, thinking that's cute. Or a group of white girls trying to figure out who's going to move off the sidewalk. None of us want to move, so we would bump shoulders, whatever, to try to push each other off the sidewalk.

Is this in transit to school?

My home or wherever I was going. Their communities had sidewalks. Of course, ours didn't, so you're walking to town and go to town for your parents or get something, whatever, and you're walking down the street and you're walking through their neighborhood. Or you're riding on your bicycle through their neighborhood and one of their dogs comes walking after you. That's why I don't like dogs. People tell me, "My dog is friendly." Please, uh-uh. I don't believe that.

Was your town segregated physically by a railroad track or river or road or some physical thing?

There was a railroad track but, yeah, there was a railroad track. It's true. But, so one, so in the western part of the town is where I lived, and it's separated by railroad track that ran north and south. Then you have the white sections of town and then another black section of town. So, I just happened to live closer to the railroad track. People who lived in the most eastern part of the town, they were white, I mean black. In the middle you had a lot of white folks.

And when you went to the white side of town, was it usually with your parents?

I don't recall myself going there. What I did was go through there so I could go downtown to get whatever my mom was sending me for or whatever. I had to go through their neighborhood to get to school sometimes. Different activities that you might get involved in. But to say, "I'm going into the white community to see someone," no, that never happened.

One time I had to go see my aunt. She was at work and my mom had to tell me, "You must go to the back door. You cannot go to the front door. Your aunt will lose her job." So, I went to the back door. I remember that. The only time I went to a white person's house in my hometown.

Your aunt was a maid.

Yes. But my mom was a stay-home mom. My father worked two jobs because he said his wife was not going to take care of white children at the neglect [of] her own children. So we had land, so we grew almost everything. We had pigs. We had a cow. We had chickens. You know, working-class people with a little land and a little, small house, but I don't ever recall wanting for anything.

So, your community, the black community in which you lived, was pretty much self-contained. The businesses were black owned.

No. There was a section downtown that was a black street, where there were black businesses.

Downtown?

Uh-uh. But not in the main, you know the white folks are here, but some of their businesses are on this street here, but you make a turn off Main Street going north and south and you go east, those are other black communities and that's where you have like a black barber shop. There was even one of those storefront churches. The only storefront church in my home town was there. Hammond Temple, I believe it was called. A five-and-dime, a place to get your hair done, and a little restaurant. And further down the street was a funeral home. There were about six or eight businesses on the black street.

And again, you never went there for a purpose except for that one time?

That's the only time I entered a white home.

And your parents weren't afraid of sending you to the white side alone?

No. As a child in the daytime I was going to take my aunt something. They would not have done that at nighttime. This was daytime and I am on a bicycle, so.

Do you have siblings?

Yes. We were eight, now we are six. Two boys and six girls.

Where did you fall in there?

I guess if there is a middle child I guess I'm it. I'm the fifth child. The only thing odd about it is that I was born eighteen months after a kid who was born in '49. She was born in February of '49, I was born in October of '50. We are the only two children that close in the family. Everybody else got two years or three years, whatever. My parents had their eight children over twenty-two years. So that makes the two of us a little bit odd from the rest of them. We both are sort of like middle kids. Because there are three born in the forties, '40, '42, and '44. Then my mom had a long period of no children and [in] '49 she has this daughter and then '50 I come. She was not happy. [Laughter] She told me she wasn't happy, which you could understand because the kid before me had asthma and she never had children that close together before. A minimum of two years between her children and the one before me was asthmatic. In the late forties and fifties, an asthmatic child could die. They didn't have the kinds of accommodations they have now. You know you could rush little black children to the hospital, to the white hospital.

So, there was no black hospital?

No. What we had since this is a small town—I was supposed to be born by a midwife. She was supposed to deliver me. She went out of town, told my mom that I had two weeks, and I decided to come during the first week of her departure and my neighbors helped my mom delivery me, and a white doctor came in and made sure I had ten toes, ten fingers, or whatever. But he did not deliver me. I look like on my birth certificate that he did, but he did not. Okay. So, the next child born three years after me, at that time we had a black doctor in town and he had a private maternity clinic, so my mother had her in that setting. The last two kids were born at the white hospital that had a black ward—a boy born in '55 and a girl born in '61. They were the only two that came into this world through white doctors delivering them.

Were there any other adults besides your parents that played a significant role in your upbringing?

My grandmother.

Paternal or maternal?

Paternal. My mother's parents died before she was twenty-two. That is because they had their children over a span of about thirty years, and there was a fifteen-year difference between her mother and father, so her parents are both dead by the time she was twenty-two. My grandmother, I am named for her, so I was close to her because I was named for her. One time in the week you get to ride to church in a car, she would show up and say "Okay, Nancy, we're walking to church." [Laughter] "Don't you get those socks dirty." "Don't you get those shoes dirty." We were walking on dirt roads.

But she would tell me things, so I did come to value that, but I was more interested in riding in the car once a week, and this old lady is taking my car ride away. We walked to school and everything. Round trip from my school was three miles, so it was a mile and a half in the morning and a mile and a half in the afternoon. That was nothing. You just ran along, skipped along, talking to friends.

You said your schools were segregated.

Oh yeah. We were all-black schools, all black teachers, principal, librarian. I think a black nurse came to give us vaccination shots because I don't remember going to a white nurse. We had a white bible teacher, Ms. Campbell.

You had a bible teacher in school?

Public school, yes. This is before that court case, and so she came once a month. It was just time not to be in the regular class. I didn't pay her any mind. Nobody got excited when she came. Nobody. She came, you did it, that was it.

Did you enjoy school?

Yes. When it got to high school, every now and then my mother would give you what you call an abracadabra day, let you stay home and help her do some work and stuff like that. You were just tired of school. But we wanted to go to school. If you didn't go to school you worked on the farm, so school was beautiful. School was exciting to us. We went to school. I'm sure we had dropouts in my community, but we preferred going to school.

Do you remember a particular teacher who had a particular influence on you?

There were two. My first grade teacher. For some reason, I reminded her of herself when she was in first grade. I was a very petite child, so I still wore high-top white shoes, Okay. And when I came home from school I put on high-top oxford colored shoes. [. . .] See I was very, very shy. They would just have to ask me, do you want water, or—I was just a very shy child. That was my coming out because she saw me, I think, as reminding her of herself, so she took a liking to me. I wasn't a teacher's pet, but I knew we had something special. And so, the next teacher that had a tremendous influence over me was Mrs. Blaylock, an English teacher in the ninth grade. Then my history teacher, civic teacher, and I had him. Blaylock was the homeroom teacher and the English teacher for the high school. He was the history and civic teacher for the high school. So those two people. She went to Spelman, and he went to Clark. So, she was trying to get me to go to Spelman, but I didn't want to go to an all-girls school because I heard it would be more strict. I didn't need that. I came from a family where you did what your parents told you to do. Okay. So, I needed something just a little bit more flexible. They showed me a map that they were across the street from each other, but I just knew it was a lie, so I went to Clark. Ended up modeling at Spelman. Had my first job at Spelman, so you just go back and forth. Had classes at Morehouse, Spelman. But those two people had the most influence on me.

How would you describe your family's beliefs and attitudes about people who were different from you, either racially, white folk, you know what I'm saying, or class-wise, or religion? Did you guys talk about that?

My father was very forthcoming, even truthful about white people. My father said something to his friends, and I was serving him coffee and I'll never forget it. He said there isn't a Negro alive that can steal as much as a white man. He said they stole us from Africa, they stole Native American land, and they still stealing our labor. My father was very political. I remember that. I wasn't even twelve or thirteen at that time. I remember that. So, my father told me the truth about white people. My mother did not work outside the family, so my mom basically showed you how to be diplomatic and to work within the black community. My father gave you what you needed to do to work amongst [. . .] white people. [. . .] You could not say the word "nigger." You could not call each other that. That was a sinful word in my family. Probably could get away with cursing better than you could calling someone nigger.

When it came to class, because we grew up in a small town, you know you don't say "middle class," "working class." I use the term "working class" now because I understand it, that concept. But then you were either better off or worse off, so everything is relative. My good friend who came from a family where both parents were teaching, they had far more material goods than we had, so they were better off than us. But I had somebody live down the street who were worse off than us and they have to borrow my shoes when they go to like a school program. Okay. So, class wasn't a big issue. What was a better issue is probably respectability. Being a respectful, dutiful person who's working, trying to take care of the family. If you weren't doing that, then people would talk about you. [. . .]

Whites were a big issue. I grew up in a town with three ethnic groups. Native Americans belonged to my county, so they came to town. They're called the Lumbee. My father grew up around Lumbees, so some of his Lumbee friends used to come to the house, and sometimes we would work on a Lumbee person's farm. They had a big farm and needed extra work hands or something like that. Sometimes we did that. What I didn't know, my mom had a Lumbee friend. They tended to live in the county, but when they lived in town they lived in the black community when I was a child. [. . .] I had lots of chores. First of all, you would have to clean, help clean the house on the weekends. When you were going to school, one of us had to get up early to help my mom make breakfast because we had freshly prepared meal for breakfast and dinner, so somebody was always in the kitchen helping her on duty. Those who weren't in the kitchen [were] helping her feed the pig, cow, or make sure the chickens were in or fetched firewood. We had a wood stove to heat the bedroom, so we worked. In summertime you worked, they used to give us like a row while we worked in our parent's garden. But they would give you a row and you would have your little corn and tomatoes, little things you would grow. And you would be like so proud of them and stuff like that. We worked. And I don't regret that.

Did you think it gave you a sense of the value of things, having to work for something?

Yeah. Oh yeah. I can remember looking out over the field sometime and seeing heat waves and thinking, "Shit, I am not going to be caught in this little town. I'm getting out of here. I don't know how I'm going to do it, but I'm getting out of here." So, but no work was good because you learned things. I never felt overworked or anything like that, but we worked. From the time I was thirteen I would work tobacco in the summer and save up money for my school books. God bless the child that's got his own. If you made money your parents bragged about you. I didn't know any lazy kids. You got a chance to work and make your own money, you did it 'cause then everybody would be praising you.

* * *

My father and some of his friends would go down to the beach and get all kinds of shellfish and shrimp and stuff and have like a craw bowl in the fall. Everybody would be out, talking, eating, and having fun. Kids running, teenagers trying to kiss each other, whatever. Adults winking and nodding at each other. Those were fun times. Going to school. I loved going to school. I loved learning. When I was little I used to look at *National Geographic*. It doesn't surprise me that I turned out to be an anthropologist because I always wanted to go see the world. I wanted to see the world beyond my hometown. But going dancing; I love dancing. To this day every Saturday night we go dancing. I loved those parties where we danced. I didn't grow up in a town where people were fighting and killing each other, young people when they go to events. Sometimes a bunch of boys from another town would ride up and start fighting our boys. Serious violence. I never was taught to fear black people, always feared violence from white people. I will never forget it. One day I was walking down a street in Harlem. It was evening, early evening. It was fall. I was walking, going to the bus stop. So these guys said, "Hey baby. How you doing?" I said, "I'm not too bad. How you all doing?" They said, "You're not from New York, right?" I asked, "Why is that important?" You got a certain ease about yourself. I went to Harlem [and] I wasn't scared of black people. I still am not scared of black people. The people I'm scared of are the people I can't fucking predict. White people. I can predict black people. I can't fucking predict white people. This fear of a people has never been of my own people. It's what those people could do to us. I remember something from my childhood that hurt me. Sometimes husbands and wives would fight, and I saw this man fighting his wife. I saw him dragging her. Two days later I see her with a bandage on her arm and sitting all up under him and everything. I said to my mama, "That will never happen to me." Somebody whip my butt and I'm going to be hugged up on them the next day. My mom said, "Honey, life isn't that simple." Life is simple to me. My mom knew my dad was a ladies' man. Sometimes it hurt her and she would be crying. I said, "I'm sorry but I would not cry for that." [. . .]

What are your worst memories?

The night the Ku Klux Klan was going to come to my hometown and threaten to shoot up black people in the late fifties. A chemical plant in my hometown was going to blow up. My best friend, my first cousin died in a car accident. She was in a coma for five or six months. Then, that happened to me in the eleventh grade. And in twelfth grade another friend was in a car accident, and she became paralyzed. When I went off to college and came back she was dead. Those are some very painful memories. Remember I told you about the cousin who I said to her, "You smell good"? That's the one that died. She was a poet. We used to talk about crazy stuff. She wanted to see the world outside as well. I remember the first time I made love; I really thought she was going to come back and ask me how it was. She would say, "Girl, did you get some? I'm dead, I'm coming back and asking you." I got scared as hell. I'm serious. I was nineteen going on twenty. I got scared. "Oh my God, is she coming?" It was a joke, but we used to say it with such intensity. Those are some of my worst moments, losing those friends.

How would you describe the importance of your southern upbringing to your character?

Well, I try to be helpful. If I can't be helpful I won't be around. My mom would say, "If you ain't got nothing good to say shut the hell up." Don't add to the craziness. Then there's an expression which is, "Honey attracts more flies than shit." That is a southern expression. A lot of people call southerners phony, but I know what they doing. They being sweet so they get what they want. It doesn't have to be something conniving or mean. "Honey," "baby," "sweetheart"—all those terms of affection. I like that stuff. I like southern culture. I know that we can talk about folks, and then they enter the room, and it's "Honey, how you doing?" The person comes in the room and I would tell my mother, "I know they been talking about me." I mean some people say the South is very two-faced, but I don't. Everybody know who's talking about who. I like the civility. I like the hospitality of the South. People in the North would say to me, "You are so southern." I would give something to someone and not think anything about it, no big deal. I would hear, "You so kind." I don't know any other way to do this. There are mean people in the South, but the South encourages you to be a kind person. You know scholars now say there's a great difference between the North and the South. Always has been. Northern cultures have been greatly influenced by northwestern European cultures: English, French, Irish, and Norwegian. The South was influenced equally by African cultures. So, this civility that we have in the South, whether white or black people, that shit comes straight out of Africa. You go over there and it tells you right away why we do the shit that's good and why we do the shit we do that's bad. 'Cause Africans be talking about your ass, you come in the room, they change the whole conversation. So, I like trying to build consensus, but at some point let's get on with it. Southerners take too long. You can't always build consensus. White people will do everything to build a consensus. We are not going to agree. Let's be respectful of each other and move on. Please. I can do that with black people more than white people.

Nora

Nora was born in Houston, Texas, in 1983. She grew up in a tumultuous family situation in which she had to become the primary caregiver for her six young siblings while her mother worked. Despite her situation, she managed to attend college. The interview took place on September 12, 2012, in Dallas, Texas.

[My childhood] was rough. [I] grew up in a lower economic status neighborhood. Half of that time, my mom was single, but . . . I'm the oldest of seven kids. She only had six before I went to college, so I helped raise the other five. I have one brother from my mom. I have another one from my dad. The rest of us are girls, so in total, like six girls, one boy.

And besides your mom, were there any other adults that played a significant role in your upbringing?

Yeah, I had a stepdad for about ten years. He's the father of the four after me. [. . .] My mom divorced my stepdad, 'cause he was really abusive. And so I just met my real dad, right before I turned thirteen, so by the end of that school year, my mom sent me to live with him so I could go to school, 'cause she had to live in a shelter for a while. And I lived in the battered women's shelter with her and the kids for, I don't know how long.

Okay. And so, your stepfather was abusive to you, more physically abusive, just verbally?

Umm-hmm. Both.

Did you witness that?

Yeah, in the beginning, when I was like three and four, I did, 'cause that's when she met him, when I was three. But after that . . . I don't know if she convinced him to, like, hit her in the bedroom, but . . . I could hear it. And so, after that point, it was kinda private. Of course, I saw, you know, the bruises, the black eyes, and stuff after that, stuff everywhere in their room, you know, after it was over. But after—yeah, after about three or four, the act, it was mostly hidden. Now, he would talk trash to her and stuff in front of us.

Did he direct any of that towards you or the other kids?

Yeah. I mean, most of his—most of it was directed towards my mom, but his first daughter—my—the sister under me, she was born, I was seven. So, there's a period of, like, four years where, like, I was his kid. But after my sister was born, it was like, "Oh, you're not my biological daughter." He never said it like that, but he used to call me his little poopoo and then that stopped once my sister was born, 'cause now she was the little poopoo. And then he would say stuff like, "Your daddy's a punk." I guess I look just like my dad, and so if my mom brought up my father, that would cause a fight. And he was really tough on my brother; I mean, our brother was just surrounded by girls, there are dolls everywhere, and he would just like—he just has a tactile thing, like, pick up a doll, play with the hair, and my stepfather was like, "You can't do that," you know, "my son's not gonna be soft," blah, blah. So . . . my brother got whoopins all the time when he was a toddler.

Just for playing with dolls, or . . . ?

Yeah. Or just even picking one up, you know. You can't touch anything that's a girl's, you know, 'cause that was his only son.

Umm-hmm. Was your stepfather an alcoholic?

Yeah. There's a story. I think in '86, he was run over by a taxi, a Houston taxicab or something is the story. And there was this big lawsuit, and he won some money that he blew. I remember we got a whole bunch of new furniture, clothes, like even in our tiny apartment. My mom wanted to invest it, you know, get a house, that sort of thing. We even took a trip to Florida to see his brother, Clay. After he blew all that money, I don't know if he got really depressed or what, but he was back to being like his old, mean self.

Oh, so while he had the money he was pleasant?

Yeah. [Laughter] And it was like, we're gonna go to Red Lobster all the time, we're gonna eat Popeye's all the time. [Laughter] You know, he was more pleasant. But after that, he was considered disabled, so he got a disability check 'cause something was wrong with his back, but he looked fine, but he was in pain a lot.

Well, obviously not enough pain to keep him from being abusive. [Laughter]

I know, yeah. And he would take on little, like, patch jobs or whatever, like working at the club up the street or he'd work the polls. And around that time is when he started drinking. [. . .] We got a new van, that's what he did with part of the money. He would be driving drunk with us in the car; he wouldn't let my mom drive because he was the man of the house, that sort of thing. So, I remember several times just praying all the way home. We'd almost get into several car accidents because we'd be driving from the south side [from] his sister's house, all the way back. And he would drive so fast and he's just like, "Oh, I'm fine." My mom's name's Glenora, and he'd just be, "I'm fine, Glenora. You don't tell me what to do." That's when he would curse or say something vulgar in front of us and my mom'd say, "Don't say that in front of the kids." I think that those times were toughest for her; she tried to hide that side from us, but we always knew. His eyes were always bloodshot, we could smell beer on him all the time. I'm not sure if he ever drank, like, hard liquor, but lots of beer. [Laughter] Lots and lots of beer. So that's probably the main reason why I didn't take a drink until I was almost twenty-two, because I was afraid of the stuff, you know, and I didn't wanna get hooked or become a monster like that. 'Cause, of course, he was the worst when he was drunk.

As a kid, how did you cope with that kind of thing going on?

Well, I think privately, I did a lot of reading. I was very studious. My mom, before she just kinda gave up on parenting, she was really big on education, and so I always had tons of books, always went to the library, so I escaped that way—writing, that sort of thing. But my main focus was taking care of the kids, because while all of this stuff was happening—I always say my childhood ended when I was eight, because that's when I learned how to and was forced to do all the laundry for us, cook for us, walk up the street to the store to get groceries . . .

At eight?

Yeah. You know, the back of pennies, 'cause we were poor. Back then there were actual food stamps, before they had the card, Lone Star card. I don't know what it's called now. So, my focus was always on holding it together for my siblings, who would be screaming, "What is Daddy doing to Mama?" and that sort of thing. So, I kinda had to, like, shut off my emotions to make sure they were okay, make sure they would stop screaming or crying or, you know, they missed my mom 'cause sometimes my stepdad'd make her sleep outside on the steps that led to the upstairs and threatened us, like, "If you open this door," you know, whatever was gonna happen to us. And then, even after my mom divorced him, my focus was taking care of them, making sure they had their homework done, they got to the bus. I washed their hair; I had their clothes ready; cooked 'em dinner. If we didn't have food, I'd have to go get something. I started working during the summer when I was fourteen, so I'd buy them school supplies, I'd buy my own clothes. It was pretty tough. I've been in a lot of therapy and that's something I still haven't worked through yet, like, that part of my childhood, 'cause it was just so tough. My mom was very loving, but she was also very neglectful. She'd check out a lot because she just couldn't handle it, and so I was always second mom. They still call me, to this day [laughter], like, "fix our problems." And even though you're 250 miles away, you know. So that's how it is.

Are they still living with your mother?

Yeah, all of 'em. I think my brother's about to move out. He's transferring to U of H, so I think he's only one about to move out. The sister, she still lives there. She has lupus and so there's a bunch of complications, so she hasn't been able to move out of the house yet. And she's gay, too, and that's really not good. [Laughter] My mom hates that, but yeah, but the rest of 'em, they're all there.

Did you enjoy school?

Yes and no. I've always like learning, you know? But even though it was a poor neighborhood, there are those poor families that the kid always has the newest Jordans. My mom was not like that. I didn't have the new nothing. I was always the tallest in my class and I grew very fast. I guess I take after my dad; by the time he was twelve, he looked like a grown man and was driving cars. [Laughter] I was like that; I looked grown really young. And so, you know, my pants were always flooding and I wore my mom's shoes. I started wearing my mom's shoes by the time I was in the third grade, and so things were not in style—too short—my mom was just like, "As long as it's clean, that's what matters," but that was tough, you know. I got picked on a lot. And I was in gifted and talented classes, and . . . all my schools were mostly black and Latino, but there were small groups of whites and Asians . . . and so most of them were in the GT [gifted and talented] classes, and I was in there with them. In my neighborhood and [at] the school overall, during lunchtime I'm around all the black kids; in the class, I'm one of the few black kids in there. So that was very awkward. I was uncomfortable: too white for the black kids, too black for the white kids, and people always saying, "Where you from, River Oaks?" or just some really rich white area outside of Houston. I was like, "Acres Homes, just like you." [Laughter] [. . .]

My mom just raised me differently—I couldn't say "ain't," I couldn't say "yeah," had to say "yes," you know. So, I may speak differently, but I'm from the same area. And so, it was always tough, not having the latest hair styles, not being like the other girls, not being as feminine as the other girls, just never having money, you know. Sometimes, if my backpack broke, all those AP books, I had to just carry on the bus, and I was the only one with books on the bus. Everyone had a rolled up folder in their back pocket, pencils where they did beats with 'em. So, I've always been different in some way. And I mean, I resented some black people for a while until I got to college and took a bunch of sociology classes and understood where a lot of things came from and learned about internalized racism, that sort of thing. So, I'm a lot more compassionate and sympathetic now, but back then, I was like, "Whatever! I'm going to college!" you know, like that meant anything. That just made me get teased more, but yeah, that was hard.

So, you enjoyed acquiring more knowledge, but it was the peer pressure that you didn't like?

I've always gotten through school—well, you know, since having to take care of the kids. I hate admitting this . . . it's something that makes me feel terrible, even though some people are like, "That's good." I got by on my natural logic or something, you know. I could really bullshit papers, basically 'cause I didn't have time to study. Once I got home, it wasn't like, "Oh, I'm gonna play on my PlayStation." I had a Nintendo; that's the only game console I ever got. [Laughter] [. . .] I got home before my siblings, but then [I would] go get them from the bus at the front of the apartments and make sure they started on their homework, make sure they're fed, make sure they're bathed, clean up and then, "Start your homework." But I was so tired all the time. And so, I never was able to, really sit down and read. The only textbook that I really, really read was my psychology book, and just 'cause I was just so intrigued by the topic. I had an AP psychology class when I was a junior. But besides that, I was just able to memorize things if I flipped through something really quickly. I could use context clues. I guess I'm a good critical thinker, and so that got me through, and I graduated top 4 percent of my class—even college, the same way. I had to have three jobs to get through college, and went half-time, so I graduated in eight years and graduated cum laude, but still felt like I was cheated, 'cause I wasn't allowed that space to really be a student, to really read the chapters. I wasn't like, "Oh, I'm going to the bar or the club," or "I'm not gonna study." No, it was like, "I'd rather be studying, but I have to go to work." And that was always hard. It was always like taking care of the kids. And of course, when it was open house night, so embarrassing. My mom went there; all these babies—one on my hip, one on her hip—we all looked different 'cause we got three or four different daddies and [laughter] . . . people were always like, "Your mom looks so young." I'm like, "She is young." My mom's only eighteen years older than me, and black don't crack, but . . . people would either pity me or make fun of me and call my mom a ho and I'd have to defend my mother. And then, kids'd call me ugly and I'd go home, my mom was like, "You're not ugly," totally disregarding any sort of problems I was having at school. But that's how that went. [Laughter]

. . . .

Keturah
Although Keturah was a bit hesitant about sharing her story for this book, after we began the interview her story seemed to flow easily. She worked

for years as a middle school teacher before stopping to devote full time to her writing, which led to the publication of her first novel. She was born in Atlanta, Georgia, on August 15, 1980, the oldest of three children. As a child she suffered with depression, due in part to her struggle with weight. She lives with her wife, Shetikka, whom I also interviewed for this book (see chapter 6). The interview took place at their home in Lithonia, Georgia, on August 8, 2012.

Do you remember where you went to elementary and middle school and high school, and friendships that you had then?

I remember elementary. I went to Cleveland Avenue at first in the city. I didn't have friends there. I was teased a lot because of my weight. I was a sensitive, creative child living in the freaking projects and living in these areas that were not conducive for you to be creative and sensitive. So [. . .] my sister and I were always in—I think me more so than her—always in fights. Always. 'Cause we were teased a lot . . . that was Cleveland Avenue. But I do remember having some friends; it just never lasted. [. . .] I spent most of my time with the boys at that age, spent most of my time with them. [. . .] That was it. And then from there, we moved to Lavonia when I was in the third or fourth grade. I went to Pinola Way Elementary and I don't remember having a lot of friends there, either. I just didn't fit in, and again, I was teased. And then I came on my cycle when I was very young, so I was like in fourth grade on my cycle, and that brought a total different dynamic into my world. And me being a child. Because I was in what, I was eight?

So, there were no other little girls who had gotten their period that early?

If they were, I didn't know them. I didn't know about it.

But I guess that's before you would've had the class. You have that in fifth grade or sixth grade, the—

Yeah, that was before that. So, my mom had to teach me those things. And it was already difficult, 'cause I had breasts at a very young age. I had hips, I had a butt, you know, I had these very mature parts of myself. And it was just difficult trying to be a kid. And now I have a cycle. And all the things that I was, was not considered pretty at that time, so I didn't feel pretty. I didn't feel attractive. And I do remember preferring to have light-skinned friends, because I wanted light-skinned friends with long hair and slim [physiques]. Because I felt that they were attractive and I was not attractive. And that was in elementary school. And I do remember being teased and bullied. That was mainly because of my weight. And I would retaliate. Like I said,

I was always in fights or I was always with people that you would not assume, if you knew me, [. . .] that I would be with. [. . .]

By the time I got to middle school, I was just tired. I was tired of being teased. Because I was bigger, there was a problem with it. So like if I wanted to run track—"How you gonna run track and you big?" It was that type of stuff that you get from kids. And I don't remember teachers being there to be a buffer for that or to protect you in any way. So, by the time I got to middle school, I started hanging out with people that reminded me more of my family. And my mom and my dad did not like it, 'cause they left that environment so we could have more, and I'm out trying to be in the streets. But that's what I did in middle school, and it was almost like, am I going to be a bully or am I going to get bullied? So, I ended up joining the bullies and the popular crowd, but at the end of the day I was not them. I could not keep it up, and then they ended up turning against me. 'Cause I just—it wasn't me. I was trying, but it wasn't me.

So, what happened in high school?

[. . .] I almost got jumped because I had a yearbook. And in my yearbook I wrote these different things by people's names. Like, I might say "bitch," I may say "ho," I may say "fuck you." [Laughter] You know, I may just say all of these things, and I let someone who I thought was my friend go through my yearbook. She went through my yearbook and then passed my yearbook around. So now all of these people are seeing these things, and so it was like a gang of them trying to fight me on the day before last day of school. I ran away a lot when I was younger. I ran away a lot.

Where would you go?

Sometimes I'd just walk and get in a car with anybody who'd pick me up. I would hide out at friends' houses. I ran away. When I tell you I was sad and frustrated and not understanding why I was here on this Earth, not wanting to be here, feeling like I was being punished—just all of these different emotions that I experienced—I wasn't happy. And then I felt like it was dysfunctional in my household. My mom and my dad didn't have friends, so I don't have family, they don't have friends, and then I'm out in this world and I'm so different. I felt so different. We didn't grow up celebrating any holidays except for our birthday. We used to go to Ohio for Thanksgiving, but then that stopped, so there was no fantasy in my childhood at all. And so, because there was no fantasy and my mom and my dad, they were very particular into making sure that we understood the reality of things: there's no Santa Claus; we didn't celebrate Halloween; we didn't celebrate anything.

So, it was hard, on top of already feeling like an outcast, and then you're in an environment where you know everybody around you is celebrating Christmas. So, you come outside, everybody in their new stuff and it was just hard. Or Halloween: the next day everybody would come back and they've trick-or-treated and we couldn't participate. So, they did a lot to my sister and I . . . they just did a lot.

· ·

Pat Hussain

Anyone who's anyone in the black LGBTQ community in Atlanta knows Pat Hussain. She has been an activist and worker for social justice for most of her life. She was also adamant that I use her first and last name! Pat was born in Atlanta, Georgia, in 1950, the second child of teacher parents. Like a number of narrators, Pat followed a traditional path of black southern women of getting married—and in her case, twice—based on the social and cultural mores of the South. Once she discovered her desire for women, however, she never turned back, despite it causing tension with her mother.

Pat is married to Cherry Hussain, whom I also interviewed for this book (see chapter 9), and the two of them were a tag team during each other's interviews, with one filling in forgotten stories for the other. They also cooked for me a hearty country breakfast of grits, eggs, and sausage— a real treat. The interview took place in Atlanta on August 9, 2012.

[My childhood] was fun. [. . .] Both of my parents were music majors. My father's instrument was the trumpet, and my mother's was the piano, and so there was always music in the house, and reading, and we rode our bikes. We lived in a segregated neighborhood clearly at that time. It was called Urban Villa. And we would just run around like idiots on our bikes. Or go into the woods and mess around in the creeks and do things that the adults would have been mortified to know that we were doing out there. But it was a good time.

What did your parents do for work?

My mother was a teacher. She was initially primary grades and became a reading specialist. Always believed she could teach a rock to read. She was an absolutely brilliant teacher, and my father was a mail carrier with the post office. He played in a band and had a paper route and was an associate editor for a magazine. He was a "BMW". black man working.

Did you have siblings?

Yes. There was my brother who was the oldest. And they wanted a boy and a girl—a boy first and then a girl—so we're eighteen months apart. And about six years later was an accident; there were identical twins.

Oh wow, that's quite an accident. [Laughter]

Oops.

So there's four of you?

Yes.

And besides your parents, did any other adults play a significant role in your upbringing?

One of my aunts, who was an economics major at the time. It might have even been home economics, but she could cook. She was known to us as Aunt Willie. Her given name was William because they had planned on having a boy, and they had picked out the name, and William was born, but Aunt Willie was just a magnificent cook. If there were things I wouldn't eat, my mother would get her involved, and however she prepared it I was ready to eat it after that. [Laughter] No grandparents on either side, and it was mostly family and the neighbors. When I go to that old neighborhood it was a time when we knew the Johnson's house or the Monroe's house and that was it. At that time that neighborhood was involved in an annual tradition and it was called Family Night. Every summer two adjoining neighbors' backyards would be used for a cookout, barbecue. And this would go on and I would go back to that as an adult, as a young adult be-cause it was going . . . because the neighborhood association would do it. And for a long time, realizing now that we shouldn't have been, we would all come back, we would all meet in the voting line because none of us had changed our precincts, just come and chat each other up while we were there. We'd catch up on each other's lives. But that community had a major influence in my life. At the time it was almost a team of surrogate parents that you were under the constraints. That Mr. Johnson's yard across the street, you knew don't step on his grass. Walk to the corner and turn. Mr. Johnson did not want anyone on his grass. That kind of thing. We all knew where the children were and who the adults were, so they had a major influence also.

So, you grew up inside the perimeter?

Yes.

And was it segregated?

Yes.

Was it a physical separation between blacks and whites like a railroad track or a highway or something? Or was it an understood imaginary segregation?

I'm not really sure. I really don't know how it developed but it was—there were lines that would morph. The neighborhood was in northwest Atlanta, and it was segregated with various socioeconomic levels within that segregated part of Atlanta. In Atlanta, a street like Boulevard crosses Ponce de Leon and becomes Monroe. Those name-change designations were a way of redlining because white people were not going to live on Boulevard where the Negroes lived; hence, the name change. You can see it also on Moreland Avenue again. When it crosses Ponce it becomes Briarcliff.

That's interesting. Do you remember where you went to elementary, middle school, and high school?

I went to several, and I'm thinking one was E. C. Clement. And I'm thinking about school because it was a time when they believed in accelerating children, "skipping a grade," as it was called then. And it was done to me and that—I've told Cherry this—it was a very difficult thing. I didn't know at the time that I was queer. But then all at once I was out of my social element, and I had been rather introspective anyway. I was the library person. And now at sixty-two and long before sixty-two, you know those lifelong friendships that go back to kindergarten, especially being in the city where I was born? They're just not there. I didn't connect. I graduated from Turner High School.

Which is still there?

No, it is now something else. The building's there but it's changed. I remember getting my class, getting ready to go register to vote at the end of that school year, and I couldn't go. I was sixteen. I already had had two heads because I was odd and library addicted, but that just made it different. I began to catch up in college because we were all aging into adulthood and a year, two years didn't make that much difference.

So how many grades did you skip?

One and I, my first school was Spelman. I went to Spelman Nursery School and I showed up ready to write, my pencil, my tablet, knew how to write my name and we were going to read, and we didn't do that. I was just so disappointed that we were not going to do that in nursery school. How can this be?

CHERRY: She didn't tell you that she was reading at three.

Cherry's a country girl. I'm the city girl and she laughs at me because one of the places, my mother was all about education and excursions and whatever would enrich us. I had to take ballet lessons, from which my father rescued me. I was not that kind of girl. And we did modern dance. I had to take piano lessons. Saturday was filled with lessons either in the basement or on the piano there. I was interested in French and I spent a summer, which it turned out to be wasted, with a family. I immersed in French with a family that was French-speaking to assist me with the language. So, she was always looking for ways to broaden whatever experience we were having or particular thing that had grabbed our interest.

Was Turner segregated?

Yes, it was. And integration of the schools began while I was in Turner. And as I recall there were letters or something that went out where you could put yourself on the list or some type of application process to be a part of this transition. I don't know; my parents probably put my name into that. My mother I'm sure did. Well, I really don't know but I was in love, I know now, of singing in the mixed chorus at Turner and I was in love with the accompanist. Her name was Sharon . . . I might be too sick to go to school and I would crawl out, go to first period which was chorus, then homeroom and maybe not even go to the homeroom and then I would go home because she had tried to pry me out before. My brother was sent to a military academy in Powhatan, Virginia: St. Emma. And they had a sister school and my mother wanted me to go. I was not leaving mixed chorus. I was [like], "No, no, no." She kept trying to get me out of there to go too. I'm in Turner and I'm here. She graduated the year before I did, so that last year I was still, chorus was okay but it wasn't a vital part of my life.

Are your parents still alive?

My father is. My mother's died. My father is eighty-seven and we siblings, now a blended family. My parents divorced. My father remarried and the mother of my heart who I call my mom—other people would call her my stepmom—but she taught me graciousness. She, not as a child as an adult, she's had a major influence on my life, and I have tried to learn from her example. Many times I'm not as good as her example, but I know that better is possible because she shows me.

Growing up, what were your family's, particularly your parents', attitudes about people that were different from you either based on religion or class or sexuality? Was there talk about people who were different from you?

There was no talk about sexuality. There were different places where my mother taught. There were children who were more economically disadvantaged, and she would bring them to the house or take them places with us. There was never a sense, though, of them and us as different. There was a lot that I didn't understand about that because their jobs made it possible for them to shield us from so much around segregation. And I knew that for instances we would go to Rich's Department Store downtown, the icon of the time. That was it. And I always wanted to go. I could see these bridges and we would go walk through them where they had food for sale. And I wanted to stop at those and we never stopped, and I'm sure now that that was because we weren't supposed to, and we rarely went. I remember going to the bathroom in that store once and it was downstairs. It was on the bottom floor, somewhere which probably I didn't see. And my guess is that there may not have been a sign that said "colored" or those that said "white only" because if something had words on it, I'd read it. That has continued all my life. And I didn't see that, but my mother was driving her car to the store so there weren't the encounters with the bus. I did ride the bus, ten years old, talking 1960, and I would ride from school and transfer downtown around that Rich's area and ride the bus out Peachtree to what was then the Emory Dental Clinic . . . I was having dental stuff done there, and I always sat in the front of the bus right behind the driver, children doing what they do. When Cherry and I discussed this later I told her that they probably were not—they didn't pay children as much attention because, you know children, because there was never a point where I was told to move or nothing like that. And Cherry brought me back down to earth real quick on that. She said, "They weren't sure about you." I didn't hear it. The hand, the hand, you know, and it began to penetrate that she was more than likely correct.

That you could pass?

Yes, and that that's what was happening. That's why I was allowed that freedom on the bus mostly. But those were encounters that happened periodically while I was having dental work done. But as a regular, on a regular basis, there was almost always one of our parents with us and we were moving about in their cars, so I just missed a lot of that . . . it was going on all around me, but I was oblivious in many ways.

· ·

Priscilla

When I think of Priscilla I smile. She has an infectious laugh—and she loves to laugh. But underneath that gregarious personality is a fierce activist who is quite serious about the freedom of queer people of color. She was born in a military hospital in San Antonio, Texas, in 1967, but was reared in East Austin. East Austin is historically African American due to segregation but is currently being gentrified. Priscilla's family has lived there for generations. She and her partner, Rose (also interviewed for this book) live within one mile of her parents' home. The interview took place on September 9, 2012.

My father was in the military until 1978. And then after that, he worked at my uncle's garage. My uncle owned a car mechanic garage, and so he worked there for a minute and then he went back into the civil service and work at Bergstrom Air Force Base until it closed. And then he got transferred to Carswell Air Force Base and lived there for maybe ten, fifteen years—actually commuted back and forth. My mom was off and on a homemaker. She also worked cleaning white folks' houses [laughter] and was a nurse's aide at a nursing home. But what I mainly remember her doing is either being home or cleaning white folks' houses.

Did you ever accompany her?

I did. [Laughter] Whoo. [Laughter] Yes, so I went to work with my mom a couple of times for Dr. Kraut, who is actually her current rheumatologist. And he had two twin daughters and he must have other children, but I only remember the two twin daughters who were just a little bit younger than I. And I remember going to work with her and her giving me a portion of the pay. Now, I don't know if this is true, but I felt like she made twenty dollars and that she gave me five dollars and I was just too through [laughter] because I felt like we ought to be halving it. [Laughter] I was like, "Well, surely I'm gonna get half that money." But I think I got five dollars. And I remember going there with her two times and saying, "Oh, no. This ain't me. This ain't me and can't be me." [Laughter]

And how old were you?

I had to probably be ten maybe. Yeah. Because she didn't do that when I got older. She actually stayed at home and wasn't really working. But I was like, "Oh, no." I think it was the money, knowing how much money [laughter] that was, and just also feeling very irritated being in the peoples' house and, you know, they just wait for you to come clean it up. [Laughter] I know that they left that shit down here till we got here, right, like you didn't clean that up all week long? You don't come here but once a week, Mama, so what the hell they doing the rest of the week? [Laughter] So yeah, I did that a couple of times and I didn't do that anymore. I remember when I got a job with the Youth Employment Services here, which is a place that hires young folks [. . .] so you can go to work—they probably called us "at-risk" children. And I remember going to one of my first jobs. And they took me to clean somebody's house. And I remember going maybe once, maybe twice, and cleaning this white woman's toilet. And deciding again, "Oh, this can't be me. And, in fact, this is not gonna be me." Because it also tied into this thing where we had to be at the facility at like 8:00 in the morning. And they put us all in a van and drove us out to the west side of town here, which is primarily white older people or white people with money. And the guys would generally be cutting peoples' yards, so we'd go all the way up in the hills and they would drop them off and then they would take me and drop me off. And I might do two hours of work but be gone until 6:00 P.M. in the day. And so, I've always been very money oriented in terms of how much money and how much time is this. And I was like, okay, that's not adding up. And then the white woman didn't like the way I cleaned her toilet, so I was done.

She told you she didn't?

Yes, in fact [she] had me go back a couple of times to do it. And it was something about her being an older white woman. And when I went with my mother, they were not home, for the most part. I didn't see the families, so nobody was saying, "Do this, do that, redo this, redo that." The kids would come home sometimes before we left . . . that's how I met the twins. But other than that, nobody was supervising. And I just didn't like no white woman telling me that that wasn't clean enough, given that that was my primary job at home, and knowing that my mother is an extremely clean person, so I know how to clean this bathroom to satisfaction. [Laughter] So I was like, "Hmm." I said, "No, I can't do that." In fact, I don't need to work. [Laughter] So I just didn't go back. Because I worked out of wanting to work, but I didn't need to work. It wasn't like I needed that, because I got allowance, but I also babysat and did other things. But my parents were well enough that I didn't have to work to have spending money.

* * *

Were your schools integrated?

No. Well, in the sixth grade, I was sent to an integrated white school. Way in Travis Heights, sixth grade school. So, kindergarten through fifth grade [was] all black. There was one Latino in the room, but everybody else was black. In sixth grade, because we were integrated, they sent two black kids from the east side—one boy, one girl—and two from the south, and they put you in the classroom, so you could integrate the classroom. And so, it's interesting now, because the girl who was in the class was named Gwen Cubit [see chapter 10], who I know now, who is a lesbian, right? [Laughter] She was from the south and I was from the east side.

And so, did they randomly just select two black kids to—?

I think what they did was they sent many more of us over there, but how they integrated the actual classroom was they put two of you from the east side, two of you from the south side, so there would be four of you. So, there was four blacks in this classroom—but I think there was probably only one busload of us [in the school].

This would have been like '78?

I got skipped up a grade, so I'm always a little off . . . I probably was ten in the sixth grade.

So '76.

That was '77. Yeah, I was born in '67, so about '77.

So before then, the schools in Austin had not been integrated?

No. And so then, we integrated the school there. By seventh grade year, I went to the school up the street here, which was primarily black, had some white kids in it. But come the eighth grade, they bused us again, and to go integrate Lamar Middle School. They cut the neighborhood in half and sent half of us to Lamar Middle School and the other folks went to Dobie Middle School. And so, we integrated Lamar Junior High. So, it wasn't integrated, [laughter] which was absolutely fine with me, because it's funny that I did so well in school and had gotten skipped up, until I went to school with white kids. And when I went to school with white kids, they started then telling my mother that I was behind. And they actually had us in those little groups by animal names, based on our reading abilities. Now, all I remember is that they had put us in the slower group, whatever that was. Gwen and I actually saw each other recently and were talking about how they would put us on the little beanbag behind the bookcase because we were in the "zebra" [group]. They had the elephant group and the zebra group and the cat group or something, based on your intelligence level. And it's interesting that we all ended up in the less intelligent group of people. [Laughter] And so there were a lot of race fights, particularly when we went to the sixth grade. But when we went to the eighth grade, one of the first things I remember was we went and they said, "On this particular day is the race fight." And what it meant was, all the black and white kids who were on the football team, but primarily the white kids, would then have a fight against all the black people that went to the school. And it was going to be very different this year apparently, because now there were enough blacks to match the white students, and so the school had to do this big interference in it. And, in fact, put us like on lockdown for the day and had an assembly and was saying, "We've heard this," coming over the loud speaker, "that this thing is going to go down," but we were ready. We were ready for the day that it was going to go down. And I hadn't been to the school the year before, so I didn't know what that looked like, but we knew we were going to be fighting. But it was mainly going to be the guys. But, of course, we were going to be fighting because we never let black guys just fight white people. [Laughter] Like, "If that's my cousin fighting, we gonna be fighting, too."

And so, there was this big day that there was going to be this race thing. And I remember the day that there was the race thing in the sixth grade and how there was an Asian guy. And they didn't know what to do with him. And he didn't speak English. And I just remember it just being like one of the worst fights I had ever seen, because they didn't know whether to treat him as a person of color and so, of course, he was just fighting everybody. He was fighting the whites and the blacks. It was just very traumatizing in that way. But yeah, integrating the schools was something that was very difficult. But also, it kind of helped me in my schooling because everybody would then, when I went to all-black schools, it was like I was trying to be white. And so, when there was this thing about I shouldn't want to be intelligent, I shouldn't want to go to school, I shouldn't want to go to class, and why didn't I skip school. And then when I went to Pierce, my friends would try to get me to skip school and I was just like, "That is so dumb." It just didn't make sense to me because I didn't like to do makeup work, you know? And it was like it didn't make sense to me. So, I did much better when I went to school when it was more integrated and there were white people because that could be the focus. I wasn't the only one, right? And I was disbursed from my neighborhood kids. But when I was in the other classes, first through fifth grade, I'm in class with the person across the street from me, right? [Laughter] And I got to go home, you know, and they's kicking my ass and chasing me every day, right? [Laughter] Or trying to kick my ass and chase me, but my mother was like, "That's enough. You all need to whoop they asses and they gonna leave you all alone." [Laughter] And so once we started doing that, it was done.

. . . .

RonAmber

RonAmber was a part of a larger group of younger women in Dallas, Texas, who are a part of the black queer artist scene. Born in Dallas in 1981, RonAmber is a spoken word poet. Much of her poetry speaks to the trials and tribulations of African Americans—both gay and straight. The interview took place on September 14, 2014, in Dallas.

I spent a lot of time outside. But at the same time   there was a lot of turmoil. My brothers were heavy into selling drugs, and so I saw a lot of that. My mom was working when she finally sort of got her life together and was working all the time. And she worked the nightshift, so overnight she was away, and so they were hustlers. So, I saw a lot of different things during my childhood.

Was your mother aware that your brothers were into drugs?

She knew. She knew that they were dealing because my father, before he died, the story goes that he is actually the one who kind of introduced them to it because he was a physical therapist. But he lost his license because he was dealing drugs out of the office and turned to selling drugs and was then, you know, a dope dealer. And we didn't have the same father. My two older brothers and my oldest sister—their father was in prison, and so they just did what they knew to do. They weren't interested in school very much, and so they were selling drugs. And my mom knew, but she had to be at work, and so I kind of became the spy of the family, so I was known as being the tattletale. I kind of reported to her about things that would happen while she was away. So, she found out, but she couldn't be in two places at one time, so she couldn't really change very much.

Right. How old were you when this was going on?

I would say between the ages of seven until maybe I was twelve. [. . .] And then my oldest brother went to prison around that time and so he was kind of out of the picture. And my oldest sister was always still selling drugs. But my mom was sometimes working the dayshift, so she was around a little bit more. But for the most part she was always at work. The majority of my childhood she was at work.

And how much older are your brothers and your sister than you?

They are . . . between seven and ten years older than me.

So, there's a big gap.

Right.

Did you see drugs?

Yeah. The most vivid memory I have . . . one time, I can't remember how old I was, I was young, though, my brother was cutting up the crack. And he left the room and me being inquisitive, I grabbed a piece of it and like tasted it with the tip of my tongue. I just remember the tip of my tongue being very, very numb and I remember then realizing, "Oh that's what happens when you chew or when you taste crack cocaine." But I knew what crack looked like. But they tried in their way to not have us in the room if they were dealing it or had it on there. But I knew it was always around somewhere.

What do you think kept you from using or selling?

Oh, I don't know. And I ask myself that a lot and they ask me, too, you know, wondering. Because my life went very different from their lives.

I think I always had this fear of just, you know, police and jail and things like that. And just sort of knowing about the things that were happening to them. My brother got shot three times and I think [. . .] I felt the danger of that life. And at a very early age . . . my great aunts were very active in our life, and we spent a lot of time in church. Me and my other sister and my little brother. And I was very afraid of God. And I really felt like there were some things that you just shouldn't do. [. . .] I was known for being a reader and a poet and just this little girl that performed. And I was really concerned about letting people down. So early on I felt that I had to do something different.

Was performing and writing sort of your escape?

It was very much my escape because [. . .] I didn't know very many other little black girls doing poetry. And so, I was really the only poet that I knew for a long time. And it was just that one thing that made me different and it made me stand out. [. . .] I cling . . . I clung . . . I clung to it. And it became, you know, part of my own little narrative.

Who exposed you to poetry?

. . . So in the first grade my sister, who is two years older than me, she was chosen to be in the oratorical contest at our elementary school, and one of my teachers pulled me out of glass to go watch her perform. And she did the Gettysburg Address. And I remember sitting there thinking, "Wow," you know, like, "That is so cool." And then so when it came for my age group to start preparing, they chose me and I did "Boa Constrictor" by Shel Silverstein. And I just remember the pressure of, you know, you're representing your class and you have to learn this poem. And this one teacher, I think her name was Dr. Harris, she was always working with me and trying to tell me how to just be expressive. And at the time . . . we missed a lot of days in school, so we weren't the popular kids. So that kind of brought me into some sort of popularity in the school. So, I think I remember being aware of people noticing me a little more . . . because I was doing something important it seemed. And my sister actually performing was the first sort of entry into like poetry that I got. And then from then on she did something else, and I was always sort of the one doing the oratorical contests. So, I like to think that she kind of handed it down to me. [Laughter] And she's, I think, a much better writer than I am, but she's not interested in writing.

What kind of things did you write about?

. . . I wrote about . . . the flowers or something, you know. Just whatever prompt I was given in school, I would write that, but I wasn't really a "journaler." Or you know, I didn't really journal very much. I learned poems. [. . .] I would come across a poem and I would just need to learn it because

I just had this sort of, I don't know, a repertoire of poetry that I knew that I could recite. And then when I got older, in my teenage years in high school, I started like taking it a little bit more seriously. I had a teacher who I was very close to. And she used to tell me to write and, you know, [she said,] "You should write" and "You have a . . . you have a gift." And it wasn't until I did ACT-SO, this competition through the NAACP, and my poem won the local competition. Actually, I didn't win that year, but they liked it so much that they invited me to go with them and I saw then that there were hundreds of other kids that would write, that were poets, and doing other kind of things. And I was like, "Wow," you know, "there are other people who have been having this same experience." It took me, you know, years until I really realized that.

What's ACT-SO?

It's a sort of a performing arts, academic of the mind, like mad science essay competition by the NAACP. And some students compete on the school level, and then they go to the city level. But I went straight into the city competition because my school wasn't really participating in it. And you can enter in the different categories. And the first couple of years I did it, I did dramatics and oratory, I think. And then my senior year I wrote a poem called "Black Man." [. . .] I did that poem and it was a hit. I didn't win. The judges didn't choose for me to win, but the organizers heard it. I didn't win, so technically I wasn't supposed to go to the nationals . . . I don't know, I didn't really technically win. [The ACT-SO organizers] called me one day and was like, "We like your poem and we have to take you to the national competition." And that year it was in New York. And so, I went to New York and I did my poem for the judges and I didn't win . . . it was really the first time that I really put my poetry out there.

What was it about? What was the poem about?

"Black Man" was just like social commentary about the different representations of black men. Like, "black man, black man, what do you see? Troubles, troubles coming after me. Look behind your back, in front of your face, we're going through the same thing, living in the same place. We can't turn to each other, so we turn against each other. Black man vs. white man, black brother vs. black mother. Quick to point them fingers, quick to place the blame, quick to get pulled over, and give them your brother's name. So you run, run, as fast as fast as you can. You can't catch me 'cause I'm a black man." And then I can't remember the rest of that part. But the next part was about, "black girl, black girl, what do you see? Troubles, troubles coming after me." And then it was about just the black woman. I have your kids, I clean your clothes. I bring you money when you in jail. Something about that. I can't remember the exact words, but I think [. . .] it was like a coming together of all the different images of black men and black women that I knew of because that was what I saw about black women and black men. You know, you're running from the police, you kicking a football, you going to take money to the jailhouse, you know? I honestly had not, before that, really, believed that it was a thing, really. I just thought, yeah, I write and I'm good at rhyming, and maybe I can come up with some great ideas. But I didn't really think it was significant until then and then still much later.

And what were your mother's thoughts about your poetry? Did she nurture that?

Yes. My mother was very supportive. She was my main audience. Whenever I would write something I would say, "Hey, I got a new poem," and you know, she'd be watching TV and she'd be like, "Oh Lord, here we go." But she would always make sure that the TV got cut off and that I had like a stage to perform. And so my family were—they were always very supportive because—well, they wanted to hear it because they knew that I was writing about them. [Laughter] So they wanted to hear how I had kind of told their story. But they were always—they responded like family. It was like, "Oh, Lord, another poem," but they always listened. I always felt like, even though I was kind of forcing them to be a part of my audience, they always were interested in hearing what I had. And so my mom was always very supportive.

. . . .

Rose

Rose was born in Roanoke, Virginia, in 1958 but now lives in Austin, Texas, with her partner, Priscilla (see above). Roanoke is located in southwest Virginia along the Blue Ridge Mountain range and has a population of ninety-eight thousand, 70 percent of whom are white. Rose was married to a man for several years, is mother to four children, and has ten grandchildren. The interview took place on September 9, 2012, in Austin.

You know it was, on one hand, kind of this upwardly mobile black country folk childhood. My mom and dad had moved to Virginia, and they were really young. And they were leaving Alabama trying to find work. Neither my mom or dad had finished high school, and I was born when my mother was eighteen. And I had an older sister already. And so, this is really fresh because my mom, my dad, my two sisters, and I just went to Salem and Roanoke a couple weeks ago to visit a great aunt who was having her ninety-eighth birthday and another great aunt. And all the stories of their migration and then their migration back to Alabama are really fresh with me because a lot of that conversation happened while I was there. But my father talks about having started working scrubbing pots at the VA Hospital, and then becoming a nurse's assistant, and getting his high school diploma. And then going to nursing school while my mom got her diploma and became a hair dresser, and you know, different things. But they bought a house. They were able to buy a house even though they were—because that's what you did. You put your money together. And so, my memory is of us—you know if you'd asked me, I'd say we were middle-class black folk. That's probably not true, right? Because I remember times when there was very little food, and I didn't know it at the time, but my mom would send one of us kids to one neighbor and ask us to get some potatoes and one of us to another neighbor's house and ask for an onion. And then she'd come back and make potato soup or something. But we were not aware because it was this little enclave. It was on a dead end street. All of the neighbors were black folk in community, and we lived there until I was ten or eleven, and it was very comfortable and very supportive, and I felt very secure there. And we moved back to Alabama.

Where in Alabama?

You know it's one of those things where you have to say the county. Because the town [is] too small. So, Tallapoosa County, Alabama. It's near Alexander City. But the actual town is called Daviston. So, we moved back there because my dad went to Vietnam. The thing that was not so wonderful about my childhood is that my father was a drinker when we were in Virginia. And I just remember, you know, a lot of things revolving around his being drunk or intoxicated, and he wasn't particularly violent to my mother. There's a story about him raising his hand to hit her once and she was in the kitchen and threw a knife at him. And you know the folklore is that it parted his hair. Right? So, you know that didn't happen anymore.

I guess not.

I guess not. And before he went to Vietnam he wasn't particularly violent with us kids, but when he came back he was viciously violent. And it was such a conflict because he was an incredibly loving man, on the one hand, and on the other hand, terribly, terribly violent with me and my sisters. Not my brother, but with my sisters. And you know I just loved him so that it was just so hard to kind of hold all of that together.

How many siblings?

There are four of us all together.

Okay, and where did you fall in that?

I was second. I am second.

Okay. And your father's violence—was it always around punishing you for something you had done, or it was unprovoked?

It was generally. At least there was a narrative of punishment for something you had done. It wasn't always easy to connect. Generally speaking, it was like, you know, for "the dishes weren't washed" or "they weren't washed right." But it was one of those things where he'd wake you at 2 A.M. and beat the fire out of—and he saw [my sisters and I] as a unit . . . and so one didn't get punished unless all of us got punished. So, if one did something we all got punished for it. It was very strange, and it seemed to be very much connected to whatever happened with and to him while he was in Vietnam.

Did you feel that your mother could protect you from the violence from your father? Did she, at any point, say to him, "Stop" or "Don't do that"?

I'm not aware that that ever happened. [. . .] I don't ever remember her being there. I don't remember her being present. And I know that that's a function of memory as opposed to reality because she had to be around. But my memory is that she wasn't there. She wasn't present. I suppose that part of why I choose to remember in that way is because then I can keep her—I could keep her in a particular—you know, if she were present and she didn't do anything, then at least my younger mind would have required that I hold her responsible. But I never did hold her responsible at all. And maybe it's [. . .] because I had to have one of them and my relationship with my mother has always been fractious. [. . .]

In Alabama I had started out in a segregated school. And my father decided that we would integrate the elementary school, and we did that about a year before the schools were integrated there. So, my dad takes his three children and puts them in the white school. The only little brown spots in there.

Now if this is before the schools had been officially integrated, how does he, like, literally do that?

I don't know. And he didn't talk about it, but you know some years later I saw a newspaper article that talked about it. And he wasn't into organized civil rights at all, which is interesting. But he had petitioned the school board or done something, and there we go. But it was at the tail end. And then so we went to the school for a full year. And then other black kids followed the year after. And so, I'm in this culture, this black culture that—where at least where I was living the notions of femininity and masculinity were not as linear and not—you know, they overlapped, at least where I lived, a great deal more. And then I went to a white school where it was really, you know, girls like this, boys like this, so it was just odd. I didn't understand it. And all I knew was like this is how I am, which was just this mix, right? You know physically strong and likes to play—but also was interested in learning to sew and to quilt and to do all the things that you know it took to—and it wasn't as if it was to be a homemaker, but they were just industrious and resourceful things. And everybody was supposed to be industrious and resourceful somehow. At something. I'm not sure that if I had not been interested in repairing cars that wouldn't have been fine, too. In fact, my father taught my sisters and I how to repair cars.

So, it was a matter of pragmatics.

Yes, it's like, "How do you get it done?"

When you were growing up both in Virginia and in Alabama were your— were both of your towns segregated?

So, as a young child in Alabama, I lived in Alabama at different times even when my family was in Virginia. So, I lived in Alabama for a year or so when I was four and then again in the family. I don't know why I was the one chosen to go stay with my grandparents, but I was. It was segregated. Alabama was absolutely segregated. And in fact, when we moved back to Alabama when I was ten or eleven, however old I was, we again moved— desegregated the white school. And again, in another year the black students came to that school. And I remember things like driving from Virginia to Alabama, being in the car. And conversations about "Where could we stop?" We'd have to use the bathroom on the side of the road. There was a time where we stopped. I remember it distinctly. And I had to be little. Stopped at a Shoney's Big Boy. They were going to get some food, and my father went in and came back cussin' and saying, "My money is green . . . if I can't get the food like everybody else, well I'll just go someplace else." And my mother is saying something like, "The kids need to eat." And he was like, "They won't eat there." So yes, Alabama was segregated and then it wasn't. But it was. And so was Virginia and then it wasn't.

And was the segregation based on a physical barrier—like a railroad track, a river, a road—or was it self-segregated as well?

You know, I have no idea, because in my young mind it was just home, right? It was just my people. But having just visited Virginia I asked my mother. I actually asked her and I said, "Were there parts of town that black people [lived]?" And she said, "Yeah, we lived in a black part of town." And then they took me to another part of town which was a black part of town, and she showed us where she had had a beauty shop there and lived in a kind of boardinghouse space before they were able to purchase the house. And Alabama was less so because it was very rural. So, where we lived in Virginia certainly wasn't urban, but it wasn't rural either. It was a little town. You know, a nice little town which is now a big town. But in Alabama it was very rural, and so folks would have their spots, you know, their little pieces of land. And sometimes their family compounds where they had gotten a piece of land and divided it up among family and they had their little wooden houses and whatnot. But the white folks may be the next plot of land over. But it was just because it was extremely rural. You bought a piece of land where you could buy a piece of land.

. . . .

Roshandra

Roshandra was born in Fort Lauderdale, Florida, in 1976. She is among several women I interviewed who attended Florida A&M University and decided to stay in Tallahassee. The interview took place on August 18, 2013, in Tallahassee, Florida.

Was your town segregated when you were growing up?

Yes. We actually even had a Cracker Day parade. [Laughter] And, you know, [when you're] young, you didn't really understand what that meant. But as you got older, you kind of understood that [. . .] it's more so geared towards whites, even though we did participate in it.

And that's what it was called: a "Cracker Day" parade?

Cracker Day, mmm-hmm, yeah. And then, after some years, I believe I had already left to come on to college. People didn't like that, so I think they either got rid of that parade or they changed it to a different name.

What was the history of the parade? What was the parade for?

You know, I honestly haven't the slightest clue. I just know my high school used to participate in it. And we would march in it, whether it be the band, you know. And that's the only high school in my city besides the private school. So, you really didn't know; you just were told you had to participate and [so] you did. [Laughter]

Okay. And it was segregated how? The blacks lived on one side and the whites lived on one side or—?

Pretty much. Most of the whites lived on the beach side and most of the blacks lived in the black areas, which is basically the MLK, Martin Luther King area. But you have a section where the majority all blacks live. And then you have an area where majority of whites live.

Sharita

Sharita was born the youngest of three in Washington, DC, in 1979. As she recounts below, she and her siblings were reared by her aunt to keep them out of foster care because her mother could not care for her children. She was also the victim of sexual abuse by her stepbrother. In addition to being the mother of a young daughter, Sharita is also happily married to her wife, Shayla (see chapter 2). The interview took place on October 5, 2013, at her home in Little Rock, Arkansas.

My childhood was typical. I was raised by my aunt from six months up until she passed away. So, I knew my mother was her sister. And I knew my dad, but I lived with her and she had two sons. One was older than me, and then she had one that was younger than me. And I mean I guess it was a struggle, if you would describe it from the outside looking in. We were poor, you know, struggling. We never technically lived in the projects, but not too far from it. And all males. Well I have one cousin; she's a female that we were really close, more like siblings. I had biological siblings, which my aunt took in. Me, I was about six months. My older brother I think he was like four or five. And she eventually got my older sister I think when she was about four or five. But she originally went with her father's side of the family. And then somehow something went some kind of way and she ended up with us as well. But I'm the only one out of my mother's children that stayed with my aunt the duration of my life.

Why did your aunt take you?

Well, we all went to foster care. And I was a baby, I was an infant, so everybody wanted to take me, but nobody wanted my siblings because they were older probably, I'm assuming. But she was the only person that was willing to take all of us. And so that's probably why: they wanted to keep us together. We all went. And my mother wanted for us to stay together because my sister went off with her side of the family. So, it left me and my oldest brother, [who] was I think five at that time. And so, it always left him being left in the system. [. . .] She didn't have anything when she got us. She did it purely out of I guess love for her sister and us, as a family unit.

Why was your mom unable to take care of you?

Well the same year that I was born, her mother passed away. I was born in August; her mother passed away in November. And I guess she had issues with that. I was told that she called the police, or somebody called the police, and they had said that she was trying to kill me. Well the police even said she was trying to kill me or that was her cry out for help. This is the story she told me. When the police got there, they said that she was holding onto me so tight that they physically had to force me out of her arms. And so, from there we went to the foster care system. I guess she went off to get help or whatever. And you know she was on and off drinking. I can't say for sure drugs, but I thought I heard coming up that she'd done drugs at a point. And then at a point she asked God [. . .] to take that from her. But she continued to drink all the time.

So, I knew of her. I seen her. She came around. But I never lived with her. Of course, by the time I was five, six, ten maybe, I would ask, "Why don't I live with my mother?" My aunt would say, "You're not old enough to know right now. I'll tell you when you get old enough you can understand." I think I was about ten years old. I remember asking her, "Why don't I live with my mother?" Well, she sat me down. She's like, "Your mother has some issues. They came in and they took you out of the way. And that's when I got you." And of course, along the way I started hearing different . . . stories. She was like, "You know, nobody wanted your brother; they always wanted you. And so, I just took both of you and your sister ended up coming along afterward." And after I got that story I was fine with it. But as I continued to get older I seen it: my aunt—she was the type of person that protected us as children. You know, [she] didn't want us to see too much, didn't like too much going on around us. But we had the [kind of] household where it was a family gathering place. [. . .] So, every time we would have a family cookout, all of the ones that were about the same age always would come over. Drinking would get involved. It would end up not so good. And as I remember growing up, when I would go to my mother's house it was usually an incident that I would have to come back early because either she got drunk or she got into an altercation. And I would go back to my aunt's. And I was fine, you know. I was a kid; I adapted. As long as I got back home and I was safe I was fine. I remember one incident . . . I went with my mother somewhere. Maybe it was a friend's house or something. And they were drinking, you know, kids being kids and she got really intoxicated, got into an altercation, and I remember them putting me in a cab to send me back to my aunt's house. I don't know why out of all of them that's the one that's most vivid in my memory.

. . . .

Tommye
I have known Tommye for over twenty-five years. I first met her during my first year of graduate school when I auditioned for a part in a film based

on the poetry of Sharon Bridgforth. At the time, Tommye was a theater
director in New Orleans and taught theater at the University of New
Orleans. I was cast in the film as a drag queen named Miss Flame. The
film was never finished, and I lost touch with Tommye for several years
until now.

Tommye was born in Orange, Texas, in 1952. Orange is the
easternmost city in Texas, sitting on the Texas-Louisiana border. While
the population of Orange is just at nineteen thousand, it is birthplace to
a number of famous people, including professional football player turned
actor Bubba Smith and rock singer Bobby Kimball, among others. While
Tommye spent her formative years in Orange, she has called New Orleans
home for most of her life. She and her partner of over twenty years have
adjoining businesses—Tommye a restaurant that features traditional
New Orleans food and jazz, and her partner a hair salon. Besides being
an entrepreneur, award-winning director, and restaurant owner, she is a
captivating storyteller. The interview took place on April 20, 2013, at her
restaurant and at her home.

Oh, man. I think I had a wonderful childhood. I had a wonderful,
wonderful childhood. I was raised by great aunt, Hilda, who was a teacher,
a principal, and a college professor. She was a spinster, and she had me
since I was one year old, so that made her my mom. She raised me and
another sister of mine who's older than I. We were her baby dolls. And
this is the fifties. I remember Aunt Hilda changing cars every other year.
I remember her dressing to the nines. She built her home from the ground
up in Pontchartrain Park, which was the first African American subdivision
in this country—subdivision in this country in an urban setting, I should say.
With my aunt we had everything. The can-can slips, patent leather shoes, the
fur coats, the fur things, kid gloves at six years old, cashmere sweaters. You
know what I'm saying? We had everything. Violin lessons, piano lessons,
dance school, charm school. That didn't work with me. [Laughter] We just
had everything. My aunt was a very, very, very, very proper lady. And I had
a wonderful childhood because even though she had . . . we were not with
our mother, who lived in Texas, there was some stipulation that said that
every summer we had to go and spend the summer months with my mom.
And this is as a kid. My mom was living with my grandmother at the time.
Shotgun house, outhouse, kerosene lamps, pumping water out of the well,
pigs, chickens . . . and my five brothers are there, too.

And where were you in the—

In the food chain? Which was also the bath chain. [Laughter] I was the third oldest, so I have two older sisters and five younger brothers. But my aunt took two of us and raised two of us, the two girls. Two of the three girls. The oldest girl, my sister Sharon Kay, she came when my aunt took the other two, but because she was older she couldn't quite make the adjustment from living with my mom and my grandmother to here. So, I had the best of two worlds because I was also a tomboy. And so being with my brothers every summer and climbing trees and riding horses, running around and playing in the dirt, and playing shoot-'em-ups, and all this other kind of stuff, and getting dirty was wonderful because I did that from like June until September. And then from September until June. So, nine months out of the year I had the finest things in life and three months out of the year I had the finer things in life, you know. And the finer things were running around with my brothers. But I was always so ready for September to come so that I could, you know, get back. I was ready for the school; I was ready for the prim and proper thing. But by the time those nine months were over with I was so ready for waddling in the dirt and running with my brothers and all of that. So, I had a wonderful childhood.

So, you didn't have chores around the house?

Mmm-hmm. Oh yeah! Oh yeah. Had chores around the house. We had a, I guess you could say, a nanny, who came in on weekends. My aunt lived with her younger sister, Aunt Annie, who's ninety-three, who I just came from seeing. My Aunt Hilda, who was the love of my life, passed before Katrina, thank God, because Katrina would have taken her out, okay? . . . The difference between Aunt Hilda's age and Annie's age was almost like eight years. And so, Aunt Hilda actually kind of raised Aunt Annie and Annie's a spinster, too. And when Aunt Hilda took [. . .] the two girls, the three girls, one went back after six months . . . [and] there was a, I don't want to say favorite. I'm told Aunt Hilda really just wanted one girl: me. But my mother said, "Take one, you've got to take them all." So, she took all three. And the oldest one, Sharon, couldn't make the adjustment. So, it was just me and Michael. Michael was two, going on three, and I was one, so what did I care, you know? Just pick me up, hug me, give me some love, and that's it.

Aunt Annie was abusive to me, I always thought because she knew that Aunt Hilda sort of kind of favored me, but my Aunt Hilda was a very fair woman. She was probably the most financially solvent of anyone in my entire family. That means cousins, aunts, ba-ba-ba-ba-ba, and independently solvent. But she never bought anything for me that she didn't buy for my sister. She never bought anything for my sister that she didn't buy for me.

Same quality, same thing. We were like matching baby dolls. Okay? And we always had the finest things in life. But whenever Aunt Hilda would leave the house, Aunt Annie was extremely, extremely abusive to me. Not overly physical abusive, but—

Verbal abuse?

—verbal . . . verbal, punished for no reason and . . . and [she] also told me that I was . . . oh, God, I was just hideous, I was just so ugly. I had . . . my lips were so thick. And my sister who, who my aunt raised, the other one, is fair skinned, more red in her skin and stuff like this. And my ears were too small, my nose was too small, my lips were too big. And so every picture of me as a kid is like me with my lips tucked. Mmm-hmm. And she used to tell me that the only thing I had going for me was my hair. That was the only thing because I had curly hair. And that was the only thing. So that went on for years and years and years, and I guess when I was about eight or nine, Aunt Annie, I guess had run out of ways to get back at me, or get back at Aunt Hilda, or whatever. But Aunt Hilda left the house one day and when she came back home I was bald. Bald! Cut off my hair. I think that's the only time I saw my Aunt Hilda absolutely lose it. I mean, I don't ever recall my aunt raising her voice until then. And never a time after that. But she lost it, absolutely lost it.

Did you cut your hair off to spite her?

Aunt Annie?

Mmm-hmm.

No, Aunt Annie cut my hair off.

(Gasps) Oh-h-h-h.

[. . .] Came home and . . . Annie had cut off my hair. And my Aunt Hilda lost it. Anyway, so when I was sixteen Aunt Hilda . . . and we used to always spend Christmas there, too. Me and my sister would go there for Christmas. This particular Christmas my Aunt Hilda and Aunt Annie drove us to Texas as they always did, but they stayed for Christmas. And Aunt Annie and I got into an argument, and the day that we were leaving, coming back, Aunt Annie told Aunt Hilda if I got in that car that we both couldn't get in that car, that Aunt Hilda had to make a choice. Now, mind you, I've been with this woman since I was a year and a half. Aunt Hilda had to make a choice, me or Annie, or her sister. [. . .] I remember getting out the car. I got out the car and I grabbed my suitcase and Aunt Hilda stood there and she says, "Get back in that car." And I said, "No." She says, "You get back in that car right now, young lady." And I said, "No." And I started running down this country road and I think they waited . . . and as night began to fall they had to get back, and I saw Aunt Hilda then get back in the car, and they just drove off. And so that's how I ended up staying in Texas. So [in the] middle of my junior year, December to May of my junior year and into my senior year, I lived in Texas with my mom. And so now I'm living with my brothers all the time. That was okay. I mean, you know. It's interesting because I didn't miss New Orleans; I only missed Aunt Hilda. I didn't miss the house because I knew that every time Aunt Hilda left I was being abused, so I never missed New Orleans or the house. I just missed Aunt Hilda, you know. Then when I graduated from high school, came back to college and I came back to New Orleans. But I didn't live with them. I lived on campus.

· ·

Xami

Xami is as cool as her name. A musician and middle school teacher, Xami was born in Hampton, Virginia, in 1957, the only child of her parents. Hampton is a coastal city in southeast Virginia, with a population of 145,000, half of which are black. It is also home of Hampton University, a prestigious historically black university. Xami is referenced in the story of another narrator in this book, but not by name. It wasn't until Xami began sharing her story with me that I began to put two and two together: Xami was a player! For years she took care of her ailing mother. The interview took place on October 31, 2014, in Pensacola, Florida.

[. . .] I think we invented something down here that kind of leaked out around 1985 to the rest of the world. And the country kind of caught up with it. The South for me on a day-to-day basis with the gay experience was very nuclear. Extraordinarily nuclear, and there was like a house. There would be a mother figure; there would be a daddy; there would be no kids—but they were protégés—young ones, babies, and they were very diligent about this mother and father figure, daddy figure. We were very diligent about how well we took care of these people. And this idea of butch femme-ness, daddy loving, you know, I could broaden it to the leather dynamics. I am so convinced it was a southern phenomenon because so much grows down here and then travels up the rails. And much like our cultural experience being African American, so much of it is born in our community and then travels the rail worldwide.

I think that the North kind of looked at this dynamic of how we expressed love, and how we lived together, and functioned with the same regionalist arrogance that they did many other things. The kind of a regionalist—I don't want to say faux pas—but I want to say retrograde, like we haven't quite caught up with the world. Where I think it was the exact opposite. This is where you found it, and you took it to where you live. And you called it your own, and that's fine, because we don't need that piece. But this is where you come every summer and enrich that piece and see how we navigate this world. Then you go up to Brooklyn and try to do that thing without getting in too much trouble. You see how to navigate out of it or you get lynched and burnt. You can live out this life if you're true to that integrity piece and not hiding behind closet doors and living as a pseudonym of yourself.

So, I'm very tied to the rich culture of the South. And not just politics . . . we brought so much of that [culture] to the nation, and sexuality I see as just another vein on that. So, I'm not sure if I have a true perspective of how the rest of the country sees southern, you know, lifestyles and sexuality per se. I can imagine from my travels. In California they'd say, "Oh you're from Mississippi," and then there it is. And then you decide if you have time to educate or not. So, it's, "Okay I'll educate you." Or not. But there's a certain kind of savoir faire that the North and the West have with the South. The East Coast has it too. I guess they need it. It's almost like a family system. And we don't care because we don't get it. And I don't get their experience as well. And so, I just say, "Don't knock it because what you live probably got lived out here first." This is where that great experiment happened first. And that's probably it. A very regionalist perspective on my part. [. . .]

I went to a historically black institution: Jackson State University. It just so happened that my mom had moved to Mississippi three years prior. And I told her I would never move to Mississippi. I was afraid of Mississippi. I thought it was everything I had read about it. And I wondered what did she think she's doing down there. But eventually came down to go to school. Again, I was out. I had to be at least twenty-two at the time. So, I was an older student. And I didn't care. At twenty-two that would have been '78–79. And so, it's new but not really. They know my personality type. The archetype but not really, not personally, so it was difficult to navigate all of the subcultures of a college, and a black college at that. But the thing of it was I was just so comfortable in my autonomy and my experience, and I had done a lot of work on me by then. Because I could easily see how many would not have survived that experience. I have so much compassion for young gay and lesbian individuals who are battling the bullying complexes that lead to self-determination and self-worth. I would love to do work in that area some day. Because I have lived it, and we have all lived it to an extent. But we have not lived it 2013 style. And it's a whole different animal. It's got to be. So, it was difficult, but I was very focused on music, the violin, and education. I knew I didn't want to do both together, but I wanted a side gig if the music didn't work out. [. . .]

What was the culture like there? Did you find that there were other LGBT students? And if there were, were they open or were they able to find each other? What was the community like there?

The men were much easier to find and embrace than the women. It just was. Because here they are living their life quite loud. They are leading the majorettes, homecoming, and they're teaching, at the bar. They're owning it. The culture, the presentation, they were our role models in the seventies. And not just drag queens. [. . .] These were gay men who were in their community and living out before we even had that language. And demonstrating how to be well and all that. And so, what it kind of came to mean for me was find a very strong supportive—not clique—of friends because you've got to make it thick, not too tentacles. But yes, you've got to put that pseudofamily around you like a cloak. And if you notice, they were never alone. So, you don't even walk to the store alone. You kind of have this first idea of what this rainbow-like family concept. It was deep. Now I hear there are houses and whatnot. We didn't have the language back then. But yes, they were often in the arts or church. And embracive. Almost like on a mission. "Yeah, you need to come over here with us and sit right here," and "Just watch this," and "Be quiet girl. You might learn something." And so that's what my college experience looked like . . .

What was the reaction of the faculty to these men?

I never saw them rejected. In fact, I saw them overloved in the African American community. They were celebrities—big time. And carried themselves as such and never disappointed. They had the height of integrity. They had the work ethic that you just dreamed for. Charming personality plus some kind of amazing talent. And I'm learning now everyone has one as a gifted teacher, and they worked very hard to find theirs, and found it and shined it. Taught me how to have the guts to get on that guitar in the middle of the stage—however many people watching me—to sing my song. Because my community as an African American girl was telling me, "Your song is not too important actually. You just sit right here and can you pass that chicken over here." Basically, you know, and you know we raised black girls in the South to be supportive, not necessarily trailblazers. And even though I come from a background of trailblazers that energy was always there. To fall in, not lead.

So why do you think that the men were (a) more open and (b) more accepted than the lesbian women?

It's a dynamic [that] until just very recently has always existed. I love history and I love to kind of get context for America. If you're going to European, Roman, you've got to get that West African. But when I look at the European/Roman and the history of gay males in our civilization, of being embraced, then slaughtered, then embraced. Then slaughtered and then embraced . . . it just shows me the fickle nature of it. [. . .]

Does Your Mama Know?
Motherhood and Mother-Daughter Relationships

2

The above title riffs on a common question that circulates among queers, especially African Americans, because of the privileged place black motherhood holds in African American communities. The embodiment and representation of the "black mother" are vexed owing to the role that black women have had to play in the nurturance and protection of children to whom they gave birth that were then taken from them under chattel slavery and to whom they did not give birth but whose care was imposed upon them—in slavery and in freedom—whom they were expected to care for because of their "innate" mothering abilities. Indeed, the trope of black motherhood has been pathologized in contradictory ways that has served whatever racist, sexist, heteropatriarchal purpose needed to maintain control over black women's bodies.

When I began conducting these oral history interviews, I had no idea that mothering would emerge as such a powerful trope, for I, too, fell into the sexist and homophobic trap of thinking that black queer women would not be invested in mothering. While I expected to meet a number of women who were themselves mothers, I had no idea how powerful the role of mothering would play in some of these women's lives. Indeed, many of the women speak passionately about their desire to have children despite, and sometimes because of, being black and queer. As noted in the introduction, gay parenting, and especially among queers of color, is more common in the South.

Not all of the women with whom I spoke had a desire to be mothers, however. In fact, there were some women, like Cherry Hussain (see chapter 9), who had children because they felt trapped by the expectations of heterosexual marriage; others, like Sharita, got pregnant through a one-night stand and felt abortion was not an option; while others, like Mary Anne Adams (see chapter 13), became de facto mothers to their siblings because of circumstances of poverty, abandonment, or death of a parent. In these instances, *being* a mother was not the same as *desiring* to be a mother. Like the character Eva in Toni Morrison's novel *Sula*, their mothering love was a "love of necessity."[1]

In addition to being a biological or adoptive mother, mother-daughter relationships emerged as a prevalent narrative among these women. Some of them speak quite movingly about their close bonds with their mothers and how their mothers accepted them when they revealed their same-sex attraction. More surprising, some of the women relay stories of how their mothers came out to them, explaining that they were not free to do so, given the time in which they lived, and resigned themselves to remaining in a heterosexual marriage. In other instances, mothers and daughters actually are both open about their same-sex attraction. Indeed, I interviewed mothers and their daughters in the same setting, revealing generational differences between how each woman came into her sexuality and the impact it had on the family. Finally, many women share heartbreaking stories about their mother's rejection of them based on their sexuality. Unsurprisingly, much of this rejection is on religious grounds. Over the course of several years, some of the women's mothers come to tacitly accept her daughter's sexuality, sometimes due simply to the passage of time, sometimes due to being won over by the partner or wife of her daughter, and sometimes by the birth or adoption of a grandchild. Whatever the case, these stories of mothering and mother-daughter relationships convey a deeply moving and complicated history of gender and sexual relations among black southern women.

. . . .

Alpha
Everybody in the black queer community in Dallas, Texas, knows Alpha. Besides being a mother and grandmother herself, she is mother to an entire community of "young heads." She is also an HIV/AIDS activist who worked for the Dallas Urban League as a public health educator in the early days of the disease and is still currently involved in HIV/AIDS care and prevention.

The eleventh child of fifteen, Alpha was born in Dallas in 1957. As she explains below, her relationship with her daughter is in striking contrast to the relationship she had with her own mother, which was strained because of what she describes as her mother's religious fanaticism, leading her to try to exorcise Alpha's homosexuality. It was not until her mother was on her deathbed that the two were able to reconcile. The interview took place on September 15, 2012, in Dallas.

You are a mother. Talk about your decision to become a mother and a little bit about your relationship with your daughter, being a black same-gender-loving woman.

Yes, I was in a relationship with a woman who—well, we both decided that we wanted another child. She had a child from a previous marriage, but we both wanted a daughter. And so, we decided that I would go through Child Protective Services as a single parent and adopt a child. So, I did. And so, that's how I became a mother. My daughter came into my life when I was—excuse me, when she was eight months old. I requested a toddler. I wanted a child between the ages of two and four, because I wanted to bypass all the diapers and a lot of that. Because I used to have issues about getting urine and fecal material on my hands. But when God blessed me with this eight-month-old child, I overcame all of that finicky stuff, okay? I started telling my daughter about me being a same-gender-loving person when she was able to talk because my partner and I made up our minds that we were going to be very open and honest with our children. Because I adopted her as an out lesbian, I was open with the state. But my partner and I, at that time we decided that we didn't want to have any secrets in our family. And we wanted both of our children to grow up in a healthy, wholesome home. So, as I said, the minute my daughter was able to talk, I started telling her, "You have two mommies." And we had books, like *Heather Has Two Mommies.* And we used to read that book to our daughter. And we also wanted to be open with her about being adopted. So, we had a book from Sesame Street that dealt with being adopted. But we've always been open and honest with our children about being same-gender loving. And then when my daughter was two, the relationship ended. My daughter came to live with us when she was eight months old and then when she was two years old, my partner decided that she wanted a husband. So, our relationship ended. So, I raised my daughter alone. Well, with the help of the community, the school, and the community.

And so, my daughter, when she was a teenager, that's when we really talked about what it means to be same-gender loving and to have a mama who is same-gender loving. Now, I'm a revolutionary, and I put that spirit in my daughter. So, I told my daughter over the years that nobody defines us, we define ourselves. We define family, not the church, not the community, not the school, not even our immediate family. You will have people who will say, "Oh, your mommy is blah, blah, blah. She's a bulldagger. She's gay. She's a freak. She a lesbian." I always taught my daughter, "Don't let that get to you. When people come at you with the poison you're not gonna be a part of that. And I want you to remember, I want you to hear my voice when the negative people come at you with this, because they're gonna come." And then I taught her what my mentor taught me about just because the wolves come for you doesn't mean they have to eat you. So, my daughter really was never teased about having a same-gender-loving mama. I locked my daughter's hair when she was two years old. And when she started school, the children teased her about her hair. But they never, ever—she never really was teased about having a same-gender-loving mama.

Now, when my daughter was in high school, she attended a single-gender school here in the Dallas community. And she started writing papers on gay adoptions and what it means to grow up in a same-gender-loving or a gay home, a gay household. And even when she went to college, she wrote papers on gay adoptions and growing up in a gay household. Actually, she did a presentation in one of her classes in college on growing up in a same-gender home, same-gender-loving home and having a same-gender-loving mama. So, as I said, she's a little revolutionary, like me. And she kind of went through this phase in college, because she attended a single-gender college in Oakland, California, Mills College. And California is very liberated. . . . So, she kind of had crushes on a few female students there. But I reminded her, I said, "Girl, let me tell you. This is nothing to play around with." She likes what she calls studs. She said, "Ooh, they're so, cute, they're like cute little boys." I said, "I want to remind you that they may be cute, dress nice, and all that, maybe look like a guy. But trust me, when she takes off her clothes, she's gonna have breasts and a pussy." I was just honest with her. And I said, "She's not gonna have a penis or a dick dangling between her legs. Now, she may have sex with you maybe with a dildo. But remember, she's still a woman. She's not a man. And I'm not teaching you to have this little fantasy in your mind about studs thinking that is she gonna be just like a guy? No." I said, "This is a very dangerous playground to play on, if you're not same-gender loving or you calling yourself bi-curious. No." I said, "You can't play on the playground like that, big girl. Somebody will hurt you possibly, because they may fall in love with you. And here you are, you just want to play house. But this person has become emotionally connected with you and maybe even loves you. And I'm telling you, it can be a very dangerous, winding road. So, you need to really know what you're doing if you're going to play on that playground, because that's nothing to play with, big girl." So, she got over her little stud fascination. So, I'm a grandmother now. My daughter has an eight-month-old child. And I stay at home and I'm helping my daughter raise her, because my daughter is a Bill Gates scholarship recipient. And I don't want her to lose that scholarship just because she's a mother. She's studying nursing. I know that that's not an easy major. So, I didn't want her to have any excuses for not being able to study and to graduate, just because she's a mom.

How old is she now?

She's twenty-one now. When there's certain things in the media about the LGBT community, she'll call me and say, "Mama, turn on channel blah, blah, blah. And blah, blah, blah is on. They're talking about gay rights or bisexuality or whatever." So, that makes me feel good, because she is open-minded. And what I wanted for her, the open-mindedness, the love, the care, the compassion, and all of that, for humanity is in her. Because I told her that in our home we have no place for discrimination, prejudice, and what have you. Because we've had other issues that we've had to deal with, like immigration. And I told her, we don't have negative attitudes or behavior towards people who don't have their legal status or whatever—no, no. So—but I'm proud of my daughter, because the things that I put into her in terms of that foundation, they're there. And they're surfacing through her behavior and even things that she says, conversations that we have. So, I'm proud of myself as a parent. I feel that I've done a great job with my daughter. And she can speak out on what it means to have a same-gender-loving mama, knowing that she was raised in a healthy, wholesome, loving environment. Her mama made her a Gates Scholar, and she graduated sixth in her class of twenty-one students, with a GPA of 3.6 on a 4.0 scale. So, I'm proud of myself, you know. And when she was a student at Mills College, she was involved in the LGBT community there at the college. So, kudos to her, I feel really good about the job I did with her.

* * *

My mother was mentally ill and she was also a religious fanatic. And we experienced a lot of emotional, psychological, spiritual, and physical abuse. So, I did not have a happy childhood.

Were you an only child?

No, I come from a family of fifteen children. I'm number eleven. I'm Alpha and I have a sister named Omega. My mother was very religious. She named all of her children from the Bible.

Really?

Yes. But my childhood was very traumatic for me.

So, did you know your father?

Yes, I come from a two-parent household. Actually, I was raised by my sister and her husband. But I did frequently visit my birth family.

So, you said you're number eleven of fifteen children?

Yes, mmm-hmm.

And what are the age ranges?

Well, my oldest brother, he's deceased, but he would probably be close to eighty. And my youngest brother is like in his early forties.

Oh, wow. Did you have chores when you were a child?

Yes, we had chores. We had to clean our house, wash dishes, wash clothes. We used to wash clothes in the bathroom on a scrub board with lye soap. And we had to do the yard work, too. And so, yes, I did have chores.

And you said that your sister and her husband raised you?

Yes, I have a sister who's seventy-seven. And she and her husband—they raised me.

How did that come about?

That came about as a result of me not wanting to live in the same household with my parents because things were so dysfunctional. [. . .] During that time, I was seven years old. And because of the dysfunctionalism that existed at home, at age seven, I made just a serious decision that I didn't want to live in that type of environment. And it was at a time when they were integrating schools. So, I used the excuse of not wanting to attend an integrated school, as opposed to telling my parents, "Y'all fight too much, and that's really why I don't want to live with you." So, with my sister and her husband, now I did not know this, but they fought, too. So, I just really jumped out of one bad situation and entered another one. But my sister and her husband economically were in a better shape than my parents because they only had one child. And so, I had my own room that I shared with a nephew. But we had plenty of food. I mean coming from a family where there are fifteen children, if we were not home at a certain time, we didn't eat. So, living with my sister and her husband, I didn't have to experience those hardships.

What did your father do for work?

He was a construction worker. And my mother, she was a domestic worker, when she worked. But most of the time, she was a stay-at-home mom.

And did you consider your sister your mother, in a way, because you moved in with her so early?

I never really considered her my mom. But my sister forced me to call her mom.

She did?

She did. Because I was telling people that she was my sister. And for whatever reason, she did not like that. So, she threatened me and told me that I better tell people that she's my mom and not my sister. So, I was terrified, and I was like, "Oh, okay."

Well, how did your mother feel about that?

Well, she wasn't really crazy about it. My mom and my sister, they really didn't get along well. Because this sister came from a previous marriage from my father. So, there was a lot of friction between my mom and my sister. We never said we were half-sisters or anything like that. Our parents just taught us that we were all sisters and brothers. But this particular sister and my mom, they had a lot of problems with each other. So, my mother wasn't happy about it, but she was a very passive woman. And she just let it be.

Growing up, what role did church or religion play in your life?

Oh, church and religion played a major role in my life. As a matter of fact, my mother was Pentecostal and we went to church every Sunday. We also went to tarrying.

What's that?

It's like in the Pentecostal church, when you spend the entire night praying. You stay up all night just praying. And so we did that. I hated church because our mother, she used religion to really shame and embarrass us.

How?

Well, she would always tell us that the devil was in us. I know now that my mother was mentally ill. But at that time growing up as a child, I didn't know that she was sick. But she used to always tell us that the devil was in us, and the devil made us do this, the devil made us do that. Mom referred so much to the devil that I always said, "If I ever meet that motherfucker in person, I'm going to kick his ass." [Laughter] That's how much I hated the devil, you know.

Did you even have a concept of who the devil was?

Not really, you know. She just always talked about the devil, and I just grew up hating him. And I always just said if I ever meet him in person, I'm going to do him a good ass whipping. [Laughter] And so, my mother was a fanatic. And as I said, I know now that she was mentally ill. And religion—it divided my parents. They used to have these religious debates a lot of times. And my mother was very committed and dedicated to the church. I mean, she put more in church than she did at home. So, yes, religion played a very big role in my life. And when I came out to my family, my mother exorcised me. And that was extremely traumatic.

How old were you?

Seventeen.

Wow. And what did she do exactly?

Well, first she told me that God made woman for man and not for another woman. And that homosexuality was of the devil and evil. And then she laid hands on me. She took her hand and put it on my head and began to speak in tongues and do this little ritual to remove the devil from me. And I grew up in a household where we were taught that everything your parents tell you is right. You never question them because they love you and they know what's best for you. So, we went through the ritual.

Who was there?

Just the two of us. We were outside in our garden. We had been picking fruit because we had fruit trees. I had just recently come out to my family. And so, she just told me, she says, "You know, you're really not a homosexual. That's a demon in you that's making you think that. And I'm going to drive that demon out of you." And so, that's when the ritual started of her placing her hand on my head and praying and speaking in tongues. And she was saying, "Come out, in the name of Jesus! Hallelujah! [Speaking in tongues]" You know. And I'm thinking, "Oh, my God." You know, I had this demon in me, because this is my mother who had me and who loves me, telling me this. "Oh, God, please." I was praying silently that the devil would come out of me. And so, we finished with the ritual. I went inside of our house and I laid down. And I was doing this self-talk. I said, "Oh, my God. I'm possessed by the devil because I'm a homosexual. Well, let me go to sleep, and when I wake up, the devil is going to be out of me." And remember, I was seventeen years old, just a kid, with nobody really to talk to and to explain to me that I was really okay. So, I laid down and went to sleep. And when I woke up, I expected to be heterosexual. But it didn't happen, it didn't work. So, I was like, "Well, you're still gay. Well, you just better accept it." But I internalized a lot of shame and fear. And that was a battle for me, you know. I just began this struggle to feel good about myself and to love myself. But I made it through, you know. I stopped going to church on and off. And I just became so very defensive about being gay that anytime I would hear people say negative things about being gay, I was ready to whoop ass, you know. And it got so bad that after I graduated from college I had difficulty functioning in the professional world because when I would hear people say negative things about gays and lesbians, I would immediately just click back in my mind to being exorcised by my mom—and also experiencing the negativity from some of my siblings because they shamed me, too. They told me they were embarrassed of me and that nobody in our family—that we didn't have homosexuals in our family. And that I was basically a disgrace.

Was that true?

Oh, no. You know, I have a brother who, he's gay, too. But he's not out; he stays away from the family. He lives in another state. But I saw him when I was twenty-one years old, in a gay bar on Halloween night, you know. And I approached him because at that time I wasn't thinking about him being gay. I was just thinking, "Well, my brother is," you know, "here probably with some buddies, just hanging out." Because there are straight people that hang out with gay folk. So, I assumed that that was what he was up to: just hanging out at the bar with some of his gay partners. And I went up to him to hug him. And he pushed me away. He says, "Get away from me. I don't know you." And I was twenty-one years old and that really hurt me. And I just began to internalize even more shame and hurt. So, that created friction between he and I. And I started going to psychotherapy because I was beginning to have some serious emotional and psychological problems. So, the therapist helped me to understand that, more than likely, my brother was gay, too. But because of his shame, he just tried to put it all off on me. And she told me that I needed to confront him. So, over the years, when I gained enough strength and courage, I wrote him a letter and I did confront him. And I told him, "How dare you attempt to spew your shame on me, when you're just like me. You're gay, too." And I just said some other different things. But he never responded to the letter. And since then, we've had some of our siblings' children come out to me. But I really do believe that my mother—both of my parents are deceased now—but I really do believe that my mother was a lesbian, too.

Really?

I do believe that. Because there was this certain look that my mom gave me. And it was like, it was a look like, "I wish I could do the things that you're doing. I wish that I could be as brave as you are." And, I mean, I just felt that connection with her. So, I believe that lesbianism is in my genes. And I don't mean my 501s. [Laughter] I believe that I inherited it from my mom. And I'm okay with myself now. It has taken me many years to learn how to feel good about myself and to be okay with who I am. And it's a great feeling. It's a really great feeling.

So, how did your relationship with your mother evolve after the exorcism? Like between then and, I don't know, say twenty-one or twenty-two? What happened in those years? Because obviously, the exorcism didn't work.

Right. Well, what happened I come from a family where we just pretended like everything was okay. So, she never mentioned anything to me about being a lesbian after that again. All she always talked about was the devil and going to hell. But there was a time over the years when I wrote my mom a letter, too. Actually, I wrote a letter to my entire family. And I did mention being lesbian in those letters. And [Mom] wrote me letters back. But every sentence was a biblical quote. That's when I really realized the sickness of my mom. Because she never really addressed any of the issues that I addressed in the letters. Everything was just scriptural quotes. And I'm like, "Oh, my God, my mom is out of touch. She's really ill." And so, we just went on from there. I just never really talked about it anymore.

And in her later years, when she was a lot older, did you and she ever sort of reconcile or come to some kind of understanding or be at peace with each other?

That never happened until my mother was dying. When she was dying, it was important to me to go to her, to make peace with her. Because I do not like shame, guilt, and fear, but especially guilt. And I did not want to live with any guilt regarding my mom. So, I took it upon myself to go to her on her deathbed and make peace with her. I told her that I love her and that I was sorry for the things that had transpired between us. And the fact that we had our differences and we never were able to get past those differences. And that I did not want her to pass away without us talking as mother-daughter. Nor did I want her to face Jesus and God with us not being able to make resolution between us. So, I asked her for forgiveness, for whatever I had done to maybe hate or to hurt her, or what have you. I just said, "Mama, please forgive me for whatever hurt or pain I've caused you. And I also want to let you know, Mom, that I forgive you for the hurt and the pain that I have experienced with you. And I just want us to have a clean slate. And I want you to have peace with me. And I want you to have serenity." And she really was unable to speak. But then she, some kind of way, I believe through the power of God, was able to say the word "serenity." And so, that's how things transpired with us. And so, today, I do have a peace of mind in reference to my mom because I was the only sibling that went to her, to make amends. And so, it was a very good feeling. But before doing that, I spent probably like an hour, an hour and a half, communicating with God, and just wailing to God, asking Him to give me what I needed, to be able to go to my mom's bedside and say the things that I needed to say to her. And I feel that God did empower me with what I needed to do that because I was able to do it, and it gave me such a peace of mind.

Bonita/Bluhe

Between the time of the interview and the publication of this book, Bonita transitioned to presenting as male, uses the pronouns "he" and "they" and goes by the name "Bluhe." The second oldest of fifteen children, Bluhe was born in 1968 in Anderson, South Carolina. Anderson is a part of the northwest region of South Carolina known as the Upstate, which consists of the cities Greenville, Spartanburg, and Anderson, the smallest of the three with a population of twenty-six thousand—a third of whom are African American. Like many of the mothers I interviewed, Bluhe's children are the product of a marriage that they felt compelled to be in based on his family's expectations. When the marriage ended, he got custody of the children, and they live with him and his current partner. Besides being a parent, Bluhe is also a poet (see chapter 5). The interview took place August 22, 2012, at his home in Winston-Salem, North Carolina.

You have children?

Yes.

Did you have them?

I HAD them, yes, and you want to know the story behind that?

I do.

Then let's get busy. Okay, growing up in the South you are taught morals and values. That's just it in a nutshell, point blank, period. They believe in the moral value system whether you want to hear it or not. This is how we're supposed to be. A man is supposed to marry a woman, and that's that and nothing else, nothing less. My grandma taught me that, as well as my family. My immediate family that I was with on my mom's side taught me the same morals, the same values. I said, "Well," you know, "I must give it a try." And I was too busy trying to satisfy my family to keep them happy instead of working on my needs in my life, So, it took place. I got involved with a young man and—

How old were you?

Twenty-two.

Young.

Yeah, twenty-one, twenty-two, somewhere along there. We got together and we got married and we had a family. I have two boys and a young girl, young lady. That was my daughter and my son [referring to the two children I had just met]. My oldest son is twenty-three, twenty-two. And I have a granddaughter. But I mean, I just went through a transition. I tried it and it just did not work. It was not for me. I tried. I tried my best to maintain it, but I couldn't.

How long were you married?

We were married from '95 to '98. We didn't stay married long.

Long enough to have the kids.

We were together longer than we were married, let's just say that. We were together longer than we were married because I really didn't want to marry him. It took me a while to walk down that aisle. And I basically did it not for me but for my children. Another decision made for somebody else to keep somebody else happy. Another wrong decision is what I say. But you know, you live and you learn and then you go on. If I had the option of doing it all over, I wouldn't have. I wouldn't have.

Do you think he had a sense that you were gay?

He knew. I told him.

Oh.

I told him in the very beginning. Yes, ma'am. Yes, sir. I told him in the very beginning. I said, "I would rather date your sister than to date you." [Laughter] He said, "What you saying?" I said, "What does it sound like I'm saying?" He said, "Oh, so, you're one of them." I said, "What's wrong with them?" He just kept talking. I said, "If you're asking me if I'm gay, I'm telling you yes. I'd rather be with a woman than to be with a man," and that was that. And he still pursued; he still pursued; he still pursued. It took him about three or four months to actually get me on a date.

So, he didn't go into this not knowing what he was getting in for.

He did not go into it not knowing. I told him straight off the bat, straight off the bat, straight off the bat.

And while you were married, do you feel that you slid into the sort of conventional wife role?

I tried. [Laughter] I'm being honest. I tried to be a good wife. I tried the role. I tried to do what I was supposed to do as a wife, and it just wasn't me. I couldn't, and I couldn't continue to be in something knowing that I was that unhappy. It was just going to cause more problems, more grief. And that's not what I needed, and that's not what my children needed, and that's most definitely not what he needed.

How was the breakup?

Pretty dramatic.

It was your decision, or was it mutual?

Well . . . okay, let me say it like this right here. There were things that I wouldn't do for him that he wanted a woman to do. So, he went out, and he had an affair, and I told him, "If you do it again . . ." I forgave him the first time. I told him, "If you do it again, then we're just not going to be a family any more." And he did it again, So, I pretty much told him that it was over. We were buying a home together. We were pretty rooted and grounded together, and all that just went kaput. I packed up, packed up my three kids, and we took off. And that was that. I told him, "You can have everything, I'm starting new. Okay?" Three days later I get a phone call: "Your husband is threatening to kill himself." So, I had to go and check on him. They said, "What do you want to do, Mrs. Parks?" I say, "I'll tell you what, you can take him on down. I'm gonna sign the papers. You know what to do with him. He needs some help. If he's threatening to kill himself over something that he already, he already knows the outcome. This is over. It's over. It's etched in stone. Bonita and Louis are over. It's over, so, if he wants to kill himself, that means he's not healthy enough to be here. So, we need to do something about that." I had him committed for three weeks. I went and took care of him, see if he needed anything while he was in the lockup. I took care of all of his bills, the house stuff, whatever that needs to be taken care of, but I told him, "When you come out of here, we're still over." "Well spend the night with me." "No. Do you need anything? I mean, I'll do everything that I'm supposed to do because you are my children's father. I'm going to see to that. But anything other than that, I just can't do it." So, that was the end of it, and he finally came around to his senses that Bonita's just not going to be around here anymore.

Do you have a relationship with him now?

I do. We still talk. We have children together, so I'm not going to close that line of communication. If he wants to close that, then that's what he wants to do, but my girlfriend, she's involved in everything. If I go and take Jeremiah and Carissa to see him, she's [his current partner] right there. I don't have any interaction with him without her. I mean, she made a comment one time when we were down there. She said, "Bonita's looking real good." Because I used to weigh over three hundred pounds, so I was kind of slimming down and he say, "She's always looked good." She was like, "Yeah, I know it, but don't get too close." [Laughter] So, yeah, I mean, it's just back and forth. So, I want her to be around to see those things because I don't want anybody saying if I drop them off over there and something takes place it's just my word against his word, so I try to keep her involved. It's the same way with her. We try to keep each other involved with our relationships with our children's fathers.

And how did your children deal with you being a lesbian?

My oldest son didn't take it too well in the beginning. He was like, "Why, Mom?" "Why" this and "why" that? I had to sit down and explain it to him that this is not who I am. "I'm me, and I don't know how to be this person that everybody wants me to be, and I can't be someone that I'm not." So, over the course of the years he's come to [terms with my sexuality.] He takes it fairly well now. My baby son asked me just last week, "Mom I thought you turned gay after you and dad broke up." So, I had to sit down once again, and explain to him, "I've always been gay." And I explained to him about morals and values, that "this is why I went through that traditional family style: just to see if it was where I needed to be. And it wasn't where I needed to be." And I had to explain that to him, and he was like, "Well, I understand that now, but I just thought." I say, "That's good that you asked because I don't want you to hold that in your mind and not know the answer to it." My daughter, it doesn't matter. Mama's baby, mama's princess forever. So, it doesn't matter.

. . . .

Emilie

I almost didn't get to interview Emilie. The first attempt was foiled by a canceled flight out of Chicago. A disgruntled worker set a fire in an air traffic control tower! I was on the phone with Emilie's assistant while at the airport trying to figure out when she would be available again so that I could reschedule my flight. It would be a month later. And it was worth the wait. Emilie's story is inspirational because it defies what one thinks is possible in the South. That is, she is the first openly lesbian dean of a school of divinity in the South. She is also the first black woman to be a dean of a school of divinity. She covers lots of "firsts" in this regard. Born to academic parents in Durham, North Carolina, in 1955, Emilie attributes part of her success to her being raised in a close-knit community. Durham is located in central North Carolina and makes up a part of the Triangle—Raleigh, Durham, and Chapel Hill. It has a long history of civil rights activism, including being the site of the first civil rights sit-in of the Civil Rights Movement in 1953 at the Royal Ice Cream Parlor. It is also the home of some of the most prominent black-owned businesses, such as North Carolina Mutual Life Insurance Company and the Mechanics & Farmers Bank. This vibrant black community was the backdrop of Emilie's childhood. Below, she tells her coming-out story to her mother and the surprising revelation that emerges from that event. She resides in Nashville, Tennessee, with her wife, who is also an academic. The interview took place on September 30, 2014, on the campus of Vanderbilt University.

My mother was a molecular biologist. My father taught exercise. [. . .] Mom was the first black woman to get a PhD in cell physiology at the University of Michigan. So, it's not something she talked about a lot. The most she would say to me was it was lonely. And she said, "And I don't care to relive that by retelling it." I knew enough to leave that one alone.

Were both of them from the South?

No. Mom was from Southern Pines, North Carolina. Dad was from Mechanicsville, Pennsylvania.

Where's Mechanicsville?

Up in the mountains, west.

How did they meet?

At North Carolina Central University.

Oh, so, they went to school.

No. They were both teaching at that point, and friends who knew them individually. The wife knew my mother; the husband knew my father. [And their friends] decided it might work if they got them together. And it sort of did. Yeah.

What were the thoughts or beliefs about people that were different from you in your household, whether that be religion, race . . . ?

What I was taught was that we're all equal. I could see differences in behavior from both my parents. Mom was a little more consistent than Dad because Dad was a homophobe. Mom was not. And I often wondered what both of them saw in the world. Because Mom was a light-skinned black woman, so much so that when I was a little kid, I thought she was white. I didn't get a spanking. The worst whipping I got in my life was when I said, "Oh mama's white," not knowing what I was saying. My dad lit into me like white on rice—so much so that mom stood by to make sure he didn't kill me. And I wasn't a child that got a lot of whippings. I didn't know what I was saying. After he finished and stormed off, that's when mom sat me down and said, "Here's what you need to know." It was my first lesson in colorism. Because dad was a dark-skinned black man. I had no idea what I had stumbled into because I was just commenting on what I saw—not having any idea of what I had opened up.

And so, you have a very light-skinned mother. When she was younger, could she have passed?

Almost, not quite. But she could have come close. There's no way Dad could pass for anything other than being black. And the two different worlds they inhabited because of that—not only because of gender but also because of color . . . has often left me wondering. Because Dad was a staunch

Methodist later. He knew what he should believe, and that's mostly what he taught me. And Mom had had more church from her mother growing up, she said she was she was working on her backlog. [Laughter] She had gotten enough growing up that she didn't need to go to church. She tithed every month, but she preferred to stay home and listen to the Duke Chapel services on the radio.

* * *

My parents were sneaky. They would leave stuff in our family library for me to find so there was the *Playboy* joke book down there, as well as Radclyffe Hall's *The Well of Loneliness*. . . . And other books. But I realized as I got older they left that down there for me to find and read. And, of course, I never told them I was reading any of it especially that *Playboy*. I didn't know what I was getting into with *The Well of Loneliness*, but I figured it out. Because my mother was very technical. She was a scientist, so when I asked her where babies come from she gave me the technical explanation. "There's a penis and a vagina and the male inserts the penis into the vagina. If the woman has eggs, the male's penis has semen, and boom, baby happens." So, I had no idea why everybody was so hopped up about sex because it's like, "That's pretty perfunctory." Until I started reading some of those books down there and I'm like, "Oh, the difference is this feels good." But that's how they taught, expanding on sex ed. Because nobody said it directly: "This stuff feels good, which is why people do it." But I know. I'm [like], "Okay, now I know what the thing is about sex. It's pleasurable." So, I never got the message it was dirty or nasty, interestingly enough. I got the message, "It was pleasurable, but you keep it to yourself." As I'm reading these books downstairs, where hardly anybody would have, except me in the library in the basement, reading.

* * *

The last night I was home [after graduating from college] it just so happened that Mom and Trisha [Emilie's sister] and I were all sitting in the kitchen, and Dad was watching TV in the living room. And I . . . well, in retrospect I realize what I did. I pulled Trisha to sit in my lap so there was somebody . . . I was Dad's favorite, Trisha was mom's favorite. So, I had her favorite in front of me. [Laughter] And I said, "Mom, I got something to tell you." And she said, "Yes?" I said, "Mom, I'm gay." Mom said, "Uh-huh." I said, "Mom, did you hear me? I just told you I'm gay." She said, "I heard you. I've known for a long time." I'm like, "Really?" She said, "Mmm-hmm.

You brought all these women . . . Yes, I knew this." I'm like, "Really, Mom?" She said, "I am so sorry but we are not gonna have drama here tonight. I know. Do not tell your father." I said, "Mmm, Mom, I kind of had thought that wouldn't be a good idea." She said, "He would not be able to handle it. You've heard what he's had to say about gay men in this house, and you two have already had words about it. Just don't do it." I said, "Okay, I can live with that." And I looked at Mom and said, "I think he knows." She said, "He probably does, but until you tell him, he doesn't. And he's happy with that." And she never said anything to him either, never told him.

Next month I'm doing laundry, getting ready to get on the road. Mom was in the family room in the basement reading. Her favorite thing was reading. She's the most avid reader I have ever seen in my life. And I was going back and forth, down the stairs, and from the couch at one point I heard, "M&M?" I knew something was important because she only used that name, it was a term of endearment, it wasn't said often, and when it was she wanted my attention. So, I stopped and I was like, "Yes, ma'am." She said, "I am afraid for you." And I said, "Oh?" She said, "The lifestyle you've chosen to lead will be dangerous, and you will have a difficult time in life. And I'm afraid for you because people get killed." And I said, "I know, Mom, but you and Dad taught me to live my life with integrity, which is why I told you." And she said, "I know. I know why you told me. And I know what you're going through because if I had had courage, I would have made the same choice as you." Which I knew. I knew because my girlfriend and I had talked about, "How queer is your mama, Emilie?" So, I got on the phone right away then. That was cool. "Thank you, Mama. But I will be careful, I will take care of myself. I want to be old when I die." And she said, "Thank you. But I just had to tell you my fears." I said, "I understand." I was cool. I just went up the steps, got in the room, and closed the door and, "Girl! You would not believe what Mama just told me!"

. . . .

Iris

I learned of Iris through Mary Anne Adams (see chapter 13), who said that Iris would be a wonderful person to talk to about her life in Atlanta and her involvement in several black lesbian organizations, including ZAMI NOBLA (National Organization of Black Lesbians on Aging). Iris, however, hedged on the interview because she didn't think she had anything to say. As I soon learned, Iris had a lot to say. In fact, I asked Iris only a few questions and the first interview went on for close to three hours!

Because I ran out of time, I had to go back for a second interview, which was close to two hours. We had a great time during both interviews. Iris also loves to bake and baked me a loaf of zucchini bread during my first visit. Since then, she has challenged me to a baking competition because she knows that I, too, love to bake.

Iris was born in Miami Beach, Florida, in 1957. She is the middle child of seven. She has taught literature at Clark Atlanta University and Spelman College, her alma mater. As she relates below, her relationship with her mother was very close and important to her. The interviews took place on August 27 and October 14, 2013, at her home in Atlanta.

My mother was always supportive, even when she didn't quite get it all. I remember the very first time we even discussed it a little bit, and that was when I sort of had the falling out with my father. And I was visiting friends in New York and I went by to his apartment. And [he] wouldn't let me in. He claimed he didn't have a daughter named Iris. [. . .] But I remember my mother distinctly saying, after she talked with him and he had mentioned to her that he thought I was gay, and I remember my mother telling him, "Well, what if she is? Who's fault would it be? . . . She is who she is." And I said, "Well, I'm glad you did say that." I said, "But one wrong word there and that is 'fault.' I don't think it's anybody's fault because it's not a fault. It's no more a fault than if I was left-handed instead of right." I said, "It's simply who I am." I said, "It only defines me to a certain extent. I am who I am." And so, she said, "Okay." Oh, my gosh, this would have been like '83 or something. And from that point on, she was supportive, if not outwardly, verbally. She'd meet my friends and be, "Okay, these are her friends." And she never said like anything negative.

For her, I guess it was sort of like a crash course. Part of it was that she was the kind of mother who her children were okay. [Laughter] I'm saying it wrong, but okay in the sense of they can only do no wrong, you know. Of course, she knew that we could do things wrong. But for her, it was always like we knew she would support us regardless. And that's always where she operated from. So, I remember several times of her meeting all my friends [at] a [reading] ZAMI put on. It was at the Existentialist Church. We called it the "E Church," over not too far from Charis bookstore. And we had people reading. So, some of it was quite risqué. And my mother had just come in from Miami, because she would go back and forth over the years since about mideighties. [. . .] And I said, "Well, Ma, I got this program with ZAMI, we're doing this." And she's like, "Fine, let's go." So, she's sitting in the audience and she's hearing poems with very much erotica. And she's cool, you know. A good one, she clapped. So, afterwards, in fact, I think it was Mary Anne who walked up to her and said, "Miss Clark, I hope you enjoyed the show. I hope you weren't too put off by the . . . " And I think her response was, "My dear, I've lived even longer than my years. And I'm okay." [Laughter] She said, "I thought the show was great." And I remember the look on Mary Anne's face was like "Okay." [Laughter] You know, not too many parents would just sort of sit there through this . . . but that was really sort of her thing.

[. . .] After she died last May, I found a lot of her papers. And she wrote just prolifically, just kind of journaled like every day. And I found something that she probably had written in the last couple of years. . . . [In] one of the last descriptions [laughter] she went down the line to describe all her children in her words. And so, my oldest brother was this "workaholic pilot." I think my next brother because he is a genius but he's also in prison, a "genius jailbird." [Laughter] So, when she got to me, I was a "gay, PhD, professor," something like that. I mean, all the way down to the youngest. [. . .] That was just my mother, these were her kids. And so, I never really worried about things like introducing her to partners and this sort of thing. Again, she was always really accepting.

. . . .

"Lady Boy"
I was introduced to "Lady Boy" through a network of black queer women in Jackson, Mississippi. "Lady Boy" is a name she chose to symbolize her gender queerness. She was born in Greenville, Mississippi, in 1973 in a middle-class family that for eighty years owned a construction company. Greenville is a river port city that sits at the heart of the Lower Mississippi River where Arkansas, Louisiana, and Mississippi come together. Of the roughly fifty thousand residents of Greenville, 70 percent are African American. The interview took place August 24, 2013, in Jackson, Mississippi, at a local university.

[My] mom left when I was five years old. So, my father raised me. And I had everything I needed. I can't say I had anything I didn't need. My family owned a construction company for like eighty years. Yeah, but what I didn't have is my mom. And so, she left at age five.

Do you know why she left?

She was progressive. Not that my father wasn't, but I think that she had some desires. She had lived abroad. She was also from Greenville, and she had lived abroad. And I think that one can't fly and the other person is kind of happy with where they are. And so, I think that was difficult for them. And my mother was an only child, and she had the best of whatever, too. And I think that she was a very education-oriented type of woman. She graduated from Wilberforce. Yeah, in social work. So, I think that her objectives became different and it was hard to mesh the relationship.

Were you an only child?

I'm my father's only child. And my mother's third child.

* * *

And I think that I was kind of subject to my past a little bit because my mom just kind of got to the point where she was dating a drug dealer, and doing this, and doing that, and then eventually she left. But people never let you forget your past. It's Peyton Place. [. . .] So, my grandmother played a role. My aunts were around, but I think one of my aunts kind of gave me a hard time because she knew I was different. I've always been a lady boy. A tomboy.

You know my mom called me when I was like fourteen and it was like, "Are you a lesbian?" And my mom hadn't even talked to me. I mean, literally, like she disappeared out of my life and I didn't know where she was. And I was kinda like, "She knows my number?" You know, like when she called I was like, "Okay, well, I know what a lesbian is," but I said no.

Why would she think that?

Well, my sister talks too much still. And the town is small. So, if you call one person in the town, everybody knows what's going on, still to this day. And I said no. And that was the first time I denied myself. And when I said no, the reason why I said no is because she said she would take me from my father. And she said, "No child of mine will ever disgrace me like that." And I'm thinking, "You left me," you know like, "You disgraced me." And I just was like, this isn't right. [. . .] And so, I struggled with that. That's when sexuality became a struggle: when my parents seemed like they weren't going to accept me.

* * *

I had a very bad temper as a kid because I never dealt with my mom leaving. And so, when me and my friend was breaking up finally it was just like I just snapped. And so I put my hand through the wall, and my dad like had me in like a full nelson, but he just couldn't hold me because I'm pretty strong. And I just was hurt. You know, I just never dealt with my mom leaving, and here's another person that I love leaving. I didn't know how to let go because I was never afforded the opportunity to let go. So, when someone hurts you like that, I think that before I hurt anybody. And this is what I do now in my relationships: I can be one foot in, one foot out a lot. I tell people. My therapist helps me tell people. Basically, she tells me to tell people.

* * *

My mother knew before she passed away. She passed away in 2004. I moved to Chicago in 2000. And I think I told her in 1996. I said, "Yeah, I'm gay. I like women. It just is what it is." And she was just like, "I don't want you to get blown up in a club." "What?" "Even though you're in a big city you can have a small mind." And even though she was a social worker and she encountered people that were same-sex loving, it didn't mean that she knew how to handle it. And so, that's what I had to realize. And so, she was like, "Get a woman that's not so fast because you're kind of slow." I'm not that slow. I'm kind of street myself. I've learned a lot by moving to Chicago. I said, "Well you're right." I said, "But I'm not attracted to the church girl." Never have been, other than to make them my slut and then keep it moving, you know, but that's just never been my thing. I need an intellect who is edgy, who is a lot of fun, who wants to do things. I'm a Scorpio. I'm spontaneous. You know, I like to just get up on a whim and go do whatever I want to do. I said [with] the at-home everyday woman, I might cheat. And so, that's what I would try to tell her. And so, I said, "You like the bad boys. Drug dealers [and] all." I mean hell, I get it, honestly. My dad as quiet as he is, he had two, three girlfriends, you know. It's the hush part of the culture of the South, and we don't put our business in the street like that. Because my mother was always worried about me putting my business in the street now that I'm out gay to her. "You can't be working that government job and having all them women." [Laughter] "Mama, they don't go to work with me you know." She was so funny, though. She was so cute. I loved her a lot— I had been on a couple audits and women have tried to say something to me, and I'd be like, "No way. Setup." You know like I can smell it. But I would tell her about that. And she was like, "You're just so cute." I said, "Whatever." You know, I mean, that's how mothers are, I think, with their kids.

So, you two reconciled after a while.

To a degree. My mother was—after some assessment and after changing fields into psychology—she's borderline personality [disorder]. I am bipolar, type II. I'm not ashamed; it is what it is. I think my father has some kind of mental stuff, too. It's in my family, both sides. And so, the awkwardness that we have comes from our struggles with mental illness. And my mother was so brilliant that I think that she rejected her mental illness because she felt like she could fix it as a clinician. The worst thing you could ever do. I know I've got to take my meds. I know that I've got to get to the psychiatrist. I know that I've got to get to the psychologist. I have to do that to be able to enter in the field of counseling. You have to counsel from a centered place. So, we were able to reconcile. But there are still some things. . . . All my life I wanted her to validate me. And I realized toward the end of her life that she couldn't do that. That's a spiritual thing. That's a God thing, that's a me-and-God thing. And I prayed her into a transition. That was one of the most difficult things I've ever had to do in my life. But she felt like God was keeping her here because she had done so many things not necessarily that she should do to me and my sister and my other sister. I found out that I had a sister when the casket was closing. My mother's best friend blurted out, "Oh So and So is your sister." "What?" My departing look was like a "Oh! What?" It was more of a "Wait a minute, you're stealing this moment for me," and all these years I felt that.

. . . .

Laurinda

I met Laurinda through her books before I met her in person. A writer of black lesbian erotica and a playwright, Laurinda is well known nationally in the black queer community. She was born in Memphis, Tennessee, in 1959, the eldest of three children. Although she resided in Atlanta for many years, she fell in love with her wife, Dedra (see chapter 1), who lived in small-town Prentiss, Mississippi. It was a move that Laurinda says she was ready to make to escape the "drama" of Atlanta after a nasty breakup and to have a simpler, more fulfilling life with her partner. Two of the themes that Laurinda discusses in her narrative that were not covered by many of the other narrators are colorism and sexual abuse by female relatives. Despite her turbulent childhood, Laurinda enjoys her life with Dedra in Mississippi and keeping up with her daughters, both of whom are grown women. The interview took place on August 22, 2013, at her wife's funeral home in Prentiss, Mississippi.

Talk a little bit about your daughter.
Which one? I have two.
I didn't know about the second one. Tell me about the second one. The same guy . . .

No. Different guys. The first daughter is a sophomore at Howard. She's very gay. She's like a little boy from the boondocks. She was always in the dresses and ribbons and stuff. [. . .] And now she's just straight up [butch]. Would I choose for my kids to be gay? No. Because I'm interested in [them] experiencing the world. Experience stuff first. She's never been with a guy. And I always told them—this will sound really crass but it's the way I put it to them: "You need to have some dick first before you decide that you want to be with a girl." And she [. . .] didn't come out to me until she was sixteen. But I knew. She told everybody else but me. I read it in her journal. So, she said, "I know what you said about . . . having sex with guys, but I don't ever see myself wanting to do [that]."

Is this your younger [daughter]?

This is my oldest girl. So, I said, "Okay, whatever." So, she's living. She's out, out. I mean they lovey-dovey, hug, kiss, walk hand in hand walking down the street, out. My words of advice to her have always been, "Everybody doesn't see the world through the same eyes as you do. Just be mindful, always be mindful of your surroundings." And so, we have a very strange emotional relationship. I've always told her, "I feel like you'll be the one to destroy me and then feel bad about it the next day." And she knows. You know I battle with her emotionally. And she's acknowledged it over the past few months that I've taken some emotional beatings from her. And I know that you're giving it to me. She said, "I know that you know I'm sorry. I don't know what it is." I'm working through it, and I just got to a point now where I'm so free in my thought process and in my life. I'm in the best place in my life than I've ever been. If she doesn't [want] to hear me I say, "I don't care." But it's really how I feel: I don't care. You know she's nineteen; she's got to go about her journey. She's going to make her mistakes, do her thing. [. . .] My younger daughter, [she's] seventeen, she goes to Dillard University. I just dropped her off Sunday. She's the total opposite—all girl. You know she's still a virgin. She told me a while ago she can never be in a relationship with another woman because there is no way I could be with somebody who feels the way I do. She said, "Because I could never have two of me walking around, I could never do that emotionally." Cool. So, she's very accepting. It took a minute. I guess when they got older and they were able to voice their opinion about it, they didn't like my ex. I mean, fourteen years is really [long], and now it's over. But they adore the space where I'm in now because they knew where I came from. They knew what it was like. So, they're very respectful of me and my marriage. Very loving and caring. They adore Dedra. They told her early on, "You gave our mother her smile back." And so, we have a good family. A good family. They're teenagers and they're going through their thing. They're pains now, but they're good girls.

. . . .

Kate [b. 1981, Winston-Salem, North Carolina]

When I was nine my mother was incarcerated. She went to federal prison. She was in Danbury and then she was in Alderson. And my mother was always really smart. I just think that having me at sixteen sort of did something to her sense of hope. It was like a scarlet letter for her, if you will, because this is the South and people are ashamed. Especially 1981. I can only imagine. And my grandmother was a diehard Christian. And so, I can only imagine what that looked like for her and her congregation, if you will. And I don't even remember [my mom] working when I was a child. I remember her staying home, and I remember she always dated these really big drug dealers. . . . People say that she looks like Sade, the singer. And so, she was always very, very beautiful. And so, every guy who had something in our neighborhood or even—because my father comes from like middle class and my mom comes from like a lower socioeconomic status. And even I always wonder how my mom and dad got together or whatever, because my dad is like the opposite of my mom. And I think he saw her somewhere, one day I think he told me.

Is he older?

Yes, he's older. And they just clicked. And yeah, so, my mom basically was incarcerated when I was nine. And she was gone until I was twenty-two. She was actually sentenced to twenty-two years in federal prison, but she only did twelve.

For drugs?

Yes. And the crazy thing is my mom has never had a speeding ticket, and she never sold any drugs. But she got wrapped up with a young man. He was from New York City and in the late eighties, early nineties there was a huge crackdown in the South on crack cocaine. [. . .] My mom tells me things, and I would say that it was weird even living in a house with him, because even though my mom dated drug dealers she never dated any that had money like he did. But even though he had money we still lived in like a housing project. And so, I never could really understand it. And then at the very moment that we moved, that's when the Feds came to our house. And I remember being that nine-year-old little girl, and that day I think placed a wound on me and my mother's relationship in two ways. The first way was that Reggie, which was his name [. . .] always thought that I hated him. [. . .] I couldn't really tell them all the things that were happening to me—including the fact that one of his friends molested me as well. You understand? And so, I didn't really—I guess I wasn't as playful with him, and I just didn't give him what he wanted, if you will. And so, he always felt like I had a problem with him.

And so, my youngest brother, Darius, had braids like Reggie. And the morning that the Feds picked them up I remember my mom coming to pick us up and Darius's hair was cut. So, immediately they blamed me. And the funny thing is, to this day Darius says, "No, I cut my own hair." . . . I didn't understand why they thought I would cut his hair. And so Reggie, in my opinion, was a very sick individual. And I say that because he then goes to the store, buys Nair, and tells my mother to put it in my hair. And he didn't even put a gun to her head and tell her to do it, which is why there are some things that me and her are going to sit down and talk about at some point, too. You understand? Because even to this day I have psoriasis on my scalp and my dermatologist absolutely knows that it had to do with that. You understand? So, I'm still affected by something that happened to me when I was nine even though I'm in the process of forgiveness on a deeper level . . . and as she was putting the Nair in my hair and washes it out, like, "What were you thinking?" is what I want to ask her. And washes it out and dries it and basically soon as she's done we get a knock at the door. She tells me to go open the door because she thinks it's Reggie. Unfortunately, it's about five Caucasian gentlemen. And they're all dressed in suits and they asked for my mother. And I say she's upstairs.

And you're there bald.

Right. She comes to the top of the stairs and she's like, "Oh shit," because she realizes something's up. And I don't even think at that moment she knew it was about the drugs. I think that she really thought maybe it was about me and she shouldn't have sent me to the door. But I was the last thing on their mind. Even though they knew I wasn't all the way bald. [. . .] And basically, they go in our home and they begin to make a mess. And they tell her to take us in a room. And at this time one of his friends actually shows up. And the friend basically takes us away. So, we don't get to see the rest of what happens. We don't really get to see our mom being taken away. I think I was the only one at the house at that time, if I'm not mistaken. So, then Q, which is his friend, takes me to my grandmother's house. And you know, basically starts explaining to my grandmother exactly what happened. And I remember Q telling my grandmother that they had gotten Reggie too. And they got him like across town. So, it was like a planned sting. They knew exactly what they were coming for.

[. . .] My mom's attorney wanted me to testify. And I don't remember exactly [. . .] what he wanted me to testify about. But I think that once he found out what happened that day to me, he knew that I absolutely would not be a good witness. But I did go and watch them sentence my mother. And I remember the district attorney telling my grandmother that they were going to make an example out of my mother because she would not cooperate with them. And they were going to make an example out of her so other young women would understand that you could not have people selling illegal drugs out of your home. Whether you're involved in it or not, you were going to get the same punishment that they basically would receive and that's exactly what happened. [. . .]

And the most interesting thing is I think my mom went to federal prison and ended up starting to date women. And now her and her partner own a very beautiful country home in Winston-Salem. And you know, even people that go there are like, "Wow, you went to federal prison?" They see this beautiful home. But her girlfriend is now one of the lead detectives. [. . .] She used to work in narcotics, but now she works in like sex crimes because she's getting ready to retire and stuff. But I just still think it's kind of weird because they're still very opposite people. And I just found out recently, too, that they're not even [out]. I mean, how do you not know that they're together? But I think like among some of her friends, the police officer's friends, they don't really like boast that they're together. [. . .] I don't really know how that works. But I think it's going to be interesting when Reggie comes home. [. . .] I can only imagine, if my mother did those things to me for him, I don't really see this relationship working out very long between her and her partner. Because she has everything she wants. You know, she drives a brand-new Volvo. She has a beautiful home. We have two dogs. You know she's in school right now. And I just think it's going to be interesting, like I said, to see how it works out when he comes home. [. . .]

That's interesting. So, did you ever have a conversation with your mother about your uncle molesting you?

When my mom was in federal prison I wrote to her and I told her. And I believe she wrote me back and she apologized. But we've never really sat down and talked about it. There have been situations where when she first came home from federal prison . . . all of her kids confronted her. Not about her going to federal prison, but at this time she was dating someone that was using drugs, and this person would leave for three and four days. And we're like, "You don't have to settle for this. You just came home. Like enjoy your life." And so, we just sat her down and like confronted her. We packed the person's clothes up and like sat them outside. And like it was serious like that. And so, it was very heated because at that time I was like twenty-four. So, I didn't really understand that even in speaking to people, I'm either [giving] love or needing love. And in that situation, I was needing love, and so, of course you know it didn't come out the way it should have. And my mom had just come home from prison, and so we were all yelling at her. And she still had that "prison mentality," if you will. You know, guards yelled at them and so she just shut down. She didn't really have anything to say. And at that time [. . .] that's when I left and moved to New York. And so, to confront her, no, we never really had the opportunity. But it's important that I tell you, too, that in that moment there was a real breakdown between my mom and I, because I felt like in that moment maybe she blamed me for being the oldest. Maybe she thought I told them to pack up the clothes when it was really one of my other brothers who had the idea. And I just was like, "Okay, I'll go along with it."

· ·

Kerrie [b. 1970, Fort Lauderdale, Florida]

Okay. So, I came out to my mother on a ride back from Mobile to New Orleans. I was in New Orleans. I was living there after New York. I moved back to New Orleans, and there was a funeral in Mobile, and it's a very short distance between the two. So, she flew into New Orleans [and] we drove to Mobile for the funeral. I was like in my midtwenties. On the way back she was asking me was I dating. This was after my divorce. And I said, "Yes." And she said, "Well, who is he?" I said, "It's a woman." She said, "You stop kidding." I was like, "No, I'm not kidding." And she said, "Well, I don't want to talk about that." I was like, "Okay." And up until that point I was very open with my mother, and I thought that she was open. And she said, "Well, do you want to go to Piccadilly and eat?" [Laughter] I was like, "Okay." So, we're in Piccadilly eating. Nothing. Nothing is said. She doesn't want to talk about it. She gets up the next morning really, really early and she's like, "I'm gonna leave now, and I just want you to know that you are not gay, you are not a dyke, and you will not be and . . ." something about, "not now, not ever." It reminded me of *The Color Purple*. [Laughter]

And so she left, and then since then I've had conversations with her about my life, my partner, who I was dating—not extended conversations. And she has not been receptive. And the last time I had it was actually about maybe six months ago. I decided—

This is over a twenty-year period?

It's a long ass time. [Laughter] It really is, you know?

Wow. Given what you've said about your mother growing up—about her not really being that religious, especially Jesus folks, and her having this really good friend who was a gay man—why do you think there's been so much resistance from her? Is it because you're her child? What do you think it's about?

I don't know. I think maybe because I'm her child. But then also I have a godmother and my godmother is my cousin, her sister's oldest daughter . . . she's gay. She's been gay. She was sixteen when my father died. She was there when that happened in Florida, spending time with them. And my mother named her my godmother. And she's a nun. She just became a nun. So, it doesn't have anything to do with religion.

It's specific to you.

It's specific to me. And I think it has a lot to do with control. Like she thinks somebody is trying to control me and that I'm under the influence.

. . . .

"Joyce"

I was actually surprised when "Joyce" indicated that she wanted to use a pseudonym for the interview because she is quite an outspoken activist in her community. Her story is truly one of triumph over tragedy, as her mother contracted HIV and passed away when "Joyce" was just thirteen years old, leaving her to take care of her younger sister, who was five. She was born in Fort Lauderdale, Florida, in 1987, the eldest of two children. The interview took place on March 19, 2013, in Tallahassee, Florida.

My mom, she had a blood transfusion because she had kidney failure, and they're saying that they think it [her HIV infection] was from that because at that time they weren't screening blood, but I don't know. And my stepdad was definitely not the most faithful person, So, I don't know; we don't know. [. . .] I had to bathe my mom. I had to dress her. I had to give her medicine. At that time she was at least on thirty to forty pills a day, so I would have to like wake up early, fix her medicine, fix her breakfast, then come home from school, make sure she had [everything]. She was also on dialysis at the time. I watched her literally change. My mom was very vibrant, very active in the community, very well known, and then she literally just got extremely sick and because of the HIV medicine and how it mixed, she developed dementia. So, she just had a lot of issues, and at the time, a lot of those medicines . . . if you miss a dose, you're not supposed to keep taking it or you have to be careful about it. Well, she didn't really follow the protocols a lot. So, she had a lot of reverse effects of the medicines because she didn't know. Some of them were so expensive. So, one month she would have it, and then the next month she couldn't get it, so it was just a lot with HIV. [. . .] My mom was young. She was thirty-seven. So, it's had a huge impact on my life.

* * *

I [came out] after my mom died when I was in high school; I was going through a lot and [I was] overwhelmed, so I went to live with one of my aunts because I bounced around a lot. And she was really, probably the best thing that ever happened to me. I went to her my tenth grade year, stayed with her until twelfth grade, and my sister lived with my dad, my stepdad, around the corner. But my aunt really took care of her. Her dad was very against her moving in with us, so that aunt is really kind of like who I consider my mom because she really took me in, she groomed me, took really good care of me. Her and my uncle were like really awesome parents. . . . When I wanted to come out I thought, "Okay, I should talk to her about it, but she's very religious." We never miss church. She's in the clergy. She has a million roles, like very, and my aunt is also the most affluent person in my family. She actually went to college. Her two children went to college. She's very big on appearances. So, I knew that this was going to be an issue with her, but I didn't expect the reaction. I actually had moved to South Korea after undergrad to teach English. So, I was living in Korea and I was like, "Well, there's a lot of distance and space, so I can tell her now. There's not much she can do." And I called her one day, and I was like, "I need to tell you something." And I told her, and she was like, "I can't hear you," and so I said it again, and she was just quiet. And she just started laughing, and she was just like, "Are you sure you're okay?" And I was like, "I'm fine," and she didn't believe me. She said, "We have to pray about it. This can't be true. I just won't accept it." So, at that time I felt really invalidated and I was like, "Okay, I don't know what to do because I told her." The conversation went on for her to like preach to me about why this can't happen, why this is a mistake. She told me to never tell anybody else that, and that she was really going to pray, and I needed to pray and then I needed to repent. And that was how our conversation ended, and we never talked about it again until recently.

And how long ago was that?

That was in 2010.

And what happened recently?

Well, it got really explosive because she's like my mom. [. . .] Before I told her, my girlfriend was with me all the time. She's very masculine. I mean if you were basing it on stereotypes and appearance, you would know that that was my girlfriend. And my aunt knew; she just kind of turned a blind eye to it, and it was one of those things we don't talk about it. So, after I came out when I was in Korea, like we went on like nothing ever happened. And I didn't feel good about it, so I actually became very distant from her. And I travel a lot, I go places all the time, so I used that as an excuse of why I didn't talk to her . . . whereas before when I was in high school, we were very close. I could have talked to her about anything. She was the nonjudgmental aunt. Everything except being gay. I could probably have been a teen parent and she would've rather that than me be a lesbian. So, in September of 2012, last year, I just kind of got to a point where I feel stifled by her judgment. And I know it's a problem because I can't bring anybody around her; I can't talk about it; and when I go home I have to be a certain kind of way. So, I called her to discuss it with her, and she refused to talk about it and said, "We're not having this conversation," and she hung up the phone. Well, I sent her a very long e-mail . . . [saying] this is my life and I will not let her control me and I am lesbian; either she can accept it or move on out of my life. And I was very direct with her, and I told her the saddest part of it all is I know if my mom were alive, my mom would accept me because I've seen her to do it for other people. And for you to take the role of my mother and to treat me like that because of one thing is a problem. And she did not like that very much. So, we did not talk for several months until probably January.

Of this year?

Mm-hmm, of 2013. We started back talking. Well, she wrote back the e-mail. It was short. She just said I was lying about everything in the e-mail and that she will not support my lifestyle. She will pray and help me get through, and I have to respect her because she's been there for me when no one else was, and she just will not accept a lesbian. That's just not going to happen. So, when we started back talking, we just act like that never happened. So, it's something that's never been addressed or dealt with since then.

· ·

Malu

Malu is one of several women I interviewed whose mother was also same-gender loving. She is the only child of Nancy, also interviewed in this book (see chapter 1) and has quite an interesting life given that she's an ordained chaplain who works in palliative care. Malu was born in Cincinnati, Ohio, in 1980 and reared for part of her early childhood in New York before her family moved permanently to North Carolina, where her mother is from, when she was a tween. The interview took place on July 30, 2013, at her mother's home in Davidson, North Carolina.

Well, my mom was on this side and she knows. And I assume my dad, being on the other side, he knew when I knew. So, I'm out. [Laughter] You know.

What was your coming-out experience like?

Oh, so dramatic. And I don't know why. [Laughter] I was so dramatic. I was crying and all. It wasn't so much of who I was with; it was the fact that I had had a sexual experience, that I was horrified to say that to my mom. I was horrified, because we'd always talked about waiting until I got older, and the responsibility of it, and what that looks like. Now, most of it was coming out of a more heteronormative context in terms of pregnancy and disease, but I didn't think about that. What I thought was, "My mama told me I should wait until I get older," and here I am, like, I think fifteen, being like, "Mama." I mean, I was so drama[tic]—oh, I cried so hard. Now, we talked about it, and she kept a straight face, and then she went to call my aunt. It was like, "Girl, Malu finally done come out." And they had a good laugh about it. [Laughter]—"Girl, please. Didn't she know she was gay?" You know, we talked about it years later. But at the time, I just remember I was so emotional, because I was so concerned that she would have feelings about that. The actual act of sex. I was like, "Oh, God, what is she gonna think?"

So, it wasn't about the fact that it was with the same sex, it was about you having sex at all.

Umm-hmm.

So, what compelled you to tell her?

I have no idea. I really don't. I do not remember anymore. Whatever it was, I felt like I needed to be . . . in intimate relationships . . . there's a certain amount of transparency and integrity that I need to have with them. And that's just who I am. I lied to my mom one time in third grade, and I came back and told her I lied and put myself on punishment, and she told me that my punishment was harsher than what she was gonna do. But she was like, "Yeah, sure, go with that. No *Cosby*, no *Different World* for like two weeks." That's serious punishment when you're eight years old. . . . I wanted to be honest about who I was. This is a big difference: whereas once I had no idea what a orgasm is, I now know what that is; I have shared it with somebody else. Like, that's a big deal. So, "Mom, you need to know that about me. But I'm also freaking out that I'm gonna tell you this." And I don't think I said all those words; I'm confident I didn't. But it's more, so just about transparency and showing up in that relationship. How can I be in a real relationship and not show up?

And at that point, she hadn't come out to you, or she had?

Oh, yeah. My mom told me that a long time ago. And my response was, "I like boys. You can be gay if you want to, but I like boys."

Really?

I was real young . . . don't remember how young I was, but I was young. And she . . . just kinda gave me the side-eye, like, "Okay," and I was like, "Alright." That was really my only question. "Does that mean I have to like girls, too?" That was kinda my thing. "No." Okay, well, whatever.

And then when you came out to her, what was her reaction?

[pursing her lips] "Um-hmm." [Laughter] It was kinda like, "right." [Laughter] I mean, I think it was kinda like, "You don't think I know that's your girlfriend? I ain't stupid." [Laughter] Like, "Yeah, I know." I mean, she didn't say that, but kinda, you know. She was like, "Okay."

* * *

My son was born in 2005, so that shifted everything. [. . .] I understood parents; I didn't understand, like, co-parent family unit. [. . .] When it came to him [Malu's son] and us [her and her ex] having that discussion about what it means to co-parent a child together and whether we could break up tomorrow, but once we say this, under the commitment to him, I understood. [. . .] I've known her since I was a teenager. She's from this area, so we've known each other off and on since I was like sixteen or seventeen. But we linked up again for dating purposes. I was twenty-four. [. . .]

So, your son? Is it a son? When you and Linda got together, you made a conscious decision that one of you would have a child?

No.

No.

[Laughter] Oh, my son, the little surprise. So, Linda had—in her own journey . . . she's raised Pentecostal; her mom's a Pentecostal missionary. Now, I mean, at this point her mom was like a whole new level. But she was raised working class, Pentecostal, missionary, with her family having some roots that are like Trinidadian, some roots that are Geechee, [and] her father happens to be Liberian. But her family context was very, very conservative, very, very holy. I mean, her mom doesn't wear pants, doesn't wear earrings.

. . . She grew up going to church all the time. So, her journey of being able to say that she was a lesbian was far more painful, I would say, than my own, especially in reaction with her family, I mean, her nuclear family. So, anyway, she had been engaged to a man there for a while; and I don't doubt that she loved him, but I think a large part of it was "I am not going to be gay." Anyway, she was engaged to him and they broke up, and as people do sometimes, you dip back into old experiences. And he [her son] was a surprise out of that. So, yeah, I was there when she learned she was pregnant. She didn't know that. We didn't know she was pregnant when we first started dating—had no idea. So, that was a funny moment . . . she wasn't feeling well, so I took her to the ER, trying to figure out [what was wrong]. 'Cause she has bad asthma. And so, I was like, "Well, you're about to have an asthma attack?" "I don't know." I'm like, "We're going to the doctor. I don't know what's about to happen."

And this little white lady, she's so funny, she said, "Well, I need to tell you something. Do you want your friend to stay?" And Linda was like, "Yeah." And she was like, "Are you sure you want your friend to stay?" And she looks at me real sweet with this look in her eyes, and I'm like, "What?" By the way she said "friend," I knew she knew. So, we're just like, "Yeah," and so the doctor says, "Well, honey, you're pregnant." And I remember they both just turned and looked at me. And I was like, [laughter] "For what? Hey, like are y'all really both staring at me?" And they did. Both just complete silence, just looking at me. And I was like, "Dang." [Laughter] You know, so I think we all kinda recovered. And then there was a lot of conversation after that, like, "What does that mean?" And "Okay, you're pregnant and are we going to stay together? Are we going to break up? Are you trying to give it one more try with this dude? I mean, you were engaged to him, like what does this look like?" It was a lot of conversation, a lot of heavy intense conversations for people so young. And I know some people don't think that's all that young, 'cause people have babies earlier than that, but when you put in the dynamic of being same-gender loving and having a surprise kid . . . I haven't heard a lot of stories that are similar, put it that way. So, a lot of conversations and I prayed a lot. And the way I talk about it is that was my first calling, like my first calling from God was to motherhood. You know, I was like, "This is my kid. Okay. Huh, Okay." So, I need to get on that and adjust my life accordingly, and figure out what it means to be a mother. "Wow. Alright." Which I didn't think I would do until . . . in my thirties somewhere. But we figured it out—not well initially, in terms of our relationship—but [our son is] always well loved, had what [he] needs and he's kinda spoiled, but . . .

Well, with three mommies now.

Right. Three mommies, two grandmas in his life on a consistent basis. But then Mika, that's his stepmom; she has a mom, so he has her; and then his biological father, even though he chose not to be in his life—which is unfortunate—he has a birth mom and adopted mom, so I think Linda has a connection with his adopted mom. She's in St. Thomas. She's in one of the Virgin Islands, so she's not here, but they chat on occasion. He's got three moms and four grandmothers, so yeah. [Laughter]

And what does he call all of y'all?

Mika, he calls by her name, he calls her Mika. Initially, I was like, "No, that's not your mama." I didn't tell him that, but I made it very clear when they first dated, I was like, "Yes, this is great. Y'all can date, that's not a problem, but that's my child." Now, six years later, very different experience. So, if he's with one of us, it's just "Mommy." But if he's with [one of them], then "Mommy Lu" or "Mommy Lin." He just distinguishes like that. [. . .] I mean when he talks about his other mom, he's gonna talk about her wherever he is. You know, if he's in the street, if he's in the store, he talks openly about his family. He'll tell people—he has even told strangers before, "I have three moms." And I'm looking at them, trying to hold my energy, 'cause I'm like, "You'd better not. I don't care what you think, you better . . ." And sometimes people are like, "Oh." And I'm just looking at 'em, smiling like, "What you?" "Well, isn't that beautiful?" Or "Aren't you special?" Or "Isn't that unique?" People have not said anything rude to him, [for] which I'm grateful. Because who knows what they're really thinking. But my thing is, whatever you think, I don't care. Just don't say it to him.

· ·

"Mary" [b. 1975, Tuscaloosa County, Alabama]

So, I was talking with my younger sister the other day, and I said, "You know, I don't think that my mother realized it, but I think that she raised us to be feminists." I don't think that was her intent; she probably didn't even know it, but my younger sister and I were talking and my partner . . . it was funny because we had some of the same things that we were saying in regards to marriage, for example. My partner wants to get married. She'd probably do it if I called her at work right now and said, "Hey, let's go." She'd probably just leave work. You know, I've never been, "Woohoo, let's get married," you know? Saw somebody tweeting, said, "Girls really . . . all young girls, they dream about getting married." I didn't. I never daydreamed about getting married, didn't really care. But maybe that's because my mom wasn't married, so I didn't really think that much about it. But we were talking about getting married and talking about changing our names. And my sister, who's heterosexual, said the same thing. She was like, "Changing my name, why would I do that?" You know? And that's the same thing I said. I was like, "Why would I do that? That's not what's on my birth certificate. I was born with this last name; I want to die with this last name." So, we were just having this conversation and my partner was like, "I wonder does your mama know she just raised two feminists. You feel like you don't need a man for anything." And I said, "But you ought to think about it like this. When we were growing up we didn't." We didn't really need . . . I mean, I wouldn't say "need," but I guess we didn't have a man around for anything, so it was never a concern. It was just second nature; if this needs to be done, we do it. And so, we had that conversation and it's like, I wonder if she knows, if she knew this whole black feminist, Afro . . . maybe not the Afrocentric part, but definitely the black feminist part—she did that. Without knowing it, she did that.

Would you say that about your mother as well?

Yeah, yeah. I really do think it's starting to bother me to a certain extent because my mother and I talk and we have good conversations, but I think in the back of my mind I'm always agitated because I think I just want to blurt out, "Okay, look, you know this is the case, so let me just say this and get it out. Now, how was work today?" So, I think that's my own little thing.

You hear about mothers, in particular, having a hard time with their sons being gay. Do you think it's equally an issue between mothers and daughters?

Mmm-hmm. Mmm-hmm. Mmm-hmm. Mmm-hmm. I think it's equally an issue between mothers and daughters because what I'm coming to find out about myself, and also in talking to other lesbians and a few mothers, is that mothers sometimes have this—and black mothers in particularly—maybe have this whole perception of who their daughters will be. You know, "You can't be a lesbian because I say that you're not. And if I say that you're not and you are, that means you're purposely defying me." You know? And so, I think that that can be a struggle. I went to a conference a couple of weeks ago, the Black Women's Wellness Conference here in Atlanta, and one of the mothers there said, "Well, that hasn't been the experience between my daughter and I at all." But she said, "But I think that that may be because we've always had a closeness where I felt like she should be whoever she is and whatever that means." She said, "I think that sometimes mothers have an issue with their daughters being gay because mothers have this authoritative parenting style where they feel like they define who the daughter is." She said, "I've never felt like I could define who my daughter was, whether that related to the music she liked or who her friends were. I never tried to define who she was. So, even though her being lesbian was a little bit more of a challenge, it was still easier for me to accept because I understood that she's my offspring, but she's not the mirror image of me." So, I'm still trying to figure out all the pieces to that, but I can see how that would be true in some cases. Probably in mine as well. Because like I said, just in thinking about how I grew up, my mother taught us to be very independent . . . very proud of whoever you are. Like I just remember her always saying she was a working-class single parent, so we didn't have some of the things that some of my friends had, but she made the thrift store look good. You know? So, it was like, "No matter what you're wearing, you hold your head high." So, she gave me all these lessons about being independent, being proud of yourself, being strong, being this, being that, but be that within this box, though. Don't be that and be lesbian. That's just too much.

. . . .

Melissa

Melissa was not only eager to be interviewed for this book but also instrumental in finding other women for me to speak with. Although she is soft-spoken and unassuming, she is committed to black LGBT rights and activism. She was born in Nashville, Tennessee, in 1979, the youngest of three children. She and her siblings were raised solely by her mother off and on but experienced emotional and physical abuse from one of the men her mother married when Melissa was five. The interview took place on August 29, 2012, at her home in Nashville.

[My first girlfriend] gave me a hickey, and I remember we were in the grocery store in Kroger's in the freezer aisle, like by the beans, and we were talking something, something about the menu we [her and her mother] were doing that week or whatever. "Melissa, what is that passion mark doing on your neck?" And I'm like, "What? Passion mark? What?" And I'm just like, "Oh, I don't know, probably it's a bruise from basketball or whatever." And I had been with her [the girlfriend] like the night before, you know what I mean. And my mother knew and she just wasn't having it. [. . .] I think she came home early one day and Jessica was there, and I was like, "Go," you know, "Run out the back door. Run out the back door." And my mom's like, "Why did I see Jessica running out the back door?" And so, I think I was like, "Um . . . " And she was like, "I don't want her coming over here anymore." And [she] just started going crazy. Like she blocked all my friends . . . like a lot of my close friends, people that are not even gay, and I've been cool with since forever . . . blocked their numbers. I'm like, "They're not even gay, what are you talking about?" "They can't call here because they support your lifestyle," you know, just like crazy, crazy, crazy, crazy, crazy. And made it, to me . . . like a place where I couldn't be. I remember one of our last conversations before I moved out . . . fast-forward, this was my senior year and Jessica had broken up with me because she just got tired of the sneaking around, and she was in college now, you know what I mean? And I was real down about it, and [my mom and I] just had it out. And I just remember her being like, "Melissa, everybody knows. Everybody knows." You know? And finally . . . I just snapped and I was like—and it's probably the one and only time that I cursed at my mother—I'm like, "You fucking bitch, it's true. It's true. Are you happy?" And like we were just like staring at each other.

Up until that time you had never had a conversation with her about it?

No. And she did take me to what I'm assuming now was like an ex-gay therapist, and at first it was just she and I talking. She left the room and then I remember him telling me that what I was doing was wrong, and I was gonna go to hell. Mind you, I still had a temper back then, and I told him what he could do.

* * *

How would you describe your current relationship with your mother and father?

So, my father's dead, but my mother . . . I feel like it's better. For example, in the last year we did a talk-back around family acceptance after the *Pariah* screening. We cofacilitated workshops on family acceptance and . . .

Your mother came to see Pariah?

She came to see *Pariah* and then we did a Q&A with the audience and talking about our relationship.

You two . . . oh, wow.

And we've cofacilitated workshops . . . we just had a Faith and Sexualities conference at Vanderbilt last spring, and we cofacilitated a workshop on family acceptance. My friend Alexis [Gumbs] and her mom did a workshop on . . . queer daughters and their mothers. And like it was a retreat. And so, we did that. And so, I feel like on both parts there's a stepping towards something different and it's a lot better than what it was. It still can be a little better because . . . sometimes she feels like this mothering has to come up. Don't try to mother me now. I'm fine. No, I'm good. You know? But a lot better now. And I alluded to the accident. So I was in a real bad car accident seven years ago and I got a traumatic brain injury, spent two days in a coma and about fourteen days in recovery. Fourteen months or so in recovery. I had short-term memory loss for ten months; I had to learn how to walk, how to talk, et cetera. And I think that it's like, you know what, "This is my child," like, "We almost lost her." Same thing with my sister, you know? Even though in that I guess she might say something like, "Okay, what's up with the tie?" whatever, but that's not like, "Oh, girl, let me put you in one of my dresses." I feel like because of what that did for all of us as far as a family unit, I had to lean on them.

. . . .

Monica J.

Monica J. is one of several "sorority sisters" of my friend Shean Atkins, who is one of the narrators in Sweet Tea. *Although she now lives in Atlanta, she was born in Houston, Texas, in 1966 and was what she describes as a "latchkey" kid because her mother, who was a single parent, was often at work while she and her younger brother were at home. Her two older sisters had already left home. The interview took place on August 6, 2012, in Atlanta.*

I remember coming out to my mom and it was tough. It was hard in that I didn't want to hurt her. Our parents . . . look for us in most cases to follow tradition or follow society norms, societal norms, and get married and have kids, blah, blah, blah, blah. And I think for parents, they don't want the stigma that comes with what their friends will say about their child. And so, that was my hesitation for my mom. I didn't want her friends whispering about her child. I didn't want her to have to suffer or have to endure that. So, that's what made it difficult to me. I didn't want to let her down. I didn't want her to be disappointed. So, it was a challenge, but I knew that I had to; I just had to tell her. I couldn't go on anymore without living my truth. And I was in my early twenties when I told her.

How did that happen? Were you just visiting home?

I was in the Navy. And I came home on a trip once. And I remember one time coming home and wanting to tell her and I just couldn't do it. And so, then on another trip, I came home. I remember we were in the living room. I think I was sitting on the floor, with my back up against the sofa. And she was probably in another chair in the room, and it was just the two of us. And I was like, "Mom there's something that I need to tell you." And she was like, "Okay." And I said, "I'm gay." And the first question she asked me was, "Who else knows?" And I told her who else knew, which was my sister, Sheila. And I think I may have told her about some friends or something that knew. And she was hurt. She was hurt that I hadn't come to her. And she said to me, "I'm your mother." She said, "And you should be able to talk to me about anything. And I'm hurt that you felt like you couldn't come and talk to me." And that was it. And over the years, I think for my mom, she heard me when I told her, but I don't know if she necessarily believed me. Or maybe because she never saw me with anyone, she was just thinking, "Oh, well, I guess maybe she said that, but that's not the case." And then I met this woman and we were dating long distance. I was here; she was in Dallas, Texas. And I was just head over heels in love and just so incredibly excited that I told my mom about this relationship. And she had the hardest time. She was crying; she was calling my sister; she was crying to my sister. And she just had a very, very, very tough time with it. And this is where we're fast-forwarding—this is like fifteen or more years after I've come out to her. And I think what it was, more than anything else, I think that she felt like she was going to lose me and lose the relationship that she and I had. I felt like I believed that she thought maybe this woman was going to take her place. Now, I remember having that conversation with her, to say that to her "Mom, we will still have the relationship we've always had. No one will ever replace you." You know, I don't know if that's what it is, but that's what I think it was because she didn't really communicate why she was having such a hard time with it, you know.

. . . .

Nancy [b. 1950, Maxton, North Carolina]

My mom left this world thinking that someday I would get right [with God] and get a man. I have been with men and had very important relationships with men. But it was always easier for me to hurt a guy. Every guy I had an intense relationship with said to me, "There's a part of you that you keep to yourself." And I would say, "I hope you got something that you keep to yourself because that don't make sense to me to give somebody everything you got. That doesn't make sense." When I met up with the right woman I would give her everything and got myself smashed in terms of my feelings, right.

I'm going to be honest with you, I stopped struggling probably in my midforties. First of all, I didn't want—I have never been dishonest with my child about [sexuality]. So, she saw me date men and women. But I was always worried about people hurting my child because of what I decided. I have always been very discreet, less discreet as I have gotten older. I am like, she's grown now and she's gay. She is that new generation where she's living her life. She doesn't give a fuck what nobody says. She is a co-parent. I am a grandmother to Aday, and they go in the classroom; they go meet the teacher and say, "We are his parents. He has two mothers, who are no longer partners, but co-parents." At first, I used to worry about Aday and what the teacher would think of him and stuff like that. This is a conservative ass part of the world. They don't mind that in New York. In fact, you ain't got to say it in New York. You just have two women show up and the person will say, "Oh, this boy got two mothers." So, I used to worry about that, but I don't anymore. He's eight, and I let that go. My sister is someone that encourages me to don't worry. He'll be okay. 'Cause I'm like, you all want to be out like that. You all need to go live in fucking Washington, New York, someplace [other than] shitty little Charlotte. They used to live in Atlanta, but they live up here now.

I resisted my sexuality for a long time. Resisted even when I accepted it. I was very, very discreet if I was dating a woman. So, then I learned to be very discreet if I was dating a guy, so there wouldn't be this imbalance. I thought that was like somehow something great. Like they don't know who I'm dating. That was bullshit. That was cowardness. I mean, it's a mean world and you got to struggle with being black, a woman, and then God's going to do something like give you a sexuality that's different from the majority of the people. That's fucking cruel. What's wrong with you, Lord? [Laughter]

I never thought it was wrong; it's just that it's what these people do. This is before I had my daughter . . . I didn't think about it. Once I had her, then I started thinking more about how people can hurt her.

• •

"Neyko"

"Neyko" has an unassuming personality that puts one at ease immediately. I was most impressed, however, by her sartorial performance. She is a dandy extraordinaire and prides herself on her fashions. "Neyko" was born the youngest of three children in Forest City, Arkansas, in 1978. Located in northeast Arkansas, Forest City is known as the "Jewel of the Delta" because it sits on Crowley's Ridge, whose elevation rises above the Mississippi Delta that surrounds it. With a population of just under fifteen thousand, the city is 60 percent African American but has a long history of racial segregation—so much so that, in order to avoid integration in the sixties, the school system eliminated school-sponsored social dances and events, prompting local families to initiate segregated proms. While "Neyko" was born in Forest City, she spent most of her childhood in the

neighboring town of Brinkley, which is one-fifth the size of Forest City, with a population of only three thousand. The interview took place on October 3, 2013, in Little Rock, Arkansas.

My mother was sick and I'm like, I can't—I don't know what this will do to her. And there was this one day I came home from school . . she was a prayerful and a spiritual lady, and she called me in the room one day, and she said, "Let me ask you a question. Do you think people are born gay?"

Your mother asked you?

Yeah. And this was a few months before she passed away. She had breast cancer. I said, "Ohhh, is this a trick question?" And she said, "No. Answer me." "Really," I said, "Yes ma'am, I do." And she said, "I do too." And she said, "Whatever it is—if there is anything about your life that you want to change, all you have to do is ask God, and he'll change it. But if you're happy with who you are, be who you are and hold your head up high." And I didn't say anything. I said, "Okay." And she said, "I just felt like I needed to tell you that." So, from that point on I kind of knew; I'm like, "She knows." And now that I'm talking I can think back at one point, I remember she was on the phone, probably when I was maybe thirteen or fourteen, with a best friend. And they were laughing and talking, and I heard her say, "I tried to make her a girl but I can't. She's just who she is." And when we go shopping I tell her, "Get one girl thing," and I let her go and do whatever else she wants to do. So, my mother, I think she knew at that point.

. . . .

Porscha

I'm not quite sure who put me in touch with Porscha, but her story had a profound impact on me. Abandoned by her mother at an early age, she was in and out of foster care for years. Her relationships with her biological and foster mothers were all contentious. Despite her childhood, she has managed to make a way for herself. She was born in Compton, California, in 1987 the youngest of three siblings, but spent her formative years in Nashville, Tennessee. The interview took place on September 9, 2013, in Nashville.

Well, my mom left California and moved. Originally she was from Memphis, Tennessee, and she moved back there and brought us with her. And I guess she was running from the state back home from California. They were trying to take us there. When we got here she got strung out on the drugs and went from marijuana to snorting base at that time, which would be considered cocaine now. But back then it was called "base." And then from there it went to heroin. By about ten years old is the time that she started to actually prostitute my two older sisters out for drug money. After that I found out that my older sister actually contracted HIV [at] about the age of thirteen years old because of that. Then that's when DSS [Department of Social Services] stepped in again in Davidson County and actually took us from there. Wound up back in state custody . . . I hid the fact that I was a lesbian in the system because I didn't know how other families would take how I was and if I would get put out. I went through probably about eight foster homes and four group homes. I remember getting into numerous fights because this girl said I was looking at this girl while she was getting undressed and looking at that girl while she was getting undressed. My foster mom did not allow it. One foster home had actually video cameras in their home because they didn't know if girls were doing girls, boys were doing boys, or it was the same—if it was opposite sex. So, they watched us real closely. I kept it to a minimum until I reached high school, and then it just was really like, hey, I'm out, everybody knows. It really didn't bother me as much when I was just out of school, but being in someone else's home that's not your biological family and living by their rules is kind of hard. I stayed with a foster mom for five years and by my second year of being with her, one thing that still sticks out in my head that she had always said to me, the first day I walked in her house, "For me in my household we will serve the Lord." So, right then and there I knew no girlfriends. Like that was an abomination right then and there.

And that was here in Nashville?

Yes, that was in Nashville. And she is originally from Sandy Bottom, Georgia. So, she was stuck in her ways.

Sandy Bottom, Georgia?

Yes. That's way down in the South. She allowed me to dress how I wanted to dress. And around my sophomore year of high school I got outed by another foster mom. I was dating *her* daughter, her foster child, which kind of made me feel cool, but then at the same time I felt weird because she only outed me because she didn't really like me because I was black.

So, she was white?

No, she was black.

But light skinned.

Yes, but black. . . . And she only took in white children. So, when she found out I was dating her daughter it made it even worse, when she found out I was dating a white girl and a black girl. So, she called my cell phone, then turned around and called my house phone, and my mom swore up and down that hey, it wasn't me, it was some other Porscha. But it was me. And I denied the whole thing. She dropped me off at the center. About three hours later she called my cell phone and told me she's coming to pick me up so we can deal with this problem. And at that time she called back—I'm guessing I had been possessed by a demon inside me that she could cast out . . . she had spoken tongues and put holy water on me as I slept that would cast out the demon. The gay demon at that. Well, that didn't happen. I'm still gayer than ever.

So, she did it. She went through that.

Yes, she went through that process of—it took a while for her to grasp. And it was never spoke of again. My cousin told me, "Hey, you better tell her that was your first girl experience and your last lesbian experience." I told her, "That was my first and last," which was never my first nor last. I told her that so she would back off, but it was kind of like my last three years there was kind of like, don't ask, don't tell.

So, you were still doing what you wanted to do?

Yes. I was definitely. You know every weekend I got to go to my biological brother's house and I had girls come over, spend the night with me. And it was my life. So, I was hiding it from her. And . . . she had me dress in a certain way when I went to church. And out of respect for her—I've always had respect for her. Well, for women period. Definitely my black sisters. I've always had respect for black sisters. And when they're older than me I've always showed that respect. So, when church came around—I don't care if it was a Wednesday night Bible study—I put on the garment that she said the Lord would want me to wear and look presentable as a woman. So, then push came to shove and it started to get kind of leaked out in the church where a deacon had came to me and said to me that he's going to get with the pastor's wife and they're going to do a makeover. Yes. And try to turn me into a woman, which I know in my mind I'm a woman and I know in my body I'm a woman. I know God created me as a woman. But in his mind and in my mom's mind . . . my foster mother, they're going to create—they're going to do a makeover. They're going to change I guess the boy Porscha to a woman Porscha. I'm not sure.

But weren't you already wearing dresses and things like that to church?

To church. Not out in the community.

Oh, so they meant . . .

Right. A full makeover. Makeup and hair flip. Whatever they thought. I don't know. So, me being the person I am, I built up the confidence and I went to my pastor's wife myself. Now this is a big church.

What denomination?

Nondenominational. A very well-known church, you know. I went to her and I told her, "Hey, this deacon is saying that he's talking about having a makeover with me with Women's Day and all of this because I identify as a lesbian. This is not feelings [that] just comes and goes. This is something that's embedded in me. This is something that I've always felt from the day that I was born. I've never had any attention for *any* guys. I never look at a guy and say oh, you know, he's cute. Never. And I felt that that's just selfless and he's not even thinking of how I want to live my life." So, she tells me, "You know when I was a young girl I had those same thoughts because I was raised in the church. My mother was a wife of the pastor and my father was pastor and my granddad." And it was on down, and when she met her husband, the feeling that she was having she never had. So, she got scared. She got mixed up, and she didn't know if [. . .] these the feelings she was supposed to be having. She was like, "At [your] age I was confused also." She was like, "Now, don't get me wrong. We have a lot of young women in our church that identify just as you that you would never know that come to me just as you are." She said, "God is going to love you no matter what, and I am too." She said, "Now if this is how you want to live your life, this is how you want to live your life. When judgment day come only you have to answer, no one else." And when she saw the deacon she told the deacon, "We're not going to do this. This is this young lady's life. This is not your child. She doesn't want it, so we're not going to do it." So, when I had the conversation with my mom in the car about what the pastor's wife said to me, she told me of course never to speak of that again.

This is your foster mother?

Yes. She told me never to speak of that incident again. No one in the church ever knew that our pastor's wife had feelings for [women] or was confused at that time. She was battling with should I be with a woman? Should I be with a man? And when I told her, she told me never to speak of it again. So, I never spoke of it again until now.

. . . .

Rose [b. 1958, Roanoke, Virginia]

This is a story that's funny to me. [. . .] I was living in Vermont and I went to visit in Alabama at my mother's house. My mom and dad weren't there, but my grandmother was there. She was living with them. And I knew I wanted to tell her. I took my partner with me. We went to visit, and she liked her a lot, she liked Susan. And I knew, though, I needed to tell her directly. [. . .] So, I'm waiting to a time when she and I have some time alone, just she and I. So, one morning before breakfast she and I are the only ones up stirring around and she snuck outside so that she could get some dirt so she can eat it. And she thinks nobody notices that she'd been eating dirt because she ain't supposed to eat dirt. But she craves dirt.

Like real dirt?

Like dirt. Yes. You never heard of dirt eaters?

No.[2]

She craved dirt, so she went out and snuck out and got her some dirt. But she got dirt all down the front of her shirt where she'd been trying to eat the dirt. So, I'm sitting there with her and she's got dirt on her front pretending like she ain't snuck out and got some dirt to eat. And I said something to her like, "Nanny, I know that you have some questions about Susan and I." And she's like, "Um-hmm." I said, "You can ask me anything you want to and I will answer you." And she said, "Okay." She said, "What is Susan to you?" I said, "She's my girlfriend." "Ohh, girlfriends. Well, you know I've never done nothing like that myself but you know Miss Mamie and Miss Susie, they was mighty close, real close, umm-hmm." And she thought a minute or two and she was like, "Oh, girlfriend." So, I waited a second and I could tell you know she's thinking, thinking. And she said, "Well, what do you all do in the bed?" And I was just about to fall out. And I can't—and I told her that I would answer her anything she asked me. And I think for a minute and I said, "Well, Nanny, do you know what you and Papa did in the bed?" And she said, "Yes." She was so proud of herself. "Umm-hmm, yes." I said, "Well that's what me and Susan do but neither one of us have a penis." And I could see her thinking: "Mmm." And I wasn't going to talk about how you can buy a penis. But it's like she said, "Mmm," and finally she said "Well, okay." You can tell she had thought it through. And so then she said, "Well, which ones of y'alls is the man and which ones of y'alls is the woman?" And again I was like, okay, how I talk to her about—right? So, I just said, "In our case we're both women." And she could not wrap her head around that. She was just thinking and thinking and I think she finally decided she'd just leave that one alone. Right? But then because she's spicy, she says "Huh." I said, "What do you want to do?" She's like, "When Susan comes downstairs I'm going to ask her all those questions." I said "Okay."

Oh my God.

So, Susan comes downstairs and she's innocent. And she asks her—she says to her, "Susan, I understand that you and Rose is girlfriends." Well, Susan don't speak country. So she says, "Yes ma'am, we're good friends. Yes, we're good friends." And Nanny said, "I said girlfriends." Susan still didn't understand. "Yes ma'am, we're good friends." "I said girlfriends, Susan." And she's like—and I look at Nanny and she says, "What do you all do in the bed?" And I'm like, "Okay, that's enough. We're going to put this poor woman in her grave." This eighty-seven-year-old woman asking those questions. And then she and I of course fall out laughing. And that's how I told my grandmother. But that was—she had told me, you know, maybe a year before that, she had said to me, she asked me if I was seeing some-body and I said no. And she said "Well girl, you're young. You need to get you somebody before all that dry up." So, I guess she thought I followed her advice.

I guess so. So, had your father passed away by this time?

No, my father is still living.

And so, how did that conversation go with him?

I don't remember ever talking to him.

Oh really.

No. And as a matter of fact, my grandmother, I didn't tell her that I had told everybody else. So, my mother called me shortly after [and] she said, "Rose, would you tell your nanny that I know." And it was like, "Why?" She said, "She walking around the house going 'I know some-thing you don't know.'" But she wouldn't tell her what she knew . . . she wasn't going to tell nobody. She wanted everybody to know she knew something. But she didn't—she was not going to tell a soul if I didn't tell her that everybody knew. Because I'm sure she thought that she wanted to protect me.

. . . .

Sharon

I have known Sharon for almost twenty years. She is a professor of literature and American culture. When she lived in Chicago for a few years, we used to cook together on the holidays. She now lives in Chapel Hill, North Carolina, and teaches at the University of North Carolina. Sharon was born in 1964 in Washington, DC, to a physician father and librarian mother. She is the only child of her mother, but she has siblings from her father's subsequent marriage. The interview took place on February 3, 2013, at her home in Chapel Hill.

I came out as questioning to my women's studies class. And I went home, and I'll never forget, I was having a scotch and soda, or whiskey and soda, or something—that's what my dad drank. [. . .] I think it was my first year at grad school. I was going to finish my papers and then I was going to go to DC. I was going to talk to my stepmom and try to find out where he was. And I never got a chance to do that. My mom called that night and said he had been found dead in his office, a self-inflicted wound. And I was holding a drink that he would drink. And for months I had been thinking that I was going to die. Like I had known since Christmas something horrible was going to happen. It was like a sight. [. . .] The minute I found out he was dead I sighed a sigh of relief. I said, "That's what it was." And I couldn't know. I was like, what's going on with this feeling, and when he died I knew.

And that precipitated my coming out because the lover that I had, Jennifer—now I think [she is] Jake or Jacob, but I might be wrong about that. But she's definitely transitioned [to male] and very happy. Her father was the vice-president of importing for Payless Shoe Stores. And so, they had bank. . . . So, she flew me out from Michigan. . . . She bought the tickets like last minute, and I was a basket case. I had no idea it was going to affect me that way. Because I didn't really live with my father. But what my mother didn't know is that I used my boyfriend as a cover to go see him after school in his office. And that was back in the days before cell phones and caller ID, so you could call somebody up . . . she would call Randy's house and say, "I'm here. I want to talk to Sharon and find out when she's coming home." And then Randy would call me at my dad's office and say, "Your mom called. You better call her back." And I would go into an office and I'd be, "Oh yeah, I'm over at Scooter's," because he would say I was over at Scooter's house, who was a good friend of Randy's. So, I could play a game with her all [of] high school. And so, I saw my dad like once a month. And my mom thought I never saw my dad in high school. She had no idea I had a relationship with him. And I had gotten to a point with him where I said, "You know, Dad, you're really a bad father. Let's face it: you suck. That is so not you." I said, "You're a really great doctor, and I really just want to get to know that person. Because I don't need you to be my dad right now, and all these things you're going to try to do are going to make us both frustrated and make me hate you." And he was always chain smoking and stuttering a little bit. And he would be like, "Good idea. Yeah, yeah, that's a good idea." And so, we would read the *New England Journal of Medicine* together, or I would go to the house, watch him cook. He was really a fantastic cook. So, we had this life that my mother never knew.

So, he died, and the first thing my mother told me, she said, "Well, you don't need to come home or anything. You can just stay up there and finish school. I just wanted to let you know." And I must say the minute she told me about it was like all the breath went out of my body. And I think it took two years for it to return. I was devastated. Devastated. When somebody who helped put you into this world you lose—you really do feel like somebody has popped a balloon. And of course you can feel the air coming out of it. And then of course I had to show up with cowgirl Jennifer, and the minute we showed up to my mother's apartment, my mother was like, "Oh hell no." And she was like, "You all can't stay here." So, then I ended up staying with my stepmother. That's how we became close. When we arrived at my stepmother['s], unlike my mother, she had a guest room waiting for us and towels out for us and everything. She adored Jennifer. She thought Jennifer was great. And Jennifer was really good that weekend with my little brother, who was twelve at the time. [. . .]

So, my mom and I, that began the long thirteen-year stretch of our estrangement, which began when she was upset because I didn't tell her I was gay. I was a lesbian. And I'm like, "I didn't tell you I was a lesbian because I was going to tell you this summer but I never had a chance because my dad killed himself." You know like, "Excuse me for the conflicting bullshit." . . . And then to be cruel, she said, "Well, if I had known you were going to be like this I wish you had never been born." And to be told that so soon after a parent's suicide is almost like an unforgivable thing. And of course, being the child that I am, you know, that twelve-year-old. . . . People think they're insulting me and then I kind of turn it around. I'm like, "Okay, let's be clear. You just said that, so I'm going to make you repeat it, so years later when I'm in therapy and maybe you join me or when we're still arguing, you will know that you said it. You won't be able to say you didn't." So, she repeated it three times. Just to be cruel. Because my mother is just very much like I am. We're stubborn. And I said, "Okay, thank you very much." And then I didn't talk to her for a while. And then, you know, every time we talked to one another, it was like something out of a Faulkner novel, the words coming like short staccato slaps. We were just, "eh eh eh," we'd try to be nice. I'd try to drive home and spend some time with her. I'd end up staying a night and leaving the next morning. I mean our relationship turned into a total, like something out of a goddamn Greek tragedy, except for it wasn't so funny. So, I felt basically like I lost both my parents within a few months of each other. And I don't talk to my mother. And I reconciled with it. And then in the wake of my divorce after being with a woman for thirteen years,

I don't know—maybe my relationship with Jennifer [another Jennifer] unfortunately angered my mother somehow, made me seem negative somehow. But we ended up having a terrible row. And it culminated in her leaving a very interesting message on my machine . . . and I thought, is she going to go on forever? Like she was basically tearing down everyone I knew. So, I just decided I just couldn't talk to her anymore. You just don't get to leave your daughter for thirteen years and just come back. And then want to leave again in a bad way. I'm like, "I'm done. If you really think I'm such an evil person, then goodbye." So, I don't think she could ever reconcile herself, and I kind of don't know why.

. . . .

"Shonda"

"Shonda" is an artist who has been writing about southern women's and queer people's experiences for over twenty years. She publishes as a short fiction writer and playwright. She was born in Columbus, Georgia, in 1959 and now lives in North Texas with her wife. The interview took place on September 12, 2013, outside of Dallas, Texas.

My childhood growing up in Columbus, Georgia, the early part of my childhood was filled with a lot of movement, I should say. I lived in three different households. I grew up with my great grandmother and great aunt in one household. And then across the street in a house was a great aunt and great uncle who I called Mom and Dad. And then in the summers I went to live with a great grandmother and great aunt in Alabama. So, I would say that it was a lot of movement and a lot of daydreaming. But I felt loved. Everybody loved me, and that's partly why I moved around a lot, because everybody wanted me. My birthmother died when I was about two and a half years old. And so, I was everybody's child. I grew up in the community being everybody's child. My mother died. She was young and beautiful when she died, and when I just mentioned her name or asked them to tell me about her, they would start crying. And these were older . . . mostly much older people. So, they were in their fifties and sixties when I was born. So, I grew up in households where there were very old people and there was me.

* * *

I still remember my mother's funeral, sitting in the back seat looking at my brand new, shiny black shoes and then somebody picking me up and holding me over the casket and asking me, "Do you know who this is?"

And I don't know if I had seen my mother in a while, but I was two and a half, almost three, but I was very little. And did they tell me that story or do I remember it? But that's probably one of the most vivid memories I have . . . and then the beginning of a sadness that would sweep over me around my birthday every year everywhere. And I just didn't know what it was. And then I finally connected to the fact that my mother died a few days before my third birthday. [. . .] When you go to church on Mother's Day you're supposed to wear a red flower if your mother's alive and a white flower if she's dead. And I remember like just being devastated that I had to wear a white flower and everybody would know my mother was dead. And so, they kind of relented and let me wear two flowers because they said, "Well, your birth mother's dead, but we're your mamas and so you could wear a red one for us."

The mother and home are two recurring themes in a lot of my work, because we went to church a lot. I would pray, and I believed that God could work all kind of miracles. [. . .] And I used to pray for my mother to come back from the dead. . . . I thought it could happen. I really believed it for a very long time. And so, when I realized that wasn't gonna happen, there was a moment, there was a rough transition. But there was a moment that I almost woke up, and I realized, "Oh my God. I must be the luckiest person on the planet ever for all time. I have not one, not two, not three, but eight mothers, plus." And that became like another theme in my life. . . . And all the big mamas have passed away, but as I was growing up and I moved and I lived in all these different places, there was always a big mama. So, a big mama doesn't have to be somebody that's related to you by blood, she don't have to be big, [laughter] but [she was] somebody who looked out for you, made sure you had food. "Do you have an umbrella?" "Do you need a Bible scripture? You're looking kind of sad." [Laughter] "Have a half of my sandwich. You're looking kind of hungry," you know? [I was] in graduate school and I was invited to the Kennedy Center for some performance, and they had gotten my train fare to go, but I didn't have any other money. And this black woman, she took one look at me, we're talking and she was trying to get information about why I was there and what was going on. She knew I was there for one of my plays. And she said, "Baby, I know they didn't give you no money," and she folded twenty dollars up and pressed it in my hand. She didn't give me a chance to say yes; she just pressed it in my hand. I almost cried. I still call her to this day, and just from time to time say hello, and just [tell] her what a difference it made to me in that moment . . . I would have just been eating like a slice of pizza a day if she hadn't pressed that twenty dollars in my hand. And so, the importance of, especially big mamas, in my life has been to this day. Everywhere I go there tends to be [a big mama]. Or maybe I'm a magnet or maybe I gravitate towards or maybe I look for it. But that is a big presence in my life: having those older women.

· ·

Sharita [b. 1979, Washington, DC]

As a mother, what fears do you have, if any—maybe I shouldn't phrase it that way. I should say, what do you hope for your daughter, and how do you teach her about sexuality? What have you talked to her about sexuality, either your own or in general?

You know, that's a good question. . . I have a lot of fears. When you said "fears" I knew exactly what you were talking about when it comes to my daughter, and Shayla [her wife] and I have had this conversation. A lot of times when it comes to her having friends, I'll distance myself when it comes to communicating with their families because I don't want to associate her with being gay because I am. And so, a lot of times in, like, talking to a family member of a friend or something I'll say, "Well, Shayla, you call." Because Shayla is what you would see as a mom. You wouldn't look at me and say, "Oh, that's a mom." You automatically see that's a lesbian. And so, you gonna say, "That's a lesbian. Is her daughter a lesbian?" And so, I don't want her social life to be affected by who I am. Because I know that ignorance is out there. I'm not oblivious to that.

And so, first of all, I teach her you want to accept everybody for who or what they are. You don't discriminate against anybody because you just only really guessing at who somebody is. Let them show you who they are before you decide I like and I dislike. And so, when it comes to sexuality she's open. She's accepting. She'll say, "Ma, my friend is gay." I said, "Well, is he gay?" "Well, he's really, really feminine." "Well, some guys are just feminine when they're younger. That doesn't mean they're going to grow up to be gay. Just let him be who he is. He thinks he's gay too, but he's probably just falling for that same stereotype where I'm feminine, I'm not masculine, then I'm gay. But y'all too young to know your sexuality. That's something that's going to evolve over time." And so, I probably do hope that she's not gay because two things are going to happen: "Well, your mother was gay, so you're probably going to be gay anyway." Because that's how you were raised. Like you were raised to be gay. And this is not a life I would want her to have. I just want her to have a normal life where you go out and have friends, and you don't always have to be thinking about what people are thinking about you. Or how people are going to relate to you once they find out that you're gay. I don't want that. Because it's tough and it's isolating.

I always commend people who can come out to be gay because it's not an easy life to live. You have to be really, really comfortable with who you are. And be comfortable with even knowing that you a lot of times are going to be on the outside. Because people are still just judgmental—regardless of what you see on TV and them trying to come up with laws—it's an isolating culture to be in. And to be black and gay is even worse because your culture is really homophobic. And then you've got to split into a smaller group of African Americans out there, and so I just—I wish, I hope, I pray—I would love her any way she is, but just for her own well-being I would not want her to be gay. I would want her to be straight. [. . .] Because I'm masculine or what they perceive as a masculine female, they obviously, when they see me, know that, "Oh, she's gay." [. . .] Some are like, "Oh, well, who is the mother?" "We are the mothers. But if you want to say biologically," and I say, "Me." They're really like, "What?" A lot of people assume that's Shayla's child. That's her mom. She's not really, but biologically I am. Somewhere that we both go [. . .] together they'll look at Shayla. And then they kind of glance at me. Like they're talking to her. But I just want her to be accepted. I don't want her to go through what I have to go through even today. I just want her to be happy.

. . . .

Shayla
Shayla was born in 1980 in Little Rock, Arkansas. She is the youngest of two children. She and Sharita (introduced in chapter 1) are married and co-parent Sharita's biological daughter. The interview took place on October 5, 2013, at her home in Little Rock.

So, you're trying to adopt a child. And does the state of Arkansas allow . . .
They do now. [. . .] It is actually worded that two people cohabitating can adopt.
When did that change?
I don't know for sure. It's been recent. Maybe within the last year and a half. I believe that's when it changed. Now, she [Sharita] could probably give you the exact date. But probably a year and a half, somewhere around there.
Okay. Well, I hope it happens for you.
I do, too. I really do.
Do you care what . . . if it's a boy or girl?

I want a girl and I guess for obvious reasons . . . I mean, when I came into Destiny's life, she was already seven, and she [has a] very strong personality, very intelligent, and not the pink bows and definitely not that. And I'd like to go and do the shopping and get the pink barrettes, and she's like, "I don't want that. No, I don't." And so, actually, I would love to have a girl. [Laughter] My partner wants a boy. [Laughter] So, it's a little conflict there, but we are trying to have a child as well.

That you would carry or she would?

That I would carry. So, we don't have any say-so with that. So, I'm just gonna pray that I have the girl that I want.

[Laughter] So, that you can make her a proper little girl.

Yes, and the little programs and the ballerina . . . I mean, I'm just a girl, I am. I'm just a girl. Love all those little cute little things and the little, uh, what is it called, the little "tutus." I would probably get on their nerves. I probably would. [Laughter]

. . . .

Tonia

I first met Tonia at a national high school student council conference in Dallas, Texas, in 1984. She was a freshman and I was a junior. After we began talking, we realized that we were distant relatives. My aunt had married one of her relatives (it's still confusing as to how he was related to her), who died when he was only twenty-five. Tonia was born in Mount Vernon, New York, in 1969 but was raised in Graham, North Carolina, where her parents continue to live. Graham only became incorporated as a city in 1961 and is located in the Piedmont of North Carolina. Tonia teaches at Johns Hopkins University and conducts research on HIV/AIDS in a human rights context. The interview took place on August 20, 2013, in Silver Spring, Maryland.

So, I came out to my parents between sophomore and junior year of college. I remember I was going back to school. Or maybe it was winter break. I was home for a break and I was going back the next day. Because I remember I was packing to get ready to go back to school, and I don't know what possessed me but I decided to tell my mom. Oh, I remember, she said, "What did you do for Valentine's Day this year? Did you spend it alone?" And I was like, "No, I went to dinner with my girlfriend." I'm a really bad liar. And Mom said, "Girlfriend." And I was like, "Yeah. Girlfriend." So, she didn't pretend to be confused by what I meant by the term "girlfriend" or anything, so then we had that conversation and she was very dramatic about it, like "You're wrong" and all that kind of stuff.

So, she wasn't confused about the word. Did that mean she already had a suspicion?

She already had a suspicion. I feel like . . . she acted shocked. But the reason I say "acted" is because maybe a year before that, my first year in college, I remember she sent me a letter. And in that letter, she talked about always being worried that I would either be a slut or that I would turn to women for love because I had bad experiences with men in life. I know, like, those are your choices right? You have bad experiences, so you can either have sex with a million people or, yeah . . .

Wow. And what about your father?

I never told my father. My mother told him. So, I'm not sure what his initial response was. I know that he had a conversation with me about it and he said it was actually surprising. He was trying to be empathetic. He was like, "You know, there was a time when I thought I was gay." And I was shocked and I was like, "You did?" He's like, "Yeah, because I didn't find any women attractive. And then I realized I hadn't met the right one." I was like, "Well, Dad it's a little different."

And so how did you work through your sexuality, particularly with your mother, given her reaction?

Yeah, I think my father was not as bothered as my mother. I mean, I think my mother saw her white wedding dresses and grandbabies disappearing, so it was rough for a while. Like, we didn't fight about it, but I couldn't really talk to her about my life. And we had been really close before then, so that was really hard. And we would try to have conversations, but this was like beyond college. We'd try to have conversations and we'd end up being sort of at each other. I was very sensitive too at the time to whatever she would say, and she was very sensitive to whatever I would say, and so it took us a long time—I'd say years. Even to the making of the film, I think was the final like, "You know what. It is what it is."

Talk about that. You were in a film about what?

I was in a documentary called *For the Bible Tells Me So* that was about basically religion and homosexuality and American families. And there were five families featured in the film, and mine was one of the them. We were the brown family amongst the white families. We were the not famous family among other famous families. But I think the filming was around 2005-ish, maybe a little before, maybe a little after. And I remember when the filmmaker contacted me and asked me if my family would be in it I said,

"I'll ask them but I'm pretty sure they'll say no." And then they said, "We want to meet him." So, they met the filmmaker and they liked him, and so they agreed to do it. They still call him their New York son. My parents will adopt—I mean they like people. They liked him. They trusted him. I think they got a sense they trusted him. And my dad was like, "I never thought anybody would see this documentary. It's a documentary. Who watches documentaries?" So, they agreed to do it, and it was over a course of about a year. There were a series of interviews with them and then with me. I don't think we were ever altogether at the same time when we're doing interviews, but we had to have those kind of conversations more often. And when the film came out, they came out. They hadn't really been out.

In terms of acknowledging that they had a lesbian daughter to their friends?

Yeah, to their friends. And I think it was an eye-opener to them, not that they would know what it's like to be gay, but to see how people responded to them. So, they actually, several years after the film came out, they showed it in my hometown. I know—I was a little shocked, too. Burlington, North Carolina, they had this film.

Where did they show it?

It was at a little theater I never even heard of.

Like a little arts theater or something?

Yeah and it was PFLAG [Parents and Friends of Lesbians and Gays] who sponsored it, and my parents had invited all of their congregation at their church to come, and not a single person showed from their congregation. It was mostly my mother, father, people from PFLAG, and a couple of my [family members], like an aunt and a cousin.

Why don't you think they showed up?

I think that they didn't think it was appropriate . . . I mean, you know how southerners are not going to say to your face, "I'm not going to go to that piece of crap." But I think that's what they were thinking, and I know my mother at least, it was clear she was very hurt by that. And I think it was an eye-opener to her about how hurtful that kind of rejection can feel.

What did they think about seeing themselves in the film?

That is a good question. I've been so self-absorbed; I kept thinking about what was it like for me to say the things they said in the film. I know that for a while afterwards, my dad at least sort of saw himself as this man that gay kids could come to whenever the film was shown. If there were black gay kids in the audience they usually wanted to talk to my parents, like if there was a panel or whatever. And I think something resonated for them, and even though they weren't wildly accepting, they didn't kick me out of the house. They didn't do horrible things to me, and some of those things had happened to those kids, and they wanted to talk to my dad about it. About what made the difference. My dad [became] like "savior of the gay kids," which was hysterical.

And what about your relationship now with your parents?

My relationship now is good. You know, I think it helps to be older and independent, you know? Their life is a little weirder, like they don't live their life the way I would want to live my life, and I don't live my life the way that they would want. I think we're all okay with that. We love each other. My dad is so funny to this day. Whenever he sees any gay people in town, like when I go home to visit, he's like, "Oh, they drive your color van." I was like, "Oh 'my color van.'"

That's a euphemism for . . .

. . . that's a euphemism for "They're gay, too."

Interesting. Do you think your parents are following "Hate the sin, love the sinner" philosophy when it comes to you? Or do you think that they embrace all of who you are?

No, I don't think they embrace all of who I am. I mean, they're probably closer to that than they used to be. I think if you asked them they would say hate the sin, love the sinner kind of thing . . . at least my mother. I have more conversations with her about it. We had this very interesting conversation. She had knee replacement surgery recently, and she said she was under the influence of pain medication, that's why she's saying this, but I asked her, "If I got married to a woman would you come?" And I remember I had a ceremony around the time the film was being made. And I talked about it in the film [about my] reasons deciding it would just be me, my partner, and her rabbi, was because I didn't want to have to invite my parents and not have them come, and that would be just too hard. So, I asked her, "If I got married today to a woman would you come?" And she was like, "I probably would. Well, I don't know. Well, don't talk to me now because I'm under the influence." So, I think she would feel she would at least give a lot of thought to coming, and feeling like she would want to be there.

. . . .

Wynee

I was introduced to Wynee by a faculty member who taught at a small liberal arts college in the Adirondacks but who is from the South. When I told her that I was working on a book about black lesbians of the South,

she said, "Oh, I need to put you in touch with Wynee. She has a story."
She was right about that! Besides having a very colorful life, Wynee is a
wonderful storyteller. She was born in Jackson, Mississippi, in 1962 into
what she describes as a middle-class family. Her parents divorced when she
was eighteen months old, so she was raised as an only child, but she learned
later that she had a sister twenty years her senior. The interview took place
on October 4, 2013, in Little Rock, Arkansas.

[My mother and I] finally moved away from my grandmother's, and we lived in apartments. And right down the strip by the apartments there was this little strip mall that consisted of a liquor store, a record shop, a grocery store, a drug store, Eckerd's or something. And I hung out at the head shop all the time. It was my favorite place to be. That's how I met my first lover and I was about sixteen. She was about twenty-one.

So, she was legal.

She was legal, yes, absolutely. She already had two kids and everything, so some of that was really taboo for me for my family to be hanging out. "Why you hanging out with this older lady with two kids? What could you possibly have in common?" "We're just friends. I just like talking to her." But it was a little more to it than that. [. . .]

And how long were you together?

I moved from Jackson to Little Rock with her because this is her home. So, high school, I was sixteen, okay, probably moved here when I was nineteen or about to be nineteen because I only spent a semester in the junior college, and I actually ran away to live with her because, you know, at this point my mom had found out. She had been to my room and she had found letters and things like that. She snooped around and found stuff, and there were things that were quite revealing on the letters that she had written me. And it was obvious that I was with this person, and I'll never forget the night. It was the night before Mother's Day, and I was hanging out with my aunt. We were shopping and I was close with my mom. So, when we got to my grandmother's house after shopping, I called and she said, "Where are you?" And I just knew the tone of her voice was different. And I said, "I'm at Mama's." She said, "Stay there. You've been fucking around with these women. I've been through your closet. I found the letters. Don't leave. I'm on my way." I said, "Okay," and my grandmother said, "What's wrong?" I said, "Mamma's on her way over here," and she said, "Why?" I said, "She found something." She [the grandmother] said, "Baby, come on with it, tell me what's going on." Of course, I broke down and I cried and I told her. And you know, there was a solemn look of dis-appointment or whatever, and my grandmother is who I loved most in the world outside of my kid, but I love her to this day because she's the person that I spent the most time with. My mother worked, so this is the person that nurtured me and this and that. My mom was only interested in what I looked like and how I act. My grandmother was the person that hugged me, kissed me, and told me that she loved me. So, my mom did come over and she brought the letters. It was me, my aunt, and my grand-mother, and we were on the front porch, and my mom passed the letters around like they were photos and they all read them. And it's the first time I'd ever been slapped, and my mom slapped me, and she wanted to know if I wanted to see a psychiatrist for just what was the problem. I was like, "I don't need to see a psychiatrist. I'm not gay." But the letters they were self-explanatory; I was.

So, you told her that you weren't.

I did, but I was lying. I mean it was just so obvious from what was on the letters and she wanted the girl's number and everything. And I had no choice but to give it to her, and she wanted to call her that night, and I was so glad when she called, she [the girl] wasn't at home. Because I wanted to warn her that my mom knew and that she would be getting a call. So, the next day I did and she was like, "Oh shit." And my mom was telling her, "I really want to kill you. If I see you walking down the street I will probably run over you." So, we had to I guess sort of break up there for a minute, and the lover lied to me and said, "Well, I'm moving back to Arkansas." So, I believed it. We didn't talk and the one day . . . I went to church by myself. Nobody in the house was going . . . so of course after church I drove through the old neigh-borhood because we moved away from the apartments at that point. And there she was walking down the street. Man, my face lit up. And I started talking to her, and she said, "No, I never left, but to protect you I had told you that to keep you out of trouble and to keep your family together." I said, "I don't care about the family at this point. I don't care about being happy with the family." So, we started our relationship back up, and I graduated and I went to this junior college or whatever. And my mom would always tell me, "Where's your boyfriend?" And I always had an excuse because there was callers, of course. "I don't like him; he's light skinned." "That bitch that you call yourself liking, she's light skinned." "Well, I don't like him." "Well what about . . . ?" "I don't like him either." I didn't like any of them. I had a high school boyfriend and . . . it's so funny because all she talked about was sex, and not being pregnant, and how sex had been around for as long as forever, and that it was something that I could wait for, and this and that. So, I finally did the sex with the guy—

In high school?

Yes, and I'm like, "Is this what they're talking about? I don't ever have to do this. My God. What is all the ranting and raving about?" But the first time I did with that girl, that's when the balloons and the whistles and the trains and everything, and I was like, [claps her hands] "This is what they're talking about." And my mama kept saying, "You can't be living here being gay. It's just out of the question." So, I kept telling this lover of mine that my mom's getting on my nerves. I'm not letting boys come by, telling me I can't live there being gay, or whatever. And like I said, she was older. She had a job at Jackson State. Her brother and her sister-in-law were doctors at Jackson State. So, they lived in a nice home in our area by the apartments, and so she suggested that we get an apartment. She said, "I'll get an apartment but don't put me out here on a limb. Don't have me get the apartment and you don't come." "Oh, I'm coming. I guarantee you."

So, everything was going on quite normal, and I always talk to my mom during the day. She always say what we're having for dinner. She always say, "Okay, we're having peas today, so go ahead and put the meat on for me. So, when I get there the only thing I have to do is cook the peas and season and everything and I'll do the meat. Take out such-and-such, this is what we're having." My stepfather would always come home for lunch like clockwork, eat him something, then leave and go on back to work, but I had planned with my best friend that she was going to be there right after lunch. So, I packed up that morning prior to him coming for lunch a duffel bag with all my belongings, a few albums that I loved. And when she came she backed up in the driveway. I threw my duffel bag in. I went in and got a few more things out of my room that was mine, and I unlocked the washroom door. I locked my mother's house, I took the key off my ring, and I put her key on the washing machine in the washroom, and I locked the door and I left.

But I made sure it was July because I really love my grandmother, and she always went to Memphis in July with the neighbor next door to visit her sister, and I didn't want to give her a heart attack. I didn't want her to come home and I didn't want her to be there when I left. I felt like it would be easier when she got back and they said, "Wynee ran. She left." Well, it was obvious that they knew where I was because one of my aunt's friends lived in the apartments that we lived in and I'd see her. So, she told and one day I went to the mailbox and there was a letter from my aunt. Scared me to death and she wrote that it's obvious that we know where you are. "We're not trying to come and get you, just want you to be okay, but what you need to do is call your grandmother. She's worried to death about you." Well, I couldn't have that. So, I built up enough courage and I called my grandmother. Lo and behold, my mother answers the phone. And she said, "Mmm, you didn't expect me to answer the phone, did you?" I said, "No, I didn't." And then she said, "Wynee, how are you?" I said, "I'm okay." Then she said, "Are you happy?" I said, "I am." She said, "Okay, well, I'm not going to hold you. I know I'm not who you wanted to talk to." She said, "But call me at home when you get a chance." Her demeanor had changed. So, I talked to my grandmother and she said, "What are you doing?" And I told her I had to leave. I told her why. She said, "I want to see you." I said, "Well, I'll come and see you." So, I did and we talked, and she said, "Do you love her?" and I said, "Yes." She said, "Yes what?" "Yes, I love her." That's the answer she was looking for, so that's the answer I gave. And she looked at me and she said, "Well, baby, you can't help who you love." So, I knew I had my grandmother in my corner.

My mom up until very, very, very recently never talked about it with me, ever. So, one day we were talking over the phone, and I don't know how the conversation presented itself, but she had said something, and I said, "Well, Mom, it's just like the gay thing here. It's like you sit down to play a hand of cards and you play to win. If you're playing spades you better have one spade in your hand, but you may have face cards, you may not, but you sit there and you play that hand because that's the hand that was dealt to you. And this is the hand that was dealt to me and I have to play it as best I can." And I said, "Right now I think I'm playing pretty well because the entire time I've been away, which is over thirty years now, I've never called, picked up the phone and asked for anything." You know, I went through some hard times of saying things that I just couldn't imagine.

Walk like a Man, Talk like a Woman
Gender Nonconformity

3

One of the prevailing stereotypes about lesbian women of any color is that they all "want to be men" or that they are all "butch." While many lesbian and queer women have a masculine self-presentation, many others fall along a spectrum of gender presentation. Indeed, many of the women I interviewed speak of crossing many gender boundaries during their lives—some settling on a more constant gender presentation that exists "masculine of center," some preferring a highly stylized feminine performance, and others preferring a more fluid gender presentation or what some refer to as "genderqueer."

The interesting (and surprising) discovery for me was the recurring narrative that gender presentation for women in the South—and especially black women who were working class—was much more fluid than what is commonly thought. Part of this had to do with the work that needed to be performed by children who live in rural areas or on farmlands. Wearing dresses was not practical for feeding animals, milking cows, planting seeds, and a host of other chores around the house. Dresses also did not accommodate the kind of play in which girls could engage in these spaces, such as climbing trees or swimming in a creek. Thus, many narrators believe that being a "tomboy" did not have the same stigma as being a "sissy" because gender-neutral or boys' clothing worn by girls was seen as a practical matter as opposed to an index of sexual orientation or even preferred gender expression. Nonetheless, the practicality of clothing for some of these women provided a guise for their budding homosexuality.

This gendered sartorial freedom was circumscribed by religion and age. No matter what girls wore during the week, on Sundays they were forced to wear dresses and have their hair done (either in pigtails or pressed and curled). And, typically, after puberty these now young women were expected to leave their tomboyish ways behind (including their overalls and pants), present themselves as young "ladies," and follow a traditional path to heteronormativity. If that transition to traditional presentation did not occur, it was then that the wages of homophobia descended. What is interesting about this trajectory is how it is caught up in the politics of black respectability, one, I might add, that is peculiar to the South because of the ways in which it is undergirded by religious doctrine.

Once adults and beyond the influence or control of parents and family, these women created even more nuanced self-presentations of gender that do and do not index their sexual identity or sexual behavior. These gender markers manifest in the form of dress, language, and sexual roles. What became clear in these interviews, however, is how these codes—while part of a larger symbol system of black female same-sex desire—do not have stagnant meanings and vary from region to region and from context to context. For instance, what reads as "femme" in one context reads as "soft butch" in another. The difference between these two readings of the same gender presentation might come down to the sartorial aesthetic in vogue in one region over another—with the wearing of lipstick by a woman dressed as a dandy marking the slide from soft butch to femme.

In general, vernacular terms that index gender performance were far fewer among the women I interviewed than what I found among the gay men in *Sweet Tea*. In fact, there were so many vernacular terms among the men that I had to create an index of terms for the reader to decipher all of them. For the women, however, the same terms for gender expression recurred across regions, with very little variation—terms such as "butch," "femme," "dominant," "aggressive," "stud," and "stem." These latter terms were more common among younger women, whereas older women usually referred to traditional terms like "dyke" and even "bulldagger," which for most younger women is offensive. Importantly, none of these terms determines a woman's sexual behavior during sex with another woman. For instance, while a "stud" presents as masculine, which presumably means that she would prefer to be the "top" during sex, some self-identified stud narrators were clear that this was not the case. Also, there are "aggressive femmes" who present as passive in public but who take on a dominant role in the bedroom. As "Lisa" recounts in chapter 5, she was duped by a high femme preacher's wife who used the guise of "church lady" to seduce women in the church.

Ultimately, these narrators confirm that gender presentation, sexual expression, and sexual identity are not one and the same. Their tales of embracing traditional gender roles belie the common belief that all budding lesbians are tomboys. Their stories of being fond of makeup while also taking charge in the bedroom undermine the narrative that feminine women are passive. And their stories of preferring a butch aesthetic while also expressing emotion and being nurturers demonstrate that there are alternative ways of being masculine—in ways that run counter to performances of masculinity by heterosexual, cisgender men. Below is just a sample of the various ways these women "play" with gender.

· ·

Dammeion

Dammeion is one of the kindest and gentlest women I met—and also one of the most masculine. She rides a motorcycle, is a mechanic, and works in manufacturing. In fact, her wife told me during the visit that when she first saw Dammeion, she thought she was a cute Puerto Rican man. Dammeion was born in 1970 in Baton Rouge, Louisiana. An aspiring basketball player out of high school, her career was forestalled when she chose to stay close to home when her mother had a brain aneurysm that left her infirm for years. She and her wife, Trenda, live in Baton Rouge, along with Trenda's children from a previous heterosexual relationship. The interview took place on April 19, 2013, in Baton Rouge.

Here in the South . . . it was a challenge because I've always known about myself, but as a kid you don't know how to put it into words. And my toughest time came when my mom found out. But other than that, I was tomboyish. My mom didn't see it that way. I was her only girl, so she dressed me as she dressed. So, I had to get smart, and I would go in and make sure all my little halter tops were dirty. [Laughter] I would do anything to get out of a dress. And then my dad started to play a role, not a major role. I grew up in the country. We call it Brusly, Louisiana [. . .] going towards Plaquemine. There's a country-living town called Tombstone. It has two streets. One goes all the way through to the levy, and the other is a dead end coming back from the levy. And that little place is where I kind of found out who I was. It's me with the sports and the majority of my life being a mechanic. Now I do something different, but everything I've done has been physical or in a "man's world," per se.

So, me growing up I was always the only girl. I played Little League Baseball in Port Allen, I was the first girl to play Little League Baseball in Port Allen. Basketball kind of took over. So, I played two years at Southern University, played four years for Broadmoor High School, and then I started coaching AU [Athletic Union] ball. I was actually going pro the week my mom fell with an aneurysm. I was leaving that Thursday, and she fell that Tuesday. She collapsed that Tuesday, and she was in a coma for two and a half weeks, and I couldn't focus. So, I never went to camp. And I regret it to a certain extent, but then I don't. So, after that, that's when I started coaching, only boys—the little girls I couldn't do it—boys AU basketball for three, four, five years. And I haven't done it lately with the job change and everything. I'm forty-two years old. I'll be forty-three in a couple of months, and I still get ID'd everything I do. [. . .] I've aged recently due to some illnesses, but I look at myself and wouldn't believe I was the age that I am, you know. My other siblings, they didn't age quite as well. [Laughter] [. . .]

My grandfather . . . in his eyes there was nothing I couldn't do. If I wanted to go hunting, I'd go hunting. If I wanted to go fishing, if I wanted to play baseball, wanted to fix bikes. My grandfather used to work for what's called JTPA in Port Allen—it's a junior training program—so he had access to a lot of tractors and lawn mowers and things like that. So, he'd bring them home all the time and to the point I had a go-cart that didn't work, so my cousin and I decided to take an engine out of a lawn mower and put it in the go-cart. So, I got in trouble. I got that good old southern ass whooping, as they call it, to the point that it didn't even bother me anymore, just take it and go on. My mother had a rule: as long as you can withstand the beatings for the consequences of your actions, whatever it is you want to do, do it. And that abided to everything except my lifestyle. When it came to that, she didn't see it that well, you know. But my grandparents were my best friends growing up. And that's why . . . even as a young kid I liked old-school music. I like some hip-hop and rap but give me Luther [Vandross], Barry White, Chaka Khan, stuff like that. And my stepfather was a graduate of Alcorn. He's been a barber my whole life; that's what he did. Never made great money, but he's been in my life since I was nine. And even now through everything with my mom I consider him a good man because he stood by when most men wouldn't have put in the time and effort. And he was into jazz and music. Seventh grade they made us learn an instrument. He said, "Why don't you try the saxophone?" So, up until my senior year in high school I played the sax. When I got to Southern [University] they didn't allow women to play in the band. I was like, psht, forget it. That's how I felt. You know, that's what I wanted to do. I did marching band in high school; I wanted to continue on. When I got in school I loved basketball, it was the center of my life. All the scoring titles and all that stuff I did, LSU and Southern didn't look at me. Even though I decided to go to Southern because I was in mechanical engineering, engineering is what I decided, and it was something I was good at. I like the way things work. Figure it out. Even if I've never done it before, I'd break it down and put it back together. It just kind of fit me.

People ask me all the time, especially women and everything, and I tell them what my name is, and they go, "Okay, what's your real name?" I'm like, "That's my real name. That's what my mom named me. I'm Dammeion and my brother is Nico." So, it's just . . . it's odd how we are so different. Because he's this big six-foot three-inch, three-hundred-and-sixty-pound guy, and he's very weak. And I'm this five-foot seven-inch, one-hundred-and-thirty-pound little woman who will fight in a second. I've always had to. I got picked on a lot younger; and my mom, the way she was raised me, was "Never start anything, but you don't let anyone push you around." So, this girl was kicking my butt every day in elementary school. So, when she beat my butt I'd come home and mom would beat my butt too, so I got tired to getting two butt whippings. So, finally, one day I put some shorts under my skirt in school and handled my business, and from that day forward that's just the way it's been. "I won't start it. Just don't you start." Period. And the way I dress now people tell me. . . . Shannon [a childhood friend] says the same thing: I look the same from when I was in high school. This is about the biggest I've been; I'm one hundred thirty pounds. That's only because I'm in a gym. And my style of dress is jeans and tee—I'm happy. But if I need to put on slacks I can hang with the best of them too. Some of the best guys, I can roll with you on that. I'm not in big fashion, but it's my sense of level with myself. And my grandparents had a big influence on that. You know, my mom was an influence as well, but she was more a disciplinarian. And my grandparents did the same thing, but they allotted me to be who I was. And that helped me to not be ashamed of who I am, you know. And I've always lived my life as I am. Just me, period. Usually I'm the girl that have the long . . . I had very long hair. It's not as long because someone didn't want to roll their hair anymore. [Laughter] I've never been the type to shave my hair and I don't identify myself as what the rest of the world does. I do what Dammeion likes to do. And if you don't like that, then I'm sorry, and that's the way it is.

. . . .

Diane

When I first met Diane in Winston-Salem, North Carolina, she was the partner of another narrator. She was present during the interview with her now ex. By the time I returned to interview her, the two had separated, but they remain good friends. Like so many of the narrators I interviewed,

Diane is a survivor of sexual violence, at the hands of her adopted brother. Her particular story, however, was one that left me in tears during the interview. The pain of that experience and her parents' denial of the event continue to haunt her.

Diane was born in Spartanburg, South Carolina, in 1977. Spartanburg is in what is considered the Upstate region of South Carolina, in the northwest corner of the state, and sits close to the North Carolina border. Of the close to forty thousand residents, almost half are African American. She and her younger sister were taken from their biological mother due to her mother's drug use and placed into foster care at the age of two. The interview took place on July 31, 2013, in Winston-Salem.

I use the term "lesbian" depending on the situation or the circumstances or whatever or whoever I'm talking to. It depends. I personally don't label myself at all. I'm just me, but I'm just a feminine me, but I have a little bit of boyish in me too, so that I don't label myself because I'm a little bit of everything. I can rock the Tims [Timberland shoes] and the fitted T [shirt] and all this stuff just like a stud can do, but I'm gonna rock it with my nails, though. You see what I'm saying? I can rock it just like you can, but I'm not going to say, "Yeah, I'm just like strictly this," and "This is what I am," and "A female can't touch this, this, and this." No, no. I'm born female. I'm a woman. Woman have woman needs and that's it. I don't particularly put myself in a category. I don't do that.

. . . .

"Doris"

I met "Doris" through a mutual friend who also is a narrator in "Sweet Tea." She and I have kept in touch over the years, and she agreed to be interviewed for this book on the condition of anonymity because of her profession. "Doris" was born in New Orleans in 1967, the eldest of four children. The interview took place on April 18, 2013, in New Orleans.

I don't have a problem with identifying as lesbian. The thing that I have and they have that's bad, I guess, within the gay community is the butch thing, the stud thing, the lipstick thing, and all of that. That thing, I don't get with all that, I don't think; to me I think it's again trying to conform to a society thing because you hear the ignorant people: "Well, which one is the man and which one is the woman?" Nobody is the man or the woman. Everybody is their gender, and no one is playing because it's like, "Well, which one is playing the role of this." Nobody's playing a role. It's like they always think it's like some kind of a movie [role] you're playing, because who playing this role. Well, nobody's playing a movie. This is somebody's life. Now, if somebody may identify more with being masculine, that's fine. I don't really get with the whole "They got to dress like a guy with a guy underwear" and all of that. I can't get with that. You know, I wouldn't say necessarily I would be feminine, but I definitely don't identify with being some butch stud thing or whatever like that. I guess people [perceive] me as being "aggressive femme" or whatever that's supposed to be. I don't identify with any of that. I'm me.

· ·

Jasmine

Jasmine is the youngest woman I interviewed for this book. I was introduced to her through Della Pollock, a colleague and former professor of mine at the University of North Carolina at Chapel Hill. She was born in 1994 in Chapel Hill but was reared for most of her life in Semora, North Carolina, which is located in north central North Carolina near the border of Virginia. Semora is unincorporated and has a population less than fifteen hundred. It is home to Red House Presbyterian Church, one of the oldest churches in the state, built in 1781. The interview took place on August 25, 2012, in Carrboro, North Carolina.

In middle school, I was such a tomboy. When my parents were married, I was like a daddy's girl. Like, my dad, he would get me up early to play a sport. I think he wanted a son. He wanted me to play sports so bad, he would make me do all of this stuff, and I would just dress tomboyish, like I would always put my hair in a ponytail. And when I went school shopping, I would get the most baggiest clothes. And my friends would be like, "You look like a dyke. You look like you're lesbian. We need to paint your nails. We need to get you in a dress." I'm just like, these are chill clothes. It would just happen so much that I eventually took all of my wardrobe and gave it to my cousin, 'cause she was like taller than me and kinda bigger than me. And she's a tomboy, but that was her. So, I mean, everything that I wore fit her perfectly.

· ·

"Jill"

"Jill" was born in Huntsville, Alabama, in 1975, the eldest of two siblings. Huntsville is located in north central Alabama close to the Tennessee state border. It has a population of 180,000, 30 percent of whom are African

American. The interview took place on September 8, 2013, in Nashville, Tennessee.

When I go back and look at some of my pictures . . . I feel like my parents . . . let me dress however. I mean, I dressed tomboyish or boyish. I dressed girlish. I felt like I was just able to be me as a child. I was able to just wear whatever I felt comfortable wearing. I don't know how it is with boys, but I think it's probably easier for girls. Well, I don't know, I think depending on your family. If you have a family that's extremely strict and where girls have to wear dresses all the time, but my family wasn't like that. I felt like I was kind of like the girl who could wear whatever. Yeah, I got my hair pressed and combed and wore pigtails and whatnot, but like when I played or whatever, my parents really didn't really want me playing in a dress. It was kind of like when I played, I played in just regular play clothes, like pants mostly, shorts. Of course, I just felt like I was the type of girl whose parents . . . weren't really strict about all of that for me and my sister. Now, I think if my brother had tried to, they would have had some problem. That's why I think it's harder for boys, because I feel like as girls it's acceptable for us to be tomboys growing up, because like kids at that age sometimes—well, for girls—it's like you're kind of like genderless almost. I don't know, it's like . . . for girls, our bodies are very boyish until we reach puberty. We don't have the boobs and all the whatnot until you get to puberty, until you become a teen. But for boys . . . it's scandalous if a boy wants to wear a dress, but if a girl wants to wear blue jeans all the time or sweatpants or whatever as a little girl, it's totally acceptable.

Once I got to high school in my teen years . . . I feel like I was receiving pressure mostly from my peers, and then maybe I probably put it on myself trying to conform to peer pressure, and then a little bit, just a little bit from my mom, just maybe because I'm growing up, I'm becoming a young woman. She was like, "Oh, you should dress this way" or "just act a certain way" or "be a certain way," but I've always been kind of like in the middle as far as like expressing my gender identity or whatever. I've been kind of in the middle all my life. I can wear dresses. I don't have a problem. I don't consider myself a stud or a femme. I mean, I consider myself in the middle. I'd probably say I'm more femme, but I really consider myself in the middle, because I'm not really like ultra femme, but I really consider myself in the middle, and I probably feel like I've been like that all my life. But I'd say I'd probably say I'm more femme as far as my identity expression. [. . .]

Did you wear makeup?

I wore it like every now and then. I probably like I wear it now. It's kind of like I really don't wear that much makeup, but if I do wear it, it's very light. I feel like more to maybe enhance, not cover up, and if I do, like on a day-to-day [basis], I'd say the most I wear would probably be tinted lip gloss or tinted ChapStick, but mostly just very neutral like I am now, but it's not like a thing that I do on a regular basis. But I do get that pressure sometimes from mom. I feel like now . . . my whole world is just all of my LGBT people. They're my whole world. We don't pressure each other. We just accept each other. We don't pressure each other to be any type of way as far as gender identity or whatever. And that's one thing I really love about . . . being gay. I mean, it's just such a relief. [. . .] In my little groups that I run with here in Tennessee, I feel like we're very accepting of . . . everybody's gender expression.

. . . .

Kerrie [b. 1970, Fort Lauderdale, Florida]

[My] grandmother Nanny from DC sent me this pink dress with lots of ruffles, and I loved that dress. I loved that dress, but I hated the color pink. But I loved that dress. And it was something about that dress that I just liked and I loved it. I have this picture of me in a chair with the dress and a bow on my head. But when my father painted my room pink when I was maybe seven or eight, I just demanded that he changed the color because I just hated pink. And I hated Barbie dolls and I hated frilly things. I liked corduroys and striped sweaters. And my mother never really said anything about it, except I know on Easter I always wore a dress.

What color did your father paint your room after you objected to pink?

I think it was yellow.

And that was okay?

And that was okay. Even though the carpet was red.

. . . .

Keturah [b. 1980, Atlanta, Georgia]

How can you tell if somebody's a lesbian?

How can I tell? I don't think I can always tell, but there are the more stereotypical lesbians.

And what's a stereotypical lesbian?

The ones that their masculine energy shows very highly on the outside—I mean, pants sagging, braids to the back. My partner even wears her hair braided to the back sometimes, I'm like, "Oh, my God." You know,

"Really?" You know, breasts strapped down—she doesn't strap her breasts down, but other women, breasts strapped down, you got on the bowtie, you got the suit. So, you see them out on the street, it's a walk that they do; they got a more masculine, cocky walk to 'em, but they still feminine at the same time—those stereotypical ones, you can identify as being gay. A lot of the more feminine ones, I can't tell unless I'm in the environment with them. But let them tell it, 'cause a group of us went out to dinner, most of us were partnered, except for two women who were there, both single and both heterosexual. And the conversation came up: based on stereotypes, who would be the gayest. So, it's like ten to twelve of us, so ten or twelve being the highest, just going through who would be the gayest. And they were going through this whole thing, and they ended up asking our waitress, "Based on stereotypes, who would you say would be the gayest and who would be the straightest?" Anne was the girl who was organizing it and she says, "And I want you to know that there's two of us here at this table who are straight. Everybody else is gay." So, the woman starts and she says, "Well, let me just get the straight women out the way first." And she says, "Well, I know you're straight," and she points at me. [Laughter] And everybody falls out laughing, 'cause they already think that. So, she's like, "I know you're straight." And then she's like, "Uh, and maybe you?" And the other one that she picked was gay. But the ones she knew who were the gayest were the ones who fit that masculine stereotype, and she knew that, and it was just hilarious. But the gay women at the table, they felt that they were edgy—like, one has this tattoo, she has a short haircut. She's feminine, but she has a short haircut and she has this tattoo on her arm here, and that, to her, shows her gayness, like there is this edginess—so all of the gay women at the table felt that there was this edginess about themselves that makes them gay. But with me, they don't see any edginess. [Laughter]

'Cause you weren't nude. [Laughter]

No, I guess not! 'Cause I used to have really long, relaxed hair, so now I wear my fro and everything, and so I was like, "Well, with my fro I don't look more edgy? I don't look gay now?" They're like, "No. Straight women wear afros now, too." And I asked my partner sometimes, "Well, what makes me so straight?" And she's like, "Baby, I don't know, you just seem that way."

. . . .

Lynn

Lynn is a firecracker. You feel her warrior spirit the minute you meet her. She is an HIV/AIDS activist in Jackson, Mississippi, and has been working to get the local and state governments to fund more prevention programs for years. She was born in Jackson in 1968, the eldest of three children. She has two sons, one of whom is also gay. The interview took place on August 13, 2013, at her office in Jackson.

"Stud on stud" is a masculine-identified woman with another masculine-identified woman. They don't like that because it's not how relationships are supposed to be. And studs getting pregnant with a . . . "big dyke." And I've been calling them big dykes for years. So, I call them . . . "BTD" for years. So, that ain't nothing new. But yeah, this whole "Why these stud girls are getting pregnant? Why these butches getting pregnant?" They want their own baby, and what's wrong with a masculine-identified woman carrying her own child? "That's gay." "No, it's not gay." Just the mind-set is so jacked up here. It is. I don't know if it's anywhere else, but here it's jacked up. The big dyke. That's the only thing that's like stud on stud. But I'm not out in the community like I used to be. Because I'm frustrated with these young folks. And older people, you know, they had a house that they invited—you know, like they're so cliquish. I don't get the invitations to certain houses because I am being too open. And if I'm around, the perception is going to be "All of them are gay."

. . . .

Melanie
Melanie was born in Mobile, Alabama, in 1976. She comes from an extremely large family with fourteen aunts and uncles—just on her mother's side of the family! The interview took place on October 14, 2013, at her home in Atlanta, Georgia.

As long as I could remember, I didn't like dresses. I know there's a thing called a tomboy where [the girl says] I don't like dresses and then when she turns fifteen she starts putting on makeup and she put on dresses. Well, for me that just never happened. I turned fifteen, sixteen, seventeen, never wanted makeup. I don't wear makeup now. I think it's weird. People were like, "I'm going to put some makeup on you." I'm like, "Why?" It's not me, you know? My dad would let me play with remote control cars, any boy toys or unisex. But they bought me a baby doll. I could care less. At the height of when people were punching each other in the face for Cabbage Patch dolls, they bought me one. Had the same birthday as me. I can't tell you where that thing is. I don't care.

I remember my sister had just been born; I was seven and they'd gone to New Orleans on a little trip for them because you know when you got two kids, you work all the time, you need parent time. They'd gone to New Orleans and they were like, "We got you a surprise!" And I was like, "Oh, yes! I love surprises." They pull this thing out and I'm like, "What the hell is this? It's a doll. You know that I don't like dolls." So, it was weird, and I know that you can say because I identified with more male aspects of things that doesn't necessarily make me gay. And it doesn't, but for me, it made me different than all of the people in my family. I was the only girl that really got hardcore. Like me and my Uncle Victor, he's the one that's two years older than me. He was like, "Let's go play cars." Okay, we play cars in the backyard where we used Popsicle sticks to draw roads in the dirt. We'd use cinder blocks as the house, and we'd have little Hot Wheels, and we'd play pretend in the backyard. We'd get dirty; we'd get scummy. I was the only girl back there. You know, when it came time to play baseball, kickball, whatever it was, I was always first in line ready to go. [. . .]

I remember one year I asked my dad to buy me some button-up shirts because you watch those eighties movies, like all the John Hughes films, you know the characters have those nice crisp polo button up shirts. He bought me one, and it had a monogram on the pocket, and I didn't wear it because I thought it was too girly. Like, it was just gross to me. But I mean, you could still be a tomboy. I half expected to grow out of it, to think, "Okay, well one day, I guess I'll like makeup, maybe I will put on a dress." I mean, it was an act of Congress even when I was a Delta [Sigma Theta Sorority]. You have to go through different ceremonies and everything. I mean, I bought one dress to just learn all the history and everything. I wore it every day. You know, all the girls would change or do this. I just never put any emphasis into that aspect of being a woman. I love being a woman. I don't feel confused about my gender, but there are just certain things I don't get, and it's not because my mom isn't feminine. She wears makeup. She's the girliest person I know, but it just was lost on me. It was just like a part that was happening to my cousins, my mom, my aunts, but it just didn't seem like it was meant for me at all.

. . . .

Michelle

While all of the women that I interviewed have compelling stories and touched me in a personal way, Michelle is one of the women who continues to be an inspiration to me and who brings a smile across my face when

I think of her. She is in touch regularly and has attended several of my lectures and performances, even speaking at some of them during the question-and-answer session. Michelle's triumph over sexual molestation at the hands of her father and uncle, drug addiction, and obesity speak to the resilience of the human spirit and, as she would put it, the grace of God. She was born in Winston-Salem, North Carolina, in 1965, the eldest of three. The interview took place on August 22, 2012, at her church in Winston-Salem.

In the sixth grade I began to play the drums. Well, my mother and them had already started riding me about this tomboyish thing. I was tomboyish. I didn't want no Barbie doll. I'll keep a Barbie doll and tear her head off. [Laughter] I didn't want that. [. . .] My sister and I are eighteen months apart . . . she lived for that, you know? And to paint the toenails and to dress them up. Give me a football. Go get me a creek, you know? I was in heaven. So, my mother was real hard on me about the tomboy thing. I liked the tube socks, I wanted some Converse, you know? That was the in thing back in the seventies; that was in, you know. "No, those what boys have, so you can't have that."

So, did you feel pressure to conform to traditional gender presentation?

Yes.

Little girls wore the dresses . . .

Yes.

And what was going on with your hair?

Um . . .

Press and curl . . .

No, I thank God, they had blessed me with a decent grade of hair, and we're talking about, what, sixth, seventh, eighth grade. I was trying to do styles. I was so whack.

I would do a lot of pulling back in the ponytail and then for picture days . . . Mama would want you to have hair rollers and all this carrying on. And back in the seventh grade, that's when I began to be real athletic. So, it was either up or it's pulled back.

What kind of sports did you play?

Softball, volleyball. I've always been a juicy kid. [Laughter] Still holding on to a little bit of my baby fat now. [. . .]

I loved playing the drums. It just gave me such energy and it was exciting, and it did have a male kind of feeling to it. [Laughter] And it had a controlled feeling to it as well, you know. Um . . . as I began to get higher in school I stopped playing because they rode me so about playing the drums. You know, I wanted to do the drum set. I really enjoyed that instrument. However, um, the percussion . . . however, I wanted to stay in music, but I needed to soften things up for their sake, they being mom and dad and all of that. So, I went to clarinet and was a very good clarinet player over the years. I started playing clarinet, I think, in the seventh grade. I still play some drums, but my principal instrument was clarinet. And I carried clarinet all the way to college. And I was a music major. Music education major.

. . . .

Monica

I had the good fortune not only to interview Monica for this book but also to listen to her play the cello in her band called Honeypot. What serendipity! Monica was born in Washington, DC, in 1977 and now resides in New Orleans. The interview took place on April 18, 2013, in New Orleans.

It's so interesting because I met so many people that have a lot of fluidity. I think there is a lot of fluidity, and depending on a person and what they are willing to experience, what they're willing to allow themselves to experience, and be open to the experience. Even if the fluidity is like, "I am really only attracted to those of the same sex." And then really go into that experience and say, "Okay, well within that, that means I might be as a woman attracted to the most traditionally feminine woman. I might also be attracted to the most non-traditionally feminine woman . . . female." Or like really giving ourselves the space to really be like, "What is it?" Because I've noticed in my becoming who I am more and more every day, it's like I definitely have come into contact with women who have been like, "Well, this is who I am. I'm a dyke and it's hardcore and it's like this and it's like that, and I thought you were a dyke too," and just getting dismissed because my experience at who I am is not their experience in who they are. Even if how we are living our lives looks the same, they found a difference or an underlying way of being different and . . . and it's like, "Okay, so how is this rigid way of expressing yourself allowing you to connect to other people? Is it hindering your ability to connect to other people? Like, what is it doing for you?" And so for me, I've just been working to give myself a whole lot of space to really be like, "What is my sexuality? How does it serve me?" So that I don't find myself boxed in in a different way than how I was once boxed in by any experience and by all this external stimuli or stories, so that I can really be fluid and present in whatever way my sexuality is showing up, you know. For instance, it's like I'm attracted to trans people, trans woman or trans man, to a more effeminate man to a very traditional worker type, carpenter kind of person, to like a very feminine woman. You know, it's just like this wide range. That just kind of is and could change in a moment. Like if I were to say, "Well, I'm only . . . ," it would change the next moment. And it's, it's like, "Okay, putting my finger on what is it? Like what is it about this type of person that I'm attracted to?" It's like, I don't even fully really know. But I'm giving myself that space to just kind of sit with it and not have to quantify it or name it in a way that would disempower it, you know. So, I think there's a lot of fluidity, and it's really beautiful to see people claim their identity within this fluidity, whatever it is, especially if they give themselves . . . if they allow themselves really their full human experience to be okay, so that they're not boxing themselves in and therefore boxing other people in. You know, because there can be this way that it's like, well, "She's a straight girl. Or he's a straight guy." Which can be diminishing of that person's experience because we diminish our own in some way. So, I've been just more and more just been noticing the fluid nature.

So, you wouldn't necessarily categorize yourself under any one label, as being more straight or bi or whatever?

Right. Lately I've been kind of going with queer, and I'm still feeling that one out to see . . . because of course as any identity it's the person or persons naming it and holding space for it. But it seems to be sticking or prismatic. A friend of mine, Michaela, likes prismatic, and it's like anywhere on the prism. You know, we might fall in anywhere along this beautiful rainbow and we're prismatic. So, yeah, I definitely know that I don't resonate with "straight" and I do not resonate with "bisexual." And for me the bisexual is . . . claims that there's only two genders. Being in this city and learning more about the Ifá tradition and Candomblé and Santería and all these things, it's like you might have a male whose head is . . . he's . . . his mom is Yemayá or Oshún. And so that means that the way he might present himself is like Yemayá or Oshún all over him. And what that might mean in the context of traditional gender . . . like it alludes up a whole 'nother avenue of like, "Oh, wow, that's a whole 'nother thing." Or how your ancestors might walk with you. I know that when I'm doing constructive things or at certain moments I'm like very like I'm feeling more masculine than I'm feeling more . . . and this is like . . . I'm like, "Oh." And that just shows up some days, and then this other thing shows up, or in moments, and it's like, "Wow, what is that?" And giving space to it is just so . . . the term "bisexual" for me really closes in that, like, "Well, there's just this. You can either pick the A or the B," and it's like, well, there are people that don't exist within that A or that B that I would am attracted to. So, what is that?

....

Nadia

I could listen to Nadia speak all day. Hers is a soft but deeply rich voice that hits nicely on the ear. She is one of several women I interviewed who are alums of Florida A&M University. She was born in Pensacola, Florida, in 1983, the only child of military parents. Pensacola is located in the Florida Panhandle and is the westernmost city, with a population of fifty-one thousand, a third of which are African American. The interview took place on August 18, 2013, in Tuscaloosa, Florida.

Speaking about gender presentation, you mentioned the term "stud." And I've talked to a number of people who have defined that term for me as well. Are there folk who come into your circle that come into their sexuality who remain feminine?

Oh yeah, absolutely. Absolutely. And that's the thing we encourage, too. We try to encourage that. You don't have to be defined by a label, you know? And unfortunately, I see that a lot in our community. We're segregated because you know the white gay and lesbian community, they date whomever, they are whomever. I see that more fluid. With us there's a label. We're confined to heterosexual dynamics. It's like, "Oh you're the stud. You're not supposed to date another stud." "You're a femme. Yeah, you can date another femme, but you're definitely supposed to date a stud," and you have to be this way, you have to be that way. And I learned that here. That was difficult when I was coming into my own, too. I thought I had to be hard because if I'm going to be a tomboy, I've got to be like this. I've got to carry myself like that, and then bagging clothes, and I got to pull on myself, and be all, you know what I'm saying. I got to talk like this and act like this with girls and then that just wasn't me. So, as I got older I got comfortable. I got comfortable with myself. I don't define myself as "stud" or da, da, da. I am more dominant in personality, but that's pretty much it. I'm not defined by who I am because when most people meet me they're like, "Oh wow, you're really feminine." Was I supposed to be a man? I don't you know. But yeah, there's a lot of segregation in that alone here. Because if you see two studs, it's just like a straight man seeing two men together. That's how the mentality is. It's like, what's wrong? They're two women. So, we promote that. It's two women. If you like another woman who's dominant like you, okay. The point is we're lesbians. We like women.

· ·

Priscilla [b. 1967, San Antonio, Texas]

I think that what I know is that I always wanted to wear my—there were particular shorts that my middle brother had that I wanted to wear. I didn't mind wearing dresses and I didn't mind wearing more feminine clothes, right? But I didn't want to wear them every day because I was a very active child, like swinging on shit, climbing in trees, very tomboyish, as they would call me, they would have called me that. And in our neighborhood, the boys and the girls played together. Like we played street football and we played with—we were young: eight, nine, and ten—playing with boys who were about fifteen, sixteen years old. We all played together. And so, you would have a divided up team, but everybody played. The feminine girls, the more masculine girls, the more athletic girls. So, there was not that thing around what you wore and everything, because that's what we did, you know. And you needed to wear clothes that allowed you to do that, right? And so, it wasn't like my parents would be. like, "Oh, you need to do this." So, from what I remember, I felt that from my aunt around wearing the dress, which [laughter] I just had no understanding for. Because I also think that my parents just really let me do whatever I wanted to do. All of us are spoiled. I'm very spoiled, but so are my two brothers, and we all know it. And so, we just got to do what we wanted to do. Now I remember my father telling me like, "Girls don't whistle and girls don't spit." So, of course, I would spit and I would whistle. And I still do it, and he still can't stand it. But I'm like, "I'm a girl and I spit and I whistle, right?" [Laughter] So, I didn't really feel that out, not until you get older and you're a teenager and then it's like, "Oh, I'm supposed to be wanting to be more effeminate." And I didn't want to be. And it took me a very long time to figure out how to wear my hair. I had long hair. Hated my hair, I mean. And I had good hair, right? [Laughter] And so I couldn't stand it, because I was like, I can't see myself doing that shit. [Laughter] Like first of all, I'm very tender-headed and so everything hurts. But also, like growing up, I never wore makeup. But I don't know if that comes from my mom didn't really wear makeup. She wore lipstick and a little, I don't even know what you call this stuff that go right here [points at her cheek].

Blush.

Yeah! See? [Laughter] I'm like, "What does she mean that go right here?" Blush. And she would do that like to church or whatever or if her and my father were going out. But yeah, I don't—I didn't—there was no pressure to wear makeup, to do the dress thing, really none. You know, I think the pressure came a little bit from me around peer groups, around trying to look more like, and dress more like my girlfriends, right? Which didn't seem to fit. [Laughter] I look at pictures now and go, "Oh, Lord." [Laughter] But I still didn't do it, though. I only wore what really made me comfortable.

. . . .

Q.

I met Q. through my artist friend Sharon Bridgforth. Among other things, Q. is a filmmaker and LGBTQ activist and was responsible for introducing me to many of the women in the Dallas area to be interviewed for this book. Q. was born in 1980 in Dallas, Texas, and was adopted with two other siblings. They are all six years apart in age. The interview took place on September 13, 2013, in Dallas, Texas.

So, my mom is a girly girl, and my dad will embarrass me sometimes when I bring friends home because they had these ruffle panties made to go over my diapers. And my name is a little soulful, so it's eight letters. And so, he brings them out, and it's like these ruffle panties with my name that goes ALL the way across because it's some baby panties. And so everything for me was like Barbie dolls and dolls and Cabbage Patch Kids. And I remember I was . . . I had to be like six or seven and I was doing something in the house in my mom's room, some kind of craft, trying to build something or make something. And I used to run around with my shirt off. And this particular day my mom was like, "You've got to put your shirt on because girls can't have their shirt off," you know? [. . .] I don't think I would be outside playing with my shirt off, but just around the house, you know? I'd be like having my shirt off. [. . .] I've always been very intuitive and observant. And so I said, "Okay, so this is how girls have to be." And then when my brother came along, he got the toys that I wanted, you know? I wanted the Ninja Turtle . . . Teenage Mutant Ninja Turtle set. It had all four Ninja Turtles; it had their little secret hiding place, and it had Splinter, which is the big rat that was their mentor, and it had all the weapons, and it had the skateboard for Michelangelo. I got a Barbie house for Christmas, and my brother got the Teenage Mutant Ninja Turtles set. Oooh, talk about mad. But I just played with them anyway. I had the Ninja Turtles in the Barbie house with the GI Joes.

But I started learning from an early age how a girl is supposed to be. But I still, in my heart, I still was the Q. you see now because I would still be out at recess, rolling up my denim skirt to play soccer and football with the boys. And it was me and another girl named Charity, and we would always be over there with the boys playing in our little skirts, and I'd get my little white ruffled socks all dirty. And the girly girls would be over there doing whatever, but I was always doing something with the real boy boys, you know?

* * *

I was dating a girl and there was a—you know how they have the gay prom?
Mmm-hmm.
And so, I called him up, I'm like, "Dad, I'm going to this prom thing and I want to wear a tie." So, I went home and we sat on the staircase, and he showed me how to tie a tie. That will forever be one of my fondest memories. Because growing up I was always in my dad's closet. I loved to sit there and watch him shave. He used the Old Spice in the can and you've got to take the powder and mix it. And he had this whole little regimen. He had this little box he would take out the closet that had the knife that he would use. He'd use a knife to open up the top of the can. He had like another little thing that he poured the powder in, add some water, mixed that up with a different knife. And then he had a little brush to brush it on. Man, I wanted to shave so bad. It was so cool. [Laughter] Yeah, so I was always in his closet. Never in my mom's closet. Like I might have played around in there just messing around, but I'd always want to be in my dad's closet and put on his shoes. He had always had the little shoe trees. He always wore Allen Edmonds. He had shoe trees in all his shoes, so I couldn't really get into those because I didn't know how to put the trees back in. But I liked to get in his old suit coats and stuff that be in the closet, and he had like leather trench coats from the seventies and I would put those on. And he had a cane from when he was in his accident, so I would be in his little trench coat with the cane, walking around and thinking I was cool. [Laughter] I don't even know if he even knows this. I need to tell him.

* * *

So, college was cool. And then I pledged [a sorority]. But I was still presenting girlie and I was starting to kind of get toward my Q ness, but I'm a legacy and I grew up always wanting to be a Delta [Sigma Theta]. My dad's an Alpha [Phi Alpha] and I have an uncle that's an Alpha and my grandmother is a AKA [Alpha Kappa Alpha]. And for me, being Greek, it was this privilege that I wanted to attain, you know? I got pictures of my dad's old college yearbook of them marching civil rights. And so, my dad was gonna pledge Omega [Psi Phi] because he said my uncle was in Omega. But he said Dr. King was Alpha. So, that's why he pledged Alpha. So, I grew up with these ideals around being Greek. You know, like it's something that you do to help society. And so, when I got to college I was like, yeah. Of course, I get to college nowadays and being Greek has its own kind of different set of issues that come along with it. But still, regardless, I still wanted to pledge, and so I kind of girlied myself up a little bit just to be on the safe side and I pledged. And for whatever reason after I crossed [over], I don't know what happened. Because I think I tried so hard to be girlie . . . I even bought a purse. Yes, I had bought a purse. I went through so many different fashions finding myself in college that I went from Erykah Badu with the Afrocentrism to all different kind of stuff. Bohemian . . . I don't know what I was going through.

This was what, between '98 and 2002?

This was like between '98 and I pledged in '01.

Okay. So, in your junior year.

Yeah, my junior year I pledged. So, after I crossed, I was like, man, fuck it, and I started just slowly transforming into my Q-ness. A friend of mind that pledged grad chapter, she dances for Dallas Black Dance Theatre. She does hair, she braids hair. I said, "I want to try something new." She said, "I want to try this out." So, she cornrowed my hair all the way back. I never had that done before, but I loved it. And then a friend of mine, her name was Bernie, we were going out one night and she was like . . . I just needed to borrow a T-shirt, so she let me borrow this gray T-shirt. So comfortable, but it was kind of big. And then I had like these big jeans that for whatever reason I put on. And I looked in the mirror and I was just like, "Wow," you know? It was like, "I feel good," you know? And I'll never forget, I started . . . because at this point I was out. I had come out and I wasn't gonna come out to my line sisters or whatever, but I had a couple women over to the Delta House. So, one day I'm walking through . . .

Oh, Deltas had a house on campus?

Yeah, we did. It's not there anymore, but Deltas and the AKAs had a house. But we both lost them. So, I'm coming through and there are some Omegas there and some of my line sisters down there chillin', and I'm walking through and I hear "dyking in the Delta House." And I went, "Oh, okay," and I didn't say anything because I didn't really care, you know? Because they would see women leaving at like 6:00 in the morning or whatever.

[Laughter] I'm like . . . when I get comfortable with myself and accept myself, it's a wrap for everybody else. I don't give a fuck. It wasn't like a whole slew of women, and I didn't care. So, I ended up moving out of Delta house. I was tired of everybody all up in my business.

So, you think when you came out and you started to embrace your gender identity that you also became a player?

Mmm, I never been a player because . . . I mean, I tried one time, but that's just not in my nature. I'm a one-woman kind of guy. It usually gets me in trouble because I've attempted to have fuck buddies, but I only know how to treat a woman one way, you know? And so, I treat the women I'm with like queens because that's who they are in my reality. So, the whole player thing doesn't work for me. [Laughter] And I don't lie very well because I don't like lying. I feel like it gives people power over you. And I'm so busy that it's expensive to be with one woman. Can you imagine? I have a really good friend that has had like . . . at one time she was juggling like four different women. I'm like what does your wallet look like? You know what I mean? [Laughter] And so I've never been a player. When I'm single, I'm single. But when I'm in a relationship, that's it. I'm faithful and respectful and all of that. But when I'm single, it's you know, I don't consider that being a player, I just consider that me mingling. [Laughter]

* * *

I would just really say I'm queer. If I had to put a thing on it, I really think I'm more two-spirited and that's something that I've really been starting to come into here recently. Because I used to say I'm half trans, half stud, but now I just feel like I just really am a combination of both. You know, I happen to be born female bodied, but I definitely am not a woman. I'm definitely, of course, not a man, but I'm definitely something . . . either a combination and a third entity, you know? And in Native American culture it's called two-spirited. And those were the healers and the shamans and very sensitive to energy. And I've been told by people that I have spiritual gifts. I'm really now at this point starting to own that and embody that. Lesbian isn't my favorite term because it's white. [Laughter] And it's antiquated. I love "masculine of center" because a good friend of mine coined that term, B. Cole with the Brown Boi Project, and it, I think, encompasses more of what I embody. I don't really know how to explain me. Two-spirited comes closest right now with masculine of center.

Have you ever felt the need to change your biology? Do you feel preoperative, in other words?

Oh, um . . . for me it would be purely vanity. Because at one point I was researching transgender and looking at—not necessarily considering transitioning—but just researching it. I don't like having a chest because I like the way I look when my chest is flat, you know?

Do you bind at all?

No, not anymore. I used to. But I'm so small, I mean, and with working out . . . and I just really hate bras and hate being restricted. I don't want people to see the shape or whatever. It was like, fuck it everybody know what titties look like, you know what I mean? And bras are so uncomfortable. And so, I don't even wear them anymore at all. Like I used to wear them when I work out. The only time I wear one is when I go swimming and that's it. So, no. But, um, other than that I'm not gonna lie, I would like to have a penis.

Your own.

Yes, my own.

That's attached to your body.

Attached to my body, a real one. But technology hasn't progressed enough. But if it had, let's say right now technology progressed and like I have a nice working one and everything . . . I still wouldn't be trans. I would just be Q. with a dick, you know what I mean?

You wouldn't miss your vagina then?

. . . no, not my vagina.

Or would you want both?

I would just want my clit to grow into a dick. How about that?

Okay.

So, it would be the same. You know? Because I love my clit, but I would love for it to be a dick because I would love for—this is like really personal [laughter]—I would love to be able to feel the inside of another woman's vagina. See, I really wouldn't need my vagina, but I just need my clit so that I can penetrate because I just love being in there. [Laughter]

. . . .

RonAmber [b. 1981, Dallas, Texas]

I like to call myself "androgynous" because I do like to walk that line of both. I don't identify as stud and I don't identify as femme, but every now and then I like to wear baggy cargo pants and a pair of Jordans. But I might throw on a pair of hoop earrings. I mean I haven't really had conversations about it, but I always get very weird imagery from other officially stud women all the time. Like almost stank attitude because . . .

Directed towards you?

Yes. My friends have said, "It's because they don't really know where to kind of put you. Because you look like a stud but then you've kind of got on tight jeans" or "You have short hair and you're wearing Jordans but your clothes are kind of baggy, so they don't really know if you are really a stud or are you trying to be a femme?" And the thing is that I'm never really trying to be anything, but at the same time I'm always trying to be like courteous and cool or whatever, but I get very like irritated sort of like energy from stud women in the club. They treat me as if I'm kind of invading—it's just weird. You know, like if you see somebody, and they act like they just got a problem with you, but you don't really know where that came from. I think a lot of people would like to just be like, "Okay, so it's very boy/girl here the way they kind of like build." And this whole idea of stud for stud is taboo. Even though I really don't think so, because, I mean, my ex from Kenya, she was very stud, too. She looked a lot like me and people would see us together and we got asked a few times if we were "stud for stud." And I didn't know what that meant. And I looked it up and I was like, "Oh that means two studs that are together." That's not what we were, but it looked like what we were. Which is something that a lot of people think is gay, is like two boys. So, it's crazy. [Laughter] [. . .]

How has the internet affected some of these gender performances in terms of the way people express their desire, like you just said "stud for stud"? I mean, in your experience? And I don't know if you've dated online or not, but do you know of websites that cater to particular desires?

Mmm-hmm. So, I've met a couple of girls online. A woman that I dated in DC, I met her online. I think I met her on Myspace back in the day. I don't know very much. I mean, I'm on Downelink, but I don't really study the like different categories. But I know that you can kind of choose. I think you can choose if you're looking for somebody that identifies as like femme or stud. But I think the internet has just sort of encouraged this division between roles because pictures just allow people to just perform and model as these things, as these like different identities and characters. And I don't think [. . .] they're really that sort of black and white. And so, I think the internet just kind of encourages it in a way. Too, how you approach a woman if a girl is femme in her profile picture and another girl is stud, then you know, it's kind of expected that the stud girl is gonna be more aggressive and be the one to kind of probably hit on the femme, as opposed to it just being like, "No, I'm interested as well, like can we both just have a conversation?"

Rose [b. 1958, Roanoke, Virginia]

The term that I use when I'm identifying myself to people is "lesbian." Occasionally I use "queer" because it feels like it's more embracing of everything. But I don't know if I'm lesbian enough. You know, there are so many rules about how we're supposed to be in everything, and I'm sure I break a whole bunch of the rules. So, I don't know if people would—if other people call me a lesbian in the same way that, you know, sometimes I'm a feminist, but it depends on who is using the word. When I'm a feminist I'm a black feminist, which is a—I think a different breed altogether. But I don't follow all those rules either.

. . . .

Roshandra [b. 1976, Fort Lauderdale, Florida]

How involved are you in the gay community here?

I can truly say the most I am is with my organization. I am in a lesbian Greek organization. And that's the most I get involved is whenever my organization is doing anything.

And this is specifically a black lesbian Greek organization?

We don't discriminate, but all of our members are black females.

And do you consider yourself a fraternity or a sorority?

A fraternity.

Fraternity. [Laughter]

Uh, yeah. [Laughter]

And do you refer to each other as brothers?

Yeah, we. do. I don't like the terminology because I'm not a man and I don't equate with being a man. And only to me, men are brothers. But we do call each other brothers.

What's the history behind the organization?

There were two young ladies who wanted to form an organization for more dominant or stud, masculine women. And they came together and they actually first emulated the Omegas. And then they got away from that and came up with their own Greek organization. And came up with a history, purpose, and everything. And we're actually incorporated. So—.

—and how old is it?

I pledged in 2000, so 1999.

So, you go through a pledge process, as well?

Oh, it's legit, yeah. It's legit. Everything is our own, bylaws and everything.

Is it national now?

Well, with our org, we're local but we're expanding. That's actually something that we're working on is expansion. So, they're getting all of the individuals who are interested in other states, so. And then we have a sister organization here, who they're national, they're like all over the US.

And who comprises—?

Those are the more feminine girls. But they have some masculine girls in their organization. But we don't never really get—well, we do have some feminine girls in our organization. But, for the most part, most of the feminine women will pledge our sister organization.

That's fascinating. Are both organizations post-undergrad?

Correct.

And how do people find out about your organization?

Word of mouth. Or people here in Tallahassee. Everyone should know who we are. But it's basically by word of mouth or through our website.

That's fascinating. Any white women in the organizations?

Not in my organization. But there is, let's see, I don't know if there's any whites in our sister org, but there's none in my organization. Everyone is African American.

. . . .

Shannon

Shannon is the ex of a friend of mine. She was born in Birmingham, Alabama, in 1976, the youngest of three. The interview took place on October 13, 2013, in Birmingham.

A "soft stud" is like she was stud but she is not just hard core. Like she might have some lipstick on. She might have a purse, or she might get her toes polished and wear her feet out, and stuff like that. Versus just a "stud," who is just, you know, don't put no polish on me, don't put no makeup on me. She might even wear boxer shorts. No panties, like that kind of thing. You know, nothing but men's clothing. So, and then you have a "femme" who is just ultra, ultra feminine. And I guess that's it. I don't know what other terms there would be. I don't know—that I know of. There might be some that I don't know about, but that's all.

Do those terms translate into what role people are going to play in the bedroom?

They can.

But they don't necessarily have to.

No. I mean, because you know there are some studs, these hard girls who feel like, "No, don't touch me. No, I don't want oral sex. No, you can't penetrate me. No, you can't strap on. Don't use a dildo, none of that." They just want to be the man. They want to do everything. They want to, and then there are some women who don't want to do any of that. They want to just lay there and get done. Then you have some studs that's "pillow queen."

What is a pillow queen?

Lying on their back on the pillow just sitting there and, "Hey do this and do that."

· ·

Sharon [b. 1964, Washington, DC]

Did you wear dresses as a little girl?

I hated them. I wanted to kill the entire minibus full of Barbies with my friend Dori Ann; we hated dresses and we hated Barbies. And there seemed to be a proliferation of both. So, we would secretly mutilate them. You know, tear their hair out and clothes. But I think all girls kind of go through that kind of serial killer thing with their dolls. But we decided we didn't want them anymore. So, we took the camper and we put Barbie and Ken in all these weird sexual positions because both our fathers were doctors and so we had been like kind of raised up on anatomy. Because my dad had this anatomy book in his office and it was like the anatomy of a pregnant woman, which I still remember to this day taking apart and putting back together. But then all kinds of books and I just loved, "Oh, look at that skin disease. What is that?" Right? And I loved learning names. And so, we put them all in this Barbie—all of our Barbies—all in that little thing and we waited. Her driver was kind of running late, and we waited for cars to go by. So, the first time we tried it the car stopped. And we were like, "Oh," you know, "sorry." And then we waited like for bigger vehicles to time it better. So, this like UPS truck, but I don't know what it was, maybe a delivery truck of some sort, was coming. And we put that thing down there and it smashed it to smithereens, and the Barbies went flying, and then we pinched each other real hard, so we could cry until our mothers came out. We looked devastated. We went through all that, and then more Barbies. And I'm like, "How many did you get?" She goes, "I got about four Kens. What did you get?" I'm like, "I got that Barbie GI Joe thing." And she said, "Oh, what are we going to do now?" But we were like, "I want to get that GI Joe" —that's all we wanted is a GI Joe. Just one GI Joe. One like combat person, right? So, I think I was different.

So, you didn't like to wear dresses, but you wore them.

I wore them, but I made sure that I messed them up. And my grandmother was just like, "Just put her in some of Joe's old clothes," and then I was happy. My dad learned that too. Like literally I would take a dress off and just walk around the house and not even wear it until somebody gave me something that I approved of. I could never close my legs. I remember my grandmother telling me, "Cross your legs. How hard is that? Everybody can see everything. Why do you have to sit like that?" I'm like, "I don't know Nana; I'm just not built like that." So, I would always remember sitting like this. So, you know my legs—my knees together and hunched over so that I wouldn't have to—wouldn't do that. So also, like I remember I got carsick with my dad when my dad came to pick me up for one of his visitation things, and I threw up all over this dress, and my mother put me in this ridiculous dress, and he was just like, "Well, I'm not going to dress you then," you know. And we went to his house and I washed up, and I got to wear like seat pants and one of his big T-shirts and I was like—I'll never forget [this]—it was one of the happiest days with my dad.

* * *

A lot of the dykes I know aren't really into those labels in their relationships. Like sometimes you'll look at folks and you'll be like, "Is that two butches together?" I feel that I'm old school because I'm always the oldest one. Like by maybe like—even like you know, not by a decade but like two or three years. Sometimes by a decade. Like some of the folks are in their late thirties. And you know, I look at them and like, "Which one of you is the girl?" So, I find myself thinking in these really stone butch patterns. I'm like, "Oh, I hate myself thinking like that." But I think nowadays there is so much queerness in the queer community. There are people who transition and don't necessarily, you know, sleep with men, sleep with women, right? They sleep with other men. There are people who transition and sleep with heterosexual women. There are people who transition and sleep with lesbians. There are people who transition and sleep with other people who transition. So, I feel like things are kind of up in the air. Those old categories of butch and femme. I am a classic. I'm a butch dandy, and I want my women like, "I would like you to wear your five-inch heels and some stockings, thank you very much." So, I definitely like—I'm not like my other friends who you know find other bois—"b-o-i's" attractive. I don't find androgynous bois attractive. I don't know what to do with them. You know, we can hang out. We could watch soccer. And then, you know, we could go shopping together. We could do a whole lot of things, but sexually I don't find them attractive.

But give me, you know, some crossed legs, a little bit of cleavage, and I am like, "Dear Lord baby Jesus. Where should I sign up?" I mean, I can't go to anyplace and like sign up for something because I'd be like, "Where's the cutest femme? I just want to be where she is." You know? I love, love, love women. I just really do. And for a while I thought maybe I didn't, but I really do, you know. And I love being a boi. I love inhabiting, being a boi for, like, maybe the first time in my lesbian life. So, I just want to kind of say that I feel like I've gone through almost every spectrum of being what it is. And I feel like every couple of years I find a new part of my queerness. Which I think is kind of cool.

. . . .

Wynee [b. 1962, Jackson, Mississippi]

Have you heard the term "stud"?

Yeah, we're studs and femmes. I'm considered stud.

Really? Do you identify as such or—?

Oh, absolutely I do. I'm a stud, but a soft butch. You know, I'm not hard at all.

How do people make those distinctions? Is it because you wear makeup?

I wear makeup because I just like it, but I don't think it has anything to do with me being soft or hard. I'm soft without my makeup. I will put on a baseball cap sometimes, you know. There are times I feel more butch than other times, but it's still pretty much like I am now. I like polo shirts. I like Daniel Cruz, I have a pair of cowboy boots, not traditional cowboy boots, but they're boots and they look like the cowboy style but they're dressy. I wear those if I dress up or whatever. I'm a big shoe fan. I like Steve Madden. I like Cole Haan shoes and Stacy's [Adams]. And that's pretty much how I dress, but I was going to wear a black shirt, so my shoes aren't matching, and my OCD is really bothering me because I don't feel like I'm matching.

I Found God in Myself and
I Loved Her Fiercely
Religion and Spirituality

4

Like many African Americans born and reared in the South, I came of age in the church. For me, church was not an option but, rather, an expectation that for me was enforced from the age of six. Soon after becoming involved in the church through the choir, usher board, Vacation Bible School, and the numerous other programs and organizations for youth, the church became a place where I did not just have to be but wanted to be. The mentoring and encouragement I received from adults who were invested in not only my spiritual growth but also my intellectual and creative growth fueled in me a passion to succeed. And as I recount in *Sweet Tea*, the church also, paradoxically, encouraged my queer gender expression and budding homosexuality.[1] I assumed, erroneously, that this might be the case for the narrators of *BQSW*, especially since women comprise the majority of members of most black churches. Over the course of interviewing dozens of women, however, I found that the church and spirituality played a very different role in the lives of black queer southern women.

More often the women I interviewed speak of having to go to church as young people, but not necessarily enjoying it or finding the church a "refuge" as so many men in *Sweet Tea* stated. Beyond developing crushes on their female Sunday school teachers or other women in authority, many narrators were bored in church and, when old enough to make their own decision about whether to go, chose not to go, in pursuit of an alternative form of spirituality. Because the notion of "God" was tied to a male figure or because the male leadership of the church upheld sexist interpretations of the Bible, these women sought out forms of worship that were more woman centered or turned inward to a self-discovery of a communion with a higher power.

This alternative consciousness around spirituality was undoubtedly influenced by black lesbian and women of color feminism of the 1970s and 1980s.[2] Ntozake Shange's choreopoem/play *for colored girls who have considered suicide / when the rainbow is enuf*, from which the title of this chapter is drawn, is one of the major texts that began to reflect what Alice Walker would go on to define as a "womanist" perspective on spirituality.[3] Shange's black women characters, who represent different colors of the rainbow (e.g., lady in red, lady in blue), recount their various struggles with patriarchy and racism throughout the play, which culminates in a communal revelation that God is within each of them and they must seek affirmation from an internal female self rather than from an external male figure. And in Walker's novel *The Color Purple*, the character Shug Avery convinces the protagonist, Celie, that "God is inside you and is inside everybody else. You come into the world with God. But only them that search for it inside find it."[4] Notably, this view of God as a part of a (female) self or a presence in nature moves beyond a strictly Christian belief system, a view that many narrators of this book embrace—whether that be a nonspecific belief system or an affinity for Buddhism or other non-Western religious forms. On the day I interviewed Julia (see chapter 4), for example, her partner was hosting an event called the "Eternal Summer of the Black Feminist Mind Potluck Series and the Queer Black Sunday School," in which black queer women were gathering in the name of poet Phillis Wheatley to meditate and share poems.[5] Similarly, Charis Books in Atlanta is cited by more than one narrator as being a place that facilitated an alternative spiritual community through the sharing of poetry, literature, and community organizing.

And even for those who remained active within traditional Christian black churches, they found ways to devise transgressive strategies to affirm their sexuality. As briefly mentioned in chapter 3, the stereotypical "church lady" image prevalent in black communities is one trope employed by "lipstick lesbians" (i.e., feminine) to signal same-sex desire within the visual economy of the black church. This dynamic is captured explicitly in Ann Allen Shockley's novel *Say Jesus and Come to Me*, through the character, Myrtle Black, an itinerate evangelist who travels the South preaching at revivals, using her charismatic style to seduce unsuspecting women during her altar calls. In the opening scene of the novel, Shockley describes in explicit detail Myrtle's seduction of a young woman who is "caught up" in the spirit:

> To mask her sexual excitement, which was causing her to breathe faster, she looked up over the girl's head at the church-goers,

although she really did not see them for she was blinded by her overwhelming passion. Maneuvering her voice to rise and gasp out the words in frenetic passion, she shouted, "Jesus loves ev-errybody. All those great and small, rich and poor, ugly and beautiful—"

At this point, she expertly pressed her thumb over the angle of Magdalen's jaw and kept it there. The girl fainted in her arms. "See, God has *struck* this child with *love!*"

[. . .]

The girl slowly opened her eyes in the arms of Myrtle, who pretended to bend over to see if she had been revived. Then she whispered without moving her lips, "Meet me afterwards?"

The girl mouthed consent.

"Bless you child," Myrtle said aloud. And under her breath: "My black Buick's parked at the back of the church." Solicitously she eased the girl back to her seat, slyly brushing her hand across her breasts.[6]

As this passage makes clear, the performative rituals of folk preaching may easily serve a dual function as they camouflage the calling of the spirit with the calling to the flesh. Spirituality and sexuality easily slip and slide into each other.[7]

Alternatively, butch or masculine women (e.g., dominants and studs) also circulate within women's organizations and clubs within the black church, but do so in ways that allow them more latitude to express their female masculinity, whether that be through offering to do manual labor (setting up tables and chairs in the fellowship hall or driving the church bus) or serving on the usher board (as opposed to singing in the choir), where the uniform is sometimes more gender neutral. Ultimately, these women draw on their own technologies of self-assertion within the confines of black southern culture to signal, build, and sustain their sexual identities.

· ·

Anita [b. 1964, Hickory, North Carolina]

I was going to this church in Newton, Word of Life Christian Center Church, and I was like, "I don't want to be gay no more." I came out and I went back in for like ten years. I stayed away from it for ten years. I was, how do you pronounce it? Celibate?

Celibate?

Yeah, celibate.

So, you didn't date men?

No, I didn't like men. I tried to go back to my high school sweetheart, and I mean I have had sex with guys, but I don't like it . . . I went through a hard relationship with this lady and at the end of it I came out. When I came out of that relationship I was just down. I had hit a bottom. That was the lowest point in my life, and I had my son and this kid is—I had gotten him from his mother who left him in a motel room when he was like three weeks old. And I had this kid and I was raising this kid and at the time my son was, I think he was maybe eight or nine and I had taken, I had drug him through this relationship with me. When I got out of that relationship, we left with trash bags. That was the lowest point of my life. That was my bottom. And when I hit that bottom I thought that it was because of the life I was living, the way I was living my life, so I didn't get back in another relationship with a female or a male or anybody.

I went to church. So, I went to church and I started saying, "I used to be gay" and "I'm not gay anymore" and "Pray the gay away." I had oil poured on my head and all this stuff and I was going to this church . . . they had this girl come in and she's an artist rapper. And she has a ministry, and her ministry is, "I was once gay and I'm not gay anymore," and I came out of it. And some of the stuff she says about how she was sitting in church with her lover and both of them were on their way to hell and dah, dah, dah. I didn't hear it because I didn't choose to go to it because of the way I feel about it. I said all that to say that I think she's one of those people that chose, that did have a choice. Everybody that's gay don't have a choice and that's what society, that's what religion, because it's not Christianity, that's what religion don't understand. You got people that's coming in that's saying, "I have a best friend," not a best friend but a friend right now that has three kids. She had a bad relationship with the kids' daddy and she broke up with the kids' daddy and she's dating a woman now. And she says, "Oh, this is just something I'm going through." But do you know what, what kind of stamp that's putting on us that can't choose? So people like you are making it look like people like us can choose and because I tried that. And I tried to choose, but what's in there is in there, and if it's not in there, it's not going to stay. As far as the question that you asked, yes I think you're born that way, and people that are born that way stay that way. And if you're not born, it's easy to walk away from something that's not a part of you anyway.

* * *

My oldest sister [. . .] she's stuck in religion—she's just like all the older generation, stuck in that belief. They believe that it supposed to be a man and a woman. That's her belief, and just like she believes that you're not supposed to divorce. So, she's being mentally abused by this guy. So, her opinion really doesn't matter to me because maybe you need a woman. [Laughter] Oh my God. I told her, I said, "Listen, I would much rather be in a relationship with a woman that works and we take care of each other, than to be in a relationship with a man that's mentally abusing me." Verbal abuse, he don't work, he's on drugs, and you will have the audacity to come out of your mouth and call it your husband. I wouldn't dare do that. You want to sit and look down on me, but look at you. She says, "I don't care! It ain't right!" I said, "Well, what you're doing is not right. You think that God would be okay for you to be verbally and mentally abused by this man and carry the load? Do you know that the Word says, 'If a man don't work, he ought not to eat'? I mean that's in the Bible, too. You know?"

It makes me mad. I'm going to tell you what. The best thing that I did was get in church for ten years and study the Bible. That's the best thing that ever happened to me because I didn't get religion; I got a relationship. And once I started studying that Bible word for word and studying those scriptures and finding out what they really mean and realizing that that same scripture, that same book that says a man ought not lie with another man for it is detestable. If you go on down, there's a whole lot of other stuff down there that everybody ignores. So why is it okay that in that same book it says a slave, a master can beat his slave for so many days as long as he don't die? This is like three verses down after the man ought not, so you mean that don't matter no more but this do still? So how can you take this little piece out and say, "Well, this still counts, but this don't"? Where do you get that from? So, the best thing I did was got a relationship with God and got an understanding and started researching. Now, I'm at peace with myself. I'm at peace with my relationship. I'm at peace with God that I have a relationship and I have with God and I'm also in a healthy relationship with my girlfriend and it don't matter. The only thing that you can give me now is your opinion, and the only reason why you can tell me you don't like is just because you don't like it, because it's not biblical. I told my dad, the statement I made to my dad, I said, "Daddy, I said you can't say that it's wrong because you don't like it." [Laughter] How would it be if I don't like red and I went through hell and high waters to get red taken out of the crayon box because I don't like red? How many people do like red? But just because I don't like red, I just want to take it out of the crayon box.

What sense does that make? Nowhere is it written that says red is bad, it's detestable, it's forbidden. I just don't like it, so I'm just going to get rid of it. And that's basically what's going on with it today. It's that people don't like it. They don't understand it and they don't like it, so they're doing what they're doing to try to get rid of it, but it ain't going nowhere.

....

Bonita/Bluhe [b. 1968, Anderson, South Carolina]

I attend church regularly. I attend an all-inclusive church, and that doesn't mean that everybody in there's gay—it just means come as you are. We going to love you if you're an addict, if you're gay, lesbian, straight, bi, trans, we going to love you. If you cracked up and you gangbanging, we going to love you. Come on up in here. That's what all-inclusive stands for. So a lot of people get that twisted. "That's the gay church." No, that's an all-inclusive church. That means you're included, you're included, I'm included, everyone is included. Bring all your stuff and come on to church. I started going to this church . . . in October.

Oh, so not that long.

Not that long, and I've been there ever since October. I don't think I've missed a Sunday.

What is it about it that you like, that keeps you going?

It's the fact that I can serve God in truth and spirit and not worry about what somebody's going to say about why's that homosexual, that lesbian, that gay person, why are they here? Didn't they get the message today? But my God, He told me He loves me regardless. The same God that you're serving. The same exact God that looks down from heaven onto this Earth is the same God I'm serving. So, I'm confused. Why is it that He can tell me He loves me but you can't say that because I'm gay? That's crazy. That's crazy to me. I been there since October and I don't think I'm going anywhere.

....

Darlcne Hudson [b. 1961, Las Vegas, Nevada (Fordyce, Arkansas)]

As long as I have been a Hudson, I have been in church, as long as I have been a Hudson. That's all my life. [. . .] I can remember Easter speeches, Christmas plays. I can remember baptism. My mama got my baptism thing in there [pointing to a box of papers], Certificate of Baptism.

Was it Baptist?

Mm-hmm, I come up Baptist. Yeah, after church we all went to the store. We did Sunday school, we did church, and we did BTU [Baptist Training Union]. That's right. We got three doses of it. *Three* in one day. You got plenty of Jesus that day, and that became my pattern, and I lived for that. That was my life. I loved church. I still love church. I never was begrudging or I didn't want to go. I *loved* church.

Why?

I loved the singing; I loved the hymns. I love hymns now, but back then I just loved singing, and you know, it really was a training ground. And I didn't know it at the time because [as] you do your speeches, you're learning to speak publicly. You going to learn your speech and you're going to get up there and [in a child's voice] "Happy Easter Day," but my sister was the biggest crybaby about that stuff. Anthony, my cousin, was the biggest crybaby in the family about saying the Easter speech, and believe it or not, as a child I was really kind of awkward and very shy. But I love church. I did.

Were you in the choir?

I most certainly was in the children's choir. As a matter of fact, when we lived in Pine Bluff, that's when the whole church world really took off. As good as I felt, I decided I wanted to. We was singing in the choir and then I had friends at other schools that was singing in choir. They would come over to *my* church when we were having rehearsal. I said, "Let's all sing together then," and honey, I formed me the citywide mass choir. I was in the seventh or eighth grade. Sure did. And the other little junior piano players came. Everybody came. After a while, that thing got pretty hot because we was steady growing up and sure did form me the citywide youth mass choir, sure did. I had people from Dolloway, Watson Chapel, had a little bit of everybody coming together. Next thing I know, honey, [snaps finger] we was jamming. And I went on to college and became the university choir director for the gospel choir, what they called, I guess now they still call them the same thing, the Ebony Singers. We were ambassadors. We traveled everywhere. And then I became a part of the Church of God in Christ. I put my membership with the New Calvary Temple Church of God in Christ in Little Rock because I went to school in Conway, Arkansas, for college.

Was that Central?

University of Central Arkansas, UCA, sure did. And I graduated from there in eighty-four, -eight. I got a thing somewhere that tells me exactly the date. And then I went and I became, I was a choir director. I mean, my bishop took me straight up to the choir and said, listen, "She's a choir director, put her to work." Those musicians looked at me, like, really? But they had to do what he said. And so, next thing I know, I was directing the choir for the bishop at this church. I didn't even understand all the pieces of it, but then I became a jurisdictional kind of choir director. I had my own region and everything and did quite well. Offered a recording contract, directed under Mattie Moss Clark, Twinkie Clark. I remember quite well those days, this whole po' Pentecostal movement that I was in. I was even part of a singing group called the Jesus Revolution. We used to hit it. We used to travel. We'd just go to church to church to church to church. Jerry Whitley. And we sang in his group: the Jesus Revolution. And then I became a part of the Thompson Singers, and I just got kind of reunited with Gerald Thompson, who is in Little Rock, and I can remember when Gerald Thompson, Kirk Franklin guy, and a boy out of Memphis and his name escapes me. I can just see him, but I remember when we all used to go in Memphis before Kirk was who he is today. I remember singing in Yolanda Adams's church, and she was like . . . we all loved her because she had a really cute song, Southeast inspirational singer. Honey, I took my choir down there to her church. We all sat together in fellowship hall, ate chicken, had a good time. It was like a one-time encounter.

But my church days, I loved them, and I must admit that I'm somewhat disappointed that here I am fifty, and I find myself out of balance with the church. And I tried to be a part of different affirming churches, but I guess I'm just like, I'm kind of like, I don't like what I see and I don't like how I'm treated. Because I feel like I've put in some good church days. I've done some good churching, I mean some good churching, and I'm not coming in as a beginner, and I don't want to be treated as such. Even if I sit in the pews, there's criticism. If I try to take some initiative and get involved, there's criticism. So, I'm like, you know what? I didn't come to church to fight with nobody. I got enough fighting out in the community that I have to do. I'm not coming to church to fight. So, on Sunday, I'm curled up in front of that TV watching a western. I'm trying to rest because Pride keeps me busy. This is my last year with that and, but I'm just saying, considering all of this time as a young child, my adolescent years, my young adult years, my adult years, all of that is filled with church. And it done matter to me, honey. Even when I was in college I participated in a Bible study. I led a Bible study, something called Soul Food. Can you believe it? So, you know it's very, and it ain't in the scriptures that you can't put out there that I don't know, because I understand that thing. I think I understand it really good. I really do. I think I'm pretty good.

So those passages of the Bible from Leviticus and so on and so forth that refer to homosexuality, how do you interpret those passages?

Well, let me tell you. It's a combination of things before I answer that question. When I got saved [. . .] I was in college and had this big spiritual revelation. As a matter of fact, my line name when I pledged Zeta Phi Beta was "Revelator" because I could see things; I could believe that I was able to look forward in time and predict, so I believed. And my friends, it was just a big running joke all the time, but you know, every time the Revelator said something it almost came to pass. Anyway, one of the mothers—two of them—that stood out in my mind that really left such an impression in my heart, Mother Byrd told me before she passed, she said, "Don't you let nobody tell you that you ain't a child of God." I mean just out of nowhere. This was the sweetest little, almost looked like Aunt Bea woman. Just as stout and just as fiery, and she would pull me up close, and she would talk to me and I was like, this is a sweet little lady and I reverenced her. She was so sweet. And the other one was Mother Bunting. She said, "I don't care what nobody else in this church say, Darlene, you are anointed and you are special in the sight of God." And that never left my heart.

So, when I became this out lesbian, and I want you to understand, there was never really a closet that I was in, it was more of an awareness that had to come about, and I thank God for the progression of how things progressed in my life and how things evolved. Maybe that's a better word, how things kind of evolved in my life, because I got my teachings in the church first. So, when this stuff came about the Leviticus and man not laying with man, I had to take it in the way that it was taught to me in the context that it was taught to me. This is the Old Testament. These were the rules that they had in place. Christ came not to do away with but to make it where you could fulfill the promises or you could fulfill the covenant. So, I don't say that it's not true. I kind of understand in the context of that day and time, who they were talking to. And I understand that everybody who was writing in the Bible wasn't so "saved" and so "Jesus" and so "sanctified" themselves. They had their own -ism. Such as Paul. Paul took issue with women. He came into an area where women were speaking all out loud, and he wasn't used to that. Remember, he was a *tax* collector, a man of power, so he took issue with that. So, he [snaps] silenced the women. "Put something over your head and hush." You know what I'm saying? I put things in context. I kind of understood what was happening in that day and time because that's how I was taught. This is what was going on in that day and time. It said about eating swine. It talks about blends being mixed. There were reasons why those people wrote those things. It was to govern that body of people. I don't think nobody in that day and time had any idea that that would be used, and rolled forward in history to become the dos and don'ts of the world for those that subscribe to it. I live with a Buddhist. She don't subscribe to all of that, but I never met a more balanced, believing, affirming person, and baby she'll nam(u) myoho renge kyo. Right now that's where they're gone. Somebody else is getting their gajanza today. She's going to do what they do, and I don't try to get all up in it, but I appreciate it.

So, you got this big Pentecostal woman here and then you got this Buddhist woman here, and you put them powers together and God has blessed us. Well you know, from what I think, God has blessed us. The universe has yielded itself very favorably for us. I got friends who been foreclosed on. I got friends who have lost. I've got friends who died. But God has been gracious enough to let me live comfortably. I don't have everything that I want, but you know what? I ain't broke right now. Right now, I ain't broke. Now, next week I might be broke, but right now, today, I am not broke. When I checked my account I was like, okay, I'm not going to pay no bills. I'm just going to feel this for a few minutes, but I got some bills paid. [Laughter] I used to sing that song, "I Let Nothing Separate Me from the Love of God." I meant that. And I told God that when it was time to do the crossover, I said, "Let me tell you something now, if this is going to put me in hell then I'm not going to do it." I never will forget, that was like a New Year's Eve night. That was a turning point for me. This girl had been working me. It was kind of cute. I was kind of liking it, but I told God, "Before I get too busy, I need to hear from you real clear," and it was just, you know. All I can tell you, honey, is the way the Lord spoke to me, people won't even believe. I've given a story about my kind of coming out, and so after I had been intimate with this woman and we were laying there, all of the sudden a radio popped on—it was my alarm. And guess what was playing? [Begins singing] "Oh It is Jesus," Shirley Caesar. I said, "Thank you!" and I ain't never looked back. Now do you believe that? That's the Gospel. That's the Gospel according to Darlene. I'm telling you that's how I came through, because I always had a close walk, even as a child moving around in the church and doing what I do. My pastor, not my very first pastor because the first two are dead, but the one that's there, that Lacy Curt Solomon, he'll tell you I was very much into the church. He didn't know where I was going with it, but he'll tell you, I was a good [churchgoer]. I attended. I was a leader. I was in the Girl Scouts. I did everything. It was through the church, and I think that today that these institutions have become so many other things. I guess trying to keep up with the times that basic things aren't being taught. I asked somebody the other day. I said, "Everybody going to church, but did anybody get saved, for real?" I'm talking about like the old-timey way. Tarry until ye be endued. You ever heard of anything like that? I read those scriptures and I wanted to study them, but I didn't care. I love God. I know God loves me, and I knew that and I know that today. And I went and took some time out once I became this lesbian person, I took the time out to kind of read the scriptures and study them. [. . .] So, I'm like I might not be able to tell you about it, but it's in here [touches her heart], and I felt like if I was doing anything against God, I would not participate in it. I don't care if I loved it. And I'm just like that. If I know, if I sense in my spirit that it's not right, I don't care what everybody else doing, I'm not participating. I'm not getting down like that. That's my little two cents on it.

. . . .

Emilie [b. 1955, Durham, North Carolina]

Both my parents were college professors. I was very comfortable, black middle class, raised in the church, but unaware of the fact that my parents were doing it significantly differently than most of their peers because . . .

You went to church differently?

They weren't even raising us or raising me in the church, and then later, nine years later, my sister . . . when they married, they decided that their children, however many, would go to the best Sunday school. Didn't matter if it was our home church or another church. Uh, but it had to be the best Sunday school, uh, in Durham. Of course, there's a color line there, so there were some restrictions. I did do Sunday school at our own church.

Well, then what did "the best" Sunday school mean?

As near as I could tell, because they never really said "the best," but the inference was, "Do you get a strong moral background for how you're to live your life?" "Do you get a sense of what the Bible is?" and not just a book. And they wouldn't have said it this way, but "Can you read and interpret? Do you learn enough to read and interpret?" Can you, in fact, get the skills to know right from wrong, that would be a support to what they were teaching at home. And what I might be getting at school. And they weren't so much concerned about were there youth group trips or opportunities to go on trips to camps or whatever. They were concerned about the moral formation of their children. They were just really clear on that because they figured that would be the most important thing they could give us is a strong sense of moral values that we live out and not just talk about.

What denomination?

United Methodist. I went to the Asbury. Our home church was Asbury Temple United Methodist Church. It's a little church by the side of the road where everybody is somebody and Christ is the Lord. [Laughter] Nine years later our home church was no longer the church that had the best Sunday school, so they sent my sister to a Presbyterian church, Covenant Presbyterian.

A Black Presbyterian church?

Mmm-hmm. Oh, yeah, there are lots of Black Presbyterian churches in the South. Originally they were not aligned with northern church, although they resided in the South. Uh, so . . .

And do you think that Sunday school was more important to them than public school? Or were they on par?

I think they were complementary. It's certainly my experience. Now, I can't get into my parents' mind because they're both gone now, but it was clear that not going was not an option. [Laughter] Until I got to high school I had to be there. In high school, I could decide whether this made sense or not.

. . . .

Julia

At the time of the interview, Julia was going through a rite of passage into Yoruba based practices. She was wearing all white and could not be touched as a part of a year-long process as an Iyawó (bride of an orisha) because of the belief that white repels negativity and symbolizes purity and touching another person makes that person susceptible to another's energy. Imagine, then, how surprised I was to learn that her father is a Baptist minister.

Julia was born the middle child of three in 1979 in Gastonia, North Carolina. Gastonia is located in the southwest part of North Carolina and is considered a part of the Charlotte, North Carolina, metropolitan area. It sits near the South Carolina border, with a population of seventy-one thousand and growing. About a third of the population is African American. The interview took place on August 26, 2012, in Durham, North Carolina.

My dad is a Baptist preacher, along with his father and almost all of his brothers and sisters and nephews.

So, a [family] history of preachers.

Mm-hmm, mm-hmm, yeah.

* * *

Choir practice wasn't play necessarily, but that was probably my favorite thing growing up was to go to choir practice and play music, listening to tapes and sing all the parts over and over again, even the instruments. And then, playing games with other little girls—doctor-type games. Yeah, that's what I think of. Basketball.

So church and religion played a significant role in your upbringing?

Mm-hmm.

Did you enjoy church?

Oh yeah, definitely. Yeah, always enjoyed church.

Besides the choir, did you participate in any other organizations? The usher board, for instance, or . . . ?

No, I didn't usher because that seemed like a lot of work. And usually the ushers were like really specific. So, no, I'm not ushering, but other leadership roles, like if there was some special occasion coming up doing speeches and so the rehearsals for that, or little skits, I enjoyed that. Vacation Bible School was always a lot of fun, particularly because like kids from around the neighborhood, or sometimes around the city who didn't necessarily come to the church, would be there. Because it's like free childcare, free food. [Laughter] So that was fun. Like the little boys who could do backflips off of walls, they would show up. So, yeah, Vacation Bible School was a hit for me. What else in church? [. . .] I think I really fully participated in the services. Usually it was my dad preaching or a relative, and once I got to the age where I could pay attention, I always paid attention and was curious about what was being said and what it meant. And whoever in the congregation that I really liked or had a crush on, like being strategic about how I could sit with them or who's got the best candy, all that kind of stuff. So, yeah, . . . I had positive, fond memories of church.

Is there anything that you want to add that I might not have covered?

I would like to add that I'm wearing all white because I was recently initiated in Ifá, which is African spirituality, so this is my [transition] year, and so I'm definitely in a place of transition and which is exciting and new. I feel like it's coming full circle. There's something about the South that feels really connected to both the continent of Africa and the Caribbean, and I feel like African spirituality kind of helps shed more light on that, like so many of the things that we did in church that I wonder about. I'm like, "Oh! That's where that came from." So, yeah, I'm excited about discovering that more and making it more visible to other people and like removing the stigma . . . removing some of the stigma from African spirituality or just African practices period.

So, you don't feel any tension between your Christian Protestant upbringing and African cosmology?

No, I feel like it brings it full circle. And like I talk a little bit with my dad about it, like, "Daddy, what do you know about seers and the Bible?" "Well yeah, prophet so-and-so was a seer and I knew somebody some time" and you know. [. . .] So, this is the way I think about it when I think about how I want to talk about it with my family—immediate and extended family. It's like all the things that I learned growing up in church and from the Bible, I was taught that that stuff was real, but we don't act like it's real in the way we practice our faith now. So then for me continually learning, reading, and discovering, and then finding a direct connection because Ifá is over six thousand years old . . . and these sort of African practices are what the people that were writing the books of the Bible, that's sort of their history, too, I think. Anyway, so it's a connection. So, it's like you taught me this and this is what I'm doing. So, what's the problem? You know? The world is opening up a whole new layer, a whole new level of literacy.

That's interesting because I know quite a few black queer women who have gone through this process. And some who went through it for whom it was a positive experience, wonderful. And others for whom it was not. And who kept like their name, the nomenclature, but don't practice because their spiritual leaders proved to be less than on the up and up and exploited them, that kind of thing.

Yeah, I've heard a lot of horror stories—even an elder that lives in Durham, a chosen grandparent of me and Alexis that's had definitely some trauma and some abuse. But my godmother is really amazing. She's an out black lesbian, organizer, activist, media mogul, I would say. So, I think that's definitely a part of it. I'm learning about this tradition and a lot of other traditions, like two-spirited people, queer people, like whatever manifestation that is, like they are gatekeepers and have a connection to spirit in a way that other people don't necessarily. And when you start abusing and just making expendable the people who have some sort of spiritual power that are supposed to ground the whole community, the whole nation or whatever, when you start chucking them out and killing them and abusing them, then that's when you end up with so much turmoil. I think that that's not a coincidence. And when I was talking about touring and the tour of superheroes, I think that that's a part of it. I think everybody is born everything, but I do think that some people maybe have a spiritual role to play. [. . .] We need to get in touch with that. Everybody does. But I think queer people in particular [need] to find out . . . your own traditions . . . go back as far as you can go back . . . tap into the spirit and get those resources back. Because I think that's what it's going to take for what seems like the way the world's ending, like if capitalism continues and multinational corporations have more rights than people. We gonna need some sort of power. [Laughter] And it ain't gonna be money. It's going to have to be some other kind of power.

. . . .

Laurinda [b. 1959, Memphis, Tennessee]

Were you raised in the church?

Yeah I was. Grew up believing that it was the most hypocritical place on the face of the earth. Because I knew the pastor of the church was sleeping with both my aunts. I walked in on him with one of them. And then on Sundays, after church both my aunts and the pastor and his wife would be in my grandma's house out the back.

Were your aunts married too?

At the time, yeah. No, no, no. When that was going on, no they weren't. But over the years they were still having dinner together like there was nothing wrong. I hated going. I would tear my pantyhose. It was my first experience with going to church without any pantyhose on because my mother was like, "Then I'll put you in the front row." So I had hairy legs. I was like a bear. They would not—my father did not believe in shaving the hair on your legs. He said a woman shouldn't shave their legs. I mean there's got to be an exception to the rule somewhere. Got to be . . . and I don't really think that it's because my mother insisted. I think it was because of who was caring for us. Okay. So the church is like right here. My grandmother lived two streets over. My great grandmother lived on the next street next to the church. And then two doors up was my father's aunt. And she kept us when my great grandmother couldn't. But they hated each other. They're both different sides of the family. So it was Vacation Bible School. It was Sunday school. It was church.

What denomination?

Baptist.

So, you weren't active in the church?

Very.

Oh, you were.

Read circle, usher boy, sang in the choir, you know, for a minute. I taught Vacation Bible School for three summers when I got to be in my late teens. And that was because I'd bring these plays for kids to do and I know they were literally lined up to be in my class. Because I did away with the manuals. I didn't use the books. We did that. But to me the Vacation Bible School was like an extension of Sunday school. You know, and whatever you couldn't do in high school you did in Vacation Bible School. You get them coconut squares and some Kool-Aid, you know, and we did that. And I mean my aunt sang. So, every Sunday you know we have records of her service. And then we'd got to my grandmother's for dinner. We'd leave there at 2:30. You know, we'd walk around in our slips and stuff. We'd leave the house at 2:30, 3:00, and go to the next service wherever it was they had to go sing. And it was done about seven, so we could go to night service at our [Anglican?] church.

And so, all day.

All day. That's why I didn't like going to my daddy's most time because I knew we had to go to church. Sunday's dinner was ready at 9:00 on Sunday morning. When we left to go to church Sunday's dinner was ready. All you had to do is come in and heat it up. And she stopped by KFC or Church's or Kentucky Fried to get a box of chicken, if she didn't have time to cook a roast. That was routine for us.

. . . .

Kei

Kei was among several younger women I interviewed who live in Tallahassee, Florida. She is an only child and was born in 1989 in Jacksonville, Florida. Located in the northeast corner of Florida and named after Andrew Jackson, it is the most populous of all the state's cities, with a population of 860,000 within the city limits and 1.5 million in the metropolitan area. The interview took place on March 21, 2013, in Tallahassee.

Growing up religious, it was definitely a switch to spiritualism because I believe in a universal higher being, not just the He anymore, and so definitely not a He anymore. I had that conversation with religious people all the time, and they're like, because He is like, and I'm like, She? [Laughter] I just like to play with that because I read the Bible still, and I'm actually kind of skeptical of the Bible still, and I grew up being like, "Why is God so vengeful? Why is he so mad at people?" If this is who God is, just whatever. If God is in control of everything, has seen everything and created everything, then he created the devil, too. Accept that; you can't . . . be a fundamentalist and pick and choose what you want to believe out of the Bible. If you want to believe the book you've got to believe all of the book.

If you're going to. I don't really believe the book, so I mean, I never met Jesus. Jesus could be like Zeus if we were Greek; then he would be a myth. It's just, for me religion is one of those things that I try to keep my mouth shut as much as possible around religious people. I don't want to disrespect anyone. I don't want to touch any wrong or push any wrong buttons, but I get them pushed all the time, so now it's just like I'll just walk away. Especially being queer and saying "I believe in God": you get a whole mouthful in the South for that. I'm there to defend it when I have to, but if I don't have to I try to stay away from the concept. There's spiritualism. If you believe in something strong and powerful and all-knowing and honest and a savior, to let it being your savior, let that concept be your savior. Stop drowning in your agony. Stop in the concepts of church and congregation. No, not my thing. It doesn't play a role at all in my life.

. . . .

Lenore

Lenore was one of several narrators who treated me like they had known me all our lives, as if we were longtime friends. In fact, she, like many others, insisted that I break bread with her before or after the interview. Before I arrived, she had prepared a wonderful Sunday dinner spread. Lenore was born in Wampee, South Carolina, in 1962. Wampee is so small that it's not even incorporated. It's located on the coast of South Carolina, just north of Myrtle Beach. I was introduced to Lenore through a former student of mine who was teaching at the University of South Carolina in Columbia and met Lenore through some LGBT activist friends. Unfortunately, Lenore passed away unexpectedly on June 13, 2014, a little over two months after our interview. The interview took place on March 31, 2014, at her home in Columbia, South Carolina.

We went every Sunday even if my mother was not there. You were there and if you didn't go, she would find out, and I learned how to read there, too. I remember the old ladies teaching us phonics and stuff. I remember that, learning to read with those pictures and doing those blends. I remember that so much because the lady was so old I could hear—I think she was a retired schoolteacher. I remember her teaching us and I can still smell her breath today. It smelled like dip. She was a dipper and I could smell that tobacco but—and her jaws would pop, she would be so old, but she really knew how to teach that stuff. So, I learned reading in church.

So, you enjoyed church?

Mm-hmm. It was a scary place, a very dark place. It was a fearful place for me. You know, if you were the first one there, it's just really quiet, but it was a scary place for me . . . very scary.

What kinds of activities did you do in church?

In church?

Did you like sing in the choir?

Mm-hmm. Yeah, I grew up doing that. Matter of fact, we had a family choir and we traveled and there was a—we would go to Wilmington, North Carolina. There was a show called *Cavalcade of Quartets*. My whole family would be on that show.

What was it called?

"Cavalcade of Quartets."

"Cavalcade of Quartets." Okay.

At that time, Reverend Bill would sometimes host that show, and I'm sure it's somewhere in the archives, but I remember being on that show and we were like this. We had on blue dresses and I'm down here looking at the camera just looking at myself. I just remember it so much, and my auntie made the dresses. The name of our group was the Macedonia Stars, because we, our church was Macedonia AME, but we were the Macedonia Stars, and it was just generations of us growing up singing. Now, my grandmother and them, they still sing. Okay?

Did you usher as well?

I didn't do too much ushering.

What denomination was the church?

AME.

AME. Oh, so it wasn't that charismatic. Y'all didn't shout and get the Holy Spirit?

Sometimes they did, but we didn't do all that like the Baptists. I kind of like to be quiet in church. I don't like all that jumping around and all that shouting. I don't care for that. I never did. Now, my cousins I noticed that they sometimes would get, they called it getting the Holy Ghost. I never really got it and I lied, and I remember when I went to revival, got down and you have to get your religion. I remember just jumping up just because everybody else did because I was tired of them pushing me and blah, blah, blah. I was tired of all that, so I faked it, and I remember the woman that was near me helping us down at the altar. She had on an orange suit. That's all I saw. I never felt a thing. I lied. I lied.

But that wouldn't have been at your church?

That was at my church.

Really?

I didn't, I never did get it.

So, the AME had revival?

Yeah, we had revival.

Okay. I never heard of the AMEs having revival.

Yes, we had revival but I never did get no religion. It's not like now how people always talking about how God speaks to them, and there's this one woman—God speaks to her every day. I don't understand it. Can you take a break and let him talk to me a little bit? [Laughter] So I don't know.

. . . .

"Lisa"

I was introduced to "Lisa" through Shean, my friend and narrator in "Sweet Tea." She is one of four of his Delta Sigma Theta sorority "sisters" to whom he connected me for this book. "Lisa" was born in 1972 in Detroit, Michigan, but was reared from the age of one in Grambling, Louisiana, the youngest of three children. Grambling is a very small town located in north central Louisiana with a population of just under five thousand, 99 percent of which are African American. It is known mostly for the football team of the historically black institution of Grambling State University. The interview took place on August 6, 2012, in Atlanta, Georgia.

What role did church and religion play in your upbringing?

Oh, man, it was strong. It was strong. Baptist through and through.

Not Catholic?

Not Catholic, Baptist through and through. Catholic is mostly south Louisiana, which you'll find in talking to people. And that's the other thing, Louisiana is like two different states. Okay?

Yeah, I know.

And so, you know, I'm from north Louisiana, then you have south Louisiana, but north Louisiana is mostly Baptist. Baptist and Methodist. And so growing up we were at church every Sunday. We were in Sunday school; we were in Vacation Bible School. Even if my mama didn't go we went, you know. [Laughter] You know, don't ask her why she's not going. And God forbid you talk in church. Oh my God, I'll never forget the second president of the university. The church I went to was the church that a lot of the university professors went to, and so the second president was R. W. Jones. We called him "Prez." I'll never forget, one Sunday I was in church clowning, acting a fool, and Prez pulled me to the side and pinched me so hard.

And I told my mom, 'cause I just knew my mom was going to cuss him out. And she whooped me. 'Cause her thing was he was supposed to. But, yeah, absolutely, very strong. Very strong. And I have very strong beliefs now. You know, I've struggled with them, I can tell you that; I've struggled because I didn't know if I was doing something that, you know, God approved of. And I still don't know. But what I do know is God is love. You know what I mean? And so my belief is that while he may not approve of my lifestyle according to the Word, I know he loves me and he knows my heart. You know. I come from a family of preachers.

Oh really?

Mm-hmm. My first cousins are preachers—my Uncle Phil's sons. My nephew is a preacher. He was actually ordained as a child minister, which is . . . not ordained, he was called as a child . . . and I think that's kind of sketchy too but, uh . . . [Laughter] You know, he truly has a gift. I tell my sister this all the time, her and her husband didn't do enough to nurture and protect that gift, and you can allow different things to come in. You know what I mean? But he truly does have a gift, it's just how he chooses to use it.

Were you active in church?

Oh, yeah, absolutely. Growing up I was active: youth choir . . . oh my God, I loved being an usher. [Laughter] We used to have so much fun. Because I'm nosey as hell and you could see everything. You know . . . [laughter] . . . you don't miss a beat. We used to love ushering, man, and there was this one guy, we called him "Chief": Jack Lane. His wife is kind of like a mentor . . . was a mentor of mine growing up. But we called him Chief because he was the chief usher, and every Sunday we ushered. On the fourth Sunday he used to always, always, always-always-always put us back in check. He's like, "Now you know y'all not supposed to act like that." You know. But I enjoyed it.

. . . .

Lynn [b. 1968, Jackson, Mississippi]

My grandmother was the mother of the church. It was the church she grew up in. [. . .] My mom grew up in the church; it was our family church. Even though it was in Clinton, Mississippi, we drove fifteen, twenty, thirty minutes to church every Sunday. And when you would hear people say we were in church all day, we were in church all day. We would leave our church and go to the church where my uncle was preaching, and we would leave his church and go to night service. So yeah, religion played a major role. And my mom was coming into herself by herself spiritually, and she would try to make us read the Bible, sit in the corner and read the Bible all day. . .

if we got in trouble that was our punishment. We would stand in the room with the Bible and we had to read the Bible and tell her what we'd read. I was like jumping out the window. And I always had sleepovers, and all my friends, they had to suffer the consequences. But we were jumping out the window like, "I'm not reading this Bible. I'm tired of this book." During the summer when we didn't have school we had to go on Vacation Bible Study. [. . .] Going into the sixth grade you had to get baptized. It was like you go and think . . . you sit in the first pew in the church for that whole week of . . . the revival. [. . .] You sit there the whole week. Then Sunday they prep you to get baptized and they want you to come . . . and say "Alleluia." I chased them out of there like, "What the hell!" I've been baptized five times in five different churches in my adult life. I went to a Pentecostal Apostolic church I guess, and they feel like if you're crying during the sermon that this is the Holy Spirit. You should be baptized right on the spot, and I did. And I didn't go back again. If you'll baptize me you'll baptize anybody. I went to another church where I didn't have to get dipped in water. They just come in . . . I mean experienced Christian. But then I started going to an LGBT church, nondenominational. It was fun. It was fun but it was very segregated. It was very white. And I was always—I felt like the token Negro in that church.

The churches you went to as a child, what denomination was that?

That was Baptist. . . . that's the only one . . . because it was like a community in the country. Everybody knew to go to Becker's Grove . . . New Mt. Zion, Pleasant . . . Shady Grove, those were the churches you were going to. Sand Hill. That's where you were going.

So, you didn't enjoy church?

No, I didn't enjoy church all day. No. I enjoyed it when we ate. When they had food. I was [like,] "We going to eat today?" Or when we took communion, but as a child you didn't take communion. You had to be baptized to take communion. And I thought it was wine. They were telling me they were drinking the bread and the wine. So, I wanted the wine. And like I said, my grandmother was the mother of the church so had—at the time we were growing up they literally had to pour the grape juice into the little glasses. And they had the . . . and they covered it up. And when they got ready for it I thought growing up that there was somebody dead under there. Because they had a white sheet covering it up, you know, covering. And I'm like, is that a body? I was just a weird child in church. I thought someone was dead. And then they took it up and I'd get mad because everybody was going around getting communion and I can't get it. I was mad because I felt like we just poured it out—"My grandmom poured it out, how come we can't have none?" Because I didn't understand. My grandmom finally, you know, told me what communion was and stuff. It didn't stop me from not wanting it, but I felt like I was in—right enough with the Lord to drink the wine.

Did they use real wine or they use grape juice?

No, they used grape juice. Our church they used grape juice. Now I went to a church where they used wine. But I was, you know, grown then so I knew that.

Did you sing in the choir?

I didn't sing or do anything. I just wanted to go to church and go home.

And your grandma didn't make you?

Not me. I told you I was the spoiled one. If I didn't want to do it, I wasn't going to do it. "I don't want to be in the choir." "Okay." "Well, you should think about doing something in church." "I do something in church. I sit there." I sit there and I listen to the sermon. . . . That's what I do. . . . go to sleep. And the church had a preacher that was a hundred years old. He was known in the church. That's what I felt church was. Until I started going to different churches, you know. I'm not going back to country ever. And I meant that. And the only time I go to that church is when somebody in our family dies.

. . . .

Malu [b. 1980, Cincinnati, Ohio (Davidson, North Carolina)]

What kind of church do you go to?

It's Wedgewood. It's a combination of American Baptist Alliance of Baptists, which is what my denomination is, and then we're also joining up with the United Church of Christ. So, it's "UCC Federated" is what they call it. But the pastor's a white guy, he's a heterosexual white guy, but our church is composed of queer folk from all the different ways you can be queer. We don't have a large Latino population—but definitely whites and blacks and multicultural families. And there's some people that go to our church that are atheists. We have atheists there and we have a few agnostics.

How does that work?

Community. Everybody in the community. So if we're singing a song about Jesus—she's actually trans—but if we're singing a song about Jesus, she doesn't stand up. If we're singing a song about people being good in the world, then she'll stand up and sing. Now, she made my ordination certificate, actually. She's an artist. But yeah, and you know, she kinda has times when she comes more, and then times when she kinda backs up and that's just the cycle of, you know. But yeah, we're a pretty radical bunch.

* * *

I am ordained. I am a chaplain, so I work in Carolina's health care system, so I work specifically with palliative care. So, it plays a large role in terms—on the outside, on the exterior—religion plays a large role in terms of my profession, my vocation, my career. Because I'm in public ministry, I am called to serve any and every one, so for me it switches more to spiritual, spirituality, than it does religious institution. So, it plays a large role and at the same time it doesn't. [. . .] For me, religion is more kind of exterior. It has much more to do with politics. Whereas spirituality has more to do with that intimate journey and the process of being yourself and being in a relationship with God, being in a relationship with others . . . so that's more of what's important to me and what that looks like. And however you get to that relationship, whatever the religion is you choose, at the core it's about creation, knowing yourself, love, actualizing that divine potential. Those are things that are meaningful for me.

What role do you think religion plays in peoples' capacity, particularly in the South, to come to terms with their sexuality?

Oh, so much. So, so, so, so much. I mean, one of the saddest things I have encountered is having a black woman say to me, "You're a lesbian. How can you be ordained?" Well, first, it was, "Wait, that's your son?" That used to, whoo! Oh, Lord, I used to be ready to fight people over that. [. . .] So first, it was questioning that call, and then questioning the second call, which was, "How could you be? But you're gay." "Umm-hmm." "Are you celibate?" No. I have a sexuality that is blessed by God. Like, it is good and God said so and God made it real good, so no. And of course, I really can't say that to everybody, they kinda think you're a heretic. [Laughter] So that's been one of the saddest things that I've ever seen. And I know people right now who are tortured, literally tortured, by this idea: "God made me. I am who I am and God made me, but I'm not right, and God can't have made me this way and God can't love me like this." I mean, that is—it is torturous. And in part, because I think it goes to the core of who we are as spiritual energy beings. Also, because [. . .] the South has a culture of Christianity, whether you're— no matter what religion you are, you are impacted by Christian culture in the South. Right? [Laughter]

So, you have the culture of Christianity. Then you have the fact that many of us as black folks are connected to the church in some way.

Like even the woman I spoke of who's Muslim, she's second-generation Muslim. Right? Well, her parents converted, so she still has a grandmother that was Baptist, another grandmother that was Episcopal, so she still grew up in and out of churches. Even with her being Muslim and being very much a Muslim woman, she also is still impacted. You see what I'm saying? And you know, our spirituality, our relationship to divine, has been not just a means by which we've gotten through all of what it means to be black in this country, but it's also been a form of resistance, a very mighty form of resistance to all of what society has said. You get it, right? So if you're alienating yourself, if in being—accepting who you are to say "No, I'm queer, and it's okay and God blesses that"—you're alienating yourself potentially from this rich community and legacy and connection. And that is torturous. It is a torturous, scary experience that most people—I mean, just talking about it, it hurts my heart. I did not have to go through that in the same way, 'cause I didn't have that belief, you see what I'm saying? But [. . .] my parenting partner, her process of coming to terms with being gay, [. . .] she in some ways has more masculine identified ways of being, so that compounds that in terms of her gender presentation. People confuse her for being a man, sometimes. So, all of that journey—it's torturous. [. . .] I think it causes mental illness, I think it causes addiction. We know it's caused suicide in people that are young enough. At the same time, there are pockets and communities of folks that are resisting that; we have churches here that are doing it. There's a unity movement, there's churches here and Atlanta and a church out in California that are—I think they're connected. There's two different unity movements that are going on, but I think they talk to each other. I don't know. Either way it goes, there are those spaces where, you know . . . I can't remember the church name, but it's Pentecostal, but it goes back to like the real roots with Azusa Street Pentecostal, which was really radical for its time, right? So kinda reclaims those roots. So, there are pockets and, you know, the Alliance of Baptists, we're not rooted in the black church experience, but we are open and affirming. So, there are pockets where you can get healing, but it's—just the process of acknowledging the wound and seeking healing is such a courageous act. I mean, and there's many people who it takes a long time to heal from that. It takes a long, long time.

. . . .

"Martha"

"Martha" was born in Fort Sill, Oklahoma, in 1982 on a military based and was reared mostly in Sikeston, Missouri. Sikeston is located in the

southeast corner of Missouri in what is known as the "Missouri Bootheel."
It has a population of sixteen thousand, a quarter of whom are African
American. The interview took place on October 4, 2013, in Little Rock,
Arkansas.

I grew up in a very religious home. My grandmother was a very religious woman, and she and I used to participate actively in church. I sang in church and, you know, was very, very active in the church.

What denomination?

We went to a Southern Baptist and then it changed to Baptist and so now my parents or actually my mother and my stepfather are actually pastors of a nondenominational church.

When I was younger I was extremely religious. I sang in the church, and singing is pretty much my life, like I love to sing. So, it plays a big impact in my life because you know I believe in a higher power and I feel that it leads and guides me and that's what I put my trust in. So, I would say it does have a big impact in my life. I've had to deal with coming to terms as far as being a lesbian and being a Christian and if I could be, if I could actually be, if I could be a lesbian and be a Christian. I felt tormented for many years after I realized that I was a lesbian that I was going to hell, am I, you know I can't be Christian and be a lesbian. This just isn't right. It took a lot of years of me accepting myself and digging deeper and just kind of doing a little bit of research theological-wise, to come to terms that God loves me the way that I am, so.

But as a kid you learned that it was wrong?

Yes.

In church?

Yes, as a child.

And that was preached from the pulpit?

Mm-hmm.

And at home too?

Yes, because when you look in the Bible you know they call it perverse and you know all of that and so that's what you see. And so, I believe that children are not born, they're taught as far as when it comes to racism, and as far as when it comes to hate and anything of that sort. It's learned. It's nothing that they're born with. It's something that's in the household that they see and are told every single day, and that's how they believe it. It takes them to step out on their own in order for them to realize, in order to make their own decisions about how they stand on certain topics.

Were there not people in your community growing up that were gay?

Growing up, not until I got into my teens that my mother's, one of her best friends was a gay man, and he actually had AIDS and he passed away from AIDS.

Really?

Yeah. My mom had always very open to gay men, but she had an issue with gay women.

Interesting. So, you were exposed to gay people all your life, but yet you were hearing in church that it was wrong, but your mother's best friends were gay.

Yeah.

How did you reconcile that?

I had to meet the person. You know, I've always been taught that it's not really the sin. You have to love the person instead of loving the sin and I realized that as I got older. But he never mistreated me. He was always nice to me. He was good to me. You know, there was times I was home by myself, my mom would say tell him, "Hey go check on her and see if she's okay," and we would talk, you know. So I mean, yeah, I was exposed to it. I never really thought much of it because I didn't know that I was gay within myself all that time and hadn't come out yet, so it really didn't affect me much. I just saw him as a friend of my mother's.

. . . .

"Mary" [b. 1975, Tuscaloosa County, Alabama]

I remember one Sunday this guy came to church . . . white guy . . . I can't remember the name of the movie, but he came and he showed a movie. I was about eleven or twelve. And in the movie there's this man who was drinking and cursing, basically end of the world. And then he gets on his motorcycle to drive away and he dies and he goes to hell. [. . .] I was eleven. Scared the shit out of me. So, I was really scared for the longest time, and I remember asking some questions about the movie and the response was always the same. And I just grew up with . . . you don't question God. I said, "But I'm not questioning God, I'm asking you. I want to know, what does this mean? I'm not questioning him." To a certain extent I really think that sometimes it was just something parents used when they didn't necessarily know how to answer it. So it was this whole fear of . . . if I have questions about Christianity or if I have questions about why shouldn't I do this or why should . . . it's interpreted as, you know, "You don't have faith in God; you're questioning God." And I just never thought that that's what it was. I just thought I was young,

I was a kid, I was inquisitive. I wanted to know. So . . . yeah, religion was a very big part.

What role does religion or church play in your life currently?

Good question. To be honest with you, I have not been to church since . . . December of 2010. Last year, New Year's Day I made a conscious decision that I was not going to attend church for one year. Just I was going to, you know, pray and meditate and practice my own sense of spirituality and just do that for a year. And, ironically, once the year was up I didn't feel that need to reconnect. I mean, every now and then, you know, when I'm watching *Sunday's Best*, I'm like, aw man, it'll be good to hear some good old . . . singing and hear some of these old hymns or whatever. But other than that, like I really didn't feel the need to . . . like, "Oh my God, I've been out of the church for a year, I've got to go back, I've got to find me a church home." I didn't and I still don't, which is one of the reasons why I was . . . sad that my son went to live with his dad, but I think that was one of the . . . one of the advantages is that living in that small little area I know he's going to church on Sunday. So . . . with his grandmother.

So, it's important to you that your son be raised in the church.

Yes. I mean . . .

Why?

And that's important . . . because I think that in the back of my mind I'm always thinking about what if, you know? "What if, what if, what if." Let's say that he turns out to say, one day he's gay? Oh, is it my fault because I didn't send him to church? Was it my fault because I'm gay? So, I'm like, okay, well, he's with his dad, he's in the church, he's doing all of those things that the straight Christians say you're supposed to do to make sure your child isn't gay. Okay. So, he's doing that. So, should he happen to be gay it's not my fault. [. . .] I feel like my Christian foundation is and always has been very beneficial to me. I always loved spirituality. I always loved the singing, always loved worshipping. I just never liked the condemnation and I never liked organized religion. You know, and I think that that has been my issue with organized religion is that I feel like, you know, it's what I call the "soap box Christians." You know, you're standing up there pointing your finger at me doing this the whole time, and when while you're pointing I see all those skeletons shaking back there that can barely be still, but you're still pointing at me, you know? So, I . . . always describe myself as a spiritual person, but . . . me and organized religion . . . we don't really see eye to eye. You know, I just say, you know, "Me and God, we good, we good." And a couple weeks ago I think I wrote something on Facebook about being a

Christian, a black feminist Christian Buddhist, and someone commented and said, "You can't be both Christian and Buddhist." I said, "Why not?" And his comment was, "Well . . . God is a jealous God. He doesn't want you worshipping other, blah, blah, blah." And I just said, "Well, for me Christianity and Buddhism . . . have two different purposes and I don't feel like living according to Buddhist principles is . . . in some sort of way a strike against living in a Christian manner." Because for me . . . the aspects of Buddhism that I feel are important are in terms of how you treat people, the meditation, your outlook on the world, the world view that I have. And I think that's very comparable to what Christianity is supposed to be. It may not be comparable to what people who practice organized religion have determined that Christianity is, but I think it's very comparable to what, you know, God intended it to be. So if you really look at religion and think about various religions as much as people don't want to say this, there is a lot more in common across all religions than . . . there is different. But . . . somebody may say you're questioning God if you believe that. So you can't believe that.

. . . .

Maryam
Maryam was born in 1977 in Washington, DC, the middle child of eight. I interviewed her and her wife, Toni, for this book. The interview took place on September 9, 2013 in Nashville.

You talked about this a little bit, because your biological father is Muslim, but what role did religion play in your upbringing?

I would say initially, when my father was around, he was, of course, probably like most Muslims are, they're very strict, disciplined. You have to do things at certain times, every day, the same way. And then you're not allowed—we couldn't—we didn't have a TV, radio. You could only read books with no pictures. So, with him around, and then I was homeschooled, when he was there, my mom homeschooled me and my older brother. And my older sister, who eventually moved when she was thirteen, because she didn't get along with my father because he was very strict. And, I mean, he physically would punish you if you didn't do something, you know, correct. So, I think six and under, it was very—you wanted to do everything right because you would get in trouble. So, when he went to prison, me and my brothers, my brother who was older and I had a younger one, we were very happy just because my mom didn't do that. And so, it was good for him to be gone. And then my stepdad came along and he was not—he was definitely not as aggressive, I would say, as my birth father. So, we were able to finally, you know, wear shorts, because we couldn't wear shorts. We couldn't go out. I couldn't go out, without being covered up, even when I was little. And I couldn't wear shorts, you know, out the house to visit people. We really couldn't visit people because we couldn't have friends, unless they were Muslim, and nobody was Muslim in rural west Tennessee.

And so, after that, again think we were happy to be out. We moved to—when he left, my mom wasn't working. So, we moved to the projects in Huntington. So again, even though it was the projects, for us it was like great, because it's all these other kids running around and playing. And now we can play and hang out. So again, it . . . was definitely different than, you know, before, my younger years.

So, after six, your biological father goes to prison. Y'all move. And your mother converts back to Christianity.

Mmm-hmm.

What church did you go to then? Or you didn't go to church?

Well, initially, I started going to church with a friend of mine. I would spend the night with her and then I'd go to church with her. And then it probably was a year or two before my mom actually started going to church and joined a church, and it was called Parker's Chapel Missionary Baptist.

. . . .

Melissa [b. 1979, Nashville, Tennessee]

I would say, in a sense, I'm still shaping what it looks like to be a spiritual activist in a sense. But nothing about proselytizing and telling people to read or do it this way, but more around, like, for example, I'm starting a group called the People's Sunday School. And so the curriculum is based on everyone that's in the group, so you know, what book or what passage do you consider sacred text. Some people might be the Bible. I might pull out a Audre Lorde poem, et cetera. And so, everyone in the group reads it and we discuss it, this idea of building a bridge. But not like proselytizing, like, "Oh, you have to believe in Allah" or this . . . you know, it's nothing like that, more around this . . . this shared value. So, I think I'm at a point of my life I'm done kind of fighting for . . . fighting against things to more like fighting for things because I feel like the frames are different and it takes different energy. I don't know, when I used to do a lot of motivational speaking, and I'm kind of leaning towards that again. And when I did guest preaching I enjoyed it somewhat, but I'm not a minister. So, I probably would look like doing more motivational speaking and then more faith work.

For example . . . in my work area there's not a lot for kids to do. It's like they need a positive outlet and it's like, oh, what about . . . we get stipends for the youth. And then on Wednesday nights I do work for . . . night schools, workshops, and a church. A local church just sponsored it and it worked well. And so to replicate that kind of work, to . . . having the church meet the need without this requirement of, "Oh, you're hungry," "Oh, you have to sit in on that one-hour ceremony," "Oh, and then we'll feed you." Well, I mean, one-hour sermon, and then we'll feed you dinner. You know, this idea of like recruitment. And so to do more work like that. I see myself doing more work like that.

. . . .

Monica J. [b. 1966, Houston, Texas]

You know, we went to church. We were probably there every Sunday. My mom was not really strict in that. During the week, there was no reading of Bible verses or anything like that. So, I really think that my mom went, kind of, more so out of it being an exercise or tradition, the thing that you're supposed to do. Because she wasn't a Bible-verse-quoting type of woman. My mom was extremely social. Back then, she smoked cigarettes. And she would have her cocktails. She would go out partying with her girlfriends and to nightclubs and stuff like that. But she did go to church. And she took us to church. I remember when I was baptized. I remember my outfit that I was dressed in before and after the baptism. I remember going in the pool and being baptized. You know, I remember all of that. But I also remember how church went long and I would get my mom's keys out of her purse. And this is probably now like around the age of maybe twelve. And getting the keys and going, sitting in the car waiting for church to be over.

And she didn't care?

No, she would not come and get me or any of that. My mom was an usher in the church, so she was active. I sang in the choir as a kid in church. I remember being taunted by some of the church—the kids at church, because I was tall. I was tall and I was thin and I had long feet. And so, I remember them taunting me about my shoes, you know. [Laughter] And it didn't feel very good. But yeah, now, my mom would not come and get me when I would get the keys and go sit in the car. And I'm probably doing it at the point where there may be maybe another thirty minutes of service left. You know, it's not like I'm sitting in there for the whole two and a half hours. But yeah, probably about thirty minutes left, I'm sitting out in the car, just waiting.

So, you didn't enjoy church?

Um, let me think about that. I didn't dislike it. It wasn't like I woke up on Sunday morning and said, "Oh, I dread that I have to do this." I just knew that it was a part of the routine. But I think what that was, was you're a child and a child's attention span only goes for so long. And back then, there was a nursery for like infants. But there was no children's church. So, for us we're in church with the adults. And I think it was just an attention span thing, you get fidgety and after a while, it's like, okay, I'm bored. But I wouldn't say that I disliked it.

And besides, you said you sang in the choir?

Yeah, I sang. I sang in the choir. And I was an usher, too, now that I think about it. So, I was like one of the little junior ushers. I remember that having to go to rehearsal for the choir and for ushering. I'm trying to think about the whole ushering piece, how did I feel about that. I don't think I was all that crazy about being an usher. But the singing in the choir part was fine. But I wasn't crazy about being an usher.

And what was church culture like? You were raised Baptist?

Right, exactly, I was raised Baptist. And I remember us having only two pastors, I think, for that church. And his name was Reverend Galloway was the name of our pastor. He had a daughter that was maybe a couple of years younger than me, because we got baptized I think at the same time. And it was a sense of family. I remember my mom was friendly with a lot of people at the church. And this one particular family, the McElroys, we would go I think like maybe once a month on Sundays, after church we would go to their house. Their mom and dad and I think it was maybe about four of them. And we would go and have Sunday dinner at their house. And I always looked forward to that, I enjoyed being at their house. Their mom cooked well and the food was good. And she would make this lemon meringue pie and it was so good that, while the adults were in some room doing something and the kids were playing, I would always sneak into the kitchen and eat more of the pie. [Laughter] You know. But church culture, and I'm looking at it through the lens of my mom, I see that my mom really enjoyed it. And those were her friends and people congregating kind of after church and talking, the adults. But for me, it was just the thing to do. You know, I hear some people say, "Oh as a kid, I remember getting the spirit" —none of that ever happened for me. I wasn't led by the spirit, you know. I was just there because I was required to be there, so I was just there.

Did you go to Sunday school?

No.

No.

No, we did not go to Sunday school. It was just church. It didn't start to resonate with me until I became older. And having grown up Baptist is—it's still a part of my roots. I remember going to—here in Atlanta, and I don't know if you would call it a gay church, I don't know. Clearly, all-inclusive. And clearly predominantly gay. And so, I went. And I just felt extremely uncomfortable, because it was probably 90 percent gay black men. And I remember—I don't know if it was the invitation where you call people to join the church and the deacons or whatever are up there. And I remember seeing one of the guys who I guess was a deacon was someone that I knew had dated a friend of mine. And his name was Chris. And I was looking and I'm like, no, that's not right. I couldn't make the connection of you're a deacon but you're gay. [. . .] And it was a challenge for me. And I remembered being so taken aback that when service was over, I went and got in my car. I had to sit in my car for a few minutes to collect myself before I could even drive off.

And so, what I know about me is I—in a church setting, I still need some semblance of the Baptist roots, meaning the choir or the mothers of the church, and that it needs to be diverse, you know. Men and women, heterosexual, gay but just kind of all one type is not—it doesn't settle well with me. I've been before and I went back recently to another church here in Atlanta, Victory. And I went and worshipped with a friend of mine on Easter Sunday. And there's more of a balance there in terms of families and men and women and heterosexuals, gays. But I was distracted because I'm looking around. I'm just looking at all of the men and that's kind of distracting me, really, from like the message. And where I've been worshiping since I moved back from Baltimore is at a church that's not far from my house, Elizabeth Baptist, and it's I guess your traditional Baptist church. So yeah, I still need that, I need some smattering, I guess, of some Baptist in there somewhere. And it was interesting because I was talking to a friend of mine. And there's like a New Thought church that some of my friends are going to here called Impact. And a friend of mine said that he had visited. He was like, "But it won't work for me because they don't have a church choir." So, I guess it's all about what you've gotten used to and what's important to you and what you need. But yeah, in terms of church, I guess just what I grew up with is still a part of me, that type of church setting. Even as far as the construct of the building goes, and as weird as it may sound, for me, there's something about walking into a church and being in an actual church, compared to maybe if it's a church that's just getting started up and they're in the school's gymnasium or they're in a hotel ballroom or something like that, for me, I feel very differently. I feel much more connected. I feel like I really am truly in the House of God when I go into a church. And I know that I've heard people say, "Well, the church resides in you and that's just a building." But there is a different feeling that comes over me when I'm actually in a church worshipping.

* * *

I think that for me, I'm at a place where I'm moving—or I shouldn't say "moving towards"—I'm trying to incorporate more I guess new thought into my spirituality. And when I say "incorporate," meaning that church still plays a part. And I'm going to get on my knees and pray every morning. Or I've found where I've said, well, I'm going to sit and I'm going to meditate. And there's a guilt that comes with that. I feel like I have to be on my knees and I have to send a prayer up to God. And when I have tried to say, "Okay, well, I'm going to sit and meditate," I feel like I'm putting that before God. And so, I will stop and I will get on my knees. And I will pray to God. And then from there, I will go to a sitting meditation. [. . .] And where I am now is again I'm going to pray every day. I will maybe a few times a month pick up my Bible and read certain scriptures. But what I am mostly now is in trying to just elevate my conscience. And being more conscious in trying to be more humane. [. . .] So that's just kind of the place that I'm in now, is just trying to be more conscious and more humane. And just asking God, "Who am I supposed to serve? How am I supposed to serve?" Let me extend love. Help me to extend love in all situations at work in my personal life, people that I meet on the street. Saturday, I went with a group of friends to Lake Lanier. We stopped to get something to eat. And there was a guy in the restaurant that looked like if he was not homeless, he was pretty close to being homeless. And I asked him if he was hungry, if he wanted something to eat. I never would have done that eight months ago, so I'm growing. I'm trying to be more conscious.

. . . .

Nancy [b. 1950, Maxton, North Carolina]

When we would go to Pentecostal church the woman preacher, her husband used to be like a ragtime pianist, and he would play that piano in church. We used to make jokes about him. Stuff like that, but that's not really. . . . Everybody knew the Presbyterians were high class, but nobody gave a damn. There weren't that many of them, but they were there. So, this is what I find fascinating when I think about my childhood. All the women that were doing something bad, I found fascinating. Because they had more freedom. There was a woman on my block, she rented from one of my neighbors, elderly couple. She rented a room from them. She would play her music loud, on her little, what do you call stereos, phonograph, or whatever. Okay. And um, she wore lipstick during the week, fingernails always polished. I suspect women didn't like her because maybe she made her living by having boyfriends, lovers, and gave her gifts. You didn't see her working a lot. Okay. When she worked she worked for somebody black. So, I thought she was fascinating. Then there was the woman that was obviously masculine in demeanor. I knew they whispered about her, but I didn't understand what that meant. But I found her fascinating too because it seemed everybody that was odd was free. There were women who married men and had babies. I don't know a lot of them who were happy. But you'd look at them and they were smiling all the time. Like women who were on the edge, I found them fascinating. You know, when you got women on the edge, women who are trying to be respectable, that bothers them. I probably heard it but it didn't sink in. I thought it was interesting.

. . . .

Michelle [b. 1965, Winston-Salem, North Carolina]

My mother was a church organist, my father was a deacon, so . . . we used to sing. [Laughter] My grandma was a Sunday school teacher. Every time that door opened, honey, we were there. Religion was a big part of . . . is a big part of black culture, you know. And in this area, especially, in the Bible Belt area practice is the big thing.

Did you enjoy church?

Coming up, I did. I didn't enjoy going all the time. [Laughter] And I really think that because of the teachings and some of the . . . religious rule, I think I missed out on some things because my parents, my dad . . . it was pretty much him . . . was very strict because of it. They were raised with a certain set of teachings, and of course, they passed those on. And I don't think they did much. So, I mean, when he had girls and it was two of us, the rope was kind of tight. And I'm taking that back to the religious guidelines and teaching that we were raised under.

I really didn't know God. I learned to mask. You learn to mask, you know. They got cute little clichés out now: "God is good," of course, "all the time." [Laughter] They didn't have those then, but you know, um . . . everything was always alright, and the more religion you wore, the higher the position in church and the . . . you know, the more clout you had. I didn't see the realness of people until they got busted doing something, you know. As I began to get older in church, and you were of age to really be accountable for your sins, then seemed like you could never get in right standings. You were always in a backslid state, no matter what, you know? Always. You can't drink, you can't smoke, you can't . . . definitely can't have no sex. You know, it's all kinds of stuff, and I understood some of that. But then you took away some of the innocence . . . of learning and being able to participate with other kids and do what they would do. Stay out late from the football game and all those. I can remember my senior prom . . . this is senior prom . . . child, I looked a hot wretched mess. Honey, when I look back, I looked a hot wretched mess, honey. [Laughter] I said, "Dad . . . " he said, "You need to be in my house at 12:30." I said, "Well, Dad, listen, the prom doesn't get over 'til 12:00 and everybody goes out to eat. You know, I need to stay . . . I want to stay out a little later, it's my senior prom." I said, "Mom, tell him." "Wright . . . " you know, she calls him Wright . . . "Wright, listen, these children don't live but one time," and da da da. He didn't care, though. She fought, fought, fought. He says, "Linda, this is my house and what I say go in this house." I said, "But Dad, everybody goes out to eat after the prom." He said, "I'm gonna tell you what you do." He said, "You go eat before you go. You better be at this house by 12:30." [Laughter] That's the senior prom. So, he was that kind of type.

. . . .

"Lady Boy" [b. 1973, Greenville, Mississippi]
I had to go every two weeks because at church in the Delta is a little bit different. Because typically that church split ministers because they were traveling ministers, you know. So we'd have church the second and fourth Sundays. And spirituality was really important . . . it was important to me then and is now. But it's a little different for me now. I'll tell you why. Then it gave me some form of structure. Going to a Catholic school and understanding how they saw spirituality was a little bit different than what my Baptist roots were. I think Baptist was more experiential. Catholic was a little more, how do you say it, I just didn't feel the spirit. I'll put it like that. I knew it was there. I knew that the liturgy meant, you know, offering God into the services. But I just didn't feel it. I don't know, it was—it became more of an order of service as opposed to just letting the spirit take over. So, spirituality has always been important. My father is a strong believer. He's a deacon in the church. My cousin who passed away led the church for many years. I gave my life to Christ in 1985. And it wasn't something that they made me do. It was

something that I wanted to do. But at that time, I didn't know that religion would become such a problem the older I got, as I competed with my . . . as I struggled with my sexuality.

I think religion is the reason why I stayed closeted so long. Religion is the reason why I had a breakdown in 2006 because I was going to a Baptist, strict Baptist church in Illinois. And at that time, I think the president was Bush, who gave the money to the black churches to start speaking out against homosexuality. And I went from enjoying the church I attended and orchestrating various functions there in a leadership capacity to hating my own skin. And I just—I just melted. With everything else that was going on in my life. And so now I would say that I'm spiritual. I understand that God loves me. I understand that He loves everyone. I understand that I have a divine purpose. I know that He used people that were totally different than what the Bible thinkers—thumpers, say in regards to religion. I know that religion is something that was used to brainwash African Americans as a whole. I understand that. It's very discerning; it's very unfortunate to me that some—as African Americans we don't understand that. And I think that that is something that we're so busy trying to assimilate that we don't—we don't take the time to do our own research and understand who Israelites and understand who God was. You know, a lot of us have white Gods in our home still. When actually God is—if we're made in the image and likeness, God looks a lot like you— whoever it pertains to at that moment, you know. And that's why I don't understand why people can't respect universal principles of love. And that's what I'm all about. So, I found myself in my adulthood really getting at pastors when they come at me. I mean, I've had to really kind of be ugly a little bit since moving back to the South because you don't determine who I love, who I am, my values, the God I serve. That is something that is personal, and when you start getting in people's bedrooms, then you totally violate the human construct of being, of individualism. And you become a collectivist mob. And that's what we have in this country right now. It's kind of discerning to me. It's kind of frustrating to me. I use discernment to see it when I'm faced with it. But I'm very bothered by it, almost annoyed you know. So that's that.

Do you attend church now?

I do. I attend a nondenominational church locally. The pastor there is amazing. He's kind of like a fallen angel. He is straight but he believes that all people should love and be loved and he's an amazing man. He's a pastor of one of the largest churches here. And he came against some things in his life and people kind of shunned him. And our community has always supported his ministry. And so, he just opened the doors to everybody. Built his own church. That's the only church that opened the doors to everybody. And it is a blessed place to be in on Sunday morning. Even now when I struggle I know that I could probably go to him and talk. But I'm so introverted that I don't. But at least I know that that's an outlook that I could have if I needed it.

Are most of the members LGBT? Or is it a mix of everybody?

A mix of everybody. It's kind of interesting because, you know, he always says that you know heaven is not going to segregate you. People segregate each other. I attended Trinity under Pastor Wright. I joined under Pastor Wright, and then I was sitting under Pastor Moss until I left. I still kind of log in every now and then just to hear what he's talking about. It's a phenomenal place. There's no place like that; you know, even though I love my church here, I miss Trinity many days, you know. I think it had gotten a little different before I left. You know, the same-sex ministry was pretty prominent. But I don't know what happened with it. I just know that it started changing. I know that when I go back I'm probably going to visit Urban Villages.

· ·

"Louise"

"Louise" was the second oldest woman I interviewed for this book. She and her partner have been together for over thirty years. She was born in Durham, North Carolina, in 1944. The interview took place on August 25, 2012, in Durham.

I don't consider myself religious. I'm not an atheist. I do believe that there is something bigger and grander and greater than I. I do believe that. I don't think that sunsets are just different molecules of color. I don't. But I don't believe that there is a God who looks at me individually every day and is so aware of me that . . . I don't think I'm that important. [Laughter] So no, I don't believe that. But I don't like what religion does to spirituality. I don't like the ritual, I don't like . . . the unwillingness to think and to challenge and to question. I don't like that you're not encouraged to do that because I think that all, that we, if nothing else, is learning. And if you're not encouraged, if you're not allowed, if you're told something like "because I said so," which is something a parent would say to a little kid, no, I don't like it. I don't like it. So, I am not religious. I am not religious. And it's been a struggle because I grew up, as I told you, in the church and I participated in all of the activities of the church. And there is something that is very communal about church. You know, you can find good friends there. It's a social thing. When I was growing up, that's why you went to church. You went to church, number one, because your mother made you, but also because your friends were there. So, it's a good place to find, I think, good people. But it is not necessarily for me a good place to find like-minded people.

. . . .

Monica [b. 1977, Washington, DC]

I go to the Mississippi River at least like three or four times a week. I love her. I sit by her to just be at peace, to just feel like that water and hear it and like what is being said, like what are the messages. So, within that work I definitely have been calling on a higher power, my creator, my ancestors. I've been asking for divine guidance, surrendering to divine . . . real and divine time. So, less church these days and more working with spirit and being obedient to spirit and listening. And when I get a feeling about someone or when I . . . it's like just acting. "Don't do that. You don't need to go there." "Okay, I won't go there. I'll do this instead." "Okay." And just being very obedient and wise and seeing what happens, which has opened up . . . it opens up a whole lot, makes life a lot easier. So, I haven't really been doing much that is religious in terms of traditional, but like there are a lot of cultures represented in this city, so in terms of Ifá and Candomblé, I've been getting readings from time to time with priests of Candomblé . . . and just having my ears like wide open for the message in however it will get to me and whomever brings it. And going back to roots, that very rooted, very practical application, earth wisdom, wind wisdom, you know. [. . .] And that New Orleans . . . is prime, fertile ground for that kind of work, and it really encourages it, you know. I mean they talk, the spirits talk. They . . . carry on here. [Laughter] They just been carrying on, which is very healing and wonderful—and also can be very heavy and present sometimes as well.

. . . .

Pat Hussain [b. 1950, Atlanta, Georgia]

Father's Lutheran and my mother was down with it all. My Aunt Doris, not here, lived in North Carolina with my nieces and nephews, and she's still a staunch Catholic. I had difficulties. When I want to annoy my wife, I'll say Immaculate Mary to her or start a Gregorian chant, anything, start saying Hail Marys. I was in tune with Catholicism, a believer, yet it was contentious because I had questions and I was used to having questions and having either answers or being pointed in the direction to find the answer by my parents. And when I questioned, for instance, the birth control pill, a papal bull was issued and that Catholics with good conscience would not engage in this form of birth control. Alright, got it. Then, there was an uprising in the Congo—Mao Mao priests killed, nuns raped, a revolution in progress. The Pope gave the nuns on the continent special dispensation to take birth control pills. And when I went to class, catechism, I thought it's outrageous so I raised the question, why have these women been given—the Pope has spoken and now he's done something different than that. Didn't understand it, and of course, it couldn't get any better. Father Christian talked about papal infallibility and that the leader of the church on the Earth, the seat of St. Peter, all that, that he has spoken, which didn't hit my sense of logic, and I told him, "Well, I think that the Pope doesn't have enough faith in God. If he wants them not to be pregnant, they will not get pregnant." End catechism for the day. There were many times when my parents . . . got the call before I got home, and they said, "Just ask us but don't ask these questions in catechism." I was down with the whole program. As I began to get older there were things that just I couldn't get into sync with my world view, and I couldn't get an answer that made sense, that made me say, "Okay, I got it" from the priest, and that started the break.

So, you didn't enjoy church?

I did for a long time. I did as a child. I enjoyed the ceremony. I loved midnight mass. I was not a confession kind of Catholic. I might go. My mother was really pissed, though, and she was choir director and organist extraordinaire and would ask the priest if I had gone to confession. He couldn't tell her, seal of the confessional and all of that. Can't even get an up or down. She was livid. [Laughter]

Given you're growing up in the South and particularly Atlanta, I'm sure all around you are Baptists and COGIC [Church of God in Christ] and Methodist. Did you feel odd being a black Catholic, or was there a large black Catholic population here as well?

There was not. My childhood was to a large degree insular. I remember once during the homily, which is the Catholic version of the sermon, and someone said really loudly—well, it was real loud in a very quiet room where we were all listening intently to the priest—"Amen!" Nothing like that was in my realm of experience. It was like a shotgun going off, and it was quiet for a few seconds and then the priest continued.

. . . .

Q. [b. 1980, Dallas, Texas]

I'm not religious. People see my spiritual practice as a religion, and that's fine, but it's more of a philosophy. And I'm Buddhist. Nichiren Daishonin

Buddhist. Most people will understand that as "Tina Turner Buddhism." [Laughter] But it's a philosophy and it's not a religion. I just believe that everyone should be happy. In order to be happy, you have to be your highest self. In order for you to be your highest self and to live in that fullness, you have to be compassionate, and you have to know what you want and be okay with that and own that and send energy to that, and know that's what you're gonna get back. And understand that everything is connected, everybody's connected, and there's energy all around, and you want to be in rhythm with that energy. And when you get in rhythm with that, then that's when you're able to receive what you want to receive. That's because you're sending out at your highest self at your most enlightened state. And what's what I strive for. So, I don't pray to anybody. I just believe in the energy of the universe and everything's connected. And that when I'm working and striving to be my highest, that's how I connect with people, and I just believe in being happy.

I'm like, I used to be so stressed out all the time, all these gray hairs I got from different things, mostly women . . . [Laughter] and always just stress. There used to always be stress. I used to suffer from migraines. I had my friend tell me to say that I'm a former migraine sufferer and to really start inviting and owning what I want instead of staying in this place of lack, you know? And so now I do say, "I'm a former migraine sufferer" and now I am. I'm not stressed. I don't let shit stress me out anymore, you know? Because I know that I have the power within me to change whatever I want to change in my environment, in my reality. You know?

And so, it's spiritual, but it's a philosophy because if I believe that I want to be happy, and I know what it takes for me to be happy and I send energy and I focus on that, then I'm gonna get that. If I spend energy and time focused on people hating on me, the kind of woman I don't want, the kind of job or career or clients that I don't want, the kind of situations that I want to avoid, then I'm gonna get all of that shit. But instead I focus on what I do want and make that happen. So, yeah, people see that particular Buddhism as a religion, but it's more of a philosophy because you can be Buddhist and be anything else. We have people that are Buddhists and Hindu, Buddhists and Christian. So, it's a philosophy, but I like it because everybody's equal. They don't care about sexuality; they don't care about anything. We just want people to be happy and our main goal is world peace. In order for world peace to happen, it has to start with the single individual because miserable people do miserable things. Hurt people hurt people. You know? So, if you're hurting you're gonna fuck up a whole bunch of shit. If you're happy and you're owning who you are and you're like working to be your highest self, then you're not gonna do anything but send out good energy. Then whoever you touch with that good energy, hopefully that'll just . . . it'll be a ripple effect. And then that's when the world peace happens.

. . . .

Roshandra [b. 1976, Fort Lauderdale, Florida]

[Religion is] the biggest platform in my life to this day. Anyone that knows me, they call me, ask me to pray for them. I have friends who ask me to pray for their pets. Anyone who knows me will tell you that's the biggest thing about me is my spirituality and . . . I try to get people to go to church even though there was a point that I wasn't in church. But I've got back into it. I just put God first in everything that I do, so.

What denomination were you raised?

I grew up Pentecostal.

Oh, wow.

Now, I am African AME. I'm AME—.

Oh, that's a big shift. [Laughter]

Oh, yeah, it's a big difference. I mean, but it's the church that I joined up here and that happened to be the denomination. [. . .]

. . . .

Shannon S.

My friend Roderick Hawkins introduced me to Shannon S. They were childhood friends. Shannon S. was born in 1972 in Baton Rouge, Louisiana, the eldest of two children. Her brother, who is twelve years younger, is also gay. The interview took place on April 19, 2013, in Baton Rouge at the home of Dammeion, another narrator in this book who also happens to be a good friend of Shannon's.

I went to church every Sunday, when she [her mother] was with me, when I didn't skip with my godbrother. I'm Catholic. I learned a lot being Catholic, catechism and stuff like that. No religion likes homosexuals. I don't care what religion it is. At nineteen I decided to be converted to Baptist just to try it, because I wanted to please my grandmother, because she was still in denial about me being gay. And I went there one Sunday, and he gave this fire in hell brimstone speech sermon about being gay, and I was, like, I can't believe a God that's so full of love would have this much hate towards things that he created. I couldn't believe it, and it broke my heart, because it's like, "Is this what my grandmother think of me?" I didn't want to be that.

Stopped going to church. Well, religion it played a big role because of the values that I have. I'm not Jesus. I ain't going to turn the other cheek, but I can love you from a distance, but it's not all bad.

Did you enjoy going to church?

I did. I did. I did. Not the Baptist church, because I don't like all that screaming and hollering. The Catholic church, they get right to the lesson . . . and you're out in forty-five minutes, which was perfect for me. The saints, I admire stuff like that. I enjoy stuff like that. I enjoy white—my light—I still light white candles to this day and pray and worship and give homage to the saints. I still do that. Every once in a while I still cross myself when I pass by a Catholic church I respect, because it wasn't all bad. It wasn't all bad, and I can only recall one time that I actually heard them mention homosexuality. One time. So, I mean, they all right. The Catholics all right by me.

* * *

I'm scared that when I walk in the church it's going to catch on fire. [Laughter] I still pass by. I just, I don't think I belong. I went to a gay church one time here, and I just don't feel like I belong really. Strange as that may sound. I listen to a lot of Joyce Meyer. I listen to a lot of Creflo Dollar. I read a lot. I read the Koran. I'm studying feng shui right now. I still read my Bible. I still read the Catholic Bible. I study different religions, Buddhism. I studied Judaism. I even studied Scientology. They all say the same thing about homosexuality. So, it's like I never belong. So, I try to keep God in my heart and be a good person. That's what I try to do. I don't do it all the time because I am human. I still pray to my saints. I still like my white lights. I just don't feel like I belong in the church, because I went to a church and I joined a church, and it always happens. I enjoy the church. I had went there and visited a couple of times. I went with my sister, Baptist Church, Greater Beulah Baptist, as a matter of fact. Ironically enough, the man went to college with my mother and my aunts, and he invited them to church. And after they told him who I was and one Sunday, the deacon, who's a closeted queen, gave "the homosexuality going to hell" [sermon]. And I was like— I just can't go somewhere where when you see me that's what you think. I got the incentive because a friend of mine killed herself when she came out, and you don't know my story. Everybody got one. Everybody's story not in Barnes and Noble's, and I just don't feel like I belong, honestly. Do I want to go to church? Yes, I do. I get invited to church a lot. A friend of mine from school invited me to her church, and my fear is always when I walk in and then scan the crowd what the sermon's going to be, and I just—it hurts, because I was raised in the church, and I think sometimes that's why I have it harder than I should, because I feel like that's God tugging at my heart, telling me, "You're still mine. I'm still yours, but you won't give me a place to go." That's how I feel. You know it's not fair, because we love God, too. We really do, because in the end that's all we have so. It's not that I don't want to. I just can't find where I belong.

. . . .

"**Shonda**" [b. 1959, Columbus, Georgia]

We went to church . . . regularly. For sure every Sunday, sometimes twice. And, of course, if you went twice on Sunday there was a big meal in between. After service there was a big meal, like a big potluck. Everybody brought cakes and pies and ribs and pork chops and fried chicken, and then you have more church into the evening. And then there was prayer service at my house, and at least every other Sunday we went with either one of my great aunts or my grandmother to the nursing home to visit the people who were in the nursing home or in hospitals who were sick. That was a regular event for me, and I got used to it. I resisted. It's boring for a kid. Like when you're sitting around with these old people, it smelled funny. But I really valued that as I grew older, too, that cycle of life. We had to pay attention to our old people and our young people and that there was so much to learn because children were to be seen and not heard. And so, I listened very, very carefully, which is how I was able to, I think, really embody some of those women when I tried to tell their stories. I was quiet so that I could hear all kinds of things that they certainly would not tell me, they would just sometimes forget that I was in the room.

Were you active in the church?

Not really. I was always taught that you had to believe unconditionally. I was given lessons every day. For example . . . I was given money every morning, every Sunday morning. You know . . . the call to the altar and . . . you bring money up and give it to the church. They pass the plate . . . and you put this little bit of money in that. But I really wanted to go buy some candy . . . cross the highway and go to the candy man and get candy. And I remember one Sunday my mother gave me a little extra money and she said, "Now you make sure you put it in there because . . . what you put out you will get back tenfold." And so, I didn't want to. [. . .] One Sunday she asked me where'd I get the candy from. She knew I was not telling the truth. So, she did that little lesson for me and then we went to visit a friend of hers. And Ms. Suzy said, "You know, oh girl, isn't it your birthday?" And I said,

"Yeah, it's coming up," and she gave me a dollar. And I remember that; it was just like . . . ding! And that was a long-lasting lesson for me. It was a very simple little thing that happened, but it was a very long lesson for me in that the more you give the more you receive. And it's not just giving to just receive, but it could come from anywhere, anytime. You give what you have and what you can and it'll come back around. So that was one lesson from the church.

The second lesson was do unto others. Treat people the way that you want to be treated. And going to those nursing homes and those old people who were sitting there . . . helpless and couldn't do anything for themselves, it's like I learned that sometimes you don't have to do anything, just your presence, showing up, is worth more than a million dollars. You know? Because some of them there's nobody to come visit them. And so . . . it was a lesson in compassion for me that I learned, patience and compassion that I carried with me through them all. But I was also taught that . . . if you don't believe completely, then you can't drink the wine, you can't take the bread. And there was revival meeting and when you come to a certain age, the children sit on the front row and you're expected to join the church. And this was the do-or-die moment. I resisted going and sitting on that front row all those years, and then there came a time I was like twelve years old or something like that, and it was either do it or not. And I just didn't believe . . . and I said, "I still have questions. I'm not sure. Humans wrote the Bible and humans are flawed. And what if they're wrong? What if they wrote this . . . what if it's a story and we're to learn things from the story, but what if it's different than what they say? I'm just not sure." I'll always believe in God because of the way that I was brought up. I will always believe in something greater than myself. I will always believe in a God.

I went to different churches, Christian . . . I've been to many of them. I've had many spiritual experiences. And so, I think I'll not ever believe that there's nothing out there. I can't not believe that. But I had so many questions I just thought, honestly and truly, I can't say without 100 percent that I believe everything they say, so I'm just gonna say no. So, I never joined the church, I didn't get baptized, and it was a scandal. It was quite a scandal. But, if I lived in their house I had to get up and go to church on Sunday. [Laughter] Even when I went to college, when I came home she said, "You have to," but I was wearing pants and I had just whatever I had, so she would always buy me a dress. So, if I wanted new clothes or a new dress I would go home and we'd go shopping for a dress and then I'd go to church the next day. And it was a place of community for my family because they were just not that far removed from slavery and sharecropping. They were the first of their generation to come to the city from being like sharecroppers and not that far from slavery in south Georgia plantations. So, church for them was a place where they got to be with their people. It was really like family and community for them.

Was it Baptists?

Baptists, yeah, Southern Baptists. Southern Baptists, yeah.

And what was the music like?

It was rousing, foot stomping, get people to the point where they would be shouting and they would get very excited.

So it was charismatic.

Very charismatic, yes

Were there instruments?

No, there were no instruments. There were different choirs, though. I remember one time somebody wanted to join the choir and they didn't want to audition. They said you don't have to . . . "I don't have to audition for God, I am singing for God. I'm singing for the glory of God, so I am not going to audition and you better just step out the way, because I am gonna be in this choir because I want to sing for the Lord on Sundays."

. . . .

Shayla [b. 1980, Little Rock, Arkansas]

We don't go to church. It was a church that we were going to before, and for me, I have to feel like I'm getting something from there. And we went a few times and neither one of us felt that we got anything. I felt an issue about church when I went to church here with a friend one time, and the comments that that pastor made about gays and lesbians and the comments were very, very strong. They were very strong, and it gave me a sense of uncomfort. And I never went to that church again. I actually got up and left out. I couldn't leave completely because me and the person I went with drove together. So I couldn't leave, but I did leave out of the building. And it was completely uncomfortable. It was very vulgar. For me, church was about loving and family and a relationship with God and accepting other people as they are, and I didn't feel any of that. I didn't feel that. I didn't feel anything but hate in that church. I had to leave. So, I would say that here in this house we're more spiritual. We believe in God, we believe in a higher power, we believe, but we don't feel like we have to go to church for that. I would like to have a church that I felt comfortable in to be able to go to, but that's just definitely nothing like I've been just really looking hard for.

Tonia [b. 1969, Mount Vernon, New York (Graham, North Carolina)]

I think my meditation group would be the closest kind of communal spiritual experience that I have. And ideally I would like to spend more time in a spiritual space and in meditation. Unfortunately, as you saw today I have to work twelve-hour days, so that makes it difficult. And I'd probably say the most spiritual times that I have on a regular basis are when I run. That's like, I'm alone and I'm not doing anything else, and I get a chance to be with myself and be in my body and be in the world.

Earlier you said that as a child you felt like you were more religious than your parents and there was a flip-flop. A lot of people talk about how, particularly gay people, when they get older, they sort of leave church or institutional, institutionalized—not institutionalized, formal structures of religion but it never leaves them, if that makes sense. Do you feel some of that? For instance, like when you listen to gospel music does it make you feel a particular way?

That's so funny when you say that because when you said it doesn't leave them it was like the only way I can think that that's true is gospel music. Like, if they could take gospel music and put it into ashram, I'd be set, because there's things that I believe that make a lot of sense about being with the here and now and the present moment and not being yelled at by some preacher about fire and brimstone. But there is something I think is always going to be deeply moving to me about black gospel music.

Tonya

Tonya was born in Richmond, Virginia, in 1965, the youngest of six children. Richmond is the capital·city of Virginia and is located in the eastern central part of the state. It is one of the oldest cities in the country and served as the capital of the Confederate States of America during the Civil War. As the fourth largest city in Virginia, it has a population of 220,000, with over half African American. The interview took place on August 20, 2013, at Tonya's home in Laurel, Maryland.

I have gone through this journey where I chose not to stay within Christianity, which was my upbringing. Baptist specifically. I explored a number of different churches, and I ended up at a Unitarian Universalist Church, and it was very open and welcoming. I have always been a person that likes to explore different cultures, so different spiritualities have always drawn me.

Now I am in an interfaith church that's also metaphysical. So, I'm very woo-woo. On top of everything else. I think it was harder to come out as woo-woo than it was as lesbian for me. It's like, "Okay, we see these people who are lesbians, we know those bull dykes. They exist and whatnot. It's shocking but it's okay." Anytime you say you're not Christian, well, you going to hell for sure now. "You need yourself some Jesus girl." I just see Christianity as a way. I can get into some Bible study; I just interpret things differently. I also want to learn about Buddhist teachings and I love the earth-based religions. I feel my Native American roots come forth. I enjoy Sufism and other mystical elements of different traditions. So, I feel, I love to explore that and learn from that and to find what works for me. You know?

Many people who have left Christianity talk about them leaving it but it not leaving them. For instance, you said you enjoy church and so on and so forth, and you still speak of that with a certain fondness. Do you find even though you no longer practice Christianity that some of the rituals or music or any of those things you used to do?

I love gospel music and I love ritual, but my ritual isn't necessarily Christian ritual, but I love a certain degree of ritual. I go to an interfaith church. I was on the board for some years. I was secretary of the board, and I serve in many different ways. Most weeks I go to church, but periodically if I skip I can go down to a river and do drumming and that will be church. I believe all of our acts can be sacred. I believe being one with God and the divine within us. Whether I go to church or not, that's a nice community for me and it's nice to hear the word, and the way in which it comes, but it may be just a ritual of hearing the beating of the drum or we might have a service where we are chanting. I know that I am open and I can tap in a number of different ways, so I like that variety. I love ritual. But gospel music stirs me. I have gone through enough healing that I will hear gospel and I can accept it and sing along. Versus I hear it, hear words that don't ring true for me and I'm trying to change the words or just stay away from it because I don't believe that. It's okay; I can enjoy this form of gospel music and feel close to God. I recently joined my choir. We actually just formed the choir. We are singing two songs out of the hymnal and I am finding myself bored to tears. It's like . . . We need to get some good old-fashion [starts singing, "We need to praise . . . "]. I love to pray, and get some clapping going and whatnot. I pray a lot. My prayers sound different. With my family I may not pull out the "mother father everything and God" but I just say "God." I may not necessarily, I don't usually say in Jesus's name. I might say bringing out the consciousness of the Christ in us all. I pray differently from my family, and they recognize that and notice that. I pray.

I meditate. I put out a meditation and prayer CD so that is something that they know I'm different now. That was a way of coming out because it's very metaphysical. New thought versus the Christian tradition. My altar doesn't look like anything that, you know, they would ever see. I had different traditions represented there and whatnot.

. . . .

"Vanessa"

"Vanessa" has a PhD in sociology, and I met her through Priscilla (see chapter 1). She was born in Austin, Texas, in 1968, the youngest of three children. The interview took place on September 9, 2012, in Austin.

[Religion] had a huge impact in some ways in the sense that my family has been involved in church, different members of my family, not just my immediate family but just extended family, have been involved in church forever, I mean, preachers, deacons, deaconess, mothers of the church, Sunday school teachers, that type of thing. I know that I fell away from the church by the time I was, for some reason when I was about maybe thirteen or so, my parents stopped making me go to church. I don't know what that was about or what, but I was just kind of out there kind of wandering in the wilderness. I would go to church with friends. I got exposed to a lot of other different churches besides just the Baptist church, but it wasn't until my adult life, like really in the last ten or fifteen years that I've actually returned to church. So, I'm very active in church now, but I can't say that my upbringing had a real big impact on like my spiritual outlook now.

But up until thirteen you did go to church every Sunday?

Yes. Sunday school, the whole nine.

And you were involved in the choir?

In the children's choir.

Did you enjoy it?

You know, I didn't quite understand it back then. I mean, I went to what some people would think would be a like a traditional black church where the minister was like whooping and hollering in the pulpit, and a lot of times I didn't always understand the message. Even like I remember when I returned to church to start going to church as an adult, there were just different, I mean, besides like stories about Easter and stories related to Christmas and all that, I really didn't remember a lot of the stories that some people who have been in church since they were born could just recite all these different Bible stories and whatnot. So much of that was so new to me, so it's like in some ways I couldn't say I really enjoyed it per se. I was kind of a precocious kid, so I could see a lot of the hypocrisy in the church in the sense that, on one hand, they're saying that women should keep their place and have a certain role. But then it's like there were men in the church that were committing adultery, and running women and different things, and just not being respectful of their families, and whatnot, that I just saw the hypocrisy in that way.

* * *

I'm also been discerning a call to ministry and whatnot. So, it's kind of like with my going in a direction and going a different path with my spiritual growth and whatnot that really kind of started, we started going on separate paths in that way. So, my thing now is really just being open to the spirit, so part of being open to the spirit means that later on when I'm ready to get back out there, because it's only been two months since she and I broke up so I mean it's very fresh.

What role does religion play in your life currently?

Huge, a huge role. I am discerning call to ministry. I've been looking at seminary. I'm very, very active in my church, and the funny thing is I'm active in a denomination that does not support ordaining GLBT people, but my local church does. I'm a United Methodist and I don't, it baffles my mind why it is this is the church that I'm with and just how things have played out the last couple years that I've been a part of the church. But again, I have a strong calling for ministry. I preached my first sermon this year, so it's a very huge role. It plays a huge part in my life.

So how did you reconcile your spirituality and your sexuality?

For me, that started actually right before I came out to my parents. One of the things I did was I educated myself about those so-called clobber passages, and I found a couple of books that talked about what the Bible really says and kind of like the history behind some of those passages in the Bible that are used against GLBT people. And I just have had a real clear understanding since then that it is okay to be gay and to have a strong sense of spirituality. It's okay to be gay and be Christian. Jesus didn't say anything at all about homosexuality, none whatsoever. When you look at some of those other passages that people use to try to support keeping gay people out of church or out of roles like being preachers and that type of thing, when you really break it down, it's all about love. It supposed to be all about acceptance. That's what Jesus was about. Jesus was one who fed the hungry, who reached out to people that were lepers. There were no boundaries in terms of his love for other people. And when I look at that, what Jesus did . . . then there's no doubt that being a Christian and having that sense of spirituality is just as much my right to do so that it is someone who is very conservative and has some very strong views about, anti views about gay people.

In your experience, is the church a place to meet other women?

Well, it depends on which church. [Laughter] At one time I was a member of Metropolitan Community Church.

Oh, MCC.

The MCC. And so, I mean, in that sense if there were single women there, it was probably easier to meet women in that type of setting. But when you start getting into more mainline churches, United Methodist, even like, say, United Church of Christ where a lot of those churches are open and affirming and whatnot, I think there are, you have to have a lot of strength, to me, to be gay and to go to a mainline church and to know that you have reconciled your spirituality and sexuality. And in that regard, to me, I feel like there's very few people who have done that. Either a person says, "To hell with church, I'm not going, people are all hypocrites, I don't want to have anything to do with it" or they struggle with continuing to go to a mainline church. I mean a lot of people that they would love to still go to like a black Baptist church or they would love to go to if they grew up Episcopal or whatnot. Even though there have been changes with the Episcopal church, we know that not all of those churches are accepting of GLBT people, so I think it takes a strong person to be able to go to, I mean a strong gay person to be able to go to a mainline church, but when you go to those churches, there's going to be very few. I go to one of the largest churches in Austin as far as United Methodist goes, and we have a couple thousand members, and there's a small number of us who are out. I mean, there's some people that even though it's a downtown church, it's a progressive church, they're still not out. Those of us who are, we're small in number, and so it makes it hard. I mean my future wife might be sitting in the next pew and I don't even know it. [Laughter]

A Taste of Honey

Sex among Women Who Love Women

5

Blues singers, honeybees, and black southern women who love women have much in common. Most of the great blues singers of the twenty-first century are referred to as "Queens," for example, "Queen of the Blues" (Koko Taylor), or are positioned as the one in charge, similar to the queen bee in a bee colony. Blues singers such as Ma Rainey and Bessie Smith often sang about same-sex attraction in songs like "Prove It on Me Blues" and "The Boy in the Boat,"[1] the former referencing female masculinity: "It's true I wear a collar and a tie . . . talk to the gals like any old man," and the latter referencing same-sex-loving desire explicitly: "When you see two women walking hand in hand, just look 'em over and try to understand: They'll go to those parties—have the lights down low—only those parties where women can go."[2] Notable among many of these blues singers is the fact that they disavowed any one sexual "identity," partly due to the times, but also due to their sexual relationships with men. A queen bee, for example, has sex with a male bee (called a drone) only once, after which the drone dies. Drones who fail to mate with a queen during mating season are kicked out of the hive, thus leaving an all-female colony. Indeed, immediately after mating and her return to the hive, where she will remain for the rest of her life, the relationship between a queen bee and her sister worker bees intensifies as they "surround her in an oval shape, licking her thorax to get her scent and feeding her now and then with more royal jelly."[3] In another context this sequence of events might sound like those in a lesbian porn film!

The point here is that the narrators' stories about sex and sexuality resemble a blues song in the sense that there is joy and pain in their stories—the joy of self-discovery of their same-sex desire and the pain and heartache of sexual violence and trauma. In most instances, similar to the worker bees who maintain the hive and care for the queen and the yet unborn, the narrators find community among their peers in times of sexual pleasure and pain. The narratives in this chapter, therefore, are divided into three sections: "'Oh to Be a Pear Tree': Sexual Awakening," "'Stirring the Honeypot': Sex and Sexuality," and "'A Girl Child Ain't Safe in a Family of Men': Sexual Violence and Trauma."

"OH TO BE A PEAR TREE": SEXUAL AWAKENING

Unlike many gay men I interviewed for *Sweet Tea*, many of the narrators in this book did not "always know" that they were attracted to women. In fact, a majority of the women had their same-sex sexual awakening later in life, sometimes after having been intimate with and married to men. A number of them speak of their first sexual encounter with another woman as being life changing because it awakened in them feelings that they had never felt with a man—ones that made them feel more of an emotional as opposed to physical connection to their sexual partner. Euphemisms such as "fireworks," "light bulbs," and "explosions" were used to describe their orgasms during sex with women that ran counter to their experiences with men, with whom many found sex boring or obligatory. How apropos that the experiences of same-sex sexual awakening these women recount parallel how Zora Neale Hurston describes the character Janie Crawford's sexual awakening in the novel *Their Eyes Were Watching God* through the metaphor of bees pollinating a pear tree:

> She was stretched on her back beneath the pear tree soaking in the alto chant of the visiting bees, the gold of the sun and the panting chant breath of the breeze when the inaudible voice of it all came to her. She saw a dust-bearing bee sink into the sanctum of a bloom; the thousand sister-calyxes arch to meet the love embrace and the ecstatic shiver of the tree from root to tiniest branch creaming in every blossom and frothing with delight. So this was a marriage! She had been summoned to behold a revelation. Then Janie felt a pain remorseless sweet that left her limp and languid.[4]

Below, the women share similar "ecstatic shivers" that leave them "limp and languid." And, as Hurston's use of metaphor through poetic language suggests, self-pleasure is a key component to some of these women's sexual awakening.

. . . .

Darlene Hudson [b. 1961, Las Vegas, Nevada (Fordyce, Arkansas)]

I guess my first encounter, my friend Alfred who's deceased now . . . said to me, "There's a sister in the church that wants to spend more time with you, and she's just coming into the church, and she looks up to you and she just . . . thinks the world [of you]." So, there was this introduction, and I started hearing that that girl was gay, but you know me, I was Miss On-my-way-to-missionary-school. She was going to get saved.

How old were you?

Mmm, must be about twenty-seven I'm thinking.

And was that the first time you had a, not encounter, I'm talking about when you first had—

Remember I was conditioned. [. . .] I didn't see a girl when I was thirteen and think, "Hmm, interesting." By that same token, I wasn't feeling that about no boy, either. You know? I was so focused on being a good musician because that's how I went to college. [. . .] I didn't even think. You ever been in a situation like if you travel somewhere and you taste this wonderful food, this wonderful cuisine and you like love it, but now three days before, you didn't even know it existed, so you couldn't desire it or want it, but now that you got it, "Hey, can I have another? Let's go back and get some more of that." So yeah, twenty-seven, twenty-eight, somewhere like in that area because I was on my own and the AIDS epidemic. [. . .] And I took a job as a public health educator with the health department. [. . .] I was one of the first people on the phone to answer what they called the Arkansas AIDS Hotline. That was all the prevention we had, buddy. We didn't have nothing else. Didn't nobody know nothing else to do, but the health department did put that in place, and then our roles began to develop, and so then came training, education and training, and stuff like that. Where I'm going with it is that it was through those efforts I began to establish networks with people, and a guy who I went to college with who I stayed in contact with, I loved him, he was my very best friend, Alfred [last name]. I was telling him all about it and everything and not even thinking that he was even exposed. He didn't know. He said, "If you really want to do some outreach, Darlene, then you need to do it over here." And that's when I found out about gay clubs, gay people. In college, I kind of got like a look at people. I knew people who were there that they said were gay, but honey, I was Miss Saved Sanctified, so we did not have relationships. So, the only way that this woman got close to me was through the church, and that woman was standing at the altar in a red dress with this little crazy hairdo poofed up, and I just looked down there and

I said, "*Damn* she look good." And I said [to myself], "What did you just say?" and I said, "Damn she looks good. Girl, you need to go to the altar, too." I'm in the choir stand having this epiphany. So, I didn't play into it too much. I didn't think too much about it. [. . .]

She had sent a message through—

Yeah, she wanted to kind of go to a church meeting like one of the state convocations. She wanted to go and she just looked so up to me and so I was like, sure, I'm about to get my missionary license, why not? I'm gonna lead her to Jesus. Next thing I know, just a series of emotions and it was no denying. I never felt happier . . . just in conversation. It wasn't nothing sexual in the beginning, but there was an attraction, and I was like, I kind of like this. I'd like to know more about it. And I remember my friend Avery, he was almost disappointed because everybody, all of his friends had already said Sister Hudson is a dyke, you just don't know it and she don't neither. They all had put that word on me. I didn't know none of them. So, when I started showing up at the club I was still "Sister Hudson." I had to explain to my bishop why I was in this club. I didn't tell him it was gay. I was just doing outreach. And it just continued, and one night I saw Wanda in the club, and she came up and asked me to dance. I said, "Now this is really going too far." [Laughter] And I thought, "Oh my goodness," but now remember, I had seen her at the altar and thought, "Boy, damn, hmm, I like that." So, I was like, "hmm."

So, before you saw her in the club, y'all were doing things?

Church things.

Church things. But you never talked about an attraction to one another.

Honey, all we talked about was Jesus, the Holy Ghost, and getting saved, being saved. That's all I really knew, and she knew that was all the conversation I had too. But you know, she would do little subtle things, and I'd be like, she just don't know how too saved I am. Little did I know how that girl was chipping it away, [laughter] just knocking the edges off [mimes chopping with a machete] as we were going. If I had thought that she was trying to pull me into something, trying to mislead me and here I was, I'm supposed to be the pillar, I'm supposed to be leading her, we wouldn't have engaged. I remember we took a road trip, went down to El Dorado, attended church, and honey, I must have shouted all over that church that night, came back, got in the truck speaking in tongues and she said didn't know what to do. I said, "You got to drive, [performs speaking in tongues] 'd-d-d-d-d.'" [Laughter] I was so full. I keep in good contact with her. She's now the dean at the University of Kansas in something to do with special education. That's what she does.

Was she older?

No, she's younger. Remember, I'm the big one.

Oh, she's younger. So, after you met in the club and you had the dance, was that like the moment you—?

We started hanging out a little bit more intensely, yeah. She would come over. I would cook dinner. She had a relationship going on, a dysfunctional relationship that she was coming out of. She'd come to my house and cook dinner. We would go out to dinner. We would talk. And she was genuinely very much interested in understanding my walk with Christ, and I was trying to share information and I just thought about this and that, sharing information with her. It would be interesting to have her point of view on all of this, but from mine, where I sit today, that's what I thought was going on. That's what was going on. I was sharing Christ with her, and so even after that dance at the club, I never will forget it this other girl who was my good friend from college . . . we were both doing the outreach together. She worked for nonprofit and I was working for the health department. We had come together to do this outreach, and so I used to say, "Girl, look over there, look at that, look at that," just looking at all the gayness going on. And so, when the girl came up and asked me, I looked at her and said, "I know she ain't talking to me." And my friend told me, "Now get on out there and dance, you know you like her." I felt like a cheap Roberta Flack song, honey, they found *all* my letters and read them out loud. [Laughter] But it was fun, and we just rolled on from there, and it didn't turn into anything sexual because that was kind of bizarre, because all I known was sex with a man. So, she said, "Well, I'll tell you, I'll show you what to do." *Excellent* teacher, boo-boo. Excellent teacher. I owe her all . . . every woman I've had ever since that, I owe it to the teachings of the Dr. [first name] Chapman! [Laughter] I will call her by her name. I will give her that credit, honey. But girl says, "You really know what you doing," I say, "I had a good teacher." My first partner was wonderful to me, she really was.

· ·

Iris [b. 1957, Miami Beach, Florida]

I'm going to call her "Sandy." But she's from Buffalo. And a very beautiful woman [. . .] just gorgeous. But very quiet. She didn't live in the same dorm as I did freshman year. [. . .] We were in Chadwick, but she lived at Abbey. And I actually met her at one of those pageant things, coronation. I think it was our sophomore year. And I remember, I was sitting behind her. And when she turned around, I thought she was stunning. So, I said, "You know, did you not consider getting in this race for the queen?" And she said, "Oh, no." [Laughter] She said, "Oh, no, no, no, no." She said, "You know, in many ways, this is a meat market." And I said, "Oh, yeah, I think I agree with you." So, we started talking and we became friends. And at this point though, I didn't have the same kind of attraction for her as I had had for Sherry. [. . .] So, by this time, I'm living off campus in my own apartment. Sandy now has moved to California, but we keep in touch by letter. And so, she's writing me about, "Oh, California is so different than being in the East. And especially being in Buffalo. And it's just so different. And people are into all kinds of different things." And so, I said, "Oh, well, I got to come for a visit, it sounds to me." She said, "Oh, yeah, you should come for a visit this summer, come out and visit me. I'm staying here." So, by this time, she had moved to—I think she was in Huntington Beach and she was going to start school. She was getting back in school at UC Irvine, I believe. So, I said, "Oh, cool." I was coming out there. So, we're writing back and forth. [. . .]

So, I get a letter in, I want to say April of '78, from Sandy. And she's talking about all the crazy stuff that's being going on. She said, "Oh, I met this person, met this person. It comes to my mind that one thing I've always wanted to do was make love to another woman." I had to put the letter down. I just said, "Oh, I can't read this right now." [Laughter] So I put the letter down, because I'm thinking, you're not really processing it, but you're think-ing, it's almost like somebody had a key. And all your life, you walked past this door, and you walked past this door, and you walked past this door. And you've seen this door and you've seen this door. And you walk past this door. And you don't go in this door; you just keep walking past this door. And it's like somebody gave you a key and said, "We're going to open this door." And that's exactly what this letter did; it actually opened the door. I remember I put the letter down. And then maybe another day passed and I came back and I read it to the end. And then the next sentence, it was something like, "Oh, I'm not saying I'm lesbian or anything like that. I'm just simply saying it seems like men seem to get such pleasure in making love." And I was thinking, "Hmm, I want to try this myself." So again, I put the letter back down. But every couple of days before I actually wrote her back, I would pick up this letter and I'd read this letter. So, I wrote back and I made it sound very sort of . . . "Oh, how you been doing out there? So-and-so and so-and-so. I got your letter. And yeah, and I see you've been having a good old time. And when you going to apply for classes?" [. . .] So it's almost like, not a specific, but just a casual segue into "Oh, by the way," so I said, "Well, you know, I've thought about that, too." I've never had a complete thought about that. That's always just been, again, that's just been in this door, sitting back behind this door. I ain't never touched it behind this door, this door has just been sitting back there. So, I send the letter off. And so, she may have called—either I called her or she called me. She said, "Well, you going to actually try to come out?" I said, "Yeah, I'm going to definitely try to come out." I wanted to see what this whole thing about one woman making love to another was headed. Now, I would be lying if I said I went with the notion that that would not happen unless it just did. I was thinking, "Hmm."

You're going make it happen.

[Laughter] Again, this door, she gave me the key, I opened the door, I gotta go in. [Laughter] I gotta go in. So, I get there. And she said, "Well, let's go get a Fatburger," which is this famous, gigantic burger they have there in LA. So, at the time, she was living in Huntington Beach. And so, [we] get up the next day and we did all the stuff that you do when [it's] your first time in a place. You look at this, and you take me around to this, and go to the beach, and all this fun kind of stuff. [. . .] So, one thing led to another. And so, when she said something about, "So I saw you were interested what I mentioned in my letter about, you know, having sex with another woman." So, I said, "Well, you know, I had thought about that. I mean something you might think about." Again, I didn't put no name on it yet, [. . .] there's no name on it. But I do remember her saying something to the effect of, "Oh, I don't think I'm lesbian. I just find it interesting. And I always noticed how men seem to get so excited when they're making love. And I just want to see what—." I said, "Oh, oh, really." Now, I did not say that I'd never had sex with a male. I think she knew this because we were relatively close. So, I couldn't come back and say, "Oh, yeah, me, too." [Laughter] I can't say that because I'd never had this experience. So, I said, "Oh," I said, "Okay. Well, that seems like that would be interesting." So, like I said, one thing led to another. I know what happened. We talked about it at the dinner table and we finished that. And I think we may have watched something on TV or—so I said, "I'm going to go take a shower." So, she's left there with her wine or whatever. So, I go take a shower. And so, I'm just taking a shower. Next thing I know, she's there, said, "You mind if I join you?" So . . . I said, "Okay. This is different." [Laughter] So, of course, my heart is going twenty-five thousand miles, I said something about that. I said I wonder if she could hear that my heart is about to beat out of my chest, because talk about nervous. So, and I told her, "Well, I've never done this before." She said, "Oh, you'll know what to do." "Really?" I said, "I don't get a blueprint? I get no map? What about the directions?" Like, do this first, and do this second kind of thing. So, of course, no you don't.

You don't get directions. And you do know what to do. But the mistake I made . . . for her it's just sex. For me, it's oh, my goodness. Because of course, I had never been in a real romantic situation, even with my little boyfriend next door, that was more [than] just, you know, we'd go to the movies, this kind of thing. Nothing anywhere near close to this. But what it did show me immediately was that, "A-ha, so I see." It's almost that thing where you can't figure out why. "Okay, all my friends are running to do this and they're doing this. Why don't I seem to have an interest?" The way I would explain it to people is that, "No, I don't have time for that." [. . .] So now, I can actually put a name on it for me. The problem that occurred was that I also tried to put a name on it for Sandy. And for Sandy, it was merely just fun and games. And this is an experiment. For me, it was much more than an experiment. So unfortunately, I made the thing sort of falling more—for me, it was much more about just a feeling than it was just sex. It was all the other stuff.

. . . .

Joy

I could have listened to Joy tell stories all day. She has a contagious laugh and a personality that lives up to her name. Joy was born in 1966 in Houston, Texas, the fifth of seven children. She served in the Army, where she was a member of the basketball team. The interview took place at her home on September 9, 2013, in Dallas, Texas.

I just liked playing sports. And when they were saying, "Oh, that bulldag-ger or that dyke" . . . those were fighting words for me. And I had a boyfriend and everything in school. My senior year, Michelle Harris was a student teacher for my history class. Nice-looking black woman and stuff . . . it was something about her—she dressed real nice and all that stuff, and there was just something about her. I would be like, "She's really nice looking." [. . .] And I would look at her in class. [Laughter] But I never acted on it. So [. . .] she started coming to my track meets. She was married and everything, but she took a liking to me, and so she started coming to my track meets and my basketball games. On Saturdays, she would come and get me and we would hang out and all this stuff. And come to find out, her sister was two years older than me but played at Eisenhower High School, which was in our district, and I remembered . . . she told me who her sister was. So we started hanging out, me and her sister.

[. . .] Around prom time me and my boyfriend go to the prom and we go to Galveston and we hanging out and we laying in the bed, and I was like,

"I miss her." And I'm like, "Girl, you crazy! You know, you thinking about another woman!" [. . .] I had never approached her, we had never . . . it was nothing. We would just hang out and go play basketball, go play volleyball, you know, just hang out, she would introduce me to her friends. And after I graduated we still hung out and everything, and it was like we played in a basketball tournament and I was real sore. And she was like, "Well, you can stay all night over at my house." This was the sister, not the teacher. [. . .] And one thing led to the other and I just turned over and we started kissing and all this stuff. [. . .]

So how did you get the—oh, the gumption [laughter] to make the first move?

Well, it was because . . . she told me that she wanted to massage me. She was like, "You sore? Take your shirt off," you know, so she's on my back and rubbing and all this stuff. And I'm starting to, you know, move and she said, "Flip over." So she's laying on top of me. So I felt like it was that connection by then.

. . . .

Laurinda [b. 1959, Memphis, Tennessee]

When I got to college I put an ad in the paper—in the city paper. And it was responded to, but the girls who responded was hideous, absolutely hideous. And I was terrified. I was like, this is not the way you do this. Then I went home one summer and this girl I had gone to high school with, she was very suave, very confident, I kind of figured she might be [gay]. It turned out that she was going through stuff, whatever; we had a moment. I thought it was repulsive because it was like, all we did was kiss and touch, that's it. She was new to it as well. [. . .] I'll never forget; it was Luther Vandross playing on the stereo, and I had to go to church the next day. And she said she was going to take me to church. After it happened that night, we didn't talk the whole next day other than she told me where to go to get to the church. So, we got back that night, and it was about the same time of night again, and I was at her house when I saw Martina Navratilova in a magazine. So, I was back in the back looking at the magazine or whatever. She has her friends all looking at porn movies. And she came back to the back. And she says, "Come look," and I said, "This is nasty. I don't do porn. That's disgusting. Nothing on that thing interests me." She said, "What does that mean?" I said, "I just don't like it. It's nasty." So, she left. By this time some more people . . . had left and we were back in the front—back in the same spot. You know the same thing happened again, but nothing. What I learned about myself was that I had never experienced an orgasm before. So, I didn't know anything about having sex. I didn't know anything about lesbian sex. I knew there was such a thing [as a] lesbian. And I knew there was a gay man. I didn't know anything about that kind of stuff other than I could kiss a girl, you know, and kissing was okay, and I still dated guys. And I knew that once I kissed her and once we had gone for that weekend, "You know what, I don't like this." And I could feel a kind of emotional pull that women go through, as lesbians . . . the dynamics of the whole thing. "I want to feel that."

. . . .

Lenore [b. 1962, Wampee, South Carolina; d. 2014]

I would go to churches, especially if I saw something that said "Women's Day." Because at the time I stopped going to church, but if I saw something that said "Women's Day," well guess what, Lenore's going to visit your church and they were in there.

This has been a common theme actually. What was it about the church that said to you, "This is where I could find other women who were same-gender loving?"

Well . . . number one, I guess there are lots of women in there with just children. Never see them with a man. I just looked at that. Lots of girlfriends go to church, and I did it kind of I guess to be—it was somewhat of a rebellion. You know, you tell me that Jesus doesn't like me, but I want to go there and I want to stir up the pot. Maybe I tried to piss the Lord off. I don't know. I don't know.

And so, when you go to these programs, how would you like literally meet women?

They would meet me. They would come after me. You know sometimes just my name. And this might sound crazy, the name "Stackhouse," it's an unusual name. If I wrote on a nametag, that's a conversation piece, and sometimes people want to talk to me just because of my name. So that was one of my experiences, and I don't know, I guess I was kind of cute, and they just want to boss me around. I find that women they used to like just want to boss me around and just tell me what to do, and I would let them.

Give me an example of how this might happen. The service is over, you're in fellowship hall, and someone just comes up to you and starts talking to you?

Okay, let me tell you, let me give you one example. I volunteered to feed the homeless one holiday, I think it was around Thanksgiving, and I met this attorney. Okay? Now, she had a daughter but she met me, and I don't know, I think my personality—I might be a little funny. I made her laugh and stuff like that, and she just wanted to make sure I didn't leave until she got my number and stuff like that. "You make sure you do this," and "You stay right here," and I would stay. She was really pretty, so I would stay and I would just do what they tell me, and they get my number and that was it.

And were some of these women married?

Mm hmm. Oh, yeah. I met one woman at work and she and her husband was having some trouble, so this one night he wasn't there. Maybe he left to go wherever he was going and I got caught in her house, had to hide in the closet and get out the neighborhood really fast, especially [because] he found out somebody was in there and it was me. So, I remember backing out that parking lot, running out the house, backing out the driveway and getting out that neighborhood. Okay? So I've been in some situations where I could've got myself hurt I guess.

The women that were coming on to you, how would you describe their presentation? Were these feminine women?

Mm hmm. Yes. Very feminine.

Was this typical?

Mm hmm. As a matter of fact, I think I love a feminine woman. That's what I love about a woman: that femininity. It's a beautiful thing.

Were some of these women what you consider church ladies?

Yes, yes. [Laughter] Yes, Patrick. They were church women. [Laughter] Highfalutin.

Older? Younger?

Yes, older. Bourgeois.

Do you think that these women just want to experiment, or do you think they had experience doing this?

I think they wanted to experiment for the most part. I think they wanted to experiment. Now there's one woman. I'm going to call her "Lady X" and she's from Charleston. We ended being together for thirteen years on and off, and she just wanted me around. She loved having me around. You know, I would babysit her kid when she was out of town. She was very promiscuous, except that she ended up marrying a man and they—and they called it a commuting marriage. About five or six years into our thirteen years, she married a man. I was very hurt.

Were you in love with her?

I was. I was. I think she was the first woman that I was in love with, older woman. Yeah, as a matter of fact, she caused me to die in my scalp. It just got dry and tight. I may have lost some hair in this spot right there.

I was just down, but you know, years later you pull yourself together, but yeah. She was the reason my sorrow, so to speak, but there came a time where after that thirteen years I had to let her go because everybody wanted a piece of her. Everybody wanted to be with her. And ultimately, she chose to be with that man, and it was hard.

. . . .

Melanie [b. 1976, Mobile, Alabama]
It felt like fireworks. It felt like my body was just a bunch of just nerves. It . . . wasn't even about having actual sex, just the touch, the kiss, the being close. It was electrifying. So, I mean, you go from [sex] where nothing in your body is on fire, like this is okay; well, I'll do this. Then you go to I crave this, I think about this, I think about you and not just you, I think about other girls, too. So, it just went from I could really take or leave having any sex at all because I was more or less thinking about having sex with men to okay, I'm with women and let's just go for it, you know. I mean I had quite a few girlfriends here and there and two-timed, lied, and all those horrible terrible things that people do, but all of it was worth it, even the drama, even the craziness. Just, whatever it was, it felt right. It felt like when straight people are fighting for their relationship. "I'm fighting for you. I love you." It felt like that on a grand scale, but the difference . . . was like night and day. I was like I was, the switch was off, and then when I started getting with women, it's like the light switch came on and my whole world was just opened.

. . . .

Monika
Monika was a part of a group of women who showed up with Shannon (see chapter 3) with whom I had scheduled an interview. She volunteered to be a part of the book after listening to my interview with Shannon. She was born in 1979 in Birmingham, Alabama. The interview took place on October 13, 2013, in Birmingham.

My first experience was with the same girl that I said moved to North Carolina. When she came back, me and her hung out all the time. And then one night in particular, we had went to the movies. And I drove my step-dad's car, so we went to the movies. So, we were just sitting there, talking and talking. And that Keith Sweat song, "Nobody," came on. That [. . .] was her favorite little song or whatever. [. . .] I was like, "Well, when this song's done, I'm gonna go." So, like when the song was getting close to the end, like she just leaned over and kissed me. And like it scared me at first because I'm like, what she doing? But then I kissed her back. So, I still was tripping about it. And so, after it was over, she got out and went in. And I sat there in the driveway for a minute, just tripping. I'm like, "I just kissed a girl," you know, like it blew my mind. So, the whole way home, I'm just like, "Wow, like I kissed a girl." And I felt some kind of way about it, I felt like I wasn't supposed to be doing it, but at the same time, it was different but it felt good. And like after that . . . it was over. Like I was ready to explore some more after that. I mean, I still talked to guys after that, but, you know, I wanted to explore that some more. [. . .]

After the little situation with the kiss, I was ready to explore. [. . .] The female who actually [this] first happened [with], she played basketball, too. So, in the summertime we used to go play basketball wherever we could play—Lawson, Montevallo—anywhere where females were playing. We used to drive to Montgomery sometimes to play basketball. Anyway, so this [woman] had told my home girl that she was feeling me or whatever. So, I'm still new to it, I'm still kind of shy, and I don't know or whatever. So anyway, we ended up talking on the phone. And so, we had went and played basketball this day, me and my home girl and her. We went to Montevallo that day. And she stayed in Montevallo. But I had drove my car and my friend drove her car. So, she went on, came on back to Birmingham, but I stayed at her house. She stayed with her mom, and they had just like a small apartment. It was like a one bedroom. Her mom had her bedroom and then like she just slept on the pullout couch. We was all watching TV. [. . .] Her mom fell asleep on the couch, so she was telling me to come on in the room. So, I'm like, "But your mom," and she was like, "Just come on." So, I go on in there with her. We were just watching TV. So, I'm sitting up there. I'm nervous, because this is something new for me. And then [her] mom in the other room. So anyway, one thing led to another. We kissed and all this. And so, she gets to like pulling my clothes down. I'm still like, "Your mom, but your mom." She was like, "Don't worry about it." So, she did her little thing. I mean [. . .] I couldn't believe it. [. . .] I don't know, it was like some crack. You know what I'm saying? I just wanted to keep on, keep on doing it. After that I had the experience with a guy. No guy had ever made me have an orgasm. That first time with a female [. . .] it just happened. Like no-brainer. So, I was hooked. I'm like, okay, I'm doing this with this guy and . . . he's getting [his] but I didn't get mine. With the female, it was like every time, every time, every time.

Nadia [b. 1983, Pensacola, Florida]

I had [my first same-sex experience] when I was eighteen. I had all those feelings throughout the years back and forth, but I didn't have any until I was eighteen with my best friend, which is almost like a typical story, you know, the closest person you were with. Me and her are still best friends to this day. It was the summer right after we graduated high school, and we were just hanging out one night. We were in Pensacola, and they have a boardwalk out there with little clubs and a little area out there. We went out there, and I had been talking to her openly for a while about it, that I kind of think I like girls. I knew I liked girls, but I was trying to play with the water a little bit and see what she thought about it. She didn't seem to care and I was like, but I was really crushing on her after a while. I was like, I think I really like my best friend. And so, after a while I got confident enough to say, "Can we just try it? Have you ever thought about it?" And like, "Just let me kiss you and see."

Had she been dating guys?

Oh yeah, dating guys. I ain't gonna call her "fast," but she was a lot then. But yeah, she dated guys all the time, and as a matter of fact, I think the conversation that really pushed it was we were talking about one of her boyfriends one time and he was saying that he wanted to do a threesome or whatever. And she was like, "I don't know any girls that would do that with me." She really was digging this guy, so she really was contemplating doing it or whatever.

But he didn't know that you—

No, he didn't know. I was thinking that was kind of my entry way to talk about it, so I kept talking about it, kept talking about it . . . and I had been talking about it for weeks and getting on her nerves so much about "We should just try and just see." So, we were on our way back. It was like one o'clock in the morning, and we were on our way back home, and there's a softball field. It's an abandoned softball field right off this beach coast area, it's called Scenic Highway. And there was this one where truckers would park there and go to sleep or whatever. And she was like, "Pull over here for a second." So, we pulled over, and she was like, "So what do you want to do?" And I was like, "What do you mean, what do I want to do?" Just totally random, didn't see it coming. And she was like, "Well, I mean, you've been asking me to do it or whatever, so let's just." And so, I was just like nervous. Oh my gosh, I was shaking so bad. I'm trying to set the mood. I had one of those little CD players on top of my car, right, the little overhead thing, so I'm reaching up trying to get it. So, I was like, okay, so I'm trying to get a CD and I remember she took her seatbelt and she reached over and I thought she was reaching over to grab a CD [. . .] and she reaches over, and she just takes my face and she kisses me. And at first I was just like, "Oh my God, did that just happen?" I had to process it for a second. And then, then I went in for a kiss after that, and we did that for a while and let the seat back, and I just took over from there. I mean it just was almost like second nature. I'd never done it, never touched another woman before, never done anything and did it that day, and after that it was a wrap for me. She, however, was like, "It was okay, it was cool, but that's not my thing." She said, "I mostly did it for you."

She didn't freak out?

No, she didn't freak out. She didn't freak out. It felt awkward for a little while. I think I made it awkward because I was feeling some crazy emotions I had never felt before, but we kind of went right back to being best friends. But yeah, that did it for me though. That was it after that. I was like, "Yeah, this is the life. No turning back."

. . . .

Tommye [b. 1952, Orange, Texas]

Now, the first time it happened that I knew what it was was when I was twenty-nine. I had a boyfriend twenty-two years older. [. . .] I was in a rehearsal for a play, and I lived in Detroit, and I lived on the sixth floor. And I got home from the rehearsal very late, and I remember this as if it were yesterday. I remember getting in the elevator and leaning up against the elevator door . . . the wall, the back. Leaning. I was truly whipped. And I heard . . . this voice says, "Hold that door." Okay? And I was on the first floor and I held the door and this woman walked in. And I remember leaning up against the thing like this [demonstrates leaning] and when I held the door, she walked in and I remember that double take. And she said, "Hi," and I said, "Hi." She said, "You live on the sixth floor, right?" And I said, "Yeah." And she says, "Oh, this is my stop." She lived on third. Her name was Betty. I went upstairs and . . . [sighs] . . . like that. [. . .] It was like after 11:00 [P.M.]. And about a half hour later, like quarter to twelve and I'm just about to get into bed, there's a knock on my door. [knocking] This is an apartment complex. And there's a knock on my door, and I said, "Who is it?" "This is Betty." And I looked and I saw it was her. And I opened the door and I said, "Yes?" And she said, "I just want you to know I saw someone trying to break into your car." I said, "Really?" And she said, "Yes." I said, "Hold on for a moment," and I closed the door and I slid on some jeans and a sweatshirt, and I ran out, and we both went downstairs, and I looked around the car and stuff like this, and she said, "I think we may have scared them off." And I said, "Thank you very much." I swear this is the truth. It sounds so bizarre, but it's the truth. And I said, "Okay." I said, "Thank you very much," went upstairs and she got off on three and I got off on six, which was the top floor.

And both of our apartments are on the front of the building, and I remember taking off my clothes and then there was a . . . [knocking] It was her again. I said, "Yes?" And she said, "Would you like some champagne?" [Laughter] [. . .] "Well, you did say if there's any way I could pay you back." It was a Friday. [. . .] She said, "Oh, come on." I said, "Okay." She came in, sat on my sofa, and we started talking. And that is the very first time at twenty-nine . . . no, I'm twenty-eight going on twenty-nine, and we talked all night long, drinking champagne. And I remember the sun because my sofa was leaning up against the window. [. . .] I can actually see Belle Isle from my window. And . . . I said, "Oh, my God, the sun is coming up." She says, "Let's go for a ride." And I'm like, "Do you know what time it is? [. . .] I have never left my house going anywhere after 11:00 at night." And she said, "It's time for change," or something like that. So, we got into the car . . . it's a new car. Got into my car. . . . [Laughter] So we go on Belle Isle, facing Canada, and we're watching the sun come up. And the music is playing and I said, "Oh, I love that song!" It was a Minnie Ripperton song. And I did something, I broke my nail, and I went, "Ah! Damn," like that. And she took my hand and she kissed my finger, and I remember sliding my hand out, and I said, "Look, Betty, I . . . I'm not . . . I'm not . . . I'm not gay." And she said, "That's okay." And I said, "I think we should go." And we left. Then we got in the elevator, it was the third floor. She didn't hit three. I hit my six first, she didn't hit three. She said, "I'll just ride up." Went to my door and when I got to my door I opened my door and I said, "Well, thank you very much." And she said, "Can I have a kiss?" I'll never forget this. She said, "Can I have a kiss?" and I said, "You're a woman." She said, "Close your eyes." And I closed my eyes and that was it. That was it. That was *it*. And she stayed. [Laughter]

And the next morning . . . well, that morning when she got up . . . when we got up and when she left . . . this is Saturday . . . I packed my bags, I grabbed my dog, and I literally drove from Detroit to New Orleans. That's how terrified I was. [. . .] And in my convertible I drove from Detroit to New Orleans and I stayed for about a week. I called in sick. I told the job that I had a family emergency. It was just too much at twenty-eight for me to wrap my head around. And I remember driving back. It was time to go, I had to go, I had to go, okay? And Ralph [her boyfriend] is constantly calling, wanting to know where I was. We weren't living together or anything. He was married, as a matter of fact. [Laughing] But he was wondering where I was and all this other kind of stuff. And I drove back, me and Star, my dog, and I'll never forget. I drove up and when I hit the elevator and I went up to my apartment and I opened up my door . . . the wall phone, the yellow wall phone in the kitchen . . . I remember standing, staring at that wall phone and saying, "Who do you call first?" And I picked up the phone and I called her. When she answered the phone, and there's no caller ID then . . . she said, "I've been waiting for you to call." She didn't even say, "Who is it? Hello?" And I said, "How'd you know it was me?" And she said, "I haven't moved from my window. I haven't moved from my window since you left." [. . .]

You have to understand something. I never wavered from that moment. And by that I mean [. . .] I knew my comfort zone. And when I say I never wavered, you know how people realize they're gay and they slowly come out or they were always gay in their minds and their hearts and so they never had to come out because they always were? I think that that is a resolve that I made on the trip back. I distinctively remember saying to myself as I was driving back, "Whoever the first one I call." And it wasn't whether or not the first one I call is Betty or Ralph, the first one I call, man or woman. You see? And the first I called was her. And I never wavered. And by that, I mean there was no hiding, there was no shame, there was no "how do I keep this from anybody." I was twenty-eight years old and I remember thinking, "For twenty-eight years I did it your way, not knowing that I was doing it your way or not knowing that I wasn't doing it my way." Put it that way. Not knowing that I wasn't doing it my way, you follow? And it wasn't until I kissed her that there was a . . . [sighs] . . . okay? I never had an orgasm with a man, even though sexually . . . I never became sexually active until I was twenty, you see. Never even fooled around, you know? Just not one of those things that was a priority to me. But my attractiveness became an albatross. And it became an albatross because I attracted so many guys, but they never saw me; they only saw my figure and they saw, you know, the face. But they never saw how talented I was, how smart I am. So, it became an albatross to the point whereby the best way to avoid it is not to put yourself in that position. [. . .] I had gotten tired of fighting guys off and so it just wasn't a thing. So, when that comfort zone with Betty came, it was like, "Oh my God. This is just so wonderful; this is so perfect. This is just so comfortable." And I remember telling my brother, one of my five brothers, and he says, "I don't understand it," told me, "I just don't understand it." And I said, "Listen, let me just put it to you this way. I see what you see. I like what you like. I love the smell of a woman. You know, I love the softness, the beauty of a woman. I love the tone of a woman. I love the passion of a woman. And if those are the things that you like about women, those are the things I like about women as well."

....

Tori

Tori is one of the youngest women I interviewed. At the time, she was a sophomore at Florida A&M University. She and her girlfriend, Lindsay, who was also interviewed for the book (see chapter 6), were planning their future together postgraduation. She was born in 1993 in Orlando, Florida. The interview took place on March 23, 2013, at the Family Tree Center, an LGBT resource center in Tallahassee, Florida.

I was fifteen and something amazing happened. Pheromones are an amazing thing. I can't even explain to you how amazing it was. But at that point I was not hitting on women, but I must have been straight-up obviously gay. I had to have been because they were hitting on me. It sounds so awful when you say it out loud; it makes me sound so arrogant.

But you would have been in ninth grade or tenth grade?

Yeah, I was young. I was in ninth grade. But there was a different girl. By then the previous girl had moved back to France. But a different girl, and she was equally amazing as everyone's equally amazing when you first start out. But she had been hinting that it was something she wanted to try.

How so?

She was mercilessly hitting on me, saying how excited she was. And she was like, "I wonder what sex feels like" and "if it's anything like how it feels when we're making out it's gonna be awesome," and just all these things and things and things, and I was scared but . . .

Did you get the sense that she had had sex with a woman before?

No. I didn't. I had the sense that she had had sex with men before but not with women. But still I feel like that's accurate. I feel like I can probably say that with confidence. But it was something of course you want to try, and we were more friends than anything else. So, you know, after talking about it, which is weird because no one talks about it beforehand, but we talked about it and I said, "Okay, you know what? Here's what we're going to do. Come over, we're going to have a sleepover, I'm gonna take care of you." And then I did. So . . . it was good times.

At the end of their interview, Bonita/Bluhe (see chapter 2) recited their poem "Pussy Juice," which reads, in part: "If eating pussy is against the law / I'm going down for the tenth round / So lock my black ass up and let all the bitches loose / Because tonight is the night for pussy juice." To say the least, I was not prepared for the graphic detail of the poem, despite them warning me that they wanted to share a poem about sex. Part of my surprise had less to do with the actual words of the poem and more to do with the fact that Bonita/Bluhe was eager to share such an explicit poem with me because I am a man—and one they had just met, to boot! As I discuss in the introduction of this book, most of the women I interviewed were not shy about talking about sex with me—even about explicit details about their own behaviors (and exploits) in bed. This was despite warnings from colleagues that these women would not be forthcoming about this aspect of their lives—I experienced just the opposite.

I was also surprised by the number of women who discussed their continual sexual attraction to men, with some of them going so far as to say that they still occasionally have sex with men, but who nonetheless still prefer sex with women. As indicated in some of the narratives above, the emotional intimacy with women during sex is what makes the difference. There are also a few women, like Wynee, who shared stories of being in sexual triangles with a male and a female partner that produced a child, or women who self-described themselves as "hos" and enjoyed sex with multiple female partners. In some cases, this disclosure was couched in a braggadocio more commonly associated with men.

Related to the issue of gender nonconformity discussed in chapter 3, many women detail how their gender presentation does not necessarily correspond with their sexual behavior. For instance, some femmes desire to be the aggressive sexual partner, while some dominants [doms] prefer to be passive. In other words, the stereotypical associations that one might confer on a "butch" woman might not actually hold once the door to the bedroom or, in one instance, the car door is closed! Indeed, these stories speak to the fluidity of sexuality and gender as expressed by these women, but also belie the narrative that women in the South are less sexual.

. . . .

Darlene Hudson [b. 1961, Las Vegas, Nevada (Fordyce, Arkansas)]
In my world gender gets checked at the door. When you come in the bedroom it's about meeting needs. It ain't no tops and bottoms. It ain't "You

get this and I got that. I can only do this." It's all about making sure each person in that relationship is pleasured, satisfied, and whatever's got to be done. Whatever my partner's pleasure is, that's my responsibility, and vice versa. And that's how I feel about that. I don't have to have it because I'm the alpha I got to be the one on top always. No, it don't have to be all that either. And I have met women who thought that's what being with me was going to be about. I said, "Oh no, honey, we check that at the door. We leave that at the door. You come in here, this is a woman's world and we do women things, on with the show." [Laughing] I guess that's about as discreet as I can get about that.

. . . .

"Lisa" [b. 1972, Detroit, Michigan (Grambling, Louisiana)]

In '99 I joined this church, [name of church]. It's interesting; [name of church] is behind [X] University. [. . .] [Name of church] was the church that all the [university] professors used to go to. But I'll never forget; I joined the church, and a couple of my sorority sisters went to church there, and they were real happy when I joined. And so, there was this one Sunday that this guy came up to me and he said, "You need to be in the youth ministry." And I was like, "Huh?" And he was real goofy, just a big, tall guy, real goofy. He was like, "You need to be in the Youth Ministry." He said, "I sit here and I watch you Sunday after Sunday; you should be in the youth ministry." My first thought was, "Why the hell you watching me?" And so, I didn't pay him any attention, you know. And so shortly after that we had a Women's Day program, and they asked me to be on the program . . . they had two services. [. . .] So, I stayed for the second service and I remember sitting in the back of the church and I felt like this lady was staring at me. I felt like this lady was just staring. She was in the choir stand; I just felt like she was staring at me. And I was like, "No, she can't be staring at me."

So, the next Wednesday or a couple weeks after that, if I remember the time frame, I was at church again; I went to youth ministry. And the guy was a youth minister, and he was also one of the associate pastors at the church. After church he introduced me to his wife. Well, it was the same lady that was staring at me in the choir stand. So, I was like, "Oh, okay, okay." And so that next Sunday she said, "You know what? I need your phone number." And so I said, "Well, [John] has all my information; get it from [John]." And, you know, just casually talking. And she's like, "Oh, okay." That following Wednesday at church she asked me for it again. She said, "You know what?" She said, "I don't have time to fool around with [John]." She said, "Girl, just give me your phone number." And so, I gave her a card and gave her my number. [. . .] And that next day she called me, and it was so funny or crazy because as we were talking—and I hadn't had a relationship with a woman in like over two years by then—we were talking she said, "You know I hope you don't take this the wrong way but I'm attracted to you." And she was like, "I don't know why, I've never been attracted to a woman before," went the whole spiel. And I remember getting off the phone with her, with [Susan], her name was [Susan]; I remember getting off the phone with [Susan] and telling my friend who worked with me . . . what had happened. And [friend's name], she was a woman preacher and her husband was a preacher and she knew about my sexuality. And, you know, she'd been trying to deliver me and everything. So, she knew . . . [laughter] they had been laying the hands over me, the whole nine yards. And so, she knew about my sexuality. And so, she said, "Lisa, you need to run." I said, "Run?" She said, "Yeah, you need to run from her." She says, "I'm telling you, you need to run." And so, I called [Larry]. I called [Larry] and I said, "[Larry], I think this lady likes me." I said, "She's married." [. . .] He said, "Resist the devil." He said, "Lisa, you gotta resist the devil and flee." I said, "Okay." Needless to say, I didn't resist, you know.

And she was married?

Yeah, she was married. She was married.

Wow, that was pretty bold.

Yes. Well [Susan] was a pretty bold woman.

And this was in church?

In church. In church.

And would you describe her as a feminine woman?

Very feminine, beautiful, oh my God, petite, very charismatic, you know, and had a voice out of this world. That woman could sing, oh my God, mm-mm-mm. She had it all. [. . .]

So, you met her somewhere?

She came to my apartment one Sunday after church.

Oh. [Laughter]

Yeah, she came to my apartment one Sunday after church, and we spent the whole day together just kind of, you know, talking, playing around. And then the next day she came back . . . because I didn't go to work that next day because I was so just kind of messed up in the head. And she came over after she got off work, and we ended up having sex. And I'll never forget [Susan] telling [me] . . . and this was so true; she said, "Once we do this we can't go back." That's what she told me. And needless to say, God, almost six years later is when we ended our relationship.

Oh wow. And she was still married?

She was still married.

Did she have children?

Yep, three kids. Three kids. Her son was in college . . . 'cause she was forty. I was twenty-seven at the time and she was forty. And she had just turned forty right before we met. [. . .] I also felt years later that I wasn't her first like she proclaimed I was.

Oh really?

'Cause she was just too good at it. You know what I mean? And [Susan] was a survivor. You know, she grew up on [X] Street in [Y city]. She was a survivor. And so, she was going to do whatever it took to survive. I just felt like I wasn't her first. [. . .] But the masquerade that we started . . . charade, rather, we had was that we were best friends, you know. So, I was always at the house and the kids loved me. You know, when he [Susan's husband] had surgery I kept the kids. I was taking dinner over there. Crazy as hell. [Laughter] You know, crazy. Need to be happy we didn't get shot, you know, really. Need to be happy we didn't get shot.

You don't think that there were other people who suspected?

I'm positive. Since I've been here one of her close friends has called me a couple of times just to kind of see how I was doing and everything. And she told me that [Susan] told her. She told me that [Susan] told her. So, I'm positive that a lot of people knew and suspected because we were just so close. I know her mom suspected.

Oh really?

Yeah, her mom suspected. And so, you know, yeah.

So, you think she was a player?

Yes, God. [Laughter] So let me tell you why. Okay? To tell you how far gone I was, [Susan] lost her job. I headed up housing for the City of [Y]. I had a secretary's position open—I hired her. It was awful. She did no work—none. She didn't do any work. But in the midst of her working for me there was this guy, a developer I was working on a project with. And I knew they were getting close, right? But I just didn't really know . . . you know, I really didn't understand how close they were getting. But I knew they were getting close. At the same time, there was this other guy that was paying her a lot of attention. So, I was like, you know, something not right. Something's going on. Well, her husband called me one day and her husband said I think [Susan]'s cheating on me. I got nervous . . .

How ironic.

Yeah. I got nervous as hell. Talking about, "Oh, shit." He said, "I really think so." He said, "I went through her phone and she has this number on her phone." And so, it turned out the number was the developer that was working with me on a project. And that was kind of the turn . . . all this happened in '04, which was leading right up to the time I was leaving. But it just kind of messed me up because I'm thinking, she don't even give a damn about me enough [that] she's trying to jeopardize my job. You know, I'm doing a deal with this guy. But then more than that—damn, she's cheating on me *and* her husband! You know? [Laughter] She's cheating on both of us. And so shortly after that she got a job at the post office, which was great. So, she ended up working at the post office at the center where they do all the mail distribution. And there was a supervisor there, which the supervisor was a white woman, [June], and her and [June] are friends to this day. I'll never forget, [John] called me one night and he said, "I'm gonna kill her." And you know, I'm still paranoid. I'm like, "You're gonna kill her?" He said, "Yeah, I'm gonna kill her." He said, "I don't know what she doing." He said, "I don't know if it's man, woman, child, what, I don't know." So, I got real nervous now because he tells me that his son heard her tell somebody that she loved them. And I said, "Okay." I said, "Well [John], you know, I don't . . . " He said, "You know, maybe you just need to talk to her." I said, "I don't think so." He said, "Well, she's not answering my phone." And so, I said, "Well, let me call her." I called her; she didn't answer my number either; she didn't answer my call.

And so, I'm sitting outside on my patio drinking. [Laughter] I'll never forget, man, I was drinking some Grey Goose and cranberry juice, smoking a cigar because I'm thinking, you know, this shit is fucked up. And I was saying, God, if you get me out of this, [laughter] . . . you ain't gotta worry about me. Just get me out of this one. And so [Susan] ends up coming by my house. Ironically, I bought a town home maybe three blocks from where she lived, okay? And so, she came by my house and she said, "I need you to go home with me." And I was like, "What?" She said, "I need you to go home with me." I said, "What's going on?" I said, "First of all, where you been?" And she said, "Well, I was with [June]." So now I'm pissed, 'cause I'm thinking, "Okay, you're dealing with [the contractor], you're doing God knows what; now you're with [June] . . . You know, what the fuck?" And she said, "Well, I think [John]'s gonna try to hurt me, but if you go with me he won't hurt you." And I'm thinking in my mind, "*I* want to hurt you." You know? [Laugher] Because [. . .] the whole time we were together I didn't have a relationship with a woman until after she did all that stuff. I always dealt with men. But she used to get so jealous even if it was guys. I mean, she used to really act out if I was with somebody, and so it was as if she wanted me just for her—you know what I mean?—while she's doing God knows what.

So, I went home with her, and true enough [John]'s livid, the kid's livid, you know, she's fussing at her son, saying, "You started all this by telling your dad that. This is all your fault." [John] is just . . . he's such a calm-tempered person. I had never seen him like that before. And I ended up spending the night over there, sleeping at the edge of the bed, although I didn't sleep. He stayed in the kitchen the entire night in a bar seat. She was the only person that slept that whole night. Everybody else up . . . [laughter] . . . you know. She slept real good that whole night. And so, I was like, "You know what?" This was during the summer of 2004. I was like, "You know what? I gotta leave this girl alone." I said this is just not gonna work for anybody. And so, you know, [John] forgave her. They tried to keep their marriage together.

. . . .

"Louise" [b. 1944, Durham, North Carolina]

I married a guy that I met in college. I liked him a lot. Very, very nice man. [. . .] He was from Alabama, had pretty much not been anywhere outside of Alabama. And I probably, in all honesty, should not have married him. Not because I was aware that I was gay, but because I didn't want to get married. And we had gone through the whole marriage thing. We were supposed to get married the year before, and I didn't want to get married, and we didn't. And then we had a tragedy in my family, and he was there. And he's just a wonderful, wonderful man. And when he asked me to marry him this time, I said okay. The first woman that I was involved with [. . .] I met [. . .] through him, as a matter of fact.

Oh, the story gets interesting. [Laughter]

Yeah, I met her through him. [. . .] He and her husband were good friends. My ex-husband was an educator, but he had a part-time job, and he met this guy who was a pharmacist. And they hit it off, and we got together, and the four of us would together. [. . .] I met this woman. It was just unbelievable. Whew. Yeah, it really was very, very intense. I thought this for a long, long time. And he asked me once at some point, he said, "Let's go over," and I said, "No, I don't want to. I have to do something." And he said, "Now, they . . . come over here and we don't go over there." So we ended up going over, and I don't know how anybody could have been in that room and not seen whatever it was that was that was going . . . I'm serious. It was that intense.

So, there was this sexual tension between the two of you.

Yes, yes.

And both of you felt it?

Yes. Yes. Yes, yes, so . . . long story short, at some point I think that I was being indiscrete and I was on the telephone with her, and he picked it up and he heard it. And we had the talk, and we agreed that we were not going to stay together. And [. . .] eventually it became very, very amicable and we separated and got a divorce.

Did the other woman tell her husband, or did your husband tell him?

I don't know, because they stayed together.

Oh, really?

Oh yeah. They stayed together and eventually, you know, candles burn out. Eventually, that kind of intensity subsided. And as we got to know each other. [. . .] We were involved with each other for three or four years, I would say, and then after that maintained a friendship.

But she never said anything to her husband?

I don't know specifically that she did because she never told me that she did.

Mmm-hmm. And you never asked.

And I never asked her. And he never changed his behavior towards me because I continued to see her and him together, you know. And he would periodically call, and we had a nice relationship. It was interesting. It was very interesting.

But your ex-husband stayed in the same town as well, or did he leave?

What happened is I left the marriage, he stayed in our home for a while and then eventually rented it, and I left the state. We were in another state, so I eventually came here and he remained there.

. . . .

Michelle [b. 1965, Winston-Salem, North Carolina]

I was thirteen. Junior high school. I liked this girl. I was in love with this girl. And I used to spend the night over at her house, and she would kiss me periodically, let me kiss her, but she really wasn't gay. I think she was just curious, just a little bit. But I really didn't know too much to do at thirteen. I just didn't know. But I knew every now and then she would kiss me. So, I guess to have *sex* sex with a woman, that was my first encounter with really kissing a woman, that little girl. The first *intimate* intimate thing, where we done knocked boobs and got busy . . . I was in college. [. . .] I knew that I was gay. I hadn't really totally come out of the closet yet, but I knew that

I was gay. Everybody else didn't totally know I was gay. And with me being in the band, you got the flaggers, you got the cheerleaders. And so I liked them and hang around and did all kinds of things. But this one girl . . . I said all that to say, the next year we called them fresh meat. It's fresh meat coming in. Well, I honed in on one from Charlotte, and she, needless to say, was kind of my first girlfriend. And she was young, I was young, too. And that probably lasted a semester or something like that . . . and I think it was just an experience for her because she turned around and started having sex with guys in the band. I'd find condoms over at my house and I'd blame my sorors. "You dirty niggers, if y'all gonna do something in here, y'all at least can clean up your mess." And they were like, "It ain't ours." So, I trusted her and that had to be my first experience. I ain't know what I was doing. [. . .] Y'all call it "having fellatio." We just called it "eating pussy." [Laughter]

[. . .] So, what I began to do was I began to become a little light ho. See, the apple don't fall far from the tree, my dad was a good ho. I was a good old ho, too. And . . . it was customary for butches to get notches in their belts, and that's what I did. Because, like I told you, I had dropped down to 175 [pounds] in the eighties, rocking the asymmetrical bob. I was kind of hot, you know. And I was charming. [. . .] And if I couldn't get you . . . if I could get your attention and captivate you, I had you. It was a game. It's just like niggers, just like men, it was a game.

* * *

When I realized I was gay and I knew that I was the butch . . . I'm butch, I'm more butch, as we call it, butch or . . . my countenance was male. It was the male and I could only mimic what I had seen the male do. So that's what I did. So, I didn't want to be made to feel feminine in any kind of way. "Don't touch my breasts. You definitely don't touch my," um . . . can I use regular words?

Mmm-hmm.

"You definitely don't touch my coochie," you know. Don't do that. No, no, no, no, no. Because I'm the dominant one.

I see.

You know. It was always about a strap-on. [. . .] I'm young, I don't know any better. And so, I held up that for some years. Even to this day, depending on where I go in Greensboro, they know me as Mikey. I'm still Mikey to some people.

That was your nickname?

That's what they called me.

Your pet name, Mikey.

Mikey. Mikey likes it, he'll eat anything.

* * *

But even in my world now, and like I say I'm going through phases. I started off real . . . about to wear BVDs stud or butch. You know what I'm saying? Really. Now, I wear panties. [Laughter] Beat my face. Finally done put on mascara, honey. My sorors taught me how to beat a face, baby. I wear eyeliner because what I understood [. . .] back in the eighties, it was hard to get a job with all this carrying on. It was very much still discrimination, whether it be race, whether it be gender identifying, or all kinds of stuff. I'm saying, it was still racist . . . it's racism. And I knew it was hard to get a job, so what I had to do was tone things down. And then in relationships I began to get women that challenged me, that were femme women, but they had desires, too. So now what do you want to do with your good, good self? [Laughter] Either you're going to supply their need or somebody will. So, there was some stretching and growing through the course of these years.

. . . .

Nancy [b. 1950, Maxton, North Carolina]

My first identity is African American. It's an ethnic cultural identity. My second identity is a woman and my third is a scholar or teacher. My fourth one is my sexuality. All this stuff is layered.

Even as a fourth category, do you . . . but do you put a name on it?

I don't want to tell people I'm bisexual so I'll just say I'm a lesbian. People see bisexual . . . straight people see bisexual people as greedy. And gay people see bisexual people as not really knowing what they are or who they are. So, I mean how many fucking layers of fighting are you going to do? You come out in your own community and you hear, "How'd you get your daughter?" Fucking married her father, had her, loved him, bum died early when she was a little girl. That was real. That was not me trying to play straight. That's the only man I ever truly, truly trusted. We started dating off and on in high school. But we would get in an argument about something and I would say, "Fuck you. I don't need you, nigger," you know. I didn't say that but I was thinking that. Even then I wouldn't say that word. But eventually we did settle down and make a family. But even before that I knew, as I told you, by the time I reached my early twenties and in New York, I'm beginning to realize what it is that's inside of me, why I'm attracted.

Then it was in New York that I had my first real love affair, and it started when I was in Africa.

Talk about that.

On a student exchange for the summer. There was Mildred, and I lived in the West Village and she lived in the East Village. We used to go to a college in Staten Island, so we would end up on the ferry going from Lower Manhattan over to Staten Island. Sometimes we would talk. It was something about the way she would look at me that would just unnerve me. Do you understand me?! That girl made me want to sweat, scream, holler, whatever. While it put me un-at-ease with it at a certain level, I wanted it. She said, "Fairley, are you going to Ghana?" I said, "Yeah." She said, "Your friend Nina is still waiting to ask her husband. Are you asking your boyfriend?" I said, "Are you stupid? I'm not asking a fucking man if I can go someplace." I told them, "I'm going to Africa. I'm trying to raise this money. I hope you can give me some." He was like, "Oh shit, that's great." I'm an adult. I'm not asking nobody if I can do something. Of course, I would if I had to with my parents, but you know what I mean. So, she started laughing and she said, "Shit you're a woman." I said, "Yeah, I'm grown." Nina and I were close friends, but Nina was obviously a straight woman who had a crush on me. I had to figure out what that was, but I didn't want to get tangled up in that. So, I was always standoffish with Nina. But sometimes we would double date. Nina married very young. She did the traditional thing, but she was going to college. So, when we got to Africa, I think I was Nina's roommate and Monica was Mildred's roommate. We started talking on the bus about life and everything, and she said, "I'm really bisexual." I said, "You are?" And she said, "Yes, right now I'm dating a guy, but if the right woman came along I'd date her." She said, "What about you?" I said, "I'm probably the same way." Everything that I had been feeling about her but trying to keep it at a distance just blew up because I'm in the homeland, the motherland. Everything was ten times more intense. That was the first place I made love with a woman: in a dormitory at the University of Ghana.

How was that different from your sexual experiences with a man?

I've always been very clear about something. If there is no effort to give me pleasure, then this isn't a relationship. This isn't happening. You've got two chances. If you isn't rockin' it by the second chance, I'm not going to be intimate with you. You can't just dump in me. This is lovemaking. Maybe you're fucking, but I'm making love. [. . .] But the intensity of the feeling of making love with a woman was so different. The intensity of it was three or four times what it was like to make love with a guy. So a guy can please me, but it is different with a woman, more intense. My body is more electrified. I sort of lose myself in the moment, where I am a little more conscious of myself making love with a man.

. . . .

Pat Hussain [b. 1950, Atlanta, Georgia]

When I don't understand something, or want to know something, I went to the library and I read a book called *A Bisexual Option* and I thought, "Hmm." I still had not reached a point where I could acknowledge or recognize my feelings. [. . .] So, I decided after doing my research, reading my book. I thought, "Well, there's only one way to find out." And I figured I'd go to a gay bar, and I selected Numbers on Cheshire Bridge, and I started going, and I loved it finally. [. . .] Numbers was just a sleazy bar. Oh, it was fabulous! [Laughter] I went to Numbers, parked, and hopped out to go see what's shaking in here. I never made it in the door. I started sweating, my hands were shaking, I got nauseous, lightheaded. I went back to my truck and tried to calm myself down. "What's the matter with you? Relax. Breathe. Breathe." [. . .] So I had approached it from an academic [approach]; I went to the library. Then I decided to go into the field and I went to Numbers. However, I couldn't continue my research because I couldn't get inside. All the emotion that had been squelched and stuffed by me for so long that I couldn't get in, and [. . .] my brother said, "Well, you might not want to tell Geri [his wife] about that because her husband left her for another man. You might not want to discuss it with her, just kind of keep it between us, Sis." And heeding my brother's warnings, I went and told her everything except that I wasn't going to Numbers. I told her I was trying to find out and I left one Friday, went, and usually I'd spend hours going through the cycle. I might be gone three or four hours and just driving. And I'd always [hear], "How was the club?" I'd say, "Oh it's fine." "Did you meet anybody?" "Nah, I didn't meet anybody." That night I went back and tried to get in once. Nothing different. Back in the truck. When I could drive I just came home. I came in the house and she said, "You're back awful early." I said, "Oh yeah, there wasn't much going on." She said, "Did you even go in?" I said, "Yeah." She said, "What's going on?" And I told her what's been going on all those months. She got her purse, she got her keys, she said, "Let's go." She followed me to Numbers.

Your sister-in-law. Wow.

She got out of her car and got to my truck, got me out, took me by the hand, and we walked into Numbers. We went to the bar. We had a drink. She said, "Are you alright now?" I said, "Yes." She said, "Well, good night." [Laughter] That was it.

And did you meet somebody that night?

It wasn't that night, but it was soon. When I'm saying my truck, I had a van. I had an F-150 van, and I met me a woman on the dance floor, and she whispered in my ear and kissed me, and my hair stood up all over my body. A first in my life. Girl, we went out to my van, and I knew then I was not bisexual. That door had closed. I never was in the closet. I was so relieved to know that I was alive, that I could feel, so incredibly relieved. I hadn't been in a place that was . . . I hadn't been in a gay bar. I hadn't been around my folk like that. And I was partying down, back. I was immersing myself in women. I was just like the kid in the candy store running wild, but I was alive and I never had a thought of going in the closet because I wouldn't trade what I was feeling and the aliveness and feeling the blood flowing through my veins for anything in the world.

. . . .

Sonja

I interviewed Sonja and her then partner, Felicia, on the same date.
Sonja was born in Troy, Alabama. in 1973, the youngest of six children.
Troy is located in southwest Alabama, just south of Montgomery. It
has a population of eighteen thousand, 40 percent of whom are African
American. It is the home of Troy University. The interview took place on
October 14, 2013, in Lithonia, Georgia.

My sexual intimacy with a man was very short. I had an orgasm and that was it. I didn't want to cuddle, coddle—anything like that. And I wanted it to be really, really quick. I wanted to get it. I didn't necessarily care about you getting yours. So that was it.

And so why bother?

Because you need that sexual release. I had to have that sexual release.

And with your female partners it was different?

Yeah, it was a lot more intimate.

Emotionally or just physically?

Both. Both. I want to take my time getting to know you in the bed. I want to take the time to know what it is that you like because I've never just had sex with one person, and we just had sex that one time. So I knew

I was going to see you again, so I wanted to make sure that things were right between us.

* * *

There's two women I don't want to date. I don't want to date someone who is ultrafeminine because I don't like high maintenance and I like for someone to look—I like for you to be able to change out. I want you to wear tennis shoes with me. We may wear some heels together, but I just don't like you to be extra—I don't like all the extra. And I don't like it if you're too masculine. And one of the reasons especially I don't like you if you're too masculine because I can't be dealing with strap-ons all the time. And [. . .] if you're ultraeffeminate, what I've heard, I can't be dealing with strap-ons all the time, either. I'm not about to put on strap-ons all the time, and I'm not about to be given a strap-on all the time.

. . . .

Tori [b. 1993, Orlando, Florida]
I identify as pansexual. I think I theoretically could have a physical attraction to a man. It hasn't happened yet, but I feel like it could only because I know for a fact I'm capable of forming romantic attachments to men. I have in the past been very close with them, and I feel like if I met a man and there was such a strong romantic attraction that I could kind of close my eyes and get it over with. But that hasn't happened. I don't think that's going to happen. I'm very happy with who I'm with. But I feel like it's possible. I feel like that that part of me is in there somewhere and it could be switched on, but it's definitely off right now. I have a very strong physical preference for women.

. . . .

Sharita [b. 1979, Washington, DC]
Sometimes the dom [dominant] female is more like the giver and not the big receiver. [. . .] And there's times where you might get in the room and she's just as feminine as the other girl. So you don't know. In my case I probably would think that I would probably take on more of the masculine role. And I like to be satisfied. I'm not a "touch-me-not" by far. But I get a lot of pleasure out of pleasing. Like that's one of my biggest turn-ons. If I know that I've satisfied you, that definitely turns me on. And probably if I get to that place you probably could do just about anything, I'd probably be a little—you know, once I get there [. . .] that makes me feel good. That's where

a lot of my excitement comes from, you know. The moaning and all that of the feminine female.

....

Wynee [b. 1962, Jackson, Mississippi]

I had already met this person at the hospital, and I didn't know she was married, and we just kind of sneaked around the hospital, a little kissing here, a little kissing there, and we'd go out to smoke together or whatever, but it never came up that she was married. And she invited me to her house one day for dinner, and she introduced me to her husband. What a shocker. We got along well.

You and the husband?

Yeah, we did. And sitting there eating dinner, Pauline [her ex-girlfriend] calls and she said, "While you're sitting down eating dinner with Wynee and enjoy[ing] yourself, I'm just calling to tell you she's fucking your wife."

How did she know?

I don't know how she knew. To this day I don't know how she knew. So, he hung up the phone, and she said, "Well, who was on the phone?" He said, "It was just Pauline." And so she said, "What'd she say?" "Oh, she just said while I'm just sitting here smiling at Wynee that y'all are fucking." Lost my appetite immediately and was ready to go home but—

And he just said it like that calm?

Just like that. Hung the phone up and wasn't going to say a thing. She said, "Who's that?" "It's Pauline." "Pauline who?" "Wynee's friend." "Well, what did she say?" She said, "While we're down here grinning and eating dinner and everything that Wynee's fucking my wife." They kept eating. I couldn't eat another bite. I was nervous. I was real nervous. I didn't know what was going to happen, you know. Nothing did. They wanted to watch a movie after dinner. Nothing else was said about that. So they asked to visit more often, and he'd be just as excited as she was. So, we all formed a friendship. We'd sit down, smoke weed, drink tequila, and everybody was happy-go-lucky. I knew his family. His brothers would come to visit. I was just a friend. Our relationship [. . .] eventually dwindled out or fizzed out or whatever, but a few years later I went to see her at the hospital. I started experimenting with drugs a little bit, whatever, so I went to see her. And she said, "Where you living?" And she said, "Oh, you mean you have an address that I can come to." I said, "Yeah." I hadn't been with Pauline in a little while, and so she started to visit, and the relationship got stronger. And eventually I had a roommate or whatever that was cheaper, so she'd, well, come on over to the house. So we had a little bachelor's pad there, you know, but I was most interested in Mariska. And when I got there, she was doing drugs, so because I had experienced it, it wasn't hard for me to start experiencing more or whatever.

So, this was more than just weed?

Right, it was cocaine.

Coke.

Yes. And her name was Mariska, and she came by, and she caught me doing it, and she said, "Let's take a ride." So, I did and she said that "I've gone through this; my husband's gone through this. I went through rehab, and I don't do this anymore, and I told him just as I'm going to tell you: I can't have you and you have cocaine." I stopped, abruptly. Even though this woman was married, I was in love with her. And she said, "As a matter of fact, I'm getting you out of this atmosphere to make sure." "Why you going to do that?" "Because you're moving in with me and Ed." "Okay." They had a spare room, so I moved to that room. Him and his brothers went back and got my furniture and brought it and set it up in that room, and that's where I lived. Half the time Mariska was in my room and half the time she was in her room until it got to a point that she didn't want to go back to that room. And then the issue came up that we wanted a baby.

We who?

[Laughter] Mariska and I. [. . .]

Did she and her husband already have children?

No. She could not have kids.

And was it your understanding that he actually knew that the two of you were [having sex]?

Well, when you're sleeping in the other room all the time, he's sleeping there by his self, he knew.

Did they have an understanding?

Obviously, because he said, "Can I watch y'all?" What straight man don't want to watch? "Yeah, you can watch, but you can't touch me." He watched. He said, "Teach me how to do that." Why would a skillful person as myself teach another person my trade? "Naw, you gotta learn on your own." And she said, "No, up until now you said it upset your stomach. Why you want to learn now? Because I told you if you wouldn't I was going to find somebody that would, and I did." And he was like, "Well, I guess you did then." I mean, that's just how calm they were. I mean their relationship was [. . .] pretty open. Maybe he went out and did things on his own. You know, I don't know, but and he was, he was quite a bit older than she was or whatever. And one night [he] told me, "Well, I don't care about y'all fucking, you know." And that was his words: "Because she loves me. You guys are just fucking."

That's what he thought?

Yeah. I said, "Yeah." So then we sat down and we wanted a baby. So we discussed that and we discussed it with him. He had a good job. He worked for the railroad. I knew that my baby would be taken care of. It wasn't going to be not just anybody up off the street because even though we were her parents, she was going to want to know who her dad was at one point in her life. So, it had to be somebody that I knew and could put my hands on at any given time. So, the three of us sat down over some joints and tequila and discussed it. Well, he was all for having a baby. I think he was more or less more excited about getting with me, you know, but I was smart. We weren't doing this in vain because it wasn't something that I liked. Ovulation tests, peeing on those little sticks for a sign. "Alright c'mon, tonight's the night, tonight's the night!" You know. So, we got loaded and we had a threesome. I got pregnant.

How long did it take?

That time. We didn't know it so we tried the next night or whatever, and I was pregnant. A couple months or maybe six or eight, maybe six weeks we're sitting down after work because Mariska always did exercise or whatever. So I was sitting in the room changing clothes and I was like, "I could start do[ing] exercise with you because my sides are getting pudgy." And she said, "You might be pregnant." I said, "Oh surely not, you know, surely not." We had already bought the home pregnancy test or whatever. "C'mon do one, c'mon do one. Let's just see." Well, these were the old-fashioned ones. You had to pee on the stick or whatever and pour the solution on it. Okay, the stick turned pink before I poured the solution on it. I said, "What do you think? Are they defective?" And we would have to get some more because these are turning pink way too quick. And then she said, "No, no, no, we're just going to wait until the morning because you can really tell then. You get that fresh morning pee." I'm thinking pee is pee. Either you are or you're not, so of course wait until morning and the same thing happened. As soon as I dipped it in the pee it was pink and it gave a positive pregnancy test. I went into work and everything. I knew all the girls that worked in the lab, all the girls everywhere, but anyway, nobody was there that night that worked. They was all off for some reason or another, so I went to the emergency room. I knew them too. So, I need somebody to draw my blood; I need a pregnancy test. They said okay, and so they did. They told me to come back in an hour and when I went back in an hour I was like, "Well?" "Go to Room 8."

Room 8, that means the doctor's coming in. And he did and he said, "You are pregnant, and you need to go on and start seeing you a doctor so he can put you on prenatal vitamins," and things of this nature.

So, I called home to confirm that the test was right, and then we had it. We had a little girl. Well, after that it was about time for him to leave. We getting about tired of him. So, she went in and put in for a divorce and he was served, and he came home and he said, "Well, I didn't want a divorce." "Well, we just think it's the best thing because we're going to raise this baby and we going to buy us a house." He just so backwooded. They're not going to let two women buy no house. Two women got income, two women got good credit, I don't know why. So, we bought our first house and we stayed there a little while. And he stayed until finally we were so gracious in helping him find a nice apartment and giving him what he wanted out of the house and everything. And told him when we move out he could move back into the house. Actually, Mariska had been to the military and bought the house with her little GI grant or whatever. So, basically it was her house except for the fact she had a husband, but there was nothing that he could with the house without her. So, it wasn't a problem for him moving back in. That's where he is now to this day. And so, we had the baby and everything. And we had talked and I told him, "This is the baby and if you want to be in her life it's up to you. I'm never going to knock on your door and drop my baby off and tell you take your baby because of this or that. If you want a relationship it's up to you to make that relationship." And he did. They're just like this [holds to fingers close together] to this day. [. . .] Yeah, so we're one big happy family. Mariska and I were together for about seventeen years.

"A GIRL CHILD AIN'T SAFE IN A FAMILY OF MEN": SEXUAL VIOLENCE AND TRAUMA

Alice Walker published her Pulitzer Prize–winning novel, *The Color Purple*, in 1982. The novel opens in the year 1910 in rural Georgia with a series of letters addressed to God written by the fourteen-year-old protagonist, Celie, who has already been a victim of rape by her stepfather, Alphonso, by whom she bears two children. He then "gives" her to a man named Albert (aka "Mr. ____"), who also sexually and physically abuses her. The 1985 film based on the novel became a cult classic, but not without stirring controversy over Walker's depiction of black men. I remember distinctly the number of public debates and talk shows that focused primarily not on the abuse that Celie and the other women characters in the novel and film suffer at the hands of men but, rather, the "negative" depiction of black men as rapists, philanderers, and physical abusers—despite the fact that most of the male characters are transformed by the novel's and film's end.

The line that serves as the title of this section is taken from the character Sofia, who delivers it to Celie, who has advised her stepson, Harpo, to beat Sofia. Preceding this line, Sofia proclaims to Celie: "All my life I had to fight. I had to fight my daddy. I had to fight my brothers. I had to fight my cousins and uncles."[5] What I came to realize in the midst of conducting these interviews is that Walker was reflecting through her character the reality of many black southern women. Never had I felt more ashamed of being a man—despite my not having sexually abused a woman—than I did while listening to tale after tale of sexual abuse at the hands of fathers, brothers, uncles, stepfathers, cousins, and even grandfathers.

Of the seventy-nine women I interviewed, sixty-six—more than 80 percent—had experienced some form of sexual abuse (e.g., rape, molestation, fondling) at the hands of a male relative. The one exception was Laurinda from Memphis, who says that she was abused by her aunt and an older male friend of the family. This high percentage among the women I interviewed seemed anomalous until I researched the national trends about sexual abuse and discovered that one in five women will be raped during her lifetime and that 46 percent of lesbians and 75 percent of bisexual women reported sexual violence other than rape during their lifetimes.[6] Even more disturbing is the fact that many of the women I interviewed report that their mothers had knowledge of the abuse and either ignored it or blamed their daughters. And in some cases the women's parents had also been the victims of sexual abuse, and thus continued the cycle. Moreover, some of the women recount instances of taking the brunt of the abuse to protect younger siblings—sometimes to no avail.

As I suggest in the introduction to this book, many of the women relived the incidents during the interview, affecting my own reaction as a listener. This was particularly true with Diane from Spartanburg, South Carolina, who actually asked to take a break while she composed herself, and with Cherry Hussain (see chapter 9), who ended up consoling me after I broke down during her testimony. In general, however, these women are survivors, many having gone to therapy and used their stories to encourage others to speak up about their abuse. Still, the scars remain visible.

Of course, the danger here is to attribute the women's sexual orientation to them having been the victims of sexual violence. Indeed, a common myth is that women sometimes "become" lesbian because of bad (sexual) experiences with men. The women themselves are the most articulate about their abuse not being the reason that they are attracted to the same sex. While some of the narrators here confirm that they made a conscious decision to embrace their same-sex attraction, none of them believes that their same-sex desire stems from their sexual abuse. In fact, many of the women had what they describe as healthy sexual relationships with men long after their sexual abuse. Nonetheless, in more than a few of the narratives, sexual abuse as a child becomes the impetus for drug, food, and alcohol addiction, sexual promiscuity, and emotional codependency that many of these women carry with them well into their adult lives.

The narratives below are only a fraction of those I collected. But as my former colleague and rape survivor Andrea Rushing once said to me, "A little rape goes a long way."

. . . .

Almah

I was introduced to Almah by my cousin Tonia (see chapter 2), who thought she would be a good person to interview. She was correct. Almah's story of sexual abuse is both similar to and distinct from those of other women in the book in that both of her parents were victims of sex abuse and also suffered from mental illness. Almah was born on April 20, 1976, in Louisville, Kentucky. She is the youngest of three children. The interview took place on August 21, 2013, in Rockville, Maryland.

What was the nature of your father's mental illness?

He is bipolar. [And he] had moments of just being institutionalized, and it could be disruptive for us at times in those kind of flares.

Do you attribute that to his molesting you?

For a long time, I did. I needed that. And I think on some degree I still do. But one of my early girlfriends was bipolar II and I guess he's bipolar I; I really don't know. In fact, when I was growing up, we called it manic depression. But she actually chafed at the notion that that makes it "You're a predator," which I respect that. I was like, "Yeah, that's a good point." I mean, I know people say that being bipolar lowers inhibitions, so I don't know. I think it helped me as a child to do that. Now, I kind of have this vacant space in that area. Like, do I think that it contributed to it? I don't know, I don't know. [. . .] So I don't want to just say, "Oh, it was that." I don't know at this point.

And at what age did this begin?

The first incident that I remember was when I was five. But there was a picture of me growing up . . . I remember when I was a kid, people would talk about this picture. It was a picture of me that people liked to pull out because it would make me cry. [. . .] I guess it's the idea that you push a button, the child cries for some reason. And years later when I saw that picture, I think I know why I cried, because my father is holding me in a way, and I was like one year old. And his hand is in my crotch in a way that seems like it's not just about the way you're holding the baby. And so I'm uncomfortable looking at the picture now, so it makes me think that it started early, it started earlier than five. [. . .]

And continued until when?

I would say thirteen. Because I remember being a teenager and putting on makeup. Like a preteen. [. . .] The reason why five is so vivid is because I kind of went through the court system at that time. And there was a period of time I had to go to court and testify and stuff.

Against him?

Yeah.

Because you told?

I did tell.

Okay. That's an important part. [Laughter]

It is important, yes, I did tell. I did tell. And it was weird because that particular incident, which I'm in no way condoning sexual abuse, it didn't feel bad, it felt weird. It felt like, "Oh, he's asking me to do these weird things." And I remember it happening, getting out of his bed. He asked me to come to his bed on my way to see cartoons. And I went to see *Woody Wood-pecker*. It was like, it was kind of strange, and so I shared it with my mother. I'm like, "This weird thing happened." And I remember her reaction was so grim. It was so grim, but no comforting of me. Like I'm, "This is wrong." But I wasn't really clear if I had done something wrong. And so, this kind of grim machinery of telling millions of people what happened. I got so tired of it. I even told her, "I wish I had never told you," because it wasn't a big deal to me. [. . .] So, I lived with my aunt in response to this. So, the idea was I could never be alone with my father for a period of time. It feels like a long time, but it's hard to know how long it was. And I had to stay with my aunt.

But your mother stayed with your father?

Yeah. And for me, I think that actually is one of the most traumatic things. It's not what happened but consistently, I feel like she's chosen him. And there's been many more examples. Because it would be nice if this story ended here. But I came back, and it continued to happen. And I told her. And that time, she told me to—I'll never forget this. She was washing dishes and her back was turned to me. And she said, "You should talk to your father about that." Yeah. So, you know how that went over. So, I went to my father. And my father grew up in a large sharecropping family where there was a lot of work to go around, but not a lot of affection. And he definitely cast himself as a victim. And said, "You know, I"—I'll never forget what he said. He said that he was—didn't have much affection and he needed it. And that's when I thought that moment, as my mother, she was useless to me. I'm just like, "Okay, you're not on my side, I'm on my own." And so, from then on, the abuse continued and I never told anyone about it. I told her again at thirteen. And again she betrayed me and said, "You're old enough now that you can do something about it."

* * *

I read so much that I kind of think I transcended a lot of borders that way. In fact, I remember reading books that were not for me when I was younger and my parents finding out and telling me, [. . .] "If I find you reading more books like this, I'm going to give you Donald Duck books." [Laughter] And I was like at that time, twelve, so that would be an insult for me to have to go back to that. But I remember my father finally sat down and talked about the birds and bees. It was like, "Are you acting like I've never seen your dick before?" It was kind of crazy. We're going to do this performance in front of everyone? You're not telling me anything I don't know—something that I haven't read or something I haven't experienced with you. And so that was weird. It was like, you know what? Adults are just so—they're on something else. Like this fakery, you know. But my mother, I remember when my period started. [. . .] I told her about it. And she came to my room, opened the door, and put a book on the bed that was very dated. And it was white women. It was so weird. And she left. And thankfully, I had already read Judy Bloom and stuff like that. So, I knew what was happening. But my mother acted like, "Oh, my God, you're on your period? Oh, I can't deal with that." And so, there was that. But it's hard to know what's like my southern upbringing and what's the fact that both of my parents are incest survivors themselves. And they have a lot of sexual wounding that is unhealed. But, you know, both my parents come from a certain era, like my father grew up a sharecropper's son. He started working with sticks on a farm in Tennessee. And my mother [is a] rural Kentucky farm girl. And they're products of their time.

How did you find out that they were incest survivors?

My father, I found out because he said one day that he was abused by his aunts. And he wonders how it affected him. [Laughter] It's like, "Oh, wow." And that was one incident. I feel like he mentioned it at other times, but I'll never forget that, because I was like, "Oh, my suffering is invisible to you? You well have become a perpetrator." Because he also abused my sister, too. Even though my sister is not his biological child. And my mother, I found out because when I moved to college and started to get concerned that younger girls in my family might be abused by my father, I wrote her a letter and tried to talk to her about that. And she was like, "You know, Vaughn," it's what they called me at the time, "You know, I—it happened to me, too, and I got over it." Which is so not true, but I come from a family that if you go into work every day, you alright. [. . .] There's a million ways to not be okay and still be kind of a functioning member of society. So, they both told me. They both told me. She told me who her perpetrator was and he told me, too. But I don't know like which aunts did it. I don't even know the aunts in question.

. . . .

Diane [b. 1977, Spartanburg, South Carolina]

I was molested by a family member from nine to fifteen, so from nine to fifteen it was just day in, day out the same thing. It was like clockwork, you know, as far as this person. They would come in do what they need to do, then leave out.

Did you tell anyone?

[Shakes her head]

No?

I didn't tell anyone because it was actually my brother. I didn't tell anyone because of the fact that my sister and I were adopted into this family, so the first thing I was thinking if I would've said something they would've took us back. So really trying to protect my sister, not so much myself, trying to protect my sister knowing that she need the stability that we were getting, I just didn't say anything. I didn't really say anything until I was about, no, I didn't say anything until about three years ago.

Oh wow. You confronted him?

No, I told my mother, his mother, our mama. I didn't say anything to him, but I told her, and I guess for me it was, I guess I was looking for something when I told her and . . . she was like, "Okay." [She begins to weep] Stop. [Long pause] Okay, I'm back.

Take some minutes. [Long pause] Do you think you'll ever confront him?

[Shakes her head]

No? So how will you deal with that pain?

I really haven't. I think I would rather leave it where it is. I would rather leave it where it is. I just . . . it's kind of like under the carpet, and that's where I want it to stay.

You don't have a relationship with him now?

We speak. We're cordial, but other than that it's not like big brother and little sister relationship.

Does he have a family?

He has a daughter. He's not married, but he does have a daughter.

Do you think he's doing anything to her?

She's eighteen now, nineteen years old. I don't personally think he has. I don't think so. But those were my thoughts at a point in time. Like, "I'm your sister," you know, not so much as him doing anything to her. "What if someone else was doing the same thing you're doing to me to her. How would you react?" You know?

So, with being adopted, being sexually abused by your brother, that really clouded your experience as a child.

It did, but a lot of people think, a few people that know the story or know some of my history ask me was that the reason why I became a lesbian. I'm like, "No." That doesn't have anything to do with it. And at the end of the day I'm at a point in my life where, to be honest, I could care less if he live or die, and some points of time in my life I was just, like, if I get in my car and run him over would I go to jail. I mean, just being honest, I really do. Those feelings I like to keep dormant. I don't like to think about it. I don't like to bring it up. It's just for me. . . . It's like for me when I see him . . . no feelings. No nothing. It's like, "Hey bro, what's up." I'm done. Next conversation. I don't like really to be around him. He does not like my lifestyle, period. And that's fine with me. I could care less.

Did you tell him?

Tell him about my lifestyle? Yeah, he know.

From you? You told him?

He knew from me, but he knew because I would bring my girlfriends around, but he does not care for my lifestyle, period. So, he doesn't deal with me, which I mean I'm fine, I'm fine with it.

Do you think your mother has had a conversation with him?

No.

Or your father?

My father doesn't know. Not unless my mom has told him. I personally don't think he knows, and that's the way I want to keep it.

Because you're afraid of what your father might do?

What he may do or what he may say. I'm not for sure because the reaction I got from her was okay and that was it, and then I don't know per se what he would say or do, so I don't know. So right now I just want to keep it the way it is, leave it the way it is. I don't like to talk about what happened. I don't like to relive it, and I bet that's one of the reasons why I don't go to counseling. I don't like it. I'm this tough person on the outside, you know? I'm a big girl, it's whatever. I don't like to feel emotions. I don't like to feel pain, I don't like to feel hurt, I don't like to feel bad, I don't like to feel anything. That's not good. So to be the person that I am now, it's like I have an electrical fence, not a wall, mine's an electrical fence. You touch it you're going to get shocked. I don't want anything in there.

Do you think you'll ever get to a point, though, because clearly it's still affecting you, because you haven't found closure, and it sounds to me that part of the reason why you went to your mom is because you were looking for some support that you didn't get, and so now the wall's gone back up again?

Right, right, right.

So, do you think it—and maybe you don't know—at some point you'll bring it up again?

Where I am right now, I don't know. Do I need to? Of course, I do. But at the same time, it's the fact of just even getting started, for wanting to take that first step, and then that means I have to open up a whole can of my life circle. I don't have the energy to deal with it, I just don't. I don't have the strength, the energy. I just want to leave it dead, even though when I talk about it I get emotional and I'm still hurting, but it's like I want it to be dead where it is. I just want to leave it dead. I want it to stay there and bury it all [. . .].

. . . .

"Doris" [b. 1967, New Orleans, Louisiana]

The guy that lived in the double next to us, he was the one that was molesting us. I think he was molesting other kids. I was really, really young, like five, six. I was young. I was very young because I don't even think we were at Robert E. Lee [elementary school]. [. . .] Robert E. Lee would've been first grade, so, and I think he may have been molesting other people in the neighborhood.

How much older was he?

I don't know. It was a man, a big man, and he was a fat man, and he used to drink. I don't remember if I was the one that told. I remember the police coming. I remember seeing him get arrested. There's like certain little things like flashes of things that I remember from childhood. I do remember him getting arrested. I don't know if it was from that or if he was abusing because he may have been hitting; I think he was married. I think I remember there being a woman that lived next door. He may have been hitting her. So, I don't know if it was that or if it was from the abuse, but I remember him not coming back. I don't remember him coming back, so I'm thinking it might have been that the story came out that he was trying to have sex with us. I think what may have happened, because I think it may have been me, and I've never talked to my mom about it. I just decided I didn't want to bring it up, but I think he might have started to try to mess with my sister. And I think I finally came forward and I said something because I wasn't about to let what he was doing to me happen to her. And I think that's actually what happened is that I came home or I was playing with friends or whatever, and I came home and I saw her because he used to make you go underneath the house. In New Orleans the houses are raised, and so you could literally sometimes like walk underneath a house or crawl comfortably under the house, so he used to do it underneath the house. And I think I saw her coming from under there, and I asked her what she was doing and you know, I got scared. And I think she told me, and this is my recollection that she told me, and I immediately told my mom. And I think that's what happened, or I may have confronted him. I don't know. Even though this was happening to me. "Now you going too far. You can do whatever you want to me but you're not going to do it to my sister."

[. . .] I think for me the reason why I probably did not like having sex with men was probably reverting back to what happened when I was a child after the experience of dealing with this person at a early age and not liking how that was. So, I think that [. . .] thought of my first experience or whatever may have been it and that's why I don't like sex with men, really. As far as I know I don't think he penetrated me. He didn't do that, but the experience of being with him or the touching me and stuff like that . . . I can still remember that smell, the smell that he had. [. . .] When I was married to a guy he came home and had that smell, and he came near me and I started screaming. He was like, "What's wrong with you?" I said, "You need to go take a shower," whatever, because I reverted right back. And it's funny how people say like if you've had an incident happen and that smell or the touch or whatever can make you go back to that place. And it did because I smelled that and I immediately was right back there as a little child underneath the house with this person. And of course, I was not there, I was somewhere else, but that smell brought me back there.

. . . .

Felicia

Felicia was born in Mobile, Alabama, in 1970. She is her mother's only child, but she has three sisters from her father's marriage to her stepmother. Both of her parents were well educated and stressed the importance of education to her. Felicia has a regal demeanor that, ironically, is more disarming than off-putting. She lives in the suburbs of Atlanta. Like many of the women I interviewed, Felicia is an incest survivor, which resulted in a pregnancy that she terminated. Despite this unfortunate event, she wishes to have a baby that she would carry because she says it would be the first child that she planned with somebody she loves. The interview took place on October 14, 2013, at her home outside Atlanta.

When I started going to Huntsville in the summers, I very clearly remember, one time there had been this incident during the school year where I was in the choir. This little boy liked me. And I think we got caught kissing in the bushes or something, and someone called my aunt, which was my dad's sister. It was like, "Dude, I think your niece was getting it on in the bushes." And I'm like, "No, we were just kissing." We may have gone there, but you know—and so I remember him asking me had I truly, officially had sex. And I told him no, but I had. And I was thinking, "Oh my God."

How old were you?

At that time I was thirteen. But I had had sex at eleven, but that's another story . . .

With a guy.

Yes. So, for me it had been two years, but I'm thinking, "Whew, well at least they only know or think that I kissed this boy in the bushes." So, I remember my father asking me, you know, "Have you had sex?" And I was thinking, "No, I haven't." And my dad knows when I'm lying because, believe it or not, I'm a lot like him. And so, I knew I would get in trouble. See, my dad's philosophy was, you don't get in trouble for things that you do that are not stupid. But you get in trouble for doing stupid things like getting caught. If you're going to do something, at least don't get caught. So, I remember him asking me and I said no. And he said, "Well, I'm going to check and see." I didn't think anything. I'm thirteen years old, thinking, "Oh my god," because I'm thinking I'm going to be discovered. So, to check he had to physically look around. I didn't think anything of it. Well, when I came out of the room [. . .] I remember [my sister] asking me what did he do? I'm thinking, "He checked." And I'm still not thinking that nothing was wrong because I knew that she had played around with a little guy, too. So, I'm thinking maybe she's asking me because she wants to know—maybe we need to get our stories together. And I remember her being like very upset, and still I didn't get it. But it took the actual occurrence for me to put two and two together and say, you know what, he's doing this to her, too. And so, I had an option of not going every summer, but I felt like I was protecting my sister. Because he would never do anything to both of us together. He would have to isolate us. And so, I had a bedroom. She had a bedroom. But I never slept in my own bedroom. I always slept in her bedroom. So, it went on for years, and I left to go to college. I had my dream scholarship to go to Auburn.

So even through high school this was happening.

When I was going just for the summer.

But what was his excuse then? Not that he was still checking you to see if you were having sex.

No, then I knew it was wrong. Then I started to know it was wrong. And my last two years I didn't go there. I was sixteen and seventeen. I didn't go those two years because at sixteen I had gone to a program at Tuskegee University. It was a minority introduction to engineering program for up-and-coming smart people, whatever you want to call it, interested in engineering. So, I went there my eleventh grade year, and my twelfth grade year I went to a similar program at Auburn. And went to college right after that. So, I didn't have to go back. So, it was really those three years that you know I would go back and be in the line of fire during that summertime.

So, you never told your mother.

I told everyone. I was twenty-four years old.

What was her reaction?

She was very quiet. And my mom is the kind of person that doesn't get loud. You can't—you don't really know how she's feeling. [. . .] But I know her well enough to know that if she is quiet it really bothered her. And because this one of the only men I've ever seen in my life that she dated. And I know she loved him. So, I told her—well, we tried to get him arrested before that. When I went off to Auburn I was there—I felt like, "Okay, I abandoned my sister," because she was now a sitting duck. I'm not there to protect her anymore. So I confided in my track coach, and I said, "Hey listen, I have to ride with my father to go home. I don't want this to happen." You know, there are other things happening. I had gotten pregnant and you know I had to confide in someone. And so—

You were pregnant by your father?

Yes.

Did he know?

Yes. And so, I told my track coach and I fell out on the field. He just said, "I wish you would have told me, but I'm here now"—I'll be your father, basically. So, he made sure I got the abortion. He made sure I was safe. He got the resident assistant involved. He put a restraining order out there. So, he basically did everything a father would do for me in that situation. And then it sent off a wave of getting involvement back at home because those kids were still minors. So, they had to come in and take them out, remove them from the home temporarily. My stepmother left him temporarily, and he didn't try to lie. He agreed that he had problems and issues.

Oh, really?

Because it came out, and we found out that he had been a victim also, and not only him, but four of his other siblings as well. And so, he agreed to counseling and, you know, those types of things. By the time my sister was graduating she was able to leave and over time my stepmother eventually came back to him, but she was gone for a while. But to make sure that I didn't have to rely on him for anything or anybody for anything at that point, I left school after my first year, my freshman year at Auburn, and I went into the military. Because to me that was going to give me stability, money, you know the things . . . a car—things that I would need so that I would not be a sitting duck or a target. [. . .] And so, I did that and never looked back. [. . .]

And he's a minister?

He became a minister some years ago. He was not at the time.

Have you interacted with him? Has he apologized for what he has done?

He has not apologized, and that's a problem that I have. He said things to allude to an apology, but I think that I am owed an apology. I have forgiven him because it will eat me up if I don't. I mean, and I don't feel like I should behave like a book says. The book says, you know, if these things happen you act like that. Well, that's not my character. That's not those seeds that were implanted in me, so I'm not like that. My thing is that if I forgive you I can move on and have a great life, and I've had that. What I have learned is what I'm not going to tolerate, what I'm not going to do, and I'm not going to put myself in those situations. And I'll never *trust* him now. Forgive is one thing, but forgetting is another. If I ever have children, they would never be around him. He went to counseling, but I just don't think people who have true issues are never really healed. And I think if you give them or if you keep feeding them the fuel, the flame, then eventually they'll take it.

And did your mother ever have a conversation with him?

That I don't know. They have an interesting situation. I remember telling her, "Listen. I have something to tell you, you're not going to like it but it's not your fault. It's not anything that you did. You raised me well. But I just think you should know because I need to move on and do some things in my life, and I need you to understand why they're going to be the way they are." And so, when I told her, she brought up two things that I—and this is how you know that people have things going on in their head but they can't really prove it or pinpoint it. She said two things. One was when I was thirteen I burned up all the clothes that he ever sent to me. I remember that. But I burned up all the clothes, and she said, "Is that why you burned up the clothes?" I said, "Yes." And then two, she said, "So that letter I found." And she reaches over and pulls out a letter that I wrote when I was thirteen years old to my best friend, Felicia, telling her about these incidents. And she said, "Do you remember this?" I said, "Yeah, I was looking for it, I dropped it. I was going to give it to Felicia." She said, "Well, I kept it," and she said, "I've been watching and monitoring and trying to see if something was really going on, but you gave me no indication." Because I was still happy. [. . .]

The letter wasn't enough?

She never asked me. My family on that side is very secretive. They're very siloed. They're very close. But if there is something going on with me, she may not approach me unless I'm going to maybe do harm or going to jail or something like that. They just don't ask a lot of questions. It's kind of don't ask, don't tell with everything. So, I was kind of the different person in the house because I'll say anything—talk about anything. I'm very open about whatever it is. And they're not. And so, it was me introducing them to something they were probably uncomfortable with at first. But they still don't really talk like that to this day.

. . . .

Jasmine [b. 1994, Chapel Hill, North Carolina]

He was my cousin. He was five or six years older than me, and now he has a brain injury. [. . .] He works, actually, but his mind is like a third-grader mind. I don't even think he remembers doing this thing to me. I see him all the time. I'm not mad at him, mostly because I can't be mad at someone who doesn't even remember anything that he's done. And so, I don't think I was ever mad at him. [. . .] I feel so weird about how this went down.

I'm more mad at his mom; his mom is my great-aunt, and I think, she walked in on us one time and she automatically blamed me.

How old were you?

I was five or six, maybe seven. And she automatically blamed me, and she told me how disgusted she was and how if she ever seen this again she would tell everybody, she would tell my mom. So when I was that age, I felt it was my fault, and I didn't know what was going on. It had happened so many times, I got used to it happening, 'cause he was my only boy cousin 'cause he had four sisters or something. So, I got used to this happening. I thought this was a thing. You know, of course, at the back of my mind I was, like, this must be wrong, but I didn't know. And so after my aunt basically went off on me I just felt it was my fault. And for a long time, I never told anybody; I didn't tell my mom until this year.

What was her reaction?

She didn't really have a reaction, which was kinda weird. I said, my mom's known for when she—her way of digesting things is putting it away . . . and never talking about them. I know my mom has had a rough childhood herself. I don't know much, I know bits and pieces. She just moves on and moves forward. I wasn't really looking for her to be—to be, like, hugging me or be emotional and all this stuff. I just felt she needed to know. It was just something she needed to know.

Did you tell her that your aunt knew about it?

Yeah, I told her. She was mad about it. And my aunt is ridiculous. So I guess when I told my mom about it, it wasn't a surprise, because my aunt's the root of evil or something. I don't know.

· ·

Kate [b. 1981, Winston-Salem, North Carolina]

Recently I was asked in an interview about my family, and I had to say some things that I think I have been avoiding for a while. When I think of them—or when I thought of them, then when I was asked this in an interview about two months ago it was definitely pain, molestation. And just really not ever feeling like I ever even knew what a family was. I had to admit that. That I had no idea what a family was. But I was very appreciative of my friends in high school. Because I was an athlete I had an opportunity to go to different people's houses, and I always felt like I was more a part of their families than I did my own. And so recently I've been doing just a lot of praying about forgiveness because I realize that something that I heard the other day, that Iyanla Vanzant said, that holding grudges is like drinking poison hoping that someone else dies. And it really touched me because I read a lot of her books and different things and I watch her on *Oprah*. And even recently finishing *A Return to Love* by Marianne Williamson, I think I look at it differently. People are either loved or needing love, and the people in my past that did the things that they did to me, they were needing love too. And even after speaking to my brother recently I realize that the things that happened to me are generational curses to my family, if you will, because it didn't just happen to me. The person that did it to me, it also happened to him, you understand. And then when you find out that the person that did it to him was the very person that brought you in this world, it gets really deep. And so now I've learned to deal with it in a way where I pray for the love of the Creator to touch their hearts, minds, body, spirit. In the same way that I believe that I am a living example of love, I pray that one day that they will be also living examples of love, and that I bear the cross so that no one else in their lives will ever have to bear that cross again. And I'm at the point in my life now where I'm okay with that.

Have you confronted him?

I haven't. And it's weird because there is a part of me that's like, okay, I do want to confront him. [. . .] Just yesterday I was riding back from Washington, DC, and I heard on the radio, they were talking about Eckhart Tolle's new book, *A New Earth*. And it said in there there are two monks and they're walking down the street, and one monk picks up a woman and takes her across the street. The other monk says five miles down the road, "Well, what did you do that for?" And he says, "That was five miles back." [. . .] And the crazy thing about it is that he's my favorite. He happens to be my favorite uncle of both uncles. And I think that so much of things that he's even offered to help me with and it's just about him feeling bad. Would I trust my child around him? Hell no. I'm just keeping it real—and that doesn't matter even if it was eons from now. [. . .] I don't really know if there is anyone that I would really trust around my child, just to be honest. Even recently there was a situation in my family which spoke again to [the] generational curse.

But let me say this before I say that: I am glad that you asked me that, though, because I do feel like molestation and rape, I feel like not talking about it in African American families has a lot to do with generational curses that possibly stem from slavery, if you will. Because here you had a person in a position of power, whether it be the master, his son, or whatever, who would physically take something—you know, to rape or molest a person. And they couldn't talk about it. And so, the mother was like, "No," you know, "Shhh." And it's still like that today in families, and not just African

American families. But that's what I relate to because that's what I am. But I just feel like that's a generational curse. [. . .] There was another situation in my family. The interesting thing about this little girl is that her mother married the great nephew of my grandfather. So, they're not really kin because she's kin to my grandmother. [. . .] There's this little girl, her mother married a guy and he wasn't her father. And she's now fourteen and she runs away at the age of fourteen and tells her grandparents that I've been being molested since I was seven. And her mother doesn't believe it. And it was hard for me because I can't even understand why my mother was gone a lot. She's a young mom. She had me when she was sixteen. So, she was still catching up on life and having fun. You know when things happened to me she absolutely was not in the home. But it was hard for me to believe that knowing their family and how close they are that my little cousin—that her mother didn't know. Because it wasn't like my situation where it was the same person happening over seven years' time. I just had a hard time believing that her mother didn't know. Because I also think women in my family carry another generational curse: for some reason they've always wanted to put their lovers before their children. And perhaps it's because they felt like they didn't get the love that they needed or deserved, or they probably have not really even admitted to themselves that they probably don't even know what love is. And they might not even know what a family is either.

I was just told recently that those are very big things to have to admit: that you don't really know what love is or what a family is. And I say that because I've always felt like your tender loving care, the people who define that for you first are your family. And I didn't get a great definition of that. [. . .] I've had great friends who really have tried to get close to me and I wouldn't allow people to get but so close. And so, like this last year and a half of my life that really changed because I really have been working on building a deeper relationship with myself and being able to understand the God within me as well as the God outside of me. And I think it's helping me to heal through a lot of those situations. But I do think at some point I am going to sit my uncle down and we're going to talk at some point. Because I think it's healthy for the both of us to talk about it. And not necessarily talk about it like a therapist. "Oh, you did this to me." We both know it happened. And who knows? He's probably dying to apologize inside. I can only imagine what it's like to do something like that. [. . .] When I lived in New York he would always call, "If you need anything you know just call. You know if you need any money or anything like that, just let me know."

Laurinda [b. 1959, Memphis, Tennessee]

I was sexually abused by an aunt when I was somewhere in that four to six range.

Was she babysitting you?

We would go stay at their house on weekends. That was my dad's sister in Atlanta. She and my other aunt lived with my grandparents. And that feeling, you know, you're not really sure what's going on, just something is different. It happened for a while. I can't give it a time frame. But I wanted out. I never talked about it. I never said a word. Then when I was nine [I was] in that environment where we go stay with a relative after school. I was staying with my great grandmother. And she was married to this man. His name was Mr. Washington, and a dirty old, crusty man. He reminded me of a slave because he always had a nasty straw hat on, and one day I'll never forget he had on a shirt—I mean, a shirt that was burgundy on the cuffs and around the neck. Kind of like a ringer shirt. But the front was an apple, was a sliced apple. And I was shocked, the pants matched. But I was reaching in the refrigerator and I remember these hands coming over my shoulders, grabbing my breasts. And I'm like, that's different, he wasn't supposed to be doing that. At the time my great grandmother still worked, so she wasn't there. My cousin Kevin, he was like probably one of the few men that I put above any other man besides Jesus, because he was just—he's just my favorite, one of my favorite people. He was there, but I mean, how do you tell him? How do you tell somebody that Mr. Washington did this to you? So, it continued. I mean it was from one thing to the next, and eventually he started asking for stuff, requesting stuff.

One day I was sick, I had a real bad cold, and I had to stay home from school, and he was the only one there. At the time I was too young to get my own [medicine]. He was giving me my medicine. I had gone to sleep and I woke up . . . and my pants and everything, my belt was undone, pants unzipped. Okay. I don't know what happened during that period of time, but he stayed on the porch the whole day. So what do you tell, if you tell?

My grandmother, my mother's mother, had had a massive heart attack one day while I was at school. At that time they all lived like within two or three streets of each other and school was across the street. And so I'd seen the paramedics and everything, fire trucks and stuff, and I didn't know they were going to my grandmother's house. When I got home from school all my other cousins were there and they were like, "Oh, you know, you're going to have to see your grandma, she in the hospital." And I'm like, "What's going on?" So, my mother called and she said, "Your grandmama is sick." She said, "I'm going to come get you all." Like we've got to come right back up here. So, we get to the hospital, and it literally became a place where I felt like we were being held hostage. We couldn't go anywhere. And my mother being the only child, she wasn't going to leave her side. So later on that week [my grandmother] had a stroke, and they didn't expect her to make it through the week. So, it became where I knew my time was going to be spent either at the hospital or around Mr. Washington. Okay. There was no ifs, ands, or buts about it, you know.

So, she was in the hospital for a while. [. . .] You had no choice. So if you didn't go there you had to go to Big Mama's house and stay with Mr. Washington. This started when I was in fourth grade. I finally told somebody when I was in seventh grade. Seventh or eighth grade. And the only reason why I told was one day we were outside playing and I saw him watching my sister. It's like, what do you do? How do you do it? And so, I had told my cousin about it, and she said, well, he had been touching her, too. And the girl across the street said the same thing. I mean, you know, my Big Mama was notorious for telling you in a minute, "Why you lie so much?" So you knew that telling her she was going to tell you that you're lying. So, I actually told a teacher, and the teacher knew my godmother, and my godmother was good friends with my parents. And so she told my dad first, and then he didn't say a whole lot, you know. Then my mother, she called me from work. She was like, "I just got a phone call." She was real cool. She said, "But I wish I could figure out why you say that." And I'm like, "Are you serious?" And she was like, "I'm just trying to figure out why you would say that about him. He's the nicest man in the world," and this, that, and the other. At that moment a lot of what I felt for my mom went out the door. My dad talked to me about it. He was still kind of like, okay, whatever. I still had to go over to Big Mama's house. And nothing changed. He didn't get in trouble for anything. He almost died. But we're still going to visit him. I still had to go to the hospital with them to go see him. And I'll never forget, I was with my mom at the hospital and I went to his room. He saw me and I saw him and I just turned away and just sat in front of the hospital. I stopped looking because I didn't want to have to go back to where he was.

So, think I was in the twelfth grade, he got sick and he died. Well, me being the oldest of all the kids, that's who they told first, [and I] had the chore of telling everybody else. He dies on Christmas Day. So I said, "Oh, Mr. Washington died." I start laughing and went about my business.

And you could feel a sigh of relief with the girls. [. . .] So I had made up my mind I wasn't going to the funeral. But my father came in my room and he said, "Out of respect for the family you will be there today. I don't want to hear nothing." I didn't cry. I just felt like a rock all day. And I can't say I hated my parents, but I didn't feel too good about them for a while because of that. I said the minute I knew I could leave Memphis and it was okay, I was gone. I did. I went to Howard [University]. And I felt like that was a different kind of life, a different kind of free.

• •

Michelle [b. 1965, Winston-Salem, North Carolina]

They had Pink Champale, and they had another one, I don't know what it was, but the pink was mine. Went to [North Carolina] A&T [State University] for freshmen orientation. My parents were not drinkers. My dad smoked cigarettes, but they were not drug users. Drugs were not a part of our family like that, not that I knew of. So, when I got there we partied. Boy, I tell you, they turned us on to these Pink Champales, and honey, I was so drunk I don't even know how many I drank. It couldn't have been that that many. But I was so drunk I couldn't get up the next morning to go take the placement test. So, my first semester of A&T I started off in remedial courses because I couldn't go place. And so, I started off with a foot on my throat, you know. It was a big transition because I came from green Winston-Salem. I was so green. I didn't get a chance to do anything. Dad held his reins so tight, and he kept saying [that] I "need to go back because I'm missing some things," as my life began to kind of transition. I began to become really rebellious, and I was angry with my father because he's the one that initially fondled me and inappropriately touched me.

And you never told your mother?

No. How do you tell? This started . . . I would say this started about seven or eight. So how do you say that? You don't know what to say. I didn't know. Because as I said, I didn't know what to say. I know one time she walked in . . . he would always come down the hall early in the morning and he would lay in the bed with me and my sister. And he would let us touch him. Oh, I know I would touch him, and then he would have an erection. Well, I'm too young to still understand really what's going on. Well, she walked in on that one morning. Later on she said, "Well, that's how little girls get pregnant by their fathers," and this, that, and the other.

She said that to you and your sister?

Yeah, she . . . she said that to me.

Mmm. But not in front of your father.

No. So as time went on and he'd make us come sit on . . . make me come sit on his lap and, you know, he'd have his fingers all up in my . . . in my stuff, and I began to be rebellious. Out of that came rebellion, and I was rebellious towards both of them. First off, because you violated me. Secondly, you didn't protect me. You know? Later on in my life I used [drugs] behind the hurt and the pain that came from that for years. I used that as one of the reasons that I got high. Because what they didn't teach us coming up was how to appropriately deal with emotions and feelings. You stuff them. You can't go ahead and cry about it. Even down to spankings. [. . .] If you get a whipping, well, then you need to shut up. They gonna whip you until you shut up. Well, this is crazy. How you gonna do this? What is going on? You know? They never taught us how to deal with emotions, how to grieve—they never taught us these things. Somebody die, you cry, you'll get over it. You know? It was nothing about a healing process. And when I look back I think they did the best they could with what they had. You know? I don't hold it against them. But they did the best they could with what they had. So now it's my job to break the curses, you know?

Did you ever have a conversation with your father about his molestation?

We haven't to this day. I'm gonna tell you how good God is, because I've had to come into my own with some things and, as it directly relates to my years of active addiction, when I really realize it was a reason why I'm using. [. . .]

Did it move beyond marijuana and alcohol?

Oh yeah, it escalated. [. . .] When I got to A&T I was drinking and found the connection over here in Winston [Salem] where you get the nickel bags. And it was a game for me. I became one of the biggest weed connoisseurs. I needed to have so many different kinds of weed, it begot friends. Because at that time I was dealing with self-esteem issues. You know, I'm a big girl, molestations, I didn't feel good about myself, inadequate, and I always found myself trying to live up to my dad's standards, and no matter what, it was nothing ever good enough. And then I was always called names, you know. "Water buffalo" and "tank," "tubby," you know, all kinds of things. So, nothing that was motivational or a builder. There were always things to break you down and so, needless to say, my self-esteem was shot to hell, it really was, if I can say that. It was shot. [. . .] But I have done some work on myself. [. . .] And that's why I opened with I'm a molestation survivor, because he fondled me. My uncle molested me. My mother's sister's husband went and he fully molested me.

And how old were you then?

I was a teenager. And my latter years in my active addiction I would use that as a form of getting my way. That was one of my ways and means. [. . .] I was already connected to him, so it was easy for me to trick. And I felt nothing for it because I hated men for doing that. I hated them. [. . .] Even though it hurt me in active addiction to be with this man, that one, that man, this one, that one or the other one, and the other one and another and another one, as my ways and my means. It was nothing to me anyhow because they were nothing to me. And it was almost like a way of getting back at them. Because [. . .] all that you can do to me has already been done to me. You can't hurt me.

So, in a way you were sort of using your sexuality against men.

Mmm-hmm. Mmm-hmm. And then at the end of that, then I get what's on the other side of it so that I could support my habit.

Oh, so you were trading sex for the drugs.

Absolutely. Absolutely. Ways and means.

Right. And because that sex didn't mean anything to you . . .

Having sex with men didn't mean absolutely nothing. My uncle took me to liquor houses and introduced me to other men and things of that nature, which in turn would become my sugar daddies, that kind of stuff.

And you were in college by this time?

Uh, yes, or out of college. But see, I was in college when it escalated to cocaine. And we were snorting powder then. They didn't have this rock and crack and stuff. I came up on rock, they got crack now. But I was introduced to powder.

Hmm. So, what was the turning point? What was the "come to Jesus," pivotal moment for you?

That got me to the point I am now?

Mmm-hmm.

I've just been in a thirteen-year relationship. Raised kids. When I got in that relationship I was thirty years old. I don't have any biological kids. I wanted kids, had boyfriends, had a fiancé. [. . .] Anyway, got in a relationship with Lisa. She had two little kids, and I was clean, had been in recovery for a minute. And never been in a relationship with children. And she said to me, "How would you have this relationship if you could?" I said, "If I could have you without them, then that's how it would be." She said, "Well, okay, we're a package deal. Now you can take all of us or you take none of us." Well, she was really the first woman that I had been with. So, I thought to myself, "Self?" and myself said, "What?" "Maybe you need to try this." And I tell you, did I try it. We went through thirteen years. All of it wasn't bad. But when you're dealing with someone with even deeper levels of brokenness than what you are, it can be challenging. And we were truly raised from two different sides, and just our viewpoints were totally, totally opposite. Even down to how we raised these children. And so, it was an in-and-out relationship, a relationship full of fighting and using. When we were on, we were on. And when we were off, I tell you, we were off. I was the one that was consistent with trying to be in here and made a promise to you and da da da da da. And she was just in and out, in and out. She'd catch a whim, "I like this," see this . . . she'd be gone. Every three, six months, boom, gone, in and out. But I loved her. How sick. I didn't love her; it was codependence, and it was still me in my sickness. Relapsed. We broke up one good final time. Every time that we broke up the hole was gaping. She took three people when she left. [She] left my heart in such an ache that I couldn't hardly make it. It would just . . . it hurt to beat. And so, I relapsed. I just said, "F it. I don't care anymore." I've taken all these years and by this time we had been in the relationship six, seven years now. I said, "I've given all I can, and I gave so much of me, I gave all of me, that I had no me left." So, when I needed me, there was no me there to show up to hold me or to help me in any way, form, [or fashion]. I was emotionally, mentally, and spiritually bankrupt. And when you get like that you're in danger. When an addict gets like that they're in danger.

At that time . . . I call them bids. I did seven years of dealing drugs after that point. The turning moment was I was at a point . . . well, I couldn't *not* use. Hunty, I couldn't *not* use. I had to have it. Thing would wake me up in the middle of the night calling me. I was a slave to the rhythm, baby. And hunty, I ran that crack, you hear what I say? I ran it. I had probably a five hundred dollar a day habit, and did what I could to make sure that I kept my habit. I would drink five 40s and if I could get liquor in between, would. If I could get wine in between them five 40s, I would. But I definitely had to have five 40s, at least a dime bag a week that I could lace with some of that crack. And that was every day.

On March the 7th, 2004, I was sitting in my backyard [begins to weep] . . . excuse me . . . it's still real. I was ready to blow my brains out. I had three options. I gave myself three options. Either I can go take another hit and I can blow my heart up, either I can go get that gun and I can blow my brains out because I'm on the cycle and I can't stop right now, or either I can try to get some help. The third one seemed so far-fetched. At that time, as I began to stand up to go and get that gun—because I needed it to end, because I couldn't end it myself—because heard this voice speaking just as clear as I'm speaking right now. And it said, "Not yet, my child, I'm not finished with you, I'm not through with you yet." And I know today that that voice was none other than the voice of God speaking to me.

It was a strong wind that night in March. Lisa and the kids had left. I was there by myself. She said, "I cooked some dinner." I said, "Alright." I was real irritable and mean, and I fell asleep. And by the time I woke up she and the kids were back. And a couple days prior to that I had said, "I want you to take me somewhere and I need to have my car because they're gonna come and repo it. I need you to take me somewhere, though." Because I had contemplated going into treatment. I told her a long time ago, "I ain't gonna always be like this. I ain't gonna always be like this." She came in and when I woke up they were there. I said, "I thought I told you I wanted you to take me somewhere." She was like, "Michelle, I'm not going out of here. This wind is too high, and I'm not gonna leave my children here by them- selves." Well, I went into a cussing tyrant. I went off. And "fuck you" and "I don't care," "You don't give a fuck about me anyhow." And "I'm leaving out. I'll take my own self." [. . .]

It was just after tax season. I owed the dope man seventeen hundred dollars. He was giving me a hundred dollars, two hundred dollars a day on crack. He was giving me that on credit because I told him that my income taxes is coming. And by that second week my income taxes hadn't gotten here. And he said, "Nigger, I'll kill you if you don't give me my money." Well, I'm gonna jump bad. "Nigger, don't you never threaten me. I don't give a fuck how much I owe you, don't you never come for me like that. What you got, I got." I was scared to death, shaking in my boots. Shaking in my boots, child. My money finally came in and I called him and I met him and when I got there to him to pay him that seventeen hundred dollars he bought me a knot like that [demonstrates the size of the bag of crack cocaine]. He knew I couldn't resist. Set me right back up again. I couldn't resist. So, after that run right there I looked like walking death. Wish I would have brought a picture. And the picture that they took of me while I was at the hospital. When I got out of the shower, went on to the hospital. I called Dad, I said, "I . . . I can't breathe and . . . and I need some help. Can you meet me?" That one that violated me, the one that talked bad about me, called me names, all kinds of stuff, was the one that met me. And I said, "I need some help, Dad." He said, "You want your mama to come?" I said, "No, don't bring her. I want you here. She can't take it." So, they checked me in. On March the 8th was when they got me upstairs, but it was late night. When I finally got up to the psych unit it was March the 8th. So, my clean date is March 8, 2004. And by God's grace and mercy I'm eight years clean. But I had five days. I had five days to make a decision. And, mind you, I had been trying to stay clean since 1990. And I finally made a conscious decision on March the 7th to check myself in. And March 8th is my clean date. So for all these years it took me all this time to have eight years clean. And I'm grateful. I don't cry over any relapse. It was part of my journey. And I'm grateful for my journey. Only by God's grace and mercy did I come before the bust or after the bust. I've never spent a day in jail. I've never been raped; I've never been beaten, though my mama, them grandmas, they prayed for me and they covered me with prayers and laid the blood of Jesus on my life because I didn't have sense enough to do so for myself. So that was my breaking point. [. . .]

I'm excellent now compared to . . . I could not even talk, have a conversation. I had to learn how to literally go flush the toilet again. I didn't have those things anymore. I wasn't employable. I literally needed somebody to guide me. That's how bad I was. In five days they started me up on an Alzheimer's unit. It was no room in what I call regular population. There was no room. So, we had an Alzheimer's unit that was big as these two rooms put together. And they put me in there. I ain't got nothing to drink. They gave me one little stick to suck on. I didn't have enough breath in my body to do a breathalyzer. You just have to blow for five seconds. I couldn't even do that. I couldn't even blow a match out. That's how bad I'd fallen. Almost dead. My godmama, when I took her to the doctor a few days prior, she said, "It was hard for me to sit in the car with you because you looked like death. I felt death on you." And as God as my witness, I felt I was headed to my grave. I knew it. I knew it. So that cry for help, that final cry, God knew what it was. Because, honey, he touched me. You hear what I say? He touched me in that final cry. [. . .] I have a picture to this day and I keep my picture and I've xeroxed several of them so I will never run out. I don't ever want that picture to leave me. I need to see myself laying there. And when I showed Pastor, he said—he calls me Wright. He said, "Wright, you look like you laying in a casket right there." I said, "My God, look there." [. . .]

By day five I said, "Okay." I said, "God, if you bless me and deliver me I will fight from now for my life. I will preach your word, teach your word, do whatever it is you want me to do. I'm yours." And from that day to this one he's kept me, he's covered me, he's even allowed my job to be about recovery.

I'm a peer support specialist, and the way I became a peer support specialist, because the streets were my life. So now I get paid for my experience being a drug addict. God has blessed me now to go back into the places that I use to recruit clients, to help people. I'm in the mental health field, and a lot of substance abuse is there. The people are . . . codependent or dual addicted. And that's what I do. So, all of my using wasn't in vain. [. . .] I thank God for birthing inward discovery, personal recovery, and affectionate outreach out of him. Because what I've found, that all of us are broken. We are the products of our environment, and I don't know of anybody's environment that wasn't dysfunctional in one way, form, or fashion. But who I learned to be shapes who I am today, how I receive, perceive information and how I deliver it, my processing. [. . .] I've literally had to learn how to reprocess things as I heal the broken places, the little red wagon places. As those places are healing and then I'm not anywhere . . . don't you think by any means have I arrived. It's an ongoing process. But when I learn who I am and in the process of growing to know who I am, then I can recover those places. So, it makes it easy for me to deacon the broken ones that come in, and it makes it easier for me to love you right where you are for just who you are. I'm a deacon every day. Even at my job I'm a deacon, they just don't know I'm a deacon. But I have to have that same love and compassion out there as I have in here for those ones that come in that door.

I've had to learn in this healing process that the ones that violated me were just as sick as I am. So, through this growing process I've had to learn to forgive. So now I humbly serve my father, I humbly serve my uncle every day. I still take care of my parents, and I take care of my aunt and uncle faithfully. Every week I go get their medication, their groceries, and anything they need in between. My mother and father, I live with them. When Lisa and I got married, a year and a half later it was over with. We were divorced. I was homeless. So, I moved home with Mom and Daddy. This November will be four years, and in that four-year time period my dad has had to go on dialysis. I couldn't get a job; I don't care if they threw it in my face. What I found out in this healing process and growing process was what happened with Lisa and I was supposed to happen because I'm on assignment and have been on assignment with my parents. [. . .] "Hey, Mom, Dad, how are y'all? You're cool?" [. . .] But God put me in that place and humbled me so that I could learn how to serve. And I needed to learn how to serve from a place of being violated. I needed to learn how to serve at home so that I could serve His people here and do it with the spirit of God.

....

Nora [b. 1983, Houston, Texas]

From fourteen to fifteen, I really heavily relied on the Bible, church, spirituality. [One of my dad's] nephews raped me, and so I was really jacked up in the head. So, I held onto that, and that really got me through. [. . .]

Did you ever tell your father about what his nephew did?

Oh, yeah, I did.

And what was his reaction?

I was fourteen or fifteen. I remember I was at Eisenhower High School, and I would stay after school a lot because at the time we didn't live by the school. We used our old address so I could go to that school, I guess, so my mom wouldn't feel so guilty for sending me off to my dad's. And so, I'd stay after school a while to wait for the bus or for my mom to pick me up. I was always in the band hall, and I walked out to the pay phone back when there were pay phones, and I called my dad at his job, so it was an 800-number, and I told him. And he pretty much [laughter] didn't believe me. It was just like, "Uh, okay, I'll talk to him." And he said that he would talk to my grandmother, too, 'cause he started molesting me at the time, 'cause actually my mom sent me to my paternal grandmother's 'cause I had a summer program at Rice University I was accepted into, and then to my dad's in Allen. So, he talked to my grandmother, 'cause that's where the stuff started—I don't know. That's why I'm guessing he talked to her. [. . .]

I used to feel really bad about telling people that I had just turned thirteen and he was already fourteen. But he was tall, he was already, like, lifting weights and stuff, and for a while I felt like that kinda invalidated everything. But I feel like I learned very well from watching my mother that whatever a guy wants, he's gonna take it, and that's how it goes, 'cause that's how it went with every relationship in my mom's family. But my dad called me back I don't know how much longer like after that, but he said that my cousin denied it and said that it was consensual, and he said that and "I just told him just never do it again." And I was like, "But that's not true that it was consensual." And he was like, "He's like a son to me. When a kid makes a mistake, you tell him 'hey, that it was a mistake' but you still love 'em." And I was like, "But I'm your actual child," you know. [Laughter] And then a few weeks later he invited him up for a barbecue. [. . .]

So, you had to see him again?

Umm-hmm. I mean, by this time, I was back in Houston, but I would go over to my grandmother's, and yeah, I had to see him.

Did you tell your mother?

Yeah, I told her around the same time, fourteen, fifteen, yeah, I think I was probably fifteen. I was doing our laundry, had a little laundromat in the apartment complex. I was in and out. And so, what I did, when I went to go take another load, I wrote it on a piece of paper, "One of my cousins raped me." And I came back in, she was laid out on the couch, just with her eyes closed and her hand over her head, just like holding it. And she was like, "Was it Boobie?" which is her nephew, my oldest cousin. I was like, "No!" I was like, "And it's not even on your side." And then I told her who it was, and it was like I just broke my mom down even further and made her feel even more guilty for sending me up there—she felt my dad didn't protect me.

But she believed you?

Yeah. She did. And it got to the point where I was so depressed and sui-cidal that she finally broke down and took me to a psychologist, 'cause you know, in my family and a lot of black families, it's like psychology, they're quacks or "that's the white man's thing," you know, "We don't get therapy, we don't go to shrinks." [Laughter] But I mean, it got to the point where it was just so bad, like, she did take me, and that became our little weekly bonding time. It was weird.

So, she went with you to the therapy?

Yeah, she went with me. I went in there alone; sometimes she would come in the session with me, but most of the time I was alone. But she'd wait and then we'd go to Exxon gas station and get a little Starbucks Frappuccino in a bottle, and that was like a treat, 'cause it was expensive, and we only got two for the two of us and drank that on the way back home. But yeah, my mom believed me.

Did you ever come to resent your father [because] he didn't believe it was rape?

Yeah. I felt like, once again, like it didn't matter that I was his kid. It's like everything just repeats itself, it's just cyclical, like we never go anywhere. Like, he was dating my mom, who's the only black woman he's ever dated. [Laughter] I think he cheated on her with my stepmom, this white lady named Becky, got her pregnant, and then married her instead. And so my sister, Makayla's two years younger than me. And then when my dad stopped coming by to pick me up and to see me and stuff, I was like, I think it's be-cause I'm not half white. So, every Christmas, I would ask for Santa to make me half white like my sister, Makayla. And then, again, I felt like, again, like I wasn't good enough—I was nothing. I was like this mistake that he made when he was a teenager and he's seventeen and knocked some girl up, even though I'm his only kid that looks like him. We have so much in common. But yeah, I resented him. I'm not as angry, but [laughter] I think to this day

I still resent him for a lot of things. A lot of things I missed out on. [. . .] Him being an introvert, my mom was an extrovert, she didn't understand my introversion, and when I met my dad, I was like, "That is why," you know, "like that is me." I don't like being around noise either, you know. But yeah, I always felt like I wasn't good enough—even when I lived with him and I was into rap he called me "ghetto" and said I wouldn't be anything listening to that hippity-hop, 'cause he just listens to country and Whitney Houston. [Laughter] And so, I think 'cause he was teased a lot, he really resents black people. [. . .] The only other black man in the neighborhood, he's also married to a white lady, and it's just like all lily-white up in there. So, yeah, they made fun of me 'cause I didn't know how to cut steak. Never had steak, I didn't know how to use a knife and fork properly. My sister and I, we used the same bathtub, and I was like, "It's Makayla's turn to clean it." You know, I was thirteen, living with him, he was like, "Well, you're darker and so your skin cells are—those are your skin cells around the tub. That's your dirt, so you clean it." And I was like, yep, [laughter] yep, more confirmation that something's wrong with me.

. . . .

Priscilla [b. 1967, San Antonio, Texas]
I didn't realize I had been sexually abused until I was in college. I mean, I knew it, but I didn't know how it impacted me until I'm taking social work classes and you're doing case studies. And you go, "Oh! That's what the fuck that was!" And then me having my meltdown, you know. It's like, "Oh, I'm about to lose my mind right now! I'm getting angry!" And having to shut all that shit down, right? [. . .] But I think being able to confront at least the one person who was the main abuser. There were many men who tried to sexually abuse me. They would try to sexually abuse a lot of us in the neighborhood, from somebody at the house to the gas station, like all of that. So constantly on the run from men as girl children. But particularly my uncle sexually abusing me. And then when I realized that, getting into therapy immediately, telling my mom. My mom confronting him. Because he has a little girl who's the same age I am at the time when I was abused. I don't like him taking her to the bathroom; it's making me nervous when I see him with her and her mother not around. Makes me nervous, makes me wonder, "Oh, he did that to me, is he doing that to his child?" Pushing me—making me tell my mother. My mother confronts him. He admits it. Tells her about his sexual abuse. She's like, "That's fine, but that don't mean—that does not make the situation alright." And not only did my mother tell him, she said,

"I'm going to tell your wife. Because I don't know if you're sexually abusing Natasha." [. . .] It had never occurred to me not talking about that could allow that to happen to somebody else, until I see him with the child. And I'm going, "Oh, shit, I can't—I can't be responsible for that. And that I'm not embarrassed by this. It is not my fault." Don't know where none of that shit came from because I was not in therapy. [Laughter] I was not in therapy yet. Don't know where, "That wasn't my fault and I'm gonna tell. I'm telling when I know to tell." [Laughter] You know, it's like I was mature in some ways. "Huh? This ain't normal? Oh!" And so, you know, she tells his wife, so the wife can keep the child safe, right? So, there's a way in which it doesn't feel like one of the worst things, because it was so suppressed. [. . .]

I got to confront him in therapy. He asked to come to therapy, because he wanted to talk to me. And I said, "You can only talk to me in my therapist's office." Said what he needed to say—not what he *needed* to say, but I got to confront him, tell him. He thought he turned me into a lesbian. He hated what he did to me because I was the way I was. My therapist was on it. "No." She said, "No, she is not a lesbian because you sexually abused her." This is a white straight woman who I feel incredibly indebted to, who did what an ally ought to do. I didn't know what to say to him. I just looked at him. Because I could have went down that road of, "Is this why I'm a lesbian?" Right? I'm fucked up then. I'm fucked up. [Laughter] Yeah, I'm fucked up. This ain't got nothing to do with my desires or what I want to do. I'm fucked up. [. . .]

The amount of violence that I was exposed to I think was probably more profound. I mean, that was part, the sexual violence that I experienced. But the violence that I witnessed, I feel like was the worst of my childhood. Because I was never part of the violence. I was never subjected to the violence. My aunts and my cousins were subjected to the violence, and I was there. And what I felt was an incredible amount of helplessness, because I was a kid, and I was small, and all I wanted to do was be bigger. All I could ever think was if I was bigger, I could stop some of this. But I was so small and such a kid. But also, not understanding why I got treated so well. My uncles by marriage, who were so abusive, were so nice to me and loving, that there's something that doesn't fit in a child's mind about what that means.

So, you think you might feel special because you were treated so nicely and loving, but I think you wonder why you not being treated like everybody else. Not that you want your ass whooped, but you don't know how to make sense of that as a child. And so yeah, the level of violence and the amount and the severity of it, I think is some of the worst stuff that I experienced. Because it still impacts me in this way about what I knew of my uncles, outside of their relationships with the people they were beating and mistreating, was that they were so nice to me. And so I don't hold the contempt against them that the kids and the ex-wives do, or hate. Because I have this multiple experience. But I know what they're capable of. And I know what they did. But they didn't do it to me. And so, I think that really impacted me, because I didn't grow up with violence in my house. I heard my parents argue once in my life, once. And I never heard them argue before that. And I thought we were fucking abnormal. So, the screaming that I had to endure and listen to, my uncles were all either alcoholics, drugs, and pimps, some of them a combination of both. [Laughter] That it just, you know, I think it made me grow up, so in ways it was good, but it was also very bad, you know, in what I had to, you know, that not physically being hurt by that, but what that does to you watching that. [. . .] What does watching violence being done on other people, how does that impact you? Not when it's done to you, but when you watch it, and you can't do anything about it.

And so, all I wanted to do was be bigger and stronger. And I was a small, skinny kid. I was small and skinny. So, as I got bigger, I never had a problem with my size and never thought, but felt like, "Oh, now I can do something." And as I got to be bigger, I did have to hold my uncle off his wife, and was very happy. Me and my mother just talked about this the other day, of how we both threw my uncle to the ground when he was choking the shit out of his wife. It was a different wife, though, because I didn't think—I was mad at her and I said, "He should have choked the shit out of her and I should have let him choke her ass." [Laughter] But recognizing that I was actually able to stop that moment and I probably was only seventeen or eighteen then, but I was very strong by then, I was very strong. And it's all I ever wanted to be, right? Like if I'm just stronger [. . .] which I'm sure has something to do with my weight right now. Like I'm big, but I don't really need to be this big, [laughter] but it probably provides me some level of comfort around being able to protect.

• •

Tonya [b. 1965, Richmond, Virginia]
I did not feel protected as a child because I had four brothers, mainly the three that were in the house. I felt like I was always fighting off men. Because their friends would come in and my father's friends would come in, and my father, being alcoholic, he hung out with other alcoholics. So, I was fighting and/or in some situations just acquiescent, not trying to rock the boat—afraid to say anything. So, I had to deal with sexual abuse at a fairly

young age. Don't know the ages, just know it was there until I finally said no to one of my older brothers who was abusing me. Then my brothers' friends each time they would try, I had my voice then, so I said, "No. *No.*" I would always say no and get in wrestling struggles or whatnot.

In the meantime, you were being molested by various men in your life. Did you ever talk with your mother about that?

Not until I was in my twenties. I told her about a man who had molested me, one of my father's friends who had recently died. So, I remember telling her about that and I was in my late twenties.

What was her response?

When my mom hears about stuff that has happened that's long gone, she had no control over or didn't know about, she may have, like, an initial crying reaction or I don't know if she feels guilt or some sort of responsibility. She felt for me, but I always go into this protective, "It's okay, it's done." One time I beat him off with a clothes hanger. Another time Terry, my brother next to me, happened to be around, and he helped pull him off of me.

So, he tried to do this publicly or in front of someone else?

Yes. And then other times I just got real creative in avoiding him. If I was ever home I would say so-and-so is down right at the tree there about to come in and whatnot. So, I really wanted to stay away from him. I shouldn't have had to. But it is what it is.

Did you ever confront any of the people who violated you?

I never confronted any of them. I've thought about it with the one brother. He was a teenager. He was doing some experimentation. I decided not to. I went through a lot of healing work to deal with that and whatnot. It wasn't until later years when there was an attempted rape by a college classmate where I confronted him at the time.

I'm Sweet on You
Stories of Love, Courtship, and Intimacy

6

One of the consistent themes across these narratives is the emotional connections that these women have with other women. Yes, these connections sometimes manifest in the form of sexual intimacy, but the emotional bonds between these women seemed to be privileged over carnal knowledge. It was actually refreshing to listen to these women talk about being open to the idea of intimacy with another human that did not necessarily have to lead to sex but made sex all the more pleasurable when there was a deep emotional, even spiritual connection.

Black southern women in particular have a long history of depending on each other, from their days of bondage to the present, and most times it was a dependency of necessity. Again, Alice Walker and Zora Neale Hurston have captured this intimacy in their work: Celie and Shug in *The Color Purple* rely on each other to help the other overcome her issues with self-esteem and paternal rejection, respectively, but also to find sexual pleasure in the other; Janie and Phoeby in *Their Eyes Were Watching God* don't share a sexual intimacy in the literal sense but nonetheless support one another through listening and bearing witness, being in each other's ear, as it were. In a world where men were unreliable or a source of aggravation, these women could find solace in one another in ways that buoyed them in a sea of despair and hopelessness. More important, the kind of intimacy that these fictional characters share mirrors many real life female bonds.

The narrators in *BQSW* reflect the close ties that black southern women have with each other, whether they are in romantic relationships or not. There is nothing like a good "sister friend" to lean on in times of trouble or to share a laugh over the "foolishness" of men, so those stories are included in this chapter as well. But to be clear, these women also love being with each other romantically. They speak of courting, seducing, and even "stealing" women from other women. What was so moving to me, however, was to see how these women care for each in their doting or literal caring when the other happened to be infirm or physically challenged. Some of these couples, like Pat and Cherry Hussain, have been together more than thirty years, while others, like Lindsay and Tori, have just started on their journey. Indeed, some of the couples fought with each other to tell the story of how they met!

Interestingly, all of these interviews took place before marriage equality became national law in 2015. Nonetheless, a few of the couples had traveled to other states where marriage was legal at the time, so that they could marry, but continued to live in their southern state where it was not. For them, the symbolism of the institution of marriage was as important as remaining in the South, which to me was a fascinating choice. Why not simply move to the state where you could be legally married and it be recognized? For many of these couples, family and a true sense of home were located in the South, not to mention that many of them could not afford to just uproot their lives and move to California or New York or another New England state where marriage was legal. Fortunately, now they do not have to compromise their right to be married with their desire to stay in a region where they are most at home.

As with all relationships, the narrators also note they had to work through issues at times based on family relations, race and class issues, and parenting. For example, some of their families were not accepting of their partners, which put a strain on the relationship. This was particularly true when the narrator was in an interracial relationship. Blended families, meaning the combining of children from previous heterosexual marriages or couplings, sometimes complicated a relationship as well—or made it stronger. No matter the case, it was clear that these women were up for the challenges of working through their situation because they were sweet on each other.

· ·

Anita [b. 1964, Hickory, North Carolina]

I'm a DJ. Actually, I've been one since we lived in the projects. I took it on after my mom died and my brother had all that equipment and I had quit school. I had nothing else to do, so I started fooling around with his equipment, and it actually paid off. [. . .] My sister had a party, and [that's where I met] my first girlfriend. That's the girlfriend that I got into relationship with after I came out the *second* time. So, I was in church and I fought it. I fought it. I fought it with everything I had. It was like, "Oh my gosh. Okay, I like this girl. No I don't. Okay, yes I do." [Laughter] I was on my knees. "Lord, take it away. I like this girl. I shouldn't." It wasn't going nowhere.

She was hanging around with one of my half sisters, so she was working at the Waffle House and I worked third shift. And I would go to the Waffle House and eat a lot, and once I saw her. We were at a party, and [when] I found out that she worked at the Waffle House, I started going to the Waffle House a lot. I started hanging out at the Waffle House, and on my breaks from work I would go eat breakfast. Or on my days off I would go sit down there. And [. . .] one night, it was Christmas Eve, and I had to go and get bicycles from one house and take them to the other house. The kids weren't asleep, they were sitting there waiting on the black Santa. [Laughter] So after I took the bikes to the kids, I went to the Waffle House, and I think that's when we had our first conversation. We started talking. We exchanged phone numbers.

Did you know she was gay?

Yeah. My half sister had told me that she was gay and she was from Detroit. She was different. There was something different about her. I knew that I had already made up my mind that if I ever got back in it that I was going to choose my mate carefully. [. . .] Most of my relationships before I actually got out of the life and stayed out for ten years, [. . .] were broken. I was young, and it was mostly me because once I decided that I wasn't going to hide it anymore, I just had girlfriends out the wazoo, I had maybe one or two at the same time. [Laughter] I was just doing me. It was like, my mom had died and I was just doing me. I went through a whole lot, and then I finally got out and went and got in church about ten years. And then when I got with her, things changed. I took this relationship serious, and I prayed about it and seeked God on it, and it's a healthy relationship.

. . . .

Emilie [b. 1955, Durham, North Carolina]

We's married. [Laughter] In the state of Connecticut. We first met each other in the nineties sometime at the American Academy of Religion [AAR] meeting. You meet people, you see people, people give papers, on and on and on. And Laurel remembers seeing me because I was part of a coup at a session. The schedule is fairly packed at AAR, as any of our professional societies, and Mary Daly had the session before in the same room. And, God bless her soul, she was so unoriented towards people; she was an animal person. Her most important relationships were with her cats, literally.

She just didn't do people well. And so, she was just going on and on and on and on and . . . it's time to start the session. We got a session full of black women because this was when this thought was still really hot in the academy. And so, people were now standing outside the doors wanting to get in because something was gonna happen. Feminists were gonna take the stage. My dear friend and colleague Katie Cannon was either the moderator or one of the key people in this next session, and we're standing in the back room, and we're all getting hot. It's like, "See, this what Audre was talking about, right here." And the moderator of the session was trying to get Mary to stop. So, Katie looks at us, gathers us together, she said, "Come you all, we're gonna take that stage." And the group of us, following Katie, marched down the aisle, and Katie's going, "Cut! Cut! Cut!" [Laughter] And I was one of the people marching. And that's where Laurel first saw me. Yeah, because she was sitting in the audience being extremely disappointed in her people. [Laughter]

A few years later I heard her do a paper at AAR, but I knew she was in a relationship, and although I thought she was really cute, I had gotten old enough to know really cute and in a relationship means you admire the cuteness and leave it alone instead of saying, like, "What can I do?" So, it wasn't until four years ago when everything lined up. We both were not in relationships. I had been relationless on purpose for six years because I had made a series of really bad decisions and I felt I needed to take a break because I clearly didn't know what the hell I was doing.

And, actually, it was Katie who said, "Why don't you take a three-month sabbatical on relationships and try to get yourself together, because this last one was a loser." And I thought she might have a point. And at the end of the first three months I was kind of liking no drama, and getting comfortable with the fact that I could be comfortable with myself. I didn't need somebody else to be there. And it just went on for six years, unintentionally. So, about maybe six months to a year before Laurel and I clicked, I was beginning to think I might be ready, that I thought I had learned enough about myself and really what I was looking for, that I might be ready to see if there's maybe somebody who I was ready to date. [. . .] All my friends were in relationships and I started telling them, "I think I'm ready." [. . .] They go, "Why? How could you do that? Your life is so peaceful that we're jealous of you. You go get in a relationship, all drama. And it's you creating it within yourself." So even that slowed down, too, because the people that I'm admiring are in relationships, but they're saying, "Mmm, mmm, girl, you got it good right like you got it right now. You might want to hold off from that idea."

So, I decided I don't have to rush. I can test the waters here and there. And so, when we were at another meeting, we started talking to each other. The first time we really started talking to each other. And somewhere in there we both admitted we had been attracted to each other for years.

And then Laurel literally ran away. And I decided, okay, I have made a foray, let me get back on the train and go back up to New Haven—because we were in New York—and keep myself out of trouble. So that's what I did. It took several months more before we dared to even talk to each other again in person. The rest was history. She showed up at my condo in these cute little white shorts, and [laughter] I thought to myself: "I'm dead."

And is she from the South as well?

No. She was born and reared in Amherst, Massachusetts. Oh God. [Laughter] She did her PhD work here at Vanderbilt. And she was like, "What the hell have I hit in this culture." So, she's sort of surprised to be back . . .

Have your families interacted?

Mmm-hmm.

And the first time they interacted, how did that go?

It was fine. The only person . . . no, that's not true. My cousin Eve and her daughter and my aunt and my sister came to our wedding. Eve's father we left in the home with her brother to take care of him while she was gone. But once I came out to mom, I didn't hide it from the rest of them. I didn't rub their noses in it, and I started looking around, going, "They've got a lot of people in that generation who are gay and less gay couples. Look at this here. Huh!" [. . .]

So, your mother had passed away before the two of you got together? Had she met Laurel?

No, she never got to meet Laurel. Mom died in '03 and we got together in '08.

Do you think she would have approved?

Yes, I do. My sister thinks so. My sister knew my mother's mind better than I did. Mom tolerated the others, and she kind of liked one, but she tolerated the others. No, she kind of liked two, but tolerated the others. When, my Aunt Agnes died three years ago, we now have a ritual in our family that when one of the family members died, none of them want funerals. None of them want memorial services. They just want us to gather around the table and remember them and then go out and have a really good meal. So that's what we were doing when my aunt died, and Laurel was there. And, we were sitting two people apart from each other. [. . .] And we were just sort of talking back and forth, and Eve was, "You know . . . I like this one." I said,

"Yeah, I think I may have finally done this right." And she said, "I think so, and I think Mommy would have liked her, too." I said, "Yeah, I think so. Looks like Aunt Helen likes her." "Yes, Aunt Helen really likes her. Look at them interacting over there." And Eve goes, "Mommy didn't like that last one." [Laughter] And then we both just fell out laughing, and people were like, "What are you doing over there?" "Nothing." I think it's because Laurel and I are now at a place in our lives where we've gotten our yayas out. It's been hard-won for both of us through very different means. And when we got married we didn't promise forever, we promised we would try. So, we didn't make a promise that we couldn't keep, and that's what binds us. We made the promise of waking up each day and trying, which most days we do. Now some days we wake up mad at each other like, "Don't talk to me." But that goes away fairly quickly. And we realize how fleeting time is now. And it is precious to find someone who needs you. We're both well respected in our fields. We both have careers. The most important challenge for us right now is that Laurel is the following spouse, which she's used to being the primary spouse. How does she make that transition and carve out her own space here at Vanderbilt.

Is she a professor?

Mmm-hmm. And she is respected and she does have a space, but she has to own it still. I need to just back off. I can't fix this. Luckily, the powers that be here at the university knew it was not gonna be a good idea to have me be her boss. She's in religious studies; I'm over here in the Divinity School. And structurally, it works. We've just got to learn to live into it. But, interesting: having an eighty-one-year-old, who we both adore, as someone not going home because she is home, has really caused an incredible shift in our lives that has made it richer.

Mmm-hmm. Is Laurel African American?

No.

Is she white?

She's very white. Her father's side is German. Her mother's side is, I think, Welsh.

Has that presented any problems? Being an interracial lesbian couple in the South?

We live in Nashville on purpose. And we live in the Vanity Bubble on purpose, because the rest of this state is not safe. We're very clear. And if we couldn't have found a house in the Vanity Bubble, we would not have moved. We would have continued our long-distance relationship even postmarriage. Because neither one of us was willing to live where we were constantly looking over our shoulders. Now it's been an odd thing to go from being married in Connecticut to unmarried in Tennessee, except the university recognizes same-sex partnerships as marriages. So, we have access to all the benefits. We just don't for the state. We do for the federal government, so we're gonna keep fighting that fight. But I think one of the things that makes it easier is that Laurel does her racial homework, and she knows you don't get it done, you keep working at it.

I was telling her a white ally story that happened on Sunday when she was away. There is a particular grocery store I go to because I like their deli counter, and I also know every time I go I'm gonna have to put up with the white people get served first. But I was wanting this particular deli meat, so I always brace, like. I can get upset and huffy puffy about it or I can just go—I'm gonna have to be ready to be patient because I got other things that I really want to expend my energy on before I die. So, sure enough, I was standing at the counter. There was a white woman somewhere near my age who was getting deli cuts for her mother-in-law and having to be very specific about them because her mother-in-law can't see well. So, she needed a particular thickness for everything. And so, she was taking a while and we just sort of glanced at each other and smiled at each other. And I was next in line. I was just standing there waiting to be [helped]. This young white woman walked up and it just so happened that the Asian woman behind the deli counter came free as this young white woman walked up. And the Asian deli counter woman said, "Who's next?" And the young white woman just started placing her order. Been there, seen it, I know it, but we didn't go there. Glad I went to the bathroom before I was standing at this deli counter. The white woman standing next to me gives me the "Can you believe this shit?" look. And I just shook my head and I said, "It happens and they really need to get a number system here, because that would really cut down on the stuff like this. But it happens all the time." So, she shook her head. The Asian woman finished the order for the young white woman. The older white woman was still doing her order. When the Asian woman looked up again and said, "Who's next," and I was just about to say, "I am," when the white woman standing next to me, "She's next. She is next. You need to help her next." And the young Asian woman was like . . . And the white woman, loud talking, says, "I was not gonna let that happen again. Not with me standing here. Just was not gonna let that happen." And I went, "Well, thank you. Thank you. I appreciate it." And the young Asian woman then starts apologizing. I said, "It's alright, it's alright. I understand," but she didn't understand what I was saying. But it was enough to get the apology, and it was even more to have a white ally.

So, I'm telling Laurel this story over breakfast this morning. This is why I love her so, because she's starting to get mad. And I'm like, "Hold it, hold it, let me tell you the end, let me tell you the end!" [Laughter] So she's like, "Alright, tell me." So, I told her the end and everything relaxed, and she said, "I'm so glad that there are more people in the world who understand the importance of being an ally." And I said, "Girl, you have no idea how relieved I was that I didn't have to swing my earring. I didn't even have on hoops. I'd have broken my neck trying to swing these earrings." So, she gets it. And she's the one, no matter who's paying the bill if we're out for dinner, she's the one who says, "You need to give the bill to her, she's paying," or when the server comes and the server's only talking to her, she stops answering. Little things, but it's the little things that make us go postal. And then the bigger things, she's there like a soldier.

. . . .

Julia [b. 1979, Gastonia, North Carolina]
I met Alexis in 2008 at Atlanta's Black Gay Pride. Her and a friend founded an organization called Quirky Black Girls. And they had a Quirky Black Girl picnic in Piedmont Park, so I went to that. It was the first one, but it's been an annual thing. And, yeah, it was cool. It was this time in my life where I was like, "I'm going to find me a partner." I'd been really specific over time of cultivating this list. So, I had a list of over fifty things. [. . .] I even had this practice of imagining the person and what a date would be like, down to the details of "I'd knock on the door" and "I'd be wearing this" and "She'd open the door and be wearing that" and "She'd say this." Anyway, I had gotten frustrated by this Pride weekend. I was like, you know what? Forget it. I'm gonna take all my money and I'm gonna buy an entertainment system and I'm going to make my movies and spend my time doing my work, whatever. Fuck 'em all! So, I was sort of in that place of frustration, but still it's like it's Pride weekend, so maybe there'll be a last little glimmer of hope. So, this is the space I'm at, at this picnic. So, I get up to fix my plate, and of course Alexis was one of the hosts, so she comes up to speak to me. And mind you, she had seen me before at an event, but she said I looked too cool for school so she didn't talk to me. So, all the people she was with I knew. I talked to all of them, but somehow we missed each other, so we didn't meet that night. But she had seen me before. So, she comes up to me and she introduces herself, and I think she was trying to strike up a conversation

but misspeaks and says that she has a partner when she doesn't. So, I was like, "Ah, okay, whatever." But, yeah, that's when we met. And I saw her a few more times because she was in Atlanta doing some research at Emory. And so, I saw her a few more times, and like, I think like two days before she was going to be leaving town we set a date to go out. [. . .] September 14th is the day we went out.

· ·

Laurinda [b. 1959, Memphis, Tennessee]

I vaguely remember seeing the friend request, given where I was in my life—my author, playwright standpoint. [. . .] I don't talk to everybody on Facebook. Contrary to what others may think, I don't have conversations with people on Facebook unless I know you or have had consistent communication with you. I remember Dedra's name, seeing it, and I remember clicking her picture and saying, "Oh, she's got beautiful hair. Her hair is so pretty." Then she was always having fun. I saw a picture of her having her face painted. She was getting her face painted. And then she had on a cowboy hat. I can remember different pictures from her family events and stuff like that. But I never accepted her friend request. At the time my ex and I, we had been together fourteen years and we were going through a really bad breakup. And I noticed that she and Dedra communicated a lot. Oh, I don't know, I really didn't want to be friends now. And I didn't. So, my ex actually . . . she had blocked me from her page. And even when we were speaking, at one point I asked her, "Why would you do that?" She said, "It's not so much for you. It's for me." So, she doesn't want to see what I'm doing. Okay, whatever. February 2011 I had already accepted Dedra's friend request and I had posted some poems from my notes that I had written. And Dedra commented on the poems. And [I was] apprehensive to say something to her because I knew she had been communicating with Charlotte. And eventually between the two of us I let her know, "I wouldn't have a whole lot to say because I know you're friends with my ex." And she asked, "What? My ex Charlotte?" Whatever, and I told her, "Yeah." So, from that moment on she was more of a confidante. You know, what can I do to help? Or here is Jennifer Hudson's "We're Going to Fight." [Laughter] I'm like, "Really?"

The end of that March I was supposed to see my ex because she was helping with one of my plays. We had still had a bad time or whatever, but Dedra called me for the first time, and we talked about an hour. And nothing crossed my mind other than she sounded very professional, very much about business. And she was very helpful. She wasn't trying to push up on me or nothing. My head wasn't there, and I think that she thought that my place in my ex's life was different than what it truly was. We weren't talking. [. . .] I had put myself in a place where I was content being secluded from everybody. I didn't want to talk or nothing. And as Dedra said, she saw another depiction of me and her, and so I said, "No, that was years, that was a while ago." And hoping by carrying the bags in the City of Atlanta, yeah, we had got to the point where we had lost everything. We lost cars, houses, money. So, the only mode of transportation was MARTA for us to get around. So, I was bitching—you've got to be carrying groceries on the bus, not that it was horrible. I just felt that I had been demeaned in such a way. I didn't go to Howard University to carry plastic bags, Walmart bags on MARTA. Okay, and that's what I'd been reduced to. [. . .]

A couple times I needed some money and she offered some money. It was always a hundred and twenty-five dollars. I'll never forget that: always a hundred and twenty-five dollars. I had talked to her about my play coming up and how I needed sponsors [. . .] so I was telling her about that. I can't do nothing like that, I got to pay taxes. [. . .] We chatted a lot on Facebook, and [. . .] she was just different. We weren't talking about [the] stuff that was aggravating me. We were just in conversations. And I kept trying to tell her in so many ways my relationship with this person or whatever, it's done. I'm healing—trying even to put myself in a position to heal right now. And this person still keeps coming at me. To me, Dedra became like a sounding board, but she was not judging. She was listening. One day out of the blue, she and I really had got comfortable. We had gone through a period of not talking and just out of the blue came over to chat. "Can I be your superwoman?" "What the hell is that?" I'm like, "Oh Lord, just when I was really getting comfortable talking to her, I'm going to delete her and I'm going to block her." I knew it was coming. I asked her, I said, "What does that mean?" She said, "I want to be your—let me be your any and everything." Oh, hell no. Delete. Block. I can't do it. And all of my friends said I can't be with this woman. One of my friends, she said, "What is that? Is that some sugar mama type business for the country?" I said, "I guess so." She said, "What did you say?" I said, "Nothing, I don't think. I just want to delete her or block her." She said, "Girl, you should. You've got to be careful. You can't just go talking to everybody." And we lost communication again.

I went through a situation with my ex and I ended up in Memphis. And I checked the voice mail after two or three days, and she popped up on it. And everyone that had called, I felt like the only one I really wanted to talk to was her. I was able to cry. I was able to hurt. I was able to just open myself completely up to her. She never passed judgment other than she really tried to embrace my wounds. And not necessarily heal them but it gave me the tools to do it. And the first thing she offered to do was to buy me a new wardrobe. Because I had gotten down to a size 14. But I didn't want anybody to do nothing for me. That's why I'm in this position: letting somebody do something for me. "Oh, but I want you to go and do so-and-so." I ain't doing it, I didn't. But after a series of events, things that she did she showed me that she cared, showed me that she was there for me and that she wasn't going anywhere unless I told her to. I started paying attention a little more.

My sister who I was staying with, she said, "Now, who's this woman in this city? [. . .] She just sent flowers to my house, roses to my house; I don't get roses in my house. I promise you if you ever meet her she gonna let you go, and I think you ought to go." And I'm like, "I don't want to do that. I want to know her." But after that I started seeing a side of Dedra that was kind. Everybody can't be kind. Everybody can't do gentle. I never heard her raise her voice. She's always very professional, very respectful of me and treated me like a woman. Not that anyone before had not. But it was different. [. . .] She called to check on me. She was making sure. She's like, "You know a woman of your stature shouldn't be doing this. A woman of your stature shouldn't be driving." "Stature?" Okay. I kind of liked that. And she just started paying attention to me. She didn't care I was an author. She didn't care about none of that. She came in. I feel like at that moment [she was] my savior [who came in] to save me from myself because I was fine being off in a box and staying in that box. I had committed to myself I was going to move to the middle of nowhere. I was going to have a two-bedroom home where I could see from the front to the back. I wanted a front porch and a back porch, and if I decided I wanted to barbecue in the front I could. If I wanted to barbecue in the back I could. I wanted to plant sunflowers. I only shared that with three people. Those three people didn't know each other.

I met this girl who was clairvoyant the following week and I was saying, "I don't believe in this," [. . .] but she said something to me about going away, going to be away from everybody: "You'll be in the middle of nowhere." And I was saying to myself, "Okay, something's gotta be going on." About two weeks after that Dedra says, "I need to talk to you about something." And we already met that first time. She said, "Well, you told me that you need to be somewhere away from people in the middle of nowhere," and she described the house to a T. It was like you had been in my house. I'm like, okay, just when this was getting really good here she come with the creepy stuff. And when I saw her house she had—it was simple but it was enough.

Dedra and Laurinda, 2014.
Courtesy of the narrator.
Photo by Elite Images Photography.

Nothing—five-thousand-square-foot homes I lived in I didn't have anymore. It was simplicity, and there was a front porch and a back porch. And there was also a side porch. She plant herself out front and out in the middle of nowhere. My internet service was in and out. Phone might work, it might not work. But that's what I wanted. And so, I feel like God heard me when I was down to absolute nothing and asked what I really wanted, what I really wanted in my heart.

So, who asked whom?

I think it was a discussion. I think it was a discussion, but I probably most likely initiated the conversation. As far as the gestures regarding securing a proposal, it was her because she was real slick about it. We had a discussion about it. And it came up from having been in relationships for extended periods of time with other people that we didn't want to marry. So, the first time I got in the car with her, she's driving and I wanted to ride into the sunset with her. No matter where something was, I'd want her with me. And I knew then. That was the first date. I felt safe in that she has the ability to make me feel safe. And no matter what's going on around me, she was able to do that, and that's what I was looking for in a spouse. I didn't believe in gay marriage before that. I didn't want to do that. So, she tricked me and proposed to me on my birthday in a real cute way. But I didn't find out until February this year she proposed, because we got married in December. I think it was always a mutual thing to get married.

Where did you go?

New York. It was our first time going.

* * *

When I came back down here and the first time I tasted sweet tea, I thought I was going to go into a diabetic coma. It was the best tea I've ever had in my life. And no one was ashamed for it. Then I met someone who was always trying to make it even sweeter than that. So, no one down here puts on airs. What you see is what you get. No one here cares. [. . .] Everybody in the town knows that she's married. And everybody in town knows that she married a high yella woman. Everybody in town knew when I came. And everybody in town knows who I am. Everybody in town respects who I am. I was wearing my baseball hats and my jeans and she said, "You ain't no boy. When everybody else see you, you gotta have your hair done, your earrings, your coat, because they know who you belong to. They know who you with." I wanna paint, I wanna do stuff. They clean for you, we had a housekeeper. Paint, we get somebody to paint. No. She made me into the whole thing about how you treat a woman, stuff like that. And our first wedding anniversary we give paper, stationery or whatever. It needs to be made of paper, fine linen. Second wedding anniversary is garnet. It's a stone. Our wedding anniversary is not until December. Our second anniversary actually of meeting she gave me some garnet and diamond earrings. No disrespect to me. How many men going to take time to look on the internet and find out what you give for this wedding anniversary? She just refined me. I was probably a diva before. Still a diva now, but she refined the diva. "A woman doesn't do this." "Okay, it's not okay for you to walk around without your hair done." So yes, damn it for me, every week. I've not had anybody to treat me that way, but it comes along with the culture. And I can appreciate that, but I've not been exposed to that. Do I need it in the North, South, East, West? Yeah, but here it's part of tradition. And for us we live openly. It's not discussed. We've never had a problem.

· ·

"Louise" [b. 1944, Durham, North Carolina]
I think that if you take away the sexual aspect of relationships with women in the South that women in the South are extremely intimate with each other. I think that southern women are very supportive. I think that southern women are very embracing, literally. I don't think that southern women are afraid to touch each other. I think they hug together, they cry together, they commiserate together. I think intimacy for southern [women] is like . . . my experience is that it's like second nature. It's so genuine and so real. And when you throw the sex in it, that's like gravy. But I think southern women are just naturally warmer and freer in terms of being able to connect with each other. I would be really curious to know if I'm right. I don't know if that's correct, but that's true. You know? That's my experience: we hug, we laugh, we cry, and that's what intimacy is about. We tell secrets, we share

stories, we curse each other out, and then hug each other the next minute. I think it's very real with southern women. I really do. I had friends who are not reared in the South who I would consider good friends, good people, but not the same level of intimacy. I have a very dear friend who is white, from Massachusetts. I always think about how we greet each other. In the South, and I am a hugger, so in the South I think that when woman hug, they hug. They really hug each other. My good friend from Massachusetts, when we hug, there was always this, um . . . there was always this, um . . . from the waist down I would be here and she would be there kind of thing. We used to always talk about that. In fact, I said to her one time, "Can I really have a real hug? I mean, what is this?" You know? I think in the South that's more natural just to embrace fully. Yeah. And, as I said, I don't know if that's correct, but it's true.

. . . .

Lindsay

Lindsay and her partner, Tori (see chapter 5), were two of the youngest women I interviewed—both students at Florida A&M University at the time. Lindsay is a talker. I would ask a question, and she would dive right in and maybe twenty minutes later I could get in another question. She was born in Jacksonville, Florida, in 1993, the eldest of four children. The interview took place on March 23, 2013, at an LGBT resource center in Tallahassee, Florida.

She is an engineering major and I am a chemistry premed major, so we don't really have classes together, but I happen to be friends with a girl who was in the anime club at the time. And she dragged me to this anime club meeting, and I didn't want to go because I'm not interested in anime at all, but I generally—

What is anime?

It's like cartoons except they're Japanese. I don't know how to describe it, I really don't. I'm not into it, but I've generally made good friends with people who are interested in anime because their personalities coincide with mine. It's just not something I'm interested in. I'll go to this meeting. Maybe I'll meet some people. I don't have any friends, whatever. So, I went to the meeting and I happened to run into a dude who was in a class with me. So, I sit there and we're talking for a minute, and of course all of his friends come over and somehow we ended up in a very warm-natured debate between him and all of his friends and me. And I'm meeting all these people, when along walks this girl who's apparently friends with him. And she comes up behind me and I know now, I couldn't hear it at the time, "Hi," to which I responded for about five minutes, at which point she then said, "Okay, bye," and walked away.

So, I blew that, but over the course of several months following that we became friends, and she was dating someone else at the time. She actually started dating someone else shortly after this first interaction, so I just really blew it. But she was dating someone else at the time, and I had to get to know her more on just a friendship level first, which I appreciate now, best friends forever. But we didn't start dating until the spring semester. This happened the fall semester my freshman year and we didn't start dating until the spring semester . . . because I was at home over Christmas and she had recently broken up. And I called up my friend from high school and I was like, "So there's this girl," and she stops me and she goes, "Okay pause. Is this one straight this time?" And I said "No," and she goes, "Okay continue." And I said, "So there's this girl, and she's really pretty and I like her a lot" and she goes, "Okay pause. Does she like you?" And I said, "I don't know. Stop asking me questions so I can tell my story." [. . .]

And it's interesting because this was right before New Year's. Actually, it was right after Christmas right before New Year's, and my grandmother always said that Christmas wishes mean absolutely nothing, it's the New Year's wishes that mean something. When you make a wish at midnight on New Year's that that's the most powerful of all because you're starting a new year, you're starting a new time, and if you actually work toward that wish, you put in some effort, then it's more likely to come true because it's turning over a new leaf. [. . .] Because I'm a very superstitious person, I of course then made a wish at midnight on New Year's that I would get to know her better and that we could have some kind of relationship, and lo and behold, six hours later at 6 A.M., she decides to text me about whether or not I watched the *Twilight Zone* marathon. And we had never actually contacted each other through texting or phones or anything because we had each other's numbers but hadn't actually talked on the phone. So, I'm like, "Yes, I always watch the *Twilight Zone* marathon on New Year's," and we just started talking. We started talking nonstop for two days until we got back to school.

And it wasn't until a week after we got back to school I was like, "So what are you doing on Saturday?" and I took her out. I didn't have any money. I was a very broke college student and I wasn't getting a full ride at the time. I was actually paying not much, like a thousand dollars a semester to go to school, but I didn't have any money, so I decided, what's the most romantic thing you can do on a budget? Let's have a picnic and go bowling at the campus bowling alley. So I was running late because I do laundry to have something to wear, so I'm running to Walgreens trying to find bread and peanut butter to make sandwiches. I'm running really super late, so I decided to buy some ready-made sandwiches just in case, so I had Coke, some Oreos, bread, peanut butter, jelly, all the stuff I needed, and I couldn't find a picnic basket. So, I made do. I ended up having to make sandwiches because she was also running late and texted me. She was like, "Could you come at 2:30 instead of 2?" So, I was like, "Yeah, okay, that works out great for me." So, I made sandwiches and shoved it all in Tupperware in a plastic bag, and we get down to the bowling alley, and it's closed because for some reason the bowling alley wouldn't be open on weekends. So, I of course smacked myself over the head repeatedly and decide to just go ahead, and go ahead with the picnic, and we ended up sitting there for six hours just talking. And bear it mind it does not take long to eat peanut butter and jelly sandwiches and some Oreos. We were sitting there down by where all the picnic benches are on campus for six hours just talking, and we only stopped because I made myself say that I was going to get her back to her dorm by a certain time because it was a first date. And I was going to be respectful because both of my parents instilled in me very, very chivalrous tendencies, especially when they found out I liked girls. So, both my parents gave me all these rules to live by.

But do you consider yourself masculine?

No, not at all. No, no. I just I believe in good old-fashioned values, and I believe in being courteous. I hold doors for everyone nondiscriminately because I don't particularly consider that chivalrous, I consider that common courtesy. So, I don't consider myself masculine, but I'm the kind of person who believes she who asks pays. And seeing as I asked her out, I was going to take the lead on the date. And so, I was determined to get her back to her dorm at a certain time, and so I kind of cut it shorter than we might have made it before, but not short at all, and walked her back, and we just started talking and dating. And it was actually interesting because we ended up having sex before our second date but not after the first date, because that would be improper. We just, it's been snowballing ever since, and it's awesome.

How do you find the climate on a historically black college being a couple?

It's interesting because I can't speak for other historically black colleges because I've never been to them, but I feel like everyone on FAMU's campus is on the DL, honestly, just about everyone. I'm not going to say everyone, but just about everyone is on the DL, but it's not really anything where you're going to get accosted. It's not anything where you're going to be physically assaulted in the hallway. I've gotten quite a few looks in the dorm especially, because we lived in the same dorm our freshman year. I've gotten a few looks. I've gotten a few people who stopped talking to me once they started seeing us in the hallway, and it wasn't anybody I was friends with originally, it was just people I would say hi to in passing if they were in a class with me, or something, a few people who just spontaneously stopped talking to me in hallways. But it was never anything terrible.

· ·

Malena

At the time of the interview, Malena was seeking a PhD in anthropology at Duke University. She contacted me about being interviewed for the book after she heard me give a talk at the University of North Carolina at Chapel Hill. She was born in 1980 in Charlotte, North Carolina, the youngest to two children. The interview took place August 1, 2013, at her home in Chapel Hill.

Anthropology PhDs take seven to nine years. [Laughter] So, I'm starting year nine. The beginning of [my] third year, it was the beginning of Laurie's first year, and a friend of mine was having a party at her house for pre-Pride, which here is in September. And Laurie had only even—she had been in Tanzania for two years doing research and had just started the program, and a friend from her program was like, "Oh, I heard about this house party, let's just go." And so, I was just being social and talking to everyone, and while was I talking to Laurie, she had mentioned she was taking an anthropology class, and I was just like, okay, went home. And so, I was asking a friend of mine who I knew was in the class, I was like, "Hey, do you know that there's a woman in—or do the public health woman who's in the class?" And somehow that question got turned into, during their next class, she was like, "Hey, Laurie, I have this friend who wants your phone number, who's in love with you," [laughter] or something like that. It was very junior high. And it turns out that Laurie's roommate, who is straight, at the time was also in the class, so she—Laurie's roommate and my friend conspired to set us up on a date. And so, we both agreed to it, and by the end of the day, I thought she was the strangest person I have ever met in my entire life.

And so, a few days afterward she sent an e-mail, it was like, "Okay, we had fun. Let's go out again, try a different restaurant or something." And I wrote back, I was like, "I think not." [Laughter] Yes, I was very mean. And so, she—but I was like, "You're pretty cool. I mean, we can hang out, but just not in that way." And so, she wrote back this e-mail, it's like, uh, "I require more of friends, and I have high standards, and you don't meet them." [Laughter]

Oh, wow. Tit for tat.

Yeah. And so, about a month later, the same friend who kind of set all this up had a Halloween party, and her Halloween parties are infamous around here. They go all out. And so she invites everyone, so of course Laurie and her roommate were invited. And at that party, Laurie's roommate was like, "Okay, tell me what's going on here." She was like, "I wanna know why you sent that e-mail." She just pretty much, she has no filter, and so I was like, "Laurie's all right." I was like, "I just thought she was kinda strange." Somehow it turned out that I agreed that I would be nice to Laurie and I would give her another chance. And it wasn't that Laurie was like pining after me or anything like that; it was more that I was like I was really rude, and that's just really not cool, and I'm not normally like that, and I should be a better person and make it up to her. And so, we had coffee and I decided, you know what, she's actually pretty cool. And then dinner and then it kept going. We still tease each other all the time. I'm like, "I don't even know why you gave me a second chance. You were crazy." [Laughter] And we actually enjoy telling that story, making fun of each other about how awful we were to each other. But yeah, it's great. Like I said, November will be six years, and yeah, we do pretty well together.

And you have introduced her to your family, but have you met her family as well?

I have.

And how did that go?

It was interesting—her approach was the same as mine. She's never actually told her parents she's gay. She's just like, "This is Malena." So, like I was telling you, my first visit to Chicago, we drove from here one Christmas up to visit her family, and—

She took you to meet her family during a holiday?

And they're white and they're from a town that has, according to Wikipedia, 0.2 percent black people. [Laughter]

And you're a black southerner at that.

Yeah, they're just polite Midwesterners, so they're like, "Oh, okay. Hi, Malena." And yeah, it was nicely awkward, [laughter] but her family's great, actually. They like me. I think mainly because of the distance and because we see my mom more, they're probably not as like, "Hey, welcome to the family," as my mom and dad are with Laurie. But they are nice. Like, one of her sisters got married, and so Laurie officiated at the wedding, and they told me to join the family picture, and I was just like, "Huh? Okay." [Laughter] And like on Facebook, a few of her siblings have like invited me to be their sister on Facebook or things like that. Or it was really funny, 'cause Laurie went to undergrad in Wisconsin, and so we went up there one time to visit, or to go to a friend's wedding in Wisconsin, and her dad currently lives in Iowa, but just across the border from Wisconsin. So, while we were in Madison, we drove over to her dad's house, and somehow, we were there for a wedding got translated into Laurie and I were there to get married, since you can get married in Iowa, and so her family thought we were coming to Iowa to get married. [Laughter] And so, they're like, "Oh, okay, that's nice." But yeah, so she's never had that conversation with them. Everyone just kind of figured it out on their own.

· ·

"**Mary**" [b. 1975, Tuscaloosa County, Alabama]

I think I have been blessed to be surrounded with some fabulous women. Like my friends and my close associates are definitely like my family. I think that we have a closeness. I haven't found it difficult at all to be intimate or to find friends or to be close to women. I know that my personality is very—I don't want to say standoffish because that's not the right word, but I'm very reserved to a certain extent. My partner always says women are drawn to me for whatever reason. And not even in a sexual [way], but just like, "Hey, I can really talk to her" type level. Because she'll introduce me to her friends and next thing, they're my friends. So, I think that the possibilities of friendship and intimate relationships among the lesbians in the South, the ones that I know at least, there's some great possibilities. And it's interesting because my friends and I were talking about pop culture's portrayal of women and their relationships and the whole "bad girl," "bad bitch," whatever stereotype that they put out just about women in general and women of color in particular. And we were just always like, I don't know people like that. I know what it was. *Basketball Wives*, the whole scenario with Jennifer and Evelyn. I was like, that would never happen with my friends and I. Because if someone does something and the other doesn't like it, we'll discuss it and we move on. But the way that they were going at each other, I can't recall any friends that I've had, any situations that will be remotely similar to something like that.

Nadia [b. 1983, Pensacola, Florida]

Her name is Rochelle. I met her almost two years ago, and we were—actually Shani, we were at her birthday party, so she swears she's a match-maker on that one. I had come out of a relationship a while. It was a short while, actually. I wasn't looking for anything, anybody. I was just trying to chill. We were actually engaged, me and my ex, but it was one of those comfortable relationships where we're just doing this because we've been together for a while and it's kind of what everybody else is doing, but it was a mutual, it was a good breakup, actually. Anyway, I was just chilling, just hanging out enjoying being single, hadn't been in a while. And Shani had a birthday party at Marriott. She [Rochelle] was working at the front desk at the time. I had met her previously about two years before because her girlfriend at the time played on the same softball team as I did. We played for a city league. We had a all-girl, all-lesbian city league team called Hotshots that Shani was on as well, so I met her there.

And it was funny because I met her, I remember putting my cleats on and she was sitting at the top of the bleachers, and I just happened to look at her and she was looking at me and we had a moment. That was like two years before, so I never really seen her again, but I just remember having that. It was so weird. So, anyway, I see her, I come to the party, and she's at the front desk, and I couldn't find the elevator. I'm like, "Do you all have an elevator?" I couldn't find it anywhere. So, I asked her where the elevator was, and I seen her face and I'm like, I've seen this girl before somewhere. I was like, "Wow, she's really cute." That's what I was thinking to myself. She told me I probably should take the stairs, and at first I thought she was being rude because she was like, "Just take the stairs." And I was like, "But I kind of want the elevator. I asked you for the elevator." She was like, "No really, just take the stairs because the elevator was all the way around the corner and five places over and all this." I was like, "Okay." So, I went up there, hung out with Shani, and had the party started, and about an hour or two later there was a knock at the door, and she had came in and she had changed clothes. She had came in, and I didn't know that she was [gay]. It was her girlfriend at the softball thing, but I didn't know she was actually gay at that time either. I just thought she was supporting or just hanging out because we had a mixture. We had women straight and gay on the team actually, and I couldn't really gauge her too well at that time either.

So, anyway, she comes in, and there's another girl there that I was cool with, and we both kind of perked up when she came into the room.

And so we run out of drinks, and I think it was a Wednesday, I think it was the middle of the week, so nothing was really open. It was like after nine. We go around looking around. She's like, "Well, Walgreens has some Moscato and some wine and stuff," and so she's like, "I'll go grab some stuff." So, me and the other girl were like, "Oh, you want us to go with you?" So, she was like, "Yeah sure, I don't know you all, but sure." [Laughter] So, we went down with her, and it was me, this other girl, and her, started automatically asking questions like, "What's your name, where you from, dah, dah, dah," and she tell us who she was. And then the other friend, not the girl that was also interested but the other one, she was just like, "So are you gay?" And she was like, "Yeah, I am," so I remember sitting there like, "Yes, yes." Me and the other chick were just like, we were really trying. We were both pulling back and forth. So, we got the drinks, we came back—we fought for the shotgun seat, by the way—got back to the place. And while I'm drinking and I'm like looking, and another girl moved in and they're sitting on the couch in the little guest area and normally I wasn't even in the mind-set. I was just sitting there and I was just like, "Damn, I really like this girl." I said I'm going to bow out because she's obviously talking to her, they're engaged in conversation. I don't know where it came over me, I just decided to get up, I walked right in the middle, I just sat myself between the two of them, and just started jumping in the conversation.

So, I started talking to her, talking back and forth, we're all talking and then I turned to her a little bit more and started talking to her, she still was engaged. By the end of the night we both walked her down to her car. I happened to park on the other side of the hotel, and they parked on that side of the hotel. So, her and her friend were talking, and everybody was trying to prolong the car conversation, and then so finally they left. And I was like, "Oh man. I parked way around the other side." And she was like, "Oh well, I'll drive you to your car." So, I got in the car with her, and she drove me over to the other side of the hotel, and then I got out and I said, "Okay, it's been a while, but I really enjoyed your conversation this evening. Can I get your phone number or whatever?" She's like, "Yeah, it's been a while for me, too. Sure. Why not?" So, we exchanged numbers. When I got back to the house I texted her to make sure she made it home safely and then I called her. Well, I texted her the next day, and I asked her was she doing anything that weekend, did she want to maybe catch a movie, or something like that. And she came over and we rented movies instead and hung out for a little bit and kind of just chitchatted from that point. And we were both very much like, okay, I don't want a relationship, just want to hang, kick it sometimes, that's all. And the more we kept saying that, the more it kept, I'm seeing you every day, hanging out, dah, dah, dah. Next thing we stumbled into a relationship. But we took our time. We actually just moved in together four months ago. Normally everybody has a U-Haul, so we actually took our time. We waited a whole year to see how it went, and then we just decided to move in recently, and I'm glad we did that.

And is she from the South?

She's from Haiti. She was born in Haiti, but she was raised in Jacksonville, so yeah, I guess you could say she's from the South, from real South, South.

. . . .

Pat Hussain [b. 1950, Atlanta, Georgia; Cherry interjects throughout.]

It was in Huntsville, Alabama. It was '85, '84. She'll clear it up. I was being transferred to take over a new store, Toys"R"Us, and I asked why. I had been engaging in a series of meaningful overnight relationships [laughter] and had included in that a number of women who were married. I wonder if it was deliberate? [Laughter] I didn't want someone for myself. I wanted someone for now. I just want to borrow someone nice. "She's a nice woman. I really like her. Thank you. Until next time." [Laughter] And, I had had some brushes . . . with men who object to that type thing. I asked the legal people. I said, "Why are you going to send a dyke to Huntsville?" I said, "It's a smaller town. It's a toy store, for God's sake. This could be a real problem." They said, "There won't be a problem." I said, "Well, if you say so," but I don't know. Atlanta's a pretty big place. Huntsville, not so much. They said I'd be fine. I said, "Okay, alright. Y'all got me, right?" Okay. So, I went, wallet in my back pocket, and the suits were there for the tour and the managers getting to meet them, and we're in the front of the store and they're introducing me around there. Cherry breaks through them and walks up, shakes my hands and says, "Hi. My name is Cherry, you're going to love me." [Laughter] They said, "Oh, that's Cherry. Don't mind her, she's one of the employees here. You'll get to meet her, and now this is so-and-so." And I thought, "Wait until you find out I'm a dyke. You just wait."

So, it escaped them what just happened?

Yes. I'm presuming that she's just talking off the top of her head. And I thought, "Yeah, I'm going to love you, really? Do you know I'm a dyke? I'm a lesbionic?" And I thought, "Wait until she finds out. If she doesn't know already, when she finds out she'll say, 'Oh my God, did I say that to her?'" Yeah, but I was just tickled. I thought, "Okay, you got it." And that's the first thing she ever said to me, "My name is Cherry and you're going to love me." And I got in and tried to get settled. "We're moving right into my blackout season, the holidays. Don't talk to me. Don't call me unless someone's died." Now it's time to make money. Now it's time to make that bottom line beautifully black, like a laser on there, and work we did. And coming out of that, I realized that I had a girlfriend in Atlanta.

CHERRY: Don't say her name.

Alright. I liked to go out with straight women or presumably straight women. A friend of mine and I would go out, a guy, a straight guy. He's really disgusting. He was really disgusting. My buddy, he would go out and meet women and tell them, "Yeah, I'm gay and I've tried to change and if I could ever meet the right woman someone who was woman enough to . . . ." He got laid so much with that horrible line. I told you he was disgusting. Anyway, we would go out, and we went to a bar. See a beautiful woman sitting there, walk in the room, and he'd say, "Alright, I'm going first." I'd say, "Go ahead. Go talk to her and get her phone number or something." [He was] shut down. He comes back, and I said, "Alright, let me show you how it's done." And what he didn't know is that I would go over and introduce myself, "My name is Pat. The gentleman that just came over and I are together, and we had a bet to see who could get your phone number, get to sit down and talk to you, and I want you to know that I'm very, very much interested in getting to know you. You're a beautiful woman." I said, "If you say no you're not interested, I'll still have my fantasies, even though I hope you don't. But I would like for you to assist me in ruining his evening. If you could just give me a big ole hug or a kiss on the cheek or something, it would just be perfect." Woo! I got kisses. I got full body hugs. I got phone numbers. [Laughter] I'd go back over to him. I said, "Thank you very much, and I will call you." "What did you say?" I said, "No, just watch and learn." [Laughter] So, I was a little predatory.

So, you might say when I got here I had a girlfriend, and once we got through the holiday season she [Cherry] was asking me out. "Let's go out and have a drink." I thought she was married. Not only married but children. I said [to myself], "You're in Huntsville, girl, and she's working for you. Slow your roll. Put a big fence around this. No." I liked it. She was bothering me at work. She was so nice. She packed up my Christmas presents for my girlfriend and sent them off on UPS because I had done apparently really badly and she had to do them so they could go. She would bring me fruit and little Hershey's chocolate kisses, and she's a hugger. She always wanted me to hug her. And one day she said, I think we were at the break room, and she said, "You hug other people. Why won't you hug me?" I said, "I just really don't want [to]." She said, "But I saw you hug so-and-so and so-and-so and so-and-so." I said, "Okay" and I hugged her. I gave her a giant hug, a meaty shoulder. The room got quiet. [Laughter] She got quiet. I hugged her alright. Mm-hmm. Yeah. Then she said I kept putting her off, but I was going out. "Where are the gay bars?" "You mean the gay bar?" The people that worked for me were saying, "Are you going to park your car in front of the bar?" I said, "I'm going in it. Yes. Yes, I am." None of the women there transferred out.

I was going home for Easter. I go home to see my girlfriend every chance I got—she was a straight woman—escorting her. My brother-in-law thought that was hilarious. And she gave me an ultimatum. She said, "This is the last time I'm going to ask you out. You go or you don't, but this is the last time. I'm not going to ask you anymore." And I thought, well, this is the mouse that roared. She said, "I can come to your place. I can cook breakfast for you." I said, "Oh, you got it. You got it." As soon as I get back from Atlanta, I think it was going to be on a Wednesday I think, and I said, "You got it, you got it. Not a problem." I said, "But you have a week to change your mind." No. She said, "Oh yeah, I'm going to set up the time." Okay, you got it. I went to Atlanta and saw my brother-in-law. My brother-in-law and I used to go out. My sister stopped us from going out together. He said I always introduced him to too many women. "Too many women, nope. That's over. I can't run." I said, "There's this sweet little thing up in Huntsville and I've been stepping around her, but she married and got two children. I'm not trying to get myself in any trouble in Huntsville, but she gave me an ultimatum and when I go back, the predator will be on the loose. I can't wait." He said, "Okay." I told my girlfriend, who would not come visit me. It was a one-way street. I told her, "I'll get you a plane ticket. I'll get you a bus ticket." She didn't like to drive, I knew that. It was one-way. And she said to me, "Well, can't you just be an adult? Be an adult and be by yourself." I said, "No, I'm not going to do that. I'm going to start going out." So, she said, "You going to be having sex with other people?" I said, "If the opportunity presents itself, yes. I'm tired of being by myself. If you want to stay in Atlanta, stay in Atlanta. I'm not a 'hear about it' kind of girl. I will tell you."

So, I came back. I was looking forward to it, and I was exhausted from the trip, went to sleep. The phone rang. She [Cherry] said, "Oh, did you change your mind?" and I said, "No." And I had just slept too late, sleeping like the dead. I said, "Give me just a minute," because I had to get up and get myself collected, and I did. I let her in. She brought in the food she was going to make. She was going to cook. When she came in I said, "Hey, how you doing?" Went around me, put all the stuff down in the kitchen. I said, "Don't I get a hug?" Nope. I thought, well, and she then was so skittish like the cat in the room full of rocking chairs and I thought, well. And she cooked a delightful breakfast of omelets. We ate, and it was just wonderful, and I had to go to a meeting. I said, "I'll go to the meeting and I'll meet you back here." She needed to go work. I said, "Do I get a hug before I go?" And she kind of gave me a hug, but she just kind of shot out the door. I thought, "Shit, okay." I went to the meeting and got back to the apartment and I was late. I got back there.

CHERRY: A friend had to call me at work.

I called a friend of hers that I knew that worked with her. I said, "Would you please call Cherry?" because she had two jobs. "Will you please call Cherry and tell her I'm running late but I'm coming." She said okay, and she did because I didn't want her to leave thinking, "Ha ha, got you to come back." And we went into the apartment, but she was so jumpy in there I thought, "Well, maybe let's go out." We went to the park, and we laid on the grass in the park, and I was just rubbing my head on her, and we had talked and talked and talked, and then she kissed me. [Whispering] Oh and it was on. It was on. That's how it began.

And how long have you been together?

Well, we had an understanding because I had been in a relationship with a woman and she was an alcoholic, which it took me a while to recognize because I drink and I wasn't getting [it]. It took a while to sink in that every time she drinks she gets drunk, which is every day, and ending that relationship was very painful. The fact that I had to get out of it didn't make me care for her any less, I just needed to drag my heart back, and the last thing I wanted was to get involved really with anyone else. And so, I told her that the relationship might last a year, maybe two, and that I was definitely nonmonogamous, and if she didn't want anything to do with me then I understood and respected that, but I didn't want to be dishonest. I wanted her to know those things about me, and she said, "I'd rather be a fool in love with you than never to have been loved by you." And somewhere along the line time just kept passing. She did have a rule, though, when we started living together that knowing now who I was that I could do anybody once, nobody twice, and there would be no strays. Don't call her house, knock on her door. "Is Pat?" No. No seconds, no strays. And after almost twenty monogamous years she unilaterally changed the terms. She said, "I'm too old for this." This is now a monogamous relationship. There'll be no first, so there'll be

Cherry and Pat Hussain,
waiting for their marriage
license in Connecticut.
Courtesy of Cherry Hussain.

no strays. Now, despite my counter and my objection that I was just about to make my move, she said, "Too late. I told you I'm too old for this. This is now monogamous." And it's been twenty-six years, it's been a long time.

And you got married?

Yes, we had a ceremony at MCC [Metropolitan Community Church] maybe fifteen to twenty years, I can't remember, and we had a ceremony joining us as a couple. We went to visit our friend in New London, Connecticut. She said, "Why don't y'all get married while you're here." I said, "Oh, I said I hadn't thought about that." I said, "Well, Cherry we don't have all the documentation. I looked online. You need a birth certificate and all this." I said we don't have any of that. I said, "But you can talk to them," because she good at talking to people. We left that day with a marriage license in hand, and we went back the next day and were married, so we married by a marriage license.

And when was that?

This was two years or three? I have to look at the marriage [certificate], three. See how I just can't remember shit—I mean stuff? And it was the idea of family. People are all over the place around gay marriage. It has like in New Orleans when they say, "Who you with?" I've always been clear about I was with you or I wasn't but we were ships passing in the night. I told her she's one of the most powerful dykes I know. She made me a mother and now a grandmother. But suppose something happens with one of the children, with the grandchildren, exclusions by stepson, by our son or by his now ex-wife, because if someone sick I took care of the oldest grandbaby, I was her primary caregiver. That's my girl. She was an infant. When I go and say my grandchild is sick, what does that mean? A marriage license changes all that. We have the papers you need, power of attorney, and will, and all that, because we seen more of it than we care to during the AIDS pandemic—[same-sex couples] that have been robbed of everything because their partner was sick when simple bedside ceremonies, marriages would've brought a stop to that. To me, like any other right, you don't have to exercise it, but it's there; it's available to you should you decide that you want to use it. So, that has been a big part in creating our family unit.

. . . .

Rose [b. 1958, Roanoke, Virginia]

It's so funny. I was with my ex-partner, my last ex-partner, and I hadn't lived here in Texas more than a year, a while. And another woman friend said, "You know, you really have to meet this person. You have so much in common, you're phenomenal." And so, she arranged for all of us to have like a happy hour thing. And I'm not a drinker. My ex-partner is not a drinker. My partner now is not a drinker. But we went to this happy hour, and I don't know, it wasn't like there was love at first sight or anything. But certainly, we connected. It was like she was drinking something. I was like, "Oh, I want what you want. I want what you got." Right? And I remember when we left my partner said to me, "Oh, you like her." I was like, "Get out of here. We'll probably be friends." But I was oblivious to any kind of attraction, but she knew. And we had had a troubled relationship for a while. And so, we didn't see each other in community here. And then I broke up with my partner. She was a college professor, and she was just here on sabbatical when I moved here. And she went back to do her gig—which was a perfect opportunity for me to break up with her [laughter] so I didn't have to look at her. And we broke up and I wasn't seeing anybody. And then I lost my job here, and P was such a friend to me in that process in the way that I needed a friend. The kind of "What do you need?" "Oh, I don't need anything." "I'll tell you what. Let me come take you to lunch because I don't think you're eating" kind of thing.

And at the time she was kind of with somebody but not really. I don't even know how to describe it. She was living with someone and their relationship had fallen apart but was reconstituting itself in a different way. It was transforming itself. But her partner or ex-partner, however she frames it, was dying. And I loved the way that she loved her, despite the reconstitution, the reconfiguring of relationship, that she could find a way to be beyond all of the prescribed ways of being in a relationship with somebody and love this person through to her death. [. . .] What I also knew was how to support her in that process in a way that didn't require a particular form of relationship. I don't know how I knew that at the time. And so, that's what we did.

Rose and Priscilla
in Anguilla, 2016.
Courtesy of the narrator.
Photo by Anne Wallace.

I supported her and she was a great friend to me. And she loved her partner, and I'm sure that she lived with love until her end. And watched her and allowed her to go in a loving way. And I didn't know that she and I could have a relationship after that. I had decided in my head that the Creator or Spirit had placed us in each other's paths for that purpose. And that when that purpose was fulfilled I really had this thought that we wouldn't have this kind of loving relationship. And she knew better. She did. She knew better. But I did, I thought that was that. Because that felt big enough, right? I was grateful for the whole experience. I didn't understand that there could be more.

And how long have you been together?

That is a hard question. Because I don't know when to count.

What date?

Right. I've been living here for two years. We've been living together for two years. [. . .] I don't know about other folks. You start a relationship when you have sex, right? So, that's the date. But I don't know. That [. . .] doesn't feel like it makes sense to me in terms of a connection that's beyond physical. It's like, okay, so this is when that kind of physical connection happened. But how is that more significant than this progression of spirit connection, of practical connection? The first time she fixed my car or something? You know what I'm saying? I don't know.

Have you met each other's families?

Yes.

And how did that go? Or how is that?

I don't know, because timing is interesting. It was like 2 A.M., 1 or 2 A.M. in the morning, and she says, "I want you to meet my mom." And I was like, "I am not going over to your mama's house at this time of morning." She's like, "She's up, she's up," and I'm like, "No, no, no." She's like, "No, no, no." She took me over to her mom's house. I walked in. Her mother was just loving and sweet, and we sat and had a conversation, and the whole time I was just like I cannot believe I walked up in this woman's house at this time in the morning. And she said that the reason why she did it is basically she couldn't contemplate any kind of relationship with somebody over the long haul until her mother had laid her eyes on her. It's like her mother had to look at you and look at your eyes, make sure you didn't have crazy eyes. Because she's like, "Mmm, that one has got crazy eyes." [. . .] So, it was interesting. So, I got the seal of approval before we were down that road.

. . . .

Sharita [b. 1979, Washington, DC]

I met my partner on Myspace. She sent me a message saying, "Hey, I was browsing profiles, and I see that you're here and you seem like a really nice person." And I thought, "Oh, okay." So, we talked for a while. And we talked over there, and so she sent me a message, and she was living with her ex-girlfriend. She said they were no longer together but they were still living in the same apartment because they had been together for like five years. And so, they were still living in the same apartment . . . but the computer was in the room that her ex-girlfriend was using, and so she was like, "Here's my number. Text me." I said, "Okay." And so we started texting or whatever. And one day I was leaving class and it was before I had to go to work. I said, "What you doing?" She said, "Nothing. I'm at home, lying down on the couch watching the rain," because she didn't go to work because she was sick that day. So I said, "Well, do you want to meet me?" And so she's like, "Yeah, I'll come and meet you."

This was going to be your first meeting?

Yeah. So, we can do it anywhere. In a public place in this case. So, we picked a parking lot—a church [. . .] with a big, open parking lot. I said, "Okay, you can meet me there." She said, "Well, okay." So, she got up, got dressed or whatever. And she was getting off the interstate, and it so happened that I was coming up the road that she was turning on. "Are you in this black car?" She was like, "Yeah." I said, "Well, I'm behind you." I said, "I can see you." She said, "Oh no, oh no, oh no. Oh my gosh, I can't do this,

I can't do this. I can't do this. No, no, no, not right now." I said, "Well, I can see you now already, so it's not a big deal." We're just meeting as friends. It's not a dating thing; we're just looking for friends. We wasn't looking to date. Because she just got out of a relationship. I just got out of a relationship, and I was trying to build this world of my own, so I wasn't looking for dates. I said, "Oh, okay, well I already see you." "You're right down the street, just keep going and I'm already behind you." "No, what if you're like a killer?" "I'm not a killer or anything. Just come on." I said, "If I was a killer I wouldn't have told you I'm following you." So, we got there. I got out of my car. I got in her car, and we sat there and talked. And despite us not looking for anything, there was already this connection between us. That's what I wanted, talking and stuff. And I guess she pointed out to me that I was growing facial hair and this car, the first time we ever met, and so she leaned over in my personal space, with her tweezers to pluck my hair. I was like, "Girl, get off of me." And she was like, "No da da da—get off. You've got facial hair." And she felt obligated to pluck it. And as she's plucking my facial hair her face was in my face, and we already had a common attraction giggly and all, like two people do—two little kids and when they meet and they like each other—and her face was in my face, and she kissed me. I said, "Oh, we kissed." And so, we kissed. I said, "Oh, my goodness."

And how long ago was this?

Six years ago. We kissed, and we kissed again, and it was like, "Oh, I've got to go to work." And she was like, "Oh, okay." I said, "Okay, I've got to go to work," and she was like, "Oh, we've got to leave, and I don't really want to, but I've got to go." So, I eventually get out of the car and leave. I called her on the phone and for her that was like a desperate plea or something. She made a call. And I'm like, "No, I just wanted to talk to you while I was on my way to work." She was like, "Oh, well." So, we talked or whatever. She disclosed this later on. She was like, "I didn't know what to think. You just called me again. I'm like definitely making sure you get where you were going and I was going to get to work." And I was like, "Well, what are you doing later?" And she was like, "Nothing." I said, "Well, Destiny go to bed about what, seven o'clock, eight o'clock. I think about eight o'clock. Destiny got to bed at eight o'clock; you can come over. Come over about then."

So, she knew you had a child.

She knew. We were friends. She knew. And well, the friendship lasted like two days. [Laughter] Yeah, the friendship lasted about two days. And so, she came over and we talked. We talked in her car until about two, three in the morning. We talked; we kissed. I believe that might have been it, so she left. I think her roommate called. Her roommate called, "Where you at?" She's like, "Oh, I'm out studying or something." "Studying? If that's just your roommate, why you got to lie?" "Well, we've been together five years, and I don't want her to feel like I just moved on like she didn't matter." So, she's like, "I was studying" or whatever. I'm like, "Okay." The next day she came back. [. . .] She came over the next day with her best friend. And she was like, "Oh, I want you to meet her." And I'm like, "Who is this?" And she's like, "Oh, that's my best friend. I just wanted her to meet you, you're so cool." She obviously was feeling me, right? She wanted to get somebody else's point of view on this person that I'm talking to. So, we all sat over there and talked and stuff. And from that moment on it was like, every minute she got extra she was in my apartment. And in the morning time she'd go to the gym. She'd say, "I'm going to the gym." She would leave home early, five o'clock in the morning, tell her roommate, "Well, I'm just going to go to the gym." And she would come to my apartment. And [. . .] it rapidly grew into a relationship.

About a month later we were like together and she was at my house or I'm at her house. She'd met my daughter. She had two nieces, and that's how the kids met. She had two nieces—three that she would have all the time. And I thought, "Well, okay, we can meet downtown," and so we all met downtown. We all played around and stuff, and so that's how my daughter met her. And she always had nieces that were my daughter's age. And so, one of her nieces and my daughter are exactly the same age, so they always hit it off, and so that all kind of went well. Probably about two months in we were living together in her apartment because it was like either one person lived in that or the other person lived in another apartment. I'm like, "Hey look, I'm cheap. Why are we paying all this in rent?" And after that first week or two were over, I started going to her apartment because my apartment where I lived they had raccoons. She is scared to death. She said, "Oh my gosh, these raccoons out here. I can't get out of the car." "The raccoons aren't bothering you."

This is in Little Rock?

Mm-hmm. She said, "No, I can't do this. No." So, we ended up going over there once my daughter had met her and we all kind of hit it off. We would go over there and spend the night or the day. Spend the night and the day, days and weeks. I'm driving my daughter to school from her apartment and stuff. And then I'm like, "Look, you're paying this much rent and I'm paying this much rent. If we're sure that this is what we want, we can just go ahead and move together, and we can save that extra money that we're spending on an apartment that's not going anywhere." I'm relationship oriented. She's more of an "Uhhhh, not so much." I don't know, she's more leery of things. I'm like, if I'm going to commit myself, I'm going to commit all that I have to the best of my ability. I'm not perfect or whatever, but I'm going to give it all. And so, we ended up moving together. Before we moved in together she had an extra key. Her ex-girlfriend had moved out by this time obviously. [. . .] Because there were times when she hadn't set her down and told her she was dating someone else. And so, she was like, "I don't want her to find out by seeing us together." I think one time we were out and ran into one of her ex-girlfriend's cousins, who called and told her that. And she's like, "Nah, that's just my friend." But by that time, they had sat down and had the conversation that I am dating somebody else and we are pretty serious. And so, they was like, "Well, it's probably best that I move out."

And so, the ex-girlfriend moved out. And I was over there at some point and I helped. I'm like, I don't have any hard feelings against her. It's just a relationship that ended. But I'm not going to treat her any kind of way because she was dating my ex. We all have a past. And I'm not a jealous type person. So, after she moved out I had had a key. I would go to her job for lunch. And I had lunch before she had lunch. I had a split shift so I would be already off, and she would meet me for lunch. And she would want me to sit outside. "I'm not sitting outside the job every day waiting for you to get out for lunch. I need a key." So, she gave me a key. She says that I got the key and never gave it back. But she never really asked for the key back. And so, after that incident of the key situation, she gave me the key; I didn't take the key. We moved in together, and then so it kind of went from there. We've been together—I mean it hasn't been perfect, but we have been together for these six years.

And so, you got married.

We got married. September the 24th was our anniversary of us dating and I was looking for an anniversary gift. And me and Destiny went to the store for an anniversary gift. "What do you think about I want to marry Shayla?" She didn't really care. And so I said, "Okay." We were out looking for an anniversary gift. It wasn't planned. I said, "Oh, let me just go in here and look at rings." So, I went in there and looked at rings and stuff. And it hit me this is what I should do. I bought her an engagement ring and took it to our anniversary dinner. We were talking about Build-A-Bears. Destiny has a Build-A-Bear. She goes, "I've never had a Build-A-Bear." [. . .] It's a store and you can go in there and you build your own bear. You pick out the bear you want. You watch them stuff it. She sticks a little heart in there. You build your own bear; you direct it however you want and stuff like that. And I'm like, "What? You never had a Build-A-Bear?" So, in my mind, "Perfect. This all comes together."

So, Destiny and I got the ring. I said, "I need a Build-A-Bear." So, we went to Build-A-Bear. I picked out the bear. I thought it was perfect, cute, something she would like. And I let them stuff it, but in it I put a personalized message in it. Because how you push the button and it talks. I picked a personalized message. And so, I said a personal little thing. And I said, "Well happy anniversary. Will you marry me?" And then I had them put that in the little bear hand, and they filled it up and I dressed the bear in a wedding outfit. And so, for our anniversary we went out to dinner and she seen this box. She was like, "Oh, what's that, what's that," and I'm like, "Nothing, nothing, nothing." She said, "I see that box." And I said, "Yeah, it's nothing." So, we ate and I gave her the Build-A-Bear. In her mind she probably expected perfume or something. Oh, I got some perfume. No. I got her a Build-A-Bear and it talks, too. You push the button; see what it says. She's like, "Oh, that's so cute." She stopped and looked. "The bear just asked me to marry it." I said, "Oh, yeah." I said, "Do it again, let me hear." So, as she did it again I pulled out the ring and said, "Would you marry me?" She's like, "Oh yeah." So, we got all that stuff started and we had our ceremony in DC.

. . . .

Shetikka

I first interviewed Shetikka's wife, Keturah (see chapter 1), and Shetikka about a year later after they had been married for nine months. Shetikka was born in 1975 in Atlanta, Georgia, the eldest of two children. She and Keturah initially wanted to remain anonymous for the book but then changed their minds after they were married. The interview took place on August 25, 2013, at their home in Lithonia, Georgia.

[I met my partner] June 5th, 2009, [at] a women's meeting group. A women's only. I don't think it was necessarily lesbian, necessarily. But it was a once-a-month meeting group for women to talk about women's issues. [. . .] And actually, it was funny because my friend at the time, a really good friend, kept trying to get me to come out [. . .] to meet this person who was running the [meeting].

Not come out as a lesbian, but just to come out to the meeting.

Right, come out to the meeting, yes. And the person who was running the meeting, she had been trying to get me to come see her. And I was like,

"No, no, no, no." And so, I had just broken up with a girlfriend about a month ago maybe. And it was a Friday night because it happened to be the first Friday of the month was when this meeting was . . . it was just me, her, my friend who invited me, and the person who was running the meeting. And the reason my friend told me to come [. . .] she was talking about my partner, and she was like, "Yo, she's got a booty on her." [. . .] She told me how attractive she is to her. And I'm just like, "Oh my gosh, yeah, if she could sit on me one more time," this, that, and the other. And I'm sitting there like, "Oh wow, like yeah." She said, "Just come out to the meeting." "It will be fun to get out," because again I'm sitting home brooding over this broken heart. [. . .] I'm just not going to spend another Friday night alone watching movies over and over again so I don't have time to think about it.

So, I went to this meeting. And when I saw my friend I was like, "Wow." I see she's gorgeous. But again, my friend is interested in her, so I'm just happy for my friend. I don't have any reason to be anything but just at the meeting and doing whatever the meeting is supposed to be about. So, we end up having a discussion about relationships or something. I can't even remember what the conversation was. But I know at the end of the day she did not like me. We argue that that's not the way it was. But she said she did not like me. I was just saying stupid things. I don't think they were stupid at the time. I think they were genuinely how I felt about the situation that we were discussing. I remember one of them being about if an ex gives you a call after ten should you take it? And my philosophy was if we're just sitting there watching TV and she calls, then I can pick up the phone and answer it. And I think she was like, "No, that's crazy." Like that's disrespectful. I'm like, how is that—like I'm not going to interrupt the conversation to answer the phone. Like if we were talking, then she's going to wait. Or I'll talk to her tomorrow. But if we're just sitting there watching TV and we're not even in the same room when she calls, yeah, I can talk to her if I want. I was stupid. She was not happy with me. She was not nice to me.

Well, I left the meeting, and I was talking to my friend about how great looking she is, and I was like, "Man, good luck with that." Again, my friend liked her, so I wasn't trying to step into that arena. And so, eventually they got on a date and it didn't go well. Well, my friend considered it a date. To her [Keturah] it wasn't a date. And she backed it up with her proof that it was not a date. But it was a date for my friend. And my friend came back [saying], "Oh, she was a bitch," and "She was horrible." And I was like, "Oh, I'm so glad you went on that date and I didn't have to go through it." Because she was like, "Oh, she was picky. She didn't want to see a picture of my kid. How rude is that?" And I was saying like, "Yeah, that's rude." And I knew how my friend felt about her daughter. She had graduated from high school and she was very proud, and she was like, "Want to see a picture of my baby?" And Keturah was like, "No. I don't want to see no kids." And so I was like, "Oh, I'm so glad that was you and not me." So, from that point forward she was eye candy. I'm like, my friend went out on a date; it didn't go well. She don't like me either, so I'm just going to look at her for a while and enjoy my once-a-month Friday meetings just looking at her. So, that's what I did for a good year and change. We didn't ever go out on a date, I think—she invited me to her birthday in August of 2010.

So, what changed? Was it the group? The group dynamic?

She won't tell me what it is. Because I had girlfriends throughout that process. I even had girlfriends going to the meeting with me. They didn't know that this was my girlfriend at the time. But I had girlfriends going to the meetings with me. And I don't know, we just—we kind of started walking, which I don't even know how that started. But I think she initiated walking. We'd walk once a week. And then I wasn't very forthcoming with my current girlfriend, off-and-on girlfriend, and so she kind of gave me an ultimatum. And so, I'm like, "Hey, we can't walk anymore," because of my current person I was with was a little jealous of her. So, I was like, "We can't walk anymore." And so, we went for a while, and I think she invited me to her birthday, and so we started talking again. And then we started dating. I was dating someone at the time too, and we started dating, and then she was like basically, "I think I like you." And then it just started from there. I don't know what happened. Whatever it was, I was thankful. I was thankful because I had been watching her for too dang long, too long.

And how long was it before you moved in together?

I think it was a year. Yeah, it was a year later we moved in. [. . .] The first thing that clicks for me [is] the financial piece. She was someone who split things 50/50. Groceries, toiletries, it was like we're going to share this. Like, "I'm going to pay half. If we're going out to dinner I'm going to pay half." I'm not just sitting there waiting for the check to get there and then looking like, "No, I'm not paying that." And after five minutes and the person is, "Are you ready for me to take this?" And there's nothing in there, [and] you're like, "Oh, I guess I'm supposed to pay." Okay. And so, I'm paying for everything. So, she was the first one who was about splitting things and equal, and I was like, "Man, like I hate this about her—like you're going to treat me to the movies?" Because I might have treated two weeks ago. She was like, "I've got this." Love it. That just blew my mind. And so, even while we weren't living together we started spending a lot more time in each other's place, and it was things she did for me to make me comfortable. And then there were things that she needed for me to have in my house, so we weren't traveling with bags in the car. I'm going to stay at your house, but I need my certain this, this and this. She's a very avid tea drinker. I was like she brought a tea contraption and all her stuff. Okay, this is what I need at your house, but it stayed at my house. It wasn't one of those things, "Oh, I've got to bring this with me." So, and I realized we had stuff in each other's houses. "We should just be living together." And so we did.

And who asked whom to marry?

Oh, that's funny. So, the technical version is I did. But I have to admit that it was so off-the-cuff that if she probably would have took me up on it I'd be like, "Oh my God, now I've got to go forward." But she asked me first. She asked me for the ring first. Like I said, [my proposal was] off-the-cuff. We were in Vegas, passing by a chapel. And I was like, "Hey, let's get married." But she asked me—I want to say it was a year later.

Did you say yes immediately?

Yes, and this is the funniest part about the story. She always makes me tell this part. It was the last day of school, I think—around that time. I know it was a holiday. I can't even remember that part, but I remember we were leaving downtown Decatur. And I think it was the last day of school and I was trying to get her to go out. And she was like, "No, I just want to go home. Let's just go home." And the Beyoncé song "Should Have Put a Ring on It" came on. And I'm in one of my, I guess, moods. Because I'm like, oh, I've got to go home again, like we're not going to go out. It's the last day of school, so now you don't have to go to work and you're off for the summer. That's no excuse. So she was like, "No, let's just go home." So the song comes on. I'm just like, "Well, I should put a ring on?"—just being annoying. And so, when we get home and I don't remember the details of this part, but I think she wanted a cherry pie. And I can't remember if she bought it or I bought it, but there is a cherry pie in the house, and she's like, "Do you love me? Take a bite of it," and I'm just like, "No." Because I don't eat fruit pie. I don't eat cooked fruit anything. And I'm just like, "No, no." And she's been asking me for the longest time to try this pie. She's like, "It's so good," and I'm just like, "No. No, like I'm not going to eat this. You are not going to make me eat this. No." And she just keep going like, "You don't love me." You know, I'm just going back and forth like, "Why do you equate love? Why do I have to eat this cherry pie?" "Just if you love me you'll take this one bite."

Under duress I eat this piece of cherry pie. And I mean it wasn't even big, but it was still like too much for me to eat. So, I eat this piece. She was like, "Okay, let me take your plate." And I'm sitting here like, what's all this extra and I'm not getting it. And she's like, "Turn around." And I turn around and [. . .] she's got a ring. And I was feeling like such an ass. I was sitting here feeling like an ass, [like] "You are the biggest ass. I should have put a ring on it." I'm going through all this with the cherry pie. And she's like, "I wanted to see what you would be willing to do." And I'm saying like, "Oh my God, imagine if I wouldn't have ate that cherry pie." Oh, I would be crying. Nothing wrong with eating that cherry pie, that could have been just like the end of my relationship right there. All based on a piece of cherry pie. But yeah, she proposed first, and we were at home by ourselves. And I was just like, I had to go to a club that night. I'll eat a whole cherry pie if you ask me to. I was like, "Yes." So, that was like great. That was like awesome.

And when did you get married?

December 12, 2012. 12-12-12. Stone Mountain. There is a resort at Stone Mountain. She's good at surprising. I like surprises. I can never surprise her, though. So, she tells me she's going to take me somewhere. I can't even remember how that came to me. But she's taking me somewhere and I'm realizing that we're going to Stone Mountain. I'm just like, "Where is she taking me?" Because we're going to eat. And we get there, and it's this buffet thing they have, and it's supposed to be really nice. So, we get there and I'm like, "Oh, I'm excited." I'm enjoying the buffet. And I'm liking my dessert, a chocolate cake. I love chocolate. So, I'm about to really get into this. And she's like, "Stop. I need you to go to the car and get something. Get the camera like right now." I'm like, "Right now?" I was just about to put that bite [in my mouth]. "Yes, stop now!" I'm like, "Oh my God! I can't finish this? We can't go get whatever it is when we get ready to leave?" She's like, "Stop now." I'm like, "Oh, God."

So, I'm upset, leaving to go get whatever it is she wants me to get out of the car. I was going to make myself like Charlie Brown. And I go to the car and she tells me it's in the trunk. I go to the trunk and I pop the trunk, and it's cold as a matter of fact. This is December, remember. So, it's cold. And I open up the trunk and I'm looking in the trunk like, "Why are my clothes in the car?" And I'm looking around. Like, am I punked or something? Like, what is this? What's going on? And then I get my phone in my pocket and it vibrates and it was like, "Grab the bags and come on, meet me at the elevator. Fourth floor of the elevator." I'm saying like, "What the hell is going on?" So, I get the clothes and I'm like, "Oh, this is an overnight bag." It's coming together. And I come up in the elevator and she's sitting at the top of whatever floor we're on. And she's like, "Okay, just follow me." And we're going down the hall and it said—I don't remember—"Haywood Suites." What? So, we walk in and the room is fabulous. It's got a fireplace. It's got a table—a dining room table that seats eight. It's got a little kitchenette. A living room. It's got two rooms, a bathroom, jet tubs. I was sitting here like, "Where am I? Who is watching me?" I had to pinch myself. This cannot be real. Champagne, chocolate-covered strawberries, and I'm like, "What? This is amazing."

So, I have to be a kid because I am a kid at heart, and so I'm running to both rooms, jumping on the bed, like this is just the greatest thing in the world. She's like, "We're gonna stay here." So, I'm excited. She said, "Yeah, we've got a late checkout." I'm like, "Okay, great." So, I'm enjoying it. I'm not going to work the next day, so I'm just like, "Hey, let's just leisurely get up. We've got a late checkout." I'm strolling and she's kind of rushing me. And I'm getting agitated because she's like, "Hurry." I'm like, "Wait a minute. They ain't closed nothing up." "So, we got massages. So, I'm having massages and I'm relaxed and we have them together. And it's all just like this is awesome. And then she tells me to go put on your clothes. It's Stone Mountain, we're going somewhere." I'm like, "I can't put on my sweats? Why do I have to put on clothes?" And she's like, "Yeah, you have to put clothes on." And then she tells me we're going to have a private ceremony on top of Stone Mountain. So, I think she does tell me that. It's just going to be me and her. We're just going to go up there. She makes me write my vows. And I'm like, okay. But I'm like, "Really? I've got to get dressed for that? It's just me and you on top of Stone Mountain. We can't wear sweats?" So, I'm getting done and I think the next thing I hear one of my favorite songs, "At Last," and I'm like, "Why is that playing?" And so, we come out. Cameras everywhere. It's decorated in the living room. Her sister is there with her niece. My sister is there with my niece and nephew. I'm all about to cry. It was beautiful, it was amazing. So, we had our ceremony there. And it was just like people I love was there.

I know for her one of the things is her parents possibly saying no to coming or being there. I'm okay with my mom not being there. If my dad doesn't come I'm still going to be okay. But I already know my mom is not going to be there. So, for me those weren't important pieces. I wanted a big wedding. She kind of shied away from that. So, for them to have to be there for that commitment ceremony for us was like—I was like at the end of the day this is all. And it was funny because she asked me to marry her first but

Keturah and Shetikka at Yellow River Park in Stone Mountain, Georgia, 2014.
Courtesy of the narrator.
Photo by Ashbea Day.

I actually asked her mom before I gave her my ring and her mom was like, "It's not a relationship—it's not something for us. It's for you and her and the Spirit." So, it was kind of one of those like blessings, and it was like at the end of the day you're right—it's just between me and her and what we have committed to each other. So, she's good—I'll tell you, oh my gosh, it's awesome. I love her. I'm over happy. I'm ecstatic.

. . . .

Tommye [b. 1952, Orange, Texas]

Actually, I met Phyllis here in my house. On the very first time that Essence had a party . . . the Essence Music Festival. I have so many friends all over this country. I had friends calling me from New York saying that they were coming, friends calling me from Chicago saying that they were coming, LA, they were coming, Detroit, they were coming. They all had hotel rooms. But all I knew is that I couldn't see them all in a three-day period. That was impossible. So, I decided what I was gonna do was to have a party. So, I had a little pool party and invited them all here. They, of course, came to town with friends of theirs. Okay? [. . .] So, of course, when you invite friends, then their friends, so I ended up having, I guess, maybe about seventy women here inside and out. I have a little pool out back and I'm the hostess, so I'm busy, busy, busy. And there was this woman who came up to me and tried to have a conversation, and it was Phyllis. And she says, "Hey," she says, "my name's Phyllis, I'm from Atlanta." And I just said, "Hey, how are you?" I said, "You must excuse me now." And that was it. I didn't have a lover or anybody, I was by myself, but still, I was the hostess and I gave this party by myself, which grew a lot bigger than I thought it was gonna be. So, this was on a Saturday night, and at any rate, finally, as the night wore on, I never got to talk to this woman. I was going out the back door and I had something in my hand. I don't know what it was, I think it was a tray of food. But this hand just grabbed my arm, and I looked down at this little woman, and she said, "Look, I'm tired of following you around all evening like a puppy dog. If you want to talk to me, I'm in the pool." That was my first time seeing her, and I saw her and I said, "Oh, okay," totally unaware that she had been following me around and stuff like this. Anyway, forty-five minutes later I finally got a break and I saw her in the pool, and I got into the pool and I said, "Hey." And she says, "Hey." And I said, "What did you say your name was?" And she said, "Phyllis." And she says, "Well, gotta go." [Laughter]

And she was gone because her friends were ready to leave, you know? They had already been there about three hours. And by the time I got out the pool and then somebody else called me, and by the time I looked around she was gone, and that was it. And the next day, which was a Sunday, I said to myself, I said, "Did I miss my blessing?" And so, I got on the phone, calling all my friends to find out who is this girl and who is she with. "Who is she staying with? Who is this woman?" And finally I called Kim, and Kim said, "Oh, that's Phyllis. They're staying at the Hyatt." And I immediately called and I said, "What's her last name?" and she didn't know. So, I just called the Hyatt and I said, "I'm looking for Phyllis um . . . [snapping fingers] can't remember her name," blah-blah-blah, and the girl at that time, she said, "Johnson?" I said, "Yes, Phyllis Johnson." And when I called Phyllis answered the phone. And the thing about it is I heard this, "Hello?" And I said, "Hello, may I speak with Phyllis?" "This is she." And I said, "Well, Phyllis, this is Tommye," and I heard this [gasps] and I said, "Whew." I heard her go like [gasps], I took her breath away and I remember smiling to my-self. And I said, "Well, I'm very sorry for my rude behavior. I was wondering if I can take you out to lunch or something like this." And she says, "Well, actually," she says, "I'm leaving today and I'm on my way to the airport." And I said, "Well, look," I said, "Can I come and take you to the airport?" And she says, "Actually, the car is downstairs, we're about to leave." I said, "Okay."

She says, "Well, give me your number and I'll call you when I get back to Atlanta." And I gave her my number and she left and that was it. About eight o'clock that night the phone rang and it was her. And then we talked for about three hours, and then the next night we talked and continued to talk. And then we talked about every other day for maybe about three weeks, and then finally I invited her to New Orleans, and she flew in and we had a wonderful time, and she left. And so, three weeks after that encounter in the pool, we finally meet the first time. [. . .]

So, this was in the nineties? When was this?

This is 1996. '96. And then I go there and she comes here. I go there and in six weeks' time—remember this was July 7th—and six weeks later she moved. And she had her own barbershop and salon right across from Morehouse College in Atlanta for years. And she closed up her business and she moved. And that was almost nineteen years ago.

. . . .

Toni

I was introduced to Toni and her partner by Melissa (see chapter 2), who was a close friend. She is strikingly beautiful and has a quiet but confident presence. She was born the oldest of two children in 1980 in Columbia, Tennessee. Columbia is located in central Tennessee and has a long history of racial violence, particularly the lynching of black men falsely accused of raping white women in the 1920s and 1930s. In 1946 the city was the site of the first major race riot after World War II. Today, it has a population of thirty-three thousand, a third of whom are African American. The interview took place on September 9, 2013, in Nashville, Tennessee.

I met her out . . . just . . . maybe seen her out with friends. But I didn't approach her until we were at a house party. And that was almost seven years ago. And I made a definite attempt because I was like—I was kind of messing around with somebody else, but I had just gotten out of a relationship like six months ago and there was just my side piece, like I don't know what I'm doing here, and she caught my eye because she just seemed like she had it together. So, I approached her at a party, and I guess you could say the rest is history, because we're still together.

Fill in some of that history. [Laughter] Like what did you say? What happened? Did you go on a date?

Let's see. I don't want you getting two stories. She's going to be coming here talking.

That's why I'm asking you. I'll ask for her version.

Alright. I met her at the house party, and I asked her could I have her number? Just real basic, not anything else. But if I want something I just—

You're very direct.

Pretty much, yeah. I mean I'm quiet but direct. You're going to know that I like you. I'm not going to hold back. So, she gave me her number, and I think I talked to her the very next day, and we went out for drinks. That was like our first somewhat date. It was off of the Momeran area, one of those bars out there. And we just talked. We just talked. I just wanted to kind of know where she was from. Because I was from Tennessee, wanted to know if she was from Tennessee. You know, basic stuff.

Was it important that she be from the South?

No. Everybody else that I had dated before her weren't from Tennessee— either from St. Louis, up north, someone was from Georgia. But never Tennessee; I had never dated a Tennessean, so that was different. I found out that we were alumni of the same university, so that was cool. And I mean we started out as friends. There was definitely an attraction there, but she kind of made me wait because I had some issues going on with this person that I was kind of dating at the time, and I told her, I said, "I'm a commitment person. If I say I want to be with you, I'm going to be with you." She was like, "I'm not going to talk to you until you get these loose ends taken care of." So, of course, I was just like, I'm not going to miss out on this so I'm going to go and take care of it. And it was probably about two or three months before we were like intimate or kissing or anything like that. So, it was pretty slow.

And how long was it before you met her family and she met your family?

I think I met her family that year. I mean, we started dating in like April, May. I should say April of 2007. And then I think I went to her family's house in West Tennessee around Christmastime.

And how did that go?

It went fine. They were nice to me. They were fine. It was totally fine.

Did that surprise you?

No. I guess I expect people to just be cordial and not be rude.

Because they're southerners. [Laughter]

Right. Talk about me after I leave, the elder thing. So, it was totally fine. I think I brought her around my parents—I know we went Thanksgiving, but probably before that because my brother played sports. I would go down often to see him play. And I would ask her if she wanted to go, and she would. My parents weren't rude to her; they'd just say, "Hi." "Oh, that's your friend." And that's it. In denial mode again, but her family has been great.

Have the two of you talked about children?

Yes.

Do you want them?

We do want them, and we have tried and haven't been successful, so it's a big thing because I know that's something she wants and I want. And I don't want it to be a stressor because we're getting older. We're getting older, so we definitely want kids, it's just, I guess it just has to be on God's time.

. . . .

Tori [b. 1993, Orlando, Florida]

We [she and her girlfriend, Lindsay] both lived on campus in the same dorm hall and as freshmen the university staff, sort of recommend that we get to know each other, and they require a lot of mixing together. And that combined with it was a hall meeting, which is also necessary for them to just talk to us about procedures and that sort of thing. It's very boring. Very, very boring. We lived on the first floor of Wheatley Hall, and at the time that was the freshman floor, so most of us were freshmen, and there were a lot of events planned by the staff at Wheatley Hall for us to get to know each other. And so, one of these things was an icebreaker right after the first hall meeting when all of us just wanted to go home. We just got done talking about something and some kind of paperwork that nobody cares about. And so, me at the time much younger and—not much younger but it feels much younger—and feeling at the time sort of predatory, I was kind of scanning the room. And I'm like, "Hmm, who's pretty, who's pretty, who's pretty, who's pretty?—Winner!" [Laughter] And so, we all had to say something that we liked to do and we went around in a circle, and when it got to her, this beautiful, beautiful person, she said that she liked to play the guitar. And so, I'm like great, music, instruments, that's something. I bleed musical notes. That's great. And so, I walk up to her after it's all said and done and I'm like, "Hi, I'm Tori, it's nice to meet you. So, I heard you like instruments. I heard you play the guitar, heard you were in a band. That's cool because I was in a band in high school." And the look on her face was very blank. [Snickering] I think she just really wanted to leave. And so, I stood there for a little while and there were no words. She was just like, "Mm-hmm." And so, I said, "Okay, great, bye"—and then left. I felt like I had gotten totally shot down. But that first meeting evolved into a friendship, evolved into something much, much more beautiful than that.

The Work My Soul Was Called to Do
Art and Activism

7

One of the glorious things about collecting the narratives for this book was being introduced to so much wonderful artistry. Whether it's Iris's baking (see chapter 2), Monica playing the cello, Bonita/Bluhe and others reciting their poetry, or listening to "Shonda" talk about her fiction, the passion with which these women discussed and demonstrated their artistry was awe-inspiring. It was not something I had expected to find when I began doing the research for the book—mainly because the art of black queer women is not always visible or celebrated, especially in the South. And yet, these women's art—in whatever form—is a vital part of the patchwork quilt that makes up the cultural representation of the black South.

What is also fascinating is how integral much of these women's art is to their political activism. This was particularly true among millennial women with whom I spoke, most of whom are spoken word poets. These women in particular found a political voice through their poetry or, in the case of Laurinda and "Shonda," both of whom are baby boomers, their fiction. Literature and reading, in general, became a conduit for self-actualization and grassroots organizing. In fact, several narrators discuss the importance of feminist and women's bookstores as the site of their consciousness raising. Charis Books, founded in Atlanta in 1974 and one of the oldest feminist bookstores still open, is one of the places that several narrators mention in their stories where they discovered their same-sex attraction and began to develop their feminist consciousness. Although the store was founded by a white feminist, Linda Bryant, the store's vision has always been antisexist *and* antiracist, providing a platform for black women who were writers, artists, and activists to commune with one another, but also to organize. It is this connection between art and activism relative to sexuality that I find so powerful, which prompted a full chapter on the topic. Like Toni Morrison's character Sula, from the novel of the same name, these women knew that artists can become "dangerous."[1]

Though art and activism are not mutually exclusive, some of the women do not consider themselves to be artists in the strictest sense of the word, and vice versa for activists. Thus, the stories are presented under two sections, the first, "'When the Rainbow Is Enuf': Art as Sexual Expression," devoted to discussions by narrators about how their art relates to their sexuality; and the second, "'Ain't I a (Quare) Woman?'": Feminist Organizing/Feminist Politics," focusing on narrators' political involvement, stances, and opinions.

"WHEN THE RAINBOW IS ENUF": ART AS SEXUAL EXPRESSION

In 1997 when I was still an assistant professor of English at Amherst College, I taught a course titled Black Gay Fiction. It was the first of its kind at Amherst and gave me an opportunity to teach and read beyond the mostly gay male authors with whom I was familiar. Poet Cheryl Clarke was one of my guest speakers in that class, but she was only one of several black lesbian writers the students and I engaged who were not as well known, such as Becky Birtha and Sharon Bridgforth. One of the keys to finding these authors was my discovery of feminist/lesbian publishers, such as Firebrand, Naiad, and RedBone, the latter whose founder I interviewed for this book. Below, the narrators—not all of whom are writers—discuss how they came to their craft and how their sexuality influences their work.

• •

Laurinda [b. 1959, Memphis, Tennessee]
Talk a little bit about how you became a writer.
I had to put it somewhere. I mean, whatever I was going through, I had to be able to put it somewhere. The ability to alter the truth played a huge factor in it, but when I started trying to tell the story at first, I couldn't tell the story by making it up. I had to put part of me in it. And I realized once I started putting a little bit of me in the story, it was easier for me to tell the story. And what I found when people started reading what I had written, I wasn't alone. Or this character wasn't alone. [. . .] They had experienced that. So, I guess when I saw the impact it had had on others and how, of course, I'm not the first black lesbian writer. But I'm the first one to really not hold my tongue. So, the point of being able to say everybody in the church is a hypocrite. So, those writers after me like Skyy, I remember seeing them at book signings. I had to get to the point where I wasn't feeling intimidated

by their presence. I had to feel like, "Hey, but you're where they came from. You made them feel like it's okay to talk, to write." And so, it's a place for me to vent and hide the truth about certain things and certain people. I can put it in a book. And if you see yourself, you see yourself. If you decide you want to sue me, you ain't going to go to court and tell people that your husband is a homo. [. . .] I've enjoyed it because it allows me to see the world through a whole other set of eyes that I don't share with everybody. I can't wait to cry about all this, my experiences. Evil eyes. I can't wait. I cannot wait.

And then you've done plays as well. How do you see the relationship between your fiction and your plays? What can you say differently in those genres? Or do you see them as just different ways of saying the same thing?

Just different ways of saying the same thing. When I did *Walk like a Man* my vision was to be able to see my character. I wondered what it would look like—I wondered what it would be like to hear this character say this, this character say that. I always wondered what it would be like to see them on stage. Always if I say I'm going to do something I do it. And I mean, six weeks later they're on stage. We opened in DC [. . .] in 2006. I had no idea— I saw a textbook. I was working at a school system as a grant writer, and I had gone by to train this lady on how to write a grant or something, and I looked in the textbook, and they were talking about writing plays and how much it would cost to do a budget and what goes in a budget or whatever. I said that's all it takes, so I sat down and turned my attention to it, putting a play on stage. I didn't know how to write scripts. The first day of rehearsals I gave them the manuscript: "Here you go." Gave them the book: "Just read that story." And they said, "What are we supposed to learn?" "Just read that story." And then I said, "So, what do we do now?" "We were waiting on a director." "Oh, okay." So we sitting around . . . and I said, "Who's the director? You?" "Oh, that ain't what I want to do." And then we were called to check on venues, and they asked about the producer's name. And my ex was like, "Who's the producer?" "I don't know." "Ask what a producer does." So, I go to the phone—the producer pays the bills. "Oh, that's us." Then well, you know, she gets on the phone, and I'm like, I didn't want to do all that. I just wanted my stuff on stage. So, over the years I had to do all of that—be producer, be director, be writer. And any given day I'll tell you I'd prefer to be the writer.

. . . .

Lisa

I have known Lisa for over twenty-five years. When we met she was a graduate student at the University of Texas at Austin and had gotten into book publishing, starting her own press, called RedBone Press, that featured the work of black lesbian writers. She named the press "RedBone" because that was a nickname she acquired when she moved to Atlanta. As she explains below, the term is used among blacks to refer to fair-skinned "high yellow" blacks. Lisa was born in 1963 in New Orleans, Louisiana, the eldest of four children. The interview took place on August 21, 2013, at her home in Silver Spring, Maryland.

I am somewhat of a public figure because of what I do. I publish books that have been seminal in people's identity, them discovering their identity or confirming their identity, but I don't think I'm a leader so much. I think my activism is in publishing. Other people might beg to differ, because people can identify me on the street, particularly during Black Gay Pride times, and like, "You did that book." I've been spotted in airports and odd places. "RedBone, that's you." I'm like, "Yeah." So, in that way, I'm kind of a public figure, but I wouldn't say I'm a leader. Wanda Sykes isn't a leader—she's a celebrity. I wouldn't say I'm a leader like a James Baldwin or Bayard Rustin or anything like that. I'm not even a Barbara Smith. I feel like I just kind of gather writers and artists together. So, I publish books. I disseminate information that way. I create synergy basically, and I get artists and writers together to feed off of each other's energy and work and create new stuff. So, in that way I also create synergy. Sometimes I call myself a midwife, because I help birth people's ideas, i.e., books. I don't know that I'm a leader. I don't think I'm a leader so much.

How did you get the idea for RedBone Press?

One of my sisters came to live with me with said nephew that just called. He was eight months old, and she was in community college, because she had to drop out of four-year college when she had the kid, and she moved out to Atlanta to live with me. I said, "You have to be in school." So, I'd pick her up occasionally from school. This one day I picked her up, and it was pouring down rain, and one of her classmates said, "Can I get a ride with you?" and my sister said, "Sure." So, she got in the car, and I said, "Well, it's pouring down rain. Where do you live?" And it was nowhere close to where I lived. I said, "Well, let's just go to my house, and we'll wait it out." She comes in the house, and she's looking at all my books, and she starts asking about books for black lesbians: "Do you have any coming out stories for black lesbians?" I'm like, this kid is coming out to me right now, and I said, "I think so," and I looked and looked, and no. Of course, there was no book, because it hadn't been done, but I remember seeing stories in different places like *Sinister Wisdom* and some of the *Common Lives/Lesbian Lives*, some journals that are now defunct, but also the original coming out stories, *Home Girls*, stuff like that, and so I was pulling these books out for her and thinking, "Oh well, I could at least collect a lot of these and put them in one place." I found out later that she had seen the pink triangle on the bumper of my car, and she just made a note to herself to talk to me. So, that's how she did it: catch a ride home.

So, that's where I got the idea to put together the book, and I put out a call for submissions over the course of a year and a half. I kept changing the date, extending the deadline, finally got enough stories, and then got permission to reprint stories from places that I read, some like "Johnnieruth," Becky Birtha's short story in *Lovers' Choice*, I think it's called. I think that was the one I reprinted it from. Also, Jewelle Gomez's stories, Makeda Silvera and one of the anthologies she edited—"Man Royals and Sodomites," I think is the name of the story. So, I got permission and set about researching how to get published, thinking that I was going to send the book to a publisher. Like, I was editing and I was just going to send it off, and all the publishers I interviewed said there's no market for it, and I was like, "No," because I lived in Atlanta, and they've got beaucoup lesbians in Atlanta. [. . .] So, I thought no, there's a market for it. So, I set about thinking, well, up to the last minute that somebody else was going to publish it, and my ex-girlfriend unbeknownst to me had been saving up the money, and she gave me the money to print it, and I said I don't have any excuse now. So, I did it myself. I had even hired a cover designer.

Why did you name the press RedBone?

Because I wanted it to be identifiable by a black person, because when I moved to Atlanta, everybody started calling me Redbone. In New Orleans nobody called me that, but they called me Red or Little Red, because my dad was Red. He had red hair, actually. He was pale with red hair, red beard anyway, and when I was a kid I had reddish hair. So, they called me, "Hey Red," like people in New Orleans do. Well, go to New Orleans, "What's up, Redbone." I'm like what the hell is a—it's a black term. Somebody with the ostensibly reddish tint, though I can't see it. Somebody who's light skinned as they say, "redbone." I think they add the bone in there to feminize it, because I never hear men being called redbone. It's always the women that's the redbone. Something about boning. I don't know. So, I named it that so that it would be identifiable to black people as a black-owned press, a black woman-owned press.

And then after your first book published under that label, why did you continue to publish?

I fell in love with it. Yeah. *Does Your Mama Know* took me all across the country hearing women's stories, hearing how it's changed their lives. The whole process, putting the books together, marketing them, distributing them, doing the sales, the accounting. I mean, I feel in love with just about all of it. The PR not so much, but it has to be done, especially this day and age. Everything's changed from when I first started in the business. I fell in love with it, and then Sharon Bridgforth sent me a manuscript and asked, "Would you ever want to publish work from someone else?" And I read it and I said, "Hell, yeah. I'll publish this." So, I put out *The Bull-Jean Stories*, and that's when I kind of hung out my shingle, because I didn't [see] myself editing another book, but I saw work that I thought deserved to be published, and Sharon told me later that she had sent it out to so many publishers, and they had all rejected her. I'm like, "Why? This is brilliant." You never know. I mean, I guess they didn't see what I saw.

And you exclusively want RedBone Press to be a platform for black lesbian writing?

I did. I did. I changed that, because I starting seeing work like by Marvin K. White, and I fell in love with that, and I was like, "Wow, I would love to publish this," which would mean I'd have to change my mission. And somebody said, "Well, you're the publisher. You can change your mission." Like, "You know, you're right. I could do that." So, I did, and started publishing men's work, but for me, my criterion is I have to fall in love with it, because I put all of myself and money and support behind it.

And you're also involved in another organization called Fire and Ink. Tell me about that.

Well, Fire and Ink came about because as I was crisscrossing the country with *Does Your Mama Know*. I was meeting lots of other authors that were self-published, and their books—self-published books have a bad reputation, with low-res covers and shoddy editing, and just doesn't look like a book ought to look sometimes. Sometimes they're very well done, but a majority of them are not, and I was a copy editor. I worked for the *Atlanta Journal Constitution* for a time, and I just thought that there's so many people doing the same kinds of work and asking me all these questions. Why can't we get everybody together? I also met G. Winston James during that time, Samiya Bashir, I met Dorothy Randall Gray—just this core group of people that felt the same way. I remember going to Outright that used to be held in Boston and everybody splitting up because of the way that the programming went. All the black stuff was at the same time, and so we had to split ourselves up and take notes and then come back together and compare to see what did I miss here, what did

I miss there, and I remember sitting in the lobby of the bar at one of those conferences, and somebody saying, "You know, we have enough black people here to have our own conference," and I was like, "Ding-ding-ding. Yeah, we do." So, we set about doing that. There were seven of us, and they kind of pushed me to the forefront as you are the leader I guess. I didn't want to be the face, but I have been the face, and I've been the face ever since.

When was the first Fire and Ink Conference?

[It was] 2002 in September, I want to say nineteenth. I can't remember the exact dates, but it was in 2002. I remember it because I had a fire in my apartment ten days before that happened, and that was in September of 2002. So, I literally had a fire before Fire and Ink and wiped me out of everything, but I went to Fire and Ink anyway, because I still had a plane ticket.

Where was it held?

University of Chicago.

And the name, how did that come about?

I'm sorry, UIC [University of Illinois at Chicago]. The name came from Dorothy Randall Gray, because we were casting about for a name and she proposed that one and we all went, "Yeah." That's it. Because we were riffing off the magazine *Fire!* that Wallace Thurman and company had put out, but we didn't want that same effect. Unfortunately, it happened to me with the fire. I guess you can't mess with fire for too long. You've got to do your best to respect it. You can't keep fire around and not expect it to act wild. You can get burnt out, pun intended, with all that fire.

. . . .

Melissa [b. 1979, Nashville, Tennessee]

I'm a poet, and so I've self-published three books of poetry, and so I still perform. I perform throughout Pride and been on an authors panel. Like two years ago or maybe it was three years . . . I did a workshop on LGBT population and mental health, and I always volunteer. Me and some of my friends, for a couple of years we did this party that's called Strawberry and Champagne, where I have an acoustic musician or two and a silent auction, some massages and gift cards to places. And then that pool of money will fund the LGBT youth eighteen and under who want to do anything in the arts.

. . . .

Monica [b. 1977, Washington, DC]

Why do you think that music was so important for your parents, for you and your sister?

I know that my mom grew up in a very traditional kind of Jamaican up-bringing and very church oriented, and so for her in church Jamaicans do a lot of anthems, a lot of very classically based church music. [. . .] So, she grew up singing, being in the choir. [. . .] I know she took some piano lessons or some organ lessons. They didn't last long, but she took a few. And so, music was very important for her growing up in church. And it was very much like, Jamaicans sing, that's their thing. The churches have a choir, and it's like people read, and it's huge. And so, I think for her having gotten a taste of playing the piano but for some reason not continuing with it into adulthood, it was in there for her in that way. And I think for my dad, very much the American experience of like, whatever music was going on . . . He's in his eighties, so whatever music was going on maybe in the thirties and forties and the dance halls that he would go to, music was very important in that way. And he is an amazing whistler [. . .] just always whistling. So, music is very important to him. I was home in February, and we're looking through these old reel to reels like of *Carmen* [. . .] We don't even know what to do with these things because they are valuable. [. . .] Where do you take these things to be valued? So, at some level it was even important to him where he had these operas on reel to reel . . . and they're still in the house. And so, I think it was really important for them to get us in music, reading it, studying it, and . . . I mean it was incredibly rigorous. I started at seven and my sister was nine, and it was like, okay, orchestra every Saturday for four hours, you know. And so, for two of those hours would be what they call sectionals, which the violins go off together, the cellos, and you go over your section, you run it. And then you have a little break, like fifteen, twenty minutes, and then you go back in and you're in orchestra going over the same parts. And that was every Saturday. And I think there was also another day of the week that we'd go in just for sectionals after school. And [. . .] the summer was nonstop. So, every week in the summer, Monday you'd get new music. You'd practice it Monday evening, Tuesday, Wednesday, Thursday. Friday you'd put on a concert (or maybe it was Saturday) of the new music. The next week, [snap] Monday new music—same thing Saturday. [. . .] So, during the days we'd do our like, internships or something, and then every night two or three hours of music. So, it was like a huge part of our upbringing. Yeah. Such discipline.

Did you take to it, or were you a little put off by it at first, or . . . ?

Yeah, I took to it very quickly. Maybe not all of the discipline of it, but then you start to own the discipline too. It's kind of like that thing where it's like, okay, well, [snap] you come, you sit, you behave. I mean kids love discipline in some ways, and so I think I definitely started to . . . it was a part of who I was, and still is a part of who I am. [. . .] People used to tell me all the time—it was very embarrassing to me at the time—that I would move. So, in orchestra at concerts they'd be like, "Oh, we saw you. You were moving around." And it's not a thing. I mean, now folks move a little bit more in orchestras, but even still unless it's like a very ethnic orchestra, like my sister's in BSO, the Baltimore Symphony Orchestra, and Soulful Symphony, they do like Michael Jackson covers. They go in. And they can wear jeans and funk their hair out and get real. So, they really encourage you to like, get in it. But then it was like very regimented. And so, my love of music, which has come out, and I'd be like responding to these like [whispers] quiet parts and the loud parts, you know. And so, people would always be like, "Oh, you're moving. You really enjoy music." And I was like, "Oh, God." Because who wants to stand out at [the age of] ten? Not really. Not in that way, like, no thank you. Just ignore me; please don't say anything about it that would embarrass me. So, I really took to it for sure.

. . . .

Q. [b. 1980, Dallas, Texas]

What's the relationship between your art and your sexuality? And if you want to throw in the South, you can throw in that.

[Laughter] [. . .] I call my art activism through art because just by me being on stage it's an activist or an activist act or a political act just by my body and the way I present and my energy being on that stage is already activism. I feel like people seeing me on stage in whatever I'm doing, it just allows them to broaden their mind as far as art and entertainment. My show [. . .] that I'm doing right now the main character is a woman-loving woman, but that's not what the story is about, that's not what the show is about. And so, I feel that by just me being on stage and people being able to connect with my character, it brings down barriers. Eventually some of the other things that I'm gonna do art-wise aren't gonna have anything to do with sexuality or being queer. Only thing that would have to do with it is just Q being on stage and that's part of who I am. And I think that that's revolutionary because a lot of people are just used to seeing a certain kind of person that presents in a specific way and is depicting a character in a specific way. So, just me being on stage transcends all of that. It fucks everybody's world up. [Laughter] So, I like to say it's activism through art because it's just by the nature of me doing it is revolutionary. And other than that, I think that's the only thing that really lies at that intersection. I do feel like queer people are extraordinarily creative, and so I appreciate how open I am and how free I am and that

I don't have any inhibitions or hesitancy around creating anything because just me getting up and putting on my clothes and going outside every day is revolutionary, you know? Whatever I'm gonna have to encounter on that day. And so, I reflect that in my art. It's like no fear.

Does the South play a role in your art at all? Can someone look at a film you made or one of your shows and know that it's southern?

Definitely. My show right now is based in the 1920s rural south. [Laughter] But as far as films and other art, I guess you could say yes, just by the nature of how deep I like to get into people's psyche. I don't know if that's specific to the South, but I feel like taking the time to really talk to somebody and asking those questions to really get a feel for that person, you kind of have to have that southern mentality. Like I'm not in a rush. And yet I want to get what I want to get and I want to enjoy my journey to that destination. And so, I know that's definitely reflected in my work because I'm not trying to rush to get it done. Because I'm actually invested in getting the highest quality. I'm invested in reaching that person at their highest. Yeah. So, you can't rush when you do that. You can't . . . you can't . . . yeah, you can't rush when you do that, you have to be patient.

What genres of art do you work in?

Multimedia. I want to say film, [but] nobody uses film anymore. [. . .] So [. . .] mainly video and graphic design online and then performance art. But I fuse it all together and a little bit of photography. I started out as a photographer, so that will always be a part of my aesthetic. So, I like to put all of it together, so performance, visual art, and video. I don't know what you call that. "Interdisciplinary" I guess is the academic term. I don't like to be limited, you know? Like people say I'm not a theater artist, because I'm not. And I'm not just a filmmaker. I don't know what it is in me and always being something other that has not been defined. [Laughter] That's just it. That's just how I am. You can't define what I do. [. . .] I'm at a point where I'm tired of being categorized. I'm tired of being in a community just because I fit that mold. I've been really getting into internal art forms here recently, the past six, seven, eight months. Tai chi, yoga. I guess I could officially say I'm a yogi. And in those communities, as well as Buddhism. Internal arts are very Buddhist, yoga and tai chi and stuff. And it's like on the same philosophy. People just accept you, and when I'm in those spaces I'm just Q. and I really enjoy that: just being Q. There's so many different things that come along with being Q., but being that I love women doesn't need to be stronger than everything else. And for a long time it's been that. And now that I'm really starting to navigate away from that, I just feel so much better and so much lighter. And so, I'm just enjoying being Q. and everything that comes with that. Yeah, I'm black, yeah, I love women. I'm also an artist, also love football. I'm a foodie. So, I like being all of me, all the time, and not having one particular thing being heightened because that's what people want to heighten. So, that's how I feel. I just really am anticipating the day where just being queer is like the same as just like being mixed, basically. It's no longer an issue.

· ·

"Shonda" [b. 1959, Columbus, Georgia]
You started writing early on, well, you started reading early on. Talk about how you developed as an artist and how being a southerner and being lesbian influenced your work.

Hmm. I think probably listening to the music of the language was a big influence. Listening to the way people talked in the church, the singing and the . . . it was very theatrical, actually. You know, the ladies shouting, their hats falling off, kicking over the benches, and the minister shouting, and he had these verbal tics that [. . .] felt like they were designed to wake me up [laughter] when I'd fall into a particularly deep daydreaming. So, the music of the South, the food of the South, I think all those things influenced my writing. And also, the ways in which people make community and make family, all these different kinds of families, I think. I wanted to capture that, I wanted to catch that because all the people that I grew up with, they died. I lost a lot of people early on, and I wanted to catch that because I felt like . . . I hadn't read it and I hadn't really seen much of it. And I thought, "Okay, well, here's your opportunity . . . to catch that and show some love to the people that really gave you the kind of love that made you think that everybody must have love like this, that this is the way the world is."

And what about lesbianism?

How has that affected my work? I think that I tend to write a lot about sexuality in my work in a very organic way. It's a part of life. It's not the biggest part of my life, but it is a part of my life. And that's the way it's been for me. For some people, it's like that is their identity. When you meet them, you see them, they talk about it, they live it, they love it, it's a beautiful thing. And for me it's one part of my life. And so, I think my desire in writing and kind of in the way that I write is to put all those kinds of ways of living and being and loving and all those ways that one can have family, I try to put that in my work, too. So, that's been the effect of that.

And what genre are you most comfortable in your writing? Is it playwriting? Is it fiction?

You know, I'm really interested in challenges, and the last thing that I wrote was a noir for a . . . because I lived on Staten Island, I was asked to write a noir piece. I'd never done one before, so I was like, "I'll try it." And so, for me, I like the challenge of different forms. And I am equally ready and willing to tackle something new and different, but I'm a storyteller. And at the end of the day I tell stories. And so, I'm most comfortable telling stories.

And do you consider yourself a part of the theatrical jazz aesthetic or not? Or elements of it?

I think definitely elements of it, but I can't say that I'm within a particular group. It's like I'm on that swing. It's like, "Hmmm, what do I feel like today? [Laughter] I feel like a novelist today. I think I'm gonna be . . . " when I'm working on a novel I'm a novelist. When I'm working on a screenplay I'm a screenwriter. When I'm working on poetry I'm a poet. And I incorporate all of the elements, all of the genres. When I'm working on anything all that comes into play in a way. All that information, all those ways of being. You know, a little bit of noir might find its way into my next novel. Music is always there. The visuals . . . the screenwriting, the elements that one uses in screenwriting, so that you can see something, I try to incorporate all the senses in my work, too. And so, it's all there in everything I put my hand to.

. . . .

Xami [b. 1957, Hampton, Virginia]

I was a little Suzuki baby. A little violin, and me playing the "Twinkle, Twinkle" in a group of thirty. That went on until I auditioned for a performance at FSU [Florida State University] at eighteen, 1974, and was quite— I had been medaled and honored and traveled and prepared and wow, the preparation was pretty intense. And I failed to make the cut at the audition. Everybody was scandalized. The whole community kind of rallied because I had always been this kind of prodigy of the school, of the community, of the city—everybody knew me. And there was a particular woman who, when I started playing "Nobody Knows the Trouble I've Seen"—I went into a Negro spiritual per my German violin teacher's suggestion after the Bach. Give them some Negro spiritual and a nice romantic . . . and after the Negro spiritual I just saw a shift in energy. I don't even understand what I was seeing, but it was just very profound, and I knew right then I had lost it, because she was the chair, the one with the key. . . . So, that was a very traumatic moment in my young life at seventeen to nineteen, twenty, because I had been raised to be this violinist, artist. I wasn't quite sure what that meant. I didn't get a lot of feedback on or support around [. . .] other avenues [. . .].

So, I went adrift with my guitar for about five, ten years. I don't know. I went out there just exploring another world [. . .] and trying to figure out what I wanted to do next.

"AIN'T I A (QUARE) WOMAN?": FEMINIST ORGANIZING/FEMINIST POLITICS

I don't think it is a coincidence that most of the narrators in this book have been involved in or are currently involved in some form of grassroots organizing or political movements. A number of the narrators, like Pat Hussain, Mary Anne Adams (see chapter 13), and Iris came of age during the late sixties and seventies on the heels of the Black Power and civil rights movements and at the beginning of the black lesbian feminist movements. Naturally, they have much to say about organizing for the civil rights of blacks, women, and lesbians. The younger narrators have the benefit of their foremothers' labor and therefore don't face some of the same challenges, and yet, they are just as politically active in speaking out against homophobia and anti-black laws. Consider, for instance, that the Black Lives Matters movement was started by three black women, Alicia Garza, Patrisse Cullors, and Opal Tometi, two of whom identify as queer. So, the young women in *BQSW* are a part of a contemporary social movement that actually allows their sexual identity to be incorporated into their antiracist work that previous generations did not have the luxury to do—or least felt as if they didn't.

Over the two years I collected these narratives—2012–14—many antigay, antifeminist, and antiblack movements were afoot, due mainly to a fomenting white nationalism ushered in with the rise of the Tea Party, the political gains of the LGBTQ community around marriage equality, and other forms of discrimination. Marriage equality in particular was a key issue that gave rise to states passing marriage bills and constitutional amendments, such as North Carolina's Amendment 1, that defined marriage as between one man and one woman, in effect disallowing queer folks to marry. This was particularly true in the southern states, such as Arkansas, Alabama, Georgia, Kentucky, Louisiana, North Carolina, South Carolina, Tennessee, and Texas—all of which had passed bans on gay marriage. While many folks in the black queer community had mixed feelings about gay marriage as *the* priority for the LGBTQ community, given that housing, employment discrimination, and a host of other issues were more pertinent to queers of color, they nonetheless were supportive of queer people having the choice to marry. Accordingly, as noted in chapter 4, a number of the narrators in this book traveled to states where gay marriage was legal, only to return to their home states where it was not recognized. Few of them believed that in 2015 the Supreme Court would overturn bans on gay marriage in every state, legitimizing their unions.

As the antigay marriage debate escalated, the politics of some businesses that were supportive of these discriminatory laws also came to light, such as Dan Cathy, the owner of the Chick-fil-A restaurant chain, confirming his support of bans on gay marriage in 2012. Because the chain is popular in the South, a number of the narrators weigh in about their decision to boycott (or not) the restaurant. Their opinions on the matter run the gamut, but none are neutral.

Many of the narrators are also active in grassroots and community organizations that assist black queer communities—both those that serve women and those that serve men. ZAMI NOBLA in Atlanta, allgo in Austin, and the Mobile Homecoming project in Durham, North Carolina, are just three of the numerous community organizations that these women help found or run that are at the forefront of social justice issues for queer people of color in general.

. . . .

Anita [b. 1964, Hickory, North Carolina]

I record all of the news, and I just bought me a iPad just to keep up, and my laptop, I'm always sitting here and I'm reading, especially just keeping up with this thing because I would like to see it happen in my lifetime but with the gay marriage, the Amendment 1, this Chick-fil-A thing.

Talk about Amendment 1.

Amendment 1, I don't get it. I don't understand. [. . .] Whether you allow it [gay marriage] or not, it's going to happen. We may not legally be able to, but you're not going to stop us from holding hands and being out in public. The only thing you can do is tell me no, I can't marry my partner. But I don't understand why [it's] such a big deal to you if you're not gay. I don't understand that. I don't understand why they're making such a big deal out of it, and the people making a big deal out of it is not gay, so why does it matter to you if I marry a woman? Because it's not going to stop it. I mean, you're still going to walk out your front door and you're going to see two women or you're going to see two men. The only way you're not going to see it is you stay in your house. So, you making all this hoopla around they're not going to get married. Why? Everything else is gonna go on. Everything else is gonna go on. We're going to be in your Chick-fil-As and we're going to be in your schools and we're going to be in the senate seats and we're going to be everywhere, but you don't want us to get married. Why? It's not stopping anything. I don't get it. I heard one of the comedians say if you don't like gay marriage, don't marry nobody gay. [Laughter] [. . .] You got heterosexuals that marry under any circumstance. They marry for money, then half of them are divorced in a year or two, but it don't matter about that. You're a man and you're a woman and you can get married. It don't matter if you want to kill each other; he's beating your ass every time or, it doesn't matter, they will marry you. But then you got two women that's in a healthy relationship that not only want to get married because they love each other but also want to get married for security purposes because if something happens to me and that's another thing, the only thing that you can stop is the medical and stuff like that. But if I choose to put my partner's name and leave everything to her when I die, you can't stop that. So, why do the little things that you're trying to control in my life? I'm not trying to control your life.

And Amendment 1, I just don't get it. And then this thing with Chick-fil-A, as many people that was at Chick-fil-A that's against it, you've got just as many that's for it. So, why was that a big deal? Oh, look at the turnout at Chick-fil-A. So? They didn't see the turnout. It pissed me off so bad that they had—I don't know if you heard about the preacher in Maiden [North Carolina] that made the statement that all homosexuals should be put behind an electrified fence and that if you leave them and just fly a plane over every now and then and feed them and then let them die off. That's what he said. A preacher in Maiden said that.

A black preacher?

A white guy, and this lady [who] wasn't even gay protested and she said we're going to protest around his church Sunday, and when she said that, that thing got so huge. They wouldn't even allow us to come to that man's church. They blocked off the whole city of Newton, and I'd give my left arm if it was more people at Chick-fil-A than it was at Newton that day, but they broadcast that [the rally of support for Chick-fil-A]. Oh, that was all over the news, Chick-fil-A, Chick-fil-A! But when they had that protest down there in Newton, they said, "Oh, we're expecting anywhere from two hundred to three hundred people." It was over three thousand, four thousand people. I met people from as far as Tennessee, Washington, DC. That was in Newton. I never seen that many gay people in my life. I was like, wow, I was like in heaven. I never been to Gay Pride. I never been to a gay club. Forty-seven years old, I'm lying maybe. I think I went. My sister took me in Winston [Salem] one year. I probably was about eighteen. I remember going one time. But that thing in Newton, it was huge. This was this summer. It was in May or June.

Did he apologize?

No, but my thing is they blew the Chick-fil-A thing up, but then when this thing happened in Newton they show it, [snaps] then they took it off. Fox News was there. Channel 3 was there. I was interviewed by *Charlotte Observer*. People, cameras was everywhere, but they didn't put it on. They didn't broadcast it. They didn't show it. [. . .] They put in the paper the crowd was bigger than they expected. That Chick-fil-A thing was on the news every day for a whole week, every day, every day they talk about Chick-fil-A, Chick-fil-A, Chick-fil-A, but that—

In terms of people supporting Chick-fil-A?

Supporting Chick-fil-A. It was all over the news. Every channel. I deleted all my news. I quit watching. I got so sick of hearing it. It wasn't just one day. That thing, in Newton, it was on a Sunday. They showed little excerpts of it Monday. They didn't have it Monday morning. If they had it Monday morning, then they didn't show it Monday evening. Chick-fil-A, it was on there 5:30 because I record the news. It was on the 5:30 A.M. news. It was on the five o'clock P.M. news, the four o'clock P.M., the five o'clock channel 9, five o'clock 36, and then eleven o'clock, and then the next morning it was on again and then Facebook. Oh my God! If I hear one more thing, and I like Chick-fil-A food, but I won't eat there again. I can't support that place. I can't support that. But they're trying to put a muzzle on people, not just the gay people but even the people that supports it that's not gay. You got a lot of people that support Amendment 1 that's not gay, but they don't, they keep it silent. They only broadcast what they want to. It's more to it than what they're showing on this news. That's just like them polls. That Amendment 1, that was a trick. They tricked people. People didn't know how to vote with that. People didn't know when to vote with that, and they say, "Oh, it won by a landslide because nobody voted." Nobody voted. If you was for Amendment 1, you had to vote no. It was a trick. You had to know it was like, no. If you were gay, you vote no, that's how it was . . . But see they had it set up to where it was like, they had to sit down and explain it to me. When you go vote, you vote no. I was like, "I ain't voting no. I'm voting yes. I'm for it." "No, you're not for it. Do you know what it means? They want to amend the constitution. That means they want to change it, and they want to fix it to where it's only legal for a man and a woman to be married, so no, you don't want them to do that." A lot of people if they did vote, they don't know how they voted. It was a trick, and that's what infuriates me about the whole thing.

Politics is so tricky. They put their little tricks and schemes just like the Chick-fil-A thing. You broadcast and you're like, "Oh the South is so for it," but you didn't broadcast Newton when it was three thousand or four thousand people down there that was against Amendment 1.

What was your sense of the chatter here in the black community around it? Were people in favor of changing the constitution or sort of half and half? What was your sense?

No, they didn't know. Half of these people around here didn't even know. It was a friend of mine had a gathering two weeks ago. We were at our house, and it was all women, and we were talking about getting married, and I asked one of my friends. She said, "I ain't getting married." I said, "Why not?" She said, "You getting married?" I said, "Yes, but I'm getting married," and I said, "Well, I guess I am now that the damn Amendment 1 thing," and that sparked the conversation. One girl said, "I didn't even know how to vote, so I didn't go vote," and then one said, "I didn't even know what it meant." So, how many other people do you think felt that way? It was a trick. They knew it was a trick. It's no different from what they're trying to do with the presidential election now where they're trying, they know that over 75 percent of blacks and Spanish don't have an ID. They know that, and they're trying to pass a law that you have to have an ID to vote. They trying to pass that.

A photo ID.

A photo ID to vote. I heard a commercial say when you go in, it's easier to get your home refinanced that it is to get a photo ID. They said you go to the DMV and they say, "Yes, we'd like to have your past driver's license, proof of your address, and a blood sample [laughter] for a photo ID." It's because of the Spanish people that has come in and kind of infiltrated this place, and they hard on it now. The politicians they know that. The Republicans know that. My son don't even have an ID. He don't have an ID. [. . .] When they started that, I got on Facebook and I said somebody help me go through at least our neighborhood, our community, and see if we can help these young black kids get an ID. And a lot of them hangs out, my brother has a little music studio over there where they record, and there be a lot of young guys hanging out over there, and I went over there and asked, "You have an ID? Do you not?" The thing is, they don't have a proof of address. "Put mine down. I don't care. We going to go get something, and you can put my address down, and it come to my house in your name and then we'll get you an ID." I was going to try to help these kids, but I think in the State of North Carolina it didn't pass. I think it got knocked down in the State of North Carolina, but some of the other states are still trying. I just saw it on

TV where this older lady is almost ninety and she marched with Martin Luther King, and she said that this will be the first year since she got her right to vote that she won't be able to vote because she don't have an ID. Now you just think of people. And it's just politics. It's the same thing. It's the same thing with the Amendment 1. It's a trick for these people to try to keep this nation and this South the American way, basically. The American way, it sucks. It does. I mean these people, America is so crooked, but they want to act like they're so religious. They really do and it just, it sickens me. Not just the South, this nation as a whole.

I know one time I got on Facebook and said, "I hate North Carolina." Then I got on there and said, "I hate the United States of America," the country as a whole. It just makes me sick. They always just doing, meddling in other people's business. They act like this country is so together, and they just so dirty. It's so dirty. They're just always trying to find a way to deny people their rights, if they feel like it's gonna, if it's gonna make them look bad in any kind of way, and it's mostly the white people. They don't want this country to look bad, but this country already looks bad when you go and you start these wars and get all these people killed for these wars that don't have no reason to take place. Politics, I don't like to talk about. I get so angry. And I never was a political person until I bought this house. Once I actually bought this house and actually got into, I guess you want to call it the "American way," I started [. . .] seeing the dirt. I had to go above and beyond just to get this house built. They didn't want to give me a loan.

Because you're black?

Because I'm black. The City of Hickory, they had the first-time homebuyers where I didn't have to put anything down, but me and him was the two that found out about it, maybe I think Cliff Hoyle was the one that came to Hickory and said, "Hey, do y'all know they have a first-time homebuyer's plan in Hickory, and they give you ten thousand dollars if you build a new house, but only the white people are getting it?" You know me and him are the only two blacks that I know of that actually has gotten through to Todd Hefner up there at that city to get under that first-time homebuyer's plan and get that ten thousand dollars and that program has been up there for years, decades, centuries, and we're just now hearing about it. The black people they think I'm rich. They really do. They think, "Anita got money; she built that house." No. I went through the hoops, the red tape. The city got money up there that belongs to you, but black people around here they so uneducated.

What was here before?

Nothing.

Just land.

Just land, just setting here. It looked like that over there [points out the window]. Just setting here. And they didn't want to give it to nobody black, and this is a black neighborhood.

It is a black neighborhood.

Yeah. The first time I applied for it, I was denied. I was denied because I had a felony. I remember it being over seven years old because I remember saying I don't see how he can deny me, how he can still hold me accountable for that thing when it's over seven years old, and I went back after three years and it was ten years old and he couldn't hold it against me. The first time I was denied.

. . . .

"Barbara"

"Barbara" seemed to be one person removed from many of the women I interviewed in Atlanta. She and her partner live in the Research Triangle in North Carolina and are very active in a number of organizations. She was born in Rutherfordton, North Carolina, in 1966, the youngest of three. Besides being a very difficult name to pronounce, Rutherfordton is located in the mountains of western North Carolina and has a population of four thousand, 84 percent of which is white and 13 percent African American. The interview took place on September 14, 2013, in Raleigh, North Carolina.

I'm very disappointed in the state of North Carolina. I believe that same-sex marriage should be legalized everywhere. I believe that we should have equal rights, as everyone else has equal rights. I think it is a civil rights issue. I don't think it's defined, "Oh, this is the black issue and that's the only civil rights issue that we have or we should fight for." I think it's the same. I think discrimination is discrimination. I do recognize that blacks have had to go through a whole lot, and I'm not saying that it's the same experience. But the idea of discrimination is the same, and so we should have equal rights. There are people that I introduced myself to in the workplace [. . .] as a black lesbian Buddhist mother. [Laughter] And I do that because I'm saying [. . .] these are the pieces of who I am. And some people have said back to me, "Duh." [Laughter] [. . .]

I don't live my life in the closet. We've been in this house for seven years, and so we have gone through all the political stuff with all the elections and all the amendments, and you see different people on the street who have different stickers and you know where it is. But there was a campaign that basically asked lesbian and gay people in North Carolina to basically talk to your neighbor, and we've done that just by living here, you know? Our neighbor here is new, so we don't really know her that much, but the people across the street . . . the woman across the street has two daughters and we've seen them grown up. They're like ten and fifteen or so now. And, it was always a, "Hi Barbara and Lily," and they'd come over here or whatever. And the neighbor next door hasn't been here that long. This is an older man who's in his seventies and his girls. [. . .] So, that's how we live our politics here, is just to be. And regardless of whether the State of North Carolina recognizes marriage, we introduce ourselves to each other's friends as wives, "This is my wife, Lily," because we're married.

So, the politics of North Carolina have affected us, but they don't affect us. And I talk to my friends about this when I talk about my marriage. We've moved so far in the past ten years. Now, Lily and I have been together thirteen years, and people know us and they think that we've been married forever, not just since 2005, that we've been married since the beginning. But when we started our relationship in the beginning there wasn't really anyplace to get married. And that was just a short time ago. But now we have quite a few states that we could go to, and people think about it and talk about it all the time. But in 2000, even though it was a short time, it wasn't very much for us to do other than walk around and say, "We're committed to each other." And now I'm happy to say in many ways that people have choices now and can say this is my partner or this is my wife or this is my husband or this is my girlfriend, this is my boyfriend. You know, we had to change that language because people [. . .] couldn't say this is my wifey anymore. "Is she really your wifey?" No, she's not, she's your girlfriend, your partner, whatever. Your fiancée, whatever you want to call it. But she's not your wife because there is now a way for us to say wife and . . . politically, that's important to me to say without doubt whether you get it or not. [. . .] Whenever I say "wife" they know immediately. When you say "partner" they're not sure because they're not sure if it's a business or, like with me and Lily, I think we have similarities, they go, "Are you sisters?" [Laughter] We go in a store and somebody will say, "You two look a lot alike. Are you sisters?" And we'll say, "No, this is my wife." After being together so long you start to look a lot like . . . you make a joke about it. And that's our politics. To be able to say that openly and freely, that's our statement. We don't have the rainbow on our car. I've had it, we both had it at points in our lives, but then we got to the point where it wasn't as important anymore. [. . .] I've got the golden retriever on the back of the car. I've got the Apple on the back of the car. The half marathon.

You know, we've become kind of suburbanites, so our identity as lesbians is not as political in the sense of rah-rah because [. . .] Lily's forty-nine, I'm forty-seven. That's part of it. But the other part of it is that we've had such a wonderful experience as a couple to be able to get together, to live in Atlanta where we were able to rent from people who were completely okay with us and we didn't have to be questioned, to have her family embrace us, to have my family embrace us without too much difficulty either, and to have our workspaces to be very normalized and be very heterogenic in that way. And everybody's like, "Oh, that's your wife." Or you put stuff on a desk and everybody's like, "Okay." We've never had to go up against that wall. So, over the years our politics have changed from being somebody that would maybe go and stand at a Pride march to just going to the grocery store or the hardware store now at the bottom of the hill. It was a little crazy the other day. I went down to get something out of the hardware store and the guy says to me, "What do you got, a honey-do list?" And I said, "Yeah, she told me I need to do this." And he says, "Well, you tell her that you can do this, but you can't do that today." And it's because I'm always up and down at the hardware store that it becomes . . . they know, and we've been in there together, that they know who we are and it becomes like, "You got a honey-do list? Well, let me get you this, but I can't get you this today because you're not gonna have time to finish that today. You tell her that you're not gonna have time to do it today." And so, just existing in their spaces gives us an opportunity to be political in that way.

* * *

I think I would be really, really depressed if I were not in a relationship because . . . I've thought about this a lot, not because I want to be in a relationship but I just think about when I see young women or women my age, because the gay and lesbian community has become so stretched out now, we're not in these little spots anymore. It can be very difficult to have friends because I don't just have you as a friend now because you're gay; I have this friend because they're my friend. And we don't necessarily share the same thing anymore because the gay experience has really expanded. But I can't sleep with my friend. I've got to find somebody to sleep with. And that used to be in the community. [. . .] But now everybody's kind of washed in now. Everybody's just kind of in the mix. Everybody's in that normal space, that homogenetic kind of mess, and so I'm happy that I'm in a relationship; I'm happy that I've gone through that struggle and settled in this space. But I think that it would be difficult to be gay and coming up now because it just doesn't mean the same thing. But it needs to mean something. It's a huge part of yourself, but it needs to mean something more, I think, in this world now than it does for individuals who are dealing with it. And in this world now we kind of assume that everybody's able to just assimilate. And so, for me, I feel like I've assimilated pretty good. So, I'm happy where I'm at right now, and that's not meaning that assimilating is the thing that makes it good for me, it just means that I'm not struggling. I'm not struggling with my identity. I've known who I was for a long time now, and I've lived my life. And as Mary Anne [Adams] would say, "You live your truth now." And I'm comfortable with that, and I'm very happy with that. I'm able to have all the things that everybody thinks that they want in this life. You know, I have my daughter, I have my wife, I have my house, I have my car, I have my golden retriever upstairs, waiting for me to take him out to go to the bathroom. You know, and . . . and so it's just a good existence right now. But I'm well aware that it could be totally, totally different. Yeah.

· ·

Darlene Hudson [b. 1961, Las Vegas, Nevada (Fordyce, Arkansas)]

I used to think that California was the place for lesbians to be until my friend Zandra moved out there and told me there wasn't no community out there, per se. It's not like it is in the South. You know, we get together for barbecues. See, that's the togetherness that can take place. They don't have that out there. You might do brunch every now and then. But if we get together we have barbecue. Honey, we sits on the back, we barbecue, we talk, we cry, we solve problems, we laugh, get drunk on the back. I used to have something in Arkansas, a little fellowship at my house every weekend called "choir rehearsal." And if you knew it was choir rehearsal time you came on. But now if you didn't know what choir rehearsal was, you might think it was something strange, you didn't need to be there no way. But everybody who was supposed to be there knew what choir rehearsal was. So, the word would go around, Darlene having choir rehearsal tonight. Remember I was a choir director. Darlene having choir rehearsal tonight. And honey, we'd get together and we'd sing Rachelle Ferrell, we'd sing what's the best of the Emotions, and oh we would just have us a good damn time. And so my house became like, when I lived in Arkansas, my house was the place where gay and lesbian people gathered. There was a girl before me who did lots of pulling people together, but because she wasn't working it was just too much, I think it became too much of a financial strain on her. And Scher, the only out lesbian that I ever knew outside of Wanda, that's where I would go to have socialization was at Annette Scher's house. But then we, I kind of wanted to step it up. I wanted some air, you know what I'm saying? I wanted to be comfortable. So I started coming to my house, and then I think in 1990 I formed Arkansas's first gay and lesbian organization called Brothers and Sisters. That's my baby.

Is it still going?

No, it's not. I believe that in the *Journal of Health Studies* I published that story.

* * *

Do you think in addition to HIV/AIDS, it's about a certain kind of gender conformity that is expected of men in the South? "Be a man" and what that entails?

Yeah, because a man is a man. Let me tell you something what I know and understand about gay men, and when I think I got like all of the facets of the community in terms of diversity, then out flips another one. But one thing that my guy in Arkansas used to say, he'd say, "You know what, Miss Darlene? I may be gay, but I ain't no punk. You know what I'm saying?" So, I said, "What does that mean?" He says, "You know what? I go to work. I don't let nobody push me around, and I'm still gay. You know what I'm saying?" And I could see the pride. Now he ain't wearing no flag, and he ain't going to let nobody punch him in his face. He ain't going to let nobody do him around. He is a hard worker, he'll lift and tote, whereas most gay men would be like, and the lesbians is toting it, you know what I'm saying? I see that a lot. That's the kind of gay man that I find most interesting. And my friend Zena challenged them. "You've got to remember that your lesbian sisters are still women and while we might come on in and we can lift and tote it, you were constructed to be those people. You can lift and tote." We weren't designed . . . you know, all our muscles hooked to right here [points to groin area], our uterus. [Laughter] I'm just kidding. They literally don't, but you know what I'm saying? All that lifting and toting my mama used to tell me, "That ain't good for you, Darlene. It ain't good for you. You going to wish a hundred times you hadn't done all of that," but I be like, "I've got to move this furniture, and I ain't looking for no man to do it. C'mon let's get it." And she the same way; my mama would move that furniture around in that house. I'm like, "Mother, call us.

We will come." I will go all the way to Arkansas to move my mama's furniture to keep her from doing it.

I think gay men struggle probably a little bit more than lesbians. Not to say that lesbians don't struggle, but I think in terms of how we see ourselves, especially my more butch sisters, my more masculine sisters. I think that there's a struggle there, so one the most and one the least, I think it kind of goes maybe in a hierarchy. [. . .] Some gay men are just gay, and they ain't the waving the flag group, they don't hold hands, they wasn't showing up at Chick-fil-A kissing. They ain't that kind of gay men. Black gay men are different to me than, say, white gay men. I think white gay men have made it so hard for our black gay men until—I want to be fair because I know this is going to be repeated, but I do think that in some cases white culture has had an impact in all of this. [. . .] From where I sit working in the South there were no Bayard Rustins, there were no James Baldwins, so we didn't get to see the cool black gays. We read about them later, but we didn't get to see that, so what did you get to see?

It was almost like in Arkansas your point of entry into the gay world was through the club. You feel what I'm saying? Even before our house and families became so big, but it was through the club. I mean, through the club was everything. Church, too. I understood that as I kind of evolved. That was the only place gay people could go and say "hallelujah" and have on a dress as a man. So, I think that that culture kind of makes it hard because when our overall black community think "gay" that's where they go in their thinking—and straight to the bedroom. "Oh, two men, no, no, no." But I think that has had some impact because I know how, I listen to some of my friends talk about my gay friends, males talk about that whole thing and how they had to say, "Wait a minute. I don't have to be like that, but this is who I am," and it just become just proud brothers look like just anybody else. Most of the time heterosexual women are trying to get with them. They just regular ole everyday brothers, and the more effeminate guys potentially have a lot of struggle because they just automatically fall into "Oh, they must be gay."

Well, I met several young men who were very effeminate. I'm going to tell you, I have an uncle who is so effeminate but I'm going to tell you my uncle is not gay, my cousin, he's like an uncle. But he's not, and he's just as southern, [in southern drawl] "Come over here, Honey" and "What's going on over there?" He's a principal. He's old now. The principal, a very respected principal, but he was very proper. He's just a southern gentleman. Very proper. And I tell you, you know the actress, Lela Rochon, it's her uncle. Her uncle is my mother's cousin, so there's a connection there. But nobody has ever rumored anything otherwise. He's been married all of his life to the same woman. They raised a daughter, spoiled rotten, but there was never any rumor of this cousin of mine, this elder cousin of mine ever being gay, but he was just the epitome of a southern gentleman to me., But people wanted him to be gay but he said, "Calm down."

[. . .] There's a university down there, UAPB [University of Arkansas at Pine Bluff], has a big homecoming and honey. I live to see my cousin, and we sit out on the deck, and we just watch everything, just people watch. He say, "Girl, look what that child got on." He told me one time, he said, "Honey, her knees need to have a meeting with her ankles and invite them on down." He said something crazy. I said, "Man, you so crazy," but we love him. That was like an example where people just think just because you're just soft and kind of cool like that that you have to be. I tell people if you want to know somebody gay, you need to ask them. And then I want to know what is the relevance of it. So, you'll know how to behave? So, you'll know what to do? Where you coming from in all that thinking?

* * *

How would you describe your involvement in the lesbian community? Are you active?

Very much so. I think that I'm quite, as a lesbian, I don't know about per se in the lesbian community but just in the black gay community, I'm very active. I'm probably more active than most people.

What do you do?

I show up. That's one thing at gay or lesbian events, transgender events, queer events, whatever. I organize the State of Black Gay America. It's in its sixth year, and I have a nice team of people I recruited to do it, to work with me. Me and Craig [Washington], we organized the Bayard Rustin breakfast. I teach in that area. I do panels and workshops, whatever they want to talk about I try to cover, usually coming from my experience, but if I need to teach, structure something, then I do. I'm an advocate. We organized the protest for when Rick Warren came here in 2009. I was one of the leads in that, pulling that piece together. I told you in Arkansas, I formulated the first African-American LGBTQ organization. I had adult brothers and sisters, and I even developed a junior board of brothers and sisters, my young queer people, because they need little place to be, too. I talk with people. I counsel with gay and lesbian people who will try and reconcile sexuality and spirituality. I've done that. So, you know . . . I campaign. I protest. I speak up. On my job I told them I'm a lesbian so if that's an issue, we need to talk about it now.

That was in 2004. I was told it's not going to be an issue. You know, when you're working with kids, you know. But it's not an issue because when I'm there it's about the kids, it's not about me, so they don't really give a damn what I am, even though some of those have grown up and are like, "Miss Darlene, are you gay?" I'm like, "Boy get out of my face, ain't none of your business. You want to have sex with me or something?" I'm not having it, so I send them on their way because I don't want them to become distracted with me when they should be focusing on their lives, and so I make it about them.

. . . .

Emilie [b. 1955, Durham, North Carolina]
How did you become the dean of a divinity school at a university in the South as an openly gay black?

[Laughter] I came from Yale, where I had been associate dean for academic affairs. And the dean there had groomed me to become the next dean. Everybody knew it, he was very clear about it. I was one of the last people to figure it out, but everybody else had figured it out, including the president. He was very clear. He was at that point in his career where he was like, "I don't have time for games." So, I was one of two finalists. Didn't get the job and was actually relieved because I had missed [. . .] two sabbaticals. So, I was tired and I knew I was gonna have to start as dean again. And so, the choice was either a full-year sabbatical or the deanship, and the sabbatical was appealing to me. I found out later that homophobia had a lot to do with why I didn't get the deanship. That's its own story. But in the process I realized, oh, I could be a dean. I do think like a dean. There's still a lot of stuff I need to learn to be a dean, but I could do this job. Nice to know, but it's really quiet as academic dean. You work your head off, but I'm not the bottom line. I kind of like that.

So, the dean who was hired and I agreed that I would go on my sabbatical and then come back into my role as academic dean. Thought that was fine, great. I think about April in that year one of the faculty members here [at Vanderbilt], after all the dust had settled at Yale, said, "You know, our dean is retiring from office. He's gonna stay on the faculty, but he's retiring, so we're looking for a new dean. Are you interested?" And my response was, "Oh, hell no, you've got to be fucking kidding me?" Although I said it with a lot more heat. [Laughter] And, she kept at it. And Laurel said, "Wait, wait, wait." Because by this time we were married. We realized we didn't like living apart. We were fine as long as we were dating, that we could do this long distance thing, but there was something about what the quality of what we wanted in our marriage that you can't do long distance or we had not had enough time to figure out how to do it. So, Laurel's point was, "Maybe you need to explore Vanderbilt so that Yale would take seriously bringing me." And I pissed her off because I said, "I can't do that unless I'm really serious about pursuing it, because it's too much energy and too much work and too much disruption at two schools. And I just in good consciousness . . . " and she was like, "You always have to take the high road. I love you for it, but this is not the time!" [. . .]

So, when the headhunter called I said to her in no uncertain terms, "Okay, you need to know I'm a black lesbian and I'm out and I just got married and I'm not in the closet and I need to know if this is gonna be an issue, because if it is, I don't need to apply and you all really need to go on and move on." She said, "I don't really think it's gonna be an issue." And I said, "You need to ask them, you need to find out, because I'm not interested, I don't need to go through that again." And so she talked to them, the provost and the search committee, and they all assured her, "Not an issue for us." I didn't know that Vanderbilt had just come through and is still coming through the blowup around the "all-comers policy" in which the university enforced that if you were getting money as a student group you can't discriminate over who's a member of your group, who is in the leadership of your group. You can elect people or not elect them, but you can't have policies that say a certain class of people can't. And this was brought to the head when a guy who was gay was in a group of guys trying to not be gay. [Laughter] And he decided that he actually liked being gay, and they told him he had to get out. So, he filed a complaint. Well, all hell broke loose. I get occasional letters [asking], "Where does the Divinity School stand on this?" And I'm like, "Well, the divinity school has had an all-comers policy for over thirty years, so the university has finally caught up with us. We don't discriminate." So, we were here for a conference, and the chair of the search committee e-mailed and said she would like to talk to me and to Laurel. And that got our attention. It was like, hmm . . . okay. So, we went in, and the first question was, "Okay, what's up with this thing around y'all being so open in approving gays and lesbians, because I need to know." And Laurel was actually more pushy about it than I was. Because I was listening. I was watching the effect and listening, because I know administrators. I could kind of tell when they're lying, [laughter] as I had to learn. And Carolyn assured us, "Not an issue, not an issue at all. We took the heat for our stand and we're still taking the heat for our stand." And we had a good conversation. Walked out and I was just saying to Laurel, "I think we're gonna have to . . . I'm gonna have to take this seriously. I think you're gonna have to think about this, too." And before I could get the whole sentence out, my cell phone goes off. It's the chair of the search committee saying, "The provost has a couple of free minutes. Would you like to meet him?" Now, I've never done a job on this level, so I had no idea how unusual it was. I thought he talks to everybody who's a candidate.

Had they even brought other people in?

No, this was an informal. "Would you please apply?" Walked in, sat down, and did our pleasantries because we're all southern. [Laughter] And, he said, "What do I have to do to get you to come to Vanderbilt?" And I looked at him and I said, "You have to offer me a job." And he said, "Well, I can't do that outright, we have to go through a search process." And it was at that point Laurel said, "And so, tell us what this is about being open and approving about gays and lesbians?" Same thing. And it turns out that one of his sons is gay. So, he had gone through a journey because it had not been, "Oh, thank God, my son is queer," when it happened. So, I looked at Laurel and said, "Okay, well, we need to take this seriously, but I don't know." So, I drug my feet in applying and finally did, because I hate writing application letters—they take so much damn time. I was on sabbatical, I was supposed to be having a good time, and here I am writing a letter of application. [. . .] I wrote it and forgot about it. And went on my fabulous sabbatical, which happened to be at Laurel's seminary near Chicago, so I was happy. Now I get to see Lake Michigan every day. I hadn't seen it in years and years and years. I was surprised when I got the e-mail that said, "We want you to come interview." I was like, interview for what? And Laurel's just rolling her eyes, like, "Emilie, come back to us." And I came down, and they had a two-step process. They invited six people to come for an hour and a half interview that they then narrowed to a list of three for a full interview. They were moving quickly, which at this point, yeah, I was going, "Whoa, whoa, whoa, whoa!" I'm like, "They are moving." I can't tell them to stop. Laurel's like, "You need to get your act together. Yeah, I know I warned you. I told you." My second day in office I went in to the new dean and said, "Vanderbilt has asked me to apply," and he said, "I was afraid of that." And so, I meet with the search committee, and I was asked a question about what are you working on in your sabbatical project. So, I started to talk about it, and this woman showed up and took over my body and proceeded to charm the entire room of the search committee, and which there were about twenty people. I mean, it was a big search committee. And I'm standing over in the corner looking at this chick going, "What the hell are you doing? This is *not* how you don't get a job." [Laughter]

Oh my God. Get back on the plane, come back. It was a day trip. The meeting with them, it was going so well the chair lost track of time and so she had to cut us off because we'd gone over half an hour. And she said, "We really have to keep this to the same amount of time for everybody and we've already violated that, so we have to stop right now." Okay. I was standing at Midway [airport] waiting for Laurel to pick me up. My phone goes off. "We want you to come back next week." And I was very clear with the search committee—"This is who I am, this is how I am, I'm not hiding it. If you got issues with it, then I'm really not your person because I know this is a southern school. So, I don't want to do anything that's gonna damage the school. That's not my mission in life." Came back and a similar thing happened. Like, who is this chick that keeps showing up? I realized about two or three weeks after I started, the person who showed up is me. And this was the me that I had to keep under wraps in the Northeast. Because it's a different way of relating there. You wanted warm, funny, witty, personable, I promised you. We got the box and I was like, "Damn." And I was happy being that person; I just didn't know I had become that person. So, the university made the decision that they could take the heat if there were any. The divinity school has a long history of being the thorn in the flesh of the university and being more progressive than the rest of the university. So, none of our alums were surprised. There'd been a few people [who said] I'm the "anti-Christ" and "Theological education is going to hell in a hand basket, [so] we need to pray and somebody needs to sprinkle oil." There had been a few of those. But by and large, even among the black community, which I was surprised at, when the newspaper interviewed one of our alumnus who is a professor that teaches at Penn, and she was very skeptical that I would receive an affirming welcome from black churches in Nashville, one of the black male lay folk in the area went out of his way to say, "That was unacceptable for the newspaper to print without asking any of us here because that's not true for most of us, at least not the people I know." And I'm like, "Oh, okay, okay. I'm not gonna get in a fight with a Tennessean."

So, I've been very fortunate. I've been very, very fortunate that I didn't know this liberal school sat in the South. I had no idea until I started looking into it that it has a long legacy. Students here were protesting segregation in the twenties and thirties, that early. Because Jim Lawson used to be a student here, and the provost was forced by the board of trust to put him out when he was organizing the civil rights protests in the city, and the majority of the faculty resigned in protest. Vanderbilt had to come down and go, "Excuse me, not in my family's name." And so they readmitted him, but he had already moved on to another school. The faculty was rehired except for the dean. The dean was the sacrifice. And the faculty and student body sat down and wrote what's called the Statement of Commitment that has been a moral guide for the school. And I have never seen a school, no matter how progressive it's been, to actually put in writing, we're antiracist, antisexist, anticlassist, antihomophobic, pro-environment. I mean [. . .] I was sitting there reading all that. I'm looking . . . this is . . . in the South?

And that's for the university or the divinity school?

Divinity school. No, the university has not made such a statement. But the divinity school. And I thought, "Okay, this might be a place." And . . . my colleagues by and large . . . now, people are gonna get on you because you're an administrator for all sorts of things. But it does not seem to have anything to do with sex and sexuality or even the color of my skin.

So, you're happy.

Very happy. I'm surprised. [Laughter] I'm still very, very surprised that this is where I landed and this is what I do and I like coming to work every day. I still do. And it's not all happy, happy times. But the faculty's at a place where it wants to grow and work together. We got great students who are committed to justice making. They don't all agree with how they're gonna do it, but they do agree that that's an important value. I've got the best staff in theological education. This is an incredible staff. You don't get this very often. And I have the support of the new provost and the chancellor—so far. I haven't really done anything to rock the boat other than ask a few inopportune questions from time to time. But I'm new, so I didn't know. I have no illusions that that will last, and I also know I am the only black dean in university central [administration]. And there may be some deans in the med school . . . I'm sure there are, or subdeans or something. But I'm a test. And I'm well aware of that, and tests are expendable. Long ago my mom and dad taught me [that] in a university, in a college environment everybody's expendable if the university feels threatened. Don't ever cast your lot with an institution. Cast your lot with people. So, that's what I've tried to do.

. . . .

Iris [b. 1957, Miami Beach, Florida]

Talk to me a little bit about ZAMI. How did you get involved with it?

[. . .] I had visited New York and many places. And had met a number of other lesbians. So, by that time, I was probably first identifying myself as such. I was not closeted, but I also was not out. I made sure the people who mattered knew. So, that included my mother, my father who I'd gotten back in touch with. I never told him, but he just sort of knew. [. . .] So, by the early eighties I was doing certain things. I hadn't really so much joined a group as it was I would go to certain events where I could meet other people. I met a few lesbians, not a great number of them. [. . .] So, I guess towards the late eighties, mideighties, there was a group called Sisters, I believe it was. But they didn't identify as lesbian. They made a point of not identifying as lesbian. They were identified as women loving women, much like the subtitle of your book. So, we did some interesting things, mostly social kinds of activities, that kind of thing. And I met a couple friends in that group. It still wasn't really doing what I wanted it to do. It wasn't really saying what I wanted to say. So, one of the books that I read in the mideighties was *Zami*, by Audre Lorde, what she called her biomythography. And it touched something in me so deeply because some of the background was familiar, because her family was from the islands as well. They were from Carriacou and immigrants to the United States, although she lived in New York and obviously a whole generation before me. But still, it was some of the things I could just see, you know, and just the way she wrote and the language and all that and the feeling, so much so that when I did my doctoral studies at Emory, I used it for a paper, a long paper. [. . .]

So, I went out to Colorado in '89 to do a fellowship out there. And when I got back in 1990, there was a group that was already meeting at the bookstore, at Charis. I forget the name, but there was an arm of the group called "women of color." And so, when we started meeting, I just felt it important, and some of the other women did, that we concentrate on issues that affected just the women. [. . .] And once we started concentrating on that women of color group, we started talking about it. And I said, "Well, you know what? Is it going to be for black women? Or is it going to be for women of color, which is very different than African American women or women of African descent." And after a lot of back and forth. [. . .] So, me and a couple of other people were very insistent on saying, "women of African descent," that our issues would be very different, say, than white women's or even women who are from Asia or women who are from the Spanish-speaking Caribbean. And we got ZAMI because we really were trying to come up with names. And again, I had been so influenced by Audre Lorde's biography that I just sort of threw it out there. I said, "Well, *Zami*," and she described it as a Carriacou name for women who live and work together as lovers and friends. So, I said,

"Well, it seems like that's what we want to basically embody in this group." So, most people hadn't heard of it, some people had heard of it, a couple other women had heard of it. And so it was almost like instantly and very much overwhelmingly, "Yes, let's do that." And I don't think there were any other names that were put out there once we got that. It just seemed to fit. It just seemed to really, really, really fit.

And how many were in the group?

The original group was about, I think it was about maybe ten, fifteen women. Because the group was very much changing. Some came in, some came out. And we really started as a more social group. But we were also doing certain things that were social, as well as political, and we would have discussions every week—every month at the bookstore. And some of them ended up being discussions of coming out and that kind of thing. Because you always had people who had this process. And then as we started doing more and more things, we moved into other things, like we did celebrations on Audre Lorde's birthday. And so, in the fifteen or so years that the group existed, it went from discussion, social to like advocacy and that kind of thing. One time, we had a little meetinghouse. We went from that to having drawing parties and that sort of thing to raise money. And then towards the early nineties or so we started—several people started getting burned out. I was one of them because that always happens when you have a few people trying to do a lot of things. So, at that point, it was when really Mary Anne [Adams] decided, okay, you know what? Why don't we just move into another direction. And that direction was with the Audre Lorde scholarship, where that was the primary purpose of the group. So, not so much social anymore or what have you, but really about raising money to give to out lesbians and colleges and universities. And then that went from that to just lesbians and gay men who were basically had the spirit of what we thought somebody like Audre Lorde [. . .] would have espoused.

I can't remember what my actual title was. I don't remember because I was never too much into all of that title stuff anyway. But like I said, when we were up and running, we really, really, really did do some very, very, very good things. And many people, I would hope, were helped, not by just the discussion groups, [but also] sort of pushing people in the way we thought might help them, if they had a specific need, that sort of thing. But it was a quite significant part of my life. And I really, really, really enjoyed it. I enjoyed it. I also enjoyed the years I worked at that same bookstore that I started visiting way back in the eighties.

Jasmine [b. 1994, Chapel Hill, North Carolina]

I've been doing this radio show for like a year, so we talk about these events all the time. I think our last show, we talked about the Chick-fil-A thing. I'm very outspoken. [. . .] I found this funny. I was just telling my mentor this: everywhere I go, I'll always talk about homosexuality. I just always find that in my conversation. It's just always in a debate between me and straight Christian people. Like, always. No matter where I go. I don't know how that ends up in the conversation, but it does. And so, I'm not afraid to be outspoken in that I believe in gay rights. I think when Amendment 1 was going on, I was down at high school, and one of my teachers was talking about how she—first of all, this class, I really never spoke out at all, but what she said really pissed me off. She was talking about how her cousin or something was gay, and she still voted for Amendment 1 because she thought that marriage should be between a man and a woman. And I never spoke in that class, so I was like, "Really?" Just like, "How dare you?" Like, first of all, you're not supposed to be talking about this. One. And second of all, how dare you? You're not God, you can't put somebody's rights in your hand and tell them that they're not allowed to marry whoever they wanna marry. [. . .] I was just really pissed off. How can you say that? How can you be religious or how can you be Christian, but you wanna tell someone they can't live the way they wanna live? You know what I'm saying? Or like, the people that really wanna talk about racism and it's 2012 and "we need to be better about loving everybody that's not the same color as us," yet you're homophobic. Like that doesn't make sense to me. You can go out and advocate for dogs that's getting ran over by cars, but you don't agree with gay rights? To me, that just doesn't make sense. You're obviously on the wrong side of the fence, or you just don't get it, because at the end of the day, it's all the same thing. You know? Race and homosexuality and animal cruelty—it's discrimination, regardless. You know what I'm saying? I don't understand why people don't get that.

What did your teacher say when you spoke back?

I mean, she didn't say nothing. [Laughter] I mean, she wasn't gonna say anything. I was just really mad, and this, this boy, he was like, "Well, it doesn't concern me." It does concern you. [. . .] I grew up in a Christian family, and I get why people don't agree with gay people. I get that. I would never tell someone that they're dumb because of what they believe from being religious. I would never tell someone that. But it's all about accepting it and knowing that's not your business. And also, just because someone does not sleep with the same person you sleep with does not mean they are not guaranteed—they're not able to have a happy life. That's not ever up to us as a human. You know what I'm saying? So, that just really bothers me. And I'm quick to snap my fingers and roll my neck to it and say what I wanna say. Like, "No, uh-uh." [Laughter] I am a black female, but I'm an empowered black female and I have a strong voice and I'm not afraid to use it.

But it wasn't until I came here to Chapel Hill for me to feel that way, for me to feel strongly about gay people. Because before, when I lived in Alamance, I really didn't consider myself a part of the queer community, so it didn't really bother me if anyone talked about gay people. I mean, no, let me change that. It bothered me regardless of who the person was being talked about—I didn't like that. But I didn't really think about it that much. I wasn't really the person that like, get snappy with people, because I didn't feel like I was a political person. When I came to Chapel Hill and we were talking about politics and stuff at my radio show, I was like, "I don't talk about politics." I don't even vote. [. . .] It really doesn't matter to me. And then this whole year, I've spent my time talking about politics every day of my life, and now I realize how much of a change I've been through. That's why I really feel strongly about being in Chapel Hill and [. . .] having these spaces where I could be to learn these things and these people that I learn from. So, I feel really blessed about that.

So, you're now eighteen. You get to vote for the first time.

Yeah.

Are you excited about that?

Yeah, I really am excited about that. I really wish I could've voted with the Amendment 1, but I don't even know if I was eighteen yet. I don't think so. But yeah, I'm really sad I couldn't vote for that. But yeah, I'm excited about voting.

. . . .

Joan

Joan was born in 1951 in Washington, DC, the eldest of five children. I was so honored when Joan agreed to be interviewed for this book. She was the first openly lesbian person to be elected as a Fulton County commissioner in Atlanta. She struggled over her lifetime with breast cancer, which catalyzed her to make health a part of her political platform. Unfortunately, she lost her battle to the disease on April 18, 2017. The interview took place on August 28, 2013, at her office in downtown Atlanta.

In 1989, Maynard Jackson, former Mayor Jackson, appointed me as a senior adviser to the lesbian and gay community. That was my entry into politics. I had just started twisting [my hair], because I had locks for eight years. Just started twisting. And I was his out black lesbian liaison. He had two white guys and me. And I remember my friends here telling me, "You don't want to be conspicuous." Oh, and here I am being conspicuous, you know. And there are only like a handful of us who are willing to be out and be ready for the *Donahue Show*, you know, all of that. [Laughter] I was like, yeah. And so, I was thrust into this role, where I was being political in a city that was predominantly black. And you had your middle-class black folk that I had to interact with. And part of me had fear about that. Because I know where it came from and I know what people think. [. . .] But while I had part fear, I knew that I had the mayor backing me up, who was taking a big chance. And he was like, "Okay, yes. I put her here. So, yes, she belongs here." And then there was the other part of me that was like, okay, but I'm not from here. So, I don't really have a whole lot to lose, because I'm not really from here. [. . .] I don't have the "Who's your mama? Who's your daddy? Where did you go to school? Where did you go to church?" I didn't have that. "Where do you go to church?" "Unitarian." [Laughter] "What is that?" You know? So, that helped me get through. But it helped me see.

And what I learned was the more comfortable and confident I felt in who I was, because when I came out, it was like, "Okay, this is who I am, y'all. I'm a black lesbian, this is who I am." But then I had to back down, because other people had gone through their coming out process and we would try to organize political LGBT stuff for the black community. And we'd get twenty-five people. But then you'd have a party over here at Texas and you'd get five hundred black lesbians out there . . . [and] we weren't out. And so, it was difficult because you didn't have that support from your community. You had a handful of folks who were there. But even then, you had to be careful, because everybody was not accepting. But when I wavered on being comfortable, then I saw that doubt in other folk. And it was like, "Okay, I need to not go there." So, you had to work through your fear and just know that you stepping out here and not everybody's comfortable with it.

And even today, even though I'm out, I ran out, I don't have any secrets about it, I still get people who will say, "Well, what do you think so-and-so will think about the gay issue?" "What do you think?" And a lot of it comes from my people, who are saying, "Well, what do you think so-and-so, the gays on the south side of town think about, the gay issue?" Well, what about the gay issue? I go out, this is who I am. But the church thing is real—it's very strong here. [. . .] It's so prevalent, especially with your choir directors, you know, stereotypical. And people in church, even in the pulpit. And we've got a minister here in town who came out a few years ago. He and his wife are head of the church. He came out. She was devastated. They have grown kids. She worked through her issues around it, realized that there was more to their relationship than this. She's worked through it, she's accepted it. She's still part of the church. She understands he has his life. But they're no longer married, they're divorced. But she has joined him in their dedication to bring the truth to ministry around homosexuality. And they are really challenging other ministers to do the same. But people resist it. And so, I've found that you've got folks here who are in high places who are very closeted, will not come out. And I've had people say to me along the way things like, "Well, you do what you do." "Gotcha," you know. And it's okay. And I've had people say to me, "Well, I am part of the family, but I've got to like. . . ." I got it. I respect people where they are. I don't out people. But once you're with me any more than fifteen minutes, you'll know who I am. So, I don't have issues with that. And I realize that I go in and out of a lot of different places, a lot of different circles. But I know that I do not have roots in the traditional solid black community here. I don't. And when I look around at who my network and support folks are, they're white lesbians.

So, do you think that that is an Achilles heel, in terms of some of the things that you want to get done in your position? Or do you think it's a benefit?

I have never looked at this as an Achilles heel. I think that I've gone through phases in my activism. I've gone from being the new out lesbian—"Oh, this is so great!"—to being, "Okay, now I can relax," because I grew up during the height of the civil rights movement. In fact, fifty years ago, I wanted to marry a politician because I wanted to tell that person what to do around policy, because I knew this was critical stuff happening in the nation's capital and in the Capitol. So, that's where I was fifty years ago. I was like, "Yes, Dr. King, I'm going to marry a politician, because I'm going to tell that person what to do." And so, I don't lead with that. I look at healthy communities and that's A to Z, that's everyone. And everyone benefits when everyone is healthy and has access to health and resources. And so, that's the way I lead. [. . .]

I always have to go back to growing up. There was all kinds of people that grew up with you in your neighborhood. So, I can go down into South Georgia or North Georgia, or City of Atlanta, and I feel that I can sit and listen and hear what people need, because bottom line, we all have the same basic needs, and we all just want to be heard, and we all want to make sure that we have the same access that everybody else has, to have a decent quality of life. That's what I'm about. That's my agenda. I can remember becoming the director of the Fund for Southern Communities, which is a social justice fund, part of a national network. [. . .] I think I must have been the first black executive director. I had black folk from South Carolina saying to me, "What? Do you think people going to give you money because you're black? Because you're gay?" I had other people saying, "Well, do you think people will think this is now a gay fund?" "Why, because I'm gay? It's like I don't represent other issues, as well?" And it's like, no, I realize that I'm black, I'm a woman, I'm gay, I'm old now, something's wrong with my foot so there's an ability issue. I had to bring all of me to the table. This is where the intersection and the connections and the intersectionality of issues came front and center for me. So, it's like I can't just advocate for gay issues. I have to advocate for feminist issues. I have to advocate for health issues. I have to advocate for employment issues, housing issues. It's all related. Gay people were being denied housing. I have to look at the total human being and where we fit in that, and bring all of that. So, I used my being gay as a platform to further social justice and civil rights. And so, that's kind of how I see it and how I've used being gay. So, I never let that stop me. I saw being gay as an entrée to sit at the table that we were never invited to. Because like I said, if you're going to be with me more than fifteen minutes, you'll know. And I took that charge very seriously.

So, there's been a lot of discussion back and forth between the gay and lesbian community, primarily white gay and lesbian community, and the black community about comparison between gay rights movement and the civil rights movement. As someone who grew up in the sixties, in DC, who's an activist and a politician, what are your thoughts about civil rights and gay rights and those movements?

Yeah. See, I look at them all as human rights. I try to look at everything from the sixty-thousand-foot level and then breaking it down. And there are differences in our cultures and in how we behave, and where we come from. But when you look at our sexuality, being LGBT people, we're just a microcosm of the whole society. And so, yes, black folk fighting for civil rights, we want to be heard, we want to participate, we want access. Gay folks, yes, we are fighting for the same types of things, but at a different level, or on a different platform. Because for the white gay folk, you already have access. You already have resources. You are the ones who made the rules to the game. And so, now that you have come out in terms of your identity, you're experiencing what it means to be denied, to being discriminated against.

As black folk, this has been part of our history since we got here, so we have had to live with that. So, you can't make a direct comparison.

And the way that I look at it is, where is the intersectionality of it? Where can we meet on a common ground about it? And please, you need to go do your homework, just like I had to do my homework about who you are and how as a black person I have to live in this culture, in this country, in this society, I have to know everything about you in order to be able to survive. You have to go do your homework. You need to learn about justice. You need to learn about the civil rights movement. And you need to be willing to advocate for me, because I'm willing to advocate for you, when I go in a room that is not an LGBT room, I am willing to bring your issues along with my issues as a woman, as a black person in this culture. And so, I look at it as not a comparison. And I can't compare my life to someone who's had a disability. Honestly, even with I have an issue with my foot, I cannot. I can't. However, I know what it feels like to be discriminated against. I know what it means to be denied access. I can take that. That's where I can go in and advocate for you, because I understand that. And I hope that you again will understand that. But I don't get into the let's compare. First of all, I don't think there's any hierarchy of oppression. We're all oppressed, because if you're the oppressor, you're affected because I'm being oppressed. And if I'm oppressed, you're being affected. And so there is a synergy there that we've got to realize and that we've got to acknowledge. But don't compare yourself.

And it's like I tell my partner all the time, we get into this and she's like, "Oh, woe is me, woe is me, woe is me." And I have to stop and say, "Look, okay, I get it. I understand where you're coming from and I respect where you're coming from. But let's broaden it a little further. You do have access," you know, and we have those kinds of conversations with each other. And she's learned a lot from my perspective. "Oh, I hadn't looked at it like that." And she tells a story, and she'll probably kill me for this, but she says she tells a story about how the first time she saw a black person with a golden retriever. As simple as that. She was young. She was like, "I saw a black person with a golden retriever and I had to like stop myself and go, 'Well, why wouldn't a black person have a golden retriever?'" Because she'd never seen a black person with a golden retriever before. And she didn't think that black people owned golden retrievers. And so, she was like, "You know," she said, "I had to stop and say, 'What kind of thinking is that?'" You know, it's the little things like that. So, I don't get into the whole comparison. Because until you walk in my shoes, then maybe we can do some comparison. But the fact that I haven't walked in your shoes, you haven't walked in my shoes, however, we are both being targeted and we are both being denied and we're both being discriminated against. So, let's look at where we have some common ground and see how we can move forward.

Just like with the decisions that just came down from the Supreme Court for gay folks. It's like, yay, DOMA [Defense of Marriage Act] is no longer legal, and we've got momentum, and we've got more states that are recognizing gay marriage. For black folk it was like, hey, we're saying that section 4 of the Civil Rights Act is no longer constitutional. It's like, okay, here is an opportunity for black folk and gay folk to come together because neither one of you have made it to the end yet. [Laughter] You still got work to do. You still got work to do. Here is an opportunity to look at where is the commonality and where can we gain some traction and come together and advocate for one another. And perhaps we'll have more of a momentum to get what we want on both sides. So, I kind of look to see where you've got some commonality. And that's kind of how I approach my work as an elected official, as well. I kind of look for the common ground. I know that some schools kind of look for the differences and where we can be different. I kind of look to see is there common ground. Because again, for me, my agenda is how can people get access. I don't care who you are, because we got just as many poor white people as we got poor black people. We got just as many poor gay people as we got black, white people who still don't have access, you know. And the whole health piece, the whole AIDS piece. And that was my entrée again into the movement and understanding, because I came in as part of the first—I was a member of the first dinner committee for the HRC [Human Rights Campaign] here in Atlanta. I was the only black on the committee. And my charge was to go out and find the black community. Up to that point, I hadn't really come across a lot of black gay and lesbian people, so I didn't know where they were. And I went to this organization called AALGA, African American Lesbian Gay Alliance. And I was like, "Oh, my God, I felt like I've come home. Where are you? How come you're not participating?" And then I had to learn. It was like, okay, so here's my family and my family had my back as I was out there. And I went back and I was like, "Look, I am not going to go do your work." They do not want to be brought in, paying all this money, and not get any benefit back. And so, that's just the deal, and I'm not going to be on this committee anymore. [Laughter] So, I went to the first dinner committee. And then I was like I'm not doing this again. I said, "You are an elitist group and you're being exclusive. We are not going to come." Of course, I continued to participate, but folks were like, "We're not spending that money. We don't have that kind of money to spend," especially when they were not out. So, it's those kinds of things.

Talk about some of your other involvement in community activism and leadership here in Atlanta around LGBT issues.

Okay. I first started out working on—Michael Lomax, who was the former chair of the Fulton County Commission, decided to run for mayor. And I had a friend recruit me to work with his campaign. That was kind of my first entrée into getting involved into politics. And then joined the primary. I think he decided not to move forward, because Maynard Jackson was running again. And then I got involved with Maynard Jackson's campaign. At the same time, I was starting to work for the Fund for Southern Communities, which is a social justice fund. And that group was actually the first to fund social justice issues in the Southeast, small grants. And I was involved with AALGA. So, with Maynard Jackson running the election and making me the liaison for—one of the liaisons for the gay and lesbian community, that means I had to keep my eye on what was going on in the gay and lesbian community. I was by then probably a cochair of AALGA, and so I was involved locally with black gays and lesbians. And then I was funding gay and lesbian issues as part of the funding for Fund for Southern Communities, so I had to know what was going on across the board in the metro area in North Carolina and South Carolina around gay communities. So, all of that was happening at once.

So, Maynard Jackson then appointed me to the License Review Board. And one of the city council members at the time appointed me as cochair of the Public Safety Committee for lesbian and gay issues for city council. And so, I was getting involved on a political level on boards and commissions, representing the gay and lesbian community, representing the mayor, and then also actively engaged in AALGA, working with African American lesbian and gay community. And then funding lesbian and gay issues, as a funding area. So, all of that was happening and on the local level. [. . .] I got involved with national funding for lesbian and gay issues as a member of the board of the Funders for Lesbian and Gay Issues. [. . .] But I was doing all of that around the same time. So, that—

And this would have been the nineties?

This was from '90 to like 2000. And so by then my reputation as a lesbian activist—oh, the other thing that happened in the mid- to late nineties was I was one of the cofounders of Southerners on New Ground, with Pat Hussain and Mandy Carter, Suzanne Barr, Mab Segrest, and Pam McMichael. That's when I really started looking at this whole intersectionality and interconnectiveness and started looking at the political ramifications of gay, lesbian, bi, transgender, queer, all of that, because I was working with some heavy hitters here. I was in the movement, but I was mostly funding the issues, representing the governmental entities, the local, not coming at it from the hardcore feminist work that my colleagues [were]. And I was like, "Oh, God, I'm a real lightweight right here." But I brought a different perspective. And so, I was doing all of that during that time.

And what was your role in ZAMI?

So, ZAMI had a couple of iterations. Sabrina Sojourner, she's in DC, she had come from California. She came to Atlanta, made a big splash, politically. She'd bring that California energy and then from DC. She was the one that actually helped me sort of get my footing. We started a Woman of Color Caucus in AALGA, because we were not getting the women to come out to the AALGA meetings, it was mostly male. It was male-founded, male-driven, dominated. And there were a few of us women who were willing to participate and be there. And so, we created a Women of Color Caucus. And what we did was we met separately, like on a Friday night, it was a potluck. And we would invite other black lesbians that we knew to come over to Sabrina's house. And we'd sit and get to know each other and network. And we'd have these five or ten minutes where we'd go around and talk about an issue, let them know what was going on, invite them to come to AALGA. And so, we did Women of Caucus for about a year or so. And then we started getting more women who were coming in. And then people started wanting to do something different. And you have some who want to do something over here, want to be real political. Others who just want to be social. And then you have folks who just want to kind of be middle of the road. And so there was a split. So, Women of Color dissolved. And then we had another group and it was called ZAMI. And that was the first iteration of ZAMI, this was pre-Mary Anne. And that didn't last because it was more social. And then there was a group who wanted to be the womanist forum because Alice Walker was doing her womanist thing. And that lasted a hot minute. And then Mary Anne came along, and there was still a couple people who were part of the initial ZAMI. And then I think Mary Anne might have been part of that, as well. And that's where ZAMI came, ZAMI that we know came together. And by that time, I had sort of backed off, because I was more interested in the whole political piece and we couldn't get a lot of traction for that. So, I participated in some of the early ZAMI meetings. But then my energy was more focused on a lot of national work and more of the governmental and neighborhood kind of stuff.

"Joyce" [b. 1987, Fort Lauderdale, Florida]

I always say I'm a triple minority: black, woman, lesbian. And I don't know if it's race. I don't know if it's sexuality. I don't know if it's because I'm a woman, or all those things coming together, but I just feel so limited here and judged, and it's been hard for me, especially attending Florida State, a predominantly white university. And just a lot of the experiences I've had there have really challenged me and kind of made me want to live in other places because I don't have those experiences when I travel.

[. . .] When I travel, a lot of what I do, I like to work in developing countries, with women and girls. That's my target and interest group, and a lot of times I really just go and I want to hear their stories. I want them to tell me what has motivated them to get to this point, and I find that I really connect with women and girls and it's easy for me. Like, over the summer I was in India and I went through FSU on a grant to do some research and I had the women and girls. I did poetry therapy with them, and we got so close on my last day we were all in tears, and these are women that they don't cry. [. . .] And the director, he's a guy, he said, "I don't know what you've done, but they don't cry." So, I actually really enjoy intimate relationships with women, and even here in Tallahassee I started a women's group where we meet every other Sunday and we just discuss life, just kind of affirm each other. And there are nine of us in the group, and I met all of them in different places, and I'm like, these are some awesome women, let's bring us all together. So, they all tell me how it's been so powerful to come together, and we've been doing that for like six months. And then I started the *for colored girls* project because I'm like, I love this play. I've read it a million times. I wanted to do one last thing before I leave Tallahassee, and my way of doing it was to do the play. So of course we have the cast, and our director is a woman, and it's an awesome project, too.

Is there much interaction between the black lesbian community and the white lesbian community here?

I think there's definitely a division, and I know myself, I prefer to be with black lesbians. [. . .] It's hard for people to understand me when I say that because they think it's ignorant. But I identify with black women. They understand where I'm coming from. It's not that I can't interact with white women, but that's just not my priority. I definitely have a few white women that have become very close friends through the women's group, so it's a challenge to me to really think about, well, why can't I connect with somebody that's not the same color? But when you look at the white lesbian community, a lot of the events are different. Like, they'll have burlesque shows. There was a meet-up group where they would meet for like coffee. I don't know if that's still going on. And the black events, there was actually a really prominent group in Tallahassee called Mix It, and they were pretty, they had rented like a pool hall and like once a month they would have this free gathering with food and drinks and spoken word. It was really, like, it was a big hit, but then it kind of fizzled out. And then you have like the gay club, which is all black. Like, you'll have different shows and stuff, but now the black community they don't do a lot, and I don't know why, like the black lesbian community here.

What do you think about the comparison that's sometimes made between the civil rights movement for African Americans and the gay rights movement? Do you think it's a fair comparison or unfair? What are your thoughts about it?

I think it's fair. I think when you think about the value of a human life, that's the value of a human life, I don't care what movement it happened in. And I think being very into Black Power and black rights, it's something I've thought a lot about. And I've been criticized by a few of my friends that are like, consider themselves pro-black and they say, "Well, it's not the same movement. It's different." And I think for me, a lot of times I think about it, it's kind of like the same thing but now with a different face because at the end of the day, the goal is to liberate people that are oppressed, and that's exactly what we were trying to do with the civil rights movement. I don't think a lot of people are aware of how gay people get a lot of heat. Like, I was in Haiti this past week, and like, gay men get stoned there, and that is not unusual. And actually like, you have police chiefs that will arrest you if you're a gay man, so you know, when I think about things like that, it is the equivalent because people are losing their life, people are being ridiculed, people are being spit on. That's a huge deal to me.

· ·

Julia [b. 1979, Gastonia, North Carolina]

I'm a filmmaker, an organizer building intergenerational community, particularly with the Mobile Homecoming project, traveling around the country finding our elders who've been organizing, living, and loving like from the eighties and before. And that has been like the most profound work of my life. [. . .] I think the longest trip that we've taken and just been on the road [. . .] was over fourteen days. It really felt like a tour of superheroes to be able to see the type of resilience and just spiritual power that people have had to discover, create, find, learn, to be able to survive as who they are for such a long time. So, I feel like that that's probably the biggest thing that I bring to the community is that awareness, those stories, and I intend that that will grow and even shift to, how do we take care of our folks as folks age and don't have access to some of the resources that other people have access to because of the choices that they made? So, whether it's that they don't have children or they're not connected to their families or they've not been able to have the types of jobs that would give them security as they age, that sort of stuff. Like figuring out the ways that we can live sustainably so that, yeah, so that we can take care of each other and have access to more of our brilliance.

So, how did you get into filmmaking, and do you see that as a vehicle for a kind of queer activism?

Hmm. Well, I say that black Baptist preaching is the making of *Thriller*, so not *Thriller* itself, but the video that was the making of *Thriller* is what called me. So, there's the language of church of being called . . . it is what called me to filmmaking.

I'm a little black girl growing up in the South. I had no idea that I could even be a filmmaker, like it never occurred to me. My mom loved movies. We had cable, we would rent movies, and still go to the movies like more than once a week. So, that was a huge part of my life. But it wasn't until I went to college that I even had access to the tools of filmmaking. But even then I didn't think . . . it never occurred to me I could be a filmmaker. I was like, "Oh, computer science, I can do animation, I can do websites." But I did get editing skills, and I really enjoyed that. And so it was when I moved to Atlanta and I met somebody that needed to have a film edited that it was like [snaps her fingers] "Wait a minute, I could do this."

I think at that point I was like twenty-three. So, that's kind of how I got into it. And then at that point it just opened up. Like my purpose, I think, just opened up. And I think that I definitely see filmmaking as a tool for our collective liberation, but I think what anybody is doing is that. You know, if you're on purpose, then that's what you're working toward. But I think particularly what I want to do is give people access to different ways of living, helping them see the things that are ridiculous but also just things that are other options, like the sort of gender constructs, like you're going to teach your sons that they shouldn't cry, shouldn't show any emotion, but then the men in your life that are emotionally just turned off you have a problem. But there's clearly a connection there, and I think just like Jesus had parables and preachers tell stories and tell history, filmmaking is a tool for that. And then also just a tool for healing, like being able to see patterns that you have that maybe you're not able to see it; maybe you can see it from somebody else's acting it out on screen. And then be able to see what options are there for healing. Or even things like compost toilets. It doesn't make sense that we are using the bathroom in water. Water is such an essential resource. We could do it in dirt. There's so much I think people have access to if they could just see an example of it. [. . .] Public education and entertainment doesn't want us to think critically, doesn't want us to know about alternatives that are here or in other countries. And so, I think film is also something that can help with that.

· ·

Kei [b. 1989, Jacksonville, Florida]

Well, for my business I would like to be like vintage and whatever donation driven. Whatever we don't use, I want to give back to LGBT homeless. I have done clothing drives for that particular group, LGBT homeless. There's a lot of that, young people that are like my age and younger whose parents just won't have them because of who they love, and I've done balls. The South is kind of one of those places where you can just jump into a little bit of everything. I've done all of the club atmospheres. I've done plenty of Prides. I've done fashion shows for Stonewall in Atlanta. I've done fashion shows for Black Gay Pride in Atlanta. I attend those often, definitely Gay Pride events. I would like to be more hands on, helping—not just show my face. A few friends that have been friends since early high school are starting a nonprofit and waiting for everybody to be done with grad school. [. . .] We call ourselves the Queer Musketeers, the Queens. It's all queer black women right now, but we want to be out there doing community service. We do walks and just anything, any service work we could show up to. We give back to women in distress, anything. Who knows where queer and gay is in the group of people who need help, you know? Like, who knows where they are in there, so I just try to help universally so that I can make sure that anybody that's like me can use that because it could be me in any situation. And I want to do more, but that's what I do now: community service. I like to dress people a lot, make them feel better, get them jobs. So, if I have a friend that knows a friend that needs help with this and that and that and I know people who need something to do, I would make sure they know that.

· ·

Lenore [b. 1962, Wampee, South Carolina; d. 2014]

I just attended the Leadership Summit. I go to the Harry Hancock Center once a month to have potluck.

What is that?

Harry Hancock Center is the gay community center. Okay, everybody is there, transgender, bisexual, gay, lesbian. Everybody comes together for just a potluck once a month. And then like I said, I go out and I'm in the parades. We were just in the St. Patrick's Day parade. I'm a deacon in my church. What else do I do?

There's a place for gay and lesbians in parades here?

Yes, and for twenty-five years we've been able to be in the St. Patrick's Day parade, and in other cities they're not allowed, so we're very—that's one thing we had to be proud of this last parade. We had a ball. Lisa did the marathon. They also have adult night out at my church where I invite people on Facebook to come and just be out. We do end up getting straight people, and we also end up bringing people together because couples meet at this thing. We usually try to do that once a month. [. . .]

Is there a Gay Pride parade here?

Yes.

Really?

Gay Pride, we're in that. We have a booth set up. We're very involved. [. . .] Anytime they have a vigil, we're going to be there, and like I said, I was telling him how I'm always the only black female for the most part. It's just sickening when I know all these black women are here in Columbia, and I do call them out on the social media sometimes and I talk about them. I do. I get a lot of ugly mail, but it's okay because I handle it. That's what I want. I want to piss them off.

. . . .

Lynn [b. 1968, Jackson, Mississippi]

People talk here, but they really don't want to do nothing. And everybody want to be a star. Everybody want to say "I did this," but nobody wants to do the work. So, . . . I'm tired. I'm obligated. I have a grant obligation right now, so when I fulfill my grant obligation in January, I'd say about March I'm going to go to California, and I think I'll stay until my birthday in July or August and come back. . . . I think I'm just going to take a hiatus and see how it is there and if this is where I really want to go. Because I—as my friends say, I don't owe Mississippi nothing.

Do you feel that there's a community here among the black LGBT?

I don't. It's so divisive. It's the have and the have-nots. It's you're too gay, I'm not gay enough kind of stuff. We have the clubbers, and you have the old folks that don't want to do anything. They say, "I don't want to go to the club," and yet they want twenty-year-olds, that sort of thing. So, you know I started creating different events. I was having a . . . night on Sunday once a month at the club. I think maybe twenty people if that many came out. Everybody—people say they want something different, but then when it's offered they don't do it. The King Edward downtown, my friend-girl lives there. So, they have a rooftop and so I had—I called it "wine and cheese" on the top. And everything came out of my pocket. We had wine, the cheese, the fruit, the music. Sent it out to everybody for thirty and older. . . . people came. And so, I just got to the point where, you know, you all don't want to do nothing. You talk about different, but you just don't want it.

Then you have people that I don't want to be separated. I want to be in here with the straight people because they get a kick out of trying to turn people out. I don't know what to say here in Mississippi. It sucks. . . . it sucks. I don't like it. I'm frustrated, and I'm getting to the point where I'm really burned out of trying. The club scene, the young kids go to the club scene. But none of the clubs give back to the community.

Are these black gay clubs?

Yeah, these are black clubs. And they charge them up the wahoo during certain events. During the football season there's a big game here in Jackson. They'll charge twenty to thirty dollars, thirty-five for these kids to come in the club, and it's like packed to capacity. And they want to be in the club. There is no shelters specifically for LGBT youth. There is nothing, nothing here. And I guess I wanted to save Mississippi, and I think that's the problem. I'm trying to do too much when people don't appreciate it. And they won't accept it. Getting these groups, trying to integrate LGBT issues in the groups, and they're not going to have it. I said, "Well, you guys . . . the group." "We don't know that." Well, they know that they're in the group and the work that I do with our legislature, legislators. I'm not out like that when it comes down to it because they're too conservative, so I have to maintain a certain lifestyle when I'm doing the work with politicians versus over here. But it's so funny that everybody just think that I do—what they say is that I'm just a social advocate for everything. So, when it come down to LGBT issues, they don't take a second look like, "You're gay?" They don't even ask that. They just [say], "She fights for everybody's rights." So, it's good in a sense, but in a sense it's I can't bring my partner with me to these events, unless she look like me. [. . .] Right now, we're having a conversation about doing a workshop, how to get a job, being a man who identifies as female. See, those kind of conversations are not being had because here you can go and work at a fast food restaurant. Of course, you can be on a police—some law enforcement work. But you can't never be a CEO unless you start your own company. So, how do you do that? How do you get past the way you look out there to get where you need to be? Because we have some very intelligent women here. Men who identify as women. I asked my son, "How do you get your more flamboyant gay men in a position of leadership?" Because he's always said, "Well, you can't stop people from being who they are." I said, "True enough, I can't." And I'm not trying to stop people from being who they are. But I'm thinking about how do you go into the work scene in Mississippi.

I dated a young lady for three years; she's an attorney. And she just wore hers [hair] short and natural. She wasn't really masculine. She was borderline. She started locking her hair. Her dad told her to cut her hair off because judges make decisions on that. Their decision . . . is based on what the lawyers look like, and that has nothing to do with sexuality. So, it's a lot of conversations, a lot of growth, a lot of education needs to be had here in the great State of Mississippi. But you know people talk about gay marriage. I'm like, "Why?" I performed—I'm not even ordained, nothing—a wedding. And I told him, "This ain't legal, number one." I said, "First of all, you're going to hell because I'm standing in front of God lying to Him, for you all." I said, "You're not even using your real name. You're using your gay name." I said, "I'm out here fighting for marriage equality for people who really want to be married, and you all are playing married." So, I asked the question, "If marriage equality was legal in Mississippi, would you be standing here today?" And they couldn't give me an answer because they don't know. So, I said, "Okay, it's play for you, but it's real for so many other people."

I was talking about the education that needs to happen in Mississippi, I think, in order to bring our community together. Like, I say it's about the have and have-nots here. People don't want to deal with this group of people. It's very cliquish. We're not accepting. We have our own internalized homophobia. And people don't have that conversation. And I'm the one that wants to have these conversations, but like I say, everything can't come from me. And so I try to pull people in, but if they're dealing with their own internalized homophobia they're not going to be able to help the community at large. Like [. . .] a lot of the younger boys feel like contracting HIV is a rite of passage for being gay. That's what they get for being gay. "That's what's going to happen because I'm gay. So, if I contract HIV I'm supposed to." [. . .] Religion has a lot to do with that. And I've been asking people to come in and do research studies on HIV/AIDS; somebody needs to see the connection between religion and homophobia and religion and how a gay person feels about themselves. Because you know we be up in the church. . . . So, they had a study that said gay people are the most religious people. When you have conflict, I want to do what the Bible say do. But over here, "I want to do this and I'm in the world," that's a conflict. So, you get people doing all kind of stuff, putting themselves at risk or whatever, because they have an internal conflict going on.

And do you think that things are getting worse or better in that regard? For instance, a lot of people suggest that blacks are more homophobic because they're more religious. Do you think that's the case? Or do you think it's more complicated than that?

It's more complicated than that to me. You know how we say, when you asked me do I think people are born gay or there's a choice? People choose to not accept people. That's a conscious decision they may base on something somebody else has told them, and based on the Old Testament. But like I say, regardless of all of this other stuff, the one rule that people should learn and live by in the Bible is "Love your neighbor as yourself." That's it. And I don't go back and forth with people about the Bible because I don't know the Bible. . . . And like I tell my kids, the devil in the Bible. So, sit down and leave me alone. Don't come to me telling me about my life. But we have so many people that want to be accepted. So, they will (1) dummy down, (2) they will live a certain life that they don't want to live just for people to like them. I think it's getting better because we've done marches. [. . .] We walked. [. . .] I say it's successful because it's cold as hell out here. Nobody aren't going to bother us.

But then, you know, we have all these groups that want to effect change. I mean . . . LGBT issues. But I said, "Well, why don't you all come to the Capitol when people are there? When the people are in session?" So, I ask the questions. That's what I do. I ask the questions. Are you doing this because you really want to see a change, or are you doing this just to say you're doing something? It's different. And I have a lot of folks I deal with just doing stuff just to say they're doing it. [. . .]

So, gay folks, they want to do stuff. Black folk not going to do nothing. If it's not a club, somebody stripping, they're not going to do nothing until they feel like they've been discriminated against. And then I need you to help me. Then I need you to do this. But I can't get you to come and sit in a forum and listen to how you can protect your wife. Even though we don't have nothing. I said, "You all don't want to come to the table." But you all want to reap the benefits. I said, "I'm going to do what I'm going to do anyway." I said, "I need to be at the table." "Well, I don't think I can do anything. I'm not smart." I say, "Shit. I'm not smart." I said, "I ain't got my degree yet. Almost, but not yet." I said, "So, don't use that for your excuse." I said, "That's what they want. They want to have meetings when they don't let you all know, and then when they let you know it's too late. But you're not coming anyway. Even if you come you're drunk" [. . .]

One of our legislators told a group of people, "Look, you don't have to come down here wearing no rainbow flag." He said, "What you do is you get to know them and they end up getting to know you, who you are." [. . .] Your sexuality or even HIV status, that's on you. But let them get to know you. Because the first thing, they're going to judge you—they already judge you. Here come the gays. Don't hide who you are. But let these folks get to know you. Don't come here talking about your boyfriend all the time. Talking about how much you all have seen. Listen, in the State Capitol people came down in booty shorts protesting and I'm just shaking my head. We were asking for $2.5 million for HIV. The gay folk, the gay marriage equality people came in talking about they wanted to get married. And if we had brought those two issues together since they think HIV is in the gay community, it would have looked good to be a cohesive force. One, to talk about it's not true to say, "Hey maybe—just maybe if we had gay marriage the prevalence of HIV wouldn't be as high." But I told them that's when gay marriage really was talked about, when the AIDS epidemic took place. You know, pretty much people saying let them marry each other, let them kill each other. I said, "So, gay marriage ain't never been about love. . . . Learn your history." And . . . you really have to go back and read this stuff. We're going to come to the end before they legalize gay marriage or even accept it because of what they see. They don't see the couples that's been together for years and have a house or buying properties or educated people. What they see is—especially black men—pants hanging out their butt. But even when you say, "Dude, they only want to see men like that, so why would you do it?" Because they think that's what being gay is about. Being a lesbian is about marrying a heterosexual man.

* * *

The United States don't abide by the human rights doctrine. I said, "But every other country that the United States give money to has this." I said, "It's not hard." And I compare stuff doing HIV work. Before the United States gives any money to any country they had to have a sketch, a plan on how they're going to combat HIV. We didn't have that plan here until 2010. But if we did that to get a strategy, why can't you do that with the LGBT community and say, "Hey, we need to get the United States on board with utilizing the declaration of human rights, universal declaration of human rights." So, it gets down to [the] political. And I hate politics, but I'm thinking of how do you make things better. And if I have to go and learn about the declaration of human rights, if I have to learn about the Constitution, which I can't stand—it's not about us for real. I had to pull out the state constitution and read that shit. It's against the law to have anal sex. It's against the law to have oral sex. And there are laws on the books. You have to know this kind of stuff. And just to educate. But people don't want to know that part. They just want to lead all willy-nilly and just be happy in the little freedom that they have. So, it was a good thing when the NAACP came out for gay rights. I appreciate that. And I appreciate the fact, like I said—and I'm a part of it—the NAACP health committee. But if we can get a LGBT human rights committee together, I'll be trying. I'll be trying. All I can do is just take it to them and say, "Let's do this." And they'll say, "How do you want to go about and do it?" That's what they say.

I know that your primary work is in HIV/AIDS prevention. Talk a little bit about the impact of HIV and AIDS on your life in a personal sense. Have you lost people?

Like I said earlier, my father [died from AIDS]. I had a couple of cousins. I was doing the work. I was doing the work for the wrong reasons in the beginning. In the beginning, it was a project for my public speaking class. And it so happened I went home . . . AIDS Day and they was talking about how HIV and AIDS impact women at that time. So, I called the health department, got the information, and the guy was like, "I'm not supposed to give you this," but he gave me not a consolidated plan, but a comprehensive statewide plan for HIV/AIDS in Mississippi. So, I started reading it and I started looking at the numbers and I started seeing the disparity between African Americans and white people with STDs. So, he said, "Well, we have free classes. You should come and get trained." So, I started going to his class. The more I learned, the more I wanted to learn, the more I wanted to tell everybody else. [. . .] And doing the work for the first organization that I worked with, I started seeing people—because I've always done case management. I started seeing people that I case managed years prior, and it just floored me. Wow. Then I started doing testing, and I was testing people that I knew, and they were testing positive. And it was just too much for me. But what I really started seeing was there were no services even they tested positive. So, I've had to get a life-changing status of many people that I love.

And my son, being a gay young man, he was going to Jackson State, so he would just bring all his friends. And he might bring five guys to get tested, three tested positive. And it bothered me to that point. So, the first job that I had in HIV work, not only does he work there, he heads my office. And he's finishing up his degree in social work. So, the fact that I was around his friends, because I was like a mother to them, and they were getting positive diagnoses, made me really want to do this work more.

But like I said, ten years after my father died, when I found out my dad died from AIDS, it made me really, really want to delve deeper into the work. I thought of doing politic stuff. Like I said, I hate politics. But when I realized there was nothing here in Mississippi [. . .] there is no services for LGBT youths, LGBT people period. Then there is no services, few services for people with HIV. So, I just look at the whole picture instead of just the HIV people because I can get two people to come in this office right now, let's say I've got two lesbians come in: one has HIV, one doesn't. Based on my funding I only deal with the one that has HIV. What do I do with the other one? So, I just couldn't just say, "Hey, you've got to go. We don't provide services for HIV-negative people. So, we can't help you." So, I just started saying we need to deal with this whole person. There's some stuff that's going on. Why do you feel like being gay you're supposed to contract HIV? Those kinds of conversations happen. You being a lesbian you don't have the fear of contracting HIV when you can. Because all you've got to do is have sex with somebody who has HIV, pretty much. And so, that's why I bring a lot of these issues together. You don't have anywhere to live because you told your mom you were gay. So, now you're out here at risk to contract HIV. You see, that's why I deal with the whole person.

If I had known my dad had HIV . . . my dad was an alcoholic. The first thing I probably would have done is try to get him at some kind of treatment facility. But they probably wouldn't take him with HIV. But it would have been something else. And when I found out about my dad, it made me want to work harder. Because I didn't get to go to my dad's funeral. I had a car accident the day of his funeral. So, I don't know where he's buried. Right now, I don't know where he's buried. Because I don't deal with his people. So, it's bothered me. And I lost this other guy, he died. He was homeless, you know. He was on drugs. But you know he'd get clean, he'd do good. And so, he became a spokesperson for me for homeless people being homeless and living with HIV. And he fought a good fight. He fought a good fight. He got turned around in so many meetings talking about housing and how if people aren't properly housed. So, when I start my housing program I'm going to name it after him. I asked his family; they said it was okay. And then recently we had two women just die. They had AIDS but they didn't die from a complication of AIDS. That's the funny thing. They had a lot of other stuff going on. And they were two powerful women. One just died; her funeral is tomorrow. She just died last week. She was the first woman to come out in Mississippi and talk about her HIV status in like the early nineties. That funeral is Saturday. So, knowing these people—getting to know people and having a relationship with them, having an attachment to them makes me want to do this work even more. But I really, really want to do a lot of LGBT work. Because believe it or not, one thing that happened in their life that put them at risk for other stuff, to be homeless, to contract HIV, get on drugs or whatever. So, I don't know. I just want to save the world. [. . .] I don't have money. I don't have a car. I really don't have a paying job. I don't think I could do anything else but what I'm doing now. And that is trying to build a better Mississippi for the LGBT community and people dealing with HIV. I don't know anything else.

. . . .

"**Mary**" [b. 1975, Tuscaloosa County, Alabama]

I think everybody should be black lesbians. I love being a black lesbian. I love being a black lesbian in the South. Love being a feminine black lesbian in the South, because sometimes I think I'm privy to some conversations that some more masculine black lesbians may not be. People say things around me sometimes because they're not thinking that I'm one of them, you know. So, those are opportunities for me to kind of . . . I don't want to say correct, but provide a different perspective, you know. So, in a sense I feel like being a black lesbian in the South is a sentence to be a cultural worker, whether you want to be one or not. If you have any sense of aware-ness about oppression and any social activist bone in your body, to be a black lesbian in the South means that you have to be a cultural worker, you have to be prepared to provide another view instead of the constant stereotypes. And, I mean, I also think that part of being a black lesbian for me is kind of what fueled me to want to do what I wanted to do in terms of the plays or the PhD. It was kind of like, "Oh, she's a lesbian, but she does have her PhD" [. . .] I've seen this happen with a young lady where everything that was wrong, it was because she was a lesbian and she wasn't living right, so God wasn't blessing her. And basically, what was wrong was that whether she was lesbian or straight, she really wasn't gonna be about shit anyway, so it didn't matter. [Laughter]

But when you're a lesbian, a black lesbian, it's like you have to be kind of like that whole, when you're black to be successful you've got to work twice as hard. So, when you add another layer of oppression to that? Oh, you got to do exponential things. And I think that may be why, like I was saying earlier, I have friends who are doing the most fabulous things. And we haven't sat down and said, "Oh, well, I feel like I have to overcompensate for being a lesbian," but it may be something to it. You can't just be average and be a lesbian, because then everything bad happens to you happens because you're a lesbian.

. . . .

Nancy [b. 1950, Maxton, North Carolina]

Some people will embrace the fact that we have different types of sexuality, and another person doesn't embrace it but doesn't give a damn because it doesn't have anything to do with me. That's the kind of feeling you get in places like New York, New Jersey, even to some extent in Washington. There's a type of anonymity that large city living gives you. The people in my apartment complex, when I lived in New York, they knew I was gay.

And you don't sense that around here?

No, these people know.

No. In terms of them being okay . . .

No. No. People have strong feelings. People still whisper. And I'm like, "Why do you have to whisper this?" I don't really give a shit what white people do. Let me go on record to say that. I think people know, but straight people aren't announcing who they sleep with, so I am not announcing who I sleep with. Some of this shit like coming out. Fuck you. I don't know you. I don't have to come out to fucking white people. There were people in school who would say, "Why don't you go work with the gay students?" I'm working with the black students, Latinos, the Asian Americans. Okay. I can't take on every fucking problem. I'm not going to do that. I am not going to be a poster child for each group. I will support gay students and things that they're doing, but I'm not going to be their adviser. I don't go to their meetings. I don't need to go and sit with a bunch of eighteen- to twenty-two-year-olds and share my experiences. I don't know you.

When there are gay kids up at the college of color who are having difficulty, my colleague, who's an administrator, he's gay phobic. He is homophobic. He does not believe that this is a lifestyle that God has deemed appropriate, and yet who's he going to send kids to? He's going to send them to me because I am going to say to them, "It's okay to be gay. You are acting out and fucking up and getting in trouble and all this shit. You're going to get kicked out of school. You have to find a way to deal with your sexuality in a positive light, in a positive way. You might have to transfer out of Davidson, but you don't have to be wilding out like this. You have to find a way to live with peace." You come in, you mean something to me, I'll share with you my life. But I am not doing this bullshit about "I'm gay." No. I told some white kids and some black and Latino kids, because if I start inviting you to my house there are no lies being told in there. You come in my house and you see someone there, you are going to see what I'm into. If I start inviting you to my house, at some point I'm going to say to you, if I'm dating a woman, "I'm dating a woman." If I'm dating a man, I'll say to you, "I'm dating that guy." But I may also share with you some of my life story about my sexuality if you are going to be around me. I have to be who I am in my own house. I can't be discreet, live discreetly in my own home. That don't make sense. I have talked with students to help them deal with their homophobic behavior up at the school. We used to get black kids just from the South, but they were so fucking homophobic it was bad. What is wrong with you people? Why don't you find something else to do? Obviously, you have you some problems. It isn't all that. Talk about somebody because the person is gay. Please. You need to stop. I don't care about your religion. What I understand from Christianity, even if you disagree with something someone's doing, you have to love them. There isn't any love in what you're saying.

What are your political perspectives regarding issues pertaining to LGBT people and pertaining to blacks?

Black community pisses me off sometimes. They know all them damn boys in church isn't going to ever grow up and marry Sally Joe's daughter. They know damn well. It's like the military: don't ask, don't tell. That's what the black church been doing. When Clinton came up with that shit I laughed. I said that's exactly what the black church does. And yet at the same time we have to be a little thankful that has been a haven for some of our brothers and sisters. It pisses me off that there's this intolerance for gay people. If I'm in a church, the pastor starts talking about gay people, I get up and walk out. I am not going to sit and listen to that. Okay. Maybe he's a little sweet. I'm like, "What?" I know damn well this man didn't say this. I'm getting my ass up and walk right out of that church. I will not tolerate that. I will not tolerate black people putting other black people down because of their sexuality. I hope I don't sound biased, but having a different sexuality in a world that's a bit homophobic—not a bit, it's very, quite homophobic—it gives you a different kind of insight into the world and a different level of creativity. I think that creativity comes from the fact that you are open like that. I don't know how to describe it. It pisses me off that we push some of our brightest people away. We can't afford that, damn it. We live under war conditions. That's how I feel about racism. That shit is war. Then you're going to push a sister or brother away because they don't sleep the way you sleep. They don't love the way you love. I don't have any tolerance for that. I get a chance to speak out and say something against homophobic stuff, I say it. That's not right, I just don't believe Jesus would say that. In the South I love to bring up Jesus.

What was it like around here during Amendment 1?

I put up in my yard don't vote for that shit. I put a sign up in my yard. My daughter came home with them and I put one up in my yard. North Carolina purposely made it confusing. I can't remember it right now, but I know it was purposely confusing, so I put a sign up in my yard against it, the amendment. None of my neighbors talked about it—the ones who mean something to me—in a negative way. What the hell is this? This is something to distract us. If people want to marry and they are adults, why should we care? [. . .]

One of the ladies up at the school said something about it's a disgrace to the establishment institution of marriage. I said, "Heterosexual marriages are fucked up by themselves." In fact, straight people don't seem to want to marry no more. It looks like gay people might save the institution of marriage. I said it in such a way that I wanted them to hear me, so I can't let my voice get as loud as it is now. I'll say think about it. Everyone's daughter or son shacking up with somebody, living with them six, seven, eight years before they get married. Some of them go and have children and don't even get married. Looks to me like gay people might be trying to save the institution of marriage. Maybe we worrying about the wrong thing. I said it like that because I want them to hear me. I don't want to rant and rave about shit. If you can't hear me what's the point of my talking. I know how southerners are. You ask them a question; you lead them into it very subtle. So, that woman now, if I'm having something in my family, she wants to be here. [. . .] She knows that Malu is coming and all her gay friends. [She] knows I'm gay and I think she thought I was going to talk about it one time. "So, who's Malu dating?" I said, "Nobody right now." I'm just waiting. I want you to ask me about my daughter, but I am not volunteering anything about my daughter when I know you are a homophobic person. I can say to Ms. Sis, "I sure hope Malu finds somebody that she likes. I want her to be with someone. She works too hard." Like that, I can say that to her. And she'll say, "Baby, just pray on it. If it's to be it will be." Right. Why am I going to share something like that to a homophobic person? I just don't do it. They don't rock my world to that extent that I need their approval. She's a black woman. I care more about what black people think about gay. I don't give a shit what white people think about gay. They start like rah, rah, rah, some crazy shit, and I say, "Oh Lord, I hope you right because if not you going to hell. Talking like that about gay people." I will say it in a friendly way, laugh, and walk on. One old man said, "You terrible." And I said, "Yep."

What do you think is the future of the black gay community here in North Carolina and the South in general? Do you think that things will get better, stay status quo?

Things are going to get better because my daughter's work is on the board of Charlotte Gay Black Pride. Two weeks ago they pulled off a Gay Pride weekend, and they had family events and meet-and-greet and had a panel and town hall discussion. They raised money for something. There were several hundred people attending each event. The ones that lived other places, they are bringing an energy with them, and they are more self-actualized. I think my daughter living in Atlanta and coming of age with her sexuality a little bit in high school, and then more when she got down to Atlanta at Spelman. I believe being in Atlanta, she went to divinity school and she's a chaplain. Being in divinity school you have to really reflect on who you are. She carries her strength that I didn't have at that time. She's thirty-two. She's known about her sexuality for years, acted on it for years, too. I was not that swift. My politics growing up was black and white. Had to do with racial politics. There was no politics of sexuality. I remember Stonewall and was happy that they turned and whipped the ass of the police officers. I was definitely happy about that. The sixties was [about] trying to get something for black people. But I think it's going to change in the South.

· ·

Pat Hussain [b. 1950, Atlanta, Georgia]

Oh, I am . . . fine with being black and being queer. I wish I had known it earlier or had a way to recognize, to see my reflection. I feel that I've made too many choices without enough information. One of those that stares out most glaringly to me in lifestyle is in moving up from the shadows of the civil rights movement and finding the strength for nonviolence and the queer movement that . . . when we lost battles we got hurt. I didn't know that when we won we got hurt too, and not having any sense of taking care of Pat emotionally, spiritually. That the concentration on the work to the exclusion and the ignoring of the wounds that were being inflicted, a friend called it "death by paper cuts," that led me to a point of being unable to not only do the work that I love but to function has led me to not be able to care for my wife and for us. There's a lifestyle of an activist if any corporation in America dared to work their employees the way we work, those who are employed in the nonprofit world and in not just queer organizing but progressive organizing, we would chain ourselves to this building, not enough hours in the day, how many committees. And I believe that that lifestyle of wanting to do something has to do with that burnout rate of people, which is one of the reasons that I do talk about what happened to me. The lack of nurturing for ourselves is one of the things I regret, to not nurture myself and those around me. One of the ways that illustrates it best for me and the lifestyle in that perspective is we run from one meeting to another and grab something to eat on the way. When this is over, I'm going to eat, and we pluck that piece of humanness out of what we do. We're all going to eat. I don't recall a meeting where they said we're going to meet at 5 o'clock, whatever you stop and get bring it to the meeting, we're going to eat it while we're here, and it just makes us a little more one-dimensional. We do this here and we do that there, even though we all do it every day.

The choice to be out and be married didn't feel like a choice. It felt like drawing breath. I've inhaled fresh air. I am not going to breathe anything else. Whatever the consequences may be, that is what I choose and too, I wish one of the choices that I make now is to apply myself more diligently to one of my first loves: history. There are so many stories. The civil rights movement in textbooks has been reduced to two lines, and there are three-dimensional people who are part of that, and I want to be part of the excavation to make that so. And when I had a good job making good money, I wish that I had sent more money to organizations that needed it. I did some. There's a volunteer on one side. There's an employee on the other. I couldn't go to the '87 march. I had to work. I had to work. I did just a little bit of organizing around that. I wrote checks. I could do that. That woman, a lesbian teaching fly fishing in Arkansas, said it most succinctly: "Know where you plant it. Do what you do when it's time for you to do that." Being a parent, being a grandparent has been amazing. Being a parent has been painful and wonderful. I never imagined myself in that kind of role and starting with children and learning to love children who hated me and not blaming them a bit, understanding because to their eyes I had to appear as the impediment to their parents' being together. I had to be the reason, transference. They loved them and I was available. Dog bites the hand closest to their mouth, the one that feeds them. I would want to learn patience more quickly and listen more closely to Cherry. She has the wisdom of the ages. We did have to come to an understanding that she knows everything but I'm always right, and it's worked, or was it the other way around?

Priscilla [b. 1967, San Antonio, Texas]

Unfortunately, I live, love, and work in the same place, which I work for a queer people of color organization in town. It's a community-based organization. And I've been there fourteen years. And so, a lot of my socializing happens there, because we do community events and activities. But it's where I get paid from. And it requires me to work with the white people on some level. But because we are an autonomous queer people of color organization, that's safe and home, for the most part. But then when we got to go out and interact with people from white culture, then we actually have to come home and debrief. [Laughter]

Is that because there's tension between the white gay community and black gay community here?

I think it's because they don't have some of the same priorities that we have, but that they also are racist and don't think that they are. Because everybody thinks Austin is liberal. And I'm like, its liberal white. Let's be clear. It is liberal here, but it is liberal white, which is very different than being liberal. [Laughter] Because everything moves from a white perspective. And so, yes, there's tension, because there are also some of the more—and I don't necessarily call them mainstream because I feel very main and very stream. [Laughter] And so, I call them the white people, because that's who leads them and that's—their priorities are very reflective of white peoples' priorities that we don't get invited. I mean, the organization I work for has been around longer than every queer organization, lesbian organization, gay organization in this town and still doesn't get the respect. It's been around twenty-seven years. And sometimes we get left out of shit, until you need some faces. Then we're brought in. So, the table is already made, and half the time they done ate half the bread. And then they're like, well, next time we'll bring the rest of the bread and then y'all can come, right? So, it's always like we're always coming in as an afterthought. Except when there's something that goes down with people of color. Then we get called to be in the lead. But what we talk about is we still people of color. And that by you taking that position, you're not recognizing the intersections. We black and queer. We Latino and queer. We are people of color queer. And those are synonymous. One don't come before the other. But they always feel like the queer trumps. And so, when black folks do something that they would consider homophobic, then they want us to go after the black folks. But you don't ask us to do that when it's something else, when it's white people. You'll take the lead and claim the credit and do everything else. And so, it's rough being involved to this level.

And that's what I would call the "visible queer activist" sort of community. Because there's a whole 'nother group of people who are not involved in any of this, that I have the privilege of being in a relationship with as a lesbian, who don't do the more political or who don't even come to allgo. And that's because I'm from here. So, I can go to a black lesbian party and see all different people, which is what I did before I got involved with allgo. I mean, allgo has been there twenty-seven years. I didn't know about it even though it was a Latino organization before. I went to an event in '92, didn't know it was the organization. Didn't know it was the organization I'm working for now. Friend of mine said, "There's a gay dance in town," we went to it. [. . .] I didn't know that it was the organization I currently work for. Didn't have a clue. So, when I went to apply, they were like, "Well, who are you?" Because they'd been in the community thirteen, twelve years, and they were looking for a case manager to work with HIV-positive black, primarily black folks, somebody who was from the community. I show up and they were like, "Where you come from?" And they're like, "Where you grow up?" I said, "East Austin." They were as shocked as I was that I'm from East Austin, they don't know me, have never seen me, and I don't know them. But we supposedly in this community. I'm hanging out with all these other people. So, for me, there's like multiple communities here, depending on what's happening and who you're talking about. Because what I know is that people that are from here are really not involved in allgo. And some of that is I think around the politics, that allgo is political and is out and is, that's not all we do is social-cultural things, but it's a political place, right? It's a place to also learn about racism, and it's also a place where black and brown people have kind of come together. And these folks tend to be more segregated in like black, right? So, all the people I was hanging around with were black lesbians. Never at a club. Out every weekend at somebody's house, playing spades. [Laughter]

But [. . .] there's a part of me that can't be me, because living, loving, and working in community is rough. You're always on. I can't go to a poetry reading without somebody saying, "What's the next thing at allgo? When's the next event?" And I'm like, "Did you get the newsletter? Call me on Monday." I'm one of the directors. And I've been there the longest. Like there's no board member or staff that's been there longer than me. And so, I hold a history, all fourteen years of history that has kind of come and gone through the doors, right? And so, I'm overly involved. [Laughter] Because I also host events here that are the organization's. We ain't got a lot of money, so what that means is that sometimes we need a space to have a brunch for an artist that we bringing in. Well, this lovely space, which I don't mind because I feel like this is an abundance of space for two people, right? Like this is a four-bedroom house [laughter], it don't make no sense to me. So, when people come to town or the artists come, okay, then all these rooms and all these people, right? And so, in that way we get invited to everything. We get invited to speak. I'm constantly a lesbian. [Laughter] It's a good thing that I'm out. [. . .]

The work I did at allgo for the first—so I started there in 1998 and we had a case management program for people of color living with HIV up until 2006, so I provided direct services to people living with HIV and AIDS. And I was also the supervisor of that program. And so, some of what happened in being in a community-based organization is that people I grew up with were my clients, which is this social work dilemma around what's ethical and what's not ethical, but recognizing that we were the organization that served people of color. What did that mean for them not to be able to get services there because I'm there. Some of what I have to think about is ethically, how culturally that's not ethically ethical to send people other places because I'm there, right? And so, there are a number of people that I grew up with who have died, men and women. And it has turned out that some of those clients have become—they're related to me. I didn't know this at the time, right? I didn't know when they're sitting in front of me. [. . .] So, I'm talking [about] people that I went to elementary school with, who became my clients as HIV-positive people. And then some folks' parents being my client. [. . .] I suspect that there are a number of people in my family who are HIV-positive, who are much closer to me, who I just don't know are HIV-positive. When I saw my aunt's husband in a picture, I said, "He's HIV-positive." I said, "Mama, who is he?" I said, "What he do?" She said, "He on disability because he has a back injury." I said, "He's HIV-positive." I just knew it. Had never seen him. He didn't look ill. He was six feet four, muscle-built, and I looked at him and went, "He's HIV-positive." And, of course, it came out later that he's HIV-positive, but at the time and he wasn't a client of mine, I just sensed it, right? And I think working in the HIV field has led my family to have a much more open conversation about HIV and AIDS, because some of the stuff that they've done around people who they thought had been HIV-positive, I've had to be like, "Excuse me, you don't need to wash the plate. You don't need Clorox. And we'd all have it. And I would be HIV-positive. Do you understand this? That I have sat in rooms with people, I've drank, of course we all have drank after somebody, you know." So, in that way just knowing the number of people who are impacted by it.

But also, I sit on a planning committee of women living with HIV and AIDS and have been on that committee since I started at allgo. [. . .] And so, it's this interesting mix of like being in the lesbian world, being in gay world, around where I'm immersed in it and where I'm holding all of this knowledge about people's status, that other people don't know, but I know because I'm a case manager and I know because I've been to the clinic with clients. And I've seen people at the clinics, where other people don't even know where the clinic is.

The other thing that it does is that I believe HIV has robbed me of having black gay men particularly in my world of a certain age. And so, when I'm with black men who are twenty-something, thirty-something, and they're having birthdays, I have to remind them or I have to ask them to please don't be ashamed of their age. Because black gay men got this thing around being old queens or being old. And reminding them that I want to grow old with them, because they're it, that all of the men my age and older who were out and black gay men are not here and I don't have them in my world. And that it's important that they know how important it is that they're still here. And so, in that way, I'm always craving black gay men, particularly black gay men. Because I just don't have them in my world. And I wonder what it would have been like over these last twenty-three, twenty-four years, if I had been around black gay men and black lesbians. So, when I think about Ebony Connection, which was a black gay men's group that was here, that was part of allgo, that all those people are gone, like what would it have been like. And I was here and I was out but I just didn't have the opportunity to be around them because they were in the more political world and not in the communities in which I was moving in. And so, I feel like I always crave that and want that.

· ·

Shannon S. [b. 1972, Baton Rouge, Louisiana]

I think Obama is full of it, and let me tell you why. I was the SGA president at my school. Student Government Association. And I went to Washington [. . .] in March of '12 and I went in September of '11, and he went to this gay and lesbian gala thing they were having, and I guess it's like everywhere else, it's local, so it's playing on the TV. And I remember him saying that he believed in people having equal rights so far as if you needed a medical decision or something like that made, but he didn't believe gay and lesbians should marry, and it struck me as kind of odd, because you needed our vote to get in. Nobody believed me when I got home that he said that. Now, the girl sleeping *next* to me, she was in awe, too, because she's one of them open-minded freaks, very open-minded. So, she was like, "Wow," because she's married. She's straight. She was like, "Wow." And some girl was, "Obama all for the gays," and I was like, "On the slick, no he's not." He's not, but when it come election time, he will be. Sure enough, he did, and all I kept remembering was this man just said in 2011 at these people's ball, you believe in equal rights but you didn't believe that we should have the right to get married, because marriage is the institution of man and woman. I heard you say it. So, I just don't know what to say about him. Nothing—I don't trust no politician. Daddy Bush sent a lot of my friends to Desert Storm, and a lot of my friends got killed. Clinton sent us to Operation Desert Thunder that nobody hears about. Baby Bush caused Iraq. I don't trust no politician because all y'all lie. People can't get past Obama's color long enough to see that he's a politician. Yes, he has done some things, but yeah, I did vote for him, because of the black in me . . . literally. Don't trust them. They lie. You learn a lot of what they do in the military. All these peace-keeping missions and all this stuff, and our country is wide open. Look what just happened in Boston. So, I personally think that the government is full of shit and it's "land of the free and home for the brave" when you're not born here. Literally, when you're not born here, and I don't think he's for us. I think he needed for our vote.

So, when he talked about how he had evolved on the topic, you think that was just politics as well?

Mm-hmm. He evolved because he needed the vote, because believe it or not, gays and lesbians have a lot of voting power, and he knew. He needed us, and the Mexicans, but getting us, because gays and lesbians are—the black community has more gays and lesbians—next to the Mexicans—we really do. So, not only would you get the minority vote, but you would get the gay and lesbian vote as well. Now, this was my question I always wanted to know: How would you know who is gay and lesbian minority that's voting for you, because they don't ask you? So, how did you know that you got the gay and lesbian vote? Was there some poll when we went in there, some scanner that tells you oh, she's a lesbian, oh, he's homosexual. How did you know that you got the gay and lesbian vote? The machines don't tell you. You see what I'm saying? So, I was like, how would he know that. How would you know you're getting the minority vote unless you do all these rallies? So, do you really care about us? See where I'm going with that? How would you know, because that machine don't say oh, African American lesbian voted for you. You just got one vote. So, isn't that kind of biased? It's like they're segregating us.

What about Don't Ask/Don't Tell? Were you happy to see—

No. No. No. Being in the military and I saw the hate crimes, and the military sweeps a lot—I saw a girl get raped in the desert. Helped her testify, and the guy got off, and they put her out.

They put her out?

They put her out. They put her out. Don't Ask/Don't Tell was a joke to me, because you put a target on people's backs, and whereas everybody else thought it was a good thing. "Oh, he finally letting us be free." No, I feel like he targeting us for like sending lambs to the slaughter, because now that they know, especially men, and if Barry Winchell didn't teach you nothing, it should've taught you that. You put this target on these people's backs. Now that they know, when they see you coming off of that deployment and you hugging your lover, they targeting you. They see you doing this. They see who is this, and then the commanding officers, believe it or not, you're going to suffer retaliation from that. I seen it. I wouldn't have done it. What you need to know that for? Who does who I'm with, what does that have to do with my ability to fight and defend this country? One has nothing to do with the other. I just didn't think that was fair. I think he was targeting soldiers, marines, sailors, air force men. I think he was targeting certain people in the military, and the suicide rate in the military has went up since then, but you don't hear about that on CNN.

Which do you think was worse: having no policy before Don't Ask/Don't Tell, having Don't Ask/Don't Tell, or the aftermath of Don't Ask/Don't Tell?

I think he could have implemented policy for same-sex couples without making it such a big broad issue, because you do get a lot of paperwork. I think that whoever you designate to make those decisions for you should be your choice and your choice alone, and if something happens to you and your partner is taking care of you or your children, ya'll children, then I think then it should always be about family first. I just never agreed with the Don't Ask/Don't Tell. I just don't think it's nobody's business. You're not going to ask a straight man who he's sleeping with, but you'll put him out for adultery if his wife is making an issue in the military. What difference does it make? Are you going to take care of this person's family that gave their life for this country? I think that if he was going to implement the policy, go ahead and implement the policy. Push everything else up under the table that you really want. You could have implemented that policy to make sure that everybody's family across the board who chose to serve this country was taken care of, but you chose to make it a spectacle because you needed votes, and that's how I feel.

What did you feel about the Chick-fil-A incident?

[Whispering] I think Chick-fil-A is great. I think that was just somebody being bold, and they standing firm on what they believe in, and there's nothing wrong with that. The problem comes in when you try to impose your views on someone else. How do you know the person that's purchasing it— what does their dollar have to do with their sexuality? That was my issue with Chick-fil-A, and you supporting these groups, but you supporting hate, but you supposed to be Christian based. You going to either serve one or you're going to serve the other. I don't understand what Bible these people are reading, because the Bible either said you're going to love one and hate the other. What you going to do? If you're going to support these people in their hate group, because that's what it is. That's what killed me, when people sugarcoat stuff. It's a *hate* group. Would you do it against blacks, and that's what I thought, or would you do it against Hispanics? What else you supporting that people don't know about? I love their sandwiches. I stopped going after that. I stopped going after that, because how many of your own employees are gay and you don't know? I watched this more than one time on the—it was *Immortal,* and the man said people have been killing men ever since they invented gods to forgive them, and I thought that was so deep. People have been promoting hate ever since they found groups that they can put a name on it, and the first thing they want to do is tack God to it. People are a trip, and it's not always the whites either. They had a lot of black supporters. Remember when all those preachers, all those black preachers, most of them from the South, did all that marching against same-sex marriage? Why you don't march like that for better schools, for better programs, to educate the inner-city hood? I don't see you all marching in the hood nowhere. I ain't never seen Al Sharpton up there. Obama either. You know? Like, my aunt used to say, "Jesus hung out with the whores, and the sluts, and the people that was doing wrong, because that's who needed Him." In her words, Jesus was a thug. That's why everybody loved him. I just don't like the fact that in the South this is one thing they do. They always tack God onto their hate. That's the first thing out they mouth, "And the Bible say . . ." It do. And the same Bible say, "Judge ye not." That same Bible say, "You reign on the just and the unjust." Then their eyes get big. Well, then I say, "You know, the devil reads the Bible, too."

[Laughter] I love it.

I said, "Well, that Bible also say you're not supposed to eat shellfish. You're probably going to a crawfish boil right now." I'm just saying, and it also say you're not supposed to cut your hair. If your cycle is on and you're a woman and you're outdoors, they should have stoned you to death. A friend of mine said she just told a coworker that. He wanted to tell her about the Bible and the homosexuality. She said, "You know what? The Bible said you should stone an adulterer. When you ready to get killed?" [Laughter] It's amazing the South mentality about some stuff and in our own community. Even in the gay and lesbian community, we not together.

· ·

Sharon [b. 1964, Washington, DC]

Well, I used to be one of those seventies lesbians, and inside I still am, where I'd be like, "Smash the state! We should have no recognition of anything. The state should have not its business in our bedrooms!" So, I'm kind of like that on gay marriage. But I also was very much involved in Amendment 1, helping to raise money through this party that I had at a friend's bar, locally. And I had people like—you know five hundred dollars a ticket, raised about ten thousand dollars, and lots of them gave who didn't even come. It was a very small group, but it was very fun. I feel this way. I do believe we're being hidden from history and that marriage is important because it allows us to be recognized. And I think that the French government is just about to take a vote to make it legal. To redefine marriage between two persons, period. I think the world is just moving that way. My sister described it this way: Things feel really hard right now because we've got the dragon by the tail. And instead of a little piece of its tail, we're up its back. So, all it can do now is turn around and try to just breathe fire. You know it's like crazy right now because it knows we won't let go. It's not a matter of when we get it. It's not a matter of if. It's a matter of when. It's going to happen. And it's started to happen, and guess what, all the places that have allowed it, you know we didn't have no Armageddon, the world didn't crash. The economies actually went up in those states. The bottom line of the GDP in the states went up. People are like, "Ohh. Gay people got a lot of disposable income." Now, we certainly do, don't we? So, I feel like politically I'm down with it in a way that I wasn't before. I understand civil rights are important, and I see it from my work's perspective. Being here in this conservative place and having no legal protection for being a queer person has been very hurtful. If I had that protection under the law, things might be different for me here in so many ways. I also believe that once it happens the offsetting of blackness and queerness and the queer community versus this conservative person-of-color community, that kind of stuff will stop—which would be nice, because I feel like that more than anything has destroyed the legacy of civil rights, that and HIV/AIDS.

Tonia [b. 1969, Mount Vernon, New York (Graham, North Carolina)]

When I went to college I went to this AIDS 101 thing for a local AIDS organization, and it was like one of those things that change your life, so I volunteered for that organization all through college. And then after college I worked at Feminist Women's Health Center, where I started an AIDS hotline there. And then I went to PA school to become a health care provider, and then I provided HIV care to people for sixteen years. And then I wanted to do more international work, and I started working for the CDC right at the beginning of the president's emergency plan for AIDS relief and have been doing international HIV work.

And so, you've been on the prevention side, the advocacy side, the research side as well, or no?

More recently research. Most of my time has been in HIV care, so just taking care of people living with HIV.

And have you had personal friends to pass from HIV?

Yeah.

Is it your belief that amongst black lesbians that they feel less susceptible to contracting HIV/AIDS because they're lesbian?

Oh yeah, I think we took a survey, actually I did take a survey. I forgot about that. So, in 1992? In 1992 I didn't know shit from Shinola about research, so I was like, "I want to [do] surveys." I made up a survey and I went to, I took it to clubs and lesbian events, and asked a bunch of black lesbians what they knew and thought about HIV, and most people were not that concerned. But I did a survey; it was a survey of 100 random people, and one of them was a lesbian with HIV, which I thought was kind of surprising, making no effort whatsoever to try to find somebody. I wish I'd done something with that. I think I carried it around in a file folder for like ten years and was like, this is ridiculous, and threw them out. But yeah, I think there's a general sense that this is a problem that affects my general community or affects people close to me but not a problem that affects me.

Tori [b. 1993, Orlando, Florida]

I'm definitely in support of full rights. I'm supportive of gay marriage. I would very much like to get married, I really would, and I don't want to call the person I'm with "my partner." I don't want to call them, my domestic something, my pants buddy, whatever. This is my wife, we are married, we have a life. I don't want to have to call it something that it's not when that's exactly what it is. I don't think my relationship with a woman would be any different from a straight man's relationship with a woman, and I don't see a reason to have to separate it. So, all the legislature, "Well, like let's call it something else." No. It is what it is. And I think that it would be great if everyone were to get to that point, but I don't see it happening anytime soon.

· ·

Xami [b. 1957, Hampton, Virginia]

In the early nineties when I was a music performer I was meeting all of these communities of lesbians who were doing community festivals and all kinds of amazing community empowerment stuff for us. I started running into this wall of rigid politics that was beginning to feel on the edge of—I won't say fascist—but it was just too much. They were telling me everything: what I need to eat, how to dress, what I need to talk about, how I need to spout my politics, how I need to relate to women. What was correct, what was socially incorrect. What was politically correct. Now that was an era in our time. I'm not sure if it's still going on quite to that level because I just divorced myself. And basically, left that behind. But it was so rigid and . . . dogmatic, is the word I want to say. I didn't want to live my life according to politics or your politics. And it started to feel like a club that had these rules that I lived outside of and wasn't going to play along with anyway. Butch-femme at the time was kind of assumed as a kind of a—not perversion but, you know, "emulated heterosexual politics too much." You know it was all this. And it was like, [in mocking voice] "What do you mean you're spanking your partner? Did you leave a bruise on her? You're out of the club. Goodbye." And this is still going on in Michigan and places like this. It just got too political for me and I didn't want to play anymore. I wanted to play a different way.

My Soul Looks Back and Wonders
Stories of Perseverance and Hope

All of the lives chronicled in *BQSW* are compelling in their own way, but there were six women's stories in particular that I had difficulty excerpting because they were so extraordinary. They are not exceptional because their stories are somehow more important or urgent; they are exceptional because of the ways in which they exist as outliers compared to the other women's life stories collected here. This is partly due to the seemingly insurmountable challenges that these women overcame, whether drug addiction and incarceration, abject poverty and child abuse, or language and culture acquisition, among other things. Indeed, some of these stories are devastating to the point that it's hard to imagine how the narrator survived the experiences of her life circumstances. And yet, they shared these experiences with me as women who persevered despite the odds being stacked against them.

The six women whose stories are chronicled in part II all hail from the Deep or Global South—Alabama, Georgia, Mississippi, Texas, and Puerto Rico. Perhaps it is a coincidence, or perhaps there is something about this region in the South in particular that predisposed these women to some of the hardships they faced. Ironically, however, for most of them these same communities offered them support during their time of struggle.

As I bore witness to these stories of extreme adversity, but also unexpected joy, the thing that amazed me the most were these women's tenacity and critical self-reflection. They were not just sharing stories; they were also offering what Patricia Hill Collins refers to as "specialized knowledge" or quotidian forms of theory about how institutionalized racism, sexism, classism, and patriarchy affected their and black queer southern women's lives.[1] Indeed, through their self-theorizing these six narrators tell us a great deal about the resilience of the human spirit.

Salsa Soul Sister

Aida Rentas

8

*Finding "Miss Aida," as she is called among her good friends,
was pure serendipity. I had just begun conducting interviews
in Atlanta in the summer of 2012, and several of the women
with whom I had spoken mentioned this person named Aida.
It just so happened that I was traveling to San Juan for
vacation during the Fourth of July. My good friend Duncan
Teague, who appears in* Sweet Tea, *sent a message to me on
Facebook suggesting that I get in touch with Aida while in
Puerto Rico and ask her to be interviewed for the book. Aida
and I connected, and it was love at first sight. I conducted
an interview with her at my hotel in Condado Beach. When
I returned to Chicago, to my dismay I discovered that none
of the interview was recorded. Later that year I attended
the American Studies Association convention, which just
happened to be held in San Juan, Puerto Rico. Once again,
Miss Aida drove from her home about forty-five minutes
away, picked me up from my hotel, and gave me a tour of San
Juan. She took me to all of her favorite haunts, including a
diner where President Obama ate when he visited the island.*

*Miss Aida is a spitfire. Quick-witted, spunky, and
beautifully devilish, she reminded me a lot of the women
from my childhood who were free-spirited and loving but also
didn't suffer fools gladly. As she recounts below, she considers
herself Latina and black, not only based on her African
diasporic ancestry but also because she became acculturated
into the United States through blackness in Spanish
Harlem. She spent a considerable number of years of her life
living in Atlanta, working with black and Latina lesbian
organizations. She is the oldest narrator in* BQSW. *The
interview took place on November 18, 2012, in San Juan.*

I was born in Santurce, Puerto Rico in 1938. [. . .] My childhood was not being able to fit anywhere because when I
was four my parents left Puerto Rico and moved to New

York City. My mother and father didn't speak English. Of course, I didn't speak English. We were in a no-man's-land. They didn't know the rules, they didn't know what was going on, and when I went to school . . . in 1938 they didn't understand. I was one of the first Latinos in the States, and so there was no training if you didn't speak English. You just went to class and got all Ds to the point where I told my mother "D" was "delightful" because she didn't know no better. "A" was awful. She caught on to that when I was about ten, but it was very frustrating until I decided to go into my own world because I couldn't see and no one knew that. I needed glasses. They discovered that when I was nine years old. So, I was just lost all around. Always been a leader, so that helped a lot because I had my own little cliques of friends, but you wonder what would have happened if you grew up understanding at least the language.

I'm the oldest of eight. And my mother had one, like I had four brothers and then two sisters. The sisters are eleven years apart but the boys came one after the other, so I went to school and came home and babysat and took care. I was mama. I tell her to this day *I* raised those boys; *you* didn't raise them boys. [. . .]

I left home when I was eighteen, but I got to girls' camp because everybody thought I was not listening. I was a bad girl. Bad girl didn't understand what the hell was going on. But it was a wonderful thing. I became a lesbian in jail because, hello, it was only girls in there, and so I discovered another sexuality. I think I was straight. I had boyfriends, and then I went away, and I'm a Scorpio, and so I started weighing the two. You have to cook for these guys and do this and do that, and I think I'd rather be a lesbian. And it was a choice that I made, which of course gave me a hard way to go again. But it was okay. I made the choice, and I was willing to do whatever it took, and I met wonderful people, older lesbians, older guys that took such good care of me. I always say thank God for the community because when we see someone lost we usually take them under our wings, and that's what happened with me. [. . .] I've always loved people because people have always been very kind to me.

They used to call me half-breed. "Where are you from?" Puerto Rico. In 1938, Puerto Rico was like, "Puerto what?" [Laughing] "You're a what?" And so, the African American kids didn't understand why I had good hair, why I spoke another language, and was I trying not to be black. They didn't know any Latinos. I was their Latino, so I adopted the African American culture heart and soul because it was easier to blend in. Years later somebody said to me, "Are you in the closet about being Latina?" I never thought of that one. And then I became more Latina because I didn't really know the customs. I didn't. And it's funny, I missed out on both sides because I didn't know American fairytales. Because who was going to tell them to me? But I didn't know Spanish fairytales. I had a lover when I was twenty-eight give me *America's Greatest Fairytales*, and I sat for I would say a month, and it was like, "Oh, this is Humpty Dumpty. Oh!" But you get joy in all the sudden you understand what people were talking about. So, I always had a positive attitude. I don't know how, but I always made things, "Hey, I'm the only one, then I'm number one," because I was the only Puerto Rican in town. So, it was like, okay, I'm top daddy. You all can't find another one like me.

Why did your parents move to the States?

My mother was twenty-one when she had me, and we lived where I live now, Sábana Seca. It's a little town now, but then it was the sticks really, and she went to San Juan to work. And my father came from Ponce and went to San Juan. He was a gardener; she was a cook. My dad is white with red hair, my mother looks like me, but they're both Puerto Rican. And when my mother got pregnant, you couldn't stay in Puerto Rico in 1938 when you weren't married and you were pregnant from a white man. [. . .] My mother was going to get rid of me, and my dad was like, "Oh, no you don't." So, what they did was they got an apartment in San Juan, and somebody was helping them. My dad went to New York, got a job, and sent for my mom. That took four years because I went when I was four. Because he was white he met up with some Jewish guy who taught him ambulance chasing because Puerto Ricans didn't speak English, didn't trust people, and there was a big need. [. . .] So, my dad always wore a white shirt, black pants, and had more money than any other dad because he was an ambulance chaser. At the end he was almost like an attorney. He was with Lefkowitz for so many years; he knew the laws, the regulations. Didn't read or write, but you couldn't beat him out of a penny.

So, what does that mean, ambulance chaser? What was he doing?

If you said my wife fell in the tub, he would go there and say you could get money because, and he would refer her to the lawyer and make sure she went to the doctor and do everything that would make them have a case.

And so, the doctor and the lawyer would give him a cut?

He got 15 percent of the attorney [fee]. And as a result, we as kids got wool coats for winter because we getting clothes from a Jewish family. My mother didn't even understand what wool was. She didn't want it because she couldn't wash it. She wasn't going to send it to the cleaners. [Laughter] So, this Jewish lady made me a deal. She said, "I will give you these clothes, and I will dry clean them for you." And she explained wool to me, which sounds crazy. But my mother, if it couldn't go in the washing machine or if she couldn't wash it by hand, because she didn't have a washing machine, we didn't use it, so in the winter we had cotton clothes with sweaters piled on. [. . .] Now Latinos are more connected; there's programs. But in those days you would see most Latin families with a big heavy winter coat and cotton clothes because they couldn't afford the dry cleaning. They didn't really understand wool, so I ended up explaining everything to my mom. Like, I had an Italian friend, and I used to go to her house, and her mother cooked spaghetti and meatballs and stuff like that. I was like, "Can I take some to my mother?" And I would say, "Mom, this is what they eat." And she would say, "What did you tell them? I don't feed you?" I was like, "No mom, but I told them I was going to bring them some rice and beans, and they would give me this food for me to show you." Lima beans? There wasn't no such thing. We ate red beans with color and flavor, and this lady gave me lima beans. I was like, "But they don't have no taste, and they don't have no color." I was like, "You need to put something in them." She said, "These are lima beans, and if you want to eat here, you've got to learn to eat the way we eat, too." So, I took ham hocks and lima beans to my mom. "Mom, look, this is what my African friends eat." So, she started indulging me and cooking like spaghetti and meatballs, but my dad always had to have white rice and some colored beans with some meat. People would come to our house, and we would be serving spaghetti and meatballs and rice and beans. There was always rice and beans in my house.

Fifty East 102nd Street in East Harlem was our first residence, which was wonderful because Mount Sinai Hospital was maybe three blocks away, the Museum of the City of New York was maybe two blocks away, Central Park was two blocks away. We used to play in the museum, the park, we had the best of health care at Mount Sinai, so the proximity to all of these things where we lived made a big difference. We lived off of Madison Avenue, which was like saying Broadway, so we got to see and meet people. If you lived in the hood, people were not coming in there. [Laughter] It's like that now. I mean, Harlem has changed. But remember when people would say New York ends on Ninety-Sixth Street because people that were not of color would not go above Ninety-Sixth Street.

And it was a mix of Latinos, blacks?

There was Spanish Harlem from 102nd to 116th [Street], from 116th up was regular Harlem, and Third Avenue East was [. . .] what was left of the real Italian neighborhood. And because one of the stops for Grand Central Station was 116th Street and the market was there, we got to see all of these other people that were like, who are they? They were like Martians, you know? [Laughter] So, it was quite a melting pot.

So, the blacks and Latinos interacted with one another?

Well, to be honest with you, someone had told my dad that black people would hurt us, so he tried to make us not have black friends, but we went to public school, and my best friend had to be the biggest, blackest girl in town. And I told my dad if he didn't like black people, why did you marry my mom? [. . .] I always made those questions that shocked him. [. . .] And I somehow found out about protection of children. I think one of my teachers [. . .] gave me the number to children's protection agency, and I called them and told them that my dad was telling me not to hang out with black folks and he was going to hit me and throw me out the house. So, they said that's a very serious accusation and you would have to go to court and say that. I was like, I'll go because I wanted them to take me out of my home and put me in one of my friend's homes. That's how my family is, going nowhere real quick and I had to take care of kids and stuff. So, instead they put me in, they used to call them "girls' homes." Saint Ann's, Saint Philomena's, Saint Germaine's because my mother was Catholic, then girls' camp. This was on and on from when I was nine until I was sixteen. When I was sixteen this Oriental woman said, "She has done nothing." I was the baby of the camp, because people knew I was there with murderers and everything else. I had done nothing. So, whenever I came back they were like, "Oh, she's back," and they would make my life wonderful. Then I didn't want to be home. But they looked out for me, and they taught me a lot. And this woman said to me, "I'm going to take you out because, if you stay after sixteen, you're going to go to Bedford. That's a woman's prison. Then you will have a record. I'm going to take you out, but you've got to live with your mom. You've got to promise me that you will do everything necessary until you're eighteen, because I took you out." Word is bond. I learned that there. So, for two years I went to school, I did whatever, I saved. I tell my mother, "What hour was I born?" Seven thirty in the morning. Seven thirty, November 14, 1956. I had my friends outside waiting. I had an apartment, a job. I made more than my dad. I had my connections. I found the gay clubs on 125th Street. I was eighteen and I was free. You know?

And what did your siblings, what happened to them since you were taking care of them?

My brothers loved that I was gay when I came back out. They would take their suits a size bigger because I came out [as] a daddy, okay? [Laughter] They would get their suits bigger so that I could fit in them. They were very proud because I told them you never judge people by what they are, because I knew I was a lesbian, and they were going to start hearing that, so I kind of trained them that everybody has a right. My brothers cook and wash laundry. They take care of themselves. Your wife is not your slave. She's your partner, and partner means you share. So, these women nowadays, they're like, "Aida, thank you." My brothers are 50/50 or more partners in anybody's life. When you visit, you bring a bottle [of wine], flowers, or something. People have invited you to their home. So, everything I was learning from being away from my mother, which I say was a good thing because I got an education at an American institute called a jail, but who cares? We had no television— none of that. And when I went away I had all of that, so I learned. And in jail there were all these cases that we knew because we knew the girls. So, I learned early about if someone accuses you of something, there's a court system and you don't have to accept it and get your reputation ruined. You have a way to fight. I grew up in that system. So, I was always a leader. "Go tell the principal. Don't fight her. Kick her ass later, but go to the principal."

So, during my years as a gay activist I was always that one that was leading the way when people were afraid. Pat Hussain and Joan [Garner] decided to do this thing, and they came to me and said, "Miss Aida, what should we do?" I was like, "Stop traffic on I-75. They'll listen." [Laughter] I also understood money and politics. I asked this guy for a raise at my job. I went to school. I couldn't go to college. I knew that. I knew education was important, so I joined this program that you went to school a half day and you worked a half day, and my first job was at Columbia Pictures, and I was thin, long hair, and pretty. A bitch. And Irwin Cohen may he rest in peace started liking me. There was a bookkeeping machine before computers that to do accounts receivable. You had to take off this thing and put accounts payable like parts, and they was so complicated, and nobody could do it. So, I said, "If you learn to do that, you will have a very good job." So, I made it my business to know how to do that.

So, I became an accountant without an education because I knew how to do the accounting machine. I had a teacher in school, she said to me— because I was like, I'm not preparing for college because I know I can't afford college. Let's be real—"Okay, you could still have a career." What the teacher is telling you, she's interpreting, but she's getting it from a book. As long as there's always books, you can learn anything from a book yourself, and what you don't understand you ask somebody, and then you sit with somebody, and you ask them if they see this as you're seeing it, because you may be getting a whole other thing. So, I'm a book fiend. She taught me self-education. So, I started accounts receivable, accounts payable, and became kind of an accountant without a degree or other education, and with this machine I was the head bookkeeper. I was the fiduciary officer of Columbia Pictures when I was eighteen years old, so I thought I should get a raise. So, I said to Irwin, "I need a raise." He said, "Girl, you want a raise? You want a title?" He said, "Let me tell you what to do, make a business card and give yourself any title you want to, and you can tell people that's what you are." But you see, he said that to the wrong person. I went and made a business card that said "accountant," [and I] started doing accounts outside of there. Next thing I knew, I left Columbia Pictures because of a racial issue, but I knew I had enough money and jobs. [. . .] Accountants in my day, woman accountant, black woman accountant, I was it, in my circle, so I did very, very well. So, I knew always to learn the latest. A lot of my friends, they don't want to pick up a computer because Facebook is for kids. I said, "You know what? You're being left behind. You're creating a divide, a digital divide." Whatever divide we create it ourselves. [. . .]

Salsa Soul Sisters became Salsa Soul because I was the Salsa. They were all my friends, and I was like, "Soul Sisters, what do you mean? Why can't I join? Because it's for African Americans?" They said, "Okay, Aida." They made it Salsa Soul Sisters. I fought for what I thought was mine, and so I had a really good life—a hard life in a sense, if you let people tell you that, but I don't ever remember thinking I had a hard life. I was one of the first hippies. I moved to San Francisco and lived in a commune and all of the rules—that's an education in itself—because they teach you seven rules. One is eliminate jealousy. They explain what jealousy is. Hexing. That you're perfect just as you are. You can be a perfect asshole. [Laughter] I heard that from the communes.

That you could be a perfect asshole?

Yes. [Laughter] If someone said, "You're an asshole" but then you say, "Yeah, but I'm perfect." So, the communes they used you, but [. . .] if you taught me something I'm learning it. I'm learning it. I've always been a good student. Victor Baranco who started Morehouse, which is the commune I belonged to, he was so good that it became a university. There's a Morehouse University in California that was a commune, but he taught different.

So, electricians, plumbers, and all of these people would move in, and it would be the commune, and nothing belonged to anyone. Whoever got up first in the morning got to choose what they were going to wear first. Whoever got first to the kitchen got to eat. I started watching because I wanted to open up my own commune, and someone said, "Aida, where you going to get the house?" And I thought, where did he get the house? And then I realized the value of real estate. You can't do anything unless you have a place to put it into. I learned that early on. So, these life lessons are so simple, and I always used to say, "Damn, they went and got a PhD to learn that?" [Laughter] Because there really were just some people that you say, okay? You know? So, I got this innately intelligent Jewish head, things that people would say about me. And I'd be, "Why does it have to be a Jewish mind? Can't I just be a smart Puerto Rican?" People didn't mean any harm, so they were like, "Oh, yeah, I guess. It's just a saying, Aida." I'm like, "Yeah, but it's a saying like black and white. White is always good, black is not. So, these are sayings that can't exist." I would be talking to teachers and employees and stuff, and so I always got the better jobs, the better positions. People didn't mess with me because I had a mouth, and it wasn't me trying to be smart, it was always fighting for equality because I grew up in the correction system and that's what you do in there, is you fight for equality.

When did you come out to your parents?

When I was nine. What happened is . . . or when I was eleven. My little sister was just born. She was learning how to talk, and I had a lover that was visiting me, and we were kissing in the living room, and my little sister told my mother that I was kissing this girl. And my mother said, "Well, they're friends." And my sister said, "No, they were kissing and muah, muah, muah." So, my sister outed me. A baby. And my mother was like, "Oh no, we can't have this." And I said, "Now wait a minute. I am what you made me. I was boy crazy, you sent me away. You could call me bisexual. You could call me . . . but you can't disown me because I'm not your child only when I'm good. I'm telling everybody you're my mother." Because, I mean, she really wanted to disown me because I was a bad influence on my brothers and sisters. I said, "Yeah, but before you knew, I was taking care of them, and my brothers and sisters know who I am. You're the only one who don't know who I am." Because my brothers knew. They knew they couldn't tell my mother. My dad was so hurt that for about two years he didn't even talk to me, and then he started loving the woman I was going with. When he died he asked her please to take care of me. [. . .]

My mother respects me because I raised her children. I raised *her*. I told *her* what to do. And so, she respects me and doesn't want me to think that she looks down on homosexuality, but she's a homophobe, but she hides it from me. But if you listen to her talking, like when Ricky Martin came out she was like, "Why is he flaunting this?" And then she would look at me like, "Oh, I forgot that you're a lesbian." [Laughter] It's so funny because my mother is my color. I'm the darkest in my family of my immediate siblings of my dad. My mother has African roots, and so we're the colors of the rainbow. But my mother will see a very dark-skinned person and not think they're pretty. She's a racist. And people go, "Aida, how can you say that?" I love her, she's my mother, but I've known her for seventy-four years. She's a racist. And when she thinks something, I get it from her, strong-willed. So, if you don't know how to defend yourself in my household, you're in trouble. [Laughter] But my mother would deny that she's a racist. She would deny that she's a homophobe. She's very much together. "Yeah, Ma, okay." But what do you do with your mother? You can't change her views. You learn to accept that. And a lot of older, definitely Puerto Ricans are homophobic [. . .] and that's in a lot of cultures, as we've been coming out.

I remember when it was you could go to jail for being gay. Now you can ask for marriage rights. I've seen it evolve, which is wonderful. Me and Pat [Hussain] used to talk about it all the time because we went to Highlander and in Highlander they taught people how to defend political views and what-not, and Pat was like, it's constantly defending who you are and what you are. With Pat and Cherry, they have that all the time, with Cherry being dark and Pat being light, you know? People respected them, but there was always those that didn't know them that would make their life miserable.

So, you were out at eleven, and you defied your mother and said, "You're not going to put me out." How did that work out over the next few years? You just had a standoff? Or—

No, it was never talked about. I went to work. I worked at Columbia Pictures, which I had the most prestigious job in my neighborhood, which meant I dressed well, I read, I was educated, I had white friends and every other kind of friends that came into my neighborhood. I was not ashamed of where I lived. And my mother was kind of afraid of me, if you want to say that, because I was like, "I'm taking care of that baby every day while you're at work, so if you don't have him respect me, how do you think I'm going to take care of him? You [. . .] can't talk about me to him, or you get another babysitter." Because she would not want them to be with me socially, but I babysat them! Hello?! You can't have it both ways. I was the one,

I was the—the other thing was that my mother is Catholic, religious, all that bullshit. I saw her go through a couple of abortions. I knew there were abortions. They would hang up the sheets and stuff. So, when she started preaching to me, I would say, "Ma, this is me. Remember? I *know* you. We grew up together." So, I said, "I'm not going to tell anybody, but don't give me any shit," you know? I was like her "keeping her in place" child. And so, we never had a close relationship. She's closer to everybody than me, but she loves and respects me because even though I was who I was because I had money, I made sure that my brothers had everything they needed and my sisters and her. So, I took care of family, and so there's a respect, and now it's amazing. I'm the one taking care of her in her old age, and she tells me she loves me a lot. I think she's trying to tell me she loves me all my life. I want to say, "Mom, that's just recently because you realize," but then she always says a mother always loves her children. She believes all that, and I'm not here to prove her wrong. But I tell you what. You sit back and watch and you say, "Life is amazing," especially when you see it from a gay perspective in a Latino family.

I have no children, so I'm worthless to my entire family, because they get married and then that family is their immediate family. And they may not say that to you, but they look at you like, "Who's going to take care of you when you're older? Who's going to take care of you when you're sick?" I'm like, "You know what? I have a family. Believe it or not, y'all don't have to worry." When they realized that I was that independent and I made a lot of money in my life, Patrick, I had a security company. I've always had stores. I was an accountant, so I knew the value of a dollar. [. . .] I'm not materialistic, and I'm not about the money. I'm never going to get a job. I'm retired. I'm going to make a living on what I have, okay? Time is very important. I can go sit by the beach. I can go do what I want to. I tell people you don't have to buy every latest fashion. When you're young that's okay. Comes a certain age, what are you trying to prove? Live within your means. If you go to my house, I have everything I need from vitamins to food to, but clothes. I have gowns. You know, Atlanta is gown city. I gave about thirty-five gowns away to, what's it called? Dress for Success. What am I going to do with them? They're getting rotten in Puerto Rico moisture. I kept two outfits, of which one I'm wearing for a wedding. It was so dressy. Well, you see how dressy Puerto Ricans get. You know it's too hot. [Laughter] Like, I paid two hundred dollars for these shoes. Now, if you told Puerto Ricans that, they'd be like, "What?" Because they're buying sexy things. These are SAS [shoes], I got bad feet. There's not a pain in my body with these shoes. My sneakers cost two hundred dollars, so I spend my money in things that I need, and that all comes from my past. Being on your own at an early age, I think it makes a big difference than when you're sheltered. I know kids that have gone to college, and they come out and they're like, "What am I going to be when I grow up?" And it's like my mother wanted me to go to this college, and they're lost.

My father, his real job was dishwasher. So, he used to leave the house like at three in the morning and, let's say, come home by three, and then he did his ambulance chasing, but he told me that he was a chef, not a dishwasher, because he was ashamed of that. Well, tell me that my dad's a chef. I told everybody my dad was a chef. [. . .] One day I said my daddy works in a restaurant, so I took my little brother. I had to be, I don't know, young. And me and my little brother got on the train and went to my dad's restaurant. I found it. I would be like, "Ma, what's the name of the restaurant dad works in? Where is it? How do you get there?" And my mother was an innocent Puerto Rican woman, submissive; she raised the children and dad did nothing. Even though she had a temper, she was still [makes hand gesture]. [. . .] And so, I went to the restaurant and I said to the guy, "We're here to see my dad." And he said, "Who's your dad?" I said, "Domingo Rentas," and they were like, "What does he do?" I say, "He's the chef." The guy sat us down and said, "I'll be right back." We're looking for my dad. There was no chef named Domingo Rentas. There was a dishwasher named Domingo Rentas. So, he brought my dad out, and I remember to this day my dad's face. He said, [whispering] "What are you doing?" I said, "We came for some dessert." The guy told my dad, he gave us dessert, he let my dad take us home, and on the way home I convinced my dad not to tell my mother that we were there. Later on in life I found out that he told her and forbid her to tell me that she knew. So, of course, she was angry with me for two weeks, which I didn't know why. I know now. But he said, "It was very wrong of you to take your brother on the train into a neighborhood you didn't know. If something happened to you . . ." and I waited for him to finish and I couldn't wait for him to finish to say, "It was very wrong of you to lie to us and tell us you were the chef when you were the dishwasher!" [Laughter] So I learned clear communication. Anybody that knows me will tell you, "She does not lie." I don't care what it is, I'll find a way to ease it to you, but don't look for me to lie to you about me. Why do I have to lie to you? I did it. Whatever reason I did it, I did it. You don't like what I'm doing, fine. I don't feel like I have to lie.

When I became the executive director of Grass Roots, my nonprofit, it was because I went for a job, I was the volunteer coordinator for the National Black Arts Festival. I was Shirley Franklin's volunteer coordinator. I was the outreach coordinator for the entire AIDS Quilt around the world, but I could not get this position because I did not have a college degree. I wanted to work for this nonprofit for children, and I was furious, and then it dawned on me: okay, when someone hires you they give you all these needs what they want; when you open your own business, you're the boss. I went about finding out how to open a nonprofit. I paid somebody eight hundred dollars to open it for me because it was too complicated, John Eden. He said, "Aida." I said, "That's what I want. Do it." He explained the whole thing to me like I was in school. I went over my nonprofit, knew what not to do ever, misuse those funds, get under the IRS scrutiny. I knew that from being a kid. Al Capone went to jail for evading the IRS, not killing. [Laughter] You don't mess with the IRS. So, I opened my own nonprofit, controlled my board and did fabulous things for ten years. They were about to take my nonprofit from me, this group of educated ladies, because I didn't have a college degree and part of the qualifications for being an executive director is this PhD. [. . .] I said, "You know what? It was my idea. These are my children, my programming. You want to be a ladder climber, you climb it somewhere else, but you're off my board." And I'd have my friends on my board explaining to them. They knew the deal. So, nobody could come and manipulate the nonprofit because people get this big money, not everybody, but you know they get these salaries. They don't care about the kids. I was just reading about the woman that started a nonprofit saying she was finding lost dogs that people were able to have left, she left them millions. Anderson Cooper was telling the story. The people that gave the money never—she used the money privately, millions. There's another one who's supposed to be helping veterans. The veterans haven't seen a penny, and people give millions because it's veterans. So just because it's nonprofit doesn't mean it's, you know. It's all about educating yourself and willing to be the person that you're wanting to be.

You told me another story about when you defied your parents and it was around you staying out all night and paying the rent. Tell me that story.

What happened is I would come out of school at 3:00 P.M. and have to be home by 3:15 P.M. or I would get beat, because my mother decided that that's the longest it should take me to pick up my brothers, collect all these kids, and bring them home.

In fifteen minutes?

Yes. And it could be done, but I used to talk to my friends, and I would always be late. [. . .] Milk used to come in glass bottles. She would half fill them with water, kneel me on rice, and if the bottles fell I was lying or whatever she wanted to accuse me of. I became very strong [whispering] because

I ain't dropping these bottles. I don't care what she said. It was my mind over her mind. She believed in witchcraft. She took me to a witchcraft woman to get rid of this boyfriend I had, and I told the woman if I lose my boyfriend I'm going to come and kill *you*, you better hope he stays with me forever. And my mother was kind of crazy, the things that she would do. She had the iron cord, the cord from the iron, and she would say, "Okay, you did this, I'm beating you twenty times with this cord, and if you raise your hands, it doesn't count." "Ma, I didn't do it!" She said, "You did it." They used to take me to the gynecologist all the time to see if I was pregnant. I was a virgin until I was eighteen, but she decided in her head because I had all these boyfriends, they were friends, that I was having sex. In her mind, she's a sexual deviant too. In her mind she imagines, like, my niece right now will lock the door to her room to our apartment with a friend in there. My mother, "And why would you lock? Okay, you are, you're a pervert." [Laughter] And so she would insist I did this and I did that, which I had not done. And I refused to let her think that she was fooling me. I was like, "Hello? I know what I did. I didn't do it. I don't care whose saint you burn or what you do, I didn't do it." So, after a while I got used to the beatings. [. . .] She's always had this [saying] [speaks in Spanish] "better your hand hurt than your heart," so she whipped you. It didn't faze me anymore. I said, "You know what? I am rushing home with these kids to get them there by fifteen minutes after. I very seldom make it, so I'm getting beat anyway." I used to leave the kids at the door, go back out, party, dance, go to the movies, do whatever I needed to do. Then people would say, "You going home yet?" "What's she going to do? Beat me? She beats me anyway." So, I got that beat-me attitude, you know what I mean? Then she realized she had to change her ways.

My dad was the nicer guy. So, one day he was telling me I had to do something I didn't want to. I said, "Dad, why"? He said, "Because I pay the rent." I see. I made more money than him. I said, "Ma, I want to pay the rent next month." My mom was a gopher. She was this country girl who you could bullshit. She said, "No honey, you're saving because you said you wanted to move when you're eighteen." I said, "Ma, I want to help. I want to pay the rent. I made more money than dad. I want to surprise him. I don't want you to tell him. I want to pay the rent." I did. I paid the rent. I think it was two hundred dollars. We lived in the government projects. We lived in these nice projects because they made them to simulate the Jewish condos. Because we lived downtown [. . .] so they didn't want us to feel poor, so then they built this Henry Street Settlement. I'm sure you heard of it. And that's where I was raised. All my art and culture comes from the Henry Street Settlement.

So, the next time my dad told me to do something I was like, "No, you do what *I* say." He said, "What?" I said, "Ask mom. I paid the rent." I really believed what he said. "You said I have to do what you said because you pay the rent. Well, I paid the rent so you do what *I* say." [Laughter] I taught them a lot about what you say. You've got to think about what you say to a child. And at the time, of course, you don't realize you're being so silly. I just was really wanting to be the boss. I said, "Shit, I got money, I'll pay the rent and I'll be in charge. Nobody has to beat me anymore." [Laughter]

And how long did you pay the rent?

Not long.

Okay, so they left you alone?

Yeah, my mom was not going to give me control.

Have you ever been married?

Gay boys, so that as a cover, like my friend Ricky. His lover went to his bank and exposed that he was gay, and he came to me and he was like hysterical. "Miss Aida, what am I going to do?" "Let's get married and take back the wedding pictures." So, we have wedding pictures. I married a guy for immigration purposes. I married a guy, he thought he was dying and he was going to leave me all his stuff because he didn't want to, what's the word, leave it all to the government. So, yep I've been married three times to men. I've had very long-term relationships with lesbians. In fact, my lover just died last year. We were together eighteen years.

When I got single, I was so tired of relationships that I said, "You know what? I'm taking a minute before I go in [another relationship]." I haven't had a relationship in about ten years. I'm enjoying my freedom because it was like you have to always be aware of the other person's needs and wants, and I just for once in my life wanted, if I want hot pink walls I want hot pink walls. [Laughter] I don't have to live with you, we can just be friends. . . . I always had these long-term relationships. They would meet Aida, "Crazy Aida," that was my nickname, and they loved it, but then once we were a couple they wanted to tame me. It was like, you know something? Mainly I've always been a social person. I had a fan club, according to my lovers, and I was always doing stuff that involved schedules outside the home, it's not that nine to five. You know, lesbians get married and they get into this thing. That was not me. I was doing my arts and culture and always in charge. I had to be there. And people really resented that.

I had a store. I had a jewelry shop. I always had a shop. My last shop was an art shop for starving artists. I would sell their art because they were beautiful, they just don't know how to market themselves, so they would leave the art with me. I would get 35 percent, and they'd come maybe once to have to teach my kids, whatever they did. So, I had an art shop in Atlanta on Edgewood Avenue. That's where I met most of the people at first. They couldn't believe the art show because it was talented people that did not know how to be that gallery. I said it don't have to be that fancy. Hang it on the wall and have a cause. Because if you were watching TV, everybody had a nonprofit—Jerry Lewis and their mother, everybody. I would say, "Why are we so different? As African Americans we give the most. We do this, but yet we don't do the owning the business, the this, the that." And people were saying, "Aida, you can't open a nonprofit. What you know about a nonprofit?" I said, "What did Clinton know about being president? You learn on the job. You hire a professional." Like, right now I'm trying to do an intentional community. What do I know about intentional community? I go on the computer. I talk to people about it. I need an electrician, a plumber, a nurse, and we contain ourselves. It doesn't have to be exactly what the guy that invented the word thought of. For me, it's just a way to be with my friends and barter. We don't need money. You're an electrician? I'm an accountant. You're a plumber, and that comes from my commune days.

Talk about your time in Atlanta. Why did you move there, and what was that community like?

When I became eighteen and I was an accountant, that was a freedom to travel around. My brother was in the Vietnam War. He told me, "Don't go to Europe. See America first. Those bridges are old. Just see America first." So, I lived in San Francisco, Denver, I used to take my entourage with me, two or three people. "You want to move to San Francisco?" And I would guarantee them an apartment. And I did that so often because I thought, okay, I've been in Miami a year, I've been in Denver a year, I've been in San Francisco a year. Next! My friends got worried about me. They were like, "Aida what's wrong? You don't stay nowhere permanently." At that time, black people, everybody was at a job for twenty years and they were buying a house, and everybody was all settled, and I was like, "I don't have any KIDS! I don't have to do any of that." And they would be like, "Yeah, but you're going to get old." And?

So, I was like this crazy woman. They called me crazy, and that really bothered me that they called me crazy, so I went to a shrink and asked them why everybody called me crazy, and she said, "When people don't have an answer for something it's not a fact, it's crazy. It doesn't mean you're right or wrong, it just means they don't get it." I was like, "Oh, thank you." [Laughter] So, then when people started calling me crazy I would say "thank you." I thought I was being unusual. It's okay. So, I always made good friends because I've always . . . Pat Hussain and Cherry had really rough times, and everybody loved them and admired them, but it's like, hello, do they have food? I went to their house, and their mortgage was behind. I went in the community that loved them so and collected their rent and gave it to them. Pat always says, "I don't know why you did that, thank you." If you love somebody, it's not about a card, it's about meeting their needs. I may never write you, Patrick, but if something's wrong with you and I could help, I maybe can't help, but if I could help, I'm going to be there for you, and so I've always been like that, I guess from raising my brothers and sisters. And so, I have these loyal friends, and I know that my friends love me. When I had an accident in 1996 and I had a store, people worked my store, they packed my store, they took care of me. My family was not involved, and I purposely didn't call them, because I was gay. The Spanish thing would be, "See, she need me." My sister came to see me as a guest to see how I was, but not to take care of me. These two gay boys in my life, Dennis Shears took care of me from my accident, and Ralph Slaughter took care of me when I broke my arm. I mean, they were more than my sons. They're gay boys. I brought Dennis to Atlanta because he wanted to come to Atlanta and didn't have a place to stay. I had this home. And Ralph Slaughter, I found him homeless. He was an artist—fabulous stuff. And I showed him a marketing technique. I said, "All you have to do is do your art. I'll sell it for you."

So, anyway, when I'm in the middle of all this madness, my friends were like, all these friends that I had made along the way, they really knew each other. I thought, my friends should know each other. That's another thing, everybody meets you, Facebook "I'm going to dinner with Patrick." Who is Patrick? [Laughter] So, everybody knows about Patrick. Why the secret? I love you. So, they all got together to plan to sabotage me to stay somewhere because they were really worried, and I said, "You know what, I promise you, the next place I move to I will stay three years because after two years in strange places I got the itch and I didn't want to be cold anymore." That's why I left New York. I didn't want to be cold. I discovered Miami Beach. I was like, "Oh, I don't have to live in a cold place." So, I moved to Atlanta and I had to stay there three years, and Sharon Redd, do you remember Sharon Redd the singer? She sang "Can You Handle It." My best friend [. . .] used to go with Sharon Redd, and Sharon had just been in Atlanta and told me how wonderful Atlanta was.

It's 1989. She told me how wonderful it was and how everybody, black women, gay people, "Oh, Aida, you would love it." That's why I moved to Atlanta. And so, she arranged it since I was moving and didn't know anybody there. She was like, "How you going to move somewhere?" I'm like, "I'm going to rent the place." And so, she called Joan Garner, and Joan was about to do a Labor Day party that she always had, and Joan hosted me as the new lesbian in town. I met all the top people, and they were like, "If we can help you." I'm like, "Okay, give me your names!" [Laughter] So, I became intimate with them right away. I called people for help. Where can I get a job? Where can I live? And I kept going in circles with Peachtree Street and I would be on Moreland and next thing I was on Briarcliff, and I was like, "Oh, I need somebody!" So, people showed me around and we became friends.

When I went to Atlanta, the AIDS Quilt had just got there. She didn't know what to do with it. I've always been known as that woman, "You don't know what to do, call Aida." Don't ask me, that's just been my thing. So, she called me. The National Black Arts Festival was having a really hard time getting volunteers because they mistreated the freaking volunteers, and one of my friends worked there and said, "Call Miss Aida. She will get this shit together for you." So, I used to have orientation. Just because you're a volunteer don't mean you come in, and I don't care if you're a nurse, a doctor, or a street cleaner. Here you're a volunteer. All the titles go away. This is the Black Arts Festival. You've got to make us look good. You can't be saying you're coming and don't come. I had every exit, every entrance covered, so I became famous for that. So, everybody who was having an event would want me to manage their event. So, I got to know John Lewis, Campbell, all of them, Diane Albright. So, I became a political leader and somehow somebody recommended me to the Victory Fund because somebody said, "You need to run for city council." I said, "Honey, I'm a jail bird." And they said, "So write a book and out yourself." I said, "What?" They said, "That's what you do." I was like, "Really?" So, they took me to Washington, the Victory Fund, and professionally trained me how to be a politician. You know about the Victory Fund, right?

So, when I came back from the Victory Fund, I was supposed to run for city council. I even have a video where they taped it to give my boss that I was gay, but as God would have it, June 23 of 1989 I broke my leg. I was in a car accident. I was in such pain. I said I can't run because all this money goes behind your being educated as a politician and all these white millionaires. I knew more millionaires in Atlanta. I couldn't believe I knew these people, but they decided I was Latina, had the personality, I opened Latinos in Acción, I was challenging everybody in Atlanta about, okay, you say you want diversity and we keep having these racism forums [. . .] but you still keep hiring all white for the gay parade, you still keep hiring all white for this.

You can't find black talent because I'll find them for you! So, to shut me up they would make me Grand Marshall and leader of this, assistant to this, so I became a leader. [. . .] I'm never going to be afraid of my power. I'm going to claim it. All I have as an older lesbian is my experience and my power. You got to be careful how you use it, but use it I will. Honey, we opened an Olympic Village for gay Olympians when the Olympics was in town in Atlanta. So much has been written about it because she thought she was under contract, they thought she was doing it for free, so she had a multimillion dollar debt as a result of it.

Who are you talking about?

Julie Rhoad who runs the AIDS Memorial Quilt. That's how we became friends, but I got her all the information. She looked like she had the finances together. I was the liaison for the lesbian community with Bill Campbell, and she was a big event planner with Coca-Cola, so I got them together, but what happened was there was another woman that was manipulating the money, but I didn't know that and I didn't need to know that. So, that's where I started, and that's how me and Pat Hussain became real close, because when I opened the center, her and Donna and this little movement started. They wanted to block the Olympics out of Cobb [County] so I said, "Fine." So, we started figuring out how we could block it because now I'm on the president's [committee], on the mayor's committee, and the this and the that, and we started working.

Well, what happens, Patrick, as much as I want to do this interview, as much as I try to be on time, I try to be punctual, I try to answer that, but if something is not good for me, if I have to go the bathroom, or if I'm hungry, or whatever, I say, "Patrick, excuse me, I have to take care of myself." What I find is—especially activists—they take it so [seriously], they don't take care of themselves. That's what happened with Pat [Hussain]. Pat would be sick, and I'd be like, "Pat." "Well, I've already made the commitment." "Pat," it's like Charis bookstore, "you can change the date." "Oh, but then they'll have to reprint." "So? You could die." And I was always trying to get people to take care of themselves because they were burnt out and I didn't understand burnout. I still don't understand burnout. Why are you going to take yourself until you burn out?

So, one of my things that I try to teach is, you know *The Four Agreements*, the book. Oh, Patrick, I'll send it to you. I have, maybe I have a hundred copies left. I bought five hundred copies of that book. I didn't really. I bought it, but it was because Marie Kaiser was a wonderful activist in Atlanta. She died but before she died one of the things she had willed Grass Roots, because

I loved to educate, was a book thing at Borders. So, when Borders was going out of business, I had to use it right away, so I bought [. . .] five hundred copies of *The Four Agreements* because they're with you. I started giving them to people. [. . .] Before you get to know me and before you and me become friends, you've got to read *The Four Agreements*. It's "Don't take it personal." "Clear communication." You know? "Word is bond." "Be the best that you can be." Simple stuff. I can't stand bullshit, and I call people on it. Privately, I'm not one of those like, [whispers] "Come here, Baby. Pardon me if you don't like what I'm about to tell you, but I mind that shit, and I know you're lying, and I'm not going to sit here, not Miss Aida." That's how I got the name "Miss Aida," because I've always been in a younger crowd because older people give up. Most of my friends are dead from AIDS, drugs, or whatever. The era I grew up with, they're gone. We had plans, we were going to do a gay retreat in Hollywood and all this, with all these boys, because I grew up in New York. They're all dead. So, then you come down to another generation and another generation, and I found that during my time gay people were being unkind to themselves a lot. There's a lot of alcoholism, a lot of drugs, a lot of unsafe sex, and I think it's because they were so ashamed. Now you got something to fight for. Now you've got examples. [. . .]

[When] Don Lemon came out I cried, because I knew he was gay. I used to meet the boy at Whole Foods, but the pain of having to be in the closet at that level, you almost want to say, come out, it's okay, but of course you don't do that. But when he came out I was like, "Oh, Don, you don't know how happy I am." [Laughter] And so you become an older lesbian that is not in the . . . modern life has changed, so that I don't care how you try to stay in, there's a generation gap. I was a letter writer or card writer. Kids text you. Don't text me. I'll read the text, but my phone doesn't have texting ability. I bought it as a phone. I'm on a budget. [. . .] And some of my friends, "I'll give you [a phone]." No, don't give me that. I don't want it. I have an e-mail, a Facebook on my computer. My phone. [. . .]

I always say don't abuse me, I'm not to be abused, but use me. I'm not going to lie about no reference for you, but if I can be of help. We don't do that enough for each other, and I'm happy to see the gay community is beginning to grow gracious. The Phil Wilsons of the world have made such an impact on our community. The Duncan Teagues. I met Duncan. He was the only male black that went to the E[xistentialist] Church. I was in search of a church because the Catholics condemn this and condemn that. The moment they condemn gay I'm out of there because I'm being a hypocrite, so the E Church was, when I went to Atlanta, open to everything and everyone, so I went to the E Church, and there was Duncan. He was like, "You're the famous Miss Aida, huh?" [Laughter] And we became friends, and we went through so much stuff, because Duncan is great. And thank God that he found David, but before that it was that hurt and anger every time you know how you guys do? [Laughter] I would be like, "Duncan, be by yourself."

So, what is your favorite memory of the South?

Hmm . . . Pride. To me, in fact, I said next year I was going to go in for Pride. It was all of the bars and stuff were downtown. Outwrite [Bookstore] had just gotten on the corner of Piedmont, which gave us a view. It was people who were coming from all over the world. It's Pride in Atlanta, and you being part of that. It was so much fun, but we also raised money for so many causes and stuff, and it was the one time where the neighborhood really accepted gays. It was Gay Pride. Straight people would come in. I mean, I went to New York Pride, but New York is so big it was Pride, and then it goes on. Atlanta was like after the Pride there were parties, before the Pride there were parties. It was the most beautiful time in the world is Pride in Atlanta because it's southern. People cook. People have events. People invite you to parties. People host people, and they really mean it. For that one weekend it's just a family that you so seldom sense that as a gay community, and I saw it evolve from an all-white thing. I was there when Black Pride opened, and I was like, "Where ya'll going?" And they was like, "Miss Aida, we need our own." And then every Black Pride opening with the Bayard Rustin breakfast. I didn't know who the hell Bayard Rustin was, so I looked it up, and then it was like, "Wow, Martin Luther King and Bayard." I'm one of those that reads and brings it to life and imagine what were they feeling, and so that Bayard Rustin breakfast in Atlanta to this day is an event that you shouldn't miss if you're in Atlanta and you're gay. It's mixed but really for Black America to go and share stories. Craig Washington. So, Pride in Atlanta to me was the weather was beautiful, people were beautiful, you felt good because you did something. I was grand marshal one year, and you don't know how proud I was. It was like, wow. And then they told me, "Miss Aida, you were unanimously picked." I was like, "Really?" That was a big thing for me because I'm not too impressed with status and all that, but that your community loves you and gives you the greatest honor, I think it's very important for my sense of being.

Tell me a little bit about Salsa Soul.

Salsa Soul Sister was an organization in New York City, and they would meet at the bottom of a church, and they were to New York what Mary Anne Adams is to Atlanta. She started ZAMI and that has become a home for so many. That was what Salsa Soul Sisters was in New York. That was forty years ago, but it gave us a place where we went, where we belonged, because there were other gay organizations, but there was one or two blacks or one or two Hispanics, but they weren't integrated yet. And somebody, I don't remember who, but somebody decided to do Salsa Soul Sisters, and that gave us a home and we met there and we shared and we did all kinds of from art classes to learning about your body to how to eat well, and I would not have missed. It would be like, "Work? Uh-uh, I got to go to Salsa." And a lot of wonderful friendships came out of that and a lot of relationships. Audre Lorde was my friend. A lot of those New York women we were friends because just now, eighty years from now when you're passed and you're famous, but they're human beings, they're living a life. And she [Audre Lorde] had two children. We would sit around and Alexis DeVeaux [. . .] she's a writer. I have Alexis's book. She made a book that was just pages clipped together, and she called it a book, and we bought it. Every time I'd look at this thing I'd go, Alexis and June Jordon and all of those. We used to meet and there were some shekere players, and they would come because there were some very intelligent deep sisters in New York City. I was very young, and they would say, "Miss Aida, sit down." I remember one day I got all excited about something I saw on TV and I was like [throws her hands in the air] it was on TV, and it was just a news thing, and while I was talking it passed and no one knew what they said, and they're like, "See, you couldn't just wait until it was over." One of my lessons in life. You cannot—just because you're excited, you wait until the proper moment to speak. If you would've tried to teach me that in another way, I don't think I would've learned it, but I got it. I was so embarrassed. [. . .] It was a friend of ours that was in jail, Eva Mavon, because the priest raped her or some stuff, and she came on and I was really excited because Eva was on. They were like, "We don't know what happened because you were just busy. . . ." So, those are the lessons. Those are the people that taught me.

Valerie Maynard was a sculptress, and when Stevie Wonder was young she would bring him in there to feel her sculpture, and I even thought she was nuts, and then I became the one to walk her. I used to go there and say, "You want some rice and beans?" because I lived in the building with them. And someone said, "Aida, you're the only one to walk Valerie." I said, "Walk her?" They said, "She's in there with all that stuff going into her lungs. She needs to get out into the air." That was the most amazing thing to me. So, I used to go every day and say, "C'mon" and get her out of there. I knew it was to get rid of me that she walked because who cared. So, you look back at these people. Then Valerie became, her sculptures are on top of I think it's Boston and it's like, I remember when I used to walk her. People used to say walk her like a dog? I would say no. So, you had such wonderful and these were my teachers. These were the people that taught me that, okay, you're gay doesn't mean you have to be out loud and piercing the street. You can be a member of your community and be gay, and now of course that has all evolved.

So, did you take Salsa Soul Sisters to Atlanta?

No. I left. I started, when I got to Atlanta with Latinos en Acción because that was the need. There was a lot of Latins coming into Atlanta and nowhere to go and nothing to do, and I formed Latinos en Acción, and then we integrated with all the other organizations. I've learned that being multicultural, adopting it, and not being a racist. I tell my friends who say, "What's up with that white woman?" I said, "That's a racist remark." Because all of us have something to contribute. It don't matter if you're white, black, Hispanic, whatever, and we are so racist and don't even know it. "That white woman thinks." Hello? Her name is Nan. You know? And she's trying to help you. She don't have to be here, you know. Because she's white, she does not have to be here. [. . .] There are days when you go like, Mitt Romney, I mean I call him the white guy. [Laughing] But you try to be a better person. And racially it's big, with the Muslims and the names that people had for them, come on. I remember when they called me a spic. Now Latinos are *in*, but that was not always the case. Now there's all this hate because we're going to become a majority instead of a minority. The other day a friend of mine was so good to me. She sent me like eight apology cards and I said, "You don't have to. I just wanted you to be aware." Because she didn't like the fact that whatever her name is [Zoe Saldana], is playing Nina Simone. I understand that, but she went and talked about spics and how they're taking over and how dare anybody think that this girl could play Nina Simone. And I said, "Hold it. Puerto Rican here. You've got to understand in spite of myself. Maybe I don't want to be Latina, let's say. I would love to be African American, but guess what? My mother and my father are Latinos so I've adopted a culture because that was where I was raised. That was my heart. Spanish Harlem, I used to run into American Harlem and my friends, and I love it, and we all come from Africa. So, I'm aware, but I'm also Latina, so what you're talking, you're beating up me. What the hell did I do to you?" She's like, "Oh Miss Aida, I'm so sorry it's just that I forget you're Spanish." And I'm like, "You don't need to remember I'm Spanish, you could just be kind as a human being. I don't need to know what your background is or who your lover is. Just be kind. That's all that it takes. It covers all the bases, you know." [. . .]

Money in the gay community did not make that much of a difference as much as respect when I was growing up, and you looked up to somebody that somehow commanded your respect. When I was growing up there was this woman named Gloria Tubby. She had a club, and she was kind to everybody, and so she was like our leader. "Tubby said . . ." you know. I never really belonged to that rough lesbian crowd. There was something about me that I didn't want to be known as that. Because I thought, okay, I'm a lesbian, but I'm not a thug [. . .] but because I had a loud voice people would kind of treat me [that way] and sometimes, and I would have to say, "Excuse me, I'm not the one." Yeah, it is important for you to know that I go to work and I am not dealing drugs or a drunk or that loud person that you don't want to be seen with because I respect myself. I want you to respect me. I never was part of that wild group. [. . .] I aspired to be with artists. [. . .] When *The Color Purple* came out, to be honest with you I had to see it five times before I really understood it and remembered it all, but I wanted to. It was so beautiful. There's nothing in Puerto Rican culture like that because we don't do culture like that. We do music and maybe now they're beginning to, but I don't remember my mom ever taking me to nothing equivalent to *The Color Purple*. [. . .] I remember going to see *Rainbow for Colored Girls* [*for colored girls who considered suicide / when the rainbow is enuf*]. I had to see that about eight times because it was like, I needed an interpreter, but I loved it. It was like, wow. So, art and culture have always been . . . so I didn't really run that much with the wild. There was a lot in my day, but I just didn't run with them.

Do you remember you first same-sex experience?

Uh-huh.

And how was that? What were the circumstances?

I was in jail in girl's camp, about eight, and I was crying for my mama because it was the first time I had been away and I was scared, and this woman named Shirley Rudd said, "I'll be your mama." And she treated me like her child and then cultivated me until I became a woman, and we kept in touch for years. Her daughter was my godchild. So kind. So kind because sexually you become gay. I was nothing. I was nine years old. They put you in and all of a sudden it's like, "Are you a top? Are you a bottom?" It's all sex oriented, and she kind of covered for me, you know? I didn't have sex until I was about twelve. I remember seeing girls in the sink with their finger under hot water. I would say, "What are they doing?" And somebody would say, "Well, she just put her finger in . . ." and they were so uneducated in ways of making love and what-not. All of us were, but I wasn't even going to try. I was like uh-uh. [Laughter] So, yes, Shirley Rudd was my first relationship, and we were friends for about eight years on and off. She became like a sister to me, and I was happy. I even would go to her house when we came out. I would go hang with her. She had a child. She was more like a sister. Then I met this woman named Ellen Shorty. I was with her for eighteen years. I was nineteen until I just . . . it was time to go.

Did you live together?

Mm-hmm.

And this was in New York?

Mm-hmm. She came into my room one day. I was ironing, and she wanted to see baseball. Everybody had a room and we shared the living room and the kitchen. Single-room occupancy, it was called. A lot of lesbians lived in single-room occupancy. I used to wear my half-slip up here [points with her hands]. I was ironing in my half-slip, and she came in, Shorty said, "Alice," who was the woman I was dating at the time, "said I could come in here and watch baseball or whatever because you don't watch television." I said, "So, you want me to turn off my music so that you can watch TV?" But she kept staring at me and staring at me, and I was like, let me go put on some clothes. [Laughter] And she said, "You don't have to." So, we went together for eighteen years, and I tell you something, I enjoyed that family life because we were like a couple. I think it made a big difference also in my life. Because I know people who say they are gay never had a relationship, they can't find a partner. I think that has to be a little sad because if you don't ever have that relationship that's going to affect you somehow.

Being Human Is a Dangerous Thing

Cherry Hussain

9

*I have never met anyone quite like Cherry Hussain. Trained
as an auto mechanic, with dyslexia that went undiagnosed
for years, Cherry has defied most odds. It was the first time I
had ever gone into the "ugly cry" during an interview—to the
point that Cherry was comforting me, rubbing my back while
I sobbed, whispering, "It's alright, baby. I'm okay." More than
just by her story, I guess I was also moved by her capacity to
forgive those who had physically abused her, mistreated her,
or taken her for granted. Her big heart was on display when
she insisted on preparing breakfast for me before I began the
interview with her and her wife, Pat Hussain (see chapters 1
and 6). She fixed up a mess of grits, eggs, and sausage that
made me want to fall asleep. Instead, I sat and listened to
her narrate an incredible story of triumph over tragedy and
forgiveness over resentment.*

*Known to most of her community as "Miss Cherry,"
one should not be fooled by her diminutive frame and mousy
voice. Behind that exterior is a warrior woman who does not
mind speaking truth to power or defending and protecting her
wife from those who might take advantage. Miss Cherry is
truly my shero. The interview took place on August 9, 2012,
in Decatur, Georgia, at her home.*

I was born in Daytona Beach, Florida, June 15, 1955, on a
Wednesday. My childhood . . . was good, I should say. I
am a survivor of sexual molestation. They were all men.
It started when I was four, and . . . I moved into my mother's house when I was six and had to stay up there, and
things started again, so it made me pretty mean. [. . .] It
was during the years of, "What did you do?" Everything was
always your fault because you're a female.

I'm the last of seven survivors now. It was eight of us.
My mom had a couple of miscarriages during that time,
but I'm the last child. [. . .] Two to six, two boys, six girls.

Cherry at age six.
Courtesy of the narrator.

I'm the last one. [. . .] Everybody say you're the baby. I say no, I am not. I'm the last child because everybody know that the first child is always the baby. My mother worked in the school cafeteria across the railroad in a white school. I don't know anything about my mother's husband.

[. . .] I grew up in South Street Projects. [. . .] My address was 60, unit 60, and we moved from 60 to unit 1, number 1 in South Street. [. . .] South Street, we lived across . . . the river. White people lived closer to the river and closer to the ocean, and we lived on the other side of the river on back. [. . .] We weren't allowed on the beach. The beach was eight miles away from my household, actually ten, and we couldn't go to the beach that was that close to us. Our parents or our friends or relatives would drive us to New Smyrna Beach. [. . .] Actually, at New Smyrna black people actually owned the property and stuff around the beach, but you know eventually all that changed.

Yeah, I'm sure. What were some of the things that as a kid you did for fun?

Oh God, in the woods, in the swamps, oranges—we thought we had found this magical forest that had oranges and grapefruits and kumquats, but it was the back side of a grove, but we didn't know that was the backside that wasn't really maintained as much. But we did, we had fun.

And what were the attitudes and beliefs in your family about people that were different from your own? Did they talk about white folk?

Well, you know, that was the number one subject, white folk. The Caucasians were always the subject. [. . .] They were called blue-eyed. My grandmother called them ghosts. Yes, and the ghost thing resonates with me to this day because I was laying out at the unit 60, it was a summer day and I had my little quilt out on the front porch, because you get your little baths and you put your little underwear on and you go outside and relax until nap, and this car came by. I can't remember if it was a cop or a cab driver, but it was dusk dark, it was dark enough, and it appeared out of the window, and it scared me. It was a white man. That's why my grandmother called them ghosts. So that was really profound for me when she called them ghosts.

My grandmother was my best friend, and all of her friends were my friends, and so as I grew, older people were my friends because that's what I knew. I would rather be around the older women than the younger women. And then when I reached a certain age, then I started trying to hang out with my own kind, but then I found myself migrating back to the older [people] because they kept me settled. [. . .] The wisdom and knowledge of those people were just amazing, and I must say I learned a whole lot from hanging around with older people. My skills as a mechanic or my skills at looking at something and figuring out how to fix it because my grandmother lived in the rural areas of Thomasville, Georgia. We had a well. We had pigs. We had chickens. It was like a farm type thing. My grandmother had a garden, so that's where the freshness comes from for fruits and vegetables and stuff.

Did you slaughter animals?

They did.

But you didn't?

No, oh no. That's why I stopped eating meat. But they slaughtered pigs and the chickens, and my grandmother would scoop up a couple of chickens because if our cousins or our neighbors were coming up for Sunday, they were going to come up for a week. My grandmother would scoop the chickens off the yard and put them up in a pen and feed them a diet of food that she wanted them to have, and that last week she also gave them baking soda I guess to cleanse. My grandmother was a root woman. I'm fifth generation. I'm proud to say it. [. . .] She was born in 1902, so that makes her parents ex-slaves, I guess you could say, and then it was just all girls in her siblings.

And they all practice . . . ?

You know, everybody gets siddity. [Laughter] But she did. She was our neighborhood healer. Used to get together and cut wood. During the wintertime everybody got together and shared chores because people needed things when the wintertime come. There was an incident once where we were all harvesting, I would say, wood cutting, and a man cut his leg with the ax, and my grandmother always wore a apron and in those apron pockets was goodies, a sewing needle, different things. Instead of a purse, it was the pockets on the apron. But she took care of that.

What did she put together?

She had something in her apron pocket. She said, "Ginny, run to the house and get my quilting basket," so that was my chore to always get stuff, water or whatever, and she took some orange powder out of her apron, and by the time I was gone, she had it. And when I came back it looked like a patch of moss and mud from my point as being as young as I was, and the things that she took out of her quilting basket was a—I remember it very well—it was a piece of black thread and a hook needle and she sewed him up, put another layer of something, then patched him up, and he sat and he did what he could do, and then three or four days later he was up and walking [. . .] and it didn't get infected or any of that, but she made sure that she always tended to the wound and then passed it on to his family to take care of.

Now did you just observe what she did, or did she actually teach you?

Some of the things she taught, and by not doing a lot of the things as I moved into my sophisticated household, you forget but little things I remember. Pat had a boil and I told her what to do for it, and she didn't believe it. She got upset stomach, she has diarrhea. I said, "Diarrhea is good for you, you need to have it all flushed." Vomiting is okay sometimes, but you dehydrate. You know some of the stuff, little minor things I can remember. [. . .]

When you on that farm, you throw on your boots, you throw on your dirty pants. You put a hat on or get a hat, and you put them gloves on, and you work that farm. You work. But then when you had to go to the city or the town or whatever it is, then you had to be, "Oh, let me get that for you." But when I'm on that farm, it's not that way, so why you want to act so uppity and so genteelly now when it's not the same when you're on the [. . .] farm. [. . .] And I tell Pat it was a difference between town and the city. Okay, in town, it's like the little general stores, little corner stores, and then the city it's the fast-paced, sophistication, the uppity folks, the siddity people. [. . .] We went to town and you hear things as a child and it pass you by, but then there was always the color code thing going on, and if you called somebody African, they wanted to cut you. If you called somebody black, they killed you. [. . .]

"You a African!" "I'm not an African!" That's a kill. And if you call somebody "black," they want to beat you up because they talk about your nose, your lip size, your shape. That's what it was when we were growing up. And kids [. . .] imitate what they see and hear, so it's passed on.

So, what did people prefer to be called? Colored, Negro?

I was born colored, raised Negro, I became black, I was an Afro-American, now I'm an African-American, now I'm colored again. So, you know what. [Laughter] I roll with the punches, but I'm still human. That's a dangerous thing, though. Being human is dangerous. The most dangerous animal on this planet is *human* because we take what we want, we kill for no reason, and if you got something I want, I'm going to take it from you. So, being human, is that good? I don't know.

What role did religion play in your upbringing?

Come to find out that my grandmother's husband was a preacher. We were brought up in the African Episcopal Methodist church, so I still couldn't figure out how can you be Episcopal and Methodist at the same time, but those are the things that got you thrown out of church. [Laughter] That's what we were brought up. My mother didn't force religions on us, but if we were in her household you went to Sunday school. She didn't care where you went just as long as you went.

Did she not go?

She would go, but she didn't go. She'd go when we had a program or something, but she didn't. She didn't. I think she was saying she was tired of working on white folks' job. That's what her thing was. On her seventh day, she's resting. [Laughter]

Did you participate in church? Were you active?

Oh, I was very active. I was the president of the junior church, and the old folks loved me. When I said what I said, they said, "Mmm, yes. Yes." I was very active in my mother's church.

You sang in the choir?

Oh God, yes, we sang in the choir. I emceed a lot of choir things. I emceed a lot of the things for the church.

When did you first realize that you had same-sex attraction?

I was a late bloomer, but I tell you my first encounter with a female was in, I was in fourth grade. I'll tell you her first name. I won't tell you her last name. Her name was Deborah. She said we're going to play mommy and daddy and I'm daddy, and she threw me down and laid on top of me, kissed all over the face, and said, "mmm, mmm, ah, ah." [Laughter] That was my first encounter.

Cherry Hussain : 421

And that was it?

That was it. And in the . . . I want to say seventh grade, I had a crush on one of the cheerleaders. I will NOT say her name. She was, I had her glove. She misplaced her glove, and I had it. I didn't know what was going on, but I slept with that glove for three days until I saw her and gave it back to her. Poof, went on out. But my thing was by me being molested, by me being passed around from men to men. I thought it was something normal. It just had to be done. I'll tell you these bastards' names that took advantage of me. One was [man's name], which was the man that lived in our household. The next one was [man's name], which was a family member that all my, my brother and siblings knew and would work for and do things for, and that was the opening of me realizing what was going on was not right.

I was in the ninth grade. Yes. I called myself, "me, M-E," because everything that was happening was happening to Cherry but M-E was the strongest one that would say no, fight back, punch, kick, tell. [Man's name] was on the phone with his brother-in-law in Jacksonville, Florida, and I heard him telling his brother-in-law, "Oh, that's no problem, I can bring her back up here, and I'll let you have her when I get back up here." I heard that conversation. The light bulb went on. I'm being passed around. That's why all these men are having sex with me. I became a very mean person after that, brutal. Men, didn't care. [. . .] I was really angry, and by me being a lesbian it had nothing to do with that. I left my household for all the wrong reasons, but it was the right thing to do because I packed up my stuff and left, just poof, pow, left my home. I love my mother. I love my sisters and brothers, but there are things where, when I registered to vote I went to another district to vote. They were upset because I was a Republican, which I wasn't. But they assumed so.

Why did they assume that?

Because I wasn't voting in the same district. So, I voted, and then I was asking them about their politics. [. . .] "There's a black man that's running, why don't you put him in the office?" "Oh, he just going to get in there and do what they do." "But why don't you just give him a chance to?" "They going to do what they going to do. We can vote for whoever they want and they're going to do it." And I said, "We can vote them out," but their politics were different than mine. I would ask different questions then they would do. I got involved with legal aid. I was working in a law office when I was in school, and I learned a lot from those white boys, and I would tell my mother. She'd say, "Well, you don't know nothing. That's just hearsay." And by me being a slow child, I had no knowledge of anything, so that's the way I presumed that they thought that I was doing, but that's another story. [. . .]

Is there a particular theory about homosexuality that you believe? Do you think people are born gay?

I know they are. I have two nephews that are gay. I had a uncle that was gay and my two nephews. One died, my uncle died, and then my other nephew is in Germany. So yeah, we were born gay. We were born and raised heterosexual. What model did I have of homosexuality in my household? Yes, we are born gay, and I think I've been knowing that as long as I can remember. But I, just like Pat, didn't know what was going on. I think I'll say this off the record after I get through talking, but my mother said it's a phase you go through—get married and have a couple kids and you can live through it.

So, you came out to your mother?

After the fact. This was when I was a teenager. There is a woman we call Auntie that was a very close friend to my mother, and she always said, "Why is she always drumming? Why does she always wear boys' clothes? Why does she do all the stuff the boys do?" She said, "She's strange. She's strange. Something's wrong with her." Margaret was her name, called her Auntie Margaret. But she probably knew way before I knew that I was a lesbian. Well, I call myself a dyke, but you know.

Wow. So, you didn't have any sexual experiences with women coming up?

No.

No, that was much later?

Yes.

When you went to high school, did you date?

Yeah, that's where I met my children's father, in high school the summer of tenth grade.

And so he was your boyfriend from the tenth grade until you got married?

Yes.

When did you get married?

Oh God, '78, 1978 I think it was. I moved away from home in '77, and we got married in '78, yeah '78.

Did you love him?

No. [Laughter]

Why'd you marry him?

I liked him. I did. I loved him, but I wasn't in love with him. Yes. And there's a difference. And I think within every female's genes there's that thing of caring because he didn't have a mother, he didn't have a father. His father killed his mother. His grandmother raised him. They were quiet enough children. They were educated kids, and I married him for all the wrong reasons, but it was a healthier reason for me because the path that I was on in my hometown of Daytona Beach, I would've either been in jail or killed, because I was a rough girl. I was a rough girl. I was a decent enough girl. I was a caring girl. Old people and children, yes. The people my age, no.

Were you fighting?

I wasn't fighting. I was maiming and hurting. [Laughter] No, I wasn't fighting. No. My violence was my mouth. My violence was my bullyness. Didn't take any names but kicked plenty ass, boys mostly. There was a few girls I hung around. I rather be around boys than I would girls because boys were more controllable, if that's understandable, and if I wanted, I'm going to say this word, if I wanted to fuck them, I'd pick them out, oh I think, I'm going to fuck him today, and I picked them. My mother asked me, she said, "Ginny, I come home and you leaving me with these young men in the house." She says, "Why you so mean to them?" I said, "Because they allow it." Raynard was my best friend. We hung out. Raynard was the kind of guy that I played sports with and we would play. It was a contest for me, and I would barely ever get close enough to win, but he was that guy that I hung out with. I could have twelve people in the house and Raynard would come and say, "Oh, you got company" and I'd say, "They not company." He'd say, "Well, I came by to see if you want to go play racquetball." I'd say, "Yeah, let's go," and they all sitting there. I had a guy knock on my door one day—and in Florida you leave your screen door open, the front door open, and you lock the screen door, and the breeze coming through—and somebody knock on the door and I'm laying on the sofa. And I looked up, and I got up, and this big old smile came on his face. I closed the door, BAM! I went and laid back down on the sofa. Mama say, "Who was that at the door?" I said, "I don't know." She said, "But you closed the door." I said, "Yes." She said, "Well, who was that?" I said, "I don't know. Somebody was at the door." So, she opened the door, and he was crawling on there, and she said, "Young man," and he said, "Well, I came by to see Miss Cherry." I didn't invite you. Why are you here? I had one guy tell me, "You broke my heart. You used me." I said, "Ain't that what a woman'll tell you?" That's how mean I was. I didn't care. I didn't have an inch of nothin'.

And so, did you get married before you graduated from high school?

No, I married after I graduated high school. I had gone to college. I went to Daytona Beach Community College and majored in automotive mechanics, small engines, and all that other good stuff.

And did you, in college, did you see other folks who were gay?

In high school I saw gay boys.

Oh really?

Yeah, one was named, oh God, what was his name? Charles, I think it was. I saw him on the beach one day, and he was out dancing on the piers, and he was in his element, he was in his zone, and I said, "Hey Charles, how you doing?" and he looked at me and said, "Well how are you?" I said, "Fine." I was just amazed by him because he was out. And at school you needed to be quiet because the bullies would bully you and beat you up, and somebody asked me, "Why are you talking to that boy?" I said, "Because he's a friend of mine, I went to school with him." "Well you know he's homosexual." Do I? And someone in one of Pat's gatherings would say that everyone has an uncle named "Peaches." There was a Peaches in my neighborhood. His mother was a hairdresser, and he was a bright-skinned, red-boned boy, beautiful boy, and they called him Peaches, and he and his friends would get together, and that was the first time I start wearing my shorts like Peaches because he cut off his jeans, and they had the little frail things on, and he put a little patch pocket on the back and patches on the front. I dress like Peaches because I thought Peaches was fabulous. [Laughter] Peaches was out, and "Oh, that's a whatchacallim boy," but that's who I knew. And then they had bulldaggers in my neighborhood. That's what they called them, bulldaggers. I think white folks call them "diesel dykes" or whatever. But [. . .] in my neighborhood it was cloakers and daggers. The boys were the cloakers and the girls were the daggers because they cloaked themselves, the boys did. The daggers would just butch out.

So those folks were in your neighborhood and out.

But they weren't out, out. You know what I'm saying?

Right, people knew.

Yes, and we had this guy named Pecan Red. Pecan was fabulous—he put on his red dress and his stilettos and a BEAUTIFUL boy when he got dressed up, but he made a better looking girl.

Where was he going?

He would go to the little holes in the walls that we hung out at in my hometown.

And nobody would bother him?

Well, they did, but, see, something about Pecan a lot of people didn't know. Pecan knew martial arts, and he would let these boys pick on him, but they wouldn't hurt him. He would let them rough him up, but if he walked us home . . . I lived over on Willy Drive. My other girlfriend might have lived over in Soul City, and then one might have lived where Pecan lived, but if we were out, he walked us home. And this particular night these boys wanted to pick on him. He said, "Y'all can pick on me, but you don't bother my girls." Oh, the F-word and all this, what you going to do? He pulled off his shoes and said, "Honey, hold these." You haven't heard of anyone else beating him up. Them boys didn't say anything about Pecan kicking their ass. [Yelling] "Hey, man, what's up? What's up Pecan? Hey, how you doing?" [Laughter]

My husband's cousin, Ronnie, bisexual woman. She slept with men and women, and her husband was a freak of the century, he didn't care, you know? I was a little afraid of him as well. He ain't never had sex, but he had oral sex with me, and I'm like, "Okay, if this is all you want, you can have it." But then I knew about bisexual women. My librarian's son was gay. My neighbor's youngest boy was gay. So I knew these people, but I still wasn't out. My friend Doris, we called her Sand, she say, "Come over and have a sleepover." I said, "Okay," because she had left and went to New York, and I hadn't seen her since I was like seven or eight, and we were real close when we were younger, and then fourteen years later she shows back up. So okay, Sand's here, we going to have a sleepover, and the girl tried to lay on me and have sex with me! I said, "What's wrong with you?" She said, "I thought, I thought, they said . . ." I said, "You thought and they said what? I ain't that kind of girl. We can lay up here and talk, and you can masturbate yourself over there. That's fine, because I'm cool with it, but no."

[. . .] I left home at twenty-one. I left home in '77. I got married in '78. I left home in '77 and moved to Alabama because William [her husband] called and said come, and I needed to go and I left. And my parents, my mother loved us so much. She would love us so much she didn't want any of us to leave home. I think my brother Lucius and my brother Alvin told my mother that they were leaving the house. I think everybody else just left. [Laughing] I think my sister told her that she was getting married and she left. My brother Lucius said that he was getting married and he left. My brother Alvin was saying he was leaving to go to the service and he left, and then my sister Linda—oh, my sister Linda. I love my sister Linda. She disappeared, and I didn't see her, and then she showed back up when I was, oh God, I don't know how old I was. I was still that wild girl, but she kept me sane. And then Norma and Gwen left, and I was at home with my mother and my mother kept a tight reign, but she gave more freedom than she did my other siblings because I was more exposed to stuff than my other siblings was because it was still segregation when they were growing up. And I remember one night my brother Lucius didn't come home before dusk dark, and my mother was pacing the floor walking because she was worried because he worked across the railroad. But something happened at the restaurant that he worked, and God knows my brother can fix anything. If the air wasn't blowing he'd find a switch and turn it on. He can fix stuff. But something happened to one of the coolers or something at work, and Lucius stayed over to help the man fix the problem, and he brought him home, and when my brother came home it was a joyful occasion because your mother worry. Her black baby out there somewhere after dusk dark, yeah. My childhood was okay. My childhood was good once I got control of it. It was real good.

So, you moved to Alabama, and when did you have your first child?

'78.

Oh, so right away?

Yeah. Yeah, it was '78. I got married, and then we had our son. Yeah. Yeah. I didn't want kids, but stuff happens. But I tell my kids to this day if I had known then what I knew now, I would not have had them. I love my children, I really do. And they were both mistakes but they were good mistakes. I love my babies, I do, and there was a reason for me having them because it kept their dad from getting killed. [Laughter] That's another story. We were both young. I married him. He was a selfish boy. [. . .] I called him one year after the divorce. I had so much stuff going on in my head. We were sleeping downstairs at that time in the room downstairs, and I woke up one morning because I was hearing people saying in order to forgive somebody you have to forgive yourself first, and I'm trying to figure out what the hell you need to forgive yourself for things that happened to you, you had no control over, you know? And I was fighting with that. How in the hell do I forgive myself? I didn't do anything to me. Everything that was done to me was done to me, but then it manifest itself. And I called him, I think it was in January or New Year's, and told him, "You know what, William? I forgive you because I forgive myself. We can be friends if you like to, and if you don't that's okay, but I still forgive you. I'll be there if you need me." I said, "But we're still the parents of our children, and you can take this as any way you want it, but letting you know that I do forgive you."

And I did, because the things that happened to me in my life gave me a better understanding of human beings, and I wouldn't be the person that I am today even though it was a lot of stuff on me, but it made me a lot kinder to people as I got older, and it made me understand abused women. It made me understand that runaway from home. It made me understand that poor boy sitting on the corner over there who done robbed this woman but sobbing because he done that. That made me aware. That gave me a wisdom I didn't have—a forgiveness—because everything happened for a reason. Might not know what it is, things happen. Things happen for you, and I think that it gave me a lot of patience, 'cause I didn't have any.

I don't like nonsense. I don't like chaos. I like order, and I demand it. It's like common courtesy. I tried to explain to a young man about common courtesy about the Negro race, colored folk, because it was a matter of life and death for us to know how to speak to Mr. Charlie and Miss Ann when they walk down the street. It was a matter of getting what you need if you were polite enough to the white folks to get what you wanted. It was a matter of survival to say, "please" and "thank you," "good morning," "excuse me," and not look those white folks in the eye when you were doing it. It was a matter of survival for us. What's wrong with common courtesy? It's just being a human being and saying "excuse me," "please," and "thank you," "good morning," "good evening," "good afternoon." What's wrong with that? It gets you what you need. Because I'll do more for you with your common courtesy than I will with your cussing and demanding what I need for you to do for me. Because if you demand anything from me, I give you what I'm supposed to give and let somebody else deal with you. But if you giving me common courtesy, I'm going to do everything I can for you and sometimes do things I'm not supposed to do to make sure that you get what you need. That's the difference between me. No nonsense. I need order, not chaos. I'm sorry. I get kind of crazy, don't I?

No, no, no. So, when you and your husband separated, did you keep the kids?

No.

They stayed with their father?

Yes. William, by us being young, by him being an educated man, he knew that I wasn't his intelligent level when we got involved. I think William liked me because of my caring of him, making sure that he had everything he needed. I think that's what he got because he didn't get that. He was a educated man, a very selfish man. I'll tell him that to his face today. In his role of thinking that he was trying to motivate or help me, he would call me dumb. He would tell me that I wasn't going to amount to anything, but the light bulb came on when this fool told me, "When I finish my degree, I'm going to take my children and I'm a leave you."

He told you that?

Yes. Now, why would a dumb person like me stay with a smart man, stay with him and he's telling me he's going to leave me? How dumb would I have been? He said, "You too dumb to even teach your children how to read or write." But every gift that I got my children were educated stuff and I would make them read the instructions. I bought this thing called Smath. It was a thing of spelling and math together thing. I said, "William, I bought this for the children. If you read the instructions, we can play this game with them." He said, "See how dumb you are? You can't even read these instructions to teach the children."

But you hear this all the time. When I was growing up I heard enough of it, but then when I married this man on an educated level that was supposed to been able to help me and bring me up, he wasn't smart enough to know how to do that. His intelligence wasn't at that level of intelligence to do that. But if a man telling you he's going to leave you, how dumb would it have been for me to sit there and wait? So I left him. But during that process of his selfishness . . . I tell you how selfish he is. I want to back up.

My first pregnancy I wore a size 9. I came from the state of Florida. We wore sandals and shorts, and if it got cold we put on a jacket. Alabama it snows. You get to zero, you get to eighteen. Okay? I'm pregnant. Man not bought me one maternity outfit. He told me, "Well, you don't need clothes. I'm a school teacher, I need clothes. You get a uniform." Sears gave me a uniform. I was working as a small engine mechanic with them then. He was upset because that first year that I worked with Sears, I made a hundred dollars more than he did. After that first years of Sears I made six hundred dollars more than he did. Okay? But he was upset with that.

Now, my first pregnancy he didn't make any effort to buy me any maternity clothes. That first winter of my pregnancy, he didn't buy me any shoes. I had sandals and socks, but I had my boots that I wore to work. The woman in the church that we were attending, I was attending, made me two dresses. One was flowery, you know they call them a [. . .] a muumuu, yes, and she made me a maroon one, and I wore those through two pregnancies. Still no maternity clothes. I'm a size 9 in jeans, I'm six months pregnant trying to squeeze into a pair of jeans. Didn't buy me any clothes. I went to the thrift store and bought some clothes. "What you buy all these old-looking clothes for?" He threw them out. Two dresses through two pregnancies that the woman in church made, and it was a Pentecostal church, which I got thrown out of, but anyway, that's another story. But that's how selfish he was.

Our son, perfect baby, didn't cry. He'd whine if he was hungry. We were in Parisians, no Pizitz. We had a Parisian and a Pizitz, and he was in the little store, and he saw these Spiderman little shoes. He had never acted, never acted up. He saw these Spiderman shoes. He wanted them, and I'm looking around like, oh my God, and I had a Pizitz card. I started getting credit for myself because in Alabama even though he didn't have credit, but my signature on stuff got him credit, because I had the better credit, so I got a Pizitz card and stuff, but every time they sent the card it says, "Mr. Williams and Mrs. Ralph Williams." So I charged this twenty-dollar pair of shoes for my son on this card. You know, I wore an ass whooping for that? Because my son had never acted out, never asked for anything, and he wanted those Spiderman shoes, and I bought them for him because it was something my son wanted. And he never acted up or acted out again for anything. He tried to wear those shoes until he was 7. [Laughing] He loved those Spiderman shoes, but I got slapped across the face for it.

He in a fraternity. He wanted to open a business. I said, "We can't afford a business." He said, "Well, we right down the street from the school and college kids." I said, "The college kids didn't have money. You know we didn't have money when we were in school. They don't have money." I said, "If you going to do this you need to go to the high schools, pass out your flyers, family reunions at the church, and try to thrive on those. We could still do this out of the house." No, he wanted to open a business. We opened a business, but he blamed me for the business being closed down. He's over in Decatur, Alabama, working. I'm on maternity leave from Sears. How can you run a business? People not coming in. He got me on my hands and knees scraping down the little things, because I couldn't use the broom. So, I'm sitting in there all day. It was nice. It had air conditioning, but anyway. You know?

We're trying to run a business, and then when Sears started laying off, first in stayed longer, last in went first, and I had only been there three years. Of course, when they start laying off, they start laying off the people that hadn't been there fifteen years get cut off, and one guy had one week to go and they cut him off. You know how they do? He blamed me for that because I got laid off. I didn't have any authority on those people. And that was Reaganomics. Hell. Bush came along, but we were in Reaganomics, and then jobs just started disappearing, and I couldn't get work, and then I got pregnant with my daughter. He was eight months old, nine months old when I got pregnant with his sister, eight or nine months pregnant. I wasn't able to work. Who was going to hire a pregnant woman? But anyway, he was working. He took me to the laundromat. He found out how much money it cost to wash, he gave me the money, but sometimes you put your money in the dryer and sometimes the dryer don't dry. Oh, I spent the money, I did something with his money, blah, blah, blah. I worked and brought my paycheck home because he paid the bills. My mother say, "He's the head of the household, he's supposed to take care of everything."

Okay. I worked three, four jobs of part-time work. I got a job at Toys"R"Us when I met Pat. I had been at Toys"R"Us maybe two years, I think, before she came I guess, because she came in '86 or '87. Yeah, she came right at the end of '86, because it was a new year in '87, yeah. But I worked. I worked, and he called me lazy. I went through postpartum depression, I didn't know what it was, with my second child. I didn't know what it was, and all I wanted to do was sleep. I didn't want her around me, not that I didn't love her, but my mind was like I wanted to hurt her, and I knew that I needed to stay away from her. I loved her, I did. I didn't want to cause my baby no harm. I guess it was four years in and I'm thankful that I got through it because it was hell. [. . .] They weren't aware, and I wasn't telling them because it was embarrassed that my mind was the way that it was, and when I was telling William he said, "Why you sleep so much?" and why you don't do this and you not doing that? I told him I was tired, and all he could say was lazy. Yeah, I was lazy. You're right. I wanted to sleep so wouldn't have to think about my child, and it was a lot to go through. It was really hard. It was really hard.

So, he kept them, they stayed with him after the divorce?

Yeah, the courts gave him custody of our children even though he was an abusive man.

Full custody?

Full custody, because he had me on abandonment. When I decided to leave my children's father, I would've taken a job in Tahiti as long as I had a job and somewhere to stay. If someone had offered me a job in Timbuktu, Egypt, I would've gone. But when I left my children's father, I went bound on the word of someone I didn't know. "Come live with me. I'll get you a place to stay and a job. Come and stay." When I left my children's father, I left my children with their father. They had room and board and clothes. They were in school. He had a job. He could feed them. He could clothe them. He could get them back and forth to where they were going. When I left, I had no place to stay. I had no job. I had no car. I had no school to put my children in, so where was the better place for my children? If I was going to be homeless, I wasn't dragging my children with that. If I was going to be homeless because of something else that had happened, yes, I would've had my children, but I was leaving their father. I wasn't leaving my children. I was leaving *him*. He was abusive to *me*, not to them. To the *mommy*, not the children. So when I left, I left them in very good hands. He got me on abandonment.

Do you think your kids felt resentful?

I don't know. My daughter says she felt abandoned.

How old was she?

She was eight. And [long pause] I did things in my mind that I thought were better for them because, you know, as we look along the way we could've did things, if I had of, ought of, should of, and other things, but my children, talking to them as life got on within they time of aging, my children were saying, "We heard a lot, mommy, we knew a lot," and I was trying not to cry out because I didn't want them to hear, but then after, they had told me their dad had started in on them. My son showed up at my door with the clothes on his back. He said he didn't want to live with him. He loved his dad. He said he was standing at the top of the steps wanting to push him off the steps. Something happened, but whatever happened, my children are adult enough and mature enough to forgive him and still have him as a part of their life. My daughter stayed too long with him because he was saying, if you leave me, you'll never get to see me. You know how they play on your emotions and being a girl, and her ways are like his, too. But that's my child. I don't like my child, but I love her. I don't like my children, but I love them. And I fault myself for their behavior because I left them too long with their father and allowed them to manipulate that guilt part of motherhood, and then after a while, it's like that rubber band. That rubber band is giving for a long time, and when it get tired of you stretching what it does is it pops your ass on it. It does. So, I have wonderful children, and I'm proud to say that I am the parent of Eugenia Afrineke Williams and Spencer Ellis Williams, because they are good people. They are caring. They are grateful, and they're giving, but that little girl is evil as hell. She was like her mama, but she has to get to the maturity age of which she has to understand it and deal with it. What's the old saying says? "With age comes wisdom, but sometimes age come alone by itself." [Laughter] My mother taught us not to be grown because everything that grew has grown. She said, "I'm raising mature adults. So, if anybody ever ask you are you grown, you tell them no, I'm a mature adult because I don't want you just to grow; I want you to mature." So, if anybody ask me if I'm grown I tell them, "Hell no. I'm a mature adult [laughing] because I have grown."

When was your first lesbian sexual experience?

Huntsville, Alabama, with a married woman with two children. [Laughing]

And how did that happen?

My friend Jessie, we hit it like this [puts her index and middle finger together] when I met her in Huntsville. She worked at the cafeteria at A&M campus. Alabama A&M in Huntsville was in Norman, but everybody say it's Huntsville. But anyway, I met her through one of my children's father's friends, one of his fraternity brothers, because he was over in the cafeteria. This loudmouth girl—we both loud. We hit it off just like that [claps]. We were sisters from another mother, and we are like that to this day. All of the little knickknacks and the signs were there, because she had girlfriends, and they all lived together, and I didn't think about anybody sleeping in a bed together. Hell, I still sleep with my sister. I didn't think anything about it, and they had a one-bedroom apartment. So what? That's normal for me. Ten children? Come on. [Laughing] I won't call the other girlfriend by name because she went through some stuff, but her other girlfriend, and then the light bulb came on—BING! She's a dyke. But she's my best friend, and that was okay. This other young lady that I met because we used to go out to the post, well, the arsenal in Huntsville and play basketball, because Jessie drove a bus for them, and we would get on, and I drove a cab. That's another story. But I met this woman through Jessie and come to find out that she was also a dyke with two kids, two beautiful girls, and wow, bells and whistles and lightning. That orgasm was just phenomenal. But I said that out loud. But yeah, her, and then I met another young lady.

And at this time were you married?

Mm-hmm still married.

What was the "bing," the click, the "ah-ha" or whatever, because you had had traumatic sexual experiences with men, but then you had children with your husband, but something was missing—what was it that happened with this woman? Was it just the sex, the difference in the sex or—

It probably was. I think it was the touching, the embrace, the gentleness, the emotional experience that you got with somebody just holding you, understanding you. I think that's what it was, because that's the only thing that I'm like, "Oh my, is this the way it feels to be touched and caressed and not forced?" Now, don't get me wrong, now, William, I taught him everything he knew. He was a good sex partner. I mean, look at all the lessons I had. You got to get it right. You gonna be with me, get it right, but sex was wonderful. I had orgasms with him, but there was something missing, and it was that emotional, that feeling was the thing that was missing. I loved him, I did. I cared for him, but I wasn't in love with him. He was my ticket away from home. That's what he was. I was graceful, grateful. You've got to excuse me;

I don't speak very well. I was grateful for the escape from home because I would've been in trouble.

So, you met this woman, bells and whistles, and you had other experiences. Did you at that moment decide, okay, I'm definitely a lesbian?

Yes, because William and I got in a battle. I told him, "You know what? I don't even like you. I like girls." And we fought. But I told him that was the last ass whooping I was ever going to take from him, and we fought, and he was one of the kind like Pat's mother: he wasn't happy unless he was screaming at the top of his voice at you. It had gotten so mental with me that at 3 o'clock no one had to tell me it was 3 o'clock, because I already knew it was 3 o'clock because I knew the beast was coming. I found myself sitting in the closet one day, and when he came home, just those few seconds of not having to see him was so wonderful. Just sitting in the closet and he hollered, calling my name, and then it dawned on me, "What's your stupid ass sitting in the closet for? Get out of this damned closet! Don't make that man make you fear him like that. Get your ass out of the closet!" So I sat on the edge of the bed, and he came in and said, "I've been calling you," and I said, "I've been sitting right here." "I didn't see you," and I said, "because you were too damned angry calling; you didn't see me sitting here." [I was] playing his cards. [. . .]

I was seeing this girl and she stopped seeing me, and it didn't hurt me because she stopped seeing me. It was just, I didn't know. I said okay, so I found another girl and I treated the girls almost—I didn't treat them as badly as I treated the boys, but I always told them the same way I walked into your life is the same way I'll leave your life. Poof, here I am. Poof, there I go. I was never mean to 'em, but in Huntsville being a very small, closeted place because all these women went to church, Pentecostal church, the old Primitive Baptist, and [claps her hands twice] they went to the churches, but they were all closeted. But the freaks come out at night.

Were they femmes?

Oh God, see that femme and all that, you a dyke or you're not, that's just the way I am. I don't care if you rough neck.

Were they like really feminine, like, wore makeup and all that stuff?

They got dressed up to go to church and stuff, but when they weren't at church they weren't dressed up to go to church and stuff.

Even though they were married, some of them?

Only the one that I was involved with was married, just that one. But girls in Huntsville, you, Pat, and myself. You dated Pat, you and Pat break up, I date you, you and I break up, then I date Pat, you know? That's the way it was. But I'm watching these women and trying to understand these women, and I'm watching and I'm saying, huh, they're confused, or they're just that narrow-minded not to expand themselves a little more, because I wanted to take one out to the orchestra. "Oh no, oh no, to the orchestra? You listen to that?" "Yeah." "Would you like to go to the ballet?" "Ballet?" Like I say, I have an intelligence. It might not be on the level of yours, but we all have an intelligence. Yes, I'm a project girl. Yes, I'm a dyslexic child, a special ed[ucation] kid, but I have what I have in my head that I like. You know? And I was like, oh my God. Then they found out, "Oh, she got a job. What can she give me? Give me, give me, give me." I don't give unless I want to. You can't demand anything from me. You can ask of me. It don't mean that I have to respond. And I'm mean, aren't I? [Laughs]

No, you're real.

It's like those girls lived in this closed quarter type thing and William told me, "Here. You call your sisters and brothers. You call them." I said, "I'll call them when I want to." "You tell them you like girls." Dialed my mother's number. I hung up the phone. I said, "You can't make me do anything anymore. I'll call when I want to." And so, he went through all that. He wants to call my sisters and brothers. I said, "You're an adult. You can do whatever you want. Pick up the phone and call them if you like." So, I called. The only person that really, really crushed my heart out of my siblings was my sister Gunh, my sister Gwen. My nieces and nephews couldn't say Gwen; they called her Gunh. And my brother Lucius. But everybody else, I would've got over it, even with my mother, but those two . . . and Linda. Linda said okay because I knew Linda. [. . .]

And I told my mama. I said, "Mama, I need to tell you something." She said, "Okay." I said, "Are you sitting down?" And she said, "Are *you* sitting down?" I said, "No, ma'am." She said, "You're walking and rubbing your head, aren't you?" And I'm not aware that I do this, and when I find myself doing it I stop because my mother brought it to my attention, and Pat did, too. And I said, "Yes." She said, "Well, what is it you need to tell me? You should sit down." I sat down and I said, "Mama, I like girls." She said, "You like girls?" I said, "Yeah." She said, "Are you happy?" I said, "No." She said, "Well, you need to find somebody that make you happy." I said, "But I wanted you to know that." She said, "Okay. Are you okay?" I said, "No." She said, "Pull it together." My mother told me that. I said, "Yes, ma'am." I called all my siblings. I have a brother that's a Church of God in Christ pastor. He said, "You're my sister." He said, "I might not approve of what you do, but you're my sister, and I still love you. Hate the sin, love the sinner." I said,

"I'm not a sinner [snaps her fingers]. I just happen to be a human being that loves women." He said, "You're my sister. I might not approve of what you do, but you're my sister, and I love you." And Gwen, she said, "Damn. I thought you had pneumonia or something." And I told them all. And my sister Patricia. If you look up the word to be Christ-like in the dictionary, you would see my sister Patricia, because she lives it. She doesn't preach at you, but if you asked her a question she'd talk to you. You know? But my siblings were okay with that, and that was good, and my nieces and nephews are just fine. "Oh, my auntie is a dyke. My auntie's a dyke!" [Laughter] You know how nieces and nephews are. But my family's okay with me, and that's all that matters.

When I took Pat home to meet my family, my mother had a list of things that she wanted to get for Pat. She said, "Ginny, let's go. We need to go to the store and get Pat's stuff." Pat's allergic to the sun, so we couldn't survive in Florida, so my mother loved this ice cream parlor called Dippity Dan. It's not around anymore. They used to make homemade ice cream and stuff, and she wanted to introduce Pat, so we had to go out, and she was getting a list of stuff. I said, "Hell, Pat's not special." She said, "Cherry." I said, "Yes, ma'am." She said, "That woman loves you. You're going to make me a promise that you're going to do everything you can to make her happy and keep her happy, because no one else is going to love you like her." My mother told me that. And I do everything I can to keep that promise to my mother because she deserve everything I can give her and all the things I wish I can give her. Because I work very hard to make sure that she gets everything that she needs and that's the promise I made to her mother.

That's really a beautiful story, and not one that I would have expected, given everything else you said. Why do you think your mother was so accepting?

I'm her child. What mother wouldn't want their child to be happy? What parent wouldn't want their child to be happy?

But you've heard the stories—folks have been thrown out of the house and disowned.

I have. And I am very honored and thankful that my ancestors gave me my mother that allowed me to be in the family that I have. I'm thankful for my ancestors for putting me with the people who love me, and I'm very thankful for that, because I've heard horror stories and I've lived some horror stories, but I'm thankful for my family. As jacked up as they are, they're mine and I love and honor them all.

You had said before, maybe it was when I was interviewing Pat, maybe she said it, that you like the word "dyke." So, do you not identify as lesbian?

Dyke is it, because I grew up with the bulldaggers.

So, tell me about that. Was that a term that has gone out of season, out of fashion now? Because a lot of the women that I talk to say they don't hear it, or they don't like it, "bulldagger."

It's like the word "Negro." It's like the word "colored." It's like the word "black." We used to call white people Caucasians. We called them the C-word. I will not use the -isms, but things evolved themselves again. It's like the [axis] that the world sits on. Everything comes full circle and fashions keep coming, right? They'll embrace "dyke" again. They will because it's going to be something that's going to empower another generation. They get the baggy pants. They were zoot suits when we were coming around, but they didn't hang them across their butt. They wore baggy pants, but they were up on their waists. The miniskirts was a twenties thing. They're back. They hadn't died. So, it'll be embraced again. I class myself with the bulldaggers because that's what I knew, and my best friend Shirley, "Ol' bulldagger!" They live right behind us over here. It was a lesbian couple that lived in the back of them, the bulldaggers, and they was trying to live their life, but who was the ones that were bothering them? The outsiders were. They still living their life, but it will be an empower thing for someone else because as we leave our history lives on, and someone else will say, "Bulldaggers, wow, I'm going to embrace that." It'll come again. But it's just this is what I knew, and that's who I embrace. Call me a dyke, I'm it. Call me a dagger, I'm it. Ole bulldagger.

Have you ever considered living outside the South?

I'm a tell you about the South. Born and raised in the South. I'd rather be in the South because at least I know who hates me. If I lived up north or somewhere else, I'd get killed because I don't know who hates me. You smile in my face, it's like the cross. You come with the cross, but you're stabbing me in the back with the point of it at the knife. So, I love the South. I do. Will I live anywhere else? I have. But the South is roots. It's my home. I like the weather better. We have winter days. They have winter months. We have rainy weeks. They get storms. The South is where I was born. If I was born in New York, I love Alabama. People talk about Alabama. Alabama is the land of beauty. It's got seas and oceans and valleys and mountains. Alabama the state is a beautiful place. Would I live there? Yes, it's a beautiful place. Georgia is also a beautiful state. I grew up in Florida. I never say never. I say I strongly do not want to move back to Florida. My reasons are my family is there. Yes, I miss them dearly and I wish I could put them in my pocket and bring them with me. There are no jobs in Florida. It's a retirement thing.

You can't get part-time work. The cost of living is too high. My wife is allergic to the sun. I love Florida, but would I want to live there? I'd rather be a tourist and visit. That's the way I feel about Florida.

So, do you think that there are other regions in the country that life would be better for a black lesbian?

I can't speak for other regions. I can only say when the South move, the whole country steps in line . . . because when integration came along and everybody was talking about it up north, "Up north we don't take this, and we don't have this up north," you lived in places they told you you could live, you worked the jobs they told you can have, you went to the schools they told you you could go to. Even though y'all might've lived in the neighborhoods with them, but y'all didn't have equal stuff that they had. At least in the South they segregated you and told you this is *it*. We knew that. But you got lured away because you had white neighbors, but did you go to their house and eat? Did you work on their jobs? Did you hold the positions they did? No. At least in the South, we know. The South move the whole nation. When the South do something, the whole nation moves.

Is there much interaction between the black lesbian community and the white lesbian community?

I think now it is, but still we have places where we all still live, and by Atlanta being such a metro mega county, and we . . . Pat said something about your friends. Who's in your Rolodex? If you have white friends in your Rolodex, who you going to hang out with? If you have a multiracial index, who you going to hang out with? We get together when there's an activity for us to get together. I can't speak for other people, but I can speak for Pat and myself, our Rolodex is multiracial. I can't speak for other people, but when I go out I see people, and we don't have to get together because there's an activity or there's something that we got to get together and vote on and have meetings with and the board of the board of the board. If we go out, we inviting our friends out to dinner, we're going to a movie, or we're going to the basketball game. We're hanging out. Come over. Sit down. Break bread with me. You know? Yes, Pat and I Rolodex is multi. I can't speak for everybody else, but I can speak for us.

What is your involvement in the gay community? Are you active?

My involvement is her [her wife, Pat], to keep her safe. Out of all the work, all the stuff that she did when she got sick, nobody came to knock on the door to find out why. Aida [Rentas] got together with some people and came over so I could buy Prozac for my wife. Aida reached out to the community and helped us. Some helped us get over a lot. I found out about my activity. I was a part of GLAAD [Gay and Lesbian Alliance against Defamation] when it first happened. Patrick started it, and I found out. Patrick was a great guy, and he took me because he said, "You will ask the question," because I didn't know. What does that mean? Why is that? What is that? Because I didn't know. The things everybody else was afraid to ask but I asked. But I found out that I was treated a certain way *before* they found out that I was Pat's wife. And *after* I became, "Oh, Pat's partner, oh Miss Cherry this, Miss Cherry that." Kiss my ass. [Claps] I told my wife this little arrogant little boy from New York, I won't call his name, I won't even give him that privilege. I say, "Oh, so now your opinion of me and the way you treat me now is different since you found out that I'm Pat's partner." "Oh yes, of course." Kiss my ass. When they found out that I'm her partner, "Oh, can you get Pat? Can you get Pat? Can you get Pat?" [CLAP! CLAP! CLAP! CLAP!]. That's my activity is to keep my wife safe from predators that prey upon her because she is a God-given caring person. If she could take her head off of her shoulders and program it and think that it would help you, she would do that, but I have to keep predators away from my wife. That's my activity. That's my involvement in the gay community. Now, if it was a bulldagger's community, it would be different. [Laughing]

What are your political views with regard to issues that involve the gay and lesbian community, like, well, you're married, so I'm assuming you're for gay marriage, and Don't Ask/Don't Tell, the new Chick-fil-A thing that happened?

My views on Chick-fil-A is that I have more power than Chick-fil-A because my hard-earned money that I work for those forty hours a week, I keep in my damn pocket. I can fry my own damn chicken. My view about Don't Ask/Don't Tell is that you didn't give a damn when it was a war on this soil, you don't give a damn if I'm a jackrabbit, orange, purple, polka dot, and got a flag hanging out of my ass. Pick up a gun and shoot! But you want to say that the morale . . . of me being a bulldagger in your [military] service is going to cause morale problems? When somebody's knocking on your door and blowing bombs at your ass, who you going to call? You don't give a damn if I'm a lesbian or not! You don't care if I'm queer or not. You don't care if I'm that bulldagger next door. If somebody causing you harm, you don't give a damn. That's what I think about Don't Ask/Don't Tell.

Do you think it's harder for black women to come out than it is for black men, or in general do you think there's no difference, it's about the same?

It's harder for my brothers. It's hard enough being a black male because girls don't get beat up like boys do. Girls will talk shit, pull your hair, might do some pranks, but black men, it's harder because then the most powerful people during the time of segregation and slavery was the white man and the black woman. Those were the two most powerful people on this planet, and when I say that people will look at me like I'm crazy because during segregation that black woman had to deal with those bill collectors that came to her door. That black woman had to deal with that white man that came looking for her husband, her child. You know? The white man had the power. The black woman had to deal with it. She had to hide her husband. She had to hide her son. She had to deal with that man coming telling her husband, you let me sleep with your wife and we'll forgive this debt. That's a strong ass black woman. Sorry, but my brothers have a hard time.

What role does religion play in your life now?

None. I am a learning practicing Buddhist. [. . .] When people [. . .] tell me they're Christian, I run like hell and I'm not turning my back on them. It's like being in prison: don't turn your back. You know I told you about that cross; it's for praying one and stabbing you in the neck? No, if you got to announce to me that you Christian, I'm running like hell. It says to be Christ-like. Jesus Christ was born, raised, and died a Jewish man. According to the Christians that he was the son of God, that God was Christ. To be Christ-like means Christ had the most powerful father ever. He was the most powerful man ever. But what did Christ do? He did what Buddha did, because Buddha depended on the grace and kindness of strangers. If you want to be Christ-like, Christ didn't have—I can't say the word—a multi range of mules waiting for him for his feet never to touch the ground. He didn't have houses lined up for him in the richest places. He walked among the poor. He slept among the poor. He ate with the poor. If you want to be Christ-like, be Christ-like, because Christ lived and died for what he believed. He didn't have a tailor coming into his office in his grand festive temple to sew robes for him. He didn't have people coming in saying, "Pastor, I want you to have this car." He didn't have a vacation spot in Hawaii. He didn't have five houses, did he? He could've had all the wonders in the world, could he not? When the devil tempted him when he was crossing across that desert, he said no. Did he not? So, if you're going to be Christ, be Christ-like. Be a good Christian and be Christ-like. Religion don't play a part on me. Call me a heathen if you want to! But what did you just say, I'm real? Don't tell me you Christian. Don't have me running. Don't have me looking behind me. Don't have me not turning my back against you because I don't trust you. Religion don't have any part of my life . . . any of it. If you Christian please be the right one.

How has HIV and AIDS affected your life?

My nephew died of AIDS. I have a sister that's HIV-positive. She's having a hard time right now. She's upset with me because I tell people that she's HIV. I love my nephew. I loved him. He was my oldest sister's only child. [Begins to cry] Sorry. My sister Linda, the one that I tell you disappeared when I was a child that kept me centered when she came back into my life, is the voice of reason for me sometimes because when I say something, she always have that other level of clarity for me. It's like with all my siblings that does that for me because I know sometimes when my grandmother was alive I used to have to call home so I could get that universe within me centered. But with my nephew and my sister, that's closer to home than anything else you can get. I had a nephew that died. I had a sister that lost her child to HIV went to AIDS, and he fought a good fight, and Linda's fighting a good fight but then your body get tired, and it's closer to me than that. I want to go home and see my sister, but I can't afford to go see her. I don't want to have to go home. I want to be able to see her while she's living because she's sick now. HIV is very close to me, and I fight for it. I worked in a pharmacy for a long time. Those medications, one pill would cost you almost ten thousand dollars. You know? It's a lot of money for that cocktail for people to have. HIV and AIDS is our black plague. The only difference between the black plague, they found out what was causing it. It was the fleas. They knew how to deal with that, but this AIDS, they don't know what's causing it. They can treat it, but they can't get rid of it. It's strong for me. It's strong. [Continues to weep] I'm sorry.

Have you lost other people?

There were people I met through Pat but I didn't know, I knew of them; I didn't know them, but I can't say that I had any friends that I know of that died of AIDS.

What are some of the health issues that face black women in the lesbian community?

[Sighs] Health issues for us? Diabetes one. Sickle cell is two. In general, with black women, not just us dykes? . . . The health issue of trust. The health issue of trust because we got to trust our brothers. That's a health issue for us. We got to be able to have that healthy trust situation to know that if I'm HIV I should tell you my sister, I'm HIV, and we got to have that health issue of trust to say, let's go to classes to find out how we can enjoy each other without infecting each other. That's my health issue with us. [More weeping] I get too emotional sometimes. I'm sorry.

No, it's not too emotional. Like I said, it's real.

But diabetes is our biggest culprit, and high blood pressure is our biggest health issue as black women, not just being dykes, as black women, and we're having more heart attacks. You don't hear of them, but we're having more heart attacks than any person. They always say the men are. Black women are dying of heart attacks. With me dealing with the health issue, I know this but it's not being said. We're dying, dropping, heart attacks.

What is your best memory of growing up in the South?

My best memory is my grandmother, waking up with her in the mornings. We had a wood-burning stove, black. Our house was one, two, three, four rooms and a hallway, one, two, three, four and the kitchen, so that was five. We had an outdoor toilet, we had a well, but my best things about my grandmother in the South was waking up with her in the mornings and curling up around that stove. She made my uncle make me a little box that he put next to that stove, and she would cook breakfast in the morning and by the time she had breakfast fixed, I was already awakened for the second time, and we sitting on that back porch, and the wood sitting at the end of that porch, and we having a cup of coffee. Yes, I drunk coffee with my grandmother and watching that sun rise, and she say, "Ginny, today is your day. Every day is your day," and I remember those days. That's my favorite of all things with my grandmother in the morning. That's my favorite. She taught me how to cook oatmeal on that stove. I knew how to make biscuits, and my mother claimed she didn't know how, but [laughing]. Oh my, those are my favorite memories of my grandmother in the South. [. . .]

Last question: what are your current feelings about being a black lesbian?

My current feelings? [Smacks her lips] I am a proud black dyke. My feelings about being a dyke, I have no feelings. I have feelings of being human, and when I told you before it's a dangerous thing, right? I am happy with me. I am happy with my wife. My feelings about being a dyke, being a black dyke, [giggles] I love me. I love Miss Cherry, you know. I can't say I have any feelings. I can say what I can feel about Miss Cherry and that's a happy Cherry. That's how I feel about being me, but not the other me. [Laughter] I hope I didn't bore you too bad.

I'm Happy as Hell

Gwen Cubit

10

I was introduced to Gwen and her partner, Lori (see chapter 11), through my friends Sharon Bridgforth and Omi Osun Joni L. Jones in Austin, Texas. Neither Sharon nor Omi indicated anything extraordinary about Gwen's life except to say that she would be a great person to interview. I had no idea that her story would turn out to be one of the most engaging in the whole book. A survivor of sexual abuse, drug addiction, and incarceration, Gwen is pragmatic about her past: she believes that these experiences were preparing her for her current situation: she is in a steady relationship with a woman she loves, and she has gone back to school to earn her degree. The interview took place on September 10, 2012, at her home in Austin, Texas.

I was born in Austin, Texas, on April 3rd, 1967. [My childhood] was crazy. It was crazy. [Laughter] It was crazy, you know. We moved around a lot, my—I started out at all-black school, went through the whole integration. My mother being a single parent, raising five kids on her own. I've experienced hunger, no gas, no electricity. So, it's been a long life. [. . .] I'm the middle child. I have two brothers older than me and then a brother and a sister younger than me.

What did your mother do for work?

She started out—as far—long as I knew, up until I was about eight, she stayed at home. And then, because she was, I guess, what they would call my stepfather worked, and she stayed at home and took care of the kids and the house. And then when I was around seven or eight, they split up, and she didn't do anything for a while, 'cause she really didn't—I guess she didn't have anything to do. She had tried to work before, but she worked at like a nursing home or something, it wasn't really anything specific. And so, when I was about nine or ten, she went to beauty school. And so, over the year—first she just went and go one thing, 'cause it didn't take as many hours. But she eventually ended up going back and became a cosmetologist.

Okay. Is that what she does now?

Actually, no, she's retired. She does absolutely nothing now. [Laughter]

Did you know your father, your biological father?

I knew a stepfather, and when I was fifteen, my real father came and told me he was my father.

So, you knew him, but you didn't know he was your father?

I knew him as my uncle.

Why was that?

Well, according to my mother, she was never gonna tell me. [. . .] And so, I think he got angry at her for whatever reason and decided that he wanted to tell me, and so when I was like fifteen, he told me. And I think it was a traumatic experience to have known you and seen you and to know that you have seen me and know that I have went without and you did nothing, and then to come and tell me that you're my dad. I was scarred.

Because he had means?

He had means to be able to help the situation. Yeah. And he was married and had another family and I—they were my cousins. I didn't know that he was my dad.

Did you ever reconcile that with him?

What has happened in the last couple of years, I've had to deal with that. Based on my own—I got some girls of my own, I got three girls, and their daddy issues brought up mine. And because it wasn't reconciled, I didn't probably make the best decisions with them and their dads. And so, as a result of that, I knew I needed to take a look at what was happening with my dad, and so we're not like the best of buddies, I don't call him regularly or any of that, but I have went there and—just so that I could be free and just forgiving him and let him off the hook. I had to do that. So that has evolved in the last year or so. 'Cause I was angry for so many years, so many years that I couldn't get past my anger. And so, because I couldn't get past the anger, I couldn't forgive him, and so then I couldn't be free. And so, it just sort of spilled over into the—my daughters' relationships with their dad, which I—and then when I'm looking at it and I'm thinking about it, it was probably a lotta jealousy 'cause their dads were really involved and always has been since they were born, and so I think there was a level of jealousy and not understanding that relationship.

[. . .] My stepfather, up until I was eight, and then even afterwards, he would come over and pick us up on occasion and he—legally, he was my, my legal guardian. He adopted me and legal rights and said that "I will take care of her." And so, he was really significant; he taught me the basics, like how to tie your shoe and how to ride a bicycle, and he was there. And so, he died when I was nineteen, and I remember thinking, that was my dad that died. But by then, everybody knew that he wasn't my dad, and so I had started being treated different.

By him?

No, he tried not to, but I don't think he had it to—to know what to do. But I had a son when I was seventeen, and when I was eighteen he was looking for me because he knew I'd had the son, and he wanted to see him and was calling him his grandson, and that was real significant for me. And then the next year he died. I guess whatever he was trying to do to make that relationship right, he died before he could, and then I wasn't old enough to really embrace it. But yeah, everybody else started to treat me different. And then he was just who he was, so I don't think he ever learned how to— I never heard him say stuff like, "I love you," or nothing like that. So, I just attribute that to now, being an adult myself, that maybe he didn't have that to give.

Hmm. Had he had another family before marrying your mom?

Yes, he had. And so, he had older kids and then he married my mom, and then I was already a baby when they got together, and then she had my brother and sister, my younger brother and sister with him.

How would you describe the racial politics of Austin when you were growing up? Was it segregated?

It was very segregated, very divided. It still was colored signs up, even in '67. And when I started going to school, all the black kids went to a school, and if you seen one or two white kids, I think they were just basically like white poor trash kinda kids. Hate to say that, but just, lived in the trailer park and really was not considered even favorable to their own race. And so, just sort of went to our school, but you really didn't see 'em. We had black teachers, everybody that worked in the cafeteria were black. So, we enjoyed the food. [Laughter] And then in 1975, which was later than most anybody else in Texas, Austin decided to integrate the school system and we got bused— which you'd have to get up an hour earlier to take a forty-five-minute to an hour bus ride to get to a school, just four or five of you, and then the teacher put you in a special class and didn't even assess you to see if you deserved to be in the special class.

Special meaning "slow"?

Yeah. They had the idea that black kids coming from there wasn't—and actually, I was well beyond what they were on. We had already done that the year before, so we were well beyond. Back then, I just think the teachers advocated more for us at the black schools because they knew we didn't have it, and so we were well above, and they just made sure, "You need to get this," because it may come a time when [. . .] we wouldn't have all-black schools. Personally, [. . .] I would send my kids to an all-black school, personally. 'Cause it just made a shift in Austin. [. . .] The divide was put up, and although technically they tried to talk about diversity and say how diverse Austin is, the divide continues to be up. And so, now [. . .] they're even pushing the black people further out. They don't even want you in Austin, so they're pushing you to the outskirts of Austin: "Y'all need to go live in Manor or Austin's Colony, those kinda places," and they're taking over the east side of town where we grew up at and now that's all pretty much white people. 'Cause all the older people have died, families evicted or have done lost their houses due to an inability to pay taxes, and so they did what they call gentrification.

My mother and them went up on 11th and 12th Street, and that's where they went to go party; but before my mother and them, my grandmother and them went to 6th Street, and that's where all the black people was. So, they just kept pushing and pushing and pushing, and so now it's no place; 11th Street is all-white now. The only reason why they didn't tear the buildings down is because they were historical and they couldn't. And so, all of that has changed from when I was coming up; we was going up there, going out. It's like they want central Austin to be white. That's what I feel, because that's what I see and that's the shift. I've been here since [Interstate] 35 was one-way and one-way, and [Interstate] 183 was the same way, and all of this was still gravel roads and on the east side and St. John, and it was nothing. Austin was still pretty country when I grew up. [Laughter] [. . .] They're so far behind Houston and Dallas and those bigger metropolitan cities anyway, because they always wanted to be a small town, even though it was made the capital. They always wanted to have a small-town feel, and so it pretty much has that. Forty people a year die here, everybody's like, "Oh, forty people!" Well, forty people a minute die other places. Come on. [Laughter] You know? It just makes news. And so, they've managed to do that by making the divide and making sure that they keep the black folks locked up and out the way, then we don't have to worry about the crime rate, we don't have to worry about those kinda things.

And so, when you were bused to these white schools, what was that like? Was there racial tension at those schools?

Very much so. And at the time, if you come from a black place, where everybody's black, all the neighbors black, everybody pass by, and you go to a place—'cause my mother was on Section 8, she was on housing and the welfare system, so the whole system got integrated, and they moved her into an all-white neighborhood. So that was like, couldn't play with the kids across the street, couldn't play with the kids up the street, and if they seen me playing with the kids, the parents would come out jack them, "You don't play with them little niggers." And I had never heard that. "Mama, what is that?" Because we come from where everybody was black. So, I hadn't experienced that. So now I'm nine years old and I can't play with my neighbors. I go to school, they talk to you at school 'cause the parents are not there. And a lot of them don't understand that. All they know is you look different. But they don't understand, you not supposed to talk to me, not supposed to play with me. And so, it was a real, "I didn't understand. Why? What was wrong with me?" I didn't understand that whole racial thing. And it took a while; I finally got, I got it. [Laughter] But you don't take long to get it, and then it was, it's 'cause you black, and I finally understood what being black meant in Austin, Texas—or in the South, even. That they would prefer it if we had stayed slaves, and I started to understand, because they still were calling black people "boy" and all of that in Texas, and Austin especially. It was like real slow city to change, to embrace black people. And I'm not sure that they embraced us totally there, but we're able to move around a little bit more.

And your older siblings, they didn't have to go to integrated schools, or did they?

Well, by then, they were in high school. Back then, Bedichek was all white, and so my brother and them, when they went off to middle school, it was all white, and I was still in elementary, and it was all white. They stopped going to school. My brothers probably stopped going to school in about the eighth or the ninth grade and never went back. That's how much they rebelled against it.

And nobody even asked them why, and that's what's really sad. My mother, she worked a lot, she had five of us, she was trying to make sure that we could eat, and so she never questioned, "What was that, why you don't go to school?" And I just can't believe that it was pure laziness, maybe just maybe they didn't like the feeling that they got there. I don't know, 'cause I didn't understand the stuff that I would go through on a daily basis. Like the teacher thinking I'm cheating if I make an A. And I ain't sitting by nobody. [Laughter] I was off, 'cause you know they gonna separate, you sitting on this row . . . all of them are over there. And so, they don't wanna say that you're separated, but if you look around, you can tell that you are. And so, then, like just accusing me. Like I—my mother has had to—had to go to the office and talk to the principal, and just accusing me of cheating. And he looked at both tests and then he was like, "The ones she missed is not the same ones this girl missed. It is no way she could've cheated." But to put me on the spot like that—why would you do that? So, you experience things. [Laughter] [. . .]

What was the talk in your community about white people? Or was there talk about white people?

Yeah, it was only one or two things: "Don't trust 'em." And so, as a result of that, if you hear that all your life, "Don't trust 'em," you can't never let your guard down, that's what you become. So, then you don't let your guard down and what I seen is, black people have the same stuff, too. So maybe it was a *people* thing and maybe not a *white* thing, but by this time I was so integrated, you can't never trust white people, they're always out to get the black people. And it was only after I became adult to just understand that everybody ain't out to get me. [. . .] I could contribute something to this equation, too. But I used to buy that, too, the white man trying to hold the black man back, all that—that's all we heard. And [. . .] our uncles and stuff, they all talked about it. "That white man, he told me" —all you ever heard was about complaining about a job, complaining about this, and that's what you saw. And we always had the low-paying jobs. We always worked the hardest, but the white man always got the credit.

And what was the talk about how to overcome that?

It probably was talk to overcome it, but not where I come from, because we were so poor, it was just trying to manage just so that we could have some food on the table. And my mother and them wasn't very politically activated, so if those talks were happening and if those things were happening, and my mother 'n'em wasn't a part of the civil rights movement and all that, although they were all well old enough to participate. I just think in the South black people just decided that, this is the way it is, this is the way it's gonna be. And so, I think a few people did, I'm not sure, like in the early sixties. I wasn't born 'til the late sixties, but the early sixties, when the civil rights movement happened, I'm sure some of those people came from the South. But did I see that in my community, did I see that in my family? I didn't. So as a result of that, I didn't learn how to advocate for the black people and how to be a spokesman. 'Cause I never heard nobody that I actually knew thought different than this is the way life is and you just need to accept your role in it and do it. [. . .]

I didn't come out and just really embrace the fact that I was gay until about five years ago. I grew up hiding it all my life. My first sexual encounter was with a girl, but I couldn't say nothing about it. And the gender role was so set in a black family, especially you gonna go, you gonna have some kids, you gonna get married, you're gonna do whatever, but being gay was not what you was gonna be. And I seen all the time seen how people treated gay people, so I surely don't wanna be treated like that. And so, I bought the hype for many a year and as a result of that, I was in many unhappy relationships. And I love my kids, and I would never change them for the world, but personally, I just don't think that was what was supposed to happen. It was just that I conformed. [. . .] I wore dresses straight up until I went to high school. I wore dresses to school until I got to high school and finally my mother bought me a pair of pants, and it was just like one or two, it wasn't a whole bunch. Because we went to church all the time. And so, you go to church in the South, church is big, and so being gay and being a part of the church was not acceptable, either. Although I thought some people in there might've been gay. . . but you don't say that. And so, as a result of that, yeah, you wore dresses, you got your hair done, your mama fixed your hair. I was thirty before anybody besides my mother done my hair. [. . .] I adapted and conformed to the whole deal . . . for most—for, like I said, around five years ago, I decided that I was gonna speak up and I was gonna be me. And when I did, it destroyed my family. We were divided for a while. What I believe is the love and God was bigger than the divide, and we just now getting on the point where people, whether they accept it or not, I don't feel the tension when I'm around. And what's really more confusing to me on most days is that I used drugs for many years, been to prison and went in and out, and that seemed more acceptable than me saying I was gay.

Really?

Don't be *that*. Be a crack head, but don't be gay. [Laughter]

Wow, that's deep.

That is very deep for me, and that is still—that is very sensitive to me. Really? Really? 'Cause I remember what I was when I used. I remember how I felt personally, and I remember how I treated others, because I had to have it. And you would prefer *that*? Because I remember you'd say, "I'm just gonna pray for you," but now I can't get no prayer? So yeah, me and my mother, more than anything—and I've always wanted to make her proud of me, 'cause I dropped out of school, got pregnant. And I think a lot of that had to do with I didn't have no role models. My mother worked so much, she—well, she was a good woman, I don't take nothing from her, but she didn't give me probably what I needed as a young girl. And I was abused in the household by my oldest brother, so that, in itself, made me always searching for somebody to protect me. But I can't never tell the truth. And so, I couldn't tell the truth about that, so I sure can't tell the truth about that, so my life just until I just started living and just being me, like I'm telling you, like maybe—now, it may have been seven years, but it ain't been, like—I'm forty-five and I just finally feel free.

Wow. So, you've covered a whole lotta ground in two minutes. So, we're gonna sort of slowly unpack some of this. But going back to your childhood, what role did church play in your upbringing? You talked about you had to go to church.

[. . .] We went to Baptist Church. My first remembrance is of going to church, a little bitty girl with the little dress on, little patent leather shoes and ruffled socks, and not really understanding why we was going, but knowing that that was the requirement. And then doing that up until I was sixteen, not missing a day. We went on Wednesdays, we went on Saturdays, we went to Sunday BTU [Baptist Training Union] training. My mother was in the mission, so we went on Monday, we was there all day Sunday. And if my uncle was a preacher or somebody we knew was preaching somewhere, we went there. And so, church was really big, and I think that played a major part in my conformity.

Did you participate in church? Were you active? Did you sing in the choir or the usher board?

I didn't sing in the choir, but I was active as such, like in the little junior church—could quote the Bible, say all the books of the Bible, led the little Sunday school troops. I was like that. And I sang in the choir, but I wasn't no lead singer or nothing, but I would sing in the little youth choir. And then, as I got older, I would lead Sunday school groups and stuff like that, like not just sitting in the pews.

And did your mother always go with you to church?

Most of the time, yeah. That was the motivation behind that. [. . .] So it was "Come on, we're going to church," and so you just do what everybody say you do. There's no refusal in that.

Did you enjoy it?

One part of me did. And it was always a part of me that struggled, and I didn't know what that was, 'cause I don't know that I believed everything they said. And I think that was my struggle; it was okay, but I don't know that

I believe everything you're telling me, but I went because it was expected and I was told to, and one thing I know that I learned was to do what you were told. And so, I did that, and so I went to church not really understanding why it was important, and they had all the rules. If you don't do this, if you do that—you're gonna go to hell if you don't do this. There's so many rules, you gotta try to remember the rules, and as a young kid you got all those rules, rules at school, you got the rules at home, and sometimes those rules conflict. So, who do I believe?

So, when you became a teenager, did you have a choice at that point, whether you went to church?

No. Not in my mother's house.

Oh, okay. So up until you were eighteen, you went to that church?

Well, no, I went 'til I was like fifteen or sixteen, we went to that church. And then we moved and so wasn't by that church, and we wasn't really going to church, and we started to slack off, but that was based on we didn't have a car, we had moved, my mother wasn't able to get us around, and so it was circumstances that made church not be . . . but I would sometimes still walk down the hill, which was a pretty good distance, to where my Auntie and them stayed and go to church with them. But that wasn't consistent, and now I was starting to get a touch of freedom, and so I didn't wanna go. And so, it was, "Oh, we're not going to church no more?" So then that was the shift. And so, around sixteen that happened, and by the time I was seventeen I was pregnant. So just in that period, I just . . . I didn't have nothing to stand on 'cause I didn't all the time believe what I was learning. So as a result of that, I was able to buy in to what you said, too.

So, when you all moved, did you stay in Austin?

Yeah. Yeah, we just moved from St. John to the east side. We moved a lot when I was a kid. We moved a lot. My mother was very unstable as far as that's concerned. I can remember going to bed, house full of furniture like this, she waking us up in the middle of the night and said, "Come on, we fixin' to go," and I'd walk down the stairs, the house is empty. And we would go to a new house, and it's all over there and we have moved.

And you never knew why?

Never knew why.

Wow. Have you had a conversation with her [laughter] since about why y'all were moving so much?

[Laughter] I don't even think she'd know why. And that's one of the things we have not addressed.

And was your stepfather moving with you?

No, this was after him and her had split. We moved a couple of times when they was together—a few times when they was together. We ended up in Oklahoma one time, we moved around in St. John's, to several houses in St. John's on different streets, so just was always moving, always moving. So what I learned as a result of that don't get comfortable. Always moving. I'm telling you, I lived in St. John, I went to Reagan I was in the ninth grade. While I was in ninth grade we moved to Fluger Hill. I went there for like two weeks; she moved us back to St. John and I went back to Reagan. I'm in the ninth grade. They had counted me present and we was—I was in a whole new school. She had to fill out that thing to say I had missed so many days, but I was not—I had to show proof that I was enrolled in a whole 'nother school. By the time I got to the tenth grade, we was on the east side and I was going to Johnston. Well, we moved in the middle of that and I went back to Reagan. And I ended up at the end of that back at Johnston. We moved a lot.

So as a kid, you must've just been so unsettled . . . moving back and forth to—and what happened to your friends?

I didn't make any. With the longest place we stayed was when we lived south, when they moved us into that neighborhood. We stayed there for three years, and so we stayed there from the time I was going into the—guess I could've—fourth, fifth, and the sixth grade we stayed there. Then when I was going to seventh grade, we moved in the summer before seventh grade. But we never stayed long at no other house. I went to two or three schools in the seventh grade, two or three schools in the eighth grade, two or three schools in the ninth grade, two or three schools in the tenth grade. By the time I got to the eleventh grade, I was on my second school and I got pregnant, but I had already been to two schools in eleventh grade.

So, did you finish high school?

No.

You didn't.

I didn't.

You went back later though?

Well, yeah, after some years, I guess when I was around twenty-one or twenty-two, I went to the Job Corps. They had a program for young women who was on Medicare, who was on welfare. You didn't have to live there, they would take you there every day so you would get a trade to try to help you get off of welfare, and I got into that program. I had two kids. And I went through there and I got a clerk typing is what it was at that time certificate, and got my GED while I was there, and my driver's license while I was there, and it just really was a good program. It was a good program.

When did you first realize that you had same-sex attraction? And what was your reaction to that realization?

I don't know, probably when I was around eight. And it was just taboo. Like I knew, it just felt wrong because that's what everybody always says, is all I always heard. And when I heard people talking about, well, so-and-so and so-and-so, and I didn't even know what gay was, but you would hear people say that and then say it was wrong.

They used the word "gay" or did they . . . use some other word?

Oh, "He a sissy." That was the word when we was coming up. [Laughter] "He a sissy." And you heard it more about men than you did about women. Sissies and bulldaggers. Those were the terms when I was coming up.

[. . .] And so, when I was around eight, I had my first sexual encounter with my cousin, of all people. [. . .] It was experimenting, but it was something that I will always remember in every sexual experience from then on. [. . .] Because she knew how to do it. I didn't know to do it. And she was a couple years younger than me. I don't know. And so, I try not to think about how she already knew what to do and telling me to lay on top of her and all that. I don't know.

And is she gay now?

No.

No. Okay. Have you all had a conversation about that?

Unh-unh. She a preacher's wife and all that now. [Laughter]

Oh. That don't mean nothing. [Laughter]

It don't. It don't, it don't. But to her, it's the title, and that thing is she is serious about it. [. . .] It happened a couple more times with other girls . . . that we would be around, and I don't know if it was the experimenting or if they were—I don't know, because what I can remember, when I was like eleven, we went to a sixth grade camp, and there was a girl there, and I guess she was attracted to me, we was attracted, and it just was like, we was holding hands and not in the friend manner. And I'm—I remember thinking, "Okay, this feels good." And then my mother had another friend who used to work with her, and she had a daughter my same age, and she would spend the night, and it would happen. And these were things, that's why I can remember 'em so vividly, because these were—they were something I enjoyed and I always was—would think about, I didn't think about it wrong. It felt natural, when we did it with whoever I did it with, it just felt so natural. But I had another friend—so by the time life happened, it was always somebody. I've always, at one point or another, had a—a woman in my life.

And so, when did you start having boyfriends?

Guess I was about thirteen when I said, "I have a boyfriend." But again, remember, I had already been being abused in the household, so I already knew what sex was because I had been sexually molested already.

Did you tell anyone about that?

I did not. Not until I was thirty-five.

And have you had a conversation with him?

No, I have not. He's in prison right now. I'm in a place spiritually in my life where I need to address that with him. Me and my mother have . . . it devastated her. We had a fight about it, then I had thought about my sister, and then my girls, who were coming up before he went off to prison—he invaded them because I never told? And I used to work, and he would be at my house, and so that is big. But what I realize through all of that, because I had therapy and I had counseling and all that, is that even with all of that, I don't hate men, I ain't a man basher. I prefer sex with women; I prefer to be in a relationship with women. So, you take that however. Fine with me. I ain't mad. I understand that what I've learned is like that wasn't my fault—I was a kid. So, it took a long time to get there, 'cause I was always thinking that I did something to . . . bring that attention on me. And so, there's always been a woman, though, involved on the down low.

Oh, even when you had a boyfriend, you still had a girlfriend?

Yeah, I had a girlfriend. Yeah.

Huh—how did that work? [Laughter]

It was awkward, it was awkward. And even here recently, like right before I came out into the world and told everybody and told my family, I was seeing a guy and I was seeing a woman, and it got pretty—and she knew I was seeing a guy, and she didn't like it. But she wanted to be with me, and so I felt like I was orchestrating that, which is all the way wrong, but that's the way it went. And then in the end, when I decided, okay, you gotta stop that, that's not fair to anybody, and then so I just didn't be with anybody for a year. And at the end of that year, I made the decision that I was gonna be honest with myself and everybody else, and that's when I came out.

And when you came out, who did you come out to?

Actually, I came out to—[laughter] which is crazy: I have another friend who's gay, and she already knew about the erratic back and forth between men and women, and so then I told her, I said, "You know what? I'm gonna stop playing with that," because it was just not good on the inside of me. "And I'm gonna tell people that I am truly gay, ain't no playing with it." And she was like, "I'll be here to support you whenever you get ready." We're still good friends, but she had been gay for a few years, so she understood. Her daughters was fifteen, sixteen. She had older daughters and had already been gay all that time. So, she understood the things that I was struggling with and so—'cause she got put out of the house for being gay, so she knew exactly how, why. She could understand why I didn't do it, 'cause there was a lotta days she wished she hadn't've, because it meant she got put out the house and really didn't have anywhere to go and all this stuff that happened after that. And that's how she married the man, because she wanted to get back in and wanted to get back in with her mother. So, she talked to me about all of that and told me how that went for her, and like they used to fight, her and the man, because she wasn't happy, she didn't know how to say she wasn't happy. And then one day it happened for her—she had a friend that she was able to tell that, and so I was able to talk to her and then after I told her that—I'm in Narcotics Anonymous now, so I make meetings and I told them in the meeting that I needed to share it out loud, I needed to get it out of my head, but not be playing around with it. And then after I got some feedback from other people who had experienced it, I had to tell my mother.

And how did that go?

Oh, I got, "The Bible say . . ." [Laughter] And I was like, "Well, Mama, I think it—"

And you were thirty-five, you said? How old were you?

I was like forty—thirty-nine or forty. And so, I called my mother . . .

Oh, you called? You didn't do it in person?

Uh-uh. She lives in Kansas. And it was like, my kids were already here, seeing it. And I told my kids, I had my two girls living with me. And they had seen me not be with anybody for a year, but they had also seen me doing that back and forth with a woman and a man in the house. So, they didn't know what was going on. And so, they heard everybody else tell them how bad that was—their dads—and so they want to go live with their other parent because it was wrong that I was gonna be gay. And my mother that was talking, too, and saying that it was abomination against God and just all of this. And it was, well, if you can't support me, then we're not gonna be talking. So we didn't talk for like three months, and Lori said, "If somebody called you and said something was wrong with your mama, right now, would you be okay with the way it is right now? Would you be able to be okay with that?" And I wouldn't. And so I called her, and we talked, and it wasn't still okay with her, but I just had to let her know that I was gonna be okay even if she wasn't okay. But I did not wanna go without talking to her and not letting her know that I loved her. And so three or four years went by, and I went to visit her in a face-to-face, and there, in that face-to-face, was the healing. And so, it's been different since that, too.

When you went, did you take Lori with you?

No. I went by myself. My daughter had went up there to stay with my mother for the summer, and me and Lori had went to pick her up and Lori wasn't welcome in her house. We stayed at a hotel. And because Lori wasn't welcome in her house, I stayed at the hotel, 'cause I just needed to be like very clear. So, when they—she would come down here and have some aunts to visit, she wasn't welcome to stay at my house because this is me and Lori's house together. And that was very distressful, just very, very harmful. And this was the—the whole family, they would be over there, I would be over here, it'd be horrible. But after that face-to-face, something changed, something changed.

What do you think it was?

I don't know.

Do you think that she came to a place where she's like, this is my child and I love you no matter what?

Yes, I think that's what happened. Think exactly what happened. And I expressed to her that, like, I have been through a lot and that, like, I had used drugs, I did all that, and you always embraced me, always said you believed in me. And then when I did this, you turned your back on me. And I think that was the jarring thing for me to be able to say to her is, you've always said you'd love me through whatever, and this is not showing it. And I think that was the jarring thing for her, it was, and so she was like, no matter what, I'm gonna love you. And if that means accepting you just where you at, that's what I'm gonna do. And so now Lori can go to the house, we can stay there for the—and it was like the first time, and everybody was comfortable and you did—you did not feel not one bit of tension in the room. And that was just beautiful.

So, what about your siblings? I know you've talked to your older brothers, but what about your sister? How did the conversation go with them?

I think my sister—she lives with my mother. [Laughter] She's a wonderful woman, but I don't know if it's because she's so selfish that it don't even matter, or that it's just best if she don't even have to think about it. So, we really never even talk about it.

Oh, really?

Umm-hmm. She never said, "Be what you gonna be." She never said nothing. But she don't treat me no different, either. She treat me the same way, just being herself, just being who she is. She's so selfish. But because she hasn't treated me no different, then I can't do nothing with that. And she accepts me. But the struggle was with my children and the separation, they went off to live with their dads and they were saying shit like, "You don't even know," and she was nine. She's fifteen now. "You was nine. You don't even know what gay is." [Laughter] "I don't like gay." "Why you don't like gay?" So, I sat her down and I tried to explain to her in terms of how she can understand what was happening and what that meant when I like a woman, not like if you like a boy, you think he cute, that's how I like women. But she was nine, you know. And I want you to understand, but for you to say that, you heard somebody else say that, and that's what came out. [. . .] Then I have another daughter, she's twenty now. And while she had friends who were gay—that was okay, but not my mama. [Laughter] And even it was okay to see a woman in my house one week and a man in my house the next week, as long as I wasn't committed and saying that I was doing that. As long as it looked like, okay, we don't know what she's doing, but so we could just say, we don't know what she's doing.

But now she's come around, too?

Oh, yeah. Like now . . . everybody now—well, I don't know that if I would call it, Patrick, on the same plane, [laughter] . . . but what I would call it is, is that we can sit down all in the same space and be at peace. Everybody has put aside whatever personal thoughts they have about it and just embraced the fact that I'm still the mama, I'm still the daughter, I'm still the sister, and just said, we still love her, whatever. And so, I think that, more than anything, is what has happened.

Is there a particular theory about homosexuality that you believe? Do you think that people are born gay?

I do. I do believe that people are born with something they cannot explain as to why. And I say that because I had a friend and we was like five years old, and he was a boy and he's my friend, he's my really good friend, still my friend right today. And when we were like five, we were gonna play house, because that's what you did. And he said, "But I'm gonna be the mama." I was like, "No, you're not. I'm gonna be the mama!" "No, I'm gonna be the mama. You gonna be . . ." I don't even know who he wanted me to be. [Laughter] You gonna be the daddy, I don't know, I don't know what. Who you want me to be? You gonna be my sister or somebody? [Laughter] But he always liked boys, and I'm talking about we were five. So how would he have that, even as a five-year-old, how would he know that about himself if it wasn't innate, or something that was already in him? Like he knew that. Like, he embraced that, and I sometimes am very jealous because of my inability to embrace that in myself. And I see people who was able to do that, and even though they life may not be even worse off and they have lived many years of people not messing with them, family not talking to them, I still know for themselves that they were able to come out and be free in their own skin, 'cause I was never in my own skin, I just struggled all the time. So that was why I did the back and forth all the time, 'cause I kept struggling, and like I would never commit, 'cause I didn't what the world or what everybody was gonna say about me—it mattered.

Do you think growing up in the South made you more naïve about sexuality in general?

I think so, because it's like a taboo subject in the South, and women and people always did things underhanded and behind closed doors. And it was never any open dialogue about sexuality, there was never any open dialogue about when you get thirteen or whatever and your body starts feeling a certain way, and so you don't know what that is. It was just never any open dialogue. My mother never said, "You gonna start feeling a little something." Like, I talk to my daughter. "If you kissing somebody and that little thing is happening, that is a powerful thing. And while you say you won't have sex, sometimes that overwhelms this." And so, like my mother never—no, we never had that conversation. It was so much incest and so much secretiveness and so much molestation that—and nobody wanted to know, and so don't nobody talk about it, and everybody just walk around and pretend like it ain't happening. 'Cause it happening in everybody's house. And so, the way they express sex, very, very unhealthy. And I used to think that it was only happening to me, until I have talked to other black women and it has happened to them—in my age range, older than me, and younger than me. Black people do not want to admit it, face it, or talk about it. And it's all about sexuality. And maybe if we were giving our kids that, or at least talking about that, and you were saying to boys, "When you start that, don't be looking at your sister, that's not who that—that's not who fixes that. That's not who—" you know what I mean? You need to be talking about that, because now it just seems it's so wrong, and so then it becomes nasty—when I don't think it was meant to be nasty. But also, we're from the South, so people say it's between man and wife, sex is only between man and wife, and so you shouldn't even be having no sexual thoughts about other people—especially if you're not married.

You talked about this a little. How would you describe your current relationship with your family?

My relationship now is so—it's really rewarding, because I have the ability to be honest. I have the ability to say what I need and to let them be just where they are, until—and I believe in God, not because I went to church but because I believe in an ultimate presence. But let that worry with the outcome, 'cause what I realized, when I'm bucking and they bucking, don't nothing get solved. [Laughter] Like, I'm gonna be who I am and you gonna be who you are, so we're not gonna talk, can't do nothing. And so, I just have to surrender and realize that, they get to feel everything they feeling, too, just like you do. You can't make them not feel what no other kinda way about you telling them that. That had to've been a shocker, and you living that, so that continues to be a shocker, and so you ought to let them make it.

And so, what's happened in the process is that we've been, me and my mother are better than we've ever been, than I can remember in all my life. We are better than we've ever been, and the love I have for her is probably like on a woman-to-woman basis, although she is my mother, but it's on a deep woman level as well. And I can understand now her struggle, where at first I just thought, oooh, you fucked me up. [Laughter] You know what I'm saying? People talkin' about, well, they did the best they could do. No, the hell you didn't. [Laughter] If that was your best, shit, I'd hate to see your worst! [Laughter] But what I realized is that's all she had. She wasn't raised by a mother figure so she always was struggling. Her life had been a struggle [. . .] started having kids at fifteen, then got five kids that you're responsible for. What you got to give at fifteen? By the time she's twenty, she done had all her kids. And when I look at myself, when I look at my daughters, shit, when you fifteen, you a kid. [Laughter] You know what I'm saying? And you trying to have a whole family? No, she didn't have it to give. I can't be mad at her for that. She gave me what she had, and it just wasn't enough. So, our relationship today is like all of that that it never was, because I get to express and she gets to. She calls me and says, "Okay, I'm just having some feelings. What you think about this?" [Laughter] And I'll be like, "This is so different." [. . .] Whatever's happening and like her past comes back and stuff that happened to her and how to get past certain situations. And I'll just be, amazed, like . . .

But do you think that, in a weird kind of way, because you are now living in your own truth—that has helped her?

I think so. To live in hers?

Yeah.

I think so.

And now y'all can live in it together? [Laughter]

Yeah. I absolutely think that's what has happened, because she sees me like that girl is standing up and being in her—she is doing that. And it gives her the courage to do the same.

Since you've come through all of what you've come through, looking back, do you think that a part of your drug addiction was about repressing your sexuality?

Yeah. It was about that, it was about the abuse, it was about never finding my place, it was about never feeling like I belonged. It was about never having enough, and I didn't know what enough was, whether it was food, 'cause we was poor. We were very poor. It was just all of that, and then not wanting to feel all of that. But especially, there was that sexual thing. 'Cause I can't never tell nobody—that is such a major secret. Like that was bigger than—once they found out I couldn't control the drug thing, that was like everybody knew somebody that had used drugs, and I told my mother, I said, "Well, you know people who got kids that's gay." "That's *they* kids. That's what they kids doing. That is not what I want for my kids."

And what was the turning point for you with your addiction? I mean, did you hit rock bottom and then have a come-to-Jesus moment, or—

No, I didn't hit rock bottom. [. . .] A lot of little things had happened right before I got clean. I had went to jail, and I had already been to the penitentiary one time, I didn't wanna go back, but it looked like I was heading back. But the motivating thing was that December my son was seventeen, and he lived with my mother, and they lived out here south of Austin in the projects, and I went there and she hadn't seen me, they hadn't seen me, I had been off using drugs. And so, I had been coming around the last couple days, "Hi, here I am," that kinda shit. And something happened around the corner, at the corner store. It was Halloween, so somebody had threw some eggs or something, and so my son was walking back from the store with a friend of his, and I was outside, and I seen the police just all swarm and just get on my son. And so, I ran down there and I was like, "What's going on? What's going on?" And the people were like, "Well, they stole something from the store and they egged the store man and hit him, and that's assault, and they was just going robbery and all that of that." Right? And so, my son's like, "Man." They like, "Where's your ID?" All right, he didn't have no ID, but he was like, "I don't know what you're talking about. That's not me." "Well, you gonna go back around here to the store, let the man look." And oh, this is horrible. And then I was like, I looked at him, I was like, "What you doing? What was you doing around there throwing eggs?" He looked at me, he said, "That wasn't me. And you don't even know me like that." And in that moment, I realized the truth of his statement, and I never wanted him to be able to say that to me again. And that next couple of months, I went to treatment. 'Cause he was so right, I did not know him, 'cause I went to prison and I left him, he was five. Now he was seventeen.

Hmm. So, between five and seventeen, you didn't see him?

I did, but I was in and out, in and out, in and out. And that's what they knew about me, and he was just letting me know. "You don't know me. I don't do stuff like that. I don't sell no drugs, you can't make me sell no drugs. I hate it. I hate anybody that's selling. I don't mess with people who sell drugs." 'Cause he hates it. And he said, "I don't steal. Who you think I am? You don't know me like that." Went back around to the store, the man was like, "No, this is my friend." He's like, "These boys good to me. No, no, no." That wasn't who it was? "Well, no, that wasn't him. I know him, I know him." And I was just like devastated, and like he just walked right outta my face, like, "You don't know me." And our relationship is just like beautiful. He went on, graduated high school, went off to the service, stayed for eight years, married, got a little grandbaby, they're doing they thing. But in the process, we've gotten to know each other, 'cause I never want him to have to tell me that no more. Shit. [Laughter]

So, he was staying with his father while you were away?

No, he was with my mother.

He was with your mother? Okay.

My two oldest kids was with my mother. She was with her other grandma, her baby—and I went and got her by the time she was five, so I done had her the last ten years. Then my other daughter's with her daddy and his mama. And so, I got her when she was eleven, and I sent her off to college. And so, she's in college in Kansas State. So, they didn't get to go through the whole brunt like my oldest kids did, not seeing me, me not being available. They went through a little piece of it, but they went through the big brunt of it.

How long have you been clean?

Ten years. It'll be eleven in January.

Wow, congratulations.

Thank you.

So, were you ever married?

Yes. I was married one time. I married out on my way to the penitentiary, and so I had my little baby and she was born with crack. The one that's in college. Thank you, God, for her mind and everything being right. She got all her toes, all her fingers. [Laughter]

She was born addicted, then?

She was addicted to crack. She had crack in her system, so by the time that that's—when she was born, CPS [Child Protective Services] had started coming to the hospitals, and kids that were born positive had to undergo some kinda treatment, and the parent had to get into treatment or you'd lose your kids. And so, I didn't tell her dad, and so they showed up at the house, 'cause I was living with him. He was just my friend, and we had sex, and I got pregnant, 'cause I wanted some money to go use drugs. That's how that happened. And so, they came to the house . . .

So, you were tricking?

Yeah.

But then you married him?

Yeah. I married him later.

Oh, okay.

I'm gonna tell you.

Okay.

CPS came to the house and [. . .] we wasn't married. While he was her father, we wasn't married. And so, when they came to the house and told him that she had been born with crack, I hadn't told him, but they had told me that at that hospital. He was devastated—I never seen him cry ever 'til that day. And so, he worked with the people with her, and I just continued to do what I was doing, and so I went to the pen—I was getting ready to go to the penitentiary, so I said, "Let's get married; then they can't—can't nobody do nothing . . . with the baby, 'cause we husband and wife and you can do anything you need to do with the baby. You don't have to try and defend being the baby daddy, none of that." And so, that's what happened. We got married in August; shit, I was in the penitentiary by December or something like that. But he raised her up until the time—I got her when she was eleven. He's a good man.

And you still have a relationship with him now?

He's my friend. We went back to being friends. I apologized. The first thing I did when I got clean was I divorced him and apologized profusely and it's, "What can I do to make it right?" He was just like, "Stay clean." And so, we were really good friends. If he needs something, I'll go out there and help him. That's just my way of saying, like, I'll never do that again. And so, I help him with his mom. She'll call me, I'll go out there and take her something, it's like that's my baby's dad and his mama, and whatever they need, I'm gonna do that. Because I can remember when they were willing to put up with whatever I was doing, too.

So, when you—you said you were in the penitentiary, that's not the same as jail?

No. It was—I was in the Texas Department of Criminal Justice, out at Gatesville.

Is that—is that all women?

Yes.

What was that experience like? And were you—were you still addicted while you were there?

Well, I stayed in the county jail long enough to where I wasn't like fiending for it. Stayed in there like ten months, and then they sentenced—they sentenced me a five-year sentence, and back then you used to do what they called parole in absentia, which you could parole out of the county jail as if you had been to the penitentiary, but you would come out on parole and not probation. And so, I was trying to do that, and they changed the law, and so they sent me to the penitentiary, and so I ended up staying three years. Then I got out, they sent me to Fort Worth. He came to Fort Worth and all of that, brought me some clothes and everything, my baby's daddy, my husband at the time. And then when I—I didn't stay clean. I didn't do the things necessary to stay clean, and so as a result of that, time passed, time passed, and I was heading back to the penitentiary.

And did you meet other women who were also addicted while you were in prison?

I'm sure I did. Yeah, most 'em. The reason why most women end up in prison is through drugs or domestic violence and they kill their husbands. They kill their abusers. You see that a lot in prison, women who have taken—been abused for so long, 'til finally they kill their abuser. And the system don't protect them; they go to prison.

And did you see a lot of lesbianism in prison?

Yeah, I had a girlfriend in there. But I already had a girlfriend before I went in there. [Laughter] So, it was like, okay, and she came to see me while I was locked up, too, and she had a man. It was just all confusing. I'm telling you, my whole sexual thing was—my whole sexual identity and my whole sexual thing was so confusing—like I lived so confusing in my sexual life because I couldn't never, put it all in what I—what I was, so I was just always living erratically, sexually.

I'm asking these questions because there's so much myth and misinformation about what goes on in prison. And you know, some people say that men will have homosexual relationships and women do, but then some people say that it's only while they're in the pen that they do. Did you think that the women that you knew who were engaging in sex in prison were only doing it because there was nobody else to have sex with?

Yeah. Yeah, I met several of 'em that—who was like that. I also met some who were just truly lesbian women, old-school bulldaggers who just ended up in prison because of their criminal lifestyle. They was doing other stuff. But they were what they—what my mother and them used to call bulldaggers. That's what they were. And a lot of women went there, and so they got with those old-school bulldaggers or whoever that was there that were already gay, and that's how they were able to pull 'em because they already— they want to, it was having sexual gratification. And so, yeah, they sought that out; and once they were outta there, they never engaged in any type of that behavior. And if you'd accused them of that, then they'd be ready to fight you. [Laughter] Men and women. [. . .] I took this course this summer, and it was talking about down-low men who actually have sex with other men and still have a wife or whatever. But they don't wanna call themselves gay, and so I don't know. [. . .]

Have you ever considered moving out of the South?

I have. I have. I definitely have, and I don't know if that's gonna be something, and I'm definitely making sure that when I'm done with school, that I put in applications in other states. I've talked to Lori about that, if I get a good job offer in another state, will she be willing to relocate. And she owns her own business, so it's like, "Oh, what you talking about? What you talking about?" And I know it'd be hard to get started in your own business somewhere else. And that's just like a question mark in our future. But I know that even in my field, that the money is better in other states, too. 'Cause Texas ain't gonna pay no social worker nothing. Doesn't matter your degree, unless I decide to go back and teach, and I wanna be in the meat and potatoes of effecting change. Yeah, I can't affect maybe if I reach enough students who go out and effect change, I can affect it, but I want to personally to get my hands dirty with it.

How and when did you meet your current partner?

I had always seen Lori at the meeting; ten years ago when I started going to the meetings, I would see her there. But it wasn't up until after I formally—I stopped seeing people for a year and admitted to—and came out to my friend, and she helped me walk through that process, that I actually saw Lori. And now, I had seen her, but I hadn't *seen* her. And so, I don't know what happened and what made the difference, and what I believe is like it was just—she was supposed to be my partner all the time, but because I wasn't ready yet, then I couldn't see her. And then once I got ready, I seen

Gwen at her college graduation
from the University of Texas.
Courtesy of the narrator.

her, and so I had already been seeing her and so we dated formally. The first thing we went to was one of Sharon's [Bridgforth] plays, and we dated and we just liked each other. And she has heard me sharing in the meetings, she had seen me, too, 'cause I got there and been clean and seeing me walk through so many things. [. . .] I went to her house one day and never left. [Laughter] She had a little apartment and I had a little apartment, and something was wrong with my apartment, and so I said the landlord couldn't figure out where the smell's coming from. I'm like, "I'm not living in here until you find that." I went to Lori's apartment, I never left. And when I went back, it was to move my stuff and we moved into another house.

And how long have you been together?

Five years, June 8th, five years. [. . .]

How would you describe your involvement in the gay community?

I'm just now getting my feet wet with that. Peers for Private School have been making sure I attend their functions. They asked me to be a ally, be on the committee, one of the people where they go into different classrooms and instead of just talking at people about the gay community, they do little plays and little skits to show how hard it is and how they feel when people identify them in a negative way. So, they asked me to do that, but my schedule's so crazy. I always try to attend allgo functions, I go to the dances, and I want to do more with that and start to volunteer, you know. I'd like to be more active. I don't know that I will be down at the Capitol and marching or nothing like that, and not because of anything other than, I intend to make a movement of my own as far as in the social work field. I haven't done that yet. Then everybody can see what I support after I make my move. And I don't want people to determine how they interact with me based on they seen me at a rally. [. . .]

How would you describe your political perspectives regarding issues that are issues in the LGBT community?

Right, right. Just like I get to choose what I decide for myself, other people do, too. And so, if Chick-fil-A don't want to sell to gay people, just don't go there. You know what I mean? And if they start to feel the sting, if they got something negative to say about and they antigay, just don't frequent them. Because I just think we get to decide where we go and what we do. And so do they. And so do whatever it is. And so, how many places that we know of personally that we don't talk about that we didn't feel comfortable when we went in there? Well, because they not a big conglomerate, and Chick-fil-A or Chili's or nothing like that, we don't make a big deal about it. But it's just this Joe Schmoe at the corner store, and then you know they treated you fine when you took your ass in there, but you don't say nothing about that. And so, I just need to be very conscious of how I'm advocating because if it's wrong, it's wrong for everybody. And that's what I feel.

And so, my political view if I could get married to you, I wanna be able to leave you my Social Security, you give me yours. I want the same benefits, the same everything. So, if gay marriage is not doing that for couples, it's really not doing anything—'cause we can stay together. We've been together. But I want the same benefits. I wanna be able to leave Lori everything that I've gained throughout my life, because I love her like that. I don't want her to have to struggle to put me away, I don't wanna have her to struggle to help finish taking care of my daughter. I want her to be able to take care of my business, but she can't. So now, people who have really ridiculed, that been down on me, as much as I love my mother, that whole dissed thing about us—about me being gay—you get to come in and decide what happens to me. So, that is what bothers me about that whole deal. And so, if you are saying that legally we can get married, are they getting all the benefits, Social Security? Is everybody agreeing that gay people can be married and now you can be on my insurance, you can go be on my Social Security? If I die, you get my Social Security? If you die—like, old people that's been married. They get each other's Social Security. Do gay people do that? So, even in the states where they said that you can get married, what did they give 'em besides the ability to be married?

See, those are the kinda things that I think needs to have a shift. Because we can just be together; when you saying that we married, what is that? But I want the full benefits of marriage. It's all of that, because I want to leave my partner in a place to be able to support herself, 'cause we've been in a union for all these years just like a couple that's married. That's the expectation that when you die, you just have our stuff. We got a house, you get it. I don't want nobody to be able to come in and talk about, "No . . . y'all wasn't married. This is her property." No. And then she gotta try to fight for that. Now, everybody know we been together all these years, but as soon as something happens, here everybody comes trying to get your shit. You know? I don't want her to have to fight for that, so I just think that if we're gonna do it, do it all the way. Don't half-ass do it. And I'm sure that's why they're just saying, "Yeah, you all just go on and get married." But that's all they getting, and y'all being satisfied with that? Just like, okay, so now you married; now what?

Yeah, 'cause federally, it doesn't mean anything.

Right. Now you's married. Okay. [Laughter] Back in the day, it was arranged marriages. People didn't even love each other, and so marriage didn't mean anything. So, it's like, when did we forget that? Even in the Bible days there was arranged marriages, and it was like, "I'll give you a cow and some chickens and you take my daughter." If we wanna go all the way back there, as black people, then that's how marriage was. It wasn't this thing you trying to make it be. And what are you fighting for? If you fighting for the ability to be able to have a full range of man/woman/husband to whoever you are, that thing—we ain't getting that. That's not what they giving us. They giving us the ability to say that we live in the same house—which we was doing that before we got married. [Laughter] And so, I think that's why I'm saying we have to know what we fighting for.

Like I really, really believe that Obama just didn't get a chance to [. . .] do everything that he could've done, because they fucking stopped him at every turn. We'll vote you in. Yeah, no, first black man, ha, ha, ha. But what has he really been able to do for us? Because every time he do something, they wanna stop it. They *have* stopped it . . . and they gonna continue to stop it. And if he don't get voted in, you can forget that Obamacare. That's gonna be OuttaThereCare. [Laughter] It wasn't supposed to take effect 'til 2014, they convinced him to wait that long so that, "Oh, you probably won't even be in office." So, if he ain't in office to defend it, it ain't going nowhere. So, it's like we gotta know what we're fighting for. I vote for you because I know that you have a vision. You didn't get to fulfill the vision. I saw the vision, and I would like to see people who don't have the ability to go to the doctor and they find out years later they got cancer, because they didn't have the ability to go to the doctor because they didn't have insurance. That's what I'd like to see happen, for those people. Why wouldn't we? Other countries are doing it and have been doing it, and it's been successful. We have the highest death rate, we have the highest mortality rate, we have the highest obesity rate—we are the highest everything in the United States. And so, politically, I just think that as for black people, we need to be looking at other stuff. We need to be really getting in touch with what's gonna help us in the long run. And so, my focus is policy in the social work school, and because I'm at the University of Texas, I'm gonna take every advantage that I can get and meet everybody that I know. 'Cause I tell you, I'm aiming for DC, 'cause I'm telling you, there is policies that are not in place that could effect these kinda changes. Then we wouldn't have to be wondering what we fighting for.

What has been the impact of HIV/AIDS on your life?

My auntie died from AIDS. Her and my best—one of my best friends died from it, so I have a personal—I've had personal attachments to it. Another good friend of mine had it, and I love her to death, and just like watching her not take care of herself in a healthy way kills me, because what I realize is they've come up with something where it may not be the healthiest for you, it prolongs your life. And I believe that people didn't know. However it got here, whoever gave it to who, whatever, people didn't know that it was here. And so, as people got it, continued to get infected, that was one thing. Now we know. Now we know, and there's not enough being done to educate, especially the black people, 'cause you cannot, absolutely cannot have unprotected sex. You just can't do it; in this day and time, you just can't do it. You cannot believe that just because she's a fifteen-year-old student that she may not be positive, just cannot believe it. So, they've taken out sex education out of the schools, so they're not getting it, and so the highest rate right now in Texas is that age range, from fifteen to twenty-one. And I know, because I did a whole report about HIV in Texas because I'm affected. It just baffles me.

I was talking about black men who go to prison and have sex with other black men and then come home to their wives and infect them. And so, that's big. Okay, well, then you need to do something in the prison. And even though you don't wanna protect, pass out condoms 'cause that means men are having sex, then what are you gonna do? Well, just infect all the niggers and then we won't have to worry about it. You know what I mean? So, as black people, we need to be proactive, like no. We need to come up with something for our brothers. If they're having sex with men in there [. . .] we need to do something with that because then they're gonna come home and infect all the women. Then what? There goes a generation that we could kill off because nobody cares. So, we just need to be coming up with other kinda ways. Put sex education back in the schools so these kids can know that, this disease is real. It affects you and it will take you outta here. But it's like people just like, "If it don't happen to me, I don't have to worry about it. If I ain't got it, it don't matter." And then there's these stars and all these people fighting the virus in Africa. I understand they don't have a lot of resources. Do you know how many people don't have resources right here in the United States that's affected? And I don't never see nobody saying we having a function and we having everybody come to sing and we coming together based out any of these places that's highly infectious—San Francisco, the community, we wanna help promote safe sex. Nothing. You don't hear that. You hear it in these little rallies, with these little organizations who don't have enough funding to really be effective. And so, HIV is really personal for me, you know. I'm not afraid of it; I'll be right up in the trenches with people who've been sick with it. I wiped asses, cleaned, I'm not afraid like that, because I just believe that you're supposed to care for who you love. Put your gloves on, do what the people say, and you'll be fine. You know what I mean? You'll be fine, but for kids and for people who are having unprotected sex, they need to know the dangers and the risk that they play to the population of black people.

Do you think that because there's a perception out there that lesbian women in particular are less susceptible to HIV/AIDS, that there's less use of protection among lesbians?

Probably so. I'm sure. Well, especially if you have a long term of being a lesbian, like you've been a lesbian long before the virus came out or whatever and so you never—or you never slept with a man, so you don't think, and then but the only way you can be safe with that is if you had the same partner and you all both is tested. How you know? You know what I mean? You don't know what she was doing, no matter what the people tell you. You know what I mean? And so, it's I've been tested, Lori—and we continue to get tested, not only because I was in relationships with men, but also because we were in drug relationships. And so, they didn't know, when the first case came out, how long that person had it. And so, now they're saying they've gotten better, where they can tell within six months and see if you got the T thing that can register that, but I just wanna be safe. You know what I mean? I wanna be safe with my partner. And so, every year, I'm gonna be tested, so if we do decide, we do have unprotected sex, well, so I wanna be protected in my household with my partner. You know what I mean? So, it's okay, let's both go, let's get tested. Let's not not get tested because we're afraid of the results. And I think *that* is a problem. People don't get tested because they're afraid of the result.

What are your favorite memories of growing up in the South?

When they used to come and cut the water fountain on. They would take the top off the fire hydrants and everybody was outside, nobody was worried about nothing. We was just playing. When I was a kid, we used to just play, and we'd just play outside until dusk. And we wasn't worried about what we was gonna eat, 'cause mama done worried about that. And just like growing up in all-black schools, I promise you, I wish we would go back to that. Just knowing that the teachers cared about what you were doing; when you went to the school cafeteria, you wanted to eat in there. [Laughter] 'Cause you knew that old black lady was putting it in there just like she was doing it at the house. You seen black people everywhere. [. . .] And so, but my fondest memory is of just not having a care in the world and being able to run free, play in the water, and eat watermelon.

What are your worst memories?

Being accused of stealing, can't go in the store without them following you around. Have to sit at the back of the restaurant because we were black, when my auntie took me downtown to Woolworth's. We had our own theater. We didn't go to other theaters—we had our own black theater, which was fun to me, but it's like being so segregated and so cut off that when you do interact, you don't know how to act. And so, then you just feel so mistreated. Like that whole swimming pool incident and like having to go swimming, we didn't have hair to be able to go swimming. You know, we had hair that our mamas have to get up every day or we got pressed on Sunday, and so we were different, but it was like, you can't be different. And so, I think that was like my worst—you cannot be different, and so I associated that with everything in my life.

How would you describe the impact your southern upbringing has had on your character?

I do believe that I have integrity, and I think a lot of that comes from being southern born and bred, because they do what they say and say what they gonna do. And I think I have that as a part of my character that I really enjoy. But I also have a level of fear, being in the South as a black person, and a level of distrust that carries over. And so, that part of my character, I can overcome it through—by just persevering. And so, that's another thing that you have to learn to do in the South is persevere through whatever hardships, whatever you face. You just keep moving. But I think that integrity, more than anything else, is a deep-seated South thing and it's bred. It's bred. And when my mother and them, they used to get stuff and or get a bill of groceries on a handshake, "We'll pay you next week." I seen that. And they went back and paid. Get a tankful of gas for work this week, "We gonna pay you next week." It was a handshake and they paid next week. So, that was like you do what you say and you say what you do, people gonna believe in you, and that was just what I saw with my stepfather and my mother and them. They was able to go—there wasn't no credit like it is now. The credit was what I said.

Your word.

Your word. And so, I think that's still important, that was bred in me.

How would you describe your current feelings about being a black lesbian?

Oh, I'm happy as hell. [Laughter] I'm happy as hell. It's like I'm free, and I get to experience being free and being black, and when I do go somewhere and it's a lot of white people around, I don't try to act white. I'm just me. And so, for the first time in my life, even just being a black person, I'm very happy, I'm not ashamed of black. I don't wanna be white. I don't think you got more than me 'cause you white. I can do whatever I wanna do. I believe that. And being a black lesbian, I'm just happy. I'm just happy. I'm happy. It took a long time for me to get in this place, and so I probably I embrace it more than most people would, because it took me so long to get here. So, being a black lesbian in the racially divided Austin, Texas, is like the best thing I probably could be right now, in this time. And I was like, I'm so happy. I'm happy with the person that I'm with, I'm happy with the person that I am, and I'm just like living life and just, okay, what's next?

What regrets do you have, if any, about the life choices you've made?

That I didn't do the college thing straight outta high school, 'cause it just required so much of you, and if I'd've had this, maybe I'd had a better job, and then I just go through that whole thing. Having a felony background just really hampers, has really hampered me throughout my life. I've been able to overcome it and be successful, but it still continues to come up, and it continues to stop me in some aspects.

Now, is that for life or is it—does it go away after a few years?

No, they don't go away. Right. I've been reading both expungement and pardon and the one, even if the governor pardons you, it doesn't come off your record. And the only way to do that is to have it expunged, and they don't expunge certain things and certain crimes. And so, I've just been looking into all of that, because I know in order to be licensed, I might have a real hard time with the licensing board to be licensed in Texas. And I may have to end up going somewhere else to be licensed, too, so that may be my reasoning for leaving Texas, 'cause Texas don't never give you a break once you've been convicted. But I'm willing to do whatever is necessary to do that. But yeah, this is some of the regrets that I have to even do that, gonna have to go through those measures. And just all the people and the men that I've damaged along the way with my inability to be honest, I think, is another one of my biggest regrets. I do not regret the kids that came out of it. That must've been the purpose, but I do regret the fact that, for some of 'em, we can't be friends. Like me and her [the daughter] daddy, we can't even talk. Especially when he heard I was gay. That was the ultimate. So, if I could've done anything different, it would've been that.

I'm Just a Black Woman in America

Lori Wilson

11

Lori entered the house at the tail end of my interview with her partner, Gwen (see chapter 10). Gwen commented to Lori that I should be a therapist because I was such a good listener. Perhaps she was preparing me for Lori's story, which was just as compelling as Gwen's and with similar experiences, especially with substance abuse.

Like Gwen, Lori takes a pragmatic view about her experience with addiction and believes it was a necessary part of her journey. She's been clean for over thirty years now but still takes one day at a time. What I love about Lori is her rugged exterior (she swears a lot) that barely camouflages her open spirit. The interview took place on September 10, 2012, at her home in Austin, Texas.

I was born in Seguin, Texas on October 22, 1962, and I think at the age of two we moved to Houston, Texas, and so primarily I was raised in Houston. I lived in Houston from that period of time until 1978, at which time I moved to Angleton, which is about forty-something miles south of Houston, in a country town called Angleton, Texas. And I lived there until 1987, and then in 1987 I moved to Austin, and I've been in Austin since then.

And how would you describe your childhood? You moved around a lot.

Well, we really didn't move around a lot, we just [moved] from Seguin to Houston. I'm sure it had a lot to do with the fact that my mother—I'm not really sure about that story, but I think my mother attempted to leave my father. I think at that time I was the third of five kids, and then my dad just moved to Houston to be with us, so of course then they ended up having like five more kids, and so it was a lot of us, and my dad was a construction worker. My mom just stayed pregnant most of the time, so she didn't work a whole lot.

473

Lori in San Antonio, 2015.
Courtesy of the narrator.

So, there was eight of you in total?

My oldest brother ended up staying in Seguin with my grandparents, my dad's parents, and so it was nine of us that came, so it's ten altogether. And so, then it was them, so a dozen eggs didn't do very much in our house. So, we lived in Houston and my dad. My mom didn't work a whole lot, and then when she did she worked as a maid, and my dad was a construction worker, and so it was just kind of in and out. So, what always stands out the most for me and my childhood is that we were just very poor. We lived in the same house for a few years, and then we moved a couple of times. So, we moved throughout Houston, and I think at one point we moved, when I was like in the fifth grade, to live in a better neighborhood and a better house or something, so I'm guessing my dad must've gotten a better job or something happened. I had a brother right under me, he went to live with my mom's mom, and then I had a sister, a younger sister, and she lived with her godmother, and then my youngest sister lived with my aunt and uncle. So, they had ten kids, but some were there and some were not. I just remember, like, "Damn, every time she go to the store she come back with a baby." [Laughter] The last baby was born at home, and so it was like, "Oh, mama done found a baby on the porch."

It was all very crazy. So, she was very sick with that baby, and every time she had these kids it's like it was so obvious in my life because every time she left I got sick.

Every time your mother left?

Every time my mother left. If she left me, it felt like she left me, and so I would get physically sick, and so people for many years thought, "Oh Lord, she ain't gonna never leave home, she just ain't gonna never leave home." Like when I went to school, I think I went to school when I was six, and so I just cried the first week. I just didn't want to be there. I just hated school and wanted to be at home with my mother, but I was actually the first one to leave home basically. So, went through that. My dad was an alcoholic, very abusive physically. He fought my mother a lot, terrorized the house most weekends, unpredictable. You didn't really know if he was going to buy everybody on the block ice cream or if he was going to come home and try to kill everybody.

Wow. And yet they were still having babies.

Yeah, they were still having babies, and actually my mother was probably tired of having babies, but at that time unless the husband consented to her having the surgery she couldn't do it, and he never consented, and with the last baby that she had at home, the doctor just did it for health reasons because she was very sick, lost a lot of blood with that baby. It was just very crazy. At some point, my mother started dating the guy that is my stepfather now, and one day we left home on the weekend and we never went back. We never went back. I was fourteen at the time. We would sneak around and leave and go be with him on the weekends sometimes, but we would always go back, but this particular weekend we left and we didn't go back. It wasn't a discussion they had with us. I guess my mom just decided she had had enough.

And how many of you kids were around at that time?

It was probably four of us at the time. Then I met this boy. I was fourteen. At the time that I met him my mother had people that had some kind of concern that I wasn't liking boys. It's like, it was cool. We played basketball, shoot marbles, steal bikes, fix bikes, go-carts; that was cool, but not really. So, when I met this boy, they just kind of got excited [laughter] that I was even interested and just kind of pushed that issue. He lived in Angleton, and so he would hitchhike and everything. I was fourteen. He was sixteen. He would hitchhike to Houston to come see me and just all of that. I turned fifteen in October. In November I got pregnant, and then that was in '77. In February of '78 I left home, went to Angleton, and never came back.

Because you were pregnant?

Basically, yeah. My mother was like, "Can't have no babies in my house, can't stay in my house having no babies," kind of stuff. She never really said that to me, but I could hear her—and never talked to me about it, never said, "Are you pregnant, what are we going to do?" any of that. But the message was just very clear, and so I was going to have to have an abortion or whatever. And so, the guy, he wanted his baby, and his mother was not up for that whole thing happening, and so she was like, "You can come live with us," and I did.

And he's seventeen at this point?

He had just turned seventeen that January. So, when I went to live in Angleton, he was actually in jail at the time for burglary of a building. So, I went there, and for me it was like being grown because I couldn't wait to be grown. I wasn't fast. I just wanted to smoke cigarettes and cuss. [Laughter] And then, of course, that's kind of like your rights of passage in this society. When you have a kid that kind of defines you as an adult: you grown and you got a baby kind of stuff. But what people don't realize is that the responsibility of having a baby don't really make you grown.

What did your mother say?

My mother was angry.

Was she angry that you left, or angry that you got pregnant, or all of the above?

She was angry that all of above, yeah. It was like, if I think about it, it should have been like, what are you thinking? You need to take your ass back home kind of stuff. But that never happened, and the relationship was like basically the carbon copy of my parents' relationship, so it was like he was abusive, he cheated, he did all of that, so we just fought like we didn't have nothing else to do most of the time.

So, you stayed together with his mother?

We stayed together with his mother, had the first baby in August of '78. So, at the age of fifteen, I started having sex, I got pregnant, I left home, and had the baby that year.

What was the baby?

It was a girl, Tanisha. [. . .] And then nine months later, I was pregnant again, another little girl. By now I'm just feeling stuck in this situation, and my mother [. . .] they never say that you can come home.

Did your mother meet the grandchild?

Oh yeah, she knew.

So, you were seeing your mother?

Yeah, yeah, yeah. She was from Angleton, and so they would periodically come to Angleton. Her sister lived in Angleton and all that kind of stuff, so she had relatives there and that kind of thing. And so, my mother was there. Me and my partner were talking about this yesterday, I think. This weekend we had these conversations about our past lives. My mother actually was at the hospital when I gave birth to my daughter. They were going to do the little epidural or whatever, and so she told people "no." You know? So, it was kind of like it led me to believe that it was in my best interest, because I wasn't going to sit still long enough, and I was going to be paralyzed, but what I later realized was that she was trying to punish me.

She wanted you to feel all that pain.

Yeah, and I did. But it wasn't enough to deter me apparently from getting pregnant again. And so, got pregnant again and just already realizing that it's not a good situation with this man.

Had you dropped out of school?

Yeah, I dropped out of school when I was in the ninth grade, which meant I had an eighth grade education. Then just kind of had the baby. She was born December of '79. I was working, started working at a nursing home, and this lady next door was supposed to watch the kids and she couldn't, and so my mother-in-law watched them. And I got home from work and the baby was dead. Actually, I came home from work, the oldest one was like [mimics a baby crying] "eh, eh," you know. I got two kids, neither one of them talked, both of them sucking bottles, both of them on Pampers, and she was wanting these crackers, and I was like, "shhh." So, I was asking my mother-in-law where's the baby at, and she was like, "The baby's in there and she's still asleep." And so, I go in there and sit on the side the bed and she's not asleep, and I'm thinking, because this baby don't sleep hard at all, like anything wakes her up so "Shhh, be quiet." And so, she's not waking up, she's not doing anything. I was just like what's going on over here. So, I shook the bed, she shook with the bed, shook the bed, and she shook with the bed, and she was dead and that was just really crazy. So, he, the dad, he was already "that ain't my baby, that ain't my baby, that ain't my baby" kind of shit.

Were y'all married?

We got married. We eventually got married when I turned eighteen and he was in jail.

Again?

Again. And on his way to prison, so the rule basically was that he couldn't have any contact visits unless we were married, so we got married. It wasn't because we was in love. [Laughter] It was convenience, that kind of thing. So, because he was like really stressing the hell out of me with this baby, and then when she died he was just devastated, and so I was just angry at him for being so devastated.

He said it wasn't even his.

Yeah, it's as recently as the night before, so that kind of thing.

Did they find out what happened? Was it sudden infant death syndrome, SIDS?

Yeah, that's what they ended up, because that was back in '80, so that's what they called it. So, they investigated and all that, and I just remember going to the hospital and riding in the ambulance with her, and that was like the longest ride of my life, and it probably was like five minutes, ten at the most, but it just seemed like a long ride. No panicking, no real emotion at this point because I'm probably by now so emotionally detached from life that I don't know what the fuck to feel. Happiness wasn't a good deal in my house. Sadness, you too poor for that. And so really the only acceptable emotion was anger, and everybody understood that, and so, of course, needless to say, I fought a lot growing up. So, you couldn't say stuff like, "My feelings are hurt," "That made me sad," you know? [. . .] Those were not my household words and nothing like that, so that's how you dealt with whatever it was, whether it was sadness, whether it was disappointment, whatever. You just got mad and everybody understood mad. So, she died, and probably a few months after that we ended up moving away from his mom's house and getting our own place.

You and your daughter?

And him.

Oh, I thought he went to jail.

He went to jail. He went to jail and got out of jail, went to jail, got out of jail. The story of his life.

Why did you stay with him?

One, I was still very young and [. . .] he was crazy too. At that point the thought, considering leaving, that wasn't an idea at that point. What would I do? So, it's like my mother had already put me away from her house and had never said you can come back. And then one of my younger sisters, actually the one under me, the sister up under me because there's six girls and four boys, she gets pregnant when she's seventeen and my daughter I guess is like three, but she gets to stay at home. She gets to stay at home. She gets to continue to go to school. The baby's born. The other grandmother lives across the street, so the baby's between their houses to make sure that their daughter and son can still go to school, finish school, and all of that, and so I was kind of resentful about that. But to this day, I've always been pretty committed to whatever it is I'm going to do, so I've always lived by own rules—good, bad, indifferent—and yes, took some bumps along the way. So, when my daughter was born, I just remember making that commitment to her, thinking it doesn't really matter. I'm going to take care of you no matter what. I decided this, and this is what this is going to be. So, we moved, and he now is trying to gather his thoughts, and he gets a job working for the railroad, and that's a pretty good job. We living in this little one-bedroom shack house kind of deal, but it's our house. So, we are very young and doing better than grown people, and I'm working, he's working, and trying to raise this kid. Plus, I think when my daughter died, I got pretty detached emotionally, and so he was still pretty attached to her and that was his baby. He didn't know as much about being a father as I knew about being a mother, but him probably even less. I had some idea because girls do, because it's real alright for us to play with dolls, so we learn that whole thing, nurturing my baby, get the bottle, change the Pampers, baby don't cry kind of dolls and shit. [. . .] So, that was all about preparation where with boys, it's like, if boys get caught playing with dolls it's like a whole meltdown in the house. [Laughter] So then they have these kids, and society expects them to be fathers, and they never learned how to nurture anything, so they don't know what to do with that. But you know, that was her daddy, and that was his baby. And we got high. We got high. We got high. We got high all the time. We got high. That was the thing that we probably had in common.

Was it reefer?

We smoked weed, drinking before I got pregnant with my oldest, I was drinking. I was like a blackout drinker.

As a teenager?

Yeah, as a teenager, when I was fourteen.

How were you getting alcohol?

My aunt, my mom's sister. It wasn't even a big deal. I look at that now, and I would just start fighting people if they did that to my kids now. You know what I'm saying? Because like, my partner has a fifteen-year-old that lives in the house, and she has a twenty-year-old that lives in Kansas that go to K [Kansas] State [University], and my daughter is thirty-four. Her husband's in the military, so they're stationed like ten miles away from K State, so they hang out, and so I'm like, "Don't be letting them be down there drinking either." And she's like, "No ma'am, can't drink. Can't drink on my watch." So, it's like that whole idea of them drinking is just like, no. [. . .] We tell them okay, you know your parents are both drug addicts, right? You might be waking up something in yourself, and you're going to have some problems, you might have some problems. You got to be careful with that. So, yeah, we got high, and I drank, and then I got pregnant, and I stopped drinking, but I still smoked weed. I smoked weed throughout my pregnancies. And thank God, they didn't do what they do now, which is test the babies. That little baby would've been over there in CPS [Child Protective Services] custody. So, smoked weed, and it was probably a couple years before I started drinking again. Well, actually the day that the baby died I remember like making a conscious decision about getting drunk and don't really remember getting drunk but drank, but I don't remember getting drunk, and so I think at that period is when I started drinking again. Not a whole lot, didn't really drink, but it got progressively worse. And then at some point, I had a bright idea—I'm always a sucker for a good idea—so I thought I would start selling weed. It was sell weed, keep some weed to smoke, sell weed, just kind of keep that going.

Were you growing it?

No, I was buying it.

And then reselling it?

Yeah. The whole intent was to just not have to buy weed, have enough to smoke and sell it, and just have enough. Well, the demand got great, and then it went from a quarter pound of weed to a half pound of weed, and from a half pound of weed to a pound of weed, and so it just kind of got bigger. But I'm still working, he's still working.

Where were you working at this point?

At this point I'm working at a nursing home, at a different nursing home, and so I was thinking earlier that day, how am I going to get home? A couple hours later, the police was coming to pick me up to take me home. [Laughter]

Really? Had they been watching you?

Yeah, apparently, and they raided the house and came and got me and took me back to the house, and it was just a mess in there. Damn, you didn't have to knock the bird cage over. Ain't nothing you can see in there, what'd you do that for? The flour, the cereal, it was just a messy mess, just a mess. [. . .] So, we have this Polaroid camera, and so I'm high, he high, we just decided we just going to take naked pictures. [Laughter] Naked pictures, lingerie, so we got like a couple of photo albums of pictures, and so the police come and they take the photo albums. I was like, "Why you got to take that?" "Well, there's pictures in here." I'm posing and smoking weed, and they like you smoking weed. I'm like, "I ain't never said I didn't smoke weed, but there ain't nothing in there showing me selling weed or anything." So, they take me on to jail, and a little while later he shows up at the jail. Somebody told him that they took me to jail.

So, they didn't arrest him?

He wasn't at home, and it wasn't him that the confidential informant got, but because he had a history and they knew that he was selling, which is who they wanted was him, just because he like to run his damned mouth all the time. He just could be a real asshole and cuss the police out, and this was a pretty small city, just a little place, and so people knew you. So, he knew the police was watching us. I didn't know that. He knew that because when he got there, the police was like, "Didn't I tell you I was going to get you?" and he was like, "Didn't I tell you to come get me?" And so, he had known that and so he laughing, "Heh, heh, heh." I'm thinking, real funny, you know he had that photo album. [Laughter] So, he just comes unglued and just starts just cussing the police, calling them all kind of perverts and everything. "Yeah, you all looking at my wife." So, he was really upset, and the man tells him that he's going to go back there and get some tape and put it on his mouth if he don't shut up, and he's like, "Yeah, go get it and put it on my mouth and then take it off and put in on my dick and then I'm going to put it on your mouth." He's that kind of nut. So, we go to jail. Because I was actually the one that was doing the dealings with the guy selling the weed, so he came and got me. He paid my bond to get out and all of that.

Where was your daughter?

With my mother-in-law, because I was at work, so she had been at Head Start, so she was there, which was good, which was a good thing. So, we go to jail, get out of jail, and go on with life, and of course now I'm thinking, "Okay, now I've got to pay this attorney. So, I got to sell some more weed." [Laughter]. And actually the weed that was in the house wasn't as much weed as I had because the majority of it was down the street at a friend's house. But what I don't know is, is that this guy is using cocaine is what I don't know. Like we had used it, we had snorted a couple of times. Back then, cocaine was mostly powder cocaine, and back then it was a rich man, white man high because it was pretty expensive. If you had a little cocaine they would talk about you was the shit. So, we could get some powder cocaine and it'd last us a couple of weeks you know? A gram of cocaine, because we just recreational with it, but I don't know that he's using cocaine and then—

This is the supplier?

No, this is my husband, so I don't know that he's actually using cocaine to the extent. Like we used it together, but he had by now started shooting dope.

And you didn't know.

And I didn't know. It was just kind of like a decline in life because there was something real attractive about that. Like, he had this guy that lived around the corner that shot dope, too, and so he would always like, because he didn't know how to hit himself, so he would always get this guy to do it. And so, this guy wasn't at home, so I guess he geeking, he tripping, so he don't give a shit at this point, so he comes to the house and he's trying to fix it and fix it and fix it, and so he's trying to hit himself and he keep missing, keep missing and I'm just like, "What are you doing?" Like what the hell? And so I say, "Okay, stop that, let me see that," and so I hit him, and the guy comes and he does it again, and so the guy, he does a shot of dope, it's like he just breaks out in a sweat, and so I just think, I don't know why, it was something appealing about that to me, and so now I want to try it, not today, but the next time he gonna do it I'm going to try it. So, I was like, "Oh yeah, I'm going to try the cocaine." And so, the first time I tried it, the needle got clogged up so that was a sign from God I'm sure: "Stop that. Stop, don't do that. Don't do that."

So, it never entered your system.

Yeah. So a couple weeks later it does, so it's just like, "Oh, oh, oooohhhh, okay," and so we started shooting dope. And so now we got a whole habit.

How can you afford it though?

We can't. We can't. [. . .] He was working, I was working, and we selling dope, and I was selling speed, and so we just had like money. I had money. Well, when you start doing that kind of shit, it's like you now shooting up your profits and that kind of stuff. Then he started stealing the weed, of course, because that's what he did, and selling it and that kind of stuff, and saying I fronted this person this or that person this, and really what he had done was sold it and got the money and bought dope. And so, never could recoup, and so of course the police come get me from work, so I lose my job. We just, it got, it got progressively worse. The drug using got bad pretty quick, and then we pretty much at a point where we're not homeless but we're living in a house where it's like no running water, and something happens and he goes back to jail, and so he's on his way to prison. [. . .] We shooting dope. We shooting dope. We killing it. We shooting dope, and I get sick, and so I go to Houston, and my aunt comes and gets me and checks me to Houston because she thinks I need to get out because my eyes had turned yellow.

Is this the same aunt that was giving you alcohol?

Yeah. [Laughter] And so she like, this is not right, something's not right with this. So, I go to Houston and I'm there, and he's coming to Houston with my mother-in-law and the baby. Well, the baby with me. He's coming to Houston and he's begging and crying and want me to come back, and she's begging and crying and wanting me to come back and this whole thing, so I go back.

I thought he was in jail at this point.

No. So I go back. He goes to jail. He gets out on bond and so he's waiting, right? And I'm out on bond, too, because we're still waiting to finish this case. And so, when I get back, I think I'm gone about a week maybe, maybe two. When I get back his mom had moved into the house and so now lights on, water running, and so I go back and we living there. He goes to prison. He gets a two-year sentence and he stays for six months, and I'm weighing probably about ninety pounds or so. It was just bad. So, he goes to prison and so life is going to be good. "We going to get this back, we'll get it back. We going to be living like we were living." So, it sounded good to me. Found Jesus. He learned his lesson. So, he gets out right before Christmas, a couple days before Christmas, and by January the 6th, which was his birthday, we were back shooting dope, and I thought, mm-mm. Got to come out, got to come out, got to come out. And so I told him, "When school is out, I'm going to leave you," because I was waiting for my daughter to get out of school. I said, "When school is out, I'm going to leave you." But before school can get out in March he goes back to jail, and so I just stay. I call the parole board, and they tell me when he's getting out, and so I got a plan how I'm going to work this out, and so I'm going to work until this point, which was supposed to be in November when he was going to get out and he got out in August, but I was pretty done with the relationship, so everything that happened the first time he went to jail and all that. He was so rowdy in the county jail they just moved him to a state facility. But he manages to get out.

That's what I don't understand, if he is so rowdy and disrespectful to authority, how is he getting out before his sentence?

That's what I'm saying. Because he's really in there on a bond, so his dad goes and gets him, and he gets an attorney and gets him after a few months. So, I'm at work and he calls me. This was like in '86 and he calls me. I'm just surprised because I'm thinking his ass is not going to be home until November. And so, I'm like, "Oh Lord." I called my father. Actually, I called my sister. I don't remember who the hell I called, but anyway, my father and my oldest sister, one of my older brothers, and a cousin came. But because my brother was an alcoholic and the side of Houston they on don't sell the damned 20/20 Orange Jubilee, they got to go back across to the other side of town to get the Orange Jubilee before they can leave. He got to have it for the ride. And so, before they can get there, he done damn near killed me. So, he tries to kill me.

By beating you?

Yeah, he tries to kill me.

Why? Because he knew you were going to leave him?

He thought that I was messing with some other people. He just angry because I'm not doing what he wanted, and that wasn't uncommon for us to be fighting, but this day he was mad. So, he tortured my ass for about an hour and a half.

No neighbors?

Nobody in the house. And so [he kept asking], "Who's number's this? Whose number's this?" I said, "I don't even know what you talking about, whose number is this. And it may have been a number to a doctor or whatever because I'm really not interested in fucking nobody, including you, especially you." But at some point, and throughout that relationship, he said, "You gay?" And I was like, "What?" Because I think he was probably watching some porn movie, and two women were in it, and I think I got aroused with that or something. Something happened, or I don't know if it was just concluded through just watching my best friend who lived down the street and we were like really close and that kind of thing. I liked her, but that was never anything that we, like that was no line to cross. She was married. She was an older woman because, hell, I'm fifteen, having kids, so everybody else is at school that's my age and I'm working, so I'm hanging out with these older people.

So anyway, he carries on for a while, then his sister comes and said my dad is supposed to be coming, and so she was like, okay. So we put these clothes in a basket, and she takes me over to my best friend's house to wait for my dad. So I get there, and I go in the bathroom, and I look in the mirror, and it was just like my face was just, like, it just had lots of knots in it. It was like, "Oh, Lord" and it was like "thump, thump, thump." I was like, what is going on with this. So, of course, I really need to get high now, smoke a joint, get me a beer, and everything. So my dad shows up, and he's with my cousin and my brother and stuff. My cousin sees me and he has a shotgun, so he tells my dad, "Let's go." So they're riding around. He's sitting on the outside of the car with a shotgun waiting, looking for this boy, wanting to kill him. Seen him, shot at him kind of stuff. They come back and get me, and I go to Houston and I leave everything except for this basket of clothes. Everything else—child, job—everything, because by now I'm working at the Sonic Drive-In, back at the Sonic, because that was my first job. So, I'm working back at the Sonic and go to Houston and live with my sister, who was a big ass drug addict and drinker, and so now I'm just done lost my whole mind up there with them because they some real people. They real. They was real, real. They had like piles of cocaine sitting around and shit. They was dealing with the Jamaicans. All kind of shit was going on up there, you know. They was snatching purses. They was real criminals. She was writing prescriptions. Yeah, so they just real criminals. My cousin and his homeboy, they over there running whores. They got prostitutes and shit going on over there. They bumping people on [Interstate] 610 and following them home and robbing them. It was just, that shit was busy. It was busy. So, we going to shooting galleries and shooting up at shooting galleries, which used to be like nightclubs kind of stuff. So, I'm in hiding. He didn't know where my sister lives, but he's over there terrorizing my mother, my youngest siblings, hiding in bushes up at the store. He was trying to find me.

And they don't tell?

They don't tell because they don't know. My younger siblings, they don't know, so they don't want them to know because they kids, so it was like, no. He wouldn't have been able to find [me], because Houston's big as hell but he didn't know where I was. So, I was in hiding about five months, and so I was just losing my mind up there, just back shooting dope, because at this point before that, I had stopped shooting dope while he was in jail. And so, it was kind like of a crossover was happening at the time from being an IV drug user to being a smoker. So, around '85, '86 that started happening. I was smoking crack in Houston. This friend of mine, the one that I've been working with, the one who's my best friend, she came to Houston and she was like, "You need to come home." So, I went back and I lived with her.

He didn't find out?

He went back to jail. He knows because he's actually involved with my best friend's daughter. So, she's telling him what's going on and all that kind of stuff. So, I go to Houston, stay for about five or six months, she comes up there, I'm just out of control. This is my every day all day thing. I'm criminal like hell, been put on probation for eight years and not doing nothing right, getting high as hell, drinking, drinking, drinking excessively, and [. . .] was real hopeless at this point. Life as I knew it was no longer, so I couldn't gather my thoughts. And so she came, and I started losing weight again. She's watching this madness.

So, I go back to Angleton and I live with her, and I go back to work and stay there, but I was smoking crack. We smoking crack. She's smoking too, but she's a different kind of crack smoker. [Laughter] So, I really appreciate[d] her because it didn't matter what the hell was going on, we was going to work the next day. We'd stay up all night and watch the sun come up and we still went to work, and that was her check. Even in my drug using, for me it was like, as long as you got a job, you can always get dope on credit, because now crack is out, so that's just coming through like a fucking tornado, and you just watching women just get butt naked for nothing for men who they never would've thought about having sex with two years ago. So, it was just like, mm-mm, can't suck no dicks, nope, nope, can't do it, can't do it. [Laughter] But I'm just working and smoking. I'm working and smoking. My daughter's still over there with my mother-in-law. So, it's just bad. It's bad. It's a bad situation. So, my commitment to my daughter, I was not living in that commitment, and so that made life worse for me, and I didn't know how I was going to come out of that. Like, what the hell am I going to do? Because there would be times that I would say I wasn't going to smoke and shit, I'd be smoking. So, I could never get a footing to get back right. [. . .]

So, I met this woman when I went to the place to get food stamps. She was there and was just something that was really inspiring about her. She was a black woman, and she was standing up there, and she was so eloquent, and she was pretty and just very eloquent. So, she was down from Houston, and she was driving back and forth doing this presentation for the, it was like this OJT [on-the-job training] kind of training deal that you had to deal if you was getting food stamps or welfare. So, I was like, "Okay." So, I met her, and we just stayed in contact, and so while I was in hiding one of the times, she said she was going to Angleton, and I said, "Well, I need to go and report." She said, "Okay." I said, "My cousin's going to take me." She said, "Well, I'll bring you back home." Okay. So, I meet her, and so we on the way home, and she said, "You know, if you stop getting high, if you stop using drugs, your life would be so much better." I said, "You know, if you started getting high, your life wouldn't be so boring." [Laughter] "Mm, why would I want to do that?" [. . .] That just didn't seem appealing to me. That just didn't seem like anything I want to do.

Because I'm on probation, they make this thing mandatory for us to go to at the courthouse, so these two guys are there from prison, and they're doing this presentation, and the one guy who was like twenty years old, and he was talking, and he's in prison for like ninety years or something like that, and he was a football player and all this stuff, and he was doing really good, and he got on probation, he'd go over and give his probation officer tickets, come see me, so he thought he was bullshitting the system and still doing shit. I think his dad was some kind of prominent attorney in Houston—black kid. Mom was a schoolteacher, so he just thought he could get away with shit, and this time it wasn't going to happen for him, so he's in front of the judge. And so, he told the judge, "I'm using drugs, I'm a drug addict," and so the judge told him, "You should've told your probation officer." I don't know why but that stayed with me. I would never report like I was supposed to, so people would always come to my job [and say], "I haven't seen you in two, three months." They used to be at my office at eight o'clock. So, I didn't do shit right in the first two years I was on probation, and so I had decided that the next time I go I'm going to tell this woman I'm a drug addict, I need some help.

And so, I go in and I said, "I'm a drug addict and I need some help." So, she's like, "Let me see your arms." When I got put on probation I had these tracks on my arms so that was like distinguishing marks on my body, and I was like, "No. I started smoking because I knew you'd be looking for that." She was like, "You don't look like it." Yep, because I understood the game this time. It was rules like eat before you start getting high so you don't lose weight so you don't have those telltale signs, so I had all these rules in place. And so, she was my second probation officer. The first lady she just couldn't send me to prison, so that's why she got rid of my ass, because she knew my situation: I was going with this crazy boy, I had this kid, I was young, and so she just couldn't do her job with me. So, the new PO [parole officer] goes and tells her, "She says she's a drug addict," and so she found me somewhere to go, which is here over at the Austin State Hospital, they got a unit over there. And I'm thinking, "Well, okay, wait a minute, that's for crazy people," and then I thought, I guess I'm crazy just smoking shit, losing my mind, over here doing all kinds of shit because I'm criminal, you know what I'm saying? I'm not going to be a prostitute, but I'm criminal, so we can do something. I'm not fixing to have sex, but I know the objective is everybody is trying to fuck somebody, and I'm not trying to be fucked, so I gotta fuck you. I just had that whole thing about myself.

So, were you stealing?

No. [. . .] My friend, she was cute and she was fine, and dudes, they like smoking with women. She didn't have a husband or anything at the time, and I lived with her, and so they would come and smoke at the house, and they would smoke with us. Well, of course, you start smoking, then they think they going to smoke you out your drawers. [. . .] So, of course, men being who they are, they would always try to get her to get me to come in the room and get butt naked with them and all that all kind of stuff, and it was like, no. But I was attracted to her but just could never get there.

Did she know?

No, nobody knew, nobody knew, because at this time it's like, you can be anything you want to be when you grow up, just don't be that. That was an unspoken thing that you knew about, but you knew that based on how they talked about people that they thought were butch or sissy or punk or whatever, dyke, bulldagger, whatever. So, you knew that that was not going to be what that was going to be. When I was in kindergarten I had a girlfriend. So, I already knew that I was attracted to females and had been.

So, I come to Austin and I go to treatment. My brother goes to treatment the year before and he got treatment, still smoked weed, but he didn't drink no more. That's good. They gave him these pills, Antabuse, and told him if he drank while he was taking them that he would get sick. So my idea of treatment was that I was going to get me some crack pills or cocaine pills or whatever, and then I could still smoke weed and drink. So, when I got to treatment it was like no, that's not how this goes. You can't do anything. I said, "Really?" I don't think this was the place I was supposed to come to. But by now, I'm just so hardened, my heart is just hard, and everything about me is just like crazy, and so I'm just very angry and pretty volatile and just really want to be left the fuck alone. Okay. I go to treatment for twenty-eight days. They say, "Okay, you can do whatever you want to do. You can go back home and smoke you some weed, but I'm telling you you're going to be smoking crack." I said, "I don't want to do that," and so I made a decision that I wasn't going to go back, and so I left there and went to a halfway house for like four months and then got an apartment and stayed in Austin.

You weren't going through any withdrawal or anything?

Not anything physical. People who did heroin, alcohol, they have really bad withdrawal. Alcohol will kill you if you try to detox if you physically addicted. You cannot detox on your own. You could go into d.t.'s [delirium tremens] and die. Heroin just makes you feel like you gonna die. Cocaine was more like psychological. For the first couple of days that I'm there I'm just hungry and tired. The withdrawal wasn't so much, it was just like my body was rested a little bit, and so it was like, "Okay, what are we doing here? Let's go." So, it's like that feeling of wanting to use, needing to use, but in this locked facility and it's not coming out, and I'm in a city where I don't know nothing. I'm just over here on these grounds, and I don't know where to go if I left. You had to be committed because it was the state hospital grounds.

So, this other friend of mine, she took me there, and the judge had to sign off on it, like I was being committed. They could take me to jail and shit, too. So, I was like, "Okay." And it was probation, but I didn't give a shit about that. I couldn't think like that. I didn't have that kind of concern. Shit, I was on probation, I didn't give a shit about probation. That was not a deterrent for me. Because by now I done went to jail myself four or five times in between that time. We go to jail one time and we somewhere sitting on the side of the road shooting dope. They come, police take us to jail. Just different times and stuff had happened, so I don't give a shit about that, and so I stayed and this friend [. . .] tells me if I stop getting high my life would be better. When I decided to go to treatment, I called her and said, "Hey, I'm fixing to go to treatment." She just was excited; she was excited about it. And she was like, "Well, when you get there and you get situated and everything, call me and let me know, and I'm going to come visit you." I was like, "Okay." "I'll be your first visitor" and everything. I called her and she came. She is still my friend today. And I've been clean for twenty-five years. [. . .]

So, now I'm clean. I'm clean and I'm in Austin and I'm in culture shock. This shit is killing me. All these white people is just killing me. It's white people everywhere. [Laughter] It's white people in the treatment center I'm in. I go to the halfway house, I'm the only black person in the damned halfway house. I go to the AA meetings, I'm the only black person in the AA meeting. This shit is just killing me. It's just country as hell, and I'm just looking around. This shit is crazy, and so it just seemed like really separate to me. The black folks seemed real oppressed to me. Crack really hadn't made it here yet. It was on the way, but it hadn't made it here, so they were still very, very country. Still standing under the tree drinking out of the same wine bottle and just country. And they stayed on the east side and they didn't go past I-35, and so I didn't understand it. I didn't understand what was going on in this city and it's just white people. White people, I worked with them but we never lived together, you know what I'm saying? When I was in Houston we lived in a black community. If white kids went to our school, it's because they was in foster care so they were just like us, so they're worst. When I lived in Angleton, we lived across the track, black people. Black people is what I knew, and that's what I knew is black people. And so, I got here and it just was like, I'm volatile as hell living in this halfway house terrorizing these white women. They just leave me on the whole suite on the end wing. There's two other bedrooms, and they don't even want to be on that side of the fucking house with me. They just like over here.

What were you doing?

You know, "Fuck you, fuck, fuck, fuck. Fuck with me if you want to" kind of shit, but the director she was just like, "Come in here." So, she could see something. Because I'm angry. I'm angry. I'm angry because I done left my job. I done left my daughter. I done left the city. I can't get high. I don't know what I'm doing with all of this, because my life is just different, and these white people, it's just white people. So, she was a white woman, and so she talked real hard to me because I'm talking. I said, "I don't really give a shit, you can just put me out of this motherfucker, whatever, I don't even really give a shit." She's like, "No, I'm not going to put you out, and you going to learn how to act. You're going to stay in here." You've got to go to all these fucking meetings, and white people sitting around there talking about this big old nigger this and this big old nigger that, and y'all want me to go in there, I'm not going back to the meetings. And she was like, "That's why there ain't no black people in the meetings, because they do the same thing you doing. They go to the meeting, they don't see no black people, so they don't go back, so next time a black person go there ain't no black people there, so you got to keep going to the meetings, so the next time a black person show up you'll be there." I was like, "It ain't my fucking responsibility. [Laughter] Why I gotta be a damned authority, no." But it made sense somewhere in my head.

So, they moved my probation up here. So, I go in to see the PO, a white woman. She just looking down. She don't look up, she don't talk to me. She look up, but the only thing she could think was that she was going to send me to prison because I was behind on my payments, I wasn't reporting. And I said, "You know what? Do whatever the hell you want to do. I'ma tell you what," so I just go all crazy and so, "I need to see your supervisor. Y'all better keep me away from her." So, the next month I went and I had a black PO. I had a black PO who had just started this specialized caseload for African American people with substance abuse issues that were on probation, with felony probation. Her name was Robin, and she basically became like my mentor. So she could get with me: "You need to stop this shit." So, she started taking me around. I'm all over at the capital and all that kind of shit, and she hooked me up with some more black people, and she started this group called Black LIFE, Living in Freedom Everyday. 'Cause crack done made it, and they got to do something. But the treatment is not designed for black folks. Nothing is. And so she created this whole thing in the community. So, she just helped me. [. . .] My mother-in-law died, and so my daughter came to live with me.

How old was she at this point?

She's nine. She's going on ten.

And you had been away for how long?

Eighteen months. So, I go to treatment, go to the halfway house, get out. I'm probably six months clean, so I call her because I got this apartment and so I want her to come and live with me. She don't want to come, so I'm just sick. And so her grandmother's like, "You going to leave Big Mama? Big Mama's going to miss you," and so she was like, "Well, I don't want to go." So, I was like, "Oh Lord, I don't need this shit here." So, it was Christmas and I was coming home for Christmas, and she wanted this Cabbage Patch doll, so I had to bring her this Cabbage Patch doll. This guy that lived here was going that way, and my mom was going to pick me up, and then we was going to go to Angleton and get my daughter. [. . .] Of course, Crazy [her husband] is not in prison at this time. He's just out of prison.

And still on drugs?

Well, not necessarily, I don't think at this point. [. . .] I get clean in '87 and I'm almost a year clean, and one of the people that worked at the treatment center that helped me get through that with success—with black people—saved me from getting kicked out, so they were really trying to keep me on track, and so she came over a Sunday morning, like 7:30, and I was like, "What are you doing?" Because the place I moved into was across the street from the state hospital where she worked at, and so she came over. "What's going on?" So, she was like, "Well, I need to talk to you." And I was like, "Okay." So, she talking and she said, "Well, your mama called me, and she said that your daughter's father is supposed to be HIV-positive, and so you need to get tested." And I said, "This motherfucker is going to kill me yet, he's still trying to kill me." And so, the only reason that I did not get high was because it was Sunday morning, and they don't sell alcohol until twelve o'clock, and I didn't know where no drugs was because I didn't know about the drug scene in Austin yet. And so, I was like, "Oh my God." So, it took probably a week or so before I decided to go get tested, and then of course that's when it took two weeks before you get the results, and so this woman who was my sponsor in recovery, she was like, "You can look at it like this, you only die once, so. . . ." [Laughter] And so I was like, "Okay." And so at this time, people find out and die. BAM! They were dying quickly. But he's in prison, right? He's in prison at this time, and he gets out, and he said that they got the name wrong, the wrong name and all this kind of stuff. So, his mom has a heart attack and dies basically in his arms, and my daughter who's living with them goes to sleep, her grandmother's living, and she wakes up and she's dead, and so she's crazy, still having a lot of anxiety around death. You know? So he said, "No, it wasn't me. They had the name wrong." So, we go on with life. I test and I'm not positive, and oh, Lord have mercy. So, I'm clean, right? And so now I've got this white woman who's sponsoring me, this first white woman. You know what a sponsor is, right?

Mm-hmm.

Like, go to AA and that kind of whole thing.

And it's usually someone who's been a user themselves.

Yeah, yeah. So, this whole sexuality thing is still on my plate, like it ain't going away. I haven't smoked, it ain't going away. I been clean, it ain't going away. It ain't going away.

So, up until this time you've never had anything with a woman.

Uh-uh. Uh-uh. So, I'm twenty-four, twenty-five at this point, and so she cute, and I tell her, and I said, "Look, let me tell you something. I am dealing with my sexuality right now, and I need to tell you this because I don't know how people are going to act or whatever, and so if you need to, like, detach yourself from me so you don't have to be rolled up in this and people don't have to think that about you, because I'm fixing to have to do some shit with this." [Laughter] So, I said, "You're attractive and I'm attracted to you." And she says, "Well, I'm attracted to you, too." I thought, really? Okay. Okay. And so, she ended up being like the first one. This was a terror in my life. This was a terror. This was a terror in my life because she was bisexual, and I didn't really understand that whole gay thing, how it worked in the first place, and then you got this bullshit going on. It's like, oh my God.

And she wasn't supposed to have that kind of relationship with you anyway.

And she was not. She was not. I'm real new to sobriety. She knew that. She knew that, you know what I'm saying?

But yet she didn't step off the case.

No, she just kept right on going right there. We had some dealings with each other, and I was pretty obsessed with her, and really, she was just *sexual*. She wasn't *bisexual* or nothing. She was just *sexual*. Whatever she wanted to be doing was what she was doing. So, that didn't really matter to her. The first three relationships I had was with white women, and it was like, because I didn't see no black people. I didn't see any black people! And I'm like, "Oh my God, this is killing me!" So, it's like in two of them that I was in a serious relationship with, that I lived with, their parents hated black folks. You know? That whole thing, and then I thought because you chose me I had to go with that because this was the first woman that I lived with. Like, it was not necessarily a blind date, but we talked and we were supposed to hook up, and I was going to go pick her up, and her friends would drop her off at a gas station because she was going to let a friend use her car. So, she gets out the car, and I'm backed in, and she gets out the car and walks in front of the car, and by the time she gets to the middle of the car I'm thinking, uh-uh. And she gets in the car and we go hang out, and I ended up being with this woman for like eighteen months, but she was real *invested* in helping me raise my daughter. So, she made more money than I did, and so she just had these ideas, and I thought, okay, well, maybe this is how this go. They choose you and you just go see why. [Laughter] So, she cheated and so we broke up. And my daughter was in Houston. It was the summer and she had went to stay at my mom's house, and her aunt had lived in Angleton, her dad's sister and shit. She came back and there was a whole new woman in there. And so, we lived together for two and a half years. We wasn't attracted to each other. Not really. I think we made it work at times where we just, okay, we need to do something. Since you here then I guess I'll be with you. But it was like more a roommate situation. Looking back at it, it was more that than anything. So, she cheated, but I was never emotionally available either, and I wasn't necessarily attracted to them. It was like, in order to be gay you had to be with somebody to make it real for the other people.

But before we even get to all of that, I sent my mother a letter, and it's on a long legal yellow page, five or six pages, and this whole, "I'm not really trying to hurt you, I'm not trying to do nothing but I'm gay. I'm a lesbian." And so, my mother being who she is, she tries to gather up my siblings so everybody can read the letter. Well, that don't work out for her, so as they came by the house she just let them read the letter. [Laughter] It was kind of split. It was a split there. The younger two they didn't really give a shit because they didn't really understand it, didn't really care. "I don't care," whatever. Two of my older sisters that were under me, they were just like, "What?" My older sister, she was like, "Hey, read the letter. You alright?" I'm like, "Mm-hmm." One of my brothers, he started crying, and then my older brother, he was like, "That's my sister's shit, I don't give a shit." My oldest brother at this point I don't even know where the hell he's at. We don't even know where he's at.

Like to this day?

To this day. Like he just decided for whatever reason that he was not coming back around, and that was, the last time I seen him is when my daughter was like two, maybe.

Wow. So you don't even know if he's alive.

No. He was in the Navy for many years, got out the Navy. So, he didn't come home when my grandparents died, the people that raised him, that kind of thing. We contacted him through the Red Cross because we didn't know where he was, and we thought if anything that would be, and he didn't. So, I don't know what the hell he's doing, so they were pretty split, and they also like, "Okay, well damn, is that what happened because you stopped smoking crack? Well, smoke some crack then, shit. [Laughs] Is that what happen? She went to Austin and stopped smoking crack, and now she a lesbian? What the hell is that?" [Laughter] So, that seemed very weird. And then my best friend, I told her. And so, my daughter, when she comes and lives with me, she's going on ten and I tell her. She's like, "Okay, can I put that picture on the wall, and you going to let me go to the pool?" So, she don't really get it, either. And she turned thirteen or so and she gets it. She gets it. She now understands what that means, and she just lose her whole mind.

I had to make a decision about my life in that moment because she was really upset, so I had to make a decision about how I was going to live. Was I going to live for her, or was I going to live for me? And so, I just said, "Well, you going to be an unhappy child." [Laughter] You know? And just proceeded to live my life. And then in '96, no, '93 is when I met Sharon [Bridgforth]. [. . .] Sharon was doing a presentation, and so I went because it was a black people thing, I was like, "Oh, black people." So, I go and I'm just like, [pretends to sing] "ahhh," this is the kind of situation for me because now I see some black people that are gay. So, I go there and they had this little thing at the Fiesta Garden. [. . .] And so, now I'm seeing some black folks, and now the white woman that I'm living with is intimidated by this because now I'm going to have my own friends and they're black, so she didn't really know what to do with that. So, it was an eclectic bunch of folks. And so, my daughter got to hang out, because I don't give a shit, you still my daughter, I'm still going to beat your ass, you still going to do what the hell I say, dammit. Be whatever you want to be, think however you want to think, but I'm still running that shit. And so she would have to go with me to places. It was like, "You want to go help us do outreach?" And so, they had her doing all this stuff, and so she got involved with them, and she's getting older.

And then her crazy daddy, I filed child support on him. He's in jail when it happens, so they don't transport him to Austin. He don't have no say-so, default. Usually it's just standard visitation, first, third, fifth weekend kind of stuff, but the judge said to give discretion, meaning he has a history of going to jail and being a drug addict, and so if you don't think it's safe, you don't have to let her [the daughter] go. I was like, "Okay." And so he gets out of jail. He's living with this woman, and he reads the letter, right? So, what he reads is, he wasn't going to ever see her again, and so he calls and he's screaming and he's hollering and he's cussing me out, and then he tells me, "I'm dying." I said, "What?" He tells me that he's HIV positive. So, I was sitting on the phone and my daughter is walking back and forth, and I can't act no certain way. I got to hold my shit together, so I'm like, "Okay, what are you talking about?"

So, that call years ago. It was true.

Yeah, it was true. So, he goes through this whole thing about how his mother died and he never did tell her the truth and the whole thing.

Do you think it was from using, or do you think he had sex in prison?

I think it was a combination of the two, and I don't think that it was in prison that he was having sex. I think he may have had sex in prison, too, but what I believe, like now, I get to Austin with the white people, and they tell you about all this stuff, and so I'm working for the University of Texas in their catering department with this white guy who's gay. He loves to go to the little peep show. That's his shit, cruising. So, I remember when we were together we used to go to Houston over on Montrose all the time to the little fuck bookstores, and in the back they always had the little peepshow room. And I remember like going in there; it was never really crowded, and it was always men, and that was very obvious to me. It was very obvious, and I just didn't think that women went to those kind of places because women wasn't talking about sex with the lights on and all that kind of stuff, but these men would always like look at me with discontent like, "Bitch, what is you doing here?" And they would like, go to the back, come back out, look at some more books, go to the back. We go to the back, and we looking to get us some rolls of quarters, and we go back there, and we looking, so when I moved to Austin I found out what it is, what it *really* is, and what I know is that it was several times that I didn't go to Houston with him. [. . .] So, it was things that had happened that when I look back it was like, mm-hmm, mmm-hmm, that's what that [was]. So, he said that it's been everything but sex with a man, and it's like, uh-uh, uh-uh, and years later I told him. I said, "I don't even really care. You got to know that for yourself. You got to be honest about that for yourself. If you don't ever say it out loud to anybody, you got to know that that's what happened."

But what did happen in some point I think like in early 2000, I found out that I had hepatitis C, and so that was a whole little crazy thing. He tells me on the phone that he's dying. [. . .] So, now I got to figure out how to tell his kid this, and she's so damned dramatic, you know? The [AIDS] movement is really big at this point in Austin. It comes out. It's attacking all the white boys, and they got money out the ass for all kind of stuff: condoms, outreach. And [. . .] Ronald Reagan had found out about Rock Hudson, and he think he might be positive so he's over there just giving away money for shit, and then Magic Johnson, so they just over there just pouring a whole lot of money into this and so they had the CARE program, Planned Parenthood, AIDS Service Austin. They would collaborate, so it was just a lot happening. And so, they just kind of helped my daughter with that and started teaching her about that whole thing and what that all meant and all that kind of stuff. So, she just learned to live with that fact with him, and he still ain't never done shit but smoke crack and go to prison. In prison as we speak.

So, he didn't die.

Hell no. [Laughter] Hell no, he didn't die. This bastard been HIV-positive for like twenty-five years, and I promise you I have never known him to be like really sick. When he ain't in prison, he ain't doing what the hell he's supposed to do—ever. He ain't eating right, smoking crack, run the streets. He doing whatever the hell he want to do. But of course when he go to prison it's like all eyes on me: "They not giving me my medication, they not giving me. . . ." All of it just becomes very important to him then. He wants you to write the damned president about him not getting his medication and all that. So, my daughter, she makes sure that he's alright. [. . .]

So, anyway, that's my daughter, and I love her, and so whatever her stress is probably going to be my stress. So, I have a couple grandkids, and the boy's fifteen, little girl is eight, and so they supposed to be coming for Thanksgiving and going to see him down in Beaumont. I said, "Let me tell you something. I know them your kids and that's their grandpa." I said, "I'm going to tell you this though, you going to do what you're going to do, I just have all kind of fucking anxiety, it just upsets the hell out of me for me to even think that you can try to take them down there to see his ass." I said, "Except for the fact that he has never tried to be their grandfather when he wasn't in prison, he's never gone out of his way to try to see them, I wouldn't be upset. But he ain't never tried, so I don't know why they got to go to the fucking penitentiary to see him. I don't know why they got to endure that. So, I would really appreciate if you did not take them there." I don't want my grandson being victimized by the system, being patted down because he's old enough now to have to go through that, and they got to check her, check my granddaughter because they got so much contraband and so much shit going on in prison now that you got to go through the same kind of shit you do at the airport—worse. When they talking about searching you and stuff like that, it's like, uh-uh, I don't want him to have to. He ain't going to jail. I don't want him to go to jail, and I don't want him to have the *experience* of none of that. Of course, some crazy ass black people, "Maybe he go down there and he have to see how it is to keep him from . . ." No. No. We going to keep him from going. It don't even have to be attractive to him in any kind of way. So, he doesn't have any reason to want to go to a prison.

How did you meet your current partner?

[. . .] I went to this conference in Fort Worth, and she was at the conference. It was a women's conference or whatever, and I'm just minding my own business because that's what I do, mind my own business. So, I was sitting on the sofa in the lobby area of the hotel that it was in, and so she came by, and she was like, "Lori, do you have to take up the whole sofa?" I said, "I'm sorry. You want to sit down? But yeah, I do, because I need to have my feet up." [. . .] But she had this other little woman running behind her, so I ain't really paying no attention. I just know her from the meeting, and so I just thought she was passing on by. And then a few months later she was speaking in Amarillo, and then a mutual friend of ours was there, and they stayed in a room together, so I was talking to my friend. So I said, well, let me talk to her, and I was going to tell her it's going to be fine, you're going to be good, you're going to do fine, just breathe. So, then the friend who's there is like, "We need to get together and go out sometime." [. . .] So, you want to go out, that's cool, we can do that. [. . .] So, they came back, and so we supposed to go out that next weekend, and so they came to the house, and I'm just sitting there and they're sitting there, and we're watching TV, and they were talking, and then they went to sleep and shit, and I left. And so the friend called me the next day and said, "Yeah, Gwen said she gonna knock you off." I say, "Oh, okay." So, I called and I said, "You telling people you been knocking me off, what is that?" And so, she was a little upset because she was just talking. You know what I'm saying? And so, we started talking, and then we hung out. Then I went over there and met the little kids and shit, and they looking at me and I'm looking at them and shit. Because I purposely did not get in a relationship with a woman that had kids, because I didn't want women that had kids, because I [will] fight your kid. Your ass tell me something wrong, I'm going to tell you no and hit your ass in the mouth, because that's what I do with kids. I don't give a shit from eight to eighty, I'll fight your ass. Hell. So, no. [Laughter] So, it's a very conscious decision because I knew she had kids even before I went in. I knew that before, because I could've just not entertained her. I had asked God that the next relationship be with somebody that I could love and somebody that would love me back and that we would just be. So, to me it just kind of came in the form of the unexpected, because we had seen each other, but we hadn't looked at each other, but she had probably been around like five years, but we hadn't looked at each other like *that*. So, we get together. So, we like each other, but we also know that this is sex. This is sex, too. So, you know, you're feeling good about that and all that. So, she is not out, but when she has this speaking engagement in Amarillo [. . .] she comes out. It just comes out of her mouth and she comes out.

During the speech?

Yeah, yeah, and so they do these cassettes and they sell them or whatever and so I listen to it. I'm like, "Whew, whew," but it's like months later that I listen to it though.

She didn't tell you?

I heard parts of it, but I didn't know how it went, but she hadn't done that. She hadn't said that. She had been bouncing, too. [. . .] She wasn't involved with anybody, but she had come to that conclusion that she needed to stop that, and she knew that she was attracted to women and didn't do anything about it because it was taboo, and she just had to do what mom 'n'em wanted, and the church, and whoever, so she just did what was acceptable, like me. So, anyway, we get together. So, I call this woman because we friendly. We still hang out. I said, "Look. Let me tell you this," because we go to the same meeting, too. I said, "You know I'm dating Gwen." And she was like, "Gwen who?" I was like, "Gwen from the meeting." "What?" And so, she thought that was a downgrade. So, I really didn't know how that was going to go because also I didn't know that I wanted to live with anybody again, not right away and definitely not at the time that we got together. And so, she has four kids and the two older ones, one was in the Navy, the oldest boy, and the oldest daughter was in college in Rhode Island. So, now this is summertime, so the daughter comes home fucking mean as a snake, just mean as a snake, just makes life miserable and just wanted to set the fucking temperature for everybody in the house like based on her. That's how things were, people were going to bounce and behave and so I'm just like . . .

She didn't know you! [Laughs]

She didn't. Her mama didn't either, because y'all the one letting her run thangs. So, she ended up being like a friend that came over and never went home. We started dating officially June 3 and July 3 she was moving into a house and I wasn't going to move in with her. I was going to help her start this group home [. . .] and then realized that it wasn't going to go as quickly as we thought it was going to go, and so I said, "I'll move in and I'll live here for six months until you get this up off the ground." And she got a client that probably would have allowed her to live there without me. So the two younger kids, ten and fifteen, sixteen at the time, so they move from North Austin to South Austin, and so they just upset because they got to change school. Well, the fifteen-year-old, she decides not to, so she's going to catch the bus, but they resentful as hell and mad. So, because of her drug using she hadn't really raised them all of their lives, and so she gets clean and she goes collect them. So, she's still trying to live out this resentment and anger and guilt and stuff and trying to make amends, but by basically making sure that she worked three jobs and they had whatever they wanted, and so they were not responsible for shit, so when they moved in at the house a chore list went up.

So, the youngest daughter, her dad, he in and out and not really doing much, and so she was like, "I think I should file child support." "Well, I think you should because my daughter's thirty-four years old and I still have a open child support case on her dad." [Laughter] And so, though I knew that he would probably never pay, that's still your responsibility. You don't get to, like, not have the responsibility of taking care of your kid, and I think you should have that responsibility. I don't care if you don't pay. She's still going to eat. She's still going to do whatever she going to do, but you got to know that you don't just get to [not pay child support], so I said, "Yeah, I think you should." So, now he don't want to pay child support, so now he's over there trying to bait her, "Come live with daddy. Daddy will get you a guinea pig. Come live with daddy. Daddy will get your hair done. Come live with daddy, take you to the nail shop." This kind of stuff. And so, then the fifteen-year-old, her dad lives in North Austin, and so she wants to live with us for a week, stay at his house for a week, live with us for a week, and stay at his house for a week. And he's sick, so we kind of agreeing to that, right? So, it's just crazy. It's crazy. [. . .]

Because she comes out, and it's like at the same time we get together, and so now it's my fault. It's my fault that life is falling apart for everybody. So, now they thinking that she's over there making these decisions about her kids with me, and so I'm just going through it. And so, I don't know if I'm fixing to go or stay, fixing to go or stay. I don't know if I'm going to kill somebody or not, because I'm telling you now, I'll fight your mama. So, it was bad. It was horrible. And so the little girl she wants to go stay with her dad, then she don't want to go stay with her dad. Then about a month later, she gets mad. "I want to go stay with my daddy. I changed my mind." And so it's like, okay, because he done set it up because he done got the papers from child support, and he didn't want to pay child support, so he'd prefer for her to come live with him because that's what he did with his sons and their mother.

So, the fifteen-year-old, her mama is telling her because she didn't do the chore she couldn't do whatever, couldn't go. "I don't know where you think you're going." So she's like, "Because I didn't do the chore? That's just stupid. That's stupid," and just started jumping up and down, and so the next thing I know, her mama is over there with her hands around her throat, and I'm just like, "Oh, my God." [Laughter] It's like a whole camp just breaks, and so she live with her dad, she go live with her dad, and my partner is in the fetal position in the bed. But before this, the twenty-one-year-old, she comes home from college, and she's over there wreaking havoc and she just over there, "Y'all don't have to do this. Y'all don't have to do that. She don't run nothing." I'm telling you what, "I'm telling you I'm running this shit right here. I'm telling you that you fixing to have to get the hell away from here. Here's what's going to happen. You cannot be in this house disrupting my household. You a grown woman. You visiting. So, since you can't follow the rules, you can go somewhere else." [Laughter] So, you can't set the temperature in my house. I'm paying the bills in here. But she was just very, very out of order, and it was just very bad.

So, now [. . .] I got this woman with kids and she's feeling rejected and mad and all this because they choose they daddy over her. So, now I got to stay. It's like I did it so now I got to go through it. So, this is a very rough time. Like we never got to do that honeymoon period. We never got that where it was good for three to six months. No. It immediately started falling apart—crazy. We weren't even really together yet. We were like right here. But for me and her it was like I knew that she loved me, and I knew that I could trust her and that she would have my back, so I knew that. I could feel that. I knew that, and she was willing to continue because her coming out process [. . .] she was at a crossroads with that, too, with her family. She could've went back and just kept doing what she'd been doing, but she was going to walk through it and move forward in her own life and just be true to herself. And so, people just in general, not her family but our friends, didn't understand, and they thought certain things, so they kind of did a lot of mumbling and talking about us and that kind of stuff. So, a lot of tears for her. But for me I started having sex at thirteen, so I've always had shit to deal with so I don't even give a shit what people think about me. I don't care. I do what I want to do, and I make choices and I live with them, and that's what I've learned in my life is that that's what I get to do, and so for me it was like having her back going through that and still having to be around people and still looking at each other and loving each other. And, of course, because she was so bouncy with these people, everybody that wasn't saying shit about her and the kids and all that was saying shit like, "She don't stay with nobody for no period of time. At least you got enough time you won't relapse." Say what? And so, "Yeah, everybody she mess with, they stay and relapse."

Relapse in terms of going back to drugs?

Yeah, like she did something to them or something. So, they had already kind of doomed it and decided it wasn't going to last, but at least she will stay clean. It was like, okay. I don't know what y'all think she got that's so powerful. [Laughter] Y'all don't know me, do you? So, this is the thing that really, really makes things work for me with her and that has been really different in my life in terms of living in the lifestyle, living in that truth of being gay is that I get to be me. I get to be me in a relationship and that has not always been the case, because most people tend to think that I'm the most dominant, I'm the male figure in the relationship because of who I am and who she is, because in order for it to make sense they have to put you somewhere. So, the closest that they can get to anything is the man/woman relationship, and so somebody got to be the man, somebody got to be the woman. We both men. That's how it works in my relationship, we both men. So, that just kind of throws people off, but for me it's like we both the women and we know that and absolutely very, very clear about that and love each other's parts, don't want other parts. If we do, then we can buy those and put them somewhere else when we get done, so that we don't really have to live in that. But when you with people in a relationship who think like that, too, then you get to be who they think you are, and for me it was just really difficult living in that space because that's not who I am. It's like this is just who I am and not this.

[. . .] I'm the most feminine woman in America, but people have ideas about who they think I am and who I'm supposed to be in a relationship. So, no, your ass will drown waiting for me to open the door for your ass trying to get in the car. You better get in the car. I'm in the car. I'm not opening doors. If we walking to the club and your door is on my side, I'll open the door and let you in first and walk around, but it ain't on purpose. I'm not walking from my side to your side and opening the door. We ain't doing all of that. You know what I'm saying? So, it's like, we take care of each other and I will open the door for her because I just want her ass to go on in the store. [. . .]

Pretty much since we been together, she has had every part of her body from head to foot, something has happened. She has had injections in the back of her head. She's had injections down her neck. She's had her foot cut open, her knees. She doesn't have any cartilage in either knee. I'm talking about she has had a little baby minor heart attacks or something or close to it or whatever, just a whole lot of physical problems. [. . .] But her story is, she used drugs. She smoked crack, prostituted, did walk the streets, went to prison, and all of that, and so when we got together and she'd get out the bed and couldn't really stand up and I was like, "What is that? What is going on with your feet?" And so, one day I looked at them and, "Ooh, [laughter] what is going on right here. You need to go to the doctor, sister. You got to work this out." [. . .] It was plantar fasciitis or something. [. . .] It was in the heel but it was like other little calluses throughout her feet. [. . .] I was like, "What is that? That don't, uh-uh. I never be trying to kiss your feet now." [Laughter] So, that was like the very first thing. She had this bunion, and then they did this thing and so they took out a chunk of her heel that was open, and so I had to change that, clean it, change that a couple times a day and the whole thing, and so that's where that whole door opening thing come from because it was like she was on crutches. [Laughter] I was like, "Come on, so I can make sure your ass ain't behind me falling." [Laughter] Shit. I'm telling you, she fell when we was going to a comedy show. She fell and broke her fucking ankle, her foot, whatever it was. It was like, "Oh my God," and so throughout our relationships, she's had a lot of medical problems. Lots of medical problems. So, that's where that whole door thing comes from.

How long have you been together?

Five years and surprisingly, because usually I be with your ass for six months thinking about how I'm going to get out of here, and it might not be for another year before I come out but I had not asked that question yet: "Oh Lord, how in the hell am I going to get out of here?"

Over the course of the conversation you've said repeatedly that you hardened, that you weren't emotionally available. Do you think Gwen cracked that open?

Nah, I don't think Gwen cracked that open. I think I got to a place in my life which was a progression, because I went to therapy. I was in therapy for like six years. I went initially to try to figure out how to let this woman that I was living with and my daughter act right. So, that was my initial thing, and so I went through that whole process and had to do a whole lot of healing in my own life, the stuff with my mother, my daughter dying, this man, just a whole lot of things that had happened. I think what cracked that for me is when my grandson was born. I think that was probably the beginning for me because it was so unconditional. I remember the moment that he was born, and that was like the first time that I ever cried spontaneously. He was just like my baby, and my love for him was so unconditional.

Gwen and Lori in
San Antonio, 2016.
Courtesy of the narrator.

And with my daughter, we had to learn how to be in a relationship, and I think that really started happening for us when she became an adult. And then she became a mother, and then she understood some things differently, and the fact that she wasn't fifteen or sixteen no more and just full of her own damned self, and realizing that the world don't revolve around her. So, she went from dealing with me being gay and that whole thing and then she became a teenager and started dealing with her own teenage stuff. Then she got pregnant and then we didn't know what to do with that and that whole thing. So, the period that she was pregnant it was like she was with me, and like I say, I went to all the doctor appointments, got to see him the moment he was born and then as he grew. Because he would be with me and also, I had this thing with kids and specifically with babies because my daughter died in her sleep, it was very difficult for me to do that. So, I had to live in that. I had to go through that, and for months I didn't sleep when he was with me. I was very tired every weekend he went home because I would just make sure that he was still breathing. He was just my baby. He was just the dude, and I'm telling you, he was my baby, and then my son-in-law he just kind of fell in. And so, he's my son, he's like my son.

So, my grandson, he didn't know me. He didn't know nothing about my lifestyle. He didn't know his granny was gay. He didn't know his granny smoked crack, he didn't know any of that, and so everything he had from me was genuine, and it was love. You know what I'm saying? He wasn't trying to figure out who's resenting this and still mad. So, that probably was the beginning for me. I had the same responsibility to him that I had to my daughter, and I still believe that. It's like he's an extension of me, and so as an adult I have a responsibility to him to provide some guidance and some support and that kind of stuff, and no matter where they are, it's like I'm still his grandma. So, he's like twelve. He said something. He told my daughter, "I hate you." My daughter called me. She was upset, crying because she was just devastated by it. I said, "Let me tell you something, boy. I will come to Hawaii and kick your ass. [Laughter] You her baby, but that's my baby, and I'm telling you I will come to Hawaii and kick your ass. Say something else to her." [Laughter]

[. . .] So, I think my grandkids probably because it doesn't matter, it didn't matter that I was in public and I was just like, "Oh this is my grandbaby," making baby noises. It didn't matter to me. It was just like he was important to me and me loving him, that was important to me. [. . .] So, that has always been important to me, my relationships with my grandchildren.

So, when you ask if Gwen played a part in that, she did, and mostly because she just allows me to be me. I'm going to be who I want to be. I'm going to be who I am, so you don't really get to give me permission, so you don't allow me to do shit, but it's like, whatever I'm trying to do she supports me in that, and who I am as a woman, she understands that. I'm a woman. I'm a woman. I'm a woman. She know she more manly than me. She knows it. I'm like, "Oh, you so manly," sitting over there thinking, "You gonna be my bitch." [Laughter] Trying to handle me, "Oh, don't rough me up," you know, that kind of stuff. She's a lot more vocal. I look like the mean one and people always think that, but she is, she is. She is. [. . .]

Out of everything you said, I want to ask you this final question. Given everything you've been through, how do you feel about the life choices that you made in relationship to being a black lesbian?

. . . I know that for me the first thing that I am is just a woman. And [. . .] how people or why people define me as a lesbian is mostly because of who I sleep with, but who I am throughout the course of my day is that I'm just a black woman in America. I have to acknowledge the black because that's what people see when they see me. That's the first thing they see is my color, and for people to say, "I don't see color when I'm talking to you," you must think that I'm clear. So, now you've denied that, too, in your efforts to be politically correct if your best friend is black or whatever. I understand that about myself, and before I really understood me as a gay, as a lesbian woman, I understood myself as a person, a female, girl, woman, just trying to live through the chaos and the confusion of the life choices that other people had made for themselves that included me. And as a child you're just really powerless. You don't have the power to leave. It's not like, "Fuck you all, I'm fixing to leave and go somewhere" when you eight years old. "I don't like what y'all doing and I can go live somewhere else." You just don't have that power, and so you have to live, and for me, living in the choices that my parents continued to make for themselves, and then having a child at such an early age, and going from one [set of] parents to somebody else's parents and then having a child, becoming a parent, my life still was not my life. So, I went from being my parents' child to my daughter's mother, this boy's live-in girlfriend to his wife, and so you just wake up, you go to work, you come home, you cook, you clean. You make sure the kid's alright, you make sure he's alright, and you do it all the same way the next day. For me that worked because it's consistency and so I knew what to expect. People call it control issues. I like to know what's happening in my life.

So, in living the lifestyle of a gay person is much like the lifestyle I lived when I was married. It's the same shit. It's like you go to work. You make sure that your family is safe, that they're taken care of, and that you do whatever you need to do to make sure that it happens. So, my goal in life, my whole thing is I want to be able to love them until I die, and those are the most important people. Prior to this relationship, I think I've gone through the motions of relationships and sometimes they loved me, sometimes I loved them, but I don't think it ever happened at the same time. I think with this relationship it's happening at the same time, and I'm older, so age and maturity always helps, and figuring out who I am as a woman.

So, the life choices that I made—because I work with adolescents and still raising adolescents—it's a responsibility to me that I have in helping you become the best person that you can be. What I know about that is that people can't see what's behind your eyes. They don't see your vision. You have to know that sometimes you may be the only person supporting your vision because people can't see what you see. So, when you start talking about doing things, people will try to talk you out of whatever that is, and I've made a lot of choices that I've had to live with that affected other people's lives, I'm sure—good, some not so good. So, I think in my drug using life, I think the person that was up close and personal with that whole thing was my daughter. My mother knew about it, my family knew about it, but they didn't really live in it, going to treatment. So, the first choice was having sex, drinking, getting high, skipping school, all that kind of stuff. Then I decided to have sex. There was a consequence in that. The consequence was that I got pregnant, and the choice that I made was to have the baby, and that created a domino effect. So, now I have this person in my life that is going to be a part of my life the rest of my life, which is her dad, and so that's a reality. So, living with him, continuing to live with him, even in the relationship and what I know about the relationship years later when you say why did I stay. It's like, years later after I got clean I had to make an amends to him because I shouldn't have. One was because I probably loved him in the sense that we got together when I was fourteen and that's what I was supposed to be doing, and we had a kid together, and so time was passing, but I also knew that I was attracted to females, and so as far as being emotionally available to him, probably not. So, I was in a relationship that was basically a lie. I didn't know it, and I didn't know that I had a choice to do anything differently. So, that whole thing.

People used to ask me about my daughter, "What about Tanisha." What about Tanisha? "Well, she going to be gay?" If she going to be with somebody like you, I hope so. [Laughter] It was like, "Well, no, no." So, people have asked me [that] especially in her younger days. And of course we get the same kind of questions with Desiree, the fifteen-year-old: how would you feel if she was gay? I would not like that for her. [. . .] If that's what she chose, then yeah, we'd roll with that. Why? Because being gay in America can be painful. That is my baby. Why would I want her to have to endure this bullshit that I done had to endure? I don't ever want her to be hurt. I don't want her to ever have to be in a position that there's something going on with her that I can't fix. So, no, I would not want her to be subjected to this bullshit and trying to live through this, because it can be hard.

So, the choices that I made for myself, I shot dope, I smoked crack, I got clean, I stayed clean and managed to get some kind of license where I can have a career, and then I made a choice to open my own business, and people didn't necessarily support that. People just haven't supported a whole lot of my decisions, but that doesn't matter to me. I don't expect you to have my best interest at heart; I have to have my own best interest at heart, and so I live in that. I'm very thoughtful about the choices that I make because I do know that they affect other people. Some days I would like to smoke a joint and drink a beer, but I don't know what the end result of that would be. I don't know that I would just smoke the joint and drink the beer. Or, I don't know if I would smoke crack. So, since I don't know, just don't even start it, and then I don't have to stop, because it's like, the rule is if I start smoking, y'all better get the hell away from me because I'm telling you, you better take everything you got because it's going down. So, I just believe in that. [. . .]

What's important to me is that my family is happy and that we don't have to struggle, and that gives me a sense of security. And they know that. [. . .] I love being in a relationship. I love the family dynamics of the relationship. I love the nesting part of the relationship. I love the fact that I love coming home and looking forward to seeing my family. So, that works for me. [. . .]

I think just growing up being poor was a good thing because it taught me how to be poor. [. . .] My kids now, life is good. They know that they can get whatever the hell they want from me most of the time, if it's reasonable. [. . .] So, they don't really know what it means to be hungry, eat leftovers, being in the dark, not having a TV, that kind of stuff, so they tend not to really appreciate life. And so, one of the first lessons that they got when me and Gwen got together, her kids, we went school shopping probably the first couple of months we been together. So, they just picking shit up, picking shit up, putting in the basket, picking shit up, putting it in the basket. "I want this, I want that," putting shit in the basket. I said okay, "Here you go." I gave this one a hundred and fifty dollars, and this one a hundred and fifty dollars. They was like, "What is this?" "That's your budget. That's how much money you got right here. Buy whatever you want." But now they got to go back and look, well, maybe not this twenty dollar dress. Let me go look at this clearance rack over here. [. . .] My granddaughter, she's eight, I sent her ten dollars for her birthday. "Granny rich. She's rich." So she watches you, and so I always have a rubber band around my money, and so she went and got her rubber band and put it around her money. So, now she got a rubber band around her money, because granny got a rubber band around her money. So, I want they ass falling in the aisle trying to get in the casket when I die. I want them to love me that much and gonna be missing me that much. I want to make sure that I make an impact on a lot of the people that love me.

I'm Alright with Who I Am

"Ida Mae"

12

"Ida Mae" is a wonderful storyteller who kept me in stitches throughout the entire interview. Standing at over six feet tall, she is an imposing presence that is softened by her sharp wit and sense of humor. Although she is officially retired from teaching, she does stand-up comedy at senior citizen homes around the country. She was born in Odenville, Alabama, in 1951. Odenville is located in north central Alabama and has a population of only three thousand, and only 2 percent of the population is African American. The interview took place on September 11, 2012, at her home in Houston, Texas.

I was born in Odenville, Alabama, in 1951, May 1, 1951. [. . .] My childhood it was like, it was an easy childhood in my eyes because my parents worked really hard to keep me in the dark about what actually was going on, because this was a civil rights thing, and my father and my mother were very protective of us and not letting us experience it. So, it was an easy childhood, and it was fun and everything; I had a really good time because you don't understand what's going on around you. So, if it's not right, you don't know it as long as the Kool-Aid's there and Santa's there, everything you need to be comfortable is there. So, that's the way it was, and I tell you it, must've been until I was about maybe in high school before I started to really realize that there was a lot of fear. There was a lot of fear in the community. And what was actually going on, you know, because I—you know how grown folks were in the South, "Y'all go on the porch." We didn't talk about it, so when it got to the point where I could understand the dialogue and I'm like, "Oh they're scared" or "Oh, they're going over here," I started to get an understanding of what actually was going on.

My mother went to Odenville because her mother lived there, and I was born in a house, okay? So, I was born at home. My mother was a resident of Birmingham, Alabama, so as soon as I got up on my feet, being premature and all, I was relocated to Birmingham, where I went to school. I went to a little school. My first year of school was at an old schoolhouse that was right not far from our house. My father was very disappointed with the level of education, so he pulled us out of that school and put me and my sisters in [name of school], which was a parochial school. I stayed there until I was an eleventh grader. And at that time, he felt that it was safe enough and the educational boundaries had balanced enough so that I could go to a public school, so I graduated from [name of school], and during that time during my childhood it was so much going on as far as civil rights was concerned. I think I was about maybe a sophomore in high school or freshman in high school when my father decided he was going to be a Baptist minister. That changed every damned thing, because he just got involved in trying to help out the civil rights movement and everything. He was a minister of the church, and pretty much it was the civil rights thing most of my childhood.

I remember we used to get the *Jet* when *Jet* was black and white. I remember seeing Medgar Evers hanging up from a meat hanger and his flesh was completely turned inside out. That's the kind of stuff that *Jet* was showing. This is what I started to understand what we're dealing with. They would find kids hung. They would find people, pull them people out of, what was the name of that river that was close by? Choctaw River or something like that. They used to find bodies in there all the time. It was really a thing. And then we had the civil rights movement, and Martin Luther King came in, and we had the boycott of the buses. I will never forget that because when my father got off work—he worked at US Steel—he would drive his car around to pick people up from work and help move people around. There was a lot of that going on in the community, in my community. There was a lot of, "Help us because we walking, we can't get on the bus." And it turned out pretty successful in that they got what they wanted. They brought that bus system to a screeching halt. I had no idea that minorities actually carried the transportation system. When they got them off the bus, it shut it down, so they won that battle. Then I remember the sadness of Dr. King dying and both the Kennedy boys dying. I remember how everything in our world just kind of stopped for a minute. It was a focusing moment. It was like, "Oh my God." People continually show you how awesome they can be, how terrible they can be, not awesome in that way, how terrible they can be, and the way that—and it just kind of like shut things down. [. . .] It kind of suck the life out of you. You know what I'm saying?

But everybody was determined to keep on because this is life how we know it. This is life how we know.

I left Birmingham in the eighties and came to Texas because there were no economic opportunities. There was no work. I graduated Miles College, and I was trained to be a teacher. I didn't want to teach because I didn't want to conform. The whole thing was killing me, and I talk about this a lot. This whole being a girl thing, you know? My mom used to make me wear a longline bra.

What's that?

A longline bra? It's this bra you put on that come way down here [points to her waist] back in the day.

Down to your waist?

This was before Spanx, okay? Then they had the metal staves in it, so you be like this. [Laughter] Then you had the damned girdle on. It came down to here [points to her mid thigh], from your waist down to here. It had metal staves in it, had a zipper on the side so you'd be like, suck it in. It was crazy, you know what I'm saying? But that was the way women dressed, and there was no pantyhose, so we had stockings. We had to put them up and then you had to hook that to some shit. So, all of it was like [gasps]. I hated it. I just couldn't conform.

I remember when I first went to Miles College. We used to always wear dresses. I was a big girl all my life, I mean really. I maxed out at four hundred [pounds], to tell you the truth, and so when I went to Miles I was about three hundred and fifty, four hundred, close to it. Shit, I was a big girl. And I had these shifts. My mom would always buy shifts for me, so I remember I was standing out there, and I had these little spoon heels, and I was so fat that they were sticking out on the side because they had that gap in 'em on the side, and there was a squishing going on every time you take a step. [Laughter] You know, that nylon being going shoop, shoop, shoop. I was the most miserable person in my freshman year in college. And I had no pants. My father did not allow us to wear pants, so I had no pants. So, it was the shift everyday with the longline girdle and the bra. It was killing me. It was killing me.

The kids in school were starting to call me "church girl," and I didn't know that they referred to me as that behind my back. And then one day I was sitting in front of the student union, and I was sitting up there. I was so uncomfortable. I was trying to read a book, just trying to fit in any goddamned way I could, excuse my language. And I'm sitting, and this guy came and sat beside me. I still say he saved me. His name was Frederick.

Everybody laughed or looked at or paid attention to Frederick, because he had his hair permed, and he had this big head of hair; it was just permed like a woman. And he had his shirt tied up under here [points to her chest], and he had on these cutoff blue jeans, and they were so short you could see the pockets, and he had on these little sandals and shit, and he come up there, "How you doing, church girl?" I'm like, "What the fuck?" You know? I mean nobody ever bothered to speak to me. I was just some strange motherfucker walking around that people were talking about.

I'm so timid I was totally out of my zone, because my father came home one day and told me—I was laying on the couch after graduation and I thought I was doing real good. I was sitting at home watching TV, and he walked in, and he said, "Look baby, every day I come home you laying on this sofa. Let me tell you what, let me tell you how this going to go now. You got three choices here: you need to find you a job, go to school, get in college, or you need to move." I'm serious. I sat straight up, because I had never thought about not being out of my father's house, and I never thought about work. For what? You said I had to finish high school. I finished high school. I'm done. Shit. I got up, went to Miles College, and enrolled in there.

So anyway, I met Frederick, and Frederick sat down and he said, "Church girl, what you up to?" And I didn't say that much to him. Every day we would meet there, and we just developed a friendship. So, I got a job with work study, and it was working with kids outside, so when I showed up at 4 o'clock to start my new job I had on the shift and the same little teaspoon shoes. He said, "Where you going?" I said, "I'm here." He said, "Oh no, honey. We out here hitting balls and bats and shit. You can't be out here." I said, "I don't have any pants." He said, "C'mon," and he took me to K-Mart and bought me my first pair of jeans. He bought me a pair of Bucks. Remember them old Bucks and things? And a shirt and a denim jacket. Yes he did. I went back to the school and I felt so free. When I was taking off that stuff, he was like "Oooh, oooh!" He just cut up, you know? [Laughter] "What the fuck? Why you got all this on?" He was just cuttin' up. He turned out to be my best friend, I swear to God. He died two years ago, and we talked every week. He had to have dialysis.

Frederick took me to my first gay bar. I was so freaked out because I was sitting on the thing, and he said, "You like her, don't you?" Because there was this girl, and I really like this girl, and I would just watch her walk across the campus, but I would never say anything. I didn't know people were watching me watch the girl. [Laughter] He say, "I see how you be looking at her. You like her, don't you?" And I looked at him, because I don't know nothing about what you're talking about, you understand? I always thought, I always liked women or girls. When everybody else was seeing little boys in second and third grade, I was seeing a little girl. I was sneaking around to Miss-What's-Her-Name's house, honey, and I would steer around there every evening. But this girl, all this stuff I'm talking to you about, I have poetry about it, okay? This girl I would meet her in her house, and we would go in her father's garage, and we'd play house. She had all the dolls out there and everything, but that girl knew so much, you know what I'm saying? And so she used to make me get on top of her. We'd fix all the food, and I'd get on top of her and grind, and then one day she pulled down her panties, and she peed and took my hand and put it in the stream, you know what I'm saying? I was shocked.

How old was she?

We was like seven. It took me until I was an adult to figure out that she had been abused, you know? That none of the shit that she had showed me, none of the stuff that we was doing we should have known. You see what I'm saying? And after I got grown I'm saying, she was abused, she was abused because she had it straight on. Either she had watched her folks because she knew about playing with the thing and shit like that. She knew all about that shit, but it didn't mean anything. It was just a ritual kind of thing. You do this and I do this, "Uh-uh, I'm going to show you what to do, I'm going to show you what to do." So, I got one of the best learnings I ever had at seven, and then one day I come home, she had moved. Her folks had done moved, and I was devastated. But this is the kind of experiences that I experienced when I was a child. I tried to get into the whole boyfriend thing, but I wasn't feeling that. You know what I'm saying? I tried to do just like everybody else around me was, but I just wasn't feeling it.

I can remember going to Sunday school because [woman's name], she wore emerald four-inch heels, and I just thought her legs looked so pretty in them damned stockings, and I had to go to Sunday school just so I could see her, with her red lipstick on her and her emerald pumps or whatever colored pumps she wanted to wear. I remember Miss [last name]. She had a nice waistline and a big ass, and she used to wear this big old fat belt with these skirts, those pencil skirts that come down to there [points to her shin]. But she had this waist cinched in and big old tits, and usually a cowl collar and some shit, and I be looking at her. Miss [last name], Miss [last name], all these were fine teachers. When my daddy jerked me out that school, I was like "Uh," I won't see these teachers no more. Went to Holy Family and went through the whole thing, but when I got to college, I had never been had a relationship, so Frederick took me to this bar. I wish I could remember the name. It was a beautiful name for a bar, but I can't think of it right now. But when I walked in there and we walked up some steps, and there was this big old carpet and everything, and they had lights and the floor would go around. Lights were up under the floor. They had this big ball so everything was moving. It was like, "Wow." But it was dark, so we walked in and he sat me down at the bar and said, "Wait a minute, I'll be right back." I'm sitting at the bar and I don't drink, I don't do nothing—

In the seventies, sixties?

This was in the sixties. This was in '69, about my second year of college. And I was sitting there. It was the Out of Focus; that was the name of that damned bar, the Out of Focus. And I was sitting at that bar, and I was just so glad to be around people and hear that music, Marvin Gaye and them in the background, because my daddy didn't allow us to listen to secular music, so all this was new to me. I had never been to a game. I had never been anywhere unsupervised. I had never been to the movies, so every damned thing I experienced in college was totally new to me, and I was too enamored, and I sat there in that club. I sat there about ten minutes and I said I wonder where he at because I started to feel nervous because I'm out of my element now. I don't have a car. My mama 'n'em don't know I'm here. I'm like, I'm out of my element. Finally, I started to notice. I started to pay attention to the folks, and it was men dancing with men and women dancing with women, and I was like [gasps]. So, I ran to tell Frederick [whispering]: "Fredrick, did you see this motherfucker?" He said, "What you think we come here for? Go on over there and sit down some damn where." He got some man. "Go on and sit down somewhere, make yourself comfortable." He sent a girl over there to talk to me. He told her, "This bitch gonna run out of here; go over there and calm her down." And it kind of calmed me down, and that woman, and she was so nice to me, and I thought she was going to be my first girlfriend, but looking back, it wasn't going to happen, but they were very nice to me, and I got to where I would come there a lot. I would always be at that club, and I started looking around trying to learn about the community, because I see I had no idea that there were other people, I knew nothing about gays. I was just a woman that was different. And then after that, I moved out of my mama's house and started dressing, like cross-dressing. I became the sharpest man that I thought my daddy was, so it was white shirts, Stacey Adams, canes and hats and shit. I was on my own. My folks forbid me to come to their house.

Really?

"Do not come here."

Did you cut your hair, too?

I did. I sure did. I had a nice little butch cut. Cut my hair, had my little shiny shoes on. I got into the drug business, became pretty much of a drug pin. It was me and Dr. Drake, and he was a doctor on the corner, and he would give me the strawberries, was the drug of choice back then. It was speed. It was speed, you know? It used to be strawberries or blackberries, or whatever them black ones. Different color pills, so we sold those. I was alienated from my family. I picked up. I met a girl. I had surgery on my knee in the hospital. I had to have a transfusion. That's how I got hepatitis. That was in '72. Then after I graduated from college, I met this woman. She was like, her name, she was five years my junior. She was an RN, so when I was having the surgery she would come in and out my room, and she put shit in the closet. I didn't know what was going on. So, one day I asked her, "What you doing? Why you keep sneaking in here?" She said, "Girl, I got my medicine in here." She was stealing drugs from the hospital.

And she was putting them in my room, so she was Jonesing. I didn't, but I didn't know anything about. See, that's why I say you should expose your kids to most everything, because if somebody else show it to them, they won't give it to them like you're going to give it to them. So, I didn't know about drugs, so I didn't know about addictions. I didn't know none of that shit. When I got out of the hospital back in the seventies they wouldn't give you no pain medication. You get your ass some Excedrin or something. They wasn't writing no prescriptions for no pain medicine. You can forget that. So, when I got home, I was in so much pain because they had removed my kneecap, so I was in pain a lot, and I would just whine and cry. One day that girl came over to my house. She said, "I know you in pain." She was not wrong, and she had the fix. She hit it. She come by and hit me every day. Pretty soon, we was into this thing so, okay, I got me a girlfriend. She was a nurse, had her own car and everything, but she was a junkie, and she took me right down that junk ass road with her. Then they caught her at the hospital, fired her ass, and then we were in downtown Birmingham looking for the drug man. You know? She turned me on to heroin. She turned me on to coke and all kinds of shit. So, that went on for about four years. Then finally, because I always said that you need a base—I resented my folks and shit for the way things went down, but you know what? [. . .] You know you used to hang your foot on the floor to keep the bed from moving? Even when I would be that fucked up, I would still be trying to say my Lord's Prayer. [Laughter] Because I was raised you don't go to sleep without saying your prayers. "Our Father"—people used to laugh at me—[slurring the words] "Who art in Heaven, hallowed it be thy Name." They'd be going, "Girl be quiet." I'd say, [slurring] "I gotta finish my prayers." But I swear I do believe that that saved me, because the shit that I went through and put myself through, I was supposed to be dead. Do you know what I'm saying?

Did you graduate from college?

I did. I graduated from college, got all of that taken care of and everything, and then after I got off the drugs, my friend Marilyn, who I still talk to every week, who was my roommate in college and she had a nervous breakdown and don't remember none of this. I tell her all the time, "Girl you saved me." She'd say, "How'd I save you?" Because she came to the apartment where I was, and I was so fucked up, she went into the hardware store and got a lock and put it on the outside. I couldn't get out of there. I was on the second floor. That bitch had me up there for three days, but when she come back I was sober and I was thinking. I was like, "Oh my God." I could look at my body. I could tell by the smell in the damned place. I could look at the puke in the corner and know that I had been somewhere. I never touched drugs again, man. She saved me. I never touched drugs, even today, I don't even want to give blood. Like when they come at me to give blood, I'm nervous because I still, I got a really bad experience in my head about that.

So, I came to Texas and I came with a friend. We left Birmingham running. She was in trouble with the law. She had wrote bad checks for groceries. I mean, it really wasn't nothing. We was in a bad place in Alabama. When you see white boys on the garbage trucks you know it's bad, because they didn't do work like that. It was all black folks, all black folks in the service area, and everything but that was gone. So, I left and she left, and we both still are here in Texas. She's with another partner. She's a lab analyst. She does lab work, and she makes very good money. There was no need for us to be unemployed. We were both highly educated; we just couldn't find work. She's doing quite well. I went over my life, several women, one, two, three women later. I run into this one woman who has vision. You know what I'm saying? But she, too, was an addict, but I recognize them when I see it now, but I didn't recognize it because she was a different kind of addict. She was a prescription drug user. Now, I didn't know nothing about them girls, but they all over the place. Them Vicodin heads, that's what I call them, Vicodin heads. To me, Vicodin is just about as bad as heroin. Anything you can't get rid of. But I didn't know that. I spent two years with her, loving her, and she was the first person to tell me, "You know you write good poetry," because she had me motivated. This chick had me writing. I was writing her love letters and shit, poems and stuff.

And so, one day she was reading this shit I had wrote for her, and she said, "You know, you're really good with this poetry thing." I was like, "Eh, that's just something I do." She would always look forward to those poems. Then one day she took me to an open mic, and then I read one of my poems, and it felt good to read it, and it felt good for people to understand what I was saying, so I just started writing. I just started writing, man. I had wrote a lot. I started doing open mics, and then I started to doing schools, published one book. I never published another one. I still got stuff stacked up to be published that are not published. I like performing my work. I wrote a play in 2000. It was called *My Story*. I think that was the name of it. *I Can Float*, that was the name of the piece. I did that play at Theater New West, and it went really well. It was a lot of hard work. I remember that it was a great deal of hard work, but for a one-woman show, I think it went really well. I still have people ask me to do that thing again, and I might get it out and shake the dust off of it one day. Who knows? And so, right now I've had the occasion to do my poetry in Asia, in Taiwan at Taipei American School. That was a wonderful experience. I have done my poetry at Rice, U of H, all of these universities around here. I've done it at most of the high schools. I enjoy doing the work. [. . .]

And what were the racial politics of your town back then? Did blacks and whites interact at all?

No, we had fountains that said "colored only." [. . .] See, back then when I was coming up it was black and white. There was no Italian or no Mexican or none of that shit. Either you was black or you was white. I didn't know the difference or begin to make the differences until after I was out of college. I was like, okay, they treat people according to their origin. It's Italian, it's Hispanics, it's Jews, because Jews are just white folks to me. Everybody was just black or white, so it was just, I don't know. I didn't understand the whole thing back then. It took me a long time to just get it, this whole diversity thing. I didn't really get into that until I come to Texas because I ain't never been around so many different people. One day I was on the elevator and I looked around and I said, "Damn," there must've been seven different tribes present on that elevator. Then I started to understand the coming of people and how we rank in the scheme of things. It took all that for me to learn.

In your hometown was the divide between black and white, was it a railroad track, was it a river? What divided the black side of town from the white side of town?

East and west, you know, like most of the blacks were on the east side of town. They would have areas. You knew that Avondale, that was a white community. We knew that Insley was a black community. There were some whites there, but they were in their houses, and they were in the shotgun houses. You could always tell where the blacks lived because there seemed to be an inordinate amount of shotgun houses. It was just, the projects. We had the projects and then there were suburbs, like the suburb we lived in in Wilding, these were soldiers that were out of the army, and they had these small community homes, and everybody would buy. It was all blacks in that community. There were no whites, so it was like after I was in college before we started to buying the houses that the white folks owned. We would get into a community and then at that time if too many blacks moved into a community, whites would just move away. Anytime the blacks would come, "Got to go, time to go." So, that's just the way it was, and I don't know if there was a track or a river or anything like that. It was developments. That's what it was. Don't get caught over there. Let it get dark and you over there, East Lake or whatever the community where the whites were, and that's how they protected their communities.

So, you never went to an integrated school.

Yes, my senior year. My senior year my father—and that was a trip because I had been so protected and always around blacks. When I got to Anderson High it was white folks, and I didn't really know how to act. You know what I'm saying? We really didn't. And even there it was a push and pull because I remember it was so many more kids at that school because the private school I was from was a small school. But there must have been two thousand to three thousand kids over there, and it was like hysterical, and I remember the first day I got there, it was a guy named Jake. Jake, he saved my ass. Jake was standing up on something high over up by the step, "All you all black folks, c'mon over here. Y'all don't have to be feeling like you don't belong. C'mon over here." He was the one that made us, because everyone was shivering. You know what I'm saying? And he said, "C'mon, we goin' in with everybody else. C'mon, we with everybody else." So, it worked out alright, but there was definitely a difference.

There were no blacks on the cheerleading squad. There were very few blacks on the football team, so it was Ensley High School integrated, but not really. It was like, you just, you had to stand out on your own. You had to make your mark or do whatever you needed to do. I made it through there alright because I'm a people person, so I would start a conversation with a white girl. I'm that kind of a person. I liked my art teacher. She was cool. She was white. [. . .] She was scared to death being there. Looking back, I could tell she was scared to death. "Hi!" [Laughter] Everybody just scared, you know? I found out that they have fears too, because their folks have been telling them things all along. That was how I could have white friends is because I could see that they were raised and taught a certain way from their fears and from what their ancestors experienced, and I was taught a certain way. "You can't trust white folks now. You can't be friends with them now. They going to let you know how you stand in the scheme of things." And that might be true, but then I'm the kind of person that I let you know where I stand in the scheme of things, too. [Laughter] So, we battling. We alright, but a person who was a little more timid might be overpowered by the whole thing, but I managed to make it on up through that. I managed to make it on up through. It was hard because I was scared to death. I was scared to death. I really was, because I didn't know what to expect. Nobody never talked to me about what to expect. Parents back then were, my mama didn't have a lot to say, but they didn't want to say it. The only thing they wanted to let you know was biblical. What's the biblical point of view? And there's more to it than that. There's much more to it than that.

You said your father became a minister. So, I assume that you had to go to church quite a bit.

Oh Lord. I mean, that's all we did was go to church with BTU [Baptist Training Union], choir rehearsal, prayer meeting, revivals. That's all there was. We sang in everybody's choir. If you need a choir, that's five of us. Choir done. [Laughter] You know what I'm saying? No problem. And it was like, I always wanted to do what other kids do. I wanted to—Miss [last name] lived behind us, they were having little parties for the kids and shit. My mama never had no parties. So, secular music. No games. No football. None of that stuff the other kids do. When the streetlight came on you were at home, and if you wasn't at home, then you got beat. It was a lot of corporal punishment going on around then. Looking back, if it was to happen today, their ass would be in court. [Laughter] There was quite a bit of that kick ass going on.

So, you didn't enjoy church?

I did because I like to sing, and I was doing fine in church until I found out that, after I found out I was gay and what that was about, and then I would sit up in church and listen to them talk about homosexuals and try to make people feel bad and "You're going to hell." I got so tired of hearing that until really I had to work on myself because I really thought that I was at odds with God. And I was mean to myself. When I was doing drugs, I was mean to myself because I really felt like, "You're damned anyway. You're not going to heaven. Your daddy told you so," which was not the truth. So, once I got the truth and could see the light. First of all, I don't even agree with organized religion. I'm not *down*. I have removed myself from organized religion pretty much. I need to step back and reassess some things because I'm not going to be a part of any institution that's going to make me feel indifferent about "Ida Mae," so I stepped away from the church. Right now, I have church here. I had to have a long talk with God about this. We did. We had to have a long discussion in my mind and my heart about church, and I told God, I said, "Listen. I won't abandon you if you won't abandon me." He let me feel in my heart that, "Yes, there's something wrong there. You're right. You got that feeling. It's right." It's something that has been tampered. It's not what it was set out to be. And my father was so damned, they were so judgmental. OMG. Like they would be like, love the, what's that thing? Love the sin, hate the sin, love the sinner, but then they still treat people crazy. You know, this one was welcome, that one wasn't. Even after I was gay and had girlfriends, they were not welcome. They didn't, they wasn't feeling no love. [Laughter] Nobody feeling no love here, you know what I'm saying?

And then my father sent so many mixed messages because him and my mama used to fight. It was a violent relationship. So, how you going to stand up in church and hug on these gals over here and make peace with these over here, and then you come home and kick my mama's ass? I ain't feeling you. It was definitely some things going on about religion early on. You know? And my father, I can tell that he was a product of his raising. I had to lighten up on him because his light was dull, because it had been dulled in his youth. He only was acting in good faith on what he thought was the truth. I just don't agree with his truth. We have a right to disagree. So, he was firm about his belief until I put him in the ground. He felt like he was on the right track. He was remorseful about some things concerning my mom, but he did tell me one day, he said, "You know, I don't know about this gay thing, 'Ida Mae.'" He was pretty old when he said that to me. I know he sat on that porch and thought about all the shit that we went through and how he could've been different, being the head of the household, to actually have more peace in the house, more togetherness. Him being the head of the house, he dropped the ball, and he knew it in the end, and he was very apologetic about it. I had to forgive him on them notes. And so my father being a minister, it didn't make it no better for me. The shit heated up because you have to look a certain way to be a minister and your kids have to look a certain way. There can't be no abhorrent behavior because you Reverend [last name]'s daughter. So, it didn't work for me.

What about your siblings? You're one of six. Where do you fall in there?
I am the second born.

And all of your siblings alive now?

Every one of them. I've got two that are flat on their backs with strokes, and I got two that are on their feet, one that had a stroke but she's still walking and then I got another one, so I got four sisters and one brother who lives in Delaware. [. . .]

When you were growing up did you know other gay people? Did the kids see gay, did they talk about gay people?

Miss Randy lived on the hill, and we tortured Miss Randy from childhood on. Miss Randy come up, and when he was seven years old he would put on an apron and his mama's hat or whatever it is. He has always been gay. Randy took care of the house when his mom and dad was at work. He cooked. He cleaned. He was Miss Randy. He always was a sissy. We called him a sissy, but I had no idea how sex played into it. I was so dumb on sex it was just ridiculous, but they kept that from me. Even after playing outside, I didn't know how significant it was. [Laughter] Randy was just a sissy. That's all. We used to call him a sissy. We tortured that boy. Then we thought Fred was a little gay, a little light, but mostly boys. But I noticed that women treated me differently in my community, and they knew I was a tomboy. Miss [last name] [. . .] loved me, honey. She stopped me, "You want a sandwich or something? Let me get you some Kool-Aid or something?" She said, "You a different little girl." She knew. And she knew because she was. You know what I'm saying? I met so many women. There was about three women in my neighborhood that I knew were gay women, but they were married to men because gay women got married. They didn't be gay. [Laughter] That's wasn't happening. But looking back on it, I could see that that was the deal.

Do you think they were tipping out even though they were married?

I do. I think people's being themselves. As quiet as it was kept, they was in there fighting about something. I don't know what they were fighting about, but everybody was fighting. Fighting was so common in households back then. I mean, "Oh Miss [last name] done got into it" or "Mr. [last name] across the street . . ." I could sit on the front porch and watch them drag motherfuckers and cut them up, and ambulance come, put them in the wagon. Wife would be right there with them. Be done cut 'em up. Come home drunk without the rent, it's on. It used to be a battle royal. There was a lot of domestic fighting going on.

What is your thoughts about homosexuality in terms of do you think people are born gay, do you think people choose to be gay, do you think it's a little of both?

I think it's a little of both, because I myself, I noticed my difference early on. I just enjoyed cutting grass. I enjoyed being under papa. I never really had that "give me a boyfriend" kind of thing. I always just admired pretty girls. Always. Even when I was little, I just admired girls. I loved pretty girls. So, I do believe people are born in their mix. I believe I was born in the mix. I ain't never entertained that whole regular shit. I've always run like a rabbit. "No! I'm not conforming. I ain't going there." Now, maybe it was because my mom and dad done fought so bad, maybe I didn't want a man because of that. I don't know. All I know is I never felt the urge to do that. [. . .] I look at gays now and I look at my friends how they have kids, they have adopted and did like that. Things have changed so radically since I was young, I wish I was young now. I would do it probably a little differently, but I'm not. But I am so glad to see, because my niece, seventeen, she's gay. I've got a nephew that's gay. So, just the fact that she can hold her girlfriend's hand and her dad ain't tripping, that's major shit, because when I was coming up it was get the whip.

I remember going in the Out of Focus one night and I got out the car and I walked across the street. You know, they had the lines and there was police sitting around, but I wasn't paying no attention because there's always the police, but when a guy was crossing the street, if you broke that line before your feet touched that sidewalk they was taking folks to jail [for jaywalking] in front of the gay bar. There were so many people, when they drug my ass off the street, "C'mon, you're under arrest," and they took me on the side of the building, and they had people lined up down the block. I hadn't noticed that. Then when the paddy wagon come, they used to have paddy wagon come and take you to jail, me and my girlfriend, they wouldn't let me in with the girls. They put me in with the boys. I had to ride down in the paddy wagon with the men. It wasn't a bad ride because they all had on makeup and shit. It was so fun. We had such a good time. Then we got to jail. They let my girlfriend go and told her that I was gone, and they had done isolated me and stuck me in a room in the back somewhere, and they wouldn't let me be with the boys nor the girls, and held me there for damned near twelve hours before she found out where I was and had to come back. Now this cost us between the two of us, we paid out over five hundred dollars to get us off us for jaywalking. That's the kind of harassment that you used to have to go through when you were gay. It was harassment. It was just straight up harassment. And they used to get away with that stuff. You had to be very careful. They would put you in jail for sneezing. [. . .] I hear the women before me used to go to jail for wearing pants. You know? You couldn't wear jeans and shit. It used to be against the law to dress like me, and now I'm like, "I'm glad I wasn't living in that moment." That was a bad moment for me. I'm like, are you serious? Yeah, you couldn't wear pants.

Was Out of Focus a black gay bar?

Umm-hmm. Sure was. I was tripped out. [. . .] And then another one used to be the Twenty-One Club, and I tell you the truth, we was a dry county so it was a lot of afterhours going on. We used to have a lot of afterhours joints, and that used to be everything. You leave the club—they'd shut it down twelve or one o'clock—go to afterhours joint, and you'd play cards and you'd eat pork chops until you fell out the door and the sun was up. I used to love them afterhours joints. They would be the death of me. There wasn't nothing in there but pretty women, liquor. You could smell the food frying because there was plenty of fried food, and they'd be there until the morning time, and then there'd be a card game in the back. You could lose all your money or win all of somebody else's. That's how they was rolling, honey. I tell you, when I moved out of my father's house, I got completely turned out because I didn't know what was going on so, I had all the crazies giving me instructions. I'm just glad to be here.

Tell me about how you came out to your father.

There wasn't no coming out. I didn't have to come out. I'm telling you, we dealt with that tomboy thing, and then when I got to college, I flipped the switch on that cross-dressing. It was like, [gasps]. I ain't telling nothing. They saw me coming. I heard my mama talking to my daddy one day about it. He said, "Look, what you want me to do?" She was trying to get him to take a hard line or something, do something. He was like, "What you want me to do? "Ida" been doing the same ever since we known her. You know she was different when she was two years old. We done talked about this." I heard him say that to her. They knew I was different that early on. You'd think somebody would of sat down and try to explain it to me. You know what I'm saying? Let me know what was going on. [. . .] Miss [last name] had to show me around the ropes. Why Miss [last name] had to be the one? Y'all could've told me something. "You're a little different" and "Don't you feel bad about yourself, you're still a good person." I didn't get no shit like that. I didn't get that. So, when I came after I changed my drag and everything, I went to my mom's house and that's when my dad told me, "You're not welcome here. Don't come here." That's cool. So, I used to have to sneak around to see my little brother. Sneak around and shit. I'd wait until my daddy go to work and I'd come and sit on the porch and talk to my mama, because she was so hurt about the whole thing. She didn't know what side to take, but she was not turning her back on me.

I remember sitting there one day. This was a turning point for me. I was sitting on the porch. I came there one day and had a bottle of wine in a brown bag because she knew I drank and I sat there with that wine. I didn't open it. I just sat it on the porch. I said, "I just wanted to see how you were doing, Mama." She said, "I'm fine, how you doing? You dragging that wine around." I said, "Well, it's my wine." I said, "You want some?" She said, "No, your dad will be home in two hours." In other words, if he hadn't come home, would she have taken that drink? So, I started to realizing that she was in a predicament, too. You know what I'm saying? She told me one day, "I didn't know I had options." I told her I was going with a girl, she said to me that day I was sitting on the porch with the wine, she said daddy's so upset about me. [. . .] And she said, "At least you figured out you had options. I never knew." You know? Shit. Then I started realizing that you somewhere you really don't want to be. You're doing something [. . .] because that's what they said you supposed to be and you're surprised about options? It blew me away. She was in a prison herself, and she had no tools because she was uneducated. She had raised all of us, and my daddy took advantage of her because she had no tools. She had no education. She didn't want to be there, but she didn't know the first thing about getting out of there. She was scared. He towered over her. I just think, I feel sorry for her. I feel sorry for my lack of understanding because, hell, I was fifty years old before I could figure out, okay, they were operating on what they had to work with. That narrowness is attributed to the fact that they were uneducated and they hadn't seen a thing. I know they was shocked that there was a Club Twenty-One. They would've been shocked too, you know.

Did your mother ever meet any of your girlfriends?

Yes, she did. My family is this kind of a family—we will be civil, but you understand that ain't no love here. So, they were civil to my friends, but you don't come here, and you won't spend no nights. So, if you coming to the family reunion, everybody else got a room. My brother got a room for his girlfriend, although they ain't married. You won't have a room here because you're gay. You go to the hotel room and you come for dinner. So, it was that kind of thing. Keep your life, that's your stuff. Keep it apart from us. Now, it was hurtful, and I tell you, I got me a therapist over at the Montrose Counseling Center and sat there and talked that shit out for about seven years, and now it's better. [Laughter] Now it's better.

What are your political views today about issues regarding the LGBT community?

My political views are I'm a Democrat, let me just say that first off. And I'm a Democrat not because my family was a Democrat. I am the underdog so I champion the underdogs, not the top 1 percent, because I'm not in the 1 percent, okay. So, I'm looking out for my people. I applaud Obama. This is not a rights thing. [. . .] See I have long figured out that the reason they don't want gays to get married is because [. . .] we pay a lot of taxes. Single people pay beaucoup taxes, so if you mess around and let gay folks get married, well, you losing a lot of revenue, and so I think it's money motivated. That's the whole motivation.

My father used to say something to me a long time ago. He said, "The path to hell is crowded," but I had no idea that it was crowded because of Christians, because I thought Christians was straight up, but that's on the path. These people have took the scripture and turned it to something that's totally ugly. So, I'm like the Pat Robertsons and all these evangelists, these TV evangelists, I just think that it's a business. They making money. This is how they make money, and this is how they keep on with the hate. They don't do it for the love of God. They do it for the love of man. So, I vote Democratic. I'd rather not be involved in politics, but I have to eat. I have to eat, and you can turn your back. There are a lot of black folks and a lot of people have died so that women might have a right to vote. I don't bullshit. I vote early. When they first open the polls, I'm sitting down, because I cherish the right to have a say. If it doesn't go my way, so be it. It won't be because I didn't have my say. And if you look at my Facebook, you see it's very political. If I see it and it moves me, I put it on there. So, yeah, that's about it.

I will go to the Democratic thing, and I'll do phone calls or I'll stuff letters. If you need a ride on election day, you call me. I'll put some gas in the car so I can roll all y'all if you all need to go. My girlfriend got a wheelchair van. We rolling. We going to vote. I believe in voting, and I hope that we have a very good turnout this year because there are some very important issues on the table. I do not understand why they do not want to give this man a second term because there is no president whether he was good or bad that they didn't give him a second chance to fuck up, you know what I'm saying? And I don't understand why they're trying to deny this man this right, because I think he's doing pretty good. I think he's made some major accomplishments, and if you got good insurance, well and good, but if copayments and out of pockets and ceilings and all that shit, if this is not worrying you, you 1 percent. I'm in a HMO, and that's the most I can afford, and the copay going up every year. You know, so what's the point of having insurance? Your ass can't afford it no way. I'm still broke. I can't afford it. It's getting to be a problem. So, if Obamacare, if that's what they want to call it instead of Affordable Care, if it works and if it'll get people to the doctor, everybody should be able to go to the doctor, man. This is getting real bad.

You know my out-of-pocket at United Healthcare is four thousand dollars. Fuck that. If I pay four thousand dollars, I'm already broke. I'm not eating fresh food. I am opening ramen noodles, and I don't eat ramen noodles. I have to eat fresh. I've got physical condition that says Miss [last name] you got to eat fresh. Your liver is compromised, you got to eat fresh. And so my struggle in life is to be able to go down and get a head of cabbage or something. That shouldn't be a struggle. My whole wheat bread is almost four dollars a damn loaf. I remember when bread was fifteen cents a loaf. Things have gotten out of hand here. You know what I'm saying, and I'm about to get priced out of it. So, I mean, politics is the only thing you got going for you. My daddy used to say, "Vote for the lesser of the two evils." I'm not saying Obama's Jesus, but he does give a shit. That's what's important to me. [. . .]

Do you think that the South is more homophobic than other regions of the country?

Yeah, but honey, Texas is fixing to be a swing state. Now do you know that's just like Jesus coming back? [Laughter] There's so many conservative rednecks down here. Texas a swing state? There's that many liberals down here that we can change this damned thing from red to blue? Hush! Things are changing. Things are changing from the church to the White House. Things are changing because people are becoming aware that they can be. These old white men in power have had this thing shaped so crazy for so long, it's too diverse now. We got people from all over the world. People ain't trying to hear this shit. Your rights got to be sitting on mine? They're not trying to hear this anymore, so I'm thinking that things are starting to change a little bit. I don't know if I'll see the total turnaround in my lifetime, but I sure am comfortable with what I'm looking at now. Miss "Ida Mae" feeling good. I'm like, yeah, honey. When I go out and see the children in the mall and they just enjoying themselves, and gay bars are becoming a thing of the past. We party with everybody else. We ain't looking for nowhere to be. We be wherever people be. I like that. I like that. That's change.

What has been the impact of HIV/AIDS on your life?

HIV/AIDS. Well, all of my boyfriends have AIDS, and I don't know if that's an impact because they seem to manage it well, but they have little side issues and stuff, so other than being impacted because my friends, I've lost so many friends. Oh Lord, you know? I just can't believe they're gone. So, that's the impact it has on me is I've lost so many people. I don't have any relatives that I know of that are positive, but you know, knowing my family it would be the ultimate secret. "Take it to your grave. Don't let nobody know." But I'm a very open kind of person. I even let my relatives on my Facebook. This is me. I'm over with secrets. I'm so done with secrets I don't know what in the world to do. You understand? This is the deal. I said it or I didn't say it. If I hurt your feelings, I apologize for it, but I am not the one. They used to say when I was a kid, "Honey, I save the ground I walk on." Damn right, I save mine too. If I owe you an apology, I apologize. If you owe me one, you apologize. I can't clean out my damned karma checkbook every year, because it's something that's going to drop by the thing, you know? If you stressing me, if you just can't get it together, anything that might cause me to have the risk on my liver, I let it go. I can't fix it. If I can't fix it, I'm moving on.

I've come to a realization. I've got some acceptance in my life. I've learned to do patience, hallelujah, and what makes me feel good is people half my age are getting there and it took me fifty years to get there. To see my niece in a yoga position meditating, that feels good to me because I didn't know what impact that had on you until I was fifty, how dangerous stress was. Control stress? What are you talking about? I had no idea what that was, but to clear out your mind for a minute and just breathe and feel the spirit of the God you serve, that is so healing. You know what I'm saying? I believe in God because I can't do it by myself, and it has worked for me. I'm sixty-two years old, and they say, "Well, you ain't rich and you ain't nothing, and your God ain't done nothing to you." Yes, it is because my God kept me peaceful while all this shit was going on. Do you know how much that's worth, just the peace? So, yeah, I'm fine. I got peace and I know that if anything go down, my first human reaction is to go [gasps]. Just be still for a minute, just be still and believe in your heart that you got angels all around you and God is working in your behalf.

Sometimes I see change that don't look right to me, but I just be still because some of the worst shit has made me a better person. You know what I'm saying? Something I perceive as totally horrible, like losing this three inches on my leg, but I have slowed down and done my writing. My life has not been terribly bad, but when I was there up in that hospital, I let my mind go places that it did not need to go. So, that's what the love of God has done for me. That's what having God in my life has done for me. It calms me down. I feel like I got a husband or a wife or whatever I need, whatever support I need. They say, "Well, your God . . ." Don't tell me nothing about my God. I give my God a lot of heavy stuff, and it's all taken care of. [. . .] God has done well by me. You know what I'm saying? I don't work nowhere. I don't have no circle or some money. I get my little check every month and I make it. That woman gave me the couch. That's a better damned couch than I had before I left here. Look at that lamp. That ain't a bad lamp. But God out there, like God be looking out for me and then my needs will be met. All I have to do is be still and believe. That's what I do.

You were cross-dressing in college, right? Were there other women who were cross-dressing as well?

No. To tell you the truth, when I was coming up through there it was like I kind of stood out a little bit. You know what I'm saying? It wasn't men and women that dared, I don't even remember other gay women at Miles. And I'm sure it was. I was the one of a kind, and I was so different. I used to have this, it wasn't a backpack, but it was an army bag. It was green and I kept my books in it, and I had it thrown across my back. I don't know, I just was so, uh, God almighty, I was just so. . . . And people went from calling me "Church Girl" to "Mack Daddy." Church girl to Mack Daddy.

So, you literally did a one-eighty.

I did a one-eighty on they ass. The minute that boy [Frederick] pulled me out that garter belt and that girdle, it was on. For years I didn't own another dress. I didn't buy them. I didn't fool with them. The discomfort of the whole thing, the whole hair straightening thing, that used to drive me nuts. Top of my ears be burning. Cut this shit off. Cut the hair off. Give me some boots. Give me a pair of jeans. Let me chill on Friday night. I'd get sharp, go out to the club, have me a few drinks, hang out at the overnight joint. Everything changed. My daddy just totally wrote me off. He was like, "You're lost, you're lost." That's the way it was, and after I finished college I did. My daddy let me live in a house that he owned. That shocked me, but he let me live there. He let me and my girlfriend live there. But my daddy, as hard as he was, I think he was more understanding of me than my mom was. I think my mom put a lot of pressure on him to do things concerning me that he would had not have done if she wasn't putting pressure on him. She told me one day, she was putting a damned chicken in the pot and pulling out a rooster, she said, "Tough as hell." [Laughter] So, stuff like that. That's the kind of shit we used to get into it about. I remember her cornering me in the room one day. "I want to know what you're doing with the women. What are you doing? They're calling all night long. What you doing?" No answer. I have no answer for that. It was a miss. It was a miss. I have no answer for that.

Then they would call me Don instead of "Ida Mae," and that just burned her nerves, honey. "Ain't no Don living here! Who you talking about?" She'd get on their nerves more. "I tried to call, but your mama wouldn't even call you to the phone." I know she won't. [Laughter] This the kind of stuff that I went through.

Is your mother still alive?

No, my mother and my father are passed. My mother passed about ten years ago, and my father passed about five, maybe four.

Did you and your mother reconcile before she passed away?

Not really. We were not enemies. I was there when she died, but she still wasn't having this gay lifestyle, honey. That was one of the things she said before she had the last stroke: "You know you're going to hell if you keep fooling with these women," and I say, "Yeah, Mama," because I have no more argument for her. She believes that. Let her take it to the grave. If that's what she believes, that's what she believes. I'm alright with that, so I just pat her on the back and say, "Yeah, mom, I know."

What about your siblings? How did they deal with you—

They cut my ass off just like my daddy said. My closest sister was [sister's name]. We were like a year apart. We were always close. She married [brother-in-law's name], and he beat her ass, and she just turned on me when she found out I was gay, and I had to find out from mama how she felt. I didn't know that she felt that way. Then one day she was coming down to San Antonio to visit my mom, and I was there, and my mom said, "[Sister's name] coming." I said, "I'll wait on her because that's my sister. I ain't seen her in a while. I'm going to wait on her." I sat there. About thirty minutes went by. Phone rang. They was just talking. I set thirty more minutes, and finally my mom said, "Look, she's not going to come as long as you here. [Sister's name] can't stand you, so you go on." Oh God, I was just devastated. I cried all the way back to Houston. Oh God, I thought that was one that was with me. My sister [sister's name] cut out on me, [sister's name] cut out on me, [sister's name] cut my ass a loose. They all cut me a loose. Now today, [sister's name], she's quiet, but I went to see her a couple months ago, and I thought she was shunning me, like didn't really want to see me, so I left. She was doing something, so I got up in my car and got up and left. She called me and apologized to the way she treated me. This was a couple months ago. My sister [sister's name], she told me one day, "You think you going to heaven; you got another thing coming." I said, "Who made you Jesus?" So, I don't pay her no attention. Me and my sister [sister's name], we can't discuss politics or religion. Other than that, we get along just fine, but we can't go there. My sister [sister's name] had the stroke, so she's flat on her back. She won't even see me, and she got six months to live with ovarian cancer, and I can't even get an audience with her. That's how deep, that's how deep that is.

Because you're gay?

Because I'm gay.

After all these years?

After all these years. And then my sister [sister's name] loves me to death now, who has always been more accepting of my friends because she always just like, "C'mon down. Y'all c'mon down. Y'all can't sleep in here because you know my husband will have a fit, but y'all come down and have dinner." She was always a little more accepting. She had a stroke. She flat on her back. I'm her best friend in the world. She called me this morning to tell me, "You coming down?" Yeah, I'm coming down and go visit with her and shit. She can't even get there and wipe her own ass. She in a diaper and shit, she laying on her back. It's just funny how things have changed with my family and the way, I'm so surprised I'm still on my feet. I thought that I would be flat on my back by now. I've had this hepatitis since the seventies. I have the degenerative joint disease. I have had thyroid problems, and I had two chemical treatments that have damn near killed me. I've been in a wreck that I tried to eat a damned steering wheel. I got all kind of shit. I got issues, you know what I'm saying, but I'm still alive, and I'm still vibrant, and I still feel good about my work.

So now, like, I'm doing the portrait thing and I'm doing a lot of good things, and I have for the past ten years, and it's been a real fun experience, and they have started to respect me because I don't go around them if they don't. So, I need some respect. I'm older now, y'all. I don't got no secrets. This is me. I'm still the same person. I think some of them are still surprised that "you still gay?" Like I was going to be something else. "Well, since you just going to die this way, c'mon. You alright. You a good old girl. You ain't never hurt nobody." I think I might be the reason that my family might be civil towards gay. I think my sister [sister's name], if the truth be known, she's gay but she chose to be, what's that word when you having no sex? Abstinent? For her life. Now that's hard. That's hard shit. I just believe that there was no choice. She's never been married. I've never seen her with a man. She thinks I'm going to hell for being an actively practicing homosexual. I don't know. I don't know. If someone in my family was gay, they'd keep it a secret. If my brother was gay, I'd never know it. He'd take it to his grave because that ain't right for the man he is and my daddy wanted him to be. So, I don't know, he's been married two or three times. I don't know nothing about him. I told him all the time I know him as a brother. He's a good brother. He's a good provider. If you want to know anything else, you going to have to ask some damn body else because I ain't never shut no doors on him. I ain't never shut no doors on none of them. In order to ignore a person, you need to shut the door, and I don't know these folks like that. These are my sisters, and I love them to death, and I would do anything for them, but I don't know. My sister had a stroke, and I went to Alabama, and somebody asked me something about what kind of music she liked. What the hell you asking? I don't know nothing about this woman. Shit. I don't know what food she like. I don't know what color she like. I don't know if she like music. All I know is that she thinks I'm going to hell. That's all I know. I don't know nothing about these folks. I really don't. Shit.

The niece that's a lesbian, whose daughter is she?

My brother's. My brother. My brother, I had a little bit of a hand in raising him, so he's never shunned me for being gay. [. . .] So, he's always been around my friends as far as me being gay, so it [. . .] it would have hurt me had he taken a hard line on his own daughter about being gay. I'm like, no way. Who you defrauding? But he didn't. His thing was, "Look, I love my daughter." Hell, at least he ain't got to worry about her getting pregnant before she finish college. That's the scope of his concern on the matter. You know what I'm saying? But he wouldn't tell my sister that she gay. I bet nobody else in the family knows she gay but me. If she don't tell them, they'll never know, because that's the family business. Family business is a mess. It'll keep you in the dark. It'll keep you away from therapy. It will keep you away from help with that secret shit. Ain't going to tell nobody. I'll tell you. You understand? If something cross my ass up in here, I'm going to pick up the phone. [. . .] "Hey, they getting ready to pull this car." Ain't no shame in my game. This is what's happening, and I had to learn that because I was raised, "Don't you tell this. This is a family secret. We're going in here. You don't tell nobody. Even when he was whooping our ass, don't you tell nobody." When it should have been a sign on the roof: "This motherfucker beating my mama." There should've been a sign on the roof, then maybe he would've backed up off her. You know?

Did you ever have a long-term relationship?

All of 'em been long term. The one I came to Texas with, I was with her for fifteen years, and the woman that I just broke up with about four years ago, I was with her for ten. So, they all have been, I have not been with a woman less than five years, so I'm one of those kind of people that locks in until it gets something on down that I can't change that's just totally unacceptable to me. Then it be time to put my shit in a bag and go head on. But see, I'm at the point in my life now where I don't think I'll ever live with another woman. I really don't, because I'm really enjoying having control over the thermostat, remote control, and shit. All this is shit I never had control over. I can say how many pictures go on the wall and what colors go up in here, because I be sitting over in a corner somewhere twiddling my thumbs while they moving shit in and out. They ask you something, "Well, what color should I paint it?" "I like that blue." "Well, we going to put the green." What's the point? I'm so easygoing. I just never raised any saying about anything. So, I guess that's why I'm not in a relationship, because I've always been too passive. I'm like, don't rock the boat. Sit down. Be still. I'm cool. You ain't got nothing but keep some fresh food in the house, pay the damned bills, put some gas in the car. I'm simple. It don't take much for me.

What are your best memories of growing up in the South?

My best memories of growing up in the South had to be centered around my grandmother, and that was very young, because my grandmother lived in Odenville. My granddaddy had a juke joint. My granddaddy sold some of the best whiskey that you can make in a field, and people would come from Tennessee, all over to get his white lightning. So, there was a lot going on in my grandmama's house. My mama used to take us there and put us in a corner, "Sit down, don't you move," because it was people moving, and he had a store on the property. He owned the lumber yard. He had school buses around that he picked up kids. He was just an entrepreneur, a straight-up businessman. I used to love to go down there because you could always hear the blues in the background. The jukebox, the Wurlitzer be going out there and shit. I used to love it. Everything seemed so light, lively, and they'd be drinking and shit. As soon as it get dark, "Honey, y'all get in the car, we leaving." Just when the fun getting started and the jukebox going and this chick's standing on the front porch shaking her ass and got goosed up and everything, "Y'all get in the car. Time to go." So, I used to like going to my grandma's house. [. . .]

I was named after her. She was such an easygoing person. She, too, was abused, but it wasn't abuse back then. You know, the way my grandfather used to talk to her or the way he used to have her to shave him after he come back from the field like she wasn't doing shit all day. And she wake up in the morning first, she had to light the damned heater sitting in the oven. They wouldn't even put their feet on the floor until she got up and made it warm and they could smell coffee. And then she fed him and everything, she would get to work. They'd leave, go do what they got to do. That chick be out there with her apron turned up like this, throwing that shit at the garden and wringing a damned chicken neck, throwing his ass over the corner, let him bleed. Take that shit in the house and wash that off, come back out with a bucket of hot water, put that motherfucker in there and get the feathers off of him, and all this shit is ready. When they come in, you can't do nothing but smell good food, and he come in there talking shit, dragging his friends ready to get drunk and shit. You know what I'm saying? She be working until her hands looked like knobs dealing with them damned wooden stoves and shit. It's just hard, and then she'd have to see about him, listen to him talk crazy to her and shit. You know? I didn't know that was abuse, but yeah, she was abused, too. He'd come in and say, "Alright, you got to fix some food for these fools." Half a dozen drunk motherfuckers, and she'd get up and run in the kitchen and start, get that oven running, going, get that stove going. You smell the pork frying and shit. Feed them motherfuckers, give them coffee, whatever they need, and they used to do shit like that. He was abusive, man. I think they ended up breaking up. They didn't end up together because he walked in one day had a bit to drink and pulled a shotgun and pointed it at her because of some shit he didn't agree with her about, and finally her son took her out of there. She had a heart attack behind that. She sure did. He scared her so bad she had a heart attack, and her son came and moved her out and put her in a trailer and told his daddy, "Don't you ever fuck with her again." My uncle did that, yeah.

This was your mother's mother?

Yes. And my father's mother, I didn't know much about them. I never really met those folks. Every now and then I'd run across uncles or something. I used to like Aunt Mamie. Aunt Mamie had hairy legs, and I used to sit there when I was a kid and I used to just rub her legs. I just rub that leg. She let me just sit there and rub that leg. I loved it. She come in the house and say, "How y'all doing?" She sit down and sit down. She'd say, "I knew you was coming," and I just sit there and rub her leg, and she just love it. [Laughter] That was Aunt Mamie. She was abused, too. I remember my mom and dad get in a fight one day, and she told my daddy, "Mamie would be alive if Willie wouldn't beat the shit out of her." [. . .] It used to run in families, and I think it still does. An abuser was raised by an abuser gives you an abuser. Here comes another abuser, and you just have to work on. Back then there wasn't no therapy. I didn't even know about AA until I was in Texas. AA? You mean they got something that will stop a motherfucker from drinking, all my whole family been died from alcohol abuse? I had no idea, AA. All of them died. All of my uncles died from drinking, drinking, drinking, and you mean to tell me that there's an organization that deals with drinking? I had no idea. I slid through by the seat of my pants on ignorance. There's so much that I did not know. That's the reason I be trying to spout information. You need to know this. Everybody needs to know something. You need to know some things. I'm always giving information. [. . .]

Even though I'm not with a church, I think my Christian upbringing helps me to be a gentler person because [. . .] I got heart. I don't know if that comes from the South or not, but I empathize with a lot of people and their suffering. I try to treat people the way I want to be treated. I believe in the Golden Rule. What go around come around, so maybe all of that being in the South has done that to me, because I never lived in the North. I don't know if would have these same beliefs or feelings if I was from somewhere else. I think that my parents helped shape me, and I got way out there. You know how you get way out there? But I look back and I knew that I was in the wrong place. I could feel it, that I was not in a place of peace, and I struggled to get back there, and I knew of a place of peace because of the way I was raised that there is such a thing. Although I didn't see it at home, but I read about it. I was a very good reader. I used to read a lot of things, and I knew that there's such a thing as peace and a way to live and treat people. I read the Bible from cover to cover—twice. I was confused when I got done reading it, but there's some things in it that stuck with me, and especially when Christ was dealing with people and their suffering. That stuff stuck with me. So, I don't condemn the Bible. I know it's been altered. I feel it. But I still keep one in my house because if you read it and you're mindful of how you feel, I think it can be very helpful.

How do you feel about the life choices that you've made in light of being a black lesbian?

How do I feel about the life choices? Let me tell you why I'm not angry with "Ida Mae" about my life choices, because I'm Ida Mae and I'm alright with who I am. If I were not alright with myself, I'd be pissed. But all that shit I went through, all that shit I put myself through was a process, and I was never alone. I can name you some times when I knew it was straight up miracles. I was never alone, and I never felt alone, even when I was at my worst. So, I have no qualms about the things that shaped me. I'm alright with it. I understand the process. So, I'm cool with that.

Books Saved My Life

Mary Anne Adams

13

In many ways Mary Anne is the central protagonist in this book. She was among the first group of women I interviewed in Atlanta in the summer of 2012, and it was through her that I was introduced to many other women. Perhaps coincidentally, she is referenced by other women that I interviewed who either live in Atlanta or did at one time. Her work as an activist social worker around LGBT health issues has put innumerable folks in her orbit. She is also the founder of ZAMI NOBLA [National Organization of Black Lesbians on Aging], an organization that focuses on black lesbians over the age of forty.

I spent much of my interview with Mary Anne with my mouth agape because the stories of her childhood were so over the top. I likened them to the southern gothic fiction of Flannery O'Connor or William Faulkner, the latter of whom was a resident of her hometown of Oxford, Mississippi. It's hard to believe that she actually survived the dysfunction of her home life. She is also a breast cancer survivor. And yet, she is one of the most cheerful and optimistic people I know—perhaps because she has dedicated her life to helping others.

I could not get the entirety of Mary Anne's story in one sitting, so I conducted two interviews with her over the course of a year. Below, the two interviews are intertwined. The first interview took place on August 9, 2012, and the second one took place on August 27, 2013, both at her home in Atlanta.

I was born in Oxford, Mississippi, in 1954. [Long pause.] As I grow, evolve, and learn more about the location of my childhood, I find myself describing it various ways at different times. But, you know, I'm certainly not going to give you these tired clichés like my childhood was really happy, because it wasn't. I would say it was challenging, at best.

Oftentimes, I felt very disconnected, very disjointed from my family. I felt as though I was in the wrong family much of the time. And wanted to be someplace else actually. Never got the opportunity, unfortunately. I just never felt different. I was left-handed. I was almost a breech birth. I was born with a caul over my face. And if you know anything about that, you know that you are told from an early age that you can see things—that you're special. And later I realized it's a membrane that's just extra. But nonetheless, I kind of grew up with that kind of hanging over me and being really afraid of it. Being actually pushed to explore it and to embrace it. But based on a lot of other things that happened in my childhood, I was afraid of that. I had a childhood very much marked by suspicion and a lot of myth. And as a childhood very much marked by death at an early age. A lot of loss, a lot of grief, a lot of poverty. And I think my saving grace was the fact that I was a bookworm. I grew up in kind of a two-generational family. There are ten of us—five girls and five boys. I'm the second oldest . . . my brother is the oldest. He insists, though, I'm the oldest, because there's a lot of responsibility that my brother certainly shrunk from. And I had a different sensibility about the world, so I always felt things very deeply. I would find myself, Patrick, literally crouching under the table in the house.

There were three of us for a long time, my brother and sister. I'm the middle child. So, people would come to the house and they would look at my brother and say, "Oh, he's so strong," because, you know, he was very rambunctious. He was just all into everything. And my sister was really cute. Then they'd look at me and say, "Oh, okay." I mean, probably not in those words, but that was the sense that I got. And so, my claim to fame became the fact that I was really smart. I was really respected for that in my community, and I can remember that I was encouraged to be smart. I got away with not doing a lot of chores because I was reading. My mother would often say all I had was book sense and no common sense, and I believed that for years. And finally, one day, I had this epiphany because I had just done something that required common sense. And I was like, "Oh, I do have some common sense." I mean, really, because I heard it so much that I internalized it. And so, after that day, it was like, "Wow, I do have some common sense." I can actually screw in a light bulb or [laughter] connect something. I don't have to go read and try to figure out step one, step two, step three, step four. So, it was that kind of childhood. Various paths along the way. It was different. It was wonderful. It was horrible. There was nothing static in my childhood.

What kinds of things did you do as a child in terms of a community of children? Games or activities?

Well, interesting question. I was left-handed. I was very much intro-verted. I was alone. Not lonely but alone, oftentimes by my own design. So, I couldn't jump rope. I couldn't play ball. I couldn't play marbles. I couldn't bat the ball. So, I don't think I ever tried to develop those skills because I couldn't do them. So, I didn't find myself oftentimes outside with the other kids, trying to do those kinds of things. I was in the house reading a book, sitting near my mother and her friends as they discussed who did what and how. I was that kind of kid who [they would tell], "You need to stop listening to grown folks' business"—so much so to the point where [they] became oblivious after a while. It was like, "Oh, it's Mary Anne," and they would continue to talk, because they just came to expect me as a fixture under the table, reading a book. After a while, that's just who I was, that was just my role in the family. Whereas my brother and my sister were out and about. But I generally was home, on the back porch, reading, under the house, in the house, that kind of thing. [. . .]

The community I grew up in was called Freeman's Town. And after Re-construction, there were black folks who lived out on the farms and stuff, and they migrated into town, into a certain area in Oxford. And they developed their own businesses. The schoolteacher lived next door to the domestic worker, to the minister. I mean, we all lived in Freeman's Town. And Free-man's Town had about maybe less than ten streets. It was a black section. There were maybe three black sections, but Freeman's Town was the first and the one that was most widely known, so education was just highly val-ued. So, the fact that I'm the little kid walking around with the book. Because we could walk to school, we could walk to downtown. We were a stone's throw away from Ole Miss, that's how close we were. So, everywhere I went, I would walk with this book in front of me.

What were you reading?

Anything. Anything I could get my hands on, Patrick. That's what I read. I would read soup cans, literally. My mother would read these *True Romance* magazines. I would read those. I would read the *Farmer's Almanac*, because that was popular, because folks were growing stuff. And I remember the first time I read it, I realized my mother and I had the same horoscope, I cried. [Laughter] I will never forget that because I did not want to have the same horoscope as my mother. [Laughter] I'm Libra, she's Libra, you know, Sep-tember 25th, she's October 7th. But I read everything. Books saved my life. It allowed me to imagine a world outside of where I saw myself kind of being stuck. And I realized there's a whole world out there. I remember when the lights would be turned off, I would be under the covers with a flashlight, reading. It was almost an addiction for me. I mean, I had to read. I could not not read. Could not not do it, really. I would go to my grandmother's every summer. She lived in Water Valley. Oxford is a town that supposedly was sold by this Choctaw woman but, of course, was stolen. There are a lot of Choctaws. Water Valley was about thirty minutes, where my grandmother lived, and we'd go every summer. And I would spend my summer sitting on the stoop, reading the Bible, that's what I did. I mean, whatever I could read. Sears catalog, I was not discriminating. [Laughter] Really, I wasn't discriminating, whatever I could read. I didn't have the luxury of having money to have books at my disposal, you know.

And we had a blast. We couldn't go to the so-called white library at the time. And there was a black library, Miss Nancy Armstead, it was a house right next to her house. I guess the black folks had gotten together and developed this little library. And I would go to my grandmother's for the summer, because during the summer there was a reading contest, whoever read the most books got a prize. You had to come to the library and read the books. I would come back maybe two weeks before school would start, go and read the books, and still win the prize, even though I hadn't been all summer. I mean, that's how I read. I was a voracious reader. Just voracious. [. . .] And then when I was in like ninth or tenth grade, we were allowed to go to the white library. And I would go, and I'm doing my black militant phase, I'd order all these books [. . .] because they didn't have them, so they would order them, like *Look Out, Whitey, Black Power's Gon' Get Your Mama!* and if you go now and at the book cart, you will see my name. But they would order stuff for me. I know the white lady—her name was Dixie. And I went back there and they were like, "Oh, Mary Anne," because I was always there. I was always working on all these things, so that they all knew me.

Freeman's Town, was there a physical barrier that separated it from the white side of Oxford? Was there a railroad track, a river?

Actually, there was an invisible barrier. If you drove through Freeman's Town and right at the edge, it's where the white streets began, so it wasn't anything physically, I mean, we did have a track. There is a railroad track. But on the other side of that were black folk. But you didn't venture down there too much. So, it was just literally at the end of this street, that's where the white housing began. There was no river. And actually, as you walked to town from Freeman's Town, there were some white families. So, you just knew not to venture onto those yards or into those houses. [Laughter] [. . .]

What did your parents do for work?

My mother worked off and on. Mostly she didn't. When she did work, she would do domestic work or she would do babysitting. She would take in ironing and do that from home, seamstress, that kind of work. Out of the ten kids, I'm the only one who ever knew her father. And there's a whole story behind that, which I'm not averse to sharing. So, I had a stepfather, who actually adopted me, and who actually went to prison when I was maybe six years old.

I remember my sister being born. My earliest memory is my sister being born, I was three. And shortly thereafter, he and my mother got married. His name was Bubba. He had just come back from the war. I was born in '54, my sister was born in '57. . . . Bubba was actually reared in Chicago, but he never really knew his father. When he came out of the military, he migrated to Oxford so that he could really spent some time with Mr. Clarence and get to know him, and he met my mother. And then they got married. My mother's maiden name is Adams, and so of course, we're going by my mother's name. And my mother had two kids at this point. And this is the first time that she was married, when she married him, because she had my brother at fifteen. And then she had me at seventeen. And I remember him coming to my school after he got out of prison and asking for me. Because he was a carpenter, so he would come and get us out of school.

Did you know why he had been in prison?

Oh, absolutely. It was funny, because when he married my mother, my mother had these two kids already, then she had a third, so they had three kids. And I remember there was a time when we didn't have a lot to eat. And then all of a sudden, one day we just had all this food. [Laughter] And it was like a feast, feast or famine—hot dogs, we were just eating hot dogs, and I later found out that there was a black minister in town, Reverend Davidson, Hamp Davidson. And he had dropped his check. And so, Bubba found the check on the sidewalk and he forged his name, because he was trying to buy food for us. Because he's a carpenter at work. So, his father, [Mr. Clarence] who . . . had a prominent place, and I guess some more people in the community and said, "Please don't press charges because, he's trying to do the best he can." And so he refused. He said, no, he was going to press charges, because he needed to teach him a lesson. And I remember my mother taking us up to the jail before they shipped him off to Parchman Prison, because he went to Parchman. And I actually have a picture I'll show you of us being at Parchman with him. [. . .] At that time they used to wear the stripes, black and white stripes. So, my mother had me in a black and white striped dress.

My sister [laughter] in a striped dress. And my brother in a striped shirt. That was my mother. And my brother in a striped shirt.

So that you could take the picture?

So, that we could feel some kind of affinity with him [laughter] is my guess.

So, she stayed loyal to him while he was in prison?

Oh, absolutely. My mother was an interesting woman. My mother had a difficult childhood herself, as did my grandmother, so a lot of that woundedness was passed down, as is wont to do, unless you get some resolution. My mother was not wanted by her mother, so my grandmother would not allow touch to enter into my mother's life. And my Aunt Sarah, who was like fourteen when my mother was born, would take my mother and hold her and hide under the bed, so my grandmother, who was her sister, would not see her holding my mother. My grandmother didn't want anybody to touch my mother. So, my grandmother had five kids and my mother was the second child. But she treated her very differently. My grandmother made my mother leave school to go take care of her in tenth grade. And my mother often, often told that story. And it was just really had a lot of pain around that. She was just treated like a stepchild. She's the child that my grandmother never wanted. And my mother was always, forever trying to get my grandmother's approval.

I remember my grandmother would come to our house when I was eight or nine, and just completely change the whole house around. It was almost as though my mother was rendered a little girl again with my grandmother. My grandmother never respected her. She didn't really have any kind of tangible relationship with my mother. Now, her grandchildren, she loved us, because the three of us—for six years, there were just the three of us—so we would go every summer, on the weekends. And my grandmother, for us, was a place of stability. It was a place where we knew we could get three hot meals. We knew the place was going to be warm. We knew that there were some institutions that were introduced to us that were church, for one, family reunions, for another. And it's just really interesting to me, this disconnect between my mother and my mother's children. My grandmother would take me, literally, Patrick, around to the neighborhood and brag about how well I could read. Now, I'm about eight or nine or ten. And these women were probably, I don't know, in their sixties or seventies. And she would say, "Give her a book, she can read it." Now, these big, old, huge, dusty books. I didn't know half these damn words, but they didn't either. So, a lot of them were illiterate. They had low literacy skills. And so, I would get these books and I would like, fake the funk until I could. And they were, "Oh, baby, oh, that's so wonderful." And I'm like [laughter]. . . . So, this is my grandmother's way of showing love to me, because my grandmother was not affectionate. She was very much the matriarch of the community.

I'm named after my grandmother. So, everybody called my grandmother, "Miss Mary," everybody. She was very prominent in the church, could bake and cook like nobody's business. Somebody was always coming to the house for her to bake them a cake, or she was also a quilt maker. I have quilts to this day. So, she had that kind of prominence for those skills in the community, and was considered to be a woman of high integrity, which is important. So, that is the picture that was painted for me, from other people, about my grandmother, early on. My aunt lived with my grandmother. And my aunt was considered at the time an old maid, that's what they called her. She taught French at the high school, and she was a librarian.

And my first classical record I heard, Beethoven, was at my grandmother's house, because my Aunt Margaret played it. She would buy these books, and I could read them there for me. I remember the first time I saw *Ebony* magazine was at my grandmother's house. I actually wrote a letter to *Ebony* magazine. So, my aunt read a lot, I read a lot. So, that was a place for me, that I would go sometimes just to feel safe. Because I didn't feel safe at my mother's house often, because often we were hungry, we were cold, the utilities were shut off. My mother just could not cope with all these children. She didn't have the education, she didn't have the skills, she did the best she could, but I think oftentimes she was overwhelmed. And I think that she probably suffered from a low-grade depression much of her life. She didn't really want kids coming to the house. Let's say we didn't go to school one day. They would come and say, "Why you didn't go to school?" "Well, it's not your business and don't talk to them." So, it was very much that whole insular kind of environment that she wanted to keep us in. But being who we were, we kind of broke out of that. But if it was left up to my mother, we would have very few friends, because my mother had very few friends. We wouldn't talk to anybody about anything that went on in the house. No, no.

So, there was three of you for six years and then seven more came?

Yes. One more came. And then the other six came. So, Bubba was in prison for about no more than two years. Bubba came out of prison. Because this was our house and the school was right there [points across the room], literally we could walk across to the school. I remember coming home for lunch, I was probably second grade—yeah, second grade, and he was home. And I remember just not really wanting to have anything to do with him, you know? I don't know if I felt abandoned. I don't know if it was because he was in prison. Because I was a kid who—I was just kind of strange. But I didn't want to have anything to do with him. But once he got home, I loved him. I mean, he was—would pick us up from school. My sister was in kindergarten. Come to the school, get my brother and I, because my mother would be at work, and he would—he was a carpenter, he was self-employed—take us home, build these big fires, we'd roast hot dogs and marshmallows. And he was a fun-loving guy. He was an alcoholic, but he was a fun-loving guy. He was a very loving guy, so when he came to the school and asked for Mary Anne Shaw, because that was his last name, and they said, "There's no Mary Anne Shaw here," he pitched a fit: "I've adopted her, her name shouldn't be Adams," and I'm sinking in my chair. [Laughter] Because I felt things very deeply. Everything embarrassed me. I was that kind of kid, you know. So, I'm like, "Oh, my God." So, for the rest of that year, I had to go by "Mary Anne Adams-Shaw." I had the first hyphenated name, because they were like, well, they had my Adams on everything and they just put Shaw, you know. And I hated that, because I was always the first person they'd call with Adams. Now, all of a sudden, I'm almost here at the back, you know what I mean? [Laughter] [. . .]

So, he must have come back in the summer, because I remember we were just really just happy. I remember when James Meredith, that whole weekend, I remember that whole weekend, because we were very close, and I remember hearing the shots. [. . .] And I tell the story about my stepfather. I'm hearing these shots, and I'm like, "What's going on?" He said, "Oh, those peckerwoods don't want this colored man to get into the university." But that didn't really mean a whole lot to me. And the next day was Monday. I was going to school. And my brother, we would walk to school. [. . .] So, one day we were walking to school, and my brother decided he wasn't going to go to school. He would walk me to school, and he was going to shoot [play] hooky. So, he'd walk me, he'd say, "You can walk that," it was probably maybe a block or so, so I was walking, and I saw all these soldiers. I mean, for me, eight years old, it was like just a million soldiers, white soldiers with these guns, right? And I walked up, and one of them said, "Little girl, there's not going to be any school today." [Laughter] I'll never forget that, as long as I live. And I turned around, I run back as fast as I could. Well, my brother had stopped to throw rocks into the squirrels or whatever, so I was able to catch up with him. And we walked back out of the town. Freeman's Town was actually shut down, all the black sections, for like a week, that week. We didn't go to school. We couldn't really go into town to shop, because people were afraid. We had had threats on the community, the black community.

So, I remember that, that time really, really well. Not knowing that eight years later, I would be entering Ole Miss myself.

October 7th is my mother's birthday. We had an elderly friend who was in the hospital, and that morning my stepfather said, "I'm going to go visit him." And my mother said, "You should not go, because I had a dream last night." And he was like, "Oh, you don't know what you're talking about." So, he walked across the track, because it was a railroad track where we were. Now, we were on one side of the track and the black folks were on the other side of the track. So, he didn't have a car, so he was going to walk to see him. And my mother told him she dreamed that something bad happened to him. Now, when he was in Parchman, he was a really smart guy, outspoken, take no prisoners. I would read the letters that he would write to my mother, because I'd read them, and just very, very, very bright, just a smart guy. But he told my mother that there was some white guys he had gotten into it with when he was at Parchman, and they told him that if they ever got out, they were going to kill him. Well, he had come home that week and told my mother he had seen those white guys in town that day, so I don't know if this was weighing on her when she dreamt about it or what, but she said he shouldn't go. He was like, "Uh." So, that night—I'll never forget, it was a Sunday night—my brother and my sister had gone to bed, and I was up with my mother. And Mr. Clarence, his father, came to tell us that he had been killed and his body was found on the tracks. So, there was some speculation: was he drinking and did he fall asleep on the tracks? My mother always believed that those white guys killed him and put him on the tracks, because he had seen them in town that day.

Had he been shot?

Well, the train had just kind of cut him, it just pulverized him.

So, he got hit by a train?

Yes. Yes, he got hit by the train. And we left the house that night and went to my grandfather's house, to their basement, because he had a house with a basement. So, we literally went to live in the basement. My mother just became, just comatose with grief. And I remember the next day, that Monday, my brother just did not go to school, but I went to school, because I guess I craved some sense of normalcy, I had to go to school. I didn't have any books with me, but I went to school. And after school—when I think back on it, it's just so insane—but his father and my mother, some other folks had all the kids together. We had a bunch of cousins and things. And we went and walked up and down the track because we were looking for his brains. Because suspicion was that if your brains are outside your body and the birds peck on them or eat them, whatever, that the spirit will not rest.

Did you find them?

Probably not. I think we were all just kind of numb with grief, didn't know what to do. We did as we were told. The adults, I don't know what they were thinking. They weren't. I guess they believed that, so that's what we did. We went to look for them. And I'm sure we did not find them. I can't imagine that we would have or could have, you know what I mean?

Did they not find his head?

I don't know. There was a lot that they exposed us to, but also a lot that they kept from us. I'm not really sure. But that was my first experience with death, at eight years old.

So, I would say by the time I was sixteen we had lived in probably eighteen different places. Moving oftentimes in the middle of the night. And we were probably moving just on the heels of eviction. But we moved a lot. And oftentimes, we would move up the street. So, we would carry stuff. Or down the street or around the corner. It was not really too far away. So, that's why today, stable housing is very, very important to me. I'll pay the mortgage before I pay anything, because nobody's going to ever tell me to leave anywhere, unless I decide that I'm going to leave. That's why I would never move in with any partner that I had. We had to move into something together, 'cause nobody was ever going to say to me, "Get out," for any reason. That's a lasting legacy from my childhood, in terms of that whole piece, you know.

What role did religion play in your upbringing?

My grandmother was very, very religious. She was a member of Avondale Baptist Church. And when I was at my grandmother's every summer, I went to Sunday school. I went to Bible training classes in the summer. I went to BTU [Baptist Training Union]. We went to church every Sunday. I remember my little crinoline slips that were scratchy, and the patent leather shoes, and the little white, turned-down socks. It was just part of our lives. And it's interesting, but I was never comfortable in church. I didn't like it. I was supposed to like it, but I just never liked it. And of course I went, I had no choice. But [. . .] I never felt comfortable in my skin in church. I think because much of the time I was afraid because there was so much shouting going on. [Laughter] And I couldn't figure out why. And when you're twelve you're supposed to sit on the mourner's bench, because that's what Jesus did. And I was sitting on the mourner's bench that week. And Aunt Sarah and all her friends that kind of sit behind me. And I remember that summer, we probably had about five or six kids in the neighborhood sitting on the mourner's bench. And everybody's getting up, because they're feeling the spirit and they shouting. And I just remember sitting there thinking, well, what's wrong with me? Why am I not feeling anything? [Laughter] I remember having this conversation with myself. And I remember Helen that came the next night, said, "Well, while Helen was at home, she was praying. And she got the spirit so she don't have to sit back on the mourner's bench." And I'm thinking, so it got to the point where it was just me pretty much. And the women in the thing were just beating it, "Baby, baby, pray."

So, at one point, somebody hit me in the back so hard that I kind of yelled, right? And they go, "Oh, right here! Right here, honey!" And I didn't even know what's going on. [Laughter] But I'm thinking to myself, well, if this is what's getting me off this bench, then okay. But I can't say to you that I felt anything, other than the pain in my back [laughter] from being hit so many times. I mean, it was just really strange. So, [they say], "Here's one," so I got up, "Baby, do you accept the church?" "Yes, sir." I'm baptized in the river. You got to wear all white. I go to the river. And it's this huge, muddy river. And at the time, the superstition was if you choked or anything, that you didn't have your religion. And I remember the men, two men, going to the muddy river. And I'm trying my best not to choke. So, I'm terrified. Because the only thing that's going through my mind is not that I'm feeling joyous and live, spiritual, and religious, and now I know Jesus and—none of that. I'm afraid that I'm going to choke and that means I ain't got nothing, I got to go sit back on the mourner's bench. [Laughter] This is what's going through my mind the entire time. The entire time. And when you think back on it, it was just really kind of torturous. You got a twelve-year-old kid, being baptized in this huge river, and the people in church telling me, "Baby, you can't choke, you can't." It's craziness. It was just craziness. It's the way it was. [Laughter]

When did you first realize that you had a same-sex attraction? And what was your reaction to that realization?

[Long pause] I think it was something that was probably gradual. I always had these really intense friendships with girls. And I always had these really intense friendships with my teachers. I wanted to be around them. I always wanted to seek their approval. I would do things so that I was in close proximity to them. But I didn't know what to name that. [. . .]

I didn't tell you this, but when I was five years old, my uncle raped me. He was sixteen and I was five, and this was my favorite uncle. And we had come from Water Valley, and my mother had come to pick us up. And she had stopped at Mr. Clarence's house because we had moved like down the street. And she told Tib to take my brother and I on to the house. And I remember him telling my brother to stand guard at the door, because my mother was coming back, to tell him if she came, if he saw her coming down the street. And I just remember him just this heavy, sweaty body on top of me. And I remember telling my mother later that my vagina was burning. I'm sure I didn't use the word "vagina." And she says, "Well, you need to put some Vaseline on it." That was her response to me. Because I used to wet the bed, so maybe she thought I had wet the bed, now, I don't know.

But you didn't tell her that—

No, I just said my vagina was burning, because I didn't know what to say, you know what I mean? So, I think after that, I really became withdrawn, you know. In my neighborhood, there was a lot of sex going on among kids. Mr. Clarence's common-law wife, she had a sister who was an alcoholic. So, she had eleven, twelve kids. So, they were always up there at the house with Miss Anne. We were all there. During the summer we were all there. We lived in the basement. And my mother was at work and Mr. Clarence went to work. The boys, they would come in the basement and have sex. My brother would have sex. I mean, that's just what you did. Everybody was just sexual. [Laughter]

And what was the age range of these kids?

Oh, I would say from—well, I was eight when we moved there. So, eight to probably twelve.

And they were having sex?

Yeah. Oh, yes. Yes, they were having sex. As a matter of fact, I was sitting on the back porch step. My sister would tell you, I would sit on the back step. My sister and my cousin were in the house having sex, they were like six. And I'm going to tell you why they were having so much sex. They used to have houses kind of high on stilts where I lived. And my brother was under the house, and a lot of kids would go under the house and have sex. He was under the house having sex with Bonnie Faye, and they were probably ten. And then Sherry Anne, who was probably fourteen, would be in the bed with me and then she would be touching me. It was just a lot of that going on.

I'm trying to wrap my head around this. Were they just exposed to a lot of that from adults and that's what caused that?

I do—yes. They were exposed to a lot of that. I think folks were having sex in the next room. There was not as though there were tons of separate rooms in the house. So, I think you're overhearing people having sex, you're just exposed to that.

And this wasn't like little experimental sex, where maybe someone's giving somebody a hand job or something, this was intercourse?

This was intercourse. As a matter of fact, after that, we had moved again. I was probably sixth grade then. My mother had gone for the weekend to my grandmother's that Sunday, and Ralph would tell me, "Be on the lookout," because he and Elizabeth were having sex. And I was sixth grade, so he was—so I was twelve, he was like fourteen. They were in the house having sex while my mother went to my grandmother's! I mean, people, they had a lot of sex. There was a lot of alcoholism around. So, I think people were having sex and not being very mindful that kids were probably in the next room or whatever. It was just a lot of sex going on. [. . .]

And I think there was just so much woundedness, like Johnny Ray, for example. Now Sherry Anne would show me a lot of attention. I didn't get a lot of attention. So, I really looked up to her, and she's fourteen, and I'm like eight, nine, ten. And then Johnny Ray got Mr. Clarence's gun and was in the house and shot her and killed her. And this is my stepfather's sister. So, we buried him and then a year later, her. She had some friends, they were probably ninth, tenth grade at the time. I remember they were fourteen, fifteen. Three of them during the summer went to swim and all three of them drowned, all three of these girls drowned. Wayne Beavers, who was my best friend's brother, he drowned. Bobby drowned. A lot of these kids, they couldn't swim, they would go out during the summers. There was just a lot of drownings. [. . .]

So, do you think that this death and violence and sex impacted your ability to come into your sexuality?

Oh, absolutely. I think it impacted it in the sense that I think I would have come into it much earlier than I did. I think that there was so much of my personhood that was not free. One of the shining lights in my life was when I was twelve years old and there was an influx of civil rights workers into Oxford. And these were young civil right workers, social workers, and Reverend Wayne Johnson, who had grown up there, who had gone away to say, I don't know where he went, Milwaukee or someplace like that, came back home. And everybody always talked about Wayne. Wayne had the gift of gab, he was so eloquent as a minister, and he really was. He commanded attention when he spoke. So, he came back home, with his wife and two kids. And he was kind of sick, I don't know what was wrong with him. But he came back home and started the Black House. [. . .]

So, if my school was here [points to one end of the couch], say across the street, maybe two houses down was the Black House. It was a house that they rented, and we all called it the Black House. And all the kids would congregate at the Black House, because we all lived in town. After school, we didn't go home, we went to the Black House. And at the Black House, it was just a hotbed of activity. A hotbed of organizing. It was during the time when the students, the black students at Ole Miss were trying to get a black student union started. So, they would come to the Black House, because Wayne was over the NAACP. And we would kind of sit at their knee. I'm like, twelve, thirteen. And there was a paper they had put out called the *Soul Force*, and we would write for the *Soul Force*. They had those mimeograph machines, so we would do that. We'd put the *Soul Force* out. We would deliver the *Soul Force*. This is '66, '67? [. . .] So, folks would always come to have meetings at the Black House. And we were allowed to be there. [. . .] We were encouraged to be there, to listen, to learn.

And there was a social worker named Joe Delaney who was from Grenada. And Joe had gone to Mississippi Valley State, and he had been thrown out for his activism. And Joe came to Oxford, because they were developing legal services at the time. And Joe came to there, and Louis, and just all these civil rights workers—black, you know. We hadn't seen these kind of folk in our neighborhood quite like this. And after school, Joe would teach black writing classes, black literature classes. For me, a kid, who loved reading and writing, and to be taught how to do this and to be encouraged and to be somebody who they treated us with respect, like we were important, we were the future generation, was pretty heady stuff. I remember I wrote a play about [Martin Luther] King's life, and Joe, we had rehearsals. And we put it on at the teen center, and after the play we all marched through the streets that night, like we were marching to Ole Miss. We never quite got there. So, that was encouraging to us, you know.

And I remember Joe would tell me at every moment, "You're beautiful," would tell all of us, "You're all beautiful." And they also taught us that you are inferior to no one. You're black, you're beautiful, you're not less than anybody. If anything, folks are less than you. I mean, this was drilled in us. And we believed that. At the point, at the end of the day, we believed that. So, I think it dissipated a lot of fear that I had around a lot of things. I think that was kind of my blossoming as a young black girl, you know. Wayne Johnson started this whole cooperative movement in Oxford. We had the co-op store, and we could go to the co-op store and work. He started the cooperative daycare centers. We would go there. So, I was literally taught how to be an activist, how to organize at twelve years old. And people say to me now,

"Well, how do you know how to do this?" And it's like, well, I was taught to do it. I mean, I was really developed early on.

And then when I went to Ole Miss and I majored in social work sociology, I learned these skill sets, you know. But I do think that that was, for me, I think, the beginning of knowing I had some kind of agency, believing that I was empowered in a particular kind of way, to really dream big, to go beyond where I was, because I didn't want to be there. To just hear these stories that they would tell, they would weave these stories. You really got rewarded for being smart, being willing to come into classes, writing. Wow, I mean, they rewarded all that stuff, you know what I mean? And it was a sense of belonging for us. We had a Black House, we had something that was ours. We had two white teachers when I was at my school. And I remember one, she was a white woman who taught English. And over the intercom, they used to say, "For those kids who are going to the Black House after school, don't forget to bring *Black Boy*," and I would never get this, I remember she said, "Oh, I guess next they're going to want you to bring black paper and black pencil." I will never forget that. [Laughter] I remember Mr. Booth, who was a white teacher, we were kind of overcrowded and we had this trailer. I was in eighth grade. And in the trailer was a picture of Shirley Chisholm. And that was the first image that I saw like that, that I could look at every single day. That was really an awakening for me in so many ways. [. . .]

So, when did you have your first same-sex encounter?

Really late. When I was nineteen years old—I went to Ole Miss when I was sixteen. [. . .] And I wanted to go to Tougaloo [College] and major in journalism, because I had written for the school paper, and I used to write stuff. But the folk at the Black House told me I needed to go to Ole Miss because that was my cross to bear. [. . .] I didn't question that, that's what you did because they said the more black students [who are] there, the better it would be for students coming after us, so it was not anything that I really questioned, you know? And when I was there, I had some really close female friends. I mean, there was a lot of sexual tension and energy with this one woman, who I'm sure if I had been bold enough to make a move, it would have culminated into something, but no. We're traditionally kind of slow, but there was a lot of sexual tension. And then when I was nineteen and I graduated, I went to live on an army base for a year, Fort Campbell, Kentucky, with my Aunt Margaret [. . .] under the guise that I was going to enter in the military. I hated the military, everything about the military. I always preached against the military and marched against the military. There was no way I was going to the military. Marched against the military. And I remember the recruiters used to come and pick me up and take me. And I kept failing tests and he would come. So, finally, my uncle said, "Mary Anne, I know you don't want to go to the military. You don't have to go to the military. You can stay here and do whatever you want to." I said, "Oh, thank you." [Laughter]

So, I stayed with them a year. I worked on the post nursery. And I came out to myself. I wrote this thirty-five page letter to my best friend back in Mississippi, coming out. [. . .] It was from the beginning of my childhood to the end, I wrote that to Jackie. And her thing was, "Well, we figured that, really." And I met this woman named Mildred. And she was also working at the nursery. And I don't know how we started talking about this, but she was from New York. She had four kids. She had a husband. And I don't know how we started, so she told me she was bisexual. She told me about her life, how she used to be with these women. And I'm like, "Wow." I'm nineteen, I ain't never heard all this stuff, right? And she essentially offered to turn me out. I considered it, but then I decided I was too much of a romantic to do that. It had to be with somebody that I loved and was in love with my first time. And I wanted to be in a relationship. But, that relationship was pivotal for me in that she would bring me books to read. And I started to be able to kind of see myself in some of those books, in some of those materials. Hearing her stories were like, in retrospect, it's probably like being at her feet, like reading ZAMI, you know. So, Mildred really, I think, was there when I needed somebody like that to be there, somebody who spoke about being lesbian, about sexual as a very positive thing. Even though she was married and had kids, it didn't sound as though something that she would not go back to. So my first conversation was very positive. It was really affirming in so many ways. [. . .]

My mother had died of ovarian cancer. And I had become guardian of my three brothers and sister. So, I was like twenty-four or twenty-five, and they were like nine, eleven, and thirteen. And the boy was eleven. And Linda was nine and Rita was nineteen. And my sister who was nine developed a rare form of rheumatic fever, where she all of a sudden couldn't walk, she couldn't talk, she couldn't do anything. At the time that my mother was in the hospital in Jackson, Linda was at the hospital in Memphis. And my grandmother and my brother would not help out. My grandmother said that my mother had cancer because she was a sinner and this was God's way. And I remember being in Memphis with my sister Linda, and the social worker calling me, saying that, "Your grandmother cannot stay in the hospital with your mother, because this is what she's saying to her. And she's upsetting her." And my sister, who is three years younger, didn't want to go to the hospital at all, no how, she just couldn't deal with it, and my brother wouldn't go. So, it was just, it was craziness. And my mother, she probably was in the hospital for about a year, yeah, for about a year. Yeah. So, essentially, it was my sister and I would take care of seven kids.

And so I had just moved to Jackson, and I was on my own, and then this happened. And so my sister and I just said, "Okay, this is what we're going to do. I'm going to stay in Jackson and work, to get money for us. You're going to take care of the kids. And on the weekends, I will come home to give you a break." And so, that's what we did. Sometimes, I would come on Friday and my sister had a boyfriend, she had a baby. She was already gone to start, [and the] little kids are at home by themselves. They were being literally like readied for me. My sister was not the type who was nurturing in that sense, you know what I mean? She would provide a place. But in terms of doing homework and all that kind of stuff. So literally, I would get home and help them and do all this. And my mother's in the hospital. So, I don't know how we made it, we just made it. And when my mother died, we decided I would take the girls, because my aunt and my grandmother, they said they wouldn't take anybody, that we should put the kids to foster care. . . . And it never crossed my mind to put these kids in foster care. So, my sister and I decided that I would take the girls. So, there were three girls. And she would take the four boys, because she already had two kids. And we were going to do that, that was our plan. Except my middle brother, one day I was going to the laundromat, he said, "I heard you going to take the girls." And he was eleven. I said, "Yeah." He said, "But I want to live with you." And I thought, my God, this kid is asking to live with me. And when I would come home to take care of them, he would always go with me. He would always be with me. So, I'm thinking, this kid is asking to live with me. So, I decided at that moment that I would take the older kids, the four older kids, she would take the three younger kids. That way, he would be included, because I had an older brother who was sixteen. So, nine, eleven, thirteen, and sixteen. Two girls and two boys. Well, he came to Jackson with me. And I didn't have any relatives in Jackson. I hadn't been in Jackson but like a few months, and I didn't have any relatives. And I had a job working for the Federation of Southern Cooperatives. [. . .]

So, I remember saving, and the kids and I got a brand new house. And we lived in Presidential Hills, which at the time was the little middle class enclave. And we lived on Abraham Lincoln Drive. [Laughter] And I really grew up, because I remember shortly after getting the kids and trying to give them the lunch money, and I had ran out of money and had to go to the bank. So, I said to my brother Dennis, I said, "I'll bring your lunch money to school, just go to school." So, I was a little late, so when I got there, he was still in the room. I said, "Why didn't you"—the teacher said, "I tried to get him to go and eat lunch, I would give him the money." So, I said, "Well, Peewee," his nickname was Peewee, "why didn't you go and eat lunch?" He said, "Because you said you were coming." I said, "Well, how did you know I was coming?" He said, "Because you said you would." And I was like, oh, shit, this is serious. This is no play now. This is—this kid, "because you said you would." I was like, "Okay," so I really grew up that day, and really reared them. "I'm your sister, I'm not your mama."

And it's interesting, Patrick, because when my mother went to the hospital and left their father, who was schizophrenic, who had been institutionalized during the time that he was with my mother, my brother Richard, who lives here [in Atlanta] now, was at some neighbor's house, and they had to light a campfire. And Richard fell into the fire and burned his arm and his hand. He was in the hospital, and Grady was there with him and just left and just was missing. Somebody at some church in some rural area saw him like a couple of days later, looking like a wild man, all scratched up and all this, so he had a history of mental illness but we didn't know that. But my mother had met him because he had come to Oxford to get a job. So, he ended up going to Whitfield, which was called the Hospital for the Criminally Insane. That's the plaque, "State Hospital for the Criminally Insane." And it was the only hospital in the state where people went. And they had Thorazine at the time, so you know when somebody had been to Whitfield, because everybody who was there all puffed up and looking a particular kind of way.

So, he was also violent, very paranoid. Monday through Friday, he worked at Ole Miss as a janitor. He would come home Fridays, and he would start drinking, primarily beer and liquor, and he was a weekend alcoholic. And he would drink, and he would get the gun out and threaten my mother and threaten us with the gun. I mean, it was just that kind of situation. But my mother never would leave him. And we would always try to get her to leave him, after we got old enough to leave that house. So, when she got sick, me and my sister went and literally took her away from the house. When they talk about peoples' hair going gray overnight, his hair [snaps fingers] literally went gray overnight. I will never forget, I had never seen anything like that before, but it happened with him. Because as dysfunctional as that situation was, that was his normalcy, you know what I mean? And these were his kids. These kids would follow him around like Pied Piper. [. . .]

I will never forget this, because my sister Rita, who is the oldest, her period came on that night, and that was the night that he died. Those two things I remember. Because he was always waving the gun around, like I told you, and drunk. Well, he was threatening his cousin. They were at the house, he and his guy friends were drinking. And he shot him and killed him. And he was in shock or whatever. And they say he woke up in jail, somebody told him what he had done, and he had a heart attack and died. So, all of a sudden he's gone. My mother is in the hospital. My sister and I are just trying to keep our heads above water, do the best we can. So, we don't have the wherewithal, the language, the counseling skills to be able to give anything to them. I can't tell you what filled that gap. I don't know. I just know. When they came to live with me, I tried to do the best that I could and raise them like I wish I had been raised. My brother, who was sixteen, after a couple of weeks, he decided he wanted to go back to Oxford with his girlfriend. So, he left and moved in with an older woman. Not older, but an old woman, like he got a room with her. So, he was sixteen, so he essentially was on his own. And then my sister had the three younger kids and then I had the three older kids. And the three younger kids ended up going back and forth between my grandmother, who had said she didn't want them, my sister said she couldn't take care of them. But the kids who were with me, they remained—stayed with me for the ten years, until they went off to college and I moved here [Atlanta]. And we made it. I mean, I was working for Legal Services as a paralegal. I also worked as their newsletter editor. I just had two or three jobs, you know. And then when they all turned sixteen and they all got a job. My sister, the oldest, she actually was diagnosed as bipolar her last year of high school. And I had to have her committed.

And actually, after I got the kids—now, I think this is a really important part of my story—I subscribed to the *Gay Community News*. And it would come every week. And it had fifty million staples in it. And I would just look for it. And I learned a lot about gay culture through the *Gay Community News*. I learned who the writers were. I learned who the activists were. I learned what was going on. And, I mean, it was just a huge education for me. It was out of New York. It was huge for me. And then I had a friend, my best friend who had gone to Ole Miss with me, who I was working with at Legal Services in Jackson at the time, had went away to some conference. And I was like, "Well, can you bring me back some books?" And I asked her to bring me back Audre Lorde's books because we didn't have them in Jackson. So, this is how I was able to kind of get literature and to get stuff to read and that kind of thing. But yeah, the *Gay Community News* was like, that was my Bible, you know. I mean, those rags were so vitally important, and people just don't know what tremendous impact they have. Particularly with somebody like me, who just didn't have a lifeline. I didn't have a lifeline. [. . .]

And how did you find life in Atlanta, once you got here?

I think initially it was somewhat challenging for me. I didn't really know anybody. Jackie was in Athens. And she'd kind of come back and forth because it wasn't that far. And then I knew Donna. But I didn't really know anybody. And it was difficult in the sense that I was really grappling with a lot of things, with being in that relationship, because based on my background for me to be with a white woman [laughter] is totally not ever anything I would ever fathom, you know. I'm "black power!" I'm reading *Lookout Whitey Black Power Gon' Get Your Mama*, just totally, totally out of my reality zone. And you always read these romance novels and hear people say, "I just fell in love." So, that was really something I really was trying to come to grips with. And I just didn't know where to place that. [. . .] I had gone to Ole Miss and I had white friends, but by and large, my world was really, really black. And I didn't know what the politics were of the black lesbians here in Atlanta. I didn't really know how to meet them. I was trying to find a job. I was just trying to find myself and situate myself someplace early on. I met the women of ZAMI because there was this white lesbian that I met who introduced me to them, actually. She had a gathering at her house, and she was the only white woman there and everybody else was black. This is a true story. And that's how I met some of the women of ZAMI. And then after I met them, I was kind of on the periphery because I just kind of saw myself as being a little bit more political than they were at the time. Lisa Moore, and there was a sister named Angel, and I did the newsletter for ZAMI. So, the three of us did that. And that kind of was my initial involvement. So, I started to feel a little bit more settled in that regard. I started to work at Emory. And started to meet people. I would say probably my second year here, yeah, second, third year here, I started to kind of get my feet under me. And started to kind of embrace the city and what it had to offer. And the relationships that I was cultivating. [. . .]

In general, what was the sort of political scene here in Atlanta, particularly around LGBT life?

Very, very positive. Very segregated in terms of gender, class, race. I was accustomed to working in coalition with men. Even though I certainly identified as a feminist and I was aware of all those issues, but I still did a lot of work with men. And it was very surprising to me that, and particularly in terms of the black queer community, there was not a lot of interaction.

And I remember just being baffled by that, quite frankly. And, would invite the brothers to stuff that we would have, and they wouldn't show up. And I would be like, "Well, why don't they show up?" Finally, one brother said to me, "Mary Anne, do you really, really want me to tell you why?" I said, "Yeah, because I'm just shocked, really. I know I'm naïve to a certain extent, but . . ." He said, "Because you got the wrong anatomy." And I'm like, "Oh." He said it a little more graphic than that. But I'm like, "Oh, okay. I got it." I mean, I got it. [Laughter] I really got it. [. . .] Because one night, I was saying, "Oh, God, there's this black gay man. He's the most beautiful black gay man I've ever seen." I'm telling this to some other brothers, bragging, and they said, "Who is that?" I said, "Craig Washington." And they was like, "He ain't all that." I was like, "Okay. Alright." [Laughter] You know. I'll never forget that.

We had a couple of collaborations with Second Sunday. We invited them, and we had some dialogue, we had some conversation. But we were always the one who were initiating the dialogues and the conversations and the gatherings and all that. So, after a while, that just got a little bit tiresome, so we just stopped doing that. Because there was just really not a lot of interest in us really doing a whole lot together. We're just very, very segregated. I mean, and folks were really, really living in the closet. There's a lot of fear, a lot of fear. And Iris started ZAMI [see chapter 7] and I'll let her tell you that story. And then she kind of dropped out. So, when I came on the scene, there were these monthly meetings at peoples' homes or Charis bookstore at one point. That was probably the most stable gathering place, outside of peoples' homes. And it would just kind of go in and out, you know. It would go on hiatus and come out of hiatus. And you might be able to find the organization one year, the next year you would not be able to. There might be a phone number, you might call that phone number. Somebody might answer, they might not answer—that whole thing, which is why it was difficult for me to make contact with them. [. . .]

Well, how did AIDS/HIV impact all that? I imagine it forced some people out of the closet. And although the impact wasn't felt, at least then, as greatly on the lesbian community, the people I've talked to [have said] lesbians played a really important role in the caregiving for a lot of men. So, how did HIV/AIDS during that time, late eighties, early nineties, impact peoples' level of outness?

I think that you're absolutely right. There were black gay men in this community, like Tony Daniels, for example, who identified as an honorary lesbian. [Laughter] He single-handedly, I think, did so much to support the scholarship funding in its infancy and who the first reception we had, it was full of brothers. There were probably more black gay men there than lesbians. That's the truth. And that was because of Tony Daniels. Tony had this thing where he would shame you into doing stuff. And he was unapologetic about it. But his thing was activism. Whatever it took, whatever face it wore, you were going to do the work, and this is how that work was going to be done. I would see Tony and Tony's like, "Mary Anne, this is what we're going to do. We're going to this, this." He was like, "We're going to start Black Gay Pride. We're going to"—and he had all these ideas. And he was a hard worker. So, he was very instrumental, I think, in bringing a lot of folk into the room who ordinarily would not be in the room and, when he died, were no longer in the room.

There was a brother who was very, very dear to us, who did die. Actually, they had his service at the First E [Existentialist] Church, Trey. ZAMI women served as ushers for Trey, because that's what he wanted. And right before he died, BJ and I went to see him. [. . .] And in Jackson, it was the first brother that I was close to, that I knew personally, who was dying of HIV. And I remember the time we went, he was living in southwest Atlanta somewhere with his mama. And when we went to see Trey, Trey had on these furry pink house shoes. [Laughter] I'll never forget it. His mom was there and it was really, really interesting. It was who he was. Just a wonderful spirit. But we were his ushers at his service. [. . .] So, I do think that as a community, the disease certainly did bring people out, you're absolutely correct. I think black gay men who ordinarily wouldn't be out. And with the scholarship fund, there were black gay men who we gave the scholarships to, and this was probably starting to be late nineties, who were positive, who had been positive for many years, who actually passed as part of our Audre Lorde family. [. . .]

Why did it [ZAMI] stop?

Because I was tired, for one thing. We kind of looked around and realized that we were aging in place, the women of ZAMI, and thought that it would be really good for us to try to focus on that. So, we kind of morphed into ZAMI NOBLA. You know that NOBLA is National Organization of Black Lesbians on Aging. And we wanted to kind of shift the paradigm a little bit and have us start the conversations about aging. Because our community, our culture is so youth-oriented, and people don't even want to talk about aging, so we want to start the conversations and shift this whole paradigm from seeing aging as this whole death and dying model, but to folk who are empowering, affirmed, and who are living their lives and doing that community. So, that's really why we stopped. We're going to do the scholarship again, but we're going to really focus this time just on black lesbians forty and older, because there are a lot of women who haven't had an opportunity to get their training or education, who really want to do that and just don't have the funds to get it done. So, that's something we know we can do, we can do that with our eyes closed. [. . .]

I'm kind of sensitive to this whole notion that I've heard often from other queer folk in other parts of the country, particularly black ones, that the black queer folk in Atlanta, we're kind of seen as not knowing how to do this. And we're backwards. We're uneducated. We're this and we're that. So, I take that very personally. So, despite the fact that we've done things here that nobody else in any other part of the country has ever done. So, we were going to make sure that Simone got elected. And we were equally going to make sure that Joan got elected. So, we could certainly have the distinction, not only that these women are extremely competent, but this is the South, we got the first. And Kecia, how could I forget Kecia Cunningham? Who was the first black commissioner—lesbian—in Decatur, city commissioner. Kecia has since come out as bisexual, but at the time, she was lesbian. So, I mean, I was just like, "Wow." [. . .]

You hear all the time that turning forty, turning fifty, turning sixty are the best times. At fifty-seven years old, I can literally say that when I entered my fifties, I am at the best place in my life than I've ever been— personally, emotionally, spiritually, professionally. I know who I am. I know what I know. I know what I don't know. I appreciate the fact that until the day I leave my body I'm going to be learning something. And most importantly, I have a willingness to learn. And that's important to me. I don't really spend a lot of time worrying about what people say about me, I really don't. I believe that the only reason we're put on this earth was to help each other, I really believe that. And that's really kind of how I try to live my life. And people who know me, if I can help you, I'm going to help you. I think my life's work is to just continue to try to build community and try to bring us together. And right now, with ZAMI NOBLA, I really want us to try to develop a new paradigm for aging. I don't think that we have to live by this whole medical model of death and dying as we age. I want us to start to begin to even have the conversation. So, many of us don't want to have the conversation, because we even look at the whole framework of aging, the next thing that we associate that with is dying. And for all the black folk who preach about God and Jesus and the pie in the sky, they're afraid of dying. They don't want to go there. That's another story for another day. But we have seasons, we're going to leave at some point, and we need to prepare ourselves for that. We need to understand that aging does not mean that you have no more dreams, you have no more goals, that you can't continue to grow. There's so many folk I see who are so—who have so much agency now, who empower me and affirm me. We have these models for what it's like to age successfully and to have a quality of life. And if we can't do it individually, we can do it collectively. I understand that. But I know together we can build something. We can have collective housing. We can help each other. So, that's what I'm trying to do. I'm just trying to build this different paradigm. And to do it in a multigenerational way, you know? I think we owe that to each other. I think we need to co-mentor. I've been trying to get this whole concept of co-mentoring out there. It's not doing very well. Because I think that in order for us to really be in conversation with each other, it's not about the fact that I'm older and I know more than you. No, it's not the fact that because you're young, you think you got—no. We need to continue to grow and learn and teach each other. And so we're working toward that, you know.

I believe in coalition politics. When I moved here, I joined the ethics board for East Point—well, I was appointed to the ethics board for three years. Because it's where I live [laughter], you know. And I think if things are better for everybody, then things, of course, are better for me. But at the same time, of course, I do queer organizing, because that's important to me. But I think we need to bring all of ourselves to the table. I need to go to the ethics board meeting as Mary Anne, the black lesbian, social worker, who works at Georgia State in research. That's important. Who works in HIV. I need to bring all of my selves to the table. So, I think it's important that we do that, and that's kind of what I try to do. And actually, I've been pretty well received. Yeah. I'm the secretary for the Home Loan Association. They all know I'm a dyke. These folks, I mean, "Can she keep the minutes?" [Laughter] But I've grown up here. I've really grown up here. In so many ways. So, so many ways. Most days it's just so much work to do, because there's Atlanta and there's Georgia. There's just so much work to do. [. . .] Because there's a pull here, I think people really appreciate community. And it's one thing I said about the black folk, queer folk. We fight, but when we need to come together, we come together. That's a fact. I mean, the men will tell you that. If there's something that we need to come together, we're going to come together. I appreciate that about this community. There's no doubt about that. If there's something, we would call each other, we're there. We're like brother and sister. [Laughter] We all know each other.

For all the angst that I experienced and that I put on myself oftentimes, at the end of the day, there were people who believed in me, who encouraged me for what I was, as opposed to what I wasn't. And I'm very clear that I became a woman in Atlanta. But in Mississippi, I do believe that the skills that I learned, the way of being in the world, is really—has been the cement and the glue for me, the moral values I learned. [. . .] That community at Ole Miss, for example. The community at the Black House. The community among my siblings. Invaluable. Priceless. I wouldn't give anything for that.

Epilogue
A Poet's Response

. . . .

Their fears kill us everywhere
but here
we are haunted by nooses and pickup trucks
the heavy thud slide of manure-stained boots
that menacing twang and slur
       all bent vowels and absent end consonants
the chilling specter of The South

To be *out* is to court a transient freedom
to embrace desire as a life or death proposition

And still
I reach for her
will always reach for her
risk it all
for the open loving that is my birthright too.[1]

In this excerpt from Omi Osun Joni L. Jones's poem "Touch," the speaker encapsulates the paradox of living as a same-sex-desiring woman in the South: the homophobia sewn in the soil and hearts of many, coupled with the defiant fortitude of lesbian women to embrace their heritage and each other *despite* the risks. This paradox seemed to recur throughout BQSW as narrator after narrator shared both the joys of desiring other women, family life, and art making and the pain of being the victims of racism, misogyny, and/or physical abuse. And yet, this paradox has been one with which all black southerners have had to contend. In this way, black southern women who love women are not exceptional. Nonetheless, their gender and sexuality are the very difference that is the exception to the rule—and thus, another paradox. In other words, the systemic racism, homophobia, and misogyny upon which white supremacist heteropatriarchy rests inordinately affect the black queer women whose lives are chronicled in this book. Their strategies for assailing these oppressive forces draw on a history of black communal resistance, but also those employed specifically by black women based on their particular experiences of racialized and intracultural gender violence.

The uniqueness of the strategies here, however, is that they draw on the experiences of women who love women—experiences heretofore gone undocumented.

In her important essay "Black (W)holes and the Geometry of Black Female Sexuality," black feminist historian Evelynn Hammonds points out the "void" and "absence" of black women's sexuality in the historical record and suggests a number of reasons for this lacuna, ranging from self-imposed strategies of resistance by black women themselves to the elision of this sexual history by academics—including black feminist theorists "due to their own status in the academy."[2] Hammonds surveys the work of renowned black feminist historians like Darlene Clark Hine and Evelyn Brooks Higginbotham—both of whom provide reasons why black women may have devised silence as a strategy of self-preservation when it came to their sexuality. Hine, for example, suggests that black women developed a "culture of dissemblance" whereby they "created the appearance of openness and disclosure but actually shielded the truth of their inner lives and selves from their oppressors."[3] Higginbotham, in tandem, suggests that black women—and especially during the Victorian age—employed a "politics of silence" as a political strategy to stave off representations of black women as sexually immoral.[4]

One woman among the many I interviewed who disavowed such strategies in relation to their sexual trauma is Michelle (see chapter 5). Although Michelle had been sober for eight years at the time of the interview, the memory of the pain of her hitting rock bottom with her drug addiction—an addiction catalyzed by her father's sexual abuse—is visceral as she's overcome with emotion, interrupting her narration to apologize to me for her tears, when she says "excuse me . . . it's still real." Despite the "realness" of the events, however, it's Michelle's desire to have someone bear witness to the telling that makes the pain of the re-memory of her sexual trauma bearable. As Jennifer L. Griffiths argues in her book *Traumatic Possessions*, "Testimony . . . depends on a relationship and a process between the survivor and the witness, as memory emerges and reunites a body and a voice severed in trauma. These fractured pieces of the survivor's self come together in the reflection of the listener, and memory comes into meaning through this bodily transaction, rather than simply creating a narrative in language."[5] In the act of performing her life history, Michelle is affirmed through her interaction with me, as I bore witness to the story being told. The healing, then, is in the survivor's desire to tell and the willingness of the listener to bear witness. It is the communion of teller and listener, the affective corporeal dynamic between two people being suspended in the liminal space of memory that solicits voicehood over silence. In this regard, dissemblance and silence are not adequate strategies of survival. Instead, speaking out about what was done to her is the only thing that allows Michelle—and sixty-five of the other women whose sexual trauma are chronicled here—to move forward.

One of Hammonds's challenges to scholars is to find a "methodology that allows us to contest rather than reproduce the ideological system that has up to now defined the terrain of black women's sexuality."[6] For me, BQSW takes up Hammonds's charge by employing oral history as a site of contestation, a place to fill the void and shatter the code of silence accorded black queer women—and particularly those in the South. Indeed, the women of BQSW, like Michelle, refuse to reinscribe silence as a mode of resistance. Rather, they speak in full-throttle voices of their loves, joys, and desires—and yes, their pain, which includes sexual trauma. Perhaps this is because the political landscape has shifted such that the strategies of silence and dissemblance no longer hold sway or have been jettisoned and replaced with what some believe to be more radical strategies of black feminist resistance.[7] Whatever the case, these women's willingness to speak and speak out represents a turn in how black queer southern women maneuver the discursive, political, and material terrain that is the South.

In addition to instantiating their subjectivity through voicehood, these women also contest the very categories they have been culled under for this book. As the narratives across these pages attest, what constitutes the signifiers "black," "queer," "southern," and "women" never land on hard and fast definitions as much as index the fluidity of identity. Aida Rentas (see chapter 8) stakes a claim on blackness and pushes the boundaries of what constitutes the South when she intuitively makes the connection between her diasporic blackness vis-à-vis the Atlantic slave trade affecting her birthplace of Puerto Rico and her kinship with New York blacks in Spanish Harlem and Atlanta. Women like Gwen Cubit and Lori Wilson (see chapters 10 and 11, respectively) find their way to queer—and to each other—after having spent years dealing with substance abuse, incarceration, and abusive relationships with men. And "Ida Mae" (see chapter 12) challenges the category "woman" by taking her gender nonconformity to an extreme once she escapes the trappings of traditional sartorial expectations for women. She, along with many of the women in chapter 3, transgress gender norms through verbal play (e.g., "stud," "stem," "dom"), dress, and sex roles in ways that crack open taken-for-granted notions about what it means to be a black woman in the South.

Upending these categories is not accidental. Indeed, many of these women take delight in the fact that they are not bound by rules of convention—despite being politically committed to racial, sexual, regional, and gender markers of difference. In other words, they understand that their quotidian forms of theory—language, dress, affect, art, and so forth—index the performativity of culture, the instability of signifiers, while at the same time they understand that those same socially constructed markers of difference have material consequences that demand that they not be naïve about how, at any given moment, race, sexuality, region, and gender potentially place them in peril. Unstable categories or not, being a black, queer, southern woman is no easy row to hoe. Nevertheless, as the speaker of Jones's poem says, these women "risk it all," for the "open loving that is [their] birthright too."

As a cisgender, black, gay, male, middle-class academic from the South, writing this book also entailed risks: of not getting the story "right," of gender appropriation, and a host of other critiques that are bound to emerge. But to quote the song "Hold On" from one of my favorite black women folk singing groups, Sweet Honey in the Rock, "I wouldn't take nothing for my journey now," for my life has forever been changed by my bearing witness to these women's stories. Whatever vulnerabilities, self-consciousness, or resistance I experienced about doing this work pale in comparison to the daily experiences of unrelenting misogyny, sexism, homophobia, and racism faced by these women. It is their love for and toward one another, then, that makes their stories so inspiring.

These stories are snapshots of larger lives hidden in plain sight. The silky smooth swearing and touches of drunken fathers, careless brothers, and unrelenting uncles trespass these somatic testimonies but ultimately falter, for these stories seek refuge and comfort in the love embrace of voluminous breasts beaded with the sweat of last night's humidity—hot and languid. These tales bend gender toward justice and just us, riding out the new revolutionary wave of femme aggressives and boi bottoms. Ancestral waters flow in the crevices of these stories, awakening a new consciousness about cis-ness in transition. Promiscuous, these stories get around, hover, and saunter past hegemony's hold on lesbionic leanings as they dip into the honey pot. These stories are of a matrilineage: they Lorde over the erotic.[8] They Walker round barefoot through summer snow.[9] They say Bogus things to throw the dogs off their scent.[10] They will not be undone. They will not be moved.

Notes

INTRODUCTION

1. See my introduction in Johnson, *Sweet Tea*, 20.

2. I use the term "quare" as opposed to "queer" to register the specific black vernacular reference to nonnormative sexuality. See my essay "'Quare' Studies."

3. "Clutching pearls" in black gay vernacular means to express surprise.

4. Boyd, "Who Is the Subject?," 178.

5. Throughout the book, I use various terms to indicate same-sex desire, including "same-sex loving," "queer," "quare," "gay," and "lesbian," because the women I interviewed identify variously among these or disavow labels altogether.

6. Other scholars, activists, and artists are also currently focusing on black lesbian life, including Alexis Pauline Gumbs and Julia Wallace, who founded the Mobile Homecoming Project that gathers the stories black queer women around the country. Filmmaker Tiona McClodden and publisher Lisa Moore are working on a film on black lesbian elders. Still, I believe the southern experience is underrepresented in the research currently being done.

7. One of the reasons that these women may have failed to show up for the interview is that all of them were college students. Some of them may have had other obligations take precedence or, for whatever reason, they decided that it was best not to participate.

8. Alexander, *Performing Black Masculinity*, xviii–xix.

9. Collins, *Black Feminist Thought*, 11.

10. Alexander, *Performing Black Masculinity*, xix.

11. See Johnson, "'Quare' Studies."

12. See Johnson, "Never Had Uh Cross Word"; and Johnson and Rivera-Servera, *solo/black/woman*. Sandra Richards and I codeveloped and team-taught a course on black feminism and black queer theory for eight years, a course I now teach by myself.

13. James, *Shadow Boxing*, 157.

14. Minister, "Feminist Frame for Interviews," 35.

15. Pollock, *Telling Bodies Performing Birth*, 23.

16. Olson and Shopes, "Crossing Boundaries, Building Bridges, 195–96.

17. Stacey, "Can There Be a Feminist Ethnography?," 117.

18. Conquergood, "Performing as a Moral Act."

19. See, for example, Taylor, *Archive and the Repertoire*.

20. Madison, *Critical Ethnography*, 37.

21. Hurston, *Their Eyes Were Watching God*, 6.

22. Etter-Lewis, "Black Women's Life Stories," 43.

23. For more on black (heterosexual) women's storytelling traditions, see Dance, *Honey Hush!*; Hill, *Black Women's Oral History Project*; Brown and Fauk, *Living with Jim Crow*; and Vaz, *Oral Narrative Research with Black Women*.

24. Salazar, "Third World Woman's Text," 98.

25. Madison, *Critical Ethnography*, 34–35; emphasis in original.

26. Christian, "Race for Theory," 68.

27. Madison, *Critical Ethnography*, 36.

PART I

1. After learning about the phrase, I discovered it was quite common and was the title of the 2013 book *G.R.I.T.S. Girls Raised in the South: An Anthology of Southern Queer Womyn's Voices and Their Allies*, edited by Poet on Watch and Amber N. Williams, and the title of several albums by rappers and country singers, including Kayo Starr, Greze, Schizophonic, Jon Miller, and Lacy Cavalier. And though it refers to food and not women, Grits and Honey is also the name of a catering company in Atlanta.

CHAPTER 2

1. See Morrison, *Sula*, 33.

2. I later found out that "pica," the term for eating dirt, is a common practice and sometimes is an indication of mineral deficiencies. See, for example, https://www.ncbi.nlm.nih.gov/books/NBK255/.

CHAPTER 4

1. See Johnson, *Sweet Tea*, 184–85.

2. See, for example, Hull, Scott, and Smith, *All the Women Are White*; Smith, *Home Girls*; Moraga and Anzaldúa, *This Bridge Called My Back*; and Bambara, *Black Woman*.

3. Walker (*In Search of Our Mothers' Gardens*, xi–xii) defines "womanist" in the following way:

1. From *womanish*. (Opp. of "girlish," i.e., frivolous, irresponsible, not serious.) A black feminist or feminist of color. From the black folk expression of mothers to female children, "you acting womanish," i.e., like a woman. Usually referring to outrageous, audacious, courageous or *willful* behavior. Wanting to know more and in greater depth than is considered "good" for one. Interested in grown up doings. Acting grown up. Being grown up. Interchangeable with another black folk expression: "You trying to be grown." Responsible. In charge. *Serious*. 2. *Also:* A woman who loves other women, sexually and/or nonsexually. Appreciates and prefers women's culture, women's emotional flexibility (values tears as natural counterbalance of laughter), and women's strength. Sometimes loves individual men, sexually and/or nonsexually. Committed to survival and wholeness of entire people, male *and* female. Not a separatist, except periodically, for health. Traditionally a universalist, as in: "Mama, why are we brown, pink, and yellow, and our cousins are white, beige and black?" Ans. "Well, you know the colored race is just like a flower garden, with every color flower represented." Traditionally capable, as in: "Mama, I'm walking to Canada and I'm taking you and a bunch of other slaves with me." Reply: "It wouldn't be the first time." 3. Loves music. Loves dance. Loves the moon. *Loves* the Spirit. Loves love and food and roundness. Loves struggle. *Loves* the Folk. Loves herself. *Regardless*. 4. Womanist is to feminist as purple is to lavender.

4. Walker, *The Color Purple*, 202.

5. To read more about this event, see Gumbs, "Pocket Poetry Prayer Meeting #1."

6. Shockley, *Say Jesus and Come to Me*, 6–7.

7. Many have noted the relationship between the sacred and the secular relative to sexuality in the black church. See, for example, Johnson, "Feeling the Spirit in the Dark"; and Dyson, *Race Rules*, esp. 77–108.

CHAPTER 5

1. The title of the song is a sexual innuendo referring to a vernacular phrase for the clitoris. In some lesbian circles, it was believed that an extended clitoris was a sign of lesbianism.

2. George Hannah, "The Boy in the Boat" lyrics, http://lyrics.wikia.com/wiki/George_Hannah:The_Boy_In_The_Boat (accessed March 29, 2018); "Prove It on Me Blues" lyrics, https://genius.com/Ma-rainey-prove-it-on-me-blues-lyrics (accessed March 29, 2018).

3. Wilson, *Hive*, 10.

4. Hurston, *Their Eyes Were Watching God*, 10–11.

5. Walker, *The Color Purple*, 42.

6. National Sexual Violence Resource Center, "Statistics about Sexual Violence."

CHAPTER 7

1. See Morrison, *Sula*, 112.

PART II

1. See Collins, *Black Feminist Thought*, 22.

EPILOGUE

1. Omi Osun Joni L. Jones, "Touch," unpublished poem, 2011, 1.

2. Hammonds, "Black (W)holes and the Geometry of Black Female Sexuality," 145.

3. Hine, "Rape and the Inner Lives of Black Women," 915.

4. Higginbotham, "African-American Women's History," 262–66.

5. Griffiths, *Traumatic Possessions*, 2.

6. Hammonds, "Black (W)holes and the Geometry of Black Female Sexuality," 144.

7. A host of contemporary black feminist theorists now focus on sexual pleasure and desire as opposed to trauma, as well as theorize the subversive possibilities of racialized sexual stereotypes of black women. See, for example, LaMonda Horton-Stallings's *Funk the Erotic*, in which she theorizes sexual "explicitness" among black women "as a rejection of the Western will to truth about sexuality, and underscores such truth as a con and joke" (xii). For treatments of black female representations of and participation in pornography, see Nash, *Black Body in Ecstasy*; and Miller-Young, *A Taste for Brown Sugar*.

8. See Lorde, "Uses of the Erotic."

9. See Walker, *In Search of Our Mothers' Garden*.

10. See Bogus, *Dyke Hands and Sutras*.

Bibliography

Alexander, Bryant Keith. *Performing Black Masculinity: Race, Culture, and Queer Identity*. New York: AltaMira Press, 2006.

Bambara, Toni Cade, ed. *The Black Woman: An Anthology*. New York: New American Library, 1970.

Bogus, SDiane. *Dyke Hands and Sutras Erotic and Lyric*. San Francisco, CA: WIM Publications, 1988.

Boyd, Nan Alamilla. "Who Is the Subject? Queer Theory Meets Oral History." *Journal of the History of Sexuality* 17, no. 2 (2008): 177–89.

Brown, Leslie, and Anne Fauk. *Living with Jim Crow: African American Women and Memories of the Segregated South*. New York: Palgrave, 2010.

Christian, Barbara. "The Race for Theory," *Feminist Studies* 14, no. 1 (1988): 67–79.

Collins, Patricia Hill. *Black Feminist Thought: Knowledge, Consciousness, and the Politics of Empowerment*. New York: Routledge, 1991.

Conquergood, Dwight. "Performing as a Moral Act: Ethical Dimensions of the Ethnography of Performance." In *Cultural Struggles: Performance, Ethnography, Praxis*, edited by E. Patrick Johnson, 1–13. Ann Arbor: University of Michigan Press, 2013.

Dance, Daryl Cumberland. *Honey Hush! An Anthology of Black Women's Humor*. New York: Norton, 1998.

Dyson, Michael Eric. *Race Rules: Navigating the Color Line*. New York: Basic Books, 1996.

Etter-Lewis, Gwendolyn. "Black Women's Life Stories: Reclaiming Self in Narrative Texts." In *Women's Word: The Feminist Practice of Oral History*, edited by Sherna Berger Gluck and Daphne Patai, 43–58. New York: Routledge, 1991.

Faderman, Lillian. *Odd Girls and Twilight Lovers: A History of Lesbian Life in Twentieth-Century America*. New York: Columbia University Press, 1991.

Griffiths, Jennifer L. *Traumatic Possessions: The Body and Memory in African American Women's Writing and Performance*. Charlottesville: University of Virginia Press, 2009.

Gumbs, Alexis. "Pocket Poetry Prayer Meeting #1: Phyllis Wheatley." *Eternal Summer of the Black Feminist Mind*, August 21, 2012, https://blackfeministmind. wordpress.com/2012/08/21/pocket-poetry-prayer-meeting-1-phillis-wheatley/.

Hammonds, Evelynn. "Black (W)holes and the Geometry of Black Female Sexuality." *differences: A Journal of Feminist Cultural Studies* 6, no. 2–3 (1994): 126–46.

Higginbotham, Evelyn Brooks. "African-American Women's History and the Metalanguage of Race." *Signs: Journal of Women in Culture and Society* 17, no. 2 (1992): 251–74.

Hill, Ruth Edmonds, ed. *The Black Women's Oral History Project*. 10 vols. Westport, CT: Meckler, 1990.

Hine, Darlene Clark. "Rape and the Inner Lives of Black Women in the Middle West." *Signs: Journal of Women in Culture and Society* 14, no. 4 (1989): 912–20.

Horton-Stallings, LaMonda. *Funk the Erotic: Transaesthetics and Black Sexual Cultures.* Champaign: University of Illinois Press, 2015.

Howard, John, ed. *Carryin' On in the Lesbian and Gay South.* New York: New York University Press, 1997.

Hull, Gloria T., Patricia Bell Scott, and Barbara Smith, eds. *All the Women Are White, All the Blacks Are Men, but Some of Us Are Brave: Black Women's Studies.* New York: Feminist Press, 1982.

Hurston, Zora Neale. *Their Eyes Were Watching God.* New York: Harper and Row, 1990.

James, Joy. *Shadow Boxing: Representations of Black Feminist Politics.* New York: Palgrave, 2002.

Johnson, E. Patrick. "Feeling the Spirit in the Dark: Expanding Notions of the Sacred in the African American Gay Community." *Callaloo* 21, no. 2 (1998): 399–416.

———. "Never Had Uh Cross Word: Feminist Practice in the Oral History of Black Domestic Worker." PhD diss., Louisiana State University, 1996.

———. "'Quare' Studies or (Almost) Everything I Know about Queer Studies I Learned from My Grandmother." In *Black Queer Studies: A Critical Anthology,* edited by E. Patrick Johnson and Mae G. Henderson, 124–57. Durham, NC: Duke University Press, 2005.

———. *Sweet Tea: Black Gay Men of the South.* Chapel Hill: University of North Carolina Press, 2008.

Johnson, E. Patrick, and Ramón Rivera-Servera, eds. *solo/black/woman: scripts, essays, and interviews.* Evanston, IL: Northwestern University Press, 2013.

Lorde, Audre. "The Uses of the Erotic." In *Sister Outsider: Essays and Speeches,* 53–59. Berkley, CA: Crossing Press, 1984.

Madison, D. Soyini. *Critical Ethnography: Method, Ethics, and Performance.* 2nd ed. Thousand Oaks, CA: Sage, 2012.

McKinley, Catherine E., and L. Joyce DeLaney, eds. *Afrekete: An Anthology of Black Lesbian Writing.* New York: Anchor Books, 1995.

Miller-Young, Mireille. *A Taste for Brown Sugar: Black Women in Pornography.* Durham, NC: Duke University Press, 2014.

Minister, Kristina. "A Feminist Frame for Interviews." In *Women's Word: The Feminist Practice of Oral History,* edited by Sherna Berger Gluck and Daphne Patai, 27–41. New York: Routledge, 1991.

Moore, Lisa C., ed. *Does Your Mama Know? An Anthology of Black Lesbian Coming Out Stories.* Decatur, GA: RedBone Press, 1997.

Moraga, Cherríe, and Gloria Anzaldúa, eds. *This Bridge Called My Back: Writings by Radical Women of Color.* New York: Kitchen Table/Women of Color Press, 1983.

Morrison. Toni. *Sula.* New York: Plume, 1976.

Nash, Jennifer Christine. *The Black Body in Ecstasy: Reading Race, Reading Pornography.* Durham, NC: Duke University Press, 2014.

National Sexual Violence Resource Center. "Statistics about Sexual Violence." http://www.nsvrc.org/sites/default/files/

publications_nsvrc_factsheet_media-packet_statistics-about-sexual-violence_0.
pdf. Accessed on August 12, 2012.

Naylor, Gloria. *The Women of Brewster Place.* New York: Penguin Books, 1983.

Olson, Karen, and Linda Shopes. "Crossing Boundaries, Building Bridges: Doing
Oral History among Working-Class Women and Men." In *Women's Word: The
Feminist Practice of Oral History*, edited by Sherna Berger Gluck and Daphne
Patai, 189–204. New York: Routledge, 1991.

Poet on Watch and Amber N. Williams, eds. *G.R.I.T.S. Girls Raised in the South:
An Anthology of Southern Queer Womyn's Voices and Their Allies.* Austin, TX:
Freeverse, 2013.

Pollock, Della. *Telling Bodies Performing Birth: Everyday Narratives of Childbirth.*
New York: Columbia University Press, 1999.

Salazar Claudia. "A Third World Woman's Text: Between the Politics of Criticism and
Cultural Politics." In *Women's Word: The Feminist Practice of Oral History*, edited by
Sherna Berger Gluck and Daphne Patai, 93–106. New York: Routledge, 1991.

Sears, James T. *Growing Up Gay in the South: Race, Gender, and Journeys of the
Spirit.* New York: Haworth Press, 1991.

———. *Lonely Hunters: An Oral History of Lesbian and Gay Southern Life,
1948–1968.* Boulder, CO: Westview Press, 1997.

———. *Rebels, Rubyfruit, and Rhinestones: Queering Space in the Stonewall South.*
New Brunswick, NJ: Rutgers University Press, 2001.

Shange, Ntosake. *for colored girls who have considered suicide / when the rainbow is
enuf.* New York: Scribner, 1997.

Shockley, Ann Allen. *Say Jesus and Come to Me.* New York: Naiad Press, 1987.

———. *Loving Her.* Boston: Northeastern University Press, 1974.

Smith, Barbara. *Home Girls: A Black Feminist Anthology.* New York: Kitchen Table:
Women of Color Press, 1983.

———. "Toward a Black Feminist Criticism." In *All the Women Are White, All the
Blacks Are Men, but Some of Us Are Brave: Black Women's Studies*, edited by Gloria
T. Hull, Patricia Bell Scott, and Barbara Smith, 157–76. New York: Feminist
Press, 1982.

Stacey, Judith. "Can There Be a Feminist Ethnography?" In *Women's Word: The
Feminist Practice of Oral History*, edited by Sherna Berger Gluck and Daphne
Patai, 111–20. New York: Routledge, 1991.

Taylor, Diana. *The Archive and the Repertoire: Performing Cultural Memory in the
Americas.* Durham, NC: Duke University Press, 2003.

Thompson, Brock. *The Un-natural State: Arkansas and the Queer South.* Fayetteville:
University of Arkansas Press, 2010.

Vaz, Kim Marie. *Oral Narrative Research with Black Women: Collecting Treasures.*
Thousand Oaks, CA: Sage, 1997.

Walker, Alice. *The Color Purple.* New York: Pocket Books, 1982.

———. *In Search of Our Mothers' Gardens: Womanist Prose.* San Diego: Harcourt
Brace Jovanovich, 1983.

Wilson, Bee. *The Hive: The Story of the Honeybee and Us.* New York: St. Martin's
Griffin, 2004.

Youngblood, Shay. *The Big Mama Stories.* New York: Firebrand Books, 1989.

Index of Narrators

Names that appear in quotation marks are pseudonyms.

Aida Rentas (b. 1938, Santurce, Puerto Rico), 393–416

Almah (b. 1976; Louisville, Ky.), 251–54

Alpha (b. 1957, Dallas, Tex.), 78–86

Anita (b. 1964, Hickory, N.C.), 21–23, 167–70, 281–82, 336–41

"Barbara" (b. 1966, Rutherfordton, N.C.), 341–44

Bonita/Bluhe (b. 1968, Anderson, S.C.), 87–90, 170

Cherry Hussain (b. 1955, Daytona Beach, Fla.), 53, 302, 304, 417–42

Dammeion (b. 1970, Baton Rouge, La.), 139–41

Darlene Hudson (b. 1961, Las Vegas, Nev.; raised in Fordyce, Ark.), 23–26, 170–75, 217–19, 233–34, 344–48

Dedra (b. 1966, Prentiss, Miss.), 26–29

Diane (b. 1977, Spartanburg, S.C.), 141–42, 254–56

"Doris" (b. 1967, New Orleans, La.), 142–43, 256–58

Emilie (b. 1955, Durham, N.C.), 90–93, 175–76, 282–87, 348–52

Felicia (b. 1970, Mobile, Ala.), 258–61

Gwen Cubit (b. 1967, Austin, Tex.), 443–72

"Ida Mae" (b. 1951, Odenville, Ala.), 508–33

Iris (b. 1957, Miami Beach, Fla.), 93–95, 219–22, 352–55

Jasmine (b. 1994, Chapel Hill, N.C.), 143, 261–62, 355–56

"Jill" (b. 1975, Huntsville, Ala.), 143–45

Joan (b. 1951, Washington, D.C.; d. 2017), 356–65

Joy (b. 1966, Houston, Tex.), 222–23

"Joyce" (b. 1987, Ft. Lauderdale, Fla.), 104–6, 364–65

Julia (b. 1979, Gastonia, N.C.), 176–79, 287–88, 365–67

Kate (b. 1981, Winston-Salem, N.C.), 29–30, 100–103, 262–64

Kei (b. 1989, Jacksonville, Fla.), 180–81, 367

Kerrie (b. 1970, Ft. Lauderdale, Fla.), 30–32, 103–4, 145

Keturah (b. 1980, Atlanta, Ga.), 48–51, 145–46

"Lady Boy" (b. 1973, Greenville, Miss.), 95–98, 199–201

"Laura" (b. 1976, Charleston, Miss.), 32–33

Laurinda (b. 1959, Memphis, Tenn.), 98–100, 179–80, 223–24, 265–67, 288–92, 324–25

Lenore (b. 1962, Wampee, S.C.; d. 2014), 181–83, 224–26, 367–68

Lindsay (b. 1993, Jacksonville, Fla.), 293–96

Lisa (b. 1963, New Orleans, La.), 325–29

"Lisa" (b. 1972. Detroit, Mich.; raised in Grambling, La.), 183–84, 234–38

Lori Wilson (b. 1962, Seguin, Tex.), 473–507

"Louise" (b. 1944; Durham, N.C.), 201–2, 238–39, 292–93

Lynn (b. 1968, Jackson, Miss.), 146–47, 184–86

Malena (b. 1980, Charlotte, N.C.), 296–98
Malu (b. 1980, Cincinnati, Ohio; raised in Davidson, N.C.), 106–10, 186–88
"Martha" (b. 1982, Fort Sill, Ok.; raised in Sikeston, Mo.), 188–90
"Mary" (b. 1975, Tuscaloosa County, Ala.), 34–36, 110–12, 190–92, 298, 375–76
Maryam (b. 1977; Washington, D.C.), 192–93
Mary Anne Adams (b. 1954, Oxford, Miss.), 534–58
Melanie (b. 1976, Mobile, Ala.), 147–48, 226
Melissa (b. 1979, Nashville, Tenn.), 112–14, 193–94, 329
Michelle (b. 1965, Winston-Salem, N.C.), 148–50, 198–99, 239–41, 267–73
Monica (b. 1977, Washington, D.C.), 150–52, 202, 329–31
Monica J. (b. 1966, Houston, Tex.), 114–15, 194–97
Monika (b. 1979, Birmingham, Ala.), 226–27

Nadia (b. 1983, Pensacola, Fla.), 152–53, 228–29, 299–301
Nancy (b. 1950, Maxton, N.C.), 36–44, 115–16, 197–98, 241–43, 376–79
"Neyko" (b. 1978, Forest City, Ark.), 116–17
Nora (b. 1983, Houston, Tex.), 44–48, 274–76

Pat Hussain (b. 1950, Atlanta, Ga.), 51–55, 202–3, 243–44, 301–6, 379–80
Porscha (b. 1987, Compton, Ca.; raised in Nashville, Tenn.), 117–20
Priscilla (b. 1967, San Antonio, Tex.), 55–59, 153–54, 276–78, 381–84

Q. (b. 1980, Dallas, Tex.), 154–58, 203–5, 331–33

RonAmber (b. 1981, Dallas, Tex.), 59–63, 158–59
Rose (b. 1958, Roanoke, Va.), 63–67, 120–22, 160, 306–8
Roshandra (b. 1976, Ft. Lauderdale, Fla.), 67, 160–61, 205

Shannon (b. 1976, Birmingham, Ala.), 161–62
Shannon S. (b. 1972; Baton Rouge, La.), 205–7, 384–88
Sharita (b. 1979, Washington, D.C.), 68–69, 127–28, 245–46, 308–12
Sharon (b. 1964, Washington, D.C.), 122–25, 162–64, 388
Shayla (b. 1980, Little Rock, Ark.), 128–29, 209
Shetikka (b. 1975, Atlanta, Ga.), 312–17
"Shonda" (b. 1959, Columbus, Ga.), 125–27, 207–9, 333–34
Sonja (b. 1973, Troy, Ala.), 244–45

Tommye (b. 1952, Orange, Tex.), 69–73, 229–32, 318–20
Toni (b. 1980, Columbia, Tenn.), 320–22
Tonia (b. 1969, Mount Vernon, N.Y.; raised in Graham, N.C.), 129–32, 210, 389
Tonya (b. 1965; Richmond, Va.), 210–12, 278–79
Tori (b. 1993, Orlando, Fla.), 232, 245, 322, 389–90

"Vanessa" (b. 1968; Austin, Tex.), 212–14

Wynee (b. 1962, Jackson, Miss.), 132–36, 164, 246–49

Xami (b. 1957, Hampton, Va.), 73–76, 334–35, 390

General Index

activism/activists, 16, 23, 51, 104, 178, 193, 410; and HIV/AIDS, 78, 146, 563n6; and LGBTQ issues, 55, 112, 154, 181, 378, 534; and race, 90, 547, 552, 555
Afrocentrism, 156
AIDS. *See* HIV/AIDS
Alexander, Bryant Keith, 9–10
allgo (Austin, Tex.), 336, 382–84, 466
androgyny, 158, 163
Anzaldúa, Gloria, 4

Baldwin, James, 326, 346
Baptist Training Union, 171, 450, 518, 543
Baranco, Victor, 399
Bashir, Samiya, 328
Birtha, Becky, 324, 327
Black House (Oxford, Miss.), 546–48, 558
Black Lives Matter, 335
Black Power movement, 335, 365, 537, 553
Bogus, SDiane, 562
Bridgforth, Sharon, 70, 154, 324, 328, 443, 465, 494
Buddhism, 23, 34, 166, 174, 192, 203–4, 206, 211, 332, 341, 440
Bush, George H. W., 385, 430
Bush, George W., 200, 385

Candomblé, 151, 202
Charis Books (Atlanta, Ga.), 94, 166, 323, 353, 410, 554
Chick-fil-A, 336–39, 346, 355, 386–87, 439, 466
Chisholm, Shirley, 548
Christian, Barbara, 15

civil rights, 65, 90, 156, 335, 341, 351, 359, 388, 508–9, 546–47; Civil Rights Act, 361; civil rights movement, 90, 335, 358–60, 365, 379–80, 448, 509
Clinton, Bill, 377, 385, 407
Clarke, Cheryl, 4, 324
class, 5–7, 9, 11, 15–16, 20–21, 37, 40–41, 54, 64, 95, 100, 108, 112, 133, 137, 175, 281, 349, 357, 550, 553; and classism, 21, 352, 391
Collins, Patricia Hill, 9, 391
colorism, 16, 91, 98, 401
Common Lives/Lesbian Lives (journal), 327
Conquergood, Dwight, 13
critical reflexivity (Alexander), 9–10
cross-dressing, 513, 522, 527
Cullors, Patrice, 335

Daly, Mary, 282–83
Defense of Marriage Act (DOMA), 361
DeLaney, L. Joyce, 7
Does Your Mama Know? (Moore), 7, 328
Dollar, Creflo, 206
Don't Ask/Don't Tell (DADT), 377, 385–86, 439

Ebony (magazine), 540
Etter-Lewis, Gwendolyn, 14
Evers, Medgar, 509

Faderman, Lillian, 6
Faulkner, William, 124, 534
feminism, 9–13, 66, 111, 160, 166, 192, 283, 323–24, 335, 339, 363, 389, 553, 561, 563n12
Fire and Ink, 528–29
Firebrand Books, 324

First Existentialist Church (Atlanta, Ga.), 94, 411–12, 555
Fund for Southern Communities, 359, 362

Garza, Alicia, 335
gay marriage, 22, 291, 305, 335–37, 361, 370, 372, 388–89, 439, 466
gender, 1–10, 12, 15, 20–21, 29, 78, 95, 137–39, 142–45, 148–49, 151–52, 157–59, 188, 215, 233; gender fluidity, 233; gender nonconformity, 137–64, 345; genderqueer, 95, 137; and "masculine of center," 137, 157; and trans/transgender identities, 87, 123, 151, 157, 363, 368; and "two-spirit," 157, 178
GLAAD (Gay and Lesbian Alliance against Defamation), 439
Gomez, Jewelle, 327
Gray, Dorothy Randall, 328
Griffiths, Jennifer L., 560

Haiti, 301, 365
Hammonds, Evelynn, 560–61
heteronormativity, 6, 107, 138
Higginbotham, Evelyn Brooks, 560
Highlander Folk School, 401
Hine, Darlene Clark, 560
HIV/AIDS, 28, 78, 104–5, 118, 129, 146, 190, 345, 370, 372–75, 382–84, 388–89, 441, 468–69, 491, 405–96, 525, 554, 555, 557; AIDS epidemic, 10, 217, 305, 372; AIDS Memorial Quilt, 404, 409–10
Home Girls (Smith), 327
homophobia, 5, 11, 20–21, 77, 128, 138, 335, 348, 370–71, 376–78, 381, 401, 525, 559
Horton-Stallings, LaMonda, 565n7 (epilogue)
Howard, John, 6
Hurston, Zora Neale, 13–14, 216, 280

Ifá, 151, 177–78, 202
intersectionality, 21, 359–60, 362, 381

James, G. Winston, 328
James, Joy, 10, 13
Jet (magazine), 509
Jones, Omi Osun Joni L., 443, 559

King, Martin Luther, Jr., 67, 156, 340, 358, 412, 509, 547

Langellier, Kristin, 13
Lawson, James, 351
Lorde, Audre, 4, 193, 353–54, 413, 552, 555, 562

Madison, D. Soyini, 4, 13–14
marriage equality, 281, 335, 370, 372
McKinley, Catherine, 7
Meredith, James, 541
Meyer, Joyce, 206
Minister, Kristina, 11
Mobile Homecoming Project (Durham, N.C.), 336, 365, 563n6
Moore, Lisa C., 7, 553, 563n6
Moraga, Cherríe, 4
Morrison, Toni, 4, 78, 324
mother/daughter relationships, 77–136
Muslims, 188, 192–93, 414
Myspace, 159, 308

NAACP (National Association for the Advancement of Colored People), 62, 373, 547
Naiad Press, 324
National Black Arts Festival, 403, 409
Navratilova, Martina, 223
Naylor, Gloria, 4–5

Obama, Barack, 384–85, 387, 393, 467, 524–25
O'Connor, Flannery, 534
Oprah Winfrey Show, 263
oral history, 1, 8, 10–14, 16, 77, 561

parenting, 77–136, 431–33, 461–64, 475–83; gay parenting, 77–81, 87–90, 98–99, 106–10, 115–16, 127–29
Pariah (film), 113

patriarchy, 5, 6, 11, 166, 391, 559
Peterson, Eric, 13
PFLAG (Parents and Friends of
  Lesbians and Gays), 113
poetry, 7, 59, 61–63, 70, 95, 166, 193,
  233, 288, 323, 329, 334, 364, 382, 512,
  515–16, 559, 562
politics of respectability, 41, 138
Pollock, Della, 12, 143

quare, 2–4, 6, 324, 335, 563n2, 563n5

race, 5, 11, 15, 21, 91, 241, 282, 320, 355,
  428, 445, 553, 562, 564n3 (chap. 4);
  and blackness, 8, 388, 393, 56; and
  gender/sexuality, 21–76, 364; and
  Latinx identity, 395–97, 409, 414
racism, 4, 16, 21, 36, 47, 77, 166, 189,
  241, 355, 378, 381–82, 391, 401, 409,
  414, 559; and segregation, 28, 33, 52,
  54–55, 66, 351, 447, 553–54
Rainey, Ma, 215
Reagan, Ronald, 430, 452, 496
RedBone Press, 324, 326–28
religion, 165–214, 543–44; and
  homosexuality, 167–68, 170–71, 173,
  184–90, 196, 200–201, 205–7, 213,
  518–19
romantic relationships, 16, 22, 78, 102,
  147, 157, 217–19, 234–35, 246–51,
  280–322
Rustin, Bayard, 326, 346–47, 412

Salazar, Claudia, 14
Santería, 151
Sears, James T., 6
sex/sexuality, 215–79; and bisexuality, 3,
  81, 151, 241–44, 250, 368, 400, 426,
  492, 549, 556; and butch/femme/
  stud sexual behaviors, 138, 142–44,
  152, 159, 163–64, 233, 240–41, 390;
  coming out, 15, 40, 90, 107, 114,
  123–24, 174, 326–27, 354, 357, 376,
  401, 488, 500, 522, 549; sexual
  awakening, 216–33, 415–16, 449,
  453, 548

Shange, Ntozake, 166, 364, 415
Shockley, Ann Allen, 5, 7, 166
Shopes, Linda, 12
Silvera, Makeda, 327
Sinister Wisdom (literary journal), 326
Smith, Barbara, 4, 326
Smith, Bessie, 215
Smith, Beverly, 4
Sojourner, Sabrina, 363
sororities, 148, 155–56, 160, 173,
  183, 234
Southerners on New Ground, 362
southernness/southern culture, 6, 9,
  19, 43, 167
Stacey, Judith, 13
Sweet Honey in the Rock, 562
Sweet Tea (Johnson), 1, 4–8, 15, 114, 138,
  142, 165, 183, 216, 393
Sykes, Wanda, 326

Taylor, Koko, 215
Thompson, Brock, 6
Tolle, Eckhart, 263
Tometi, Opel, 335
trauma/sexual abuse, 7, 12, 29, 83, 98,
  249–79, 396, 417, 458, 544

Vacation Bible School, 165, 177, 179–80,
  183
Vanzant, Iyanla, 262

Walker, Alice, 4–5, 7, 166, 249–50, 280,
  363, 562, 564n3 (chap. 4)
Warren, Rick, 347
White, Marvin K., 328
Williamson, Marianne, 263
womanism, 166, 363, 564n3 (chap. 4)
Women's Day, 120, 224, 234
Wright, Jeremiah, 201

Youngblood, Shay, 7

ZAMI (Atlanta, Ga.), 94, 352–53, 363,
  412, 553–55; ZAMI NOBLA (National
  Organization of Black Lesbians on
  Aging) (Atlanta, Ga.), 93, 336, 555–56

MIX
Paper from
responsible sources
FSC® C013483